The Complete
Conversations with God
an uncommon dialogue

The Complete Conversations with God

• an uncommon dialogue •

contains the entire text of
book 1, book 2, & book 3

Neale Donald Walsch

HAMPTON ROADS
PUBLISHING COMPANY, INC.

G. P. PUTNAM'S SONS
NEW YORK

A joint publication of

Hampton Roads Publishing Company, Inc.
1125 Stoney Ridge Road, Charlottesville, VA 22902
www.hamptonroadspub.com

and

G. P. PUTNAM'S SONS
Publishers Since 1838
Published by the Penguin Group
Penguin Group (USA) Inc., 375 Hudson Street, New York, New York 10014, USA
Penguin Group (Canada), 90 Eglinton Avenue East, Suite 700, Toronto, Ontario M4P 243, Canada
(a division of Pearson Penguin Canada Inc.)
Penguin Books Ltd, 80 Strand, London WC2R 0RL, England
Penguin Ireland, 25 St Stephen's Green, Dublin 2, Ireland (a division of Penguin Books Ltd)
Penguin Group (Australia), 250 Camberwell Road, Camberwell, Victoria 3124, Australia
(a division of Pearson Australia Group Pty Ltd)
Penguin Books India Pvt Ltd, 11 Community Centre, Panchsheel Park, New Delhi–110 017, India
Penguin Group (NZ), Cnr Airborne and Rosedale Roads, Albany, Auckland 1310, New Zealand
(a division of Pearson New Zealand Ltd)
Penguin Books (South Africa) (Pty) Ltd, 24 Sturdee Avenue, Rosebank, Johannesburg 2196, South Africa
Penguin Books Ltd, Registered Offices: 80 Strand, London WC2R 0RL, England

An application has been submitted to register this book with the Library of Congress.

ISBN 0-399-15329-2

Printed in the United States of America
3 5 7 9 10 8 6 4

This book is printed on acid-free paper. ∞

Book design by Marjoram Productions
Index by Leonard S. Rosenbaum
Box design by Matthew & Jonathan Friedman
Box photo copyright © ThinkStock

While the author has made every effort to provide accurate telephone numbers and
Internet addresses at the time of publication, neither the publisher nor the author
assumes any responsibility for errors, or for changes that occur after publication.
Further, the publisher does not have any control over and does not assume any
responsibility for author or third-party websites or their content.

Introduction

It was ten years ago that *Conversations with God, Book 1* first made its way to bookstores. Within weeks of its appearance, thousands of copies had been sold. Rapidly, it became a publishing phenomenon, resting on the *New York Times* bestseller list for 137 weeks. That's more than two and a half years. *Conversations with God, Book 2* and *Book 3* also made the bestseller list.

Since then, the books have been translated into 34 languages and can now be found on the shelves of bookstores almost anywhere in the world, placing them among the most widely read contemporary spiritual books of modern times, selling in the multimillions. In many of the world's countries it is difficult to find a person who has not at least heard about these extraordinary texts.

How is it that this has come to pass? Why has this occurred?

This has occurred not because I am a good writer, nor even because some consider my source to be unimpeachable. It has occurred because humanity has begun to lose patience with itself. To people everywhere, it is becoming very clear that human beings cannot continue living the way they have been living.

We cannot continue holding the opinions we have been holding, embracing the beliefs we have been embracing, saying the things we have been saying, and exhibiting the behaviors we have been exhibiting. Something's got to change, or everything's going to change, irrevocably, and not for the better. Something's got to stop before everything stops.

People know this, and so, they are looking for answers. *Conversations with God* came along at precisely the right time.

Now comes this 10th Anniversary Collector's Edition, with all three books in one, and it, too, is perfectly timed. The world has become more aware than ever, not only of the problems facing us, but of the nature of those problems.

On June 23, 2004, a most interesting press release hit the wire services. The story indicated that a scientific survey conducted by Harris Interactive the previous month had determined that 69 percent of adult Americans believe *religious differences are the biggest hurdle to achieving global peace.*

Nothing could be closer to the truth—and most people know it. And that is why books like *Conversations with God* shoot to the bestseller lists in every country in which they are published. People may not know the answer to life's biggest questions, but they know that the answers we have been giving ourselves up until now are not working.

So now that we have finally come to understand what's going wrong (and been able to admit it), we can take a look at some alternative ideas about God and Life and Each Other (they all fall like dominos once the first belief is changed), and we can at last seek a newer world.

This trilogy is full of such ideas. As I have said many times before, it is not necessary for you to believe that I had an actual conversation with God to find value here. I have never asked people to believe in my experience, merely to review the material and, irrespective of its source, explore the ideas offered here with an open mind and an open heart.

More than 100,000 people have written me personal notes, letters, and e-mails since these books have been published, telling me that their lives have been impacted in very positive ways by this material. Outlooks have brightened, attitudes have changed, guilt has fallen away, relationships have been spectacularly enhanced, sexuality has been un-shamed, marriages have been saved, right livelihood has been created, parenting has been elevated, self-esteem has been reclaimed, physical, mental and spiritual health has been improved, and faith in God has been restored.

Did you hear that? *Faith in God has been restored.*

That's been the purpose and the aim of all of this. Not to create a belief system that confounds religion, and rejects it. Not to put forth ideas that contradict religion, and replace it. But to *reopen the discussion* about God in a way that refreshes and reinvigorates our relationship with the Divine.

I can't tell you how many of those thousands of letters have contained comments like, "For the first time in 25 years my heart is open to God again," or, "My husband says, 'At last! Now this is a God I can believe in.'" The most memorable of these letters came from Rita Curtis, of Portland, Oregon, who put in her note, given to me ten years ago, fourteen words that I will never forget:

"Thank you for introducing me to a God I can fall in love with."

That pretty much sums it up. "A God I can fall in love with" is the only God that can save our world. That is the God you will find here.

If you have read part or all of this material before, this revisiting of the wonderful message that has touched your soul was meant to occur right now. It is time for you to get back in touch with the magic and the wonder of your friendship with God.

If this is the first time you have come across this material and you think that you have come across it by accident or happenstance, think again. This material came to you at exactly the right time, in exactly the right way, in answer to your mind's search and your heart's prayer and your soul's invitation.

Believe it.

Nothing happens by chance.

Nothing.

Neale Donald Walsch
Ashland, Oregon
May 2005 – Ten Years Later

Book 1

for

ANNE M. WALSCH
Who not only taught me that God exists,
but opened my mind to the wondrous truth
that God is my best friend;
and who was far more than a mother to me,
but gave birth *in* me
to a longing for and a love of God,
and all that is good.
Mom was
my first meeting
with an angel.

and for

ALEX M. WALSCH
Who told me repeatedly throughout my life,
"There's nothing to it,"
"You don't have to take No for an answer,"
"You make your own luck,"
and
"There's more where that came from."
Dad was
my first experience
of fearlessness.

Acknowledgments

First, last, and always, I want to acknowledge the Source of everything that is in this book, everything that is life—and of life itself.

Second, I want to thank my spiritual teachers, who include the saints and sages of all religions.

Third, it is clear to me that all of us could produce a list of people who have touched our lives in ways so meaningful and so profoundly as to defy categorization or description; people who have shared with us their wisdom, told us their truth, suffered us our faults and our foibles in their infinite patience, and who have seen us through all of it; seeing the best in us there was to see. People who, in their acceptance of us, as well as their *refusal* to accept the parts of us they knew we really didnt choose, caused us to grow; to get *bigger* somehow.

The people, in addition to my parents, who have been there for me in that way include Samantha Gorski, Tara-Jenelle Walsch, Wayne Davis, Bryan Walsch, Martha Wright, the late Ben Wills Jr., Roland Chambers, Dan Higgs, C. Berry Carter II, Ellen Moyer, Anne Blackwell, Dawn Dancing Free, Ed Keller, Lyman W. (Bill) Griswold, Elisabeth Kübler-Ross, and dear, dear Terry Cole-Whittaker.

I want to include in this group my former mates, whose privacy I wish to respect by not naming them here, but whose contributions to my life are deeply grasped and appreciated.

And as gratitude for the gifts I have received from all these wonderful people swells my heart, I am especially warmed by the thought of my helpmate, spouse, and partner, Nancy Fleming Walsch, a woman of extraordinary wisdom, compassion and love, who has shown me that my highest thoughts about human relationships do not have to remain fantasies, but can be dreams come true.

Fourth and finally, I want to recognize some people I have never met, but whose lives and work have impacted me with such force that I cannot let this moment pass without thanking them from the depth of my being for the moments of exquisite pleasure, insight into the human condition, and pure, simple *Lifegefeelkin* (I made up that word!) they have given me.

You know what it is when someone has given you a taste, a glorious moment, of what *is really true about life?* For me, most of these have been creative or performing artists, because it is from art that I receive inspiration, to which I retreat in moments of reflection, and in which I find that which we call God most beautifully expressed.

And so I want to thank . . . John Denver, whose songs touch my soul and fill it with new hope about how life could be; Richard Bach, whose writings reach into my life as if they were my own, describing so much of what has been my experience; Barbra Streisand, whose directing, acting, and musical artistry grips my heart time and time again, causing it to *feel* what is true, not merely know it; and the late Robert Heinlein, whose visionary literature has raised questions and posed answers in ways no one else has dared even approach.

Introduction

You are about to have an extraordinary experience. You are about to have a conversation with God. Yes, yes. I know . . . that's not possible. You probably think (or have been taught) *that's not possible*. One can talk *to* God, sure, but not *with* God. I mean, God is not going to *talk back*, right? At least not in the form of a regular, everyday kind of conversation!

That's what I thought, too. Then this book happened to me. And I mean that literally. This book was not written *by* me, it happened *to* me. And in your reading of it, it will happen to you, for *we are all led to the truth for which we are ready*.

My life would probably be much easier if I had kept all of this quiet. Yet that wasn't the reason it happened to me. And whatever inconveniences the book may cause me (such as being called a blasphemer, a fraud, a hypocrite for not having lived these truths in the past, or—perhaps worse—a holy man), it is not possible for me to stop the process now. Nor do I wish to. I have had my chances to step away from this whole thing, and I haven't taken them. I've decided to stick with what my instincts are telling me, rather than what much of the world will tell me, about the material here.

Those instincts say this book is not nonsense, the overworking of a frustrated spiritual imagination, or simply the self-justification of a man seeking vindication from a life misled. Oh, I've thought of all of those things—every one of them. So I gave this material to a few people to read while it was still in manuscript form. They were moved. And they cried. And they laughed for the joy and the humor in it. And their lives, they said, changed. They were transfixed. They were empowered.

Many said they were transformed.

That's when I knew this book was for everyone, and that it *had* to be published; for it is a wonderful gift to all those who truly want answers and who truly care about the questions; for all those who have embarked upon quests for truth with sincerity of heart, longing of soul, and openness of mind. And that's pretty much *all of us.*

This book addresses most, if not all, of the questions we have ever asked about life and love, purpose and function, people and relationships, good and evil, guilt and sin, forgiveness and redemption, the path to God and the road to hell . . . *everything.* It directly discusses sex, power, money, children, marriage, divorce, life work, health, the hereafter, the before-now . . . *everything.* It explores war and peace, knowing and not knowing, giving and taking, joy and sorrow. It looks at the concrete and the abstract, the visible and the invisible, the truth and the untruth.

You could say that this book is "God's latest word on things," although some people might have a little trouble with that, particularly if they think that God stopped talking 2,000 years ago or that, if God has continued communicating, it's been only with holy men, medicine women, or someone who has been meditating for 30 years, or good for 20, or at least half-decent for 10 (none of which categories includes me).

The truth is, God talks to everybody. The good and the bad. The saint and the scoundrel. And certainly all of us in between. Take you, for instance. God has come to you many ways in your life, and this is another of them. How many times have you heard the old axiom: When the student is ready, the teacher will appear? This book is our teacher.

Shortly after this material began happening to me, I knew that I was talking with God. Directly, personally. Irrefutably. And that God was responding to my questions in direct proportion to my ability to comprehend. That is, I was being answered in ways, and with language, that God knew I would understand. This accounts for much of the colloquial style of the writing and the occasional references to material I'd gathered from other sources and prior experiences in my life. I know now that everything that has ever come to me in my life *has come to me from God,* and it was now being drawn together, pulled together, in a magnificent, complete response to *every question I ever had.*

And somewhere along the way I realized a book was being produced—a book intended for publication. Indeed, I was told specifically during the latter part of the dialogue (in February 1993) that *three* books would actually be produced, and that:

1. The first would deal mainly with personal topics, focusing on an individual's life challenges and opportunities.

2. The second would deal with more global topics of geopolitical and metaphysical life on the planet, and the challenges now facing the world.

3. The third would deal with universal truths of the highest order, and the challenges and opportunities of the soul.

This is the first of those books, completed in February 1993. For clarity I should explain that, as I transcribed this dialogue by hand, I underlined or circled words and sentences which came to me with particular emphasis—as if God were booming them out—and these were later placed in italics by the typesetter.

I need now to say that I am—having read and reread the wisdom contained here—deeply embarrassed by my own life, which has been marked by continued mistakes and misdeeds, some very shameful behaviors, and some choices and decisions which I'm certain others consider hurtful and unforgivable. Though I have profound remorse that it was through others' pain, I am unspeakably grateful for all that I have learned, and found that I have still *yet* to learn, because of the people in my life. I apologize to everybody for the slowness of that learning. Yet I am encouraged by God to grant myself forgiveness for my failings and not to live in fear and guilt but to always keep trying—keep on trying—to live a grander vision.

I know that's what God wants for all of us.

Neale Donald Walsch
Central Point, Oregon
Christmas 1994

1

In the spring of 1992—it was around Easter as I recall—an extraordinary phenomenon occurred in my life. God began talking with you. Through me.

Let me explain.

I was very unhappy during that period, personally, professionally, and emotionally, and my life was feeling like a failure on all levels. As I'd been in the habit for years of writing my thoughts down in letters (which I usually never delivered), I picked up my trusty yellow legal pad and began pouring out my feelings.

This time, rather than another letter to another person I imagined to be victimizing me, I thought I'd go straight to the source; straight to the greatest victimizer of them all. I decided to write a letter to God.

It was a spiteful, passionate letter, full of confusions, contortions, and condemnations. And a *pile* of angry questions.

Why wasn't my life working? What would it take to *get* it to work? Why could I not find happiness in relationships? Was the experience of adequate money going to elude me forever? Finally—and most emphatically—*What had I done to deserve a life of such continuing struggle?*

To my surprise, as I scribbled out the last of my bitter, unanswerable questions and prepared to toss my pen aside, my hand remained poised over the paper, as if held there by some invisible force. Abruptly, the pen began *moving on its own.* I had no idea what I was about to write, but an idea seemed to be coming, so I decided to flow with it. Out came . . .

> Do you really want an answer to all these questions, or are you just venting?

I blinked, and then my mind came up with a reply. I wrote that down, too.

Both. I'm venting, sure, but if these questions have answers, I'd sure as hell like to hear them!

> You are "sure as hell" . . . about a lot of things. But wouldn't it be nice to be *"sure as Heaven"*?

And I wrote:

What is that supposed to mean?

Before I knew it, I had begun a conversation . . . and I was not writing so much as *taking dictation.*

That dictation went on for three years, and at the time, I had no idea where it was going. The answers to the questions I was putting on paper never came to me until the question was completely written and I'd put my *own thoughts away.* Often the answers came faster than I could write, and I found myself scribbling to keep up. When I became confused, or lost the feeling that the words were coming from somewhere else, I put the pen down and walked away from the dialogue until I again felt inspired—sorry, that's the only word which truly fits—to return to the yellow legal pad and start transcribing again.

These conversations are still going on as I write this. And much of it is found on the pages which follow . . . pages which contain an astounding dialogue which at first I disbelieved, then assumed to be of personal value, but which I now understand was meant for more than just me. It was meant for you and everyone else who has come to this material. For my questions are your questions.

I want you to get into this dialogue as soon as you can, because what's really important here is not *my* story, but *yours.* It is *your* life story which brought you here. It is *your* personal experience to which this material has relevance. Otherwise you would not be here, with it, right now.

So let's enter the dialogue with a question I had been asking for a very long time: How does God talk, and to whom? When I asked this question, here's the answer I received:

> I talk to everyone. All the time. The question is not to whom do I talk, but who listens?

Intrigued, I asked God to expand on this subject. Here's what God said:

> First, let's exchange the word *talk* with the word *communicate.* It's a much better word, a much fuller, more accurate one. When we try to speak to each other—Me to you, you to Me, we are immediately constricted by the unbelievable limitation of words. For this reason, I do not communicate by words alone. In fact, rarely do I do so. My most common form of communication is through *feeling.*
> *Feeling is the language of the soul.*

If you want to know what's true for you about something, look to how you're *feeling* about it.

Feelings are sometimes difficult to discover—and often even more difficult to acknowledge. Yet hidden in your deepest feelings is your highest truth.

The trick is to get to those feelings. I will show you how. Again. If you wish.

I told God that I did wish, but that right now I wished even more for a complete and full answer to my first question. Here's what God said:

I also communicate with *thought*. Thought and feelings are not the same, although they can occur at the same time. In communicating with thought, I often use images and pictures. For this reason, thoughts are more effective than mere words as tools of communication.

In addition to feelings and thoughts, I also use the vehicle of *experience* as a grand communicator.

And finally, when feelings and thoughts and experience all fail, I use *words*. Words are really the least effective communicator. They are most open to misinterpretation, most often misunderstood.

And why is that? It is because of what words *are*. Words are merely utterances: *noises* that *stand for* feelings, thoughts, and experience. They are symbols. Signs. Insignias. They are not Truth. They are not the real thing.

Words may help you understand something. Experience allows you to know. Yet there are some things you cannot experience. So I have given you other tools of knowing. And these are called feelings. And so too thoughts.

Now the supreme irony here is that you have all placed so much importance on the Word of God, and so little on the experience.

In fact, you place so little value on experience that when what you *experience* of God differs from what you've *heard* of God, you automatically *discard the experience and own the words,* when it should be just the other way around.

Your experience and your feelings about a thing represent what you factually and intuitively know about that thing. Words can only seek to *symbolize* what you know, and can often *confuse* what you know.

These, then, are the tools with which I communicate, yet they are not the methods, for not all feelings, not all thoughts, not all experience, and not all words are from Me.

Many words have been uttered by others, in My name. Many thoughts and many feelings have been sponsored by causes not of My direct creation. Many experiences result from these.

The challenge is one of discernment. The difficulty is knowing the difference between messages from God and data from other sources. Discrimination is a simple matter with the application of a basic rule:

Mine is always your Highest Thought, your Clearest Word, your Grandest Feeling. Anything less is from another source.

Now the task of differentiation becomes easy, for it should not be difficult even for the beginning student to identify the Highest, the Clearest, and the Grandest.

Yet will I give you these guidelines:

The Highest Thought is always that thought which contains joy. The Clearest Words are those words which contain truth. The Grandest Feeling is that feeling which you call love.

Joy, truth, love.

These three are interchangeable, and one always leads to the other. It matters not in which order they are placed.

Having with these guidelines determined which messages are Mine and which have come from another source, the only question remaining is whether My messages will be heeded.

Most of My messages are not. Some, because they seem too good to be true. Others, because they seem too difficult to follow. Many, because they are simply misunderstood. Most, because they are not received.

My most powerful messenger is experience, and even this you ignore. Especially this you ignore.

Your world would not be in its present condition were you to have simply listened to your experience. The result of your not listening to your experience is that you keep re-living it, over and over again. For My purpose will not be thwarted, nor My will be ignored. You will get the message. Sooner or later.

I will not force you to, however. I will never coerce you. For I have given you a free will—the power to do as you choose—and I will never take that away from you, ever.

And so I will continue sending you the same messages over and over again, throughout the millennia and to whatever corner of the

14

universe you occupy. Endlessly will I send you My messages, until you have received them and held them close, calling them your own.

My messages will come in a hundred forms, at a thousand moments, across a million years. You cannot miss them if you truly listen. You cannot ignore them once truly heard. Thus will our communication begin in earnest. For in the past you have only talked *to* Me, praying to Me, interceding with Me, beseeching Me. Yet now can I talk *back* to you, even as I am doing here.

How can I know this communication is from God? How do I know this is not my own imagination?

What would be the difference? Do you not see that I could just as easily work through your imagination as anything else? I will bring you the *exact* right thoughts, words or feelings, at any given moment, suited precisely to the purpose at hand, using one device, or several.

You will know these words are from Me because you, of your own accord, have never spoken so clearly. Had you already spoken so clearly on these questions, you would not be asking them.

To whom does God communicate? Are there special people? Are there special times?

All people are special, and all moments are golden. There is no person and there is no time one more special than another. Many people choose to believe that God communicates in special ways and only with special people. This removes the mass of the people from responsibility for hearing My message, much less *receiving* it (which is another matter), and allows them to take someone else's word for everything. You don't *have* to listen to Me, for you've already decided that others have heard from Me on every subject, and you have *them* to listen to.

By listening to what *other* people think they heard Me say, *you* don't have to *think at all*.

This is the biggest reason for most people turning from My messages on a personal level. If you acknowledge that you are receiving My messages *directly*, then you are responsible for interpreting them. It is far safer and much easier to accept the interpretation of others (even others who have lived 2,000 years ago) than seek to interpret the message you may very well be receiving in this moment now.

Yet I invite you to a new form of communication with God. A *two-way* communication. In truth, it is you who have invited Me. For I have come to you, in this form, right now, in *answer to your call.*

Why do some people, take Christ, for example, seem to hear more of Your communication than others?

Because some people are willing to actually listen. They are willing to hear, and they are willing to remain *open* to the communication even when it seems scary, or crazy, or downright wrong.

We should listen to God even when what's being said seems wrong?

Especially when it seems wrong. If you think you are right about everything, who needs to talk with God?

Go ahead and act on all that you know. But notice that you've all been doing that since time began. And look at what shape the world is in. Clearly, you've missed something. Obviously, there is something you don't understand. That which you *do* understand must seem right to you, because "right" is a term you use to designate something with which you agree. What you've missed will, therefore, appear at first to be "wrong."

The only way to move forward on this is to ask yourself, "What would happen if everything I thought was 'wrong' was actually 'right'?" Every great scientist knows about this. When what a scientist does is not working, a scientist sets aside all of the assumptions and starts over. All great discoveries have been made from a willingness, and ability, to *not be right*. And that's what's needed here.

You cannot know God until you've stopped telling yourself that you *already* know God. You cannot hear God until you stop thinking that you've already heard God.

I cannot tell you My Truth until you stop telling Me yours.

But my truth about God comes from *You*.

Who said so?

Others.

What others?

Leaders. Ministers. Rabbis. Priests. Books. The *Bible*, for heaven's sake!

Those are not authoritative sources.

They *aren't*?

No.

Then what *is*?

Listen to your *feelings*. Listen to your Highest Thoughts. Listen to your experience. Whenever any one of these differ from what you've been told by your teachers, or read in your books, forget the words. *Words are the least reliable purveyor of Truth.*

There is so much I want to say to You, so much I want to ask. I don't know where to begin.

For instance, why is it that You do not reveal Yourself? If there really is a God, and You are It, why do You not reveal Yourself in a way we can all understand?

I have done so, over and over. I am doing so again right now.

No. I mean by a method of revelation that is incontrovertible; that cannot be denied.

Such as?

Such as appearing right now before my eyes.

I am doing so right now.

Where?

Everywhere you look.

No, I mean in an incontrovertible way. In a way no man could deny.

What way would that be? In what form or shape would you have Me appear?

In the form or shape that you actually have.

That would be impossible, for I have no form or shape you understand. I could *adopt* a form or shape that you *could* understand, but then everyone would assume that what they have seen is the one and only form and shape of God, rather than a form or shape of God—one of many.

People believe I am what they see Me as, rather than what they do *not* see. But I am the Great Unseen, not what I cause Myself to be in any particular moment. In a sense, I am what I *am not*. It is from the *am-notness* that I come, and to it I always return.

Yet when I come in one particular form or another—a form in which I think people can understand Me—people *assign Me that form forevermore.*

And should I come in any other form, to any other people, the first say I did not appear to the second, because I did not look to the second as I did to the first, nor say the same things—so how could it have been Me?

You see, then, it matters not in what form or in what manner I reveal Myself—*whatever* manner I choose and *whatever form* I take, *none* will be incontrovertible.

But if You did something that would evidence the truth of who You are beyond doubt or question . . .

. . . there are still those who would say, it is of the devil, or simply someone's imagination. Or any cause other than Me.

If I revealed myself as God Almighty, King of Heaven and Earth, and moved mountains to prove it, there are those who would say, "It must have been Satan."

And such is as it should be. For God does not reveal Godself to Godself from or through outward observation, but through inward experience. And when inward experience has revealed Godself, outward observation is not necessary. And if outward observation is necessary, inward experience is not possible.

If, then, revelation is requested, it cannot be had, for the act of asking is a statement that it is not there; that nothing of God is now being revealed. Such a statement produces the experience. For your thought about something is *creative*, and your word is *productive*, and your thought and your word together are magnificently effective in giving birth to your reality. Therefore shall you experience that *God is not now revealed*, for if God *were*, you would not *ask* God to be.

Does that mean I cannot ask for anything I want? Are You saying that praying for something actually *pushes it away from us*?

This is a question which has been asked through the Ages—and has been answered whenever it has been asked. Yet you have not heard the answer, or will not believe it.

The question is answered again, in today's terms, and today's language, thusly:

You will not have that for which you ask, nor can you have anything you want. This is because your very request is a statement of lack, and your saying you want a thing only works to produce that precise experience—wanting—in your reality.

The correct prayer is therefore never a prayer of supplication, but a prayer of gratitude.

When you thank God in advance for that which you choose to experience in your reality, you, in effect, acknowledge that it is there . . . *in effect*. Thankfulness is thus the most powerful statement to God; an affirmation that even before you ask, I have answered.

Therefore never supplicate. *Appreciate*.

But what if I am grateful to God in advance for something, and it never shows up? That could lead to disillusionment and bitterness.

Gratitude cannot be used as a tool with which to *manipulate* God; a *device* with which to fool the universe. You cannot lie to yourself. Your mind knows the truth of your thoughts. If you are saying "Thank you, God, for such and such," all the while being very clear that it isn't *there* in your present reality, you can't expect God to be *less clear* than you, and so produce it for you.

God knows what you know, and what you know is what appears as your reality.

But how then can I be truly grateful for something I *know is not there?*

Faith. If you have but the faith of a mustard seed, you shall move mountains. You come to know it is there because I *said* it is there; because I *said* that, even before you ask, I shall have answered; because I *said*, and have said to you in every conceivable way, through every teacher you can name, that whatsoever you shall choose, choosing it in My Name, so shall it be.

Yet so many people say that their prayers have gone unanswered.

No prayer—and a prayer is nothing more than a fervent statement of *what is so*—goes unanswered. Every prayer—every
thought, every statement, every feeling—is creative. To the degree
that it is fervently held as truth, to that degree will it be made manifest in your experience.

When it is said that a prayer has not been answered, what has
in actuality happened is that the most fervently held thought, word,
or feeling has become *operative*. Yet what you must know—and
here is the secret—is that always it is the thought behind the
thought—what might be called the Sponsoring Thought—that is
the controlling thought.

If, therefore, you beg and supplicate, there seems a much smaller chance that you will experience what you think you are
choosing, because the Sponsoring Thought behind every supplication is that you do *not have now* what you wish. *That Sponsoring
Thought becomes your reality.*

The only Sponsoring Thought which could override this thought
is the thought held in faith that God will grant whatever is asked,
without fail. Some people have such faith, but very few.

The process of prayer becomes much easier when, rather than
having to believe that God will always say "yes" to every request,
one understands intuitively that *the request itself is not necessary.
Then the prayer is a prayer of thanksgiving. It is not a request at all,
but a statement of gratitude for what is so.*

**When you say that a prayer is a statement of what is so, are you say-
ing that God does nothing; that everything which happens after a prayer
is a result of the *prayer's* action?**

If you believe that God is some omnipotent being who hears all
prayers, says "yes" to some, "no" to others, and "maybe, but not
now" to the rest, you are mistaken. By what rule of thumb would
God decide?

If you believe that God is the *creator and decider of all things* in
your life, you are mistaken.

God is the *observer*, not the creator. And God stands ready to
assist you in living your life, but not in the way you might expect.

*It is not God's function to create, or uncreate, the circumstances
or conditions of your life.* God created you, in the image and likeness of God. *You* have created the rest, through the power God has

given you. God created the process of life and life itself as you know it. Yet God gave you free choice, to do with life as you will.

In this sense, *your will for you is God's will for you.*

You are living your life the way you are living your life, and *I have no preference in the matter.*

This is the grand illusion in which you have engaged: that God *cares* one way or the other what you do.

I do *not* care what you do, and that is hard for you to hear. Yet do you care what your children do when you send them out to play? Is it a matter of consequence to you whether they play tag, or hide and seek, or pretend? No, it is not, because you know they are perfectly safe. You have placed them in an environment which you consider friendly and very okay.

Of course, you will always hope that they do not *hurt* themselves. And if they do, you will be right there to help them, heal them, allow them to feel safe again, to be happy again, to go and play again another day. But whether they choose hide and seek or pretend will not matter to you the next day, either.

You will tell them, of course, which games are dangerous to play. But you cannot stop your children from doing dangerous things. Not always. Not forever. Not in every moment from now until death. It is the wise parent who knows this. Yet the parent never stops caring about the *outcome*. It is this dichotomy—not caring deeply about the process, but caring deeply about the result—that comes close to describing the dichotomy of God.

Yet God, in a sense, does not even care about the outcome. Not the *ultimate outcome*. This is because the ultimate outcome is assured.

And this is the second great illusion of man: that the outcome of life is in doubt.

It is this doubt about ultimate outcome that has created your greatest enemy, which is fear. For if you doubt outcome, then you must doubt Creator—you must *doubt* God. And if you doubt God, you *must* live in fear and guilt all your life.

If you doubt God's intentions—and God's ability to produce this ultimate result—then how can you ever relax? How can you ever truly find peace?

Yet God has *full power* to match intentions with results. You cannot and will not believe in this (even though you claim that God is all-powerful), and so you have to create in your imagination a *power equal to God*, in order that you may find a way for *God's will to be thwarted*. And so you have created in your mythology the being you call "devil." You have even imagined a God at *war* with this being (thinking that God solves problems the way you do). Finally, you have actually imagined that God could *lose* this war.

All of this violates everything you say you know about God, but this doesn't matter. You live your illusion, and thus feel your fear, all out of your decision to doubt God.

But what if you made a new decision? What then would be the result?

I tell you this: you would live as the Buddha did. As Jesus did. As did every saint you have ever idolized.

Yet, as with most of those saints, people would not understand you. And when you tried to explain your sense of peace, your joy in life, your inner ecstasy, they would listen to your words, but not hear them. They would try to repeat your words, but would add to them.

They would wonder how you could have what they cannot find. And then they would grow jealous. Soon jealousy would turn to rage, and in their anger they would try to convince you that it is you who do not understand God.

And if they were unsuccessful at tearing you from your joy, they would seek to harm you, so enormous would be their rage. And when you told them it does not matter, that even death cannot interrupt your joy, nor change your truth, they would surely *kill* you. Then, when they saw the peace with which you accepted death, they would call you saint, and love you again.

For it is the nature of people to love, then destroy, then love again that which they value most.

But why? Why do we *do* that?

All human actions are motivated at their deepest level by one of two emotions—fear or love. In truth there are only two emotions—only two words in the language of the soul. These are the opposite ends of the great polarity which I created when I produced the universe, and your world, as you know it today.

These are the two points—the Alpha and the Omega—which allow the system you call "relativity" to be. Without these two points, without these two ideas about things, no other idea could exist.

Every human thought, and every human action, is based in either love or fear. There *is* no other human motivation, and all other ideas are but derivatives of these two. They are simply different versions—different twists on the same theme.

Think on this deeply and you will see that it is true. This is what I have called the Sponsoring Thought. It is either a thought of love or fear. This is the thought behind the thought *behind* the thought. It is the first thought. It is prime force. It is the raw energy that drives the engine of human experience.

And here is how human behavior produces repeat experience after repeat experience; it is why humans love, then destroy, then love again: always there is the swing from one emotion to the other. Love sponsors fear sponsors love sponsors fear . . .

. . . And the reason is found in the first lie—the lie which you hold as the truth about God—that God cannot be trusted; that God's love cannot be depended upon; that God's acceptance of you is conditional; that the ultimate outcome is thus in doubt. For if you cannot depend on *God's* love to always be there, on whose love *can* you depend? If God retreats and withdraws when you do not perform properly, will not mere mortals also?

. . . And so it is that in the moment you pledge your highest love, you greet your greatest fear.

For the first thing you worry about after saying "I love you" is whether you'll hear it back. And if you hear it back, then you begin immediately to worry that the love you have just found, you will lose. And so all action becomes a reaction—defense against loss— *even as you seek to defend yourself against the loss of God.*

Yet if you knew Who You Are—that you are the most magnificent, the most remarkable, the most splendid being God has ever created—you would never fear. For who could reject such wondrous magnificence? Not even God could find fault in such a being.

But you do not know Who You Are, and you think you are a great deal less. And where did you get the idea of how much less than magnificent you are? From the only people whose word you would take on *everything. From your mother and your father.*

These are the people who love you the most. Why would they lie to you? Yet have they not told you that you are too much of this, and not enough of that? Have they not reminded you that you are to be seen and not heard? Have they not scolded you in some of the moments of your greatest exuberance? And, did they not encourage you to set aside some of your wildest imagining?

These are the messages you've received, and though they do not meet the criteria, and are thus not messages from God, they might as well have been, for they have come from the gods of your universe surely enough.

It was your parents who taught you that love is conditional—you have felt their conditions many times—and that is the experience you take into your own love relationships.

It is also the experience you bring to Me.

From this experience you draw your conclusions about Me. Within this framework you speak your truth. "God is a loving God," you say, "but if you break His commandments, He will punish you with eternal banishment and everlasting damnation."

For have you not experienced the banishment of your own parents? Do you not know the pain of their damnation? How, then, could you imagine it to be any different with Me?

You have forgotten what it was like to be loved without condition. You do not remember the experience of the love of God. And so you try to imagine what God's love must be like, based on what you see of love in the world.

You have projected the role of "parent" onto God, and have thus come up with a God Who judges and rewards or punishes, based on how good He feels about what you've been up to. But this is a simplistic view of God, based on your mythology. It has nothing to do with Who I Am.

Having thus created an entire thought system about God based on human experience rather than spiritual truths, you then create an entire reality around love. It is a fear-based reality, rooted in the idea of a fearful, vengeful God. Its Sponsoring Thought is wrong, but to deny that thought would be to disrupt your whole theology. And though the new theology which would replace it would *truly* be your salvation, you cannot accept it, *because the idea of a God Who is not to be feared, Who will not judge, and Who has no cause to punish is simply too magnificent to be embraced within even your grandest notion of Who and What God is.*

This fear-based love reality dominates your experience of love; indeed, actually creates it. For not only do you see yourself *receiving* love which is conditional, you also watch yourself *giving* it in the same way. And even while you withhold and retreat and set your conditions, a part of you knows this is not what love really is. Still, you seem powerless to change the way you dispense it. You've learned the hard way, you tell yourself, and you'll be damned if you're going to leave yourself vulnerable again. Yet the truth is, you'll be damned if you don't.

[By your own (mistaken) thoughts about love do you damn yourself never to experience it purely. So, too, do you damn yourself never to know Me as I really am. Until you do. For you shall not be able to deny Me forever, and the moment will come for our Reconciliation.]

Every action taken by human beings is based in love or fear, not simply those dealing with relationships. Decisions affecting business, industry, politics, religion, the education of your young, the social agenda of your nations, the economic goals of your society, choices involving war, peace, attack, defense, aggression, submission; determinations to covet or give away, to save or to share, to unite or to divide—every single free choice you ever undertake arises out of one of the only two possible thoughts there are: a thought of love or a thought of fear.

Fear is the energy which contracts, closes down, draws in, runs, hides, hoards, harms.

Love is the energy which expands, opens up, sends out, stays, reveals, shares, heals.

Fear wraps our bodies in clothing, love allows us to stand naked. Fear clings to and clutches all that we have, love gives all that we have away. Fear holds close, love holds dear. Fear grasps, love lets go. Fear rankles, love soothes. Fear attacks, love amends.

Every human thought, word, or deed is based in one emotion or the other. You have no choice about this, because there is nothing else from which to choose. But you have free choice about which of these to select.

You make it sound so easy, and yet in the moment of decision fear wins more often than not. Why is that?

You have been taught to live in fear. You have been told about the survival of the fittest and the victory of the strongest and the success of the cleverest. Precious little is said about the glory of the most loving. And so you strive to be the fittest, the strongest, the cleverest—in one way or another—and if you see yourself as something less than this in any situation, you fear loss, for you have been told that to be less is to lose.

And so of course you choose the action fear sponsors, for that is what you have been taught. Yet I teach you this: when you choose the action love sponsors, then will you do more than survive, then will you do more than win, then will you do more than succeed. Then will you experience the full glory of Who You Really Are, and who you can be.

To do this you must turn aside the teachings of your well-meaning, but misinformed, worldly tutors, and *hear the teachings of those whose wisdom comes from another source.*

There are many such teachers among you, as always there have been, for I will not leave you without those who would show you, teach you, guide you, and remind you of these truths. Yet the greatest reminder is not anyone outside you, but the voice within you. This is the first tool that I use, because it is the most accessible.

The voice within is the loudest voice with which I speak, because it is the closest to you. It is the voice which tells you whether everything *else* is true or false, right or wrong, good or bad as you have defined it. It is the radar that sets the course, steers the ship, guides the journey if you but let it.

It is the voice which tells you right now whether the very words you are reading are words of love or words of fear. By this measure can you determine whether they are words to heed or words to ignore.

You said that when I always choose the action that love sponsors, then I will experience the full glory of who I am and who I can be. Will you expand on this please?

There is only one purpose for all of life, and that is for you and all that lives to experience fullest glory.

Everything else you say, think, or do is attendant to that function. There is nothing else for your soul to do, and nothing else your soul *wants* to do.

The wonder of this purpose is that it is never-ending. An ending is a limitation, and God's purpose is without such a boundary. Should there come a moment in which you experience yourself in your fullest glory, you will in that instant imagine an ever greater glory to fulfill. The more you are, the more you can become, and the more you can become, the more you can yet be.

The deepest secret is that life is not a process of discovery, but a process of creation.

You are not discovering yourself, but creating yourself anew. Seek, therefore, not to find out Who You Are, seek to determine Who You Want to Be.

There are those who say that life is a school, that we are here to learn specific lessons, that once we "graduate" we can go on to larger pursuits, no longer shackled by the body. Is this correct?

It is another part of your mythology, based on human experience.

Life is not a school?

No.

We are not here to learn lessons?

No.

Then why *are* we here?

To remember, and re-create, Who You Are.

I have told you, over and over again. You do not believe Me. Yet that is well as it should be. For truly, if you do not *create* yourself as Who You Are, that you cannot be.

Okay, You've lost me. Let's go back to this school bit. I've heard teacher after teacher tell us that life is a school. I'm frankly shocked to hear You deny that.

School is a place you go if there is something you do not know that you want to know. It is not a place you go if you already know a thing and simply want to *experience your knowingness*.

Life (as you call it) is an opportunity for you to *know experientially* what you already know *conceptually*. You need *learn nothing* to do this. You need merely remember what you already know, and *act on it*.

I'm not sure I understand.

Let's start here. The soul—your soul—knows all there is to know all the time. There's nothing hidden to it, nothing unknown. Yet knowing is not enough. The soul seeks to *experience*.

You can *know* yourself to be generous, but unless you *do* something which displays generosity, you have nothing but a concept. You can *know* yourself to be kind, but unless you *do* someone a kindness, you have nothing but an *idea* about yourself.

It is your soul's only desire to turn its grandest *concept* about itself into its greatest *experience*. Until concept becomes experience, all there is is speculation. I have been speculating about Myself for a long time. Longer than you and I could collectively remember. Longer than the age of this universe times the age of the universe. You see, then, how young is—how *new* is—My experience of Myself!

You've lost me again. Your experience of Yourself?

Yes. Let me explain it to you this way:

In the beginning, that which *Is* is all there was, and there was nothing else. Yet All That Is could not know itself—because All That Is is all there was, and there was *nothing else*. And so, All That Is . . . was *not*. For in the absence of something else, All That Is, is *not*.

This is the great Is/Not Is to which mystics have referred from the beginning of time.

Now All That Is *knew* it was all there was—but this was not enough, for it could only know its utter magnificence *conceptually*, not *experientially*. Yet the *experience* of itself is that for which it longed, for it wanted to know what it felt like to be so magnificent. Still, this was impossible, because the very term "magnificent" is a relative term. All That Is could not know what it *felt* like to be magnificent unless *that which is not* showed up. In the absence of *that which is not*, that which IS, is *not*.

Do you understand this?

I think so. Keep going.

Alright.

The one thing that All That Is knew is that there was *nothing else*. And so It could, and would, *never* know Itself from a reference point outside of Itself. Such a point did not exist. Only one reference point existed,! and that was the single place within. The "Is-Not Is."; The Am-NotAm.

Still, the All of Everything chose to know Itself *experientially*.

This *energy*—this pure, unseen, unheard, unobserved, and therefore unknown-by-anyone-else energy—chose to experience

Itself as the utter magnificence It was. In order to do this, It realized It would have to use a reference point *within*.

It reasoned, quite correctly, that any *portion* of Itself would necessarily have to be *less than the whole*, and that if It thus simply *divided* Itself into portions, each portion, being less than the whole, could look back on the rest of Itself and see magnificence.

And so All That Is divided Itself—becoming, in one glorious moment, that which is *this*, and that which is *that*. For the first time, *this* and *that* existed, quite apart from each other. And still, both existed simultaneously. As did all that was *neither*.

Thus, *three elements* suddenly existed: that which is *here*. That which is *there*. And that which is *neither here nor there*—but which *must exist* for *here and there* to exist.;

It is the nothing which holds the everything. It is the non-space which holds the space. It is the all which holds the parts.

Can you understand this?

Are you following this?!

I think I am, actually. Believe it or not, you have used such a clear illustration that I think I'm actually understanding this.

I'm going to go further. Now this *nothing* which holds the *everything* is what some people call God. Yet that is not accurate, either, for it suggests that there is something God is *not*—namely, everything that is not "nothing." But I am *All Things*—seen and unseen—so this description of Me as the Great Unseen—the No-Thing, or the Space Between, an essentially Eastern mystical definition of God, is no more accurate than the essentially Western practical description of God as all that is seen. Those who believe that God is All That Is *and* All That Is Not, are those whose understanding is correct.

Now in creating that which is "here" and that which is "there," God made it possible for God to know Itself. In the moment of this great explosion from within, God created *relativity*—the greatest gift God ever gave to Itself. Thus, *relationship* is the greatest gift God ever gave to you, a point to be discussed in detail later.

From the No-Thing thus sprang the Everything—a spiritual event entirely consistent, incidentally, with what your scientists call The Big Bang theory.

As the elements of all raced forth, *time* was created, for a thing was first *here*, then it was *there*—and the period it took to *get* from here to there was measurable.

Just as the parts of Itself which are seen began to define themselves, "relative" to each other, so, too, did the parts which are unseen.

God knew that for love to exist—and to know itself as *pure love*—its exact opposite had to exist as well. So God voluntarily created the great polarity—the absolute opposite of love—everything that love is not—what is now called fear. In the moment fear existed, love could exist *as a thing that could be experienced*.

It is this *creation of duality* between love and its opposite which humans refer to in their various mythologies as the *birth of evil*, the fall of Adam, the rebellion of Satan, and so forth.

Just as you have chosen to personify pure love as the character you call God, so have you chosen to personify abject fear as the character you call the devil.

Some on Earth have established rather elaborate mythologies around this event, complete with scenarios of battles and war, angelic soldiers and devilish warriors, the forces of good and evil, of light and dark.

This mythology has been mankind's early attempt to understand, and tell others in a way *they* could understand, a cosmic occurrence *of which the human soul is deeply aware, but of which the mind can barely conceive.*

In rendering the universe as a *divided version of Itself*, God produced, from pure energy, all that now exists—both seen and unseen.

In other words, not only was the physical universe thus created, *but the metaphysical universe as well*. The part of God which forms the second half of the Am/Not Am equation also exploded into an infinite number of units smaller than the whole. These energy units you would call spirits.

In some of your religious mythologies it is stated that "God the Father" had many spirit children. This parallel to the human experiences of life multiplying itself seems to be the only way the masses could be made to hold in reality the idea of the sudden appearance—the sudden existence—of countless spirits in the "Kingdom of Heaven."

In this instance, your mythical tales and stories are not so far from ultimate reality—for the endless spirits comprising the totality of Me *are*, in a cosmic sense, My offspring.

My divine purpose in dividing Me was to create sufficient parts of Me so that I could *know Myself experientially*. There is only one way for the Creator to know Itself experientially as the Creator, and that is to create. And so I gave to each of the countless parts of Me (to all of My spirit children) the *same power to create* which I have as the whole.

This is what your religions mean when they say that you were created in the "image and likeness of God." This doesn't mean, as some have suggested, that our physical bodies look alike (although God can adopt whatever physical form God chooses for a particular purpose). It does mean that our essence is the same. We are composed of the same stuff. We ARE the "same stuff"! With all the same properties and abilities—including the ability to create physical reality out of thin air.

My purpose in creating you, My spiritual offspring, was for Me to know Myself as God. I have no way to do that *save through you.* Thus it can be said (and has been, many times) that My purpose for you is that *you* should know yourself as *Me.*

This seems so amazingly simple, yet it becomes very complex—because there is only one way for you to know yourself as Me, and that is for you *first* to know yourself as *not Me.*

Now try to follow this—fight to keep up—because this gets very subtle here. Are you ready?

I think so.

Good. Remember, you've asked for this explanation. You've waited for it for years. You've asked for it in layman's terms, not theological doctrines or scientific theories.

Yes—I know what I've asked.

And having asked, so shall you receive.

Now, to keep things simple, I'm going to use your children of God mythological model as a basis for discussion, because it is a model with which you are familiar—and in many ways it is not that far off.

So let's go back to how this process of self-knowing must work.

There is one way I could have caused all of My spiritual children to know themselves as parts of Me—and that was simply to tell them. This I did. But you see, it was not enough for Spirit to simply know Itself as God, or part of God, or children of God, or inheritors of the kingdom (or whatever mythology you want to use).

As I've already explained, knowing something, and *experiencing* it, are two different things. Spirit longed to know Itself experientially (just as I did!). Conceptual awareness was not enough for you. So I devised a plan. It is the most extraordinary idea in all the universe—and the most spectacular collaboration. I say collaboration because *all of you are in it with Me.*

Under the plan, you as pure spirit would enter the physical universe just created. This is because *physicality* is the only way to know experientially what you know conceptually. It is, in fact, the reason I created the physical cosmos to begin with—and the system of relativity which governs it, and all creation.

Once in the physical universe, you, My spirit children, could experience what you know of yourself—but first, you had to *come to know the opposite.* To explain this simplistically, you cannot know yourself as tall unless and until you become aware of short. You cannot experience the part of yourself that you call fat unless you also come to know thin.

Taken to ultimate logic, you cannot experience yourself as what you are until you've encountered what you are *not.* This is the purpose of the theory of relativity, and all physical life. It is by that which you are *not* that you yourself are defined.

Now in the case of the ultimate knowing—in the case of knowing yourself as the Creator—you cannot *experience* your Self as creator unless and until you *create.* And you cannot create yourself until you *un-create* yourself. In a sense, you have to first "not be" in order to be. Do you follow?

I think. . . .

Stay with it.

Of course, there is no way for you to not be who and what you are—you simply *are* that (pure, creative spirit), have been always, and always will be. So, you did the next best thing. You *caused yourself to forget* Who You Really Are.

Upon entering the physical universe, you *relinquished your remembrance of yourself.* This allows you to *choose* to be Who You Are, rather than simply wake up in the castle, so to speak.

It is in the act of choosing to be, rather than simply being told that you are, a part of God that you *experience* yourself as being at total choice, which is what, by definition, God is. Yet how can you have a choice about something over which there *is* no choice? You cannot *not* be My offspring no matter how hard you try—but you can *forget*.

You are, have always been, and will always be, a *divine* part of the *divine whole, a member of the body.* That is why the act of rejoining the whole, of returning to God, is called *remembrance.* You actually choose to *re-member* Who You Really Are, or to join together with the various parts of you to experience the all of you—which is to say, the All of *Me.*

Your job on Earth, therefore, is not to *learn* (because you *already know*), but to *re-member* Who You Are. And to re-member who everyone else is. That is why a big part of your job is to remind others (that is, to *re-mind* them), so that they can re-member also.

All the wonderful spiritual teachers have been doing just that. It is *your* sole purpose. That is to say, your *soul purpose.*

My God, this is so simple—and so . . . *symmetrical*. I mean, it all fits *in!* It all suddenly *fits!* I see, now, a picture I have never quite put together before.

Good. That is good. That is the purpose of this dialogue. You have asked Me for answers. I have promised I would give them to you.

You will make of this dialogue a book, and you will render My words accessible to many people. It is part of your work. Now, you have many questions, many inquiries to make about life. We have here placed the foundation. We have laid the groundwork for other understandings. Let us go to these other questions. And do not worry. If there is something about what we've just gone through you do not thoroughly understand, it will all be clear to you soon enough.

There is so much I want to ask. There are so many questions. I suppose I should start with the big ones, the obvious ones. Like, why is the world in the shape it's in?

Of all the questions man has asked of God, this is the one asked most often. From the beginning of time man has asked it. From the first moment to this you have wanted to know, *why must it be like this?*

The classic posing of the question is usually something like: If God is all-perfect and all-loving, why would God create pestilence and famine, war and disease, earthquakes and tornados and hurricanes and all manner of natural disaster, deep personal disappointment, and worldwide calamity?

The answer to this question lies in the deeper mystery of the universe and the highest meaning of life.

I do not show My goodness by creating only what you call perfection all around you. I do not demonstrate My love by not allowing you to demonstrate yours.

As I have already explained, you cannot demonstrate love until you can demonstrate *not* loving. A thing cannot exist without its opposite, except in the world of the absolute. Yet the realm of the absolute was not sufficient for either you or Me. I existed there, in the always, and it is from where you, too, have come.

In the absolute there is no experience, only knowing. Knowing is a divine state, yet the grandest joy is in being. *Being* is achieved only after experience. The evolution is this: *knowing, experiencing, being.* This is the Holy Trinity—the Triune that is God.

God the Father is *knowing*—the parent of all understandings, the begetter of all experience, for you cannot experience that which you do not know.

God the Son is *experiencing*—the embodiment, the acting out, of all that the Father knows of Itself, for you cannot be that which you have not experienced.

God the Holy Spirit is *being*—the *dis*embodiment of all that the Son has experienced of Itself; the simple, exquisite is-ness possible only through the memory of the knowing and experiencing.

This simple being is bliss. It is God-state, after knowing and experiencing Itself. It is that for which God yearned in the beginning.

Of course, you are well past the point where you must have it explained to you that the father-son descriptions of God have nothing to do with gender. I use here the picturesque speech of your most recent scriptures. Much earlier holy writings placed this metaphor in a mother-daughter context. Neither is correct. Your mind can best hold the relationship as: parent-offspring. Or: that-which-gives-rise-to, and that-which-is-risen.

Adding the third part of the Trinity produces this relationship:

That which gives rise to / That which is risen / That which is.

This Triune Reality is God's signature. It is the divine pattern. The three-in-one is everywhere found in the realms of the sublime. You cannot escape it in matters dealing with time and space, God and consciousness, or any of the subtle relationships. On the other hand, you will *not* find the Triune Truth in any of life's gross relationships.

The Triune Truth is recognized in life's subtle relationships by everyone dealing with such relationships. Some of your religionists have described the Triune Truth as Father, Son, and Holy Ghost. Some of your psychiatrists use the terms superconscious, conscious, and subconscious. Some of your spiritualists say mind, body, and spirit. Some of your scientists see energy, matter, ether. Some of your philosophers say a thing is not true for you until it is true in thought, word, and deed. When discussing time, you speak of three times only: past, present, future. Similarly, there are three moments in your perception—before, now, and after. In terms of spatial relationships, whether considering the points in the universe, or various points in your own room, you recognize here, there, and the space in between.

In matters of gross relationships, you recognize *no* "in-between." That is because gross relationships are always dyads, whereas relationships of the higher realm are invariably triads. Hence, there is left-right, up-down, big-small, fast-slow, hot-cold, and the greatest dyad ever created: male-female. There are no *in-betweens* in these dyads. A thing is either *one thing or the other,* or some greater or lesser *version* in relationship to one of these polarities.

Within the realm of gross relationships, nothing conceptualized can exist without a conceptualization of its *opposite*. Most of your day-to-day experience is foundationed in this reality.

Within the realm of sublime relationships nothing which exists *has* an opposite. All Is One, and everything progresses from one to the other in a never-ending circle.

Time is such a sublime realm, in which what you call past, present, and future exist *inter-relationally.* That is, they are not *opposites,* but rather parts of the same whole; progressions of the same idea; cycles of the same energy; aspects of the same immutable Truth. If you conclude from this that past, present, and future exist at one and the same "time," you are right. (Yet now is not the moment to discuss that. We can get into this in much greater detail when we explore the whole concept of time—which we will do later.)

The world is the way it is because it could not be any *other* way and still exist in the gross realm of physicality. Earthquakes and hurricanes, floods and tornados, and events that you call natural disasters are but movements of the elements from one polarity to the other. The whole birth-death cycle is part of this movement. These are the rhythms of life, and everything in gross reality is subject to them, because life *itself* is a rhythm. It is a wave, a vibration, a pulsation at the very heart of the All That Is.

Illness and disease are opposites of health and wellness, and are made manifest in your reality at your behest. You cannot be ill without at some level causing yourself to be, and you can be well again in a moment by simply deciding to be. Deep personal disappointments are responses which are chosen, and worldwide calamities are the result of worldwide consciousness.

Your question infers that I choose these events, that it is My will and *desire* they should occur. *Yet I do not will these things into being, I merely observe you doing so.* And I do nothing to stop them, because to do so would be to *thwart your will.* That, in turn, would deprive you of the God experience, which is the experience you and I have chosen together.

Do not condemn, therefore, all that you would call bad in the world. Rather, ask yourself, what about this have you judged bad, and what, if anything, you wish to do to change it.

Inquire within, rather than without, asking: "What part of my Self do I wish to experience now in the face of this calamity? What aspect of being do I choose to call forth?" For all of life exists as a tool of your own creation, and all of its events merely present themselves as opportunities for you to decide, and be, Who You Are.

This is true for *every* soul, and so you see there are no victims in the universe, only creators. The Masters who have walked this planet all knew this. That is why, no matter which Master you might name, none imagined themselves to be victimized—though many were truly crucified.

Each soul is a Master—though some do not remember their origins or their heritages. Yet each creates the situation and the circumstance for its own highest purpose and its own quickest remembering—in each moment called now.

Judge not, then, the karmic path walked by another. *Envy not success, nor pity failure, for you know not what is success or failure in the soul's reckoning.* Call not a thing calamity, nor joyous event, until you decide, or witness, how it is *used.* For is a death a calamity if it saves the lives of thousands? And is a life a joyous event if it has caused nothing but grief? Yet even this you should not judge, but keep always your own counsel, and allow others theirs.

This does not mean ignore a call for help, nor the urging of your own soul to work toward the change of some circumstance or condition. It does mean avoiding labels and judgment while you do whatever you do. For each circumstance is a gift, and in each experience is hidden a treasure.

There once was a soul who knew itself to be the light. This was a new soul, and so, anxious for experience. "I am the light," it said. "I am the light." Yet all the knowing of it and all the saying of it could not substitute for the experience of it. And in the realm from which this soul emerged, there was nothing *but* the light. *Every* soul was grand, every soul was magnificent, and every soul shone with the brilliance of My awesome light. And so the little soul in question was as a candle in the sun. In the midst of the grandest light—of which it was a part—it could not see itself, nor experience itself as Who and What it Really Is.

Now it came to pass that this soul yearned and yearned to know itself. And so great was its yearning that I one day said, "Do you know, Little One, what you must do to satisfy this yearning of yours?"

"Oh, what, God? What? I'll do *anything*!" The little soul said.

"You must separate yourself from the rest of us," I answered, "and then you must call upon yourself the darkness."

"What is the darkness, o Holy One?" the little soul asked.

"That which you are not," I replied, and the soul understood.

And so this the soul did, removing itself from the All, yea, going even unto another realm. And in this realm the soul had the power to call into its experience all sorts of darkness. And this it did.

Yet in the midst of all the darkness did it cry out, "Father, Father, why hast Thou forsaken me?" Even as have you in your blackest times. Yet I have never forsaken you, but stand by you always, ready to remind you of Who You Really Are; ready, always ready, to call you home.

Therefore, be a light unto the darkness, and curse it not.

And forget not Who You Are in the moment of your encirclement by that which you are not. But do you praise to the creation, even as you seek to change it.

And know that what you do in the time of your greatest trial can be your greatest triumph. For the experience you create is a statement of Who You Are—and Who You Want to Be.

I have told you this story—the parable of the little soul and the sun—so that you might better understand why the world is the way it is—and how it can change in an instant the moment everyone remembers the divine truth of their highest reality.

Now there are those who say that life is a school, and that these things which you observe and experience in your life are for your learning. I have addressed this before, and I tell you again:

You came into this life with nothing to learn—you have only to demonstrate what you already know. In the demonstration of it will you function it out, and create yourself anew, through your experience. Thus do you justify life, and give it purpose. Thus do you render it holy.

Are you saying that all the bad things that happen to us are things of our own choosing? Do you mean that even the world's calamities and disasters are, at some level, created by us so that we can "experience the opposite of Who We Are"? And, if so, isn't there some less painful way—less painful to ourselves and others—to create opportunities for us to experience ourselves?

You've asked several questions, and they are all good ones. Let's take them one at a time.

No, not all the things which you call bad which happen to you are of your own choosing. Not in the conscious sense—which you mean. They *are* all of your own *creation*.

You are *always* in the process of *creating*. Every moment. Every minute. Every day. *How* you can create we'll go into later. For now, just take my word for it—you are a big creation machine, and you are turning out a new manifestation literally as fast as you can think.

Events, occurrences, happenings, conditions, circumstances—all are created out of consciousness. Individual consciousness is powerful enough. You can imagine what kind of creative energy is unleashed whenever two or *more* are gathered in My name. And *mass* consciousness? Why, *that* is so powerful it can create events and circumstances of worldwide import and planetary consequences.

It would not be accurate to say—not in the way *you* mean it—that *you* are *choosing* these consequences. You are not choosing them anymore than I am choosing them. Like Me, you are observing them. And deciding Who You Are *with regard to them*.

Yet there are no victims in the world, and no villains. And neither are you a victim of the choices of others.

At some level you have *all* created that which you say you detest—and, having created it, you have *chosen* it.

This is an advanced level of thinking, and it is one which all Masters reach sooner or later. For it is only when they can accept responsibility for *all* of it that they can achieve the power to change *part* of it.

So long as you entertain the notion that there is something or someone else out there "doing it" to you, you disempower yourself to do anything about it. Only when you say "I *did* this" can you find the power to change it.

It is much easier to change what you are doing than to change what another is doing.

The first step in changing *anything* is to know and accept that you have chosen it to be what it is. If you can't accept this on a personal level, agree to it through your understanding that We are all One. Seek then to create change not because a thing is wrong, but because it no longer makes an accurate statement of Who You Are.

There is only one reason to do anything: as a statement to the universe of Who You Are.

Used in this way, life becomes Self creative. You use life to create your *Self* as Who You Are, and Who You've Always Wanted to Be. There is also only one reason to *un*-do anything: because it is *no longer* a statement of Who You Want to Be. It does not reflect you. It does not represent you. (That is, it does not *re-present* you. . . .)

If you wish to be accurately re-presented, *you must work to change anything in your life which does not fit into the picture of you that you wish to project into eternity.*

In the largest sense, all the "bad" things that happen *are* of your choosing. The mistake is not in choosing them, but in calling them bad. For in calling them bad, you call your Self bad, since you created them.

This label you cannot accept, so rather than label your Self bad, you *disown your own creations*. It is this intellectual and spiritual dishonesty which lets you accept a world in which conditions are as they are. If you had to accept—or even felt a deep inner sense of—*personal responsibility* for the world, it would be a far different place. This would *certainly* be true if *everyone* felt responsible. That this is so patently obvious is what makes it so utterly painful, and so poignantly ironic.

The world's natural calamities and disasters—its tornados and hurricanes, volcanoes and floods—its physical turmoils—are not created by you specifically. What *is* created by you is the degree to which these events touch your life.

Events occur in the universe which no stretch of the imagination could claim you instigated or created.

These events are created by the combined consciousness of man. All of the world, co-creating together, produces these experiences. What each of you do, individually, is move through them, deciding what, if anything, they mean to you, and Who and What You Are in relationship to them.

Thus, you create collectively, and individually, the life and times you are experiencing, for the soul purpose of evolving.

You've asked if there is a less painful way to undergo this process—and the answer is yes—yet nothing in your outward experience will have changed. The way to reduce the pain which you associate with earthly experiences and events—both yours and those of others—is *to change the way you behold them.*

You cannot change the outer event (for that has been created by the lot of you, and you are not grown enough in your consciousness to alter individually that which has been created collectively), so you must change the inner experience. This is the road to mastery in living.

Nothing is painful in and of itself. Pain is a result of wrong thought. It is an error in thinking.

A Master can disappear the most grievous pain. In this way, the Master heals.

Pain results from a judgment you have made about a thing. Remove the judgment and the pain disappears.

Judgment is often based upon previous experience. Your idea about a thing derives from a prior idea about that thing. Your prior idea results from a still prior idea—and that idea from another, and so forth, like building blocks, until you get all the way back in the hall of mirrors to what I call first thought.

All thought is creative, and no thought is more powerful than original thought. That is why this is sometimes also called original sin.

Original sin is when your first thought about a thing is in error. That error is compounded many times over when you have a second or third thought about a thing. It is the job of the Holy Spirit to inspire you to new understandings, which can free you from your mistakes.

Are you saying that I shouldn't feel bad about the starving children of Africa, the violence and injustice in America, the earthquake that kills hundreds in Brazil?

There are no "shoulds" or "shouldn'ts" in God's world. Do what you want to do. Do what reflects you, what re-presents you as a grander version of your Self. If you want to feel bad, feel bad.

But judge not, and neither condemn, for you know not why a thing occurs, nor to what end.

And remember you this: that which you condemn will condemn you, and that which you judge, you will one day become.

Rather, seek to change those things—or support others who are changing those things—which no longer reflect your highest sense of Who You Are.

Yet, bless all—for all is the creation of God, through life living, and that is the highest creation.

Could we just stop here for a moment and let me catch my breath? Did I hear you say there are no "shoulds" or "should nots" in God's world?

That is correct.

How can that be? If there are none in *Your* world, where *would* they be?

Indeed—where. . . ?

I repeat the question. Where else would "shoulds" and "should nots" appear, if not in Your world?

In your *imagination*.

But those who have taught me all about the rights and wrongs, the dos and don'ts, the shoulds and shouldn'ts, told me all those rules were laid down by *You*—by God.

Then those who taught you were wrong. I have never set down a "right" or "wrong," a "do" or a "don't." To do so would be to strip you completely of your greatest gift—the opportunity to do as you please, and experience the results of that; the chance to create yourself anew in the image and likeness of Who You Really Are; the space to produce a reality of a higher and higher you, based on your grandest idea of what it is of which you are capable.

To say that something—a thought, a word, an action—is "wrong" would be as much as to tell you not to do it. To tell you not to do it would be to prohibit you. To prohibit you would be to restrict you. To restrict you would be to deny the reality of Who You Really Are, as well as the opportunity for you to create and experience that truth.

There are those who say that I have given you free will, yet these same people claim that if you do not obey Me, I will send you to hell. What kind of free will is that? Does this not make a mockery of God—to say nothing of any sort of true relationship between us?

Well, now we're getting into another area I wanted to discuss, and that's this whole business about heaven and hell. From what I'm gathering here, there is no such thing as hell.

There is hell, but it is not what you think, and you do not experience it for the reasons you have been given.

What is hell?

It is the experience of the worst possible outcome of your choices, decisions, and creations. It is the natural consequence of any thought which denies Me, or says no to Who You Are in relationship to Me.

It is the pain you suffer through wrong thinking. Yet even the term "wrong thinking" is a misnomer, because there is no such thing as that which is wrong.

Hell is the opposite of joy. It is unfulfillment. It is knowing Who and What You Are, and failing to experience that. It is being *less*. That is hell, and there is none greater for your soul.

But hell does not exist as this *place* you have fantasized, where you burn in some everlasting fire, or exist in some state of everlasting torment. What purpose could I have in that?

Even if I did hold the extraordinarily unGodly thought that you did not "deserve" heaven, why would I have a need to seek some kind of revenge, or punishment, for your failing? Wouldn't it be a simple matter for Me to just dispose of you? What vengeful part of

Me would require that I subject you to eternal suffering of a type and at a level beyond description?

If you answer, the need for justice, would not a simple denial of communion with Me in heaven serve the ends of justice? Is the unending infliction of pain also required?

I tell you there *is* no such experience after death as you have constructed in your fear-based theologies. Yet there is an experience of the soul so unhappy, so incomplete, so less than whole, so *separated* from God's greatest joy, that to your soul this would *be* hell. But I tell you *I* do not *send* you there, nor do I cause this experience to be visited upon you. You, yourself, create the experience, whenever and however you separate your Self from your own highest thought about you. You, yourself, create the experience, whenever you deny your Self; whenever you reject Who and What You Really Are.

Yet even this experience is never eternal. It *cannot* be, for it is not My plan that you shall be separated from Me forever and ever. Indeed, such a thing is impossibility—for to achieve such an event, not only would *you* have to deny Who You Are—I would have to as well. This I will never do. And so long as one of us holds the truth about you, the truth about you shall ultimately prevail.

But if there is no hell, does that mean I can do what I want, act as I wish, commit any act, without fear of retribution?

Is it *fear* that you need in order to be, do, and have what is intrinsically right? Must you be *threatened* in order to "be good"? And what is "being good"? Who gets to have the final say about that? Who sets the guidelines? Who makes the rules?

I tell you this: *You* are your own rule-maker. You set the guidelines. And *you* decide how well you have done; how well you are doing. For you are the one who has decided Who and What You Really Are—and Who You Want to Be. And *you* are the *only* one who can assess how well you're doing.

No one else will judge you ever, for why, and how, could God judge God's own creation and call it bad? If I wanted you to be and do everything perfectly, I would have left you in the state of total perfection whence you came. The whole point of the process was for you to discover yourself, *create* your Self, as you truly are—and as you truly wish to be. Yet you could not be that unless you also had a choice to *be something else.*

Should I therefore punish you for making a choice that I Myself have laid before you? If I did not want you to make the second choice, why would I create other than the first?

This is a question you must ask yourself before you would assign Me the role of a condemning God.

The direct answer to your question is, yes, you may do as you wish without fear of retribution. It may serve you, however, to be aware of consequences.

Consequences are results. Natural outcomes. These are not at all the same as retributions, or punishments. Outcomes are simply that. They are what results from the natural application of natural laws. They are that *which* occurs, quite predictably, as a consequence of what *has* occurred.

All physical life functions in accordance with natural laws. Once you remember these laws, and apply them, you have mastered life at the physical level.

What seems like punishment to you—or what you would call evil, or bad luck—is nothing more than a natural law asserting itself.

Then if I were to know these laws, and obey them, I would never have a moment's trouble again. Is that what you're telling me?

You would never experience your Self as being in what you call "trouble." You would not understand any life situation to be a problem. You would not encounter any circumstance with trepidation. You would put an end to all worry, doubt, and fear. You would live as you fantasize Adam and Eve lived—not as disembodied spirits in the realm of the absolute, but as embodied spirits in the realm of the relative. Yet you would have all the freedom, all the joy, all the peace, and all the wisdom, understanding and power of the Spirit you are. You would be a fully realized being.

This is the goal of your soul. This is its purpose—to fully realize itself while in the body; to become the *embodiment* of all that it really is.

This is My plan for you. This is My ideal: that I should become realized through you. That thus, concept is turned into experience, that I might know my Self *experientially*.

The Laws of the Universe are laws that I laid down. They are perfect laws, creating perfect function of the physical.

Have you ever seen anything more perfect than a snowflake? Its intricacy, its design, its symmetry, its conformity to itself and originality from all else—all are a mystery. You wonder at the miracle of this awesome display of Nature. Yet if I can do this with a single snowflake, what think you I can do—have *done*—with the universe?

Were you to see the symmetry of it, the perfection of its design—from the largest body to the smallest particle—you would not be able to hold the truth of it in your reality. Even now, as you get glimpses of it, you cannot yet imagine or understand its implications. Yet you can know there are implications—far more complex and far more extraordinary than your present comprehension can embrace. Your Shakespeare said it wonderfully: *There are more things in Heaven and Earth, Horatio, than are dreamt of in your philosophy.*

Then how can I know these laws? How can I learn them?

It is not a question of learning, but of remembering.

How can I remember them?

Begin by being still. Quiet the outer world, so that the inner world might bring you sight. This in-*sight* is what you seek, yet you cannot have it while you are so deeply concerned with your outer reality. Seek, therefore, to go within as much as possible. And when you are not going within, come *from* within as you deal with the outside world. Remember this axiom:

If you do not go within, you go without.

Put it in the first person as you repeat it, to make it more personal:

> If I do not
> go within
> I
> *go without*

You have been going without all your life. Yet you do not have to, and never did.

There is nothing you cannot be, there is nothing you cannot do. There is. nothing you cannot have.

That sounds like a pie-in-the-sky promise.

What other kind of promise would you have God make? Would you believe Me if I promised you less?

For thousands of years people have disbelieved the promises of God for the most extraordinary reason: they were too good to be true. So you have chosen a lesser promise—a lesser love. For the highest promise of God proceeds from the highest love. Yet you cannot conceive of a perfect love, and so a perfect promise is also inconceivable. As is a perfect person. Therefore you cannot believe even in your Self.

Failing to believe in any of this means failure to believe in God. For belief in God produces belief in God's greatest gift—unconditional love—and God's greatest promise—unlimited potential.

May I interrupt you here? I hate to interrupt God when He's on a roll . . . but I've heard this talk of unlimited potential before, and it doesn't square with the human experience. Forget the difficulties encountered by the average person—what about the challenges of those born with mental or physical limitations? Is *their* potential unlimited?

You have written so in your own Scripture—in many ways and in many places.

Give me one reference.

Look to see what you have written in Genesis, chapter 11, verse 6, of your Bible.

It says, "And the Lord said, 'Behold, the people are one, and they have all one language; and this is only the beginning of what they will do: and now nothing will be restrained from them, which they have imagined to do.'"

Yes. Now, can you trust that?

That does not answer the question of the feeble, the infirm, the handicapped, those who are limited.

Do you think they are limited, as you put it, not of their choice? Do you imagine that a human soul encounters life challenges—*whatever* they may be—by *accident*? Is *this* your imagining?

Do you mean a soul chooses what kind of life it will experience ahead of time?

No, that would defeat the *purpose* of the encounter. The purpose is to *create* your experience—and thus, create your *Self*—in the glorious moment of Now. You do not, therefore, choose the life you will experience ahead of time.

You may, however, select the persons, places, and events—the conditions and circumstances, the challenges and obstacles, the opportunities and options—with which to *create* your experience. You may select the colors for your palette, the tools for your chest, the machinery for your shop. What you create with these is your business. That *is* the business of life.

Your potential *is* unlimited in all that you've chosen to do. Do not assume that a soul which has incarnated in a body which you call limited has not reached its full potential, for you do not know what that soul was *trying to do*. You do not understand its *agenda*. You are unclear as to its *intent*.

Therefore *bless every* person and condition, and give thanks. Thus you affirm the perfection of God's creation—and show your faith in it. For nothing happens by accident in God's world, and there is no such thing as coincidence. Nor is the world buffeted by random choice, or something you call fate.

If a snowflake is utterly perfect in its design, do you not think the same could be said about something as magnificent as your life?

But even Jesus healed the sick. Why would he heal them if their condition was so "perfect"?

Jesus did not heal those he healed because he saw their condition as imperfect. He healed those he healed because he saw those souls asking for healing as part of their process. He saw the perfection of the process. He recognized and understood the soul's intention. Had Jesus felt that all illness, mental or physical, represented imperfection, would he not have simply healed everyone on the planet, all at once? Do you doubt that he could do this?

No. I believe he could have.

Good. Then the mind begs to know: Why did he not do it? Why would the Christ choose to have some suffer, and others be healed? For that matter, why does God allow any suffering at anytime? This question has been asked before, and the answer remains the same. There is perfection in the process—and all life arises out of *choice*. It is not appropriate to interfere with choice, nor to question it. It is particularly inappropriate to condemn it.

What *is* appropriate is to observe it, and then to do whatever might be done to assist the soul in seeking and making a *higher choice*. Be watchful, therefore, of the choices of others, but not judgmental. Know that their choice is perfect for them in this moment now—yet stand ready to assist them should the moment come when they seek a newer choice, a different choice—a higher choice.

Move into communion with the souls of others, and their purpose, their intention, will be clear to you. This is what Jesus did with those he healed—and with *all* those whose lives he touched. Jesus healed all those who came to him, or who sent others to him supplicating for them. He did not perform a random healing. To have done so would have been to violate a sacred Law of the Universe:

Allow each soul to walk its path.

But does that mean we must not help anyone without being asked? Surely not, or we would never be able to help the starving children of India, or the tortured masses of Africa, or the poor, or the downtrodden anywhere. All humanitarian effort would be lost, all charity forbidden. Must we wait for an individual to cry out to us in desperation, or for a nation of people to plead for help, before we are allowed to do what is obviously right?

You see, the question answers itself. If a thing is obviously right, do it. But remember to exercise extreme judgment regarding what you call "right" and "wrong."

A thing is only right or wrong because you say it is. A thing is not right or wrong intrinsically.

It isn't?

"Rightness" or "wrongness" is not an intrinsic condition, it is a subjective judgment in a personal value system. By your subjective judgments do you create your Self—by your personal values do you determine and demonstrate Who You Are.

The world exists exactly as it is so that you may make these judgments. If the world existed in perfect condition, your life process of Self creation would be terminated. It would end. A lawyer's career would end tomorrow were there no more litigation. A doctor's career would end tomorrow were there no more illness. A philosopher's career would end tomorrow were there no more questions.

And God's *career* would end tomorrow were there *no more problems!*

Precisely. You have put it perfectly. We, all of us, would be through creating were there nothing more to create. We, all of us, have a vested interest in *keeping the game going*. Much as we all say we would like to solve all the problems, we dare not solve *all* the problems, or there will be nothing left for us to do.

Your industrial-military complex understands this very well. That is why it opposes mightily any attempt to install a war-no-more government—anywhere.

Your medical establishment understands this, too. That is why it staunchly opposes—it *must*, it *has to* for its own survival—any new miracle drug or cure—to say nothing of the possibility of miracles themselves.

Your religious community also holds this clarity. That is why it attacks uniformly any definition of God which does not include fear, judgment and retribution, and any definition of Self which does not include *their own idea of the only path to God.*

If I say to you, you *are* God—where does that leave religion? If I say to you, you *are* healed, where does that leave science, and medicine? If I say to you, you shall live in peace, where does that leave the peacemakers? If I say to you, the world is fixed—where does that leave the world?

What, now, of plumbers?

The world is filled with essentially two kinds of people: those who give you things you want, and those who fix things. In a sense, even those who simply give you things you want—the butchers, the bakers, the, candlestick makers—are also fixers. For to have a desire for something is often to have a *need* for it. That is why addicts are said to need a *fix*. Be careful, therefore, that desire not become *addiction*.

Are you saying the world will always have problems? Are you saying that you actually *want it that way?*

I am saying that the world exists the way it exists—just as a snowflake exists the way it exists—quite by design. *You* have created it that way—just as you have created your life exactly as it is.

I want what *you* want. The day you really want an end to hunger, there will be no more hunger. I have given you all the resources with which to do that. You have all the tools with which to make that choice. You have not made it. Not because you *cannot* make it. The world could end world hunger tomorrow. You *choose* not to make it.

You claim that there are good reasons that 40,000 people a day must die of hunger. There are no good reasons. Yet at a time when you say you can do nothing to stop 40,000 people a day from dying of hunger, you bring 50,000 people a day into your world to begin a new life. And this you call love. This you call God's plan. It is a plan which totally lacks logic or reason, to say nothing of compassion.

I am showing you in stark terms that the world exists the way it exists because *you have chosen for it to*. You are systematically destroying your own environment, then pointing to so-called natural disasters as evidence of God's cruel hoax, or Nature's harsh ways. You have played the hoax on yourself, and it is your ways which are cruel.

Nothing, *nothing* is more gentle than Nature. And nothing, *nothing* has been more cruel to Nature than man. Yet you step aside from all involvement in this; deny all responsibility. It is not your fault, you say, and in this you are right. It is not a question of *fault*, it is a matter of *choice*.

You can choose to end the destruction of your rain forests tomorrow. You can choose to stop depleting the protective layer hovering over your planet. You can *choose* to discontinue the ongoing onslaught of your earth's ingenious ecosystem. You can seek to put the snowflake back together—or at least to halt its inexorable melting—but will you do it?

You can similarly end *all war tomorrow*. Simply. Easily. All it takes—all it has *ever* taken—is for all of you to agree. Yet if *you* cannot all agree on something as basically simple as ending the killing of each other, how can you call upon the heavens with shaking fist to put your life in order?

I will do nothing for you that you will not do for your Self. *That* is the law and the prophets.

The world is in the condition it is in because of *you*, and the choices you have made—or failed to make.

(Not to decide is to decide.)

The Earth is in the shape it's in because of *you*, and the choices you have made—or failed to make.

Your own life is the way it is because of *you*, and the choices you have made—or failed to make.

But I did not choose to get hit by that truck! I did not choose to get mugged by that robber, or raped by that maniac. People could say that. There are people in the world who could say that.

You are *all* at root cause for the conditions which exist which create in the robber the desire, or the perceived need, to steal. You have all created the consciousness which makes rape possible. It is when you *see in yourself* that which caused the crime that you begin, at last, to heal the condition from which it sprang.

Feed your hungry, give dignity to your poor. Grant opportunity to your less fortunate. End the prejudice which keeps masses huddled and angry, with little promise of a better tomorrow. Put away your pointless taboos and restrictions upon sexual energy—rather, help others to truly understand its wonder, and to channel it properly. Do *these* things and you will go a long way toward ending robbery and rape forever.

As for the so-called "accident"—the truck coming around the bend, the brick falling from the sky—learn to greet each such incident as a small part of a larger mosaic. You have come here to work out an individual plan for your own salvation. Yet salvation does not mean saving yourself from the snares of the devil. There is no such thing as the devil, and hell does not exist. You are saving yourself from the oblivion of non-realization.

You cannot lose in this battle. You cannot fail. Thus it is not a battle at all, but simply a process. Yet if you do not know this, you will see it as a constant struggle. You may even *believe in the struggle* long enough to create a whole religion around it. This religion will teach that *struggle is the point of it all*. This is a false teaching. It is in *not* struggling that the process proceeds. It is in surrendering that the victory is won.

Accidents happen because they do. Certain elements of the life process have come together in a particular way at a particular time, with particular results—results which you choose to call unfortunate, for your own particular reasons. Yet they may not be unfortunate at all, given the agenda of your soul.

I tell you this: There *is* no coincidence, and *nothing* happens "by accident." Each event and adventure is called *to* your Self *by* your Self in order that you might create and experience Who You Really Are. All true Masters know this. That is why mystic Masters remain unperturbed in the face of the worst experiences of life (as *you* would define them).

The great teachers of your Christian religion understand this. They know that Jesus was not perturbed by the crucifixion, but expected it. He could have walked away, but he did not. He could have stopped the process at any point. He had that power. Yet he did not. He *allowed himself to be crucified* in order that he might stand as man's eternal salvation. *Look*, he said, *at what I can do*. Look at what is *true*. And know that these things, and more, shall you also do. For have I not said, ye are gods? Yet you do not believe. If you cannot, then, believe in your*self*, believe in *me*.

Such was Jesus' compassion that he begged for a way—and created it—to so impact the world that all might come to heaven (Self realization)—if in no other way, then through *him*. For he defeated misery and death. And so might you.

The grandest teaching of Christ was not that you *shall* have everlasting life—but that you *do*; not that you *shall* have brotherhood in God, but that you *do*; not that you *shall* have whatever you request, but that you *do*.

All that is required is to *know this*. For you are the creator of your reality, and life can show up no other way for you than that way in which you *think* it will.

You *think* it into being. This is the first step in creation. God the Father is thought. Your thought is the parent which gives birth to all things.

This is one of the laws we are to remember.

Yes.

Can you tell me others?

I have told you others. I've told you them all, since the beginning of time. Over and over have I told you them. Teacher after teacher have I sent you. You do not listen to my teachers. You kill them.

But *why*? Why do we kill the holiest among us? We kill them or dishonor them, which is the same thing. *Why*?

> Because they stand against every thought you have that would deny Me. And deny Me you must if you are to deny your Self.

Why would I want to deny You, *or* me?

> Because you are afraid. And because My promises are too good to be true. Because you cannot accept the grandest Truth. And so you must reduce yourself to a spirituality which teaches fear and dependence and intolerance, rather than love and power and acceptance.
>
> You are *filled* with fear—and your biggest fear is that My biggest promise might be life's biggest lie. And so you create the biggest fantasy you can to defend yourself against this: You claim that any promise which gives you the power, and guarantees you the love of God must be the *false promise of the devil*. God would never make such a promise, you tell yourself, only the devil would—to tempt you into denying God's true identity as the fearsome, judgmental, jealous, vengeful, and punishing entity of entities.
>
> Even though this description better fits the definition of a devil (if there *were* one), you have assigned *devilish characteristics* to God in order to convince yourself not to accept the God-like promises of your Creator, or the God-like qualities of the Self.
>
> Such is the power of fear.

I am trying to let go of my fear. Will You tell me—again—more of the laws?

> The First Law is that you can be, do, and have whatever you can imagine. The Second Law is that you attract what you fear.

Why is that?

> *Emotion* is the power which attracts. That which you fear strongly, you will experience. An animal—which you consider a lower form of life (even though animals act with more integrity and greater consistency than humans)—knows immediately if you are afraid of it. Plants—which you consider an even *lower* form of life—respond to people who love them far better than to those who couldn't care less.

None of this is by coincidence. There *is* no coincidence in the universe—only a grand design; an incredible "snowflake."

Emotion is energy in motion. When you move energy, you create effect. If you move enough energy, you create matter. Matter is energy conglomerated. Moved around. Shoved together. If you manipulate energy long enough in a certain way, you get matter. Every Master understands this law. It is the alchemy of the universe. It is the secret of all life.

Thought is pure energy. Every thought you have, have ever had, and ever will have is creative. The energy of your thought never ever dies. Ever. It leaves your being and heads out into the universe, extending forever. A thought is forever.

All thoughts congeal; all thoughts meet other thoughts, crisscrossing in an incredible maze of energy, forming an ever-changing pattern of unspeakable beauty and unbelievable complexity.

Like energy attracts like energy—forming (to use simple words) "clumps" of energy of like kind. When enough similar "clumps" criss-cross each other—run into each other—they *"stick to"* each other (to use another simple term). It takes an incomprehensibly huge amount of similar energy "sticking together," thusly, to form matter. But matter *will* form out of pure energy. In fact, that is the only way it *can* form. Once energy becomes matter, it remains matter for a very long time—unless its construction is *disrupted* by an opposing, or dissimilar, form of energy. This dissimilar energy, acting upon matter, actually dismembers the matter, releasing the raw energy of which it was composed.

This is, in elementary terms, the theory behind your atomic bomb. Einstein came closer than any other human—before or since—to discovering, explaining, and functionalizing the creative secret of the universe.

You should now better understand how people of *like mind* can work together to create a favored reality. The phrase "Wherever two or more are gathered in My name" becomes much more meaningful.

Of course, when entire *societies* think a certain way, very often astonishing things happen—not all of them necessarily desirable. For instance, a society living in fear, very often—actually, *inevitably*—produces in form that which it fears most.

Similarly, large communities or congregations often find miracle-producing power in combined thinking (or what some people call common prayer).

And it must be made clear that even individuals—if their thought (prayer, hope, wish, dream, fear) is amazingly strong—can, in and of themselves, produce such results. Jesus did this regularly. He understood how to manipulate energy and matter, how to rearrange it, how to redistribute it, how to utterly control it. Many Masters have known this. Many know it now.

You can know it. Right now.

This is the knowledge of good and evil of which Adam and Eve partook. Until they understood this, there could be no life *as you know it*. Adam and Eve—the mythical names you have given to represent First Man and First Woman—were the Father and Mother of the human experience.

What has been described as the fall of Adam was actually his upliftment—the greatest single event in the history of humankind. For without it, the world of relativity would not exist. The act of Adam and Eve was not original sin, but, in truth, first blessing. You should thank them from the bottom of your hearts—for in being the first to make a "wrong" choice, Adam and Eve *produced the possibility* of making *any choice at all*.

In your mythology you have made Eve the "bad" one here—the temptress who ate of the fruit, the knowledge of good and evil—and coyly invited Adam to join her. This mythological set-up has allowed you to make woman man's "downfall" ever since, resulting in all manner of warped realities—not to mention distorted sexual views and confusions. (How can you feel so *good* about something so *bad*?)

What you most fear is what will most plague you. Fear will draw it *to* you like a magnet. All your holy scriptures—of every religious persuasion and tradition which you have created—contain the clear admonition: fear not. Do you think this is by accident?

The Laws are very simple.

1. Thought is creative.
2. Fear attracts like energy.
3. Love is all there is.

Oops, you got me on that third one. How can love be all there is if fear attracts like energy?

Love is the ultimate reality. It is the only. The all. The feeling of love is your experience of God.

In highest Truth, love is all there is, all there was, and all there ever will be. When you move into the absolute, you move into love.

The realm of the relative was created in order that I might experience My Self. This has already been explained to you. This does not make the realm of the relative *real*. It is a *created reality* you and I have devised and continue to devise—in order that we may know ourselves experientially.

Yet the creation can seem very real. Its *purpose* is to seem so real, we *accept* it as truly existing. In this way, God has contrived to create "something else" other than Itself (though in strictest terms this is impossible, since God is—I AM—All That Is).

In creating "something else"—namely, the realm of the relative—I have produced an environment in which you may *choose* to be God, rather than simply be *told* that you are God; in which you may experience Godhead as an act of creation, rather than a conceptualization; in which the little candle in the sun—the littlest soul—can know itself as the light.

Fear is the *other end* of love. It is the *primal polarity*. In creating the realm of the relative, I first created the opposite of My Self. Now, in the realm in which you live on the physical plane, there are only *two places of being:* fear and love. Thoughts rooted in fear will produce one kind of manifestation on the physical plane. Thoughts rooted in love will produce another.

The Masters who have walked the planet are those who have discovered the secret of the relative world—and refused to acknowledge its reality. In short, *Masters are those who have chosen only love. In every instance. In every moment. In every circumstance.* Even as they were being killed, they loved their murderers. Even as they were being persecuted, they loved their oppressors.

This is very difficult for you to understand, much less emulate. Nevertheless, it is what *every Master has ever done*. It doesn't matter what the philosophy, it doesn't matter what the tradition, it doesn't matter what the religion—it is what *every Master has done*.

This example and this lesson has been laid out so clearly for you. Time and time again, over and over has it been shown to you. Through all the ages and in every place. Through all your lifetimes and in every moment. The universe has used every contrivance to place this Truth before you. In song and story, in poetry and dance, in words and in motion—in pictures of motion, which you call motion pictures, and in collections of words, which you call books.

From the highest mountain it has been shouted, in the lowest place its whisper has been heard. *Through the corridors of all human experience has this Truth been echoed:* Love is the answer. *Yet you have not listened.*

Now come you to this book, asking God again what God has told you countless times in countless ways. Yet I will tell you again—*here*—in the context of *this* book. Will you listen now? Will you truly hear?

What do you think brought you to this material? How does it come to pass that you are holding it in your hands? Do you think I know not what I am doing?

There are no coincidences in the universe.

I have heard the crying of your heart. I have seen the searching of your soul. I *know* how deeply you have desired the Truth. In pain have you called out for it, and in joy. Unendingly have you beseeched Me. *Show* Myself. *Explain* Myself. *Reveal* Myself.

I am doing so here, in terms so plain, you cannot misunderstand. In language so simple, you cannot be confused. In vocabulary so common, you cannot get lost in the verbiage.

So go ahead now. Ask Me anything. *Anything.* I will contrive to bring you the answer. The whole universe will I use to do this. So be on the lookout. This book is far from My only tool. You may ask a question, then *put this book down.* But watch. Listen. The words to the next song you hear. The information in the next article you read. The story line of the next movie you watch. The chance utterance of the next person you meet. Or the whisper of the next river, the next ocean, the next breeze that caresses your ear—*all these devices* are Mine; all these avenues are open to Me. I will speak to you if you will listen. I will come to you if you will invite Me. I will show you then that I have *always* been there. *All ways.*

2

"Thou wilt show me the path of life:
in thy presence is fullness of joy;
at thy right hand there are
pleasures forevermore."

—Psalm 16:11

I've searched for the path to God all my life—

I know you have—

—and now I've found it and I can't believe it. It feels like I'm sitting here, writing this to myself.

You are.

That does not seem like what a communication with God would feel like.

You want bells and whistles? I'll see what I can arrange.

You know, don't You, that there are those who will call this entire book a blasphemy. Especially if You keep showing up as such a wise guy.

Let Me explain something to you. You have this idea that God shows up in only one way in life. That's a very dangerous idea.

It stops you from seeing God all over. If you think God looks only one way or sounds only one way or *is* only one way, you're going to look right past Me night and day. You'll spend your whole life looking for God and not finding Her. Because you're looking for a *Him*. I use this as an example.

It has been said that if you don't see God in the profane and the profound, you're missing half the story. That is a great Truth.

God is in the sadness and the laughter, in the bitter and the sweet. There is a divine purpose behind everything—and therefore a divine presence *in* everything.

I once began writing a book called *God is a Salami Sandwich.*

That would have been a very good book. I gave you that inspiration. Why did you not write it?

It felt like blasphemy. Or at the very least, horribly irreverent.

You mean *wonderfully* irreverent! What gave you the idea that God is only "reverent"? God is the up *and* the down. The hot *and* the cold. The left *and* the right. The reverent *and* the irreverent!

Think you that God cannot laugh? Do you imagine that God does not enjoy a good joke? Is it your knowing that God is without humor? I tell you, God *invented* humor.

Must you speak in hushed tones when you speak to Me? Are slang words or tough language outside My ken ? I tell you, you can speak to Me as you would speak with your best friend.

Do you think there is a word I have not heard? A sight I have not seen? A sound I do not know?

Is it your thought that I despise some of these, while I love the others? *I tell you, I despise nothing. None of it is repulsive to Me.* It is *life,* and *life is the gift;* the unspeakable treasure; the holy of holies.

I am life, for I am the stuff life *is.* Its every aspect has a divine purpose. Nothing exists—*nothing*—without a reason understood and approved by God.

How can this be? What of the evil which has been created by man?

You cannot create a *thing*—not a thought, an object, an event— no experience of *any kind*—which is outside of God's plan. For God's plan is for you to create *anything—everything—whatever you want.* In such freedom lies the experience of God being God— and this is the experience *for which I created You.* And life itself.

Evil is that which you *call* evil. Yet even that I love, for it is only through that which you call evil that you can know good; only through that which you call the work of the devil that you can know and do the work of God. I do not love hot more than I love cold, high more than low, left more than right. It is *all relative.* It is all part of *what is.*

I do not love "good" more than I love "bad." *Hitler went to heaven.* When you understand this, you will understand God.

But I have been raised to believe that good and bad *do* exist; that right and wrong *are* opposed; that some things are not okay, not alright, not acceptable in the sight of God.

> *Everything* is "acceptable" in the sight of God, for how can God not accept that which is? To reject a thing is to deny that it exists. To say that it is not okay is to say that it is not a part of Me—and that is impossible.
>
> Yet hold to your beliefs, and stay true to your values, for these are the values of your parents, of your parents' parents; of your friends and of your society. They form the structure of your life, and to lose them would be to unravel the fabric of your experience. Still, examine them one by one. Review them piece by piece. Do not dismantle the house, but look at each brick, and replace those which appear broken, which no longer support the structure.
>
> Your ideas about right and wrong are just that—ideas. They are the thoughts which form the shape and create the substance of Who You Are. There would be only one reason to change any of these; only one purpose in making an alteration: if you are not happy with Who You Are.
>
> Only you can know if you are happy. Only you can say of your life—"This is my creation (son), in which I am well pleased."
>
> If your values serve you, hold to them. Argue for them. Fight to defend them.
>
> Yet seek to fight in a way which harms no one. Harm is not a necessary ingredient in healing.

You say "hold to your values" at the same time you say our values are all wrong. Help me with this.

> I have not said your values are wrong. But neither are they right. They are simply judgments. Assessments. Decisions. For the most part, they are decisions made not by you, but by someone else. Your parents, perhaps. Your religion. Your teachers, historians, politicians.
>
> Very few of the value judgments you have incorporated into your truth are judgments you, yourself, have made based on your own experience. Yet experience is what you came here for—and out of your experience were you to create yourself. *You* have created yourself out of the experience of *others.*
>
> *If there were such a thing as sin, this would be it: to allow yourself to become what you are because of the experience of others.* This is the "sin" you have committed. All of you. You do not await

your own experience, you accept the experience of *others* as gospel (literally), and then, when you encounter the *actual experience* for the first time, you overlay what you think you *already know* onto the encounter.

If you did not do this, you might have a wholly different experience—one that might render your original teacher or source *wrong*. In most cases, you don't want to make your parents, your schools, your religions, your traditions, your holy scriptures wrong—so you *deny your own experience* in favor of what you have been *told to think*.

Nowhere can this be more profoundly illustrated than in your treatment of human sexuality.

Everyone knows that the sexual experience can be the single most loving, most exciting, most powerful, most exhilarating, most renewing, most energizing, most affirming, most intimate, most uniting, most recreative *physical* experience of which humans are capable. Having discovered this experientially, you have chosen to accept instead the prior judgments, opinions, and ideas about sex promulgated by *others*—all of whom have a vested interest in how you think.

These opinions, judgments, and ideas have run directly contradictory to your own experience, yet because you are *loathe to make your teachers wrong,* you convince yourself it must be your *experience* that is wrong. The result is that you have betrayed your true truth about this subject—with devastating results.

You have done the same thing with money. Every time in your life that you have had lots and lots of money, you have felt great. You felt great receiving it, and you felt great spending it. There was nothing bad about it, nothing evil, nothing inherently "wrong." Yet you have so deeply ingrained within you the teachings of *others* on this subject that you have *rejected* your experience in favor of "truth."

Having adopted this "truth" as your own, you have formed thoughts around it—thoughts which are *creative*. You have thus created a personal reality around money which pushes it away from you—for why would you seek to attract that which is not good?

Amazingly, you have created this same contradiction around God. Everything your heart experiences about God tells you that God is good. Everything your teachers teach you about God tells you God is bad. Your heart tells you God is to be loved without fear. Your teachers tell you God is to be feared, for He is a vengeful God. You are to live in fear of God's wrath, they say. You are to tremble in His presence. Your whole life through you are to fear the judgment of the Lord. For the Lord is "just," you are told. And God knows, you will be in trouble when you confront the terrible justice of the Lord. You are, therefore, to be "obedient" to God's commands. Or else.

Above all, you are not to ask such logical questions as, "If God wanted strict obedience to His Laws, why did He create the possibility of those Laws being violated?" Ah, your teachers tell you—because God wanted you to have "free choice. "Yet what kind of choice is free when to choose one thing over the other brings condemnation? How is "free will" free when it is not your will, but someone else's, which must be done? Those who teach you this would make a hypocrite of God.

You are told that God is forgiveness, and compassion—yet if you do not ask for this forgiveness in the "right way," if you do not "come to God" *properly*, your plea will not be heard, your cry will go unheeded. Even this would not be so bad if there were only one proper way, but there are as many "proper ways" being taught as there are teachers to teach them.

Most of you, therefore, spend the bulk of your adult life searching for the "right" way to worship, to obey, and to serve God. *The irony of all this is that I do not want your worship, I do not need your obedience, and it is not necessary for you to serve Me.*

These behaviors are the behaviors historically demanded of their subjects by monarchs—usually ego-maniacal, insecure, tyrannical monarchs at that. They're not Godly demands in any sense—and it seems remarkable that the world hasn't by now concluded that the demands are counterfeit, having nothing to do with the needs or desires of Deity.

Deity has *no needs. All That Is* is exactly that: *all that is.* It therefore wants, or lacks, nothing—by definition.

If you choose to believe in a God who somehow *needs* something—and has such hurt feelings if He doesn't get it that He punishes those from whom He expected to receive it—then you choose to believe in a God much smaller than I. You truly are Children of a Lesser God.

No, my children, please let Me assure you again, through this writing, that I am without needs. I require nothing.

This does not mean I am without *desires. Desires* and *needs* are not the same thing (although many of you have made them so in your present lifetime).

Desire is the beginning of all creation. It is first thought. It is a grand feeling within the soul. It is God, choosing what next to create.

And what is God's desire?

I desire first to know and experience Myself, in all My glory—to know Who I Am. Before I invented you—and all the worlds of the universe—it was impossible for Me to do so.

Second, I desire that you shall know and experience Who You Really Are, through the power I have given you to create and experience yourself in whatever way you choose.

Third, I desire for the whole life process to be an experience of constant joy, continuous creation, never-ending expansion, and total fulfillment in each moment of now.

I have established a perfect system whereby these desires may be realized. They are being realized now—in this very moment. The only difference between you and Me is that *I know this.*

In the moment of your total knowing (which moment could come upon you at anytime), you, too, will feel as I do always: totally joyful, loving, accepting, blessing, and grateful.

These are the *Five Attitudes* of God, and before we are through with this dialogue, I will show you how the application of these attitudes in your life now can—and *will*—bring you to Godliness.

All of this is a very long answer to a very short question.

Yes, hold to your values—so long as you experience that they serve you. Yet look to see whether the values *you* serve, with your thoughts, words, and actions, bring to the space of your experience the highest and best idea you ever had about you.

Examine your values one by one. Hold them up to the light of public scrutiny. If you can tell the world who you are and what you believe without breaking stride or hesitating, you are happy with yourself. There is no reason to continue much further in this dialogue with Me, because you have created a Self—and a life *for* the Self—which needs no improvement. You have reached perfection. Put the book down.

My life is not perfect, nor is it close to being perfect. I am not perfect. I am, in fact, a bundle of imperfections. I wish—sometimes I wish with all my heart—that I could correct these imperfections; that I knew what causes my behaviors, what sets up my downfalls, what keeps getting in my way. That's why I've come to You, I guess. I haven't been able to find the answers on my own.

I am glad you came. I have always been here to help you. I am
here now. You don't have to find the answers on your own. You
never had to.

Yet it seems so . . . *presumptuous* . . . to simply sit down and dialogue
with You this way—much less to imagine that You—*God*—are responding—I mean, this is *crazy.*

I see. The authors of the Bible were all sane, but *you* are crazy.

The Bible writers were witnesses to the life of Christ, and faithfully
recorded what they heard and saw.

Correction. Most of the New Testament writers never met or
saw Jesus in their lives. They lived many years after Jesus left the
Earth. They wouldn't have known Jesus of Nazareth if they walked
into him on the street.

But . . .

The Bible writers were great believers and great historians. They
took the stories which had been passed down to them and to their
friends by others—elders—from elder to elder, until finally a written record was made.
*And not everything of the Bible authors was included in the final
document.*
Already "churches" had sprung up around the teachings of
Jesus—and, as happens whenever and wherever people gather in
groups around a powerful idea, there were certain individuals
within these churches, or enclaves, who determined what parts of
the Jesus Story were going to be told—and how. This process of
selecting and editing continued throughout the gathering, writing,
and publishing of the gospels, and the Bible.
Even several *centuries* after the original scriptures were committed to writing, a High Council of the Church determined yet one
more time which doctrines and truths were to be included in the
then-official Bible—and which would be "unhealthy" or "prema-
ture" to reveal to the masses.
And there have been other holy scriptures as well—each placed
in writing in moments of inspiration by otherwise ordinary men,
none of whom were any more crazy than you.

Are you suggesting—you're not suggesting, are you—that *these* writings might one day become "holy scriptures"?

> My child, *everything in life is holy.* By that measure, yes, these are holy writings. But I will not quibble with you over words, because I know what you mean.
>
> No, I do not suggest that this manuscript will one day become holy scripture. At least, not for several hundred years, or until the language becomes outmoded.
>
> You see, the problem is that the language here is too colloquial, too conversational, too contemporary. People assume that if God were to talk directly with you, God would not sound like the fella next door. There should be some unifying, if not to say deifying, structure to the language. Some dignity. Some sense of Godliness.
>
> As I said earlier, that's part of the problem. People have a sense of God as "showing up" in only one form. Anything which violates that form is seen as blasphemy.

As I said earlier.

> As you said earlier.
>
> But let's drive to the heart of your question. Why do you think it's crazy for you to be able to have a dialogue with God? Do you not believe in prayer?

Yes, but that's different. Prayer for me has always been one-way. I ask, and God remains immutable.

> God has never answered a prayer?

Oh yes, but never *verbally*, you see. Oh, I've had all *kinds* of things happen in my life that I was convinced were an answer—a very direct answer—to prayer. But God has never *spoken* to me.

> I see. So this God in which you believe—this God can *do* anything—It just cannot speak.

Of *course* God can speak, if God wants to. It just doesn't seem probable that God would want to speak to *me*.

This is the root of every problem you experience in your life—for you do not consider yourself worthy enough to be spoken to by God.

Good heavens, how can you ever expect to hear My voice if you don't imagine yourself to be deserving enough to even be spoken to?

I tell you this: I am performing a miracle right now. For not only am I speaking to you, but to every person who has picked up this book and is reading these words.

To each of them am I now speaking. I know who every one of them is. I know now who will find their way to these words—and I know that (just as with all My other communications) some will be able to hear—and some will be able to only listen, but will *hear nothing*.

Well, that brings up another thing. I am already thinking of publishing this material even now, as it's being written.

Yes. What's "wrong" with that?

Can't it be argued that I am creating this whole thing for profit? Doesn't that render the whole thing suspect?

Is it your motive to write something so that you can make a lot of money?

No. That's not why I started this. I began this dialogue on paper because my mind has been plagued with questions for 30 years—questions I've been hungry—*starving* to have answered. The idea that I would have all this made into a book came later.

From Me.

From You?

Yes. You don't think I was going to let you waste all these marvelous questions and answers, do you?

I hadn't thought about that. At the outset, I just wanted the questions answered; the frustration to end; the search to be over.

Good. So stop questioning your motives (you do it incessantly) and let's get *on* with it.

3

Well, I have a hundred questions. A thousand. A *million*. And the problem is, I sometimes don't know where to begin.

> Just list the questions. Just start *somewhere*. Go ahead, right now. Make a list of the questions that occur to you.

Okay. Some of them are going to seem pretty simple, pretty plebeian.

> Stop making judgments against yourself. Just list them.

Right. Well, here are the ones that occur to me now.

1. When will my life finally take off? What does it take to "get it together," and achieve even a modicum of success? Can the struggle ever end?

2. When will I learn enough about relationships to be able to have them go smoothly? Is there any way *to* be happy in relationships? Must they always be constantly challenging?

3. Why can't I ever seem to attract enough money in my life? Am I destined to be scrimping and scraping for the rest of my life? What is blocking me from realizing my full potential in this regard?

4. Why can't I do what I really *want* to do with my life and still make a living?

5. How can I solve some of the health problems I face? I have been the victim of enough chronic problems to last a lifetime. Why am I having them all now?

6. What is the karmic lesson I'm supposed to be learning here? What am I trying to master?

7. Is there such a thing as reincarnation? How many past lives have I had? What was I in them? Is "karmic debt" a reality?

8. I sometimes feel very psychic. Is there such a thing as "being psychic"? Am I that? Are people who claim to be psychic "trafficking with the devil"?

9. Is it okay to take money for doing good? If I choose to do healing work in the world—God's work—can I do that and become financially abundant, too? Or are the two mutually exclusive?

10. Is sex okay? C'mon—what is the real story behind this human experience? Is sex purely for procreation, as some religions say? Is true holiness and enlightenment achieved through denial—or transmutation—of the sexual energy? Is it okay to have sex without love? Is just the physical sensation of it okay enough as a reason?

11. Why did you make sex so good, so spectacular, so powerful a human experience if all we are to do is stay away from it as much as we can? What gives? For that matter, why are all fun things either "immoral, illegal, or fattening"?

12. Is there life on other planets? Have we been visited by it? Are we being observed now? Will we see evidence—irrevocable and indisputable—of extraterrestrial life in our lifetime? Does each form of life have its own God? Are you the God of It All?

13. Will Utopia ever come to the planet Earth? Will God ever show Himself to Earth's people, as promised? Is there such a thing as the Second Coming? Will there ever be an End of the World—or an apocalypse, as prophesied in the Bible? Is there a one true religion? If so, which one?

These are just a few of my questions. As I said, I have a hundred more. Some of these questions embarrass me—they seem so sophomoric. But answer them, please—one at a time—and let's "talk" about them.

Good. Now we're getting to it. Don't apologize for these questions. These are the questions men and women have been asking for hundreds of years. If the questions were so silly, they wouldn't be asked over and over again by each succeeding generation. So let's go to question one.

I have established Laws in the universe that make it possible for you to have—to create—exactly what you choose. These Laws cannot be violated, nor can they be ignored. You are following these Laws right now, even as you read this. You cannot not follow the Law, for these are the ways things work. You cannot step aside from this; you cannot operate outside of it.

Every minute of your life you have been operating *inside* of it—and everything you have ever experienced you have thusly created.

You are in a partnership with God. We share an eternal covenant. My promise to you is to always give you what you ask. Your promise is to ask; to understand the process of the asking and the answering. I've already explained this process to you once. I'll do so again, so that you clearly understand it.

You are a three-fold being. You consist of *body, mind,* and *spirit.* You could also call these the *physical,* the *non-physical,* and the *meta-physical'. This is the Holy Trinity, and it has been called by many names.*

That which you are, I am. I am manifested as Three-in-One. Some of your theologians have called this Father, Son, and Holy Spirit.

Your psychiatrists have recognized this triumvirate and called it conscious, subconscious, and superconscious.

Your philosophers have called it the id, the ego, and the super ego.

Science calls this energy, matter, and antimatter.

Poets speak of mind, heart, and soul. New Age thinkers refer to body, mind, and spirit.

Your time is divided into past, present, and future. Could this not be the same as subconscious, conscious, and superconscious?

Space is likewise divided into three: here, there, and the space between.

It is defining and describing this "space between" that becomes difficult, elusive. The moment you begin defining or describing, the space you describe becomes "here" or "there." Yet we *know* this "space between" exists. It is what holds "here" and "there" in place—just as the eternal now holds "before" and "after" in place.

These three aspects of you are actually three energies. You might call them *thought, word,* and *action.* All three put together produce a *result*—which in your language and understanding is called a feeling, or experience.

Your soul (subconscious, id, spirit, past, etc.) *is the sum total of every feeling you've ever had (created).* Your awareness of some of these is called your memory. When you have a memory, you are said to re-member. That is, to put back together. To reassemble the parts.

When you reassemble all of the parts of you, you will have re-membered Who You Really Are.

The process of creation starts with thought—an idea, conception, visualization. Everything you see was once someone's idea. Nothing exists in your world that did not first exist as pure thought.

This is true of the universe as well.

Thought is the first level of creation.

Next comes the *word*. Everything you say is a thought expressed. It is creative and sends forth creative energy into the universe. Words are more dynamic (thus, some might say more creative) than thought, because words are a different level of vibration from thought. They disrupt (change, alter, affect) the universe with greater impact.

Words are the second level of creation.

Next comes *action*.

Actions are words moving. Words are thoughts expressed. Thoughts are ideas formed. Ideas are energies come together. Energies are forces released. Forces are elements existent. Elements are particles of God, portions of All, the stuff of everything.

The beginning is God. The end is action. Action is God creating—or God experienced.

Your thought about yourself is that you are not good enough, not wondrous enough, not sinless enough, to be a part of God, in partnership with God. You have denied for so long Who You Are that you have *forgotten* Who You Are.

This has not occurred by coincidence; this is not happenstance. It is all part of the divine plan—for you could not claim, create, experience—Who You Are if you already were it. It was necessary first for you to release (deny, forget) your connection to Me in order to fully experience it by fully creating it—by calling it forth. For your grandest wish—and My grandest desire—was for you to experience yourself as the part of Me you are. You are therefore in the process of experiencing yourself by creating yourself anew in every single moment. As am I. Through you.

Do you see the partnership? Do you grasp its implications? It is a holy collaboration—truly, a holy communion.

Life will "take off" for you, then, when you choose for it to. You have not so chosen as yet. You have procrastinated, prolonged, protracted, protested. Now it is time that you promulgated and produced what you have been promised. To do this, you must believe the promise, and live it. *You must live the promise of God.*

The promise of God is that you are His son. Her offspring. Its likeness. His equal.

Ah . . . here is where you get hung up. You can accept "His son," "offspring," "likeness," but you recoil at being called "His equal." It is too much to accept. Too much bigness, too much wonderment—too much *responsibility*, for if you are God's *equal*, that means nothing is being done *to* you—and all things are created *by* you. *There can be no more victims and no more villains*—only outcomes of your thought about a thing.

I tell you this: all *you see in your world is the outcome of your idea about it.*

Do you want your life to truly "take off"? Then change your idea about it. About you. Think, speak, and act as the *God You Are*.

Of course this will separate you from many—most—of your fellow men. They will call you crazy. They will say you blaspheme. They will eventually have enough of you, and they will attempt to crucify you.

They will do this not because they think you are living in a world of your own illusions (most men are gracious enough to allow you your private entertainments), but because, sooner or later, others will become *attracted* to your truth—for the promises it holds for *them*.

Here is where your fellow men will interfere—for here is where you will begin to threaten them. For your simple truth, simply lived, will offer more beauty, more comfort, more peace, more joy, and more love of self and others than anything your earthly fellows could contrive.

And that truth, adopted, would mean the end of their ways. It would mean the end of hatred and fear and bigotry and war. The end of the condemning and killing that has gone on in *My name*. The end of might-is-right. The end of purchase-through-power. The end of loyalty and homage through fear. The end of the world as they know it—and as you have created it thus far.

So be ready, kind soul. For you will be vilified and spat upon, called names, and deserted, and finally they will accuse you, try you, and condemn you—all in their own ways—from the moment you accept and adopt your holy cause—the realization of Self.

Why, then, do it?

Because you are no longer concerned with the acceptance or approval of the world. You are no longer satisfied with what that has brought you. You are no longer pleased with what it has given others. You want the pain to stop, the suffering to stop, the illusion to end. You have had enough of this world as it presently is. You seek a newer world.

Seek it *no longer.* Now, *call it forth.*

Can you help me to better understand how to do that?

Yes. Co first to your Highest Thought about yourself. Imagine the you that you would be if you lived that thought every day. Imagine what you would think, do, and say, and how you would respond to what others do and say.

Do you see any difference between that projection and what you think, do, and say now?

Yes. I see a great deal of difference.

Good. You should, since we know that right now you are not living your highest vision of yourself. Now, having seen the differences between where you are and where you want to be, begin to change—consciously change—your thoughts, words, and actions to match your grandest vision.

This will require tremendous mental and physical effort. It will entail constant, moment-to-moment monitoring of your every thought, word, and deed. It will involve continued choice-making—consciously. This whole process is a massive move to consciousness. What you will find out if you undertake this challenge is that *you've spent half your life unconscious.* That is to say, unaware on a conscious level of *what you are choosing* in the way of thoughts, words, and deeds until you experience the aftermath of them. Then, when you experience these results, you deny that your thoughts, words, and deeds had anything to do with them.

This is a call to stop such unconscious living. It is a challenge to which your soul has called you from the beginning of time.

That kind of continual mental monitoring seems as though it might be terribly exhausting—

It could be, until it becomes second nature. In fact, it *is* your second nature. It is your first nature to be unconditionally loving. It is your second nature to choose to express your first nature, your true nature, consciously.

Excuse me, but wouldn't this kind of non-stop editing of everything I think, say, and do "make Jack a dull boy"?

Never. Different, yes. Dull, no. Was Jesus dull? I don't think so. Was the Buddha boring to be around? People flocked, begged, to be in his presence. No one who has attained mastery is dull. Unusual, perhaps. Extraordinary, perhaps. But never dull.

So—do you want your life to "take off"? *Begin at once to imagine it the way you want it to be—and move into that. Check every thought, word, and action that does not fall into harmony with that. Move away from those.*

When you have a thought that is not in alignment with your higher vision, *change to a new thought,* then and there. When you say a thing that is out of alignment with your grandest idea, make a note not to say something like that again. When you do a thing that is misaligned with your best intention, decide to make that the last time. And make it right with whomever was involved if you can.

I've heard this before and I've always railed against it, because it seems so dishonest. I mean, if you're sick as a dog, you're not supposed to admit it. If you're broke as a pauper, you're never supposed to say it. If you're upset as hell, you're not supposed to show it. It reminds me of the joke about the three people who were sent to hell. One was a Catholic, one was a Jew, one was a New Ager. The devil said to the Catholic, sneeringly, "Well, how are you enjoying the heat?" And the Catholic sniffled, "I'm offering it up." The devil then asked the Jew, "And how are *you* enjoying the heat?" The Jew said, "So what else could I expect but more hell?" Finally, the devil approached the New Ager. "Heat?" the New Ager asked, perspiring. "What heat?"

That's a good joke. But I'm not talking about ignoring the problem, or pretending it isn't there. I'm talking about noticing the circumstance, and then telling your highest truth about it.

If you're broke, you're broke. It's pointless to lie about it, and actually debilitating to try to manufacture a story about it so as not to admit it. Yet it's your thought about it—"Broke is bad," "This is horrible," "I'm a bad person, because good people who work hard and really try *never* go broke," etc.—that rules how you *experience* "broke-ness." It's your words about it—"I'm broke," "I haven't a dime," "I don't have any money"—that dictates how long you *stay* broke. It's your actions surrounding it—feeling sorry for yourself, sitting around despondent, not trying to find a way out because "What's the use, anyway?"—that create your long-term reality.

The first thing to understand about the universe is that no condition is "good" or "bad." It just *is*. So stop making value judgments.

The second thing to know is that all conditions are temporary. Nothing stays the same, nothing remains static. Which way a thing changes depends on you.

Excuse me, but I have to interrupt you again here. What about the person who is sick, but has the faith that will move mountains—and so thinks, says, and *believes* he's going to get better . . . only to die six weeks later. How does *that* square with all this positive thinking, affirmative action stuff?

That's good. You're asking the tough questions. That's good. You're not simply taking My word for any of this. There is a place, on down the line, when you'll *have* to take My word for this—because eventually you'll find that we can discuss this thing forever, you and I—until there's nothing left to do but to "try it or deny it." But we're not at that place yet. So let's keep the dialogue going; let's keep talking—

The person who has the "faith to move mountains," and dies six weeks later, has moved mountains for six weeks. That may have been enough for him. He may have decided, on the last hour of the last day, "Okay, I've had enough. I'm ready to go on now to another adventure." You may not have known of that decision, because he may not have told you. The truth is, he may have made that decision quite a bit earlier—days, weeks earlier—and not have told you; not have told anyone.

You have created a society in which it is very not okay to want to die—very not okay to be very okay with death. Because you don't want to die, you can't imagine *anyone* wanting to die—no matter what their circumstances or condition.

But there are many situations in which death is preferable to life—which I know you can imagine if you think about it for even a little bit. Yet, these truths don't occur to you—they are not that self-evident—when you are looking in the face someone else who is choosing to die. And the dying person knows this. She can feel the level of acceptance in the room regarding her decision.

Have you ever noticed how many people wait until the room is empty before they die? Some even have to tell their loved ones—"No, really, go. Get a bite to eat." Or "Go, get some sleep. I'm fine. I'll see you in the morning." And then, when the loyal guard leaves, so does the soul from the body of the guarded.

If they told their assembled relatives and friends, "I just want to die," they would really hear it. "Oh, you don't mean that," or "Now, don't talk that way," or "Hang in there," or "Please don't leave me."

The entire medical profession is trained to keep people alive, rather than keeping people comfortable so that they can die with dignity.

You see, to a doctor or a nurse, death is failure. To a friend or relative, death is disaster. Only to the soul is death a relief—a release.

The greatest gift you can give the dying is to let them die in peace—not thinking that they must "hang on," or continue to suffer, or worry about *you* at this most crucial passage in their life.

So this is very often what has happened in the case of the man who says he's going to live, believes he's going to live, even prays to live: that at the soul level, he has "changed his mind." It is time now to drop the body to free the soul for other pursuits. When the soul makes this decision, nothing the body does can change it. Nothing the mind thinks can alter it. It is at the moment of death that we learn who, in the body-mind-soul triumvirate, is running things.

All your life you think you are your body. Some of the time you think you are your mind. It is at the time of your death that you find out Who You Really Are.

Now there are also times when the body and the mind are just not *listening* to the soul. This, too, creates the scenario you describe. The most difficult thing for people to do is hear their own soul. (Notice that so few do.)

Now it happens often that the soul makes a decision that it is time to leave the body. The body and the mind—ever servants of the soul—hear this, and the process of extrication begins. Yet the mind (ego) doesn't want to accept. After all, this is the end of its existence. So it instructs the body to resist death. This the body does gladly, since it too does not want to die. The body and the mind (ego) receive great encouragement, great praise for this from the outside world—the world of its creation. So the strategy is confirmed.

Now at this point everything depends on how badly the soul wants to leave. If there is no great urgency here, the soul may say, "Alright, you win. I'll stick around with you a little longer." But if the soul is very clear that staying does not serve its higher agenda—that there is no further way it can *evolve* through this body—the soul is going to leave, and nothing will stop it—nor should anything try to.

The soul is very clear that its purpose is evolution. That is its *sole* purpose—and its *soul* purpose. It is not concerned with the achievements of the body or the development of the mind. These are all meaningless to the soul.

The soul is also clear that there is no great tragedy involved in leaving the body. In many ways, the tragedy is being *in* the body. So you have to understand, the soul sees this whole death thing differently. It, of course, sees the whole "life thing" differently, too— and that is the source of much of the frustration and anxiety one feels in one's life. The frustration and anxiety comes from not listening to one's soul.

How can I best listen to my soul? If the soul is the boss, really, how can I make sure I get those memos from the front office?

The first thing you might do is get clear about what the soul is after—and stop making judgments about it.

I'm making judgments about my own soul?

Constantly. I just showed you how you judge yourself for wanting to die. You also judge yourself for wanting to live—truly *live*. You judge yourself for wanting to laugh, wanting to cry, wanting to win, wanting to lose—for wanting to experience joy and love— *especially* do you judge yourself for that.

I do?

Somewhere you've come across the idea that to *deny* yourself joy is Godly—that *not* to celebrate life is heavenly. Denial, you have told yourself, is goodness.

Are you saying it is bad?

It is neither good nor bad, it is simply denial. If you feel good after denying yourself, then in your world that is goodness. If you feel bad, then it's badness. Most of the time, you can't decide. You deny yourself this or that because you tell yourself you are supposed to. Then you say that was a good thing to do—but wonder why you don't *feel* good.

And so the first thing to do is to stop making these judgments against yourself. Learn what is the soul's desire, and go with that. Go with the soul.

What the soul is after is—the highest feeling of love you can imagine. This is the soul's desire. This is its purpose. The soul is after the feeling. Not the knowledge, but the feeling. It already has the knowledge, but knowledge is conceptual. Feeling is experiential. The soul wants to feel itself, and thus to know itself *in its own experience.*

The highest feeling is the experience of unity with All That Is. This is the great return to Truth for which the soul yearns. This is the feeling of perfect love.

Perfect love is to feeling what perfect white is to color. Many think that white is the *absence* of color. It is not. It is the inclusion of all color. White is *every other color that exists,* combined.

So, too, is love not the absence of an emotion (hatred, anger, lust, jealousy, covetousness), but the summation of all feeling. It is the sum total. The aggregate amount. The everything.

Thus, for the soul to experience perfect love, it must experience *every human feeling.*

How can I have compassion on that which I don't understand? How can I forgive in another that which I have never experienced in Myself? So we see both the simplicity and the awesome magnitude of the soul's journey. We understand at last what it is up to:

The purpose of the human soul is to experience all of it—so that it can be all of it.

How can it be up if it has never been down, left if it has never been right? How can it be warm if it knows not cold, good if it denies evil? Obviously the soul cannot choose to be anything *if there is nothing to choose from.* For the soul to experience its grandeur, it must *know what grandeur is.* This it cannot do if there is nothing *but* grandeur. And so the soul realizes that grandeur only exists in the space of that which is *not* grand. The soul, therefore, never condemns that which is not grand, but blesses—seeing *in* it a *part of itself* which *must exist* for another part of itself to manifest.

The job of the soul, of course, is to cause us to choose the grandeur—to select the best of Who You Are—without condemning that which you do not select.

This is a big task, taking many lifetimes, for you are wont to rush to judgment, to call a thing "wrong" or "bad" or "not enough," rather than to bless what you do not choose.

You do worse than condemn—you actually seek to do harm to that which you do not choose. You seek to destroy it. If there is a person, place, or thing with which you do not agree, you attack it. If there is a religion that goes against yours, you make it wrong. If there is a thought that contradicts yours, you ridicule it. If there is an idea other than yours, you reject it. In this you err, for you create only half a universe. And you cannot even understand *your* half when you have *rejected out of hand* the other.

This is all very profound—and I thank you. No one has ever said these things to me. At least, not with such simplicity. And I am trying to understand. Really, I am. Yet some of this is difficult to grapple with. You seem to be saying, for instance, that we should love the "wrong" so that we can know the "right." Are you saying we must embrace the devil, so to speak?

How else do you heal him? Of course, a real devil does not exist—but I reply to you in the idiom you choose.

Healing is the process of accepting all, then choosing best. Do you understand that? You cannot *choose* to be God if there is nothing else to choose *from*.

Oops, hold it! Who said anything about choosing to *be God?*

The highest feeling is perfect love, is it not?

Yes, I should think so.

And can you find a better description of God?

No, I cannot.

Well, your soul seeks the highest feeling. It seeks to experience—to *be*—perfect love.

It *is* perfect love—and it *knows this.* Yet it wishes to do *more* than *know* it. It wishes to *be* it *in its experience.*

Of *course* you are seeking to be God! What else did you think you were up to?

I don't know. I'm not sure. I guess I just never thought of it that way. There just seems to be something vaguely blasphemous about that.

Isn't it interesting that you find nothing blasphemous about seeking to be like the devil, but seeking to be like God offends you—

Now wait minute! Who's seeking to be like the devil?

You are! You *all* are! You've even created religions that tell you that you are born in sin—that you are *sinners at birth*—in order to convince yourselves of your own evil. Yet if I told you you are born of God—that you are pure Gods and Goddesses at birth—*pure love*—you would reject me.

All your life you have spent convincing yourself that you are bad. Not only that you are bad, but that the things you want are bad. Sex is bad, money is bad, joy is bad, power is bad, having a lot is bad—a lot *of anything*. Some of your religions have even got you believing that *dancing* is bad, *music* is bad, celebrating *life* is bad. Soon you'll agree that smiling is bad, laughing is bad, *loving* is bad.

No, no, my friend, you may not be very clear about many things, but about one thing you are clear: you, and most of what you desire, are *bad*. Having made this judgment about yourself, you have decided that your job is to *get better*.

It's okay, mind you. It's the same destination in any event—it's just that there's a faster way, a shorter route, a quicker path.

Which is?

Acceptance of Who and What You Are right now—and demonstration of that.

This is what Jesus did. It is the path of the Buddha, the way of Krishna, the walk of every Master who has appeared on the planet.

And every Master has likewise had the same message: What I am, you are. What I can do, you can do. These things, and *more*, shall you also do.

Yet you have not listened. You have chosen instead the far more difficult path of *one who thinks he is the devil,* one who *imagines he is evil.*

You say it is difficult to walk the path of Christ, to follow the teachings of the Buddha, to hold the light of Krishna, to be a Master. Yet I tell you this: it is far more difficult to deny Who You Are than to accept it.

You are goodness and mercy and compassion and understanding. You are peace and joy and light. You are forgiveness and patience, strength and courage, a helper in time of need, a comforter in time of sorrow, a healer in time of injury, a teacher in times of confusion. You are the deepest wisdom and the highest truth; the greatest peace and the grandest love. You *are* these things. And in moments of your life you have *known* yourself as these things.

Choose now to know yourself as these things always.

4

Whew! You inspire me!

Well, if God can't inspire you, who in hell can?

Are You always this flip?

I meant that not as flippancy. Read it again.

Oh. I see.

Yes.
However, it would be okay if I were being flip, wouldn't it?

I don't know. I'm used to my God being a little more serious.

Well, do Me a favor, and don't try to contain Me. By the way, do yourself the same favor.

It just so happens I have a great sense of humor. I'd say you'd have to when you see what you've all done with life, wouldn't you? I mean, sometimes I have to just laugh at it.

It's alright, though, because you see, I know it'll all come out all right in the end.

What do You mean by that?

I mean you can't lose in this game. You can't go wrong. It's not part of the plan. There's no way not to get where you are going. There's no way to miss your destination. If God is your target, you're in luck, because *God is so big, you can't miss.*

That's the big worry, of course. The big worry is that somehow we'll mess up and not get to ever see You, be with You.

You mean "get to heaven"?

Yes. We're all afraid of going to hell.

So you've placed yourself there to begin with in order to avoid *going* there. Hmmmmm. Interesting strategy.

There You are, being flip again.

I can't help it. This whole hell thing brings out the worst in Me!

Good grief, You're a regular *comedian*.

It took you this long to find *that* out? You looked at the world lately?

Which brings me to another question. Why don't You *fix* the world, instead of allowing it to go to hell?

Why don't you?

I don't have the power.

Nonsense. You've the power and the ability right now to end world hunger this minute, to cure diseases this instant. What if I told you your own medical profession *holds back cures*, refuses to approve alternative medicines and procedures because they threaten the very structure of the "healing" profession? What if I told you that the governments of the world do not *want* to end world hunger? Would you believe me?

I'd have a hard time with that. I know that's the populist view, but I can't believe it's actually true. No doctor wants to deny a cure. No countryman wants to see his people die.

No *individual* doctor, that's true. No *particular* countryman, that's right. But doctoring and politicking have become *institutionalized*, and it's the institutions that fight these things, sometimes very subtly, sometimes even unwittingly, but inevitably . . . because to those institutions it's a matter of survival.

And so, to give you just one very simple and obvious example, doctors in the West deny the healing efficacies of doctors in the East because to accept them, to admit that certain alternate modalities might just provide some healing, would be to tear at the very fabric of the institution as it has structured itself.

This is not malevolent, yet it is insidious. The profession doesn't do this because it is evil. It does it because it is scared.

All attack is a call for help.

I read that in A Course in Miracles.

I put it there.

Boy, You have an answer for everything.

Which reminds Me, we only just started getting to your questions. We were discussing how to get your life on track. How to get it to "take off." I was discussing the process of creation.

Yes, and I kept interrupting.

That's alright, but let's just get back, because we don't want to lose the thread of something that's very important.

Life is a creation, not a discovery.

You do not live each day to *discover* what it holds for you, but to *create* it. You are creating your reality every minute, probably without knowing it.

Here's why that is so, and how that works.

1. I have created you in the image and likeness of God.

2. God is the creator.

3. You are three beings in one. You can call these three aspects of being anything you want: Father, Son, and Holy Ghost; mind, body, and spirit; superconscious, conscious, subconscious.

4. Creation is a process that proceeds from these three parts of your body. Put another way, you create at three levels. The tools of creation are: thought, word, and deed.

5. All creation begins with thought ("Proceeds from the Father"). All creation then moves to word ("Ask and you shall receive, speak and it shall be done unto you"). All creation is fulfilled in deed ("And the Word was made flesh, and dwelt among us").

6. That which you think of, but thereafter never speak of, creates at one level. That which you think of and speak of creates at another level. That which you think, speak, and do becomes made manifest in your reality.

7. To think, speak, and do something which you do not truly believe is impossible. Therefore, the process of creation must include belief, or knowing. This is absolute faith. This is *beyond* hoping. This is *knowing of a certainty* ("By your faith shall ye be healed"). Therefore, the doing part of creation always includes knowing. It is a gut-level clarity, a total certainty, a complete *acceptance as reality* of something.

8. This place of knowing is a place of intense and incredible gratitude. It is a *thankfulness* in *advance*. And that, perhaps, is the biggest key to creation: to be grateful *before*, and for, the creation. Such taking for granted is not only condoned, but encouraged. It is the *sure sign of mastery*. All Masters *know in advance that the deed has been done.*

9. Celebrate and enjoy all that you create, have created. To reject any part of it is to reject a part of yourself. Whatever it is that is now presenting itself as part of your creation, own it, claim it, bless it, be thankful for it. Seek not to condemn it ("God damn it!"), for to condemn it is to condemn yourself.

10. If there is some aspect of creation you find you do not enjoy, bless it and simply change it. Choose again. Call forth a new reality. Think a new thought. Say a new word. Do a new thing. Do this magnificently and the rest of the world will follow you. Ask it to. Call for it to. Say, "I am the Life and the Way, follow me."

This is how to manifest God's will "on Earth as it is in Heaven."

If it is all as simple as that, if these ten steps are all we need, why does it not work that way for more of us?

It *does* work that way, for *all* of you. Some of you are using the "system" consciously, with full awareness, and some of you are using it unconsciously, without even knowing what you are doing.

Some of you are walking in wakefulness, and some of you are sleepwalking. Yet *all* of you are creating your reality—*creating*, not *discovering*—using the power I have given you, and the process I've just described.

So, you've asked when your life will "take off," and I've given you the answer.

You get your life to "take off" by first becoming very clear in your thinking about it. Think about what you want to be, do, and have. Think about it often until you are very clear about this. Then, when you are very clear, *think about nothing else.* Imagine no other possibilities.

Throw all negative thoughts out of your mental constructions. Lose all pessimism. Release all doubts. Reject all fears. Discipline your mind to hold fast to the original creative thought.

When your thoughts are clear and steadfast, begin to speak them as truths. Say them out loud. Use the great command that calls forth creative power: I am. Make I-am statements to others. "I am" is the strongest creative statement in the universe. Whatever you think, whatever you say, after the words "I am" sets into motion those experiences, calls them forth, brings them to you.

There is no other way the universe knows how to work. There is no other route it knows to take. The universe responds to "I am" as would a genie in a bottle.

You say "Release all doubts, reject all fears, lose all pessimism" as if you're saying "pick me up a loaf of bread." But these things are easier said than done. "Throw all negative thoughts out of your mental constructions" might as well read "climb Mt. Everest—before lunch." It's rather a large order.

Harnessing your thoughts, exercising control over them, is not as difficult as it might seem. (Neither, for that matter, is climbing Mt. Everest.) It is all a matter of discipline. It is a question of intent.

The first step is learning to monitor your thoughts; to *think about* what you are thinking about.

When you catch yourself thinking negative thoughts—thoughts that negate your highest idea about a thing—think again! I want you to do this, *literally.* If you think you are in a doldrum, in a pickle, and no good can come of this, *think again.* If you think the world is a bad place, filled with negative events, *think again.* If you think your life is falling apart, and it looks as if you'll never get it back together again, *think again.*

You *can* train yourself to do this. (Look how well you've trained yourself *not* to do it!)

Thank you. I've never had the process set out for me so clearly. I wish it were as easily done as said—but now I at least understand it clearly—I think.

Well, if you need a review, we have several lifetimes.

5

What is the true path to God? Is it through renunciation, as some yogis believe? And what of this thing called suffering? Is suffering and service the path to God as many ascetics say? Do we earn our way to heaven by "being good," as so many religions teach? Or are we free to act as we wish, violate or ignore any rule, set aside any traditional teachings, dive into any self-indulgences, and thus find Nirvana, as many New Agers say? Which is it? Strict moral standards, or do-as-you-please? Which is it? Traditional values, or make-it-up-as-you-go-along? Which is it? The Ten Commandments, or the Seven Steps to Enlightenment?

> You have a great need to have it be one way or the other, don't you. . . . Could it not be all of these?

I don't know. I'm asking You.

> I will answer you, then, as you can best understand—though I tell you now that your answer is within. I say this to all people who hear My words and seek My Truth.
> Every heart which earnestly asks, Which is the path to God? is shown. Each is given a heartfelt Truth. Come to Me along the path of your heart, not through a journey of your mind. You will never find Me in your mind.
> *In order to truly know God, you have to be out of your mind.*
> Yet your question begs an answer, and I will not step aside from the thrust of your inquiry.
> I will begin with a statement that will startle you—and perhaps offend the sensitivities of many people. *There are no such things as the Ten Commandments.*

Oh, My God, there aren't?

No, there are not. Who would I command? Myself? And why would such commandments be required? Whatever I want, is. *N'est-ce pas?* How is it therefore necessary to command anyone?

And, if I did issue commandments, would they not be automatically kept? How could I wish something to be so badly that I would command it—and then sit by and watch it not be so?

What kind of a king would do that? What kind of a ruler?

And yet I tell you this: I am neither a king nor a ruler. I am simply—and awesomely—the Creator. Yet the Creator does not rule, but merely creates, creates—and keeps on creating.

I have created you—blessed you—in the image and likeness of Me. And I have made certain promises and commitments to you. I have told you, in plain language, how it will be with you when you become as one with Me.

You are, as Moses was, an earnest seeker. Moses too, as do you now, stood before Me, begging for answers. "Oh, God of My Fathers," he called. "God of my God, deign to show me. Give me a sign that I may tell my people! How can we know that we are chosen?"

And I came to Moses, even as I have come to you now, with a divine covenant—an everlasting promise—a sure and certain commitment. "How can I be sure?" Moses asked plaintively. "Because I have told you so," I said. "You have the Word of God."

And the Word of God was not a commandment, but a covenant. These, then, are the . . .

TEN COMMITMENTS

You shall *know* that you have taken the path to God, and you shall *know* that you have *found* God, for there will be these signs, these indications, these *changes* in you:

1. You shall love God with all your heart, all your mind, all your soul. And there shall be no other God set before Me. No longer will you worship human love, or success, money, or power, nor any symbol thereof. You will set aside these things as a child sets aside toys. Not because they are unworthy, but because *you have outgrown them.*

And, you shall *know* you have taken the path to God because:

2. You shall not use the name of God in vain. Nor will you call upon Me for frivolous things. You will understand the *power* of words, and of thoughts, and you would not *think* of invoking the name of God in an unGodly manner. You shall not use My

name in vain because you *cannot*. For My name—the Great "I Am"—is *never* used in vain (that is, without result), *nor can it ever be*. And when you have found God, you shall *know this*.

And, I shall give you these other signs as well:

3. You shall remember to keep a day for Me, and you shall call it holy. This, so that you do not long stay in your illusion, but cause yourself to remember who and what you are. And then shall you soon call *every* day the Sabbath, and *every* moment holy.

4. You shall honor your mother and your father—and you will *know* you are the Son of God when you honor your Father/Mother God in all that you say or do or think. And even as you so honor the Mother/Father God, and your father and mother on Earth (for they have given you *life*), so, too, will you honor *everyone*.

5. You *know* you have found God when you observe that you will not murder (that is, willfully kill, without cause). For while you will understand that you cannot *end* another's life in any event (all life is eternal), you will not choose to terminate any particular incarnation, nor change any life energy from one form to another, without the most sacred justification. Your new reverence for life will cause you to honor *all* life forms—including plants, trees and animals—and to impact them only when it is for the highest good.

And these other signs will I send you also, that you may know you are on the path:

6. You will not defile the purity of love with dishonesty or deceit, for this is adulterous. I promise you, when you have found God, *you shall not commit this adultery*.

7. You will not take a thing that is not your own, nor cheat, nor connive, nor harm another to have any thing, for this would be to steal. I promise you, when you have found God, *you shall not steal*.

Nor shall you . . .

8. Say a thing that is not true, and thus bear false witness.

Nor shall you . . .

9. Covet your neighbor's spouse, for why would you want your *neighbor's* spouse when you know *all* others are your spouse?

10. Covet your neighbor's goods, for why would you want your *neighbor's* goods when you know that *all* goods can be yours, and all your goods belong to the world?

You will *know* that you have found the path to God when you see these signs. For I promise that no one who truly seeks God shall any longer do these things. It would be impossible to continue such behaviors.

These are your *freedoms*, not your *restrictions*. These are my *commitments*, not my *commandments*. For God does not order about what God has created—God merely tells God's children: this is how you will know that you are coming home.

Moses asked in earnest—"How may I know? Give me a sign." Moses asked the same question that you ask now. The same question all people everywhere have asked since time began. My answer is likewise eternal. But it has never been, and never will be, a commandment. For who shall I command? And who shall I punish should My commandments not be kept?

There is only Me.

So I don't have to keep the Ten Commandments in order to get to heaven.

There is no such thing as "getting to heaven." There is only a knowing that you are already there. There is an accepting, an understanding, not a working for or a striving.

You cannot go to where you already are. To do that, you would have to leave where you are, and that would defeat the whole purpose of the journey.

The irony is that most people think they have to leave where they are to get to where they want to be. And so they leave heaven in order to *get* to heaven—and go through hell.

Enlightenment is understanding that there is nowhere to go, nothing to do, and nobody you have to be except exactly who you're being right now.

You are on a journey to nowhere.

Heaven—as you call it—is nowhere. Let's just put some space between the *w* and the *h* in that word and you'll see that heaven is now . . . here.

Everyone says that! Everyone says that! It's driving me crazy! If "heaven is now here," how come I don't see that? Why don't I feel that? And why is the world such a mess?

I understand your frustration. It's almost as frustrating trying to understand all this as it is trying to *get* someone to understand it.

Whoa! Wait a minute! Are you trying to say that God gets frustrated?

Who do you suppose *invented* frustration? And do you imagine that you can experience something I cannot?

I tell you this: every experience you have, I have. Do you not see I am experiencing my Self *through you?* What else do you suppose all this is for?

I could not know Myself were it not for You. I *created* you that I might know Who I Am.

Now I would not shatter *all* of your illusions about Me in one chapter—so I will tell you that in My most sublime form, which you call God, I do *not* experience frustration.

Whew! That's better. You scared me there for a minute.

But that's not because I can't. It's simply because I don't choose to. You can make the same choice, by the way.

Well, frustrated or not, I still wonder how it can be that heaven is right here, and I don't experience it.

You cannot experience what you don't know. And you don't know you are in "heaven" right now because you have not experienced it. You see, for you it is a vicious circle. You cannot—have not found a way yet to—experience what you do not know, and you do not know what you have not experienced.

What Enlightenment asks you to do is to know something you have not experienced and thus experience it. Knowing opens the door to experience—and you imagine it is the other way around.

Actually, you know a great deal more than you have experienced. You simply don't know that you know.

You know that there is a God, for instance. But you may not know that you know that. So you keep *waiting around* for the experience. And all the while you keep *having it*. Yet you are having it without knowing—which is like not having it at all.

Boy, we're going around in circles here.

Yes, we are. And instead of going around in circles, perhaps we should be the circle itself. This doesn't have to be a vicious circle. It can be a sublime one.

Is renunciation a part of the truly spiritual life?

Yes, because ultimately all Spirit renounces what is not real, and nothing in the life you lead is real, save your relationship with Me. *Yet renunciation in the classic sense of self-denial is not required.*

A true Master does not "give up" something. A true Master simply sets it aside, as he would do with anything for which he no longer has any use.

There are those who say you must overcome your desires. I say you must simply change them. The first practice feels like a rigorous discipline, the second, a joyful exercise.

There are those who say that to know God you must overcome all earthly passions. Yet to understand and accept them is enough. *What you resist persists. What you look at disappears.*

Those who seek so earnestly to overcome all earthly passions often work at it so hard that it might be said, *this* has become their passion. They have a "passion for God"; a passion to know Him. But passion is passion, and to trade one for the other does not eliminate it.

Therefore, judge not that about which you feel passionate. Simply notice it, then see if it serves you, given who and what you wish to be.

Remember, you are constantly in the act of creating yourself. You are in every moment deciding who and what you are. You decide this largely through the choices you make regarding who and what you feel passionate about.

Often a person on what you call a spiritual path *looks like* he has renounced all earthly passion, all human desire. What he has done is understand it, see the illusion, and step aside from the passions that do not serve him—all the while loving the illusion for what it has brought to him: the chance to be wholly free.

Passion is the love of turning being into action. It fuels the engine of creation. It changes concepts to experience.

Passion is the fire that drives us to express who we really are. Never deny passion, for that is to deny Who You Are and Who You Truly Want to Be.

The renunciate never denies passion—the renunciate simply denies attachment to results. Passion is a love of doing. Doing is being, *experienced*. Yet what is often created as part of doing? *Expectation*.

To live your life without *expectation*—without the need for specific results—*that* is freedom. That is Godliness. That is how *I* live.

You are not attached to results?

Absolutely not. My joy is in the creating, not in the aftermath. Renunciation is *not* a decision to deny action. Renunciation is a decision to deny a need for a particular *result*. There is a vast difference.

Could you explain what You mean by the statement, "Passion is the love of turning being into action"?

Beingness is the highest state of existence. It is the purest essence. It is the "now-not now," the "all-not all," the "always-never" aspect of God.

Pure being is pure God-ing.

Yet it has never been enough for us to simply *be*. We have always yearned to *experience* What We Are—and that requires a whole other aspect of divinity, called doing.

Let us say that you are, at the core of your wonderful Self, that aspect of divinity called love. (This is, by the way, the Truth of you.)

Now it is one thing to *be* love—and quite another thing to *do* something loving. The soul longs to do something about what it is, in order that it might know itself in its own experience. So it will seek to realize its highest idea through action.

This urge to do this is called passion. Kill passion and you kill God. Passion is God wanting to say "hi."

But, you see, once God (or God-in-you) does that loving thing, God has realized Itself, and needs nothing more.

Man, on the other hand, often feels he needs a *return* on his investment. If we're going to love somebody, fine—but we'd better get some love back. That sort of thing.

This is *not* passion. This is *expectation*.

This is the greatest source of man's unhappiness. It is what separates man from God.

The renunciate seeks to end this separation through the experience some Eastern mystics have called *samadhi*. That is, oneness and union with God; a melding with and melting into divinity.

The renunciate therefore *renounces results*—but never, *ever* renounces passion. Indeed, the Master knows intuitively that passion is the path. It is the way to Self realization.

Even in earthly terms it can be fairly said that if you have a passion for nothing, you have no life at all.

You have said that "what you resist persists, and what you look at disappears." Can You explain that?

You cannot resist something to which you grant no reality. The act of resisting a thing is the act of granting it life. When you resist an energy, you place it there. The more you resist, the more you make it real—*whatever* it is you are resisting.

What you open your eyes and look at disappears. That is, *it ceases to hold its illusory form.*

If you look at something—truly *look* at it—you will see *right through it,* and right through any illusion it holds for you, leaving nothing but ultimate reality in your sight. In the face of ultimate reality your puny illusion has no power. It cannot long hold you in its weakening grip. You see the *truth* of it, and the truth sets you free.

But what if you don't *want* the thing you are looking at to disappear?

You should *always* want it to! There is nothing in your reality to hold onto. Yet if you *do choose* the illusion of your life over ultimate reality, you may simply *recreate it*—just as you created it to begin with. In this way you may have in your life what you *choose to have* and eliminate from your life what you no longer wish to experience.

Yet never resist *anything*. If you think that by your resistance you will eliminate it, *think again.* You only plant it more firmly in place. Have I not told you *all thought* is creative?

Even a thought that says I don't want something?

If you don't want it, why think about it? Don't give it a second thought. Yet if you *must* think about it—that is, if you cannot *not* think about it—then do not resist. Rather, look at whatever it is *directly*—accept the reality as your creation—then choose to keep it or not, as you wish.

What would dictate that choice?

Who and What you think you Are. And Who and What you choose to Be.

This dictates *all* choice—every choice you have made in your life. And ever *will* make.

And so the life of a renunciate is an incorrect path?

That is not a truth. The *word* "renunciate" holds such wrongful meaning. In truth, you can not *renounce anything*—because what you *resist persists*. The true renunciate does not renounce, but simply *chooses differently*. This is an act of moving toward something, not away from something.

You cannot move away from something, because it will chase you all over hell and back. Therefore resist not temptation—but simply turn from it. Turn toward Me and away from anything unlike Me.

Yet know this: there is no such thing as an incorrect path—for on this journey you cannot "not get" where you are going.

It is simply a matter of speed—merely a question of *when* you will get there—yet even that is an illusion, for there is no *"when,"* neither is there a "before" or "after." There is only now; an eternal moment of always in which you are experiencing yourself.

Then what is the point? If there is no way *not* to "get there," what is the point of life? Why should we worry at all about anything we do?

Well, of course, you *shouldn't*. But you *would do well* to be observant. Simply notice who and what you are being, doing, and having, and see whether it serves you.

The point of life is not to get anywhere—it is to notice that you are, and have always been, already there. You are, always and for-ever, in the moment of pure creation. The point of life is therefore to create—who and what you are, and then to experience *that.*

6

And what of suffering? Is suffering the way and the path to God? Some say it is the *only* way.

> I am not pleased by suffering, and whoever says I am does not know Me.
>
> Suffering is an unnecessary aspect of the human experience. It is not only unnecessary, it is unwise, uncomfortable, and hazardous to your health.

Then why is there so much suffering? Why don't You, if You *are* God, put an *end* to it if You dislike it so much?

> I have put an end to it. You simply refuse to use the tools I have given you with which to realize that.
>
> You see, suffering has nothing to do with events, but with one's reaction to them.
>
> *What's happening is merely what's happening. How you feel about it is another matter.*
>
> I have given you the tools with which to respond and react to events in a way which reduces—in fact, *eliminates*—pain, but you have not used them.

Excuse me, but why not eliminate the *events*?

> A very good suggestion. Unfortunately, I have no control over them.

You have *no control* over events?

> Of course not. Events are occurrences in time and space which you produce out of choice—and I will never interfere with choices. To do so would be to obviate the very reason I created you. But I've explained all this before.
>
> Some events you produce willfully, and some events you draw to you—more or less unconsciously. Some events—major natural

95

disasters are among those you toss into this category—are written off to "fate."

Yet even "fate" can be an acronym for "from all thoughts every-where." In other words, the consciousness of the planet.

The "collective consciousness."

Precisely. Exactly.

There are those who say the world is going to hell in a handbasket. Our ecology is dying. Our planet is in for a major geophysical disaster. Earthquakes. Volcanoes. Maybe even a tilting of the Earth on its axis. And there are others who say collective consciousness can change all that; that we can save the Earth with our thoughts.

Thoughts put into action. If enough people everywhere believe something must be done to help the environment, you will save the Earth. But you must work fast. So much damage has already been done, for so long. This will take a major attitudinal shift.

You mean if we don't, we *will* see the Earth—and its inhabitants—destroyed?

I have made the laws of the physical universe clear enough for anyone to understand. There are laws of cause and effect which have been sufficiently outlined to your scientists, physicists, and, through them, to your world leaders. These laws don't need to be outlined once more here.

Getting back to suffering—where did we ever get the idea that suffering was *good?* That the saintly "suffer in silence"?

The saintly *do* "suffer in silence," but that does not mean suffering is good. The students in the school of Mastery suffer in silence because they understand that suffering is not the way of God, but rather a sure sign that there is still something to *learn* of the way of God, still something to remember.

The *true* Master does not suffer in silence at all, but only appears to be suffering without complaint. The reason that the true Master does not complain is that the true Master is *not suffering,* but simply experiencing a set of circumstances that *you* would call insufferable.

A practicing Master does not speak of suffering simply because a Master practicing *clearly understands* the *power of the Word—* and so chooses to simply *not say a word about it.*

We make real that to which we pay attention. The Master knows this. The Master places himself *at choice* with regard to that which she chooses to make real.

You have all done this from time to time. There is not a one among you who has not made a headache disappear, or a visit to the dentist less painful, *through your decision about it.*

A Master simply makes the same decision about larger things.

But why have suffering at all? Why have even the *possibility* of suffering?

You cannot know, and become, that which you are, in the absence of that which you are not, as I have already explained to you.

I still don't understand how we ever got the idea that suffering was *good.*

You are wise to be insistent in questioning that. The original wisdom surrounding suffering in silence has become so perverted that now many believe (and several religions actually *teach*) that suffering is *good,* and *joy* is *bad.* Therefore, you have decided that if someone has cancer, but keeps it to himself, he is a saint, whereas if someone has (to pick a dynamite topic) robust sexuality, and celebrates it openly, she is a sinner.

Boy, You did pick a dynamite topic. And You cleverly changed the pronoun, too, from male to female. Was that to make a point?

It was to show you your prejudices. You don't like to think of women *having* robust sexuality, much less celebrating it openly.

You would rather see a man dying without a whimper on the battlefield than a woman making love with a whimper in the street.

Wouldn't YOU?

I have no judgment one way or the other. But you have all sorts of them—and I suggest that it is your judgments which keep you from joy, and your expectations which make you unhappy.

All of this put together is what causes you dis-ease, and therein begins your suffering.

How do I know that what You are saying is true? How do I know this is even God speaking, and not my overactive imagination?

You've asked that before. My answer is the same. What difference does it make? Even if everything I've said is "wrong," can you think of a better way to live?

No.

Then "wrong" is *right*, and "right" is *wrong!*

Yet I'll tell you this, to help you out of your dilemma: believe *nothing* I say. Simply *live* it. *Experience* it. Then live whatever other paradigm you want to construct. Afterward, look to your *experience* to find your truth.

One day, if you have a great deal of courage, you will experience a world where making love *is* considered better than making war. On that day will you rejoice.

_7_

Life is so scary. And so confusing. I wish things could be more clear.

> There is nothing scary about life, if you are not attached to results.

You mean if you don't want anything.

> That's right. _Choose,_ but don't want.

That's easy for people who don't have anybody depending on them. What if you have a wife and children?

> The path of the householder has always been a most challenging path. Perhaps _the_ most challenging. As you point out, it is easy to "want nothing" when you are only dealing with yourself. It is natural, when you have others you love, to want only the best for them.

It hurts when you can't give them all that you want them to have. A nice home, some decent clothes, enough food. I feel as though I've been struggling for 20 years just to make ends meet. And I still have nothing to show for it.

> You mean in terms of material wealth?

I mean in terms of just some of the basics that a man would like to pass on to his children. I mean in terms of some of the very simple things a man would like to provide for his wife.

> I see. You see it as your job in life to provide all these things. Is that what you imagine your life to be about?

I'm not sure I'd state it that way. This is not what my life is _about,_ but it sure would be nice if this could be a _by-product_, at least.

Well, let's go back, then. What *do* you see your life being about?

That's a good question. I've had a lot of different answers to that through the years.

What is your answer now?

It feels as though I have two answers to that question; the answer I'd *like* to see, and the answer I'm seeing.

What's the answer you'd *like* to see?

I'd like to see my life being about the evolution of my soul. I'd like to see my life being about expressing and experiencing the part of me I love most. The part of me that is compassion and patience and giving and helping. The part of me that is knowing and wise, forgiving and . . . love.

Sounds like you've been reading this book!

Yes, well it's a beautiful book, on an esoteric level, but I'm trying to figure out how to "practicalize" that. The answer to your question that I see being real in my life is that it's about day-to-day survival.

Oh. And you think one thing precludes the other? Well. . . .
You think esoterics preclude survival?

The truth is, I'd like to do more than just survive. I've been *surviving* all these years. I notice I'm still here. But I'd like the *struggle* for survival to end. I see that just getting by from day to day is still a struggle. I'd like to do more than just survive. I'd like to *prosper.*

And what would you call prospering?

Having enough that I don't have to worry where my next dollar is coming from; not having to stress and strain just to make the rent, or handle the phone bill. I mean, I hate to get so mundane, but we're talking *real life* here, not the airy-fairy, spiritually romanticized picture of life you draw throughout this book.

Do I hear a little anger there?

Not anger so much as frustration. I've been at the spiritual game for over 20 years now, and look where it's gotten me. One paycheck away from the poorhouse! And now I've just lost my job, and it looks like the cash flow has stopped *again*. I'm getting really tired of the struggle. I'm 49 years old, and I'd like to have some *security* in life so that I *could* devote more time to "God stuff," to soul "evoluting," etc. That's where my heart is, but it's not where my life allows me to go. . . .

Well, you've said a mouthful there, and I suspect you're speaking for a whole lot of people when you share that experience.

I'm going to respond to your truth one sentence at a time, so that we can easily track, and dissect, the answer.

You have not been "at this spiritual game" for 20 years, you have been barely skirting the edges of it. (This is not a "spanking," by the way, this is just a statement of the truth.) I'll concede that for two decades you've been *looking* at it; *flirting* with it; *experimenting* now and then . . . but I haven't felt your true—your truest—*commitment* to the game until just recently.

Let's be clear that *"being at the spiritual game" means dedicating your whole mind, your whole body, your whole soul to the process of creating Self in the image and likeness of God.*

This is the process of Self realization about which Eastern mystics have written. It is the process of salvation to which much Western theology has devoted itself.

This is a day-to-day, hour-to-hour, moment-to-moment act of supreme consciousness. It is a choosing and a re-choosing every instant. It is ongoing creation. *Conscious* creation. Creation with a *purpose*. It is using the tools of creation we have discussed, and using them with awareness and sublime intention.

That is "playing this spiritual game." Now, how long have you been at this?

I haven't even begun.

Don't go from one extreme to the other, and don't be so hard on yourself. You *have* been dedicated to this process—and you're actually engaged in it more than you'll give yourself credit for. But you haven't been doing so for 20 years—or anything close to that. Yet the truth is, how long you have been engaged in it is not important. Are you engaged in it *now?* That's all that matters.

Let's move on with your statement. You ask us to "look where it's gotten you," and you describe yourself as being "one step away from the poorhouse." I look at you and see a quite different thing. I see a person who is one step away from the rich house! You feel you are one paycheck from oblivion, and I see you as one paycheck from Nirvana. Now much depends, of course, on what you see as your "pay"—and to what end you are working.

If the object of your life is to acquire what you call security, I see and understand why you feel you are "one paycheck from the poorhouse." Yet even this assessment is open to correction. Because with My pay, *all* good things come to you—including the experience of feeling secure in the physical world.

My pay—the payoff you get when you "work for" Me—provides a great deal more than spiritual comfort. *Physical* comfort, too, can be yours. Yet the ironic part about all this is that, once you experience the kind of spiritual comfort My payoff provides, the last thing you'll find yourself worrying about is physical comfort.

Even the physical comfort of members of your family will no longer be a concern to you—for once you rise to a level of God consciousness you will understand that you are not responsible for any other human soul, and that while it is commendable to wish every soul to live in comfort, each soul must choose—*is choosing*—its own destiny this instant.

Clearly, it is not the highest action to deliberately abuse or destroy another. Clearly, it is equally inappropriate to neglect the needs of those you have caused to be dependent on you.

Your job is to render them *independent*; to teach them as quickly and completely as possible *how to get along without you.* For you are no blessing to them so long as they need you to survive, but bless them truly only in the moment they realize you are unnecessary.

In the same sense, God's greatest moment is the moment you realize you *need no God.*

I know, I know . . . this is the antithesis of everything you've ever been taught. Yet your teachers have told you of an angry God, a jealous God, a God who needs to be needed. And that is not a God at all, but a neurotic substitute for that which would be a deity.

A true Master is not the one with the most students, but one who creates the most Masters.

A true leader is not the one with the most followers, but one who creates the most leaders.

A true king is not the one with the most subjects, but one who leads the most to royalty.

A true teacher is not the one with the most knowledge, but one who causes the most others to have knowledge.

And a true God is not One with the most servants, but One who serves the most, thereby making Gods of all others.

For this is both the goal and the glory of God: that His subjects shall be no more, and that all shall know God not as the unattainable, but as the unavoidable.

I would that you could this understand: your happy destiny is *unavoidable.* You cannot *not* be "saved." There is no hell except not knowing this.

So now, as parents, spouses, and loved ones, seek not to make of your love a glue that binds, but rather a magnet that first attracts, then turns around and repels, lest those who are attracted begin to believe they must stick to you to survive. Nothing could be further from the truth. Nothing could be more damaging to another.

Let your love *propel* your beloveds into the world—and into the full experience of who they are. In this will you have truly loved.

It is a great challenge, this path of the householder. There are many distractions, many worldly concerns. The ascetic is bothered by none of these. He is brought his bread and water, and given his humble mat on which to lie, and he can devote his every hour to prayer, meditation, and contemplation of the divine. How easy to see the divine under such circumstances. How simple a task! Ah, but give one a spouse, and children! See the divine in a baby who needs changing at 3 A.M. See the divine in a bill that needs paying by the first of the month. Recognize the hand of God in the illness that takes a spouse, the job that's lost, the child's fever, the parent's pain. Now we are talking saintliness.

I understand your fatigue. I know you are tired of the struggle. Yet I tell you this: When you follow Me, the struggle disappears. Live in your God space and the events become blessings, one and all.

How can I get to my God space when I've lost my job, the rent needs paying, the kids need a dentist, and being in my lofty, philosophical space seems the least likely way to solve any of this?

Do not forsake Me when you need Me most. Now is the hour of your greatest testing. Now is the time of your greatest chance. It is the chance to prove everything that has been written here.

When I say "don't forsake Me," I sound like that needy, neurotic God we talked about. But I'm not. You can "forsake Me" all you want. I don't care, and it won't change a thing between us. I merely say this in answer to your questions. It is when the going gets tough that you so often forget *Who You Are,* and the *tools* I have given you for creating the life that you would choose.

Now is the time to go to your God space more than ever. First, it will bring you great peace of mind—and from a peaceful mind do great ideas flow—ideas which could be solutions to the biggest problems you imagine yourself to have.

Second, it is in your God space that you Self realize, and that is the purpose—the *only* purpose—of your soul.

When you are in your God space, you know and understand that all you are now experiencing is temporary. I tell you that heaven and Earth shall pass away, but *you* shall not. This everlasting perspective helps you to see things in their proper light.

You can define these present conditions and circumstances as what they truly are: temporary and temporal. You may then use them as tools—for that is what they are, temporary, temporal tools—in the creation of present experience.

Just who do you think you are? In relationship to the experience called lose-a-job, who do you think you are? And, perhaps more to the point, who do you think *I am?* Do you imagine this is too big a problem for Me to solve? Is getting out of this jam too big a miracle for Me to handle? I understand that you may think it's too big for you to handle, even with all the tools I have given you—but do you really think it's too big for Me?

I know intellectually that no job is too big for God. But emotionally I guess I can't be sure. Not whether You *can* handle it, but whether You *will.*

I see. So it's a matter of faith.

Yes.

You don't question My ability, you merely doubt My desire.

You see, I still live this theology that says there may be a lesson in here somewhere for me. I'm still not sure I'm *supposed* to have a solution. Maybe I'm supposed to have the *problem.* Maybe this is one of those "tests" my theology keeps telling me about. So I worry that this problem may *not* be solved. That this is one of those *You're* going to let me hang here with. . . .

Perhaps this is a good time to go over once more how it is that I interact with you, because you think it is a question of My desire, and I'm telling you it's a question *of yours.*

I want for you what *you* want for you. Nothing more, nothing less. I don't sit here and make a judgment, request by request, whether something should be granted you.

My law is the law of cause and effect, not the law of We'll See. There is *nothing* you can't have if you choose it. Even before you ask, I will have given it to you. Do you believe this?

No. I'm sorry. I've seen too many prayers go unanswered.

Don't be sorry. Just always stay with the truth—the truth of your experience. I understand that. I honor that. That's okay with Me.

Good, because I *don't* believe that whatever I ask, I get. My life has not been a testimony to that. In fact, I *rarely* get what I ask for. When I do, I consider myself damned lucky.

That's an interesting choice of words. You have an option, it seems. In your life, you can either be damned lucky, or you can be blessing lucky. I'd rather you be blessing lucky—but, of course, I'll never interfere with your decisions.

I tell you this: You *always* get what you create, and you are *always creating.*

I do not make a judgment about the creations that you conjure, I simply empower you to conjure more—and more and more and more. If you don't like what you've just created, *choose again.* My job, as God, is to *always give you that opportunity.*

Now you are telling Me that you haven't always gotten what you've wanted. Yet I am here to tell you that you've *always* gotten what you called forth.

Your Life is always a result of your thoughts about it—including your obviously creative thought that you seldom get what you choose.

Now in this present instance you see yourself as the victim of the situation in the losing of your job. Yet the truth is that you no longer chose that job. You stopped getting up in the morning in anticipation, and began getting up with dread. You stopped feeling happy about your work and began feeling resentment. You even began fantasizing *doing something else.*

You think these things mean nothing? You misunderstand your power. I tell you this: *Your Life proceeds out of your* intentions *for it.*

So what is your intention now? Do you intend to prove your theory that life seldom brings you what you choose? Or do you intend to demonstrate Who You Really Are and Who I Am?

I feel chagrined. Chastised. Embarrassed.

Does that serve you? Why not simply acknowledge the truth when you hear it, and move toward it? There is no need to recriminate against yourself. Simply notice what you've been choosing and choose again.

But why am I so ready to always choose the negative? And then to spank myself for it?

What can you expect? You were told from your earliest days that you're "bad." You accept that you were born in "sin." Feeling guilty is a *learned response.* You've been told to feel guilty about yourself for things you did before you could even do anything. You have been taught to feel shame for being born less than perfect.

This alleged state of imperfection in which you are said to have come into this world is what your religionists have the gall to call original sin. And it *is* original sin—but not yours. It is the first sin to be perpetrated upon you by a world which knows nothing of God if it thinks that God would—or *could*—create *anything* imperfect.

Some of your religions have built up whole theologies around this misconception. And that is what it is, *literally*: a *misconception. For anything I conceive—all that to which I give life—is perfect; a perfect reflection of perfection itself, made in the image and likeness of Me.*

Yet, in order to justify the idea of a punitive God, your religions needed to create something for Me to be angry about. So that even those people who lead exemplary lives somehow need to be saved. If they don't need to be saved from themselves, then they need to be saved from their own *built-in imperfection.* So (these religions say) you'd better do something about all of this—and fast—or you'll go straight to hell.

This, in the end, may do nothing to mollify a weird, vindictive, angry God, but it does give life to weird, vindictive, angry *religions.* Thus do religions perpetuate themselves. Thus does power remain concentrated in the hands of the few, rather than experienced though the hands of the many.

Of *course* you choose constantly the lesser thought, the smaller idea, the tiniest concept of yourself and your power, to say nothing of Me and Mine. You've been *taught* to.

My God, how can I undo the teaching?

A good question, and addressed to just the right person!

You can undo the teaching by reading and re-reading this book. Over and over again, read it. Until you understand every passage. Until you're familiar with every word. When you can quote its passages to others, when you can bring its phrases to mind in the midst of the darkest hour, then you will have "undone the teaching."

Yet there is still so much I want to ask You; still so much I want to know.

Indeed. You began with a very long list of questions. Shall we get back to it?

8

When will I learn enough about relationships to be able to have them go smoothly? Is there a way to *be* happy in relationships? Must they be constantly challenging?

You have nothing to learn about relationships. You have only to demonstrate what you already know. There *is* a way to be happy in relationships, and that is to use relationships for their intended purpose, not the purpose you have designed. Relationships are constantly challenging; constantly calling you to create, express, and experience higher and higher aspects of yourself, grander and grander visions of yourself, ever more magnificent *versions* of yourself. Nowhere can you do this more immediately, impactfully, and immaculately than in relationships. In fact, without relationships, *you cannot do it at all.*

It is *only* through your relationship with other people, places, and events that you can even exist (as a knowable quantity, as an identifiable *something*) in the universe. Remember, absent everything *else*, you are *not*. You only are what you are relative to another thing that is not. That is how it is in the world of the relative, as opposed to the world of the absolute—where I reside.

Once you clearly understand this, once you deeply grasp it, then you intuitively bless each and every experience, all human encounter, and especially personal human relationships, for you see them as constructive, in the highest sense. You see that they can be used, must be used, *are* being used (whether you want them to be or not) to *construct* Who You Really Are.

That construction can be a magnificent creation of your own conscious design, or a strictly happenstance configuration. You can choose to be a person who has resulted simply from what has happened, or from what you've chosen to *be* and *do* about what has happened. It is in the latter form that creation of Self becomes conscious. It is in the second experience that Self becomes realized.

Bless, therefore, *every* relationship, and hold each as special and formative of Who You Are—and now choose to be.

Now your inquiry has to do with individual human relationships of the romantic sort, and I understand that. So let Me address Myself specifically, and at length, to human love relationships—these things which continue to give you such trouble!

When human love relationships fail (relationships never truly fail, except in the strictly human sense that they did not produce what you want), they fail because they were entered into for the wrong reason.

("Wrong," of course, is a relative term, meaning something measured against that which is "right"—whatever *that* is! It would be more accurate in your language to say "relationships fail—change—most often when they are entered into for reasons not wholly beneficial or conducive to their survival.")

Most people enter into relationships with an eye toward what they can get out of them, rather than what they can put into them.

The purpose of a relationship is to decide what part of yourself you'd like to see "show up," not what part of another you can capture and hold.

There can be only one purpose for relationships—and for all of *life*: to be and to decide Who You Really Are.

It is very romantic to say that you were "nothing" until that special other came along, but it is not true. Worse, it puts an incredible pressure on the other to be all sorts of things he or she is not.

Not wanting to "let you down," they try very hard to be and do these things until they cannot anymore. They can no longer complete your picture of them. They can no longer fill the roles to which they have been assigned. Resentment builds. Anger follows.

Finally, in order to save themselves (*and* the relationship), these special others begin to reclaim their real selves, acting more in accordance with Who They Really Are. It is about this time that you say they've "really changed."

It is very romantic to say that now that your special other has entered your life, you feel complete. *Yet the purpose of relationship is not to have another who might complete you; but to have another with whom you might share your completeness.*

Here is the paradox of all human relationships: You have no need for a particular other in order for you to experience, fully, Who You Are, *and* . . . without another, you are nothing.

This is both the mystery and the wonder, the frustration and the joy of the human experience. It requires deep understanding and total willingness to live within this paradox in a way which makes sense. I observe that very few people do.

Most of you enter your relationship-forming years ripe with anticipation, full of sexual energy, a wide-open heart, and a joyful, if eager, soul.

Somewhere between 40 and 60 (and for most it is sooner rather than later) you've given up on your grandest dream, set aside your highest hope, and settled for your lowest expectation—or nothing at all.

The problem is so basic, so simple, and yet so tragically misunderstood: your grandest dream, your highest idea, and your fondest hope has had to do with your beloved *other* rather than your beloved *Self*. The test of your relationships has had to do with how well the other lived up to *your* ideas, and how well you saw yourself living up to *his* or *hers*. Yet the only true test has to do with how well you live up to *yours*.

Relationships are *sacred* because they provide life's grandest opportunity—indeed, its only opportunity—to create and produce the *experience* of your highest conceptualization of Self. Relationships fail when you see them as life's grandest opportunity to create and produce the *experience* of your highest conceptualization of *another*.

Let each person in relationship worry about *Self*—what *Self* is being, doing, and having; what *Self* is wanting, asking, giving; what *Self* is seeking, creating, experiencing, and all relationships would magnificently serve their purpose—*and* their participants!

Let each person in relationship worry not about the other, but only, only, only about Self.

This seems a strange teaching, for you have been told that in the highest form of relationship, one worries *only* about the other. Yet I tell you this: your focus upon the other—your *obsession* with the other—is what causes relationships to fail.

What is the other being? What is the other doing? What is the other having? What is the other saying? Wanting? Demanding? What is the other thinking? Expecting? Planning?

The Master understands that it doesn't *matter* what the other is being, doing, having, saying, wanting, demanding. It doesn't *matter* what the other is thinking, expecting, planning. It only matters what *you* are being in *relationship* to that.

The most loving person is the person who is Self-centered.

That *is* a radical teaching. . . .

Not if you look at it carefully. If you cannot love your Self, you cannot love another. Many people make the mistake of seeking love of Self *through* love for another. Of course, they don't realize they are doing this. It is not a conscious effort. It's what's going on in the mind. Deep in the mind. In what you call the subconscious.

They think: "If I can just love others, they will love me. Then I will be lovable, and *I* can love me."

The reverse of this is that so many people hate themselves because they feel there is not another who loves them. This is a sickness—it's when people are truly "lovesick" because the truth is, other people *do* love them, but it doesn't matter. No matter how many people profess their love for them, it is not enough.

First, they don't believe you. They think you are trying to manipulate them—trying to get something. (How could you love them for who they truly are? No. There must be some mistake. You must want something! Now what do you want?)

They sit around trying to figure out how anyone could actually love them. So they don't believe you, and embark on a campaign to make you *prove* it. You have to prove that you love them. To do this, they may ask you to start altering your behavior.

Second, if they finally come to a place where they *can* believe you love them, they begin at once to worry about how long they can *keep* your love. So, in order to hold onto your love, they start altering *their* behavior.

Thus, two people literally lose themselves in a relationship. They get into the relationship hoping to find themselves, and they lose themselves instead.

This losing of the Self in a relationship is what causes most of the bitterness in such couplings.

Two people join together in a partnership hoping that the whole will be greater than the sum of the parts, only to find that it's less. They feel *less* than when they were single. Less capable, less able, less exciting, less attractive, less joyful, less content.

This is because they *are* less. They've given up most of who they are in order to be—and to stay—in their relationship.

Relationships were never meant to be this way. Yet this is how they are experienced by more people than you could ever know.

Why? *Why?*

It is because people have lost touch with (if they ever *were* in touch with) the *purpose* of relationships.

When you lose sight of each other as sacred souls on a sacred journey, then you cannot see the purpose, the reason, behind all relationships.

The soul has come to the body, and the body to life, for the purpose of evolution. You are *evolving*, you are *becoming*. And you are using your relationship with *everything* to decide *what* you are becoming.

This is the job you came here to do. This is the joy of creating Self. Of knowing Self. Of becoming, consciously, what you wish to be. It is what is meant by being Self conscious.

You have brought your Self to the relative world so that you might have the tools with which to know and experience Who You Really Are. Who You Are is who you create yourself to be in relationship to all the rest of it.

Your personal relationships are the most important elements in this process. Your personal relationships are therefore holy ground. They have virtually nothing to do with the other, yet, because they involve another, they have *everything* to do with the other.

This is the divine dichotomy. This is the closed circle. So it is not such a radical teaching to say, "Blessed are the Self-centered, for they shall know God." It might not be a bad goal in your life to know the highest part of your Self, and to *stay centered* in that.

Your first relationship, therefore, must be with your Self. You must first learn to honor and cherish and love your Self.

You must first see your Self as worthy before you can see another as worthy. You must first see your Self as blessed before you can see another as blessed. You must first know your Self to be holy before you can acknowledge holiness in another.

If you put the cart before the horse—as most religions ask you to do—and acknowledge another as holy before you acknowledge yourself, you will one day resent it. If there is one thing none of you can tolerate, it is someone being *holier than thou*. Yet your religions force you to call others holier than thou. And so you do it—for a while. Then you crucify them.

You have crucified (in one way or another) all of My teachers, not just One. And you did so not because they were holier than thou, but because you *made them out to be*.

My teachers have all come with the same message. Not "I am holier than thou," but "You are as holy as am I."

This is the message you have not been able to hear; this is the truth you have not been able to accept. And that is why you can never truly, purely, fall in love with another. You have never truly, purely fallen in love with your Self.

And so I tell you this: be now and forever centered upon your Self. Look to see what *you* are being, doing, and having in any given moment, not what's going on with another.

It is not in the action of another, but in your re-action, that your salvation will be found.

I know better, but somehow this makes it sound as though we should not mind what others do to us in relationships. They can do anything, and so long as we hold our equilibrium, keep our Self centered, and all that good stuff, nothing can touch us. But others *do* touch us. Their actions *do* sometimes hurt us. It is when the hurt conies into relationships that I don't know what to do. It's all very well to say "stand aside from it; cause it to mean nothing," but that's easier said than done. I *do* get hurt by the words and actions of others in relationships.

The day will come when you will not. That will be the day on which you realize—and actualize—the true meaning of relationships; the true reason for them.

It is because you have forgotten this that you react the way you do. But that is alright. That is part of the growth process. It is part of evolution. It is Soul Work you are up to in relationship, yet that is a grand understanding, a grand remembering. Until you remember this—and remember then also how to *use* relationship as a tool in the creation of Self—you must work at the level at which you are. The level of understanding, the level of willingness, the level of remembrance.

And so there are things you can do when you react with pain and hurt to what another is being, saying, or doing. The first is to admit honestly to yourself and to another exactly how you are feeling. This many of you are afraid to do, because you think it will make you "look bad." Somewhere, deep inside of you, you realize that it probably *is* ridiculous for you to "feel that way." It probably *is* small of you. You are "bigger than that." But you can't *help* it. You still *feel that way.*

There is only one thing you can do. You must honor your feelings. For honoring your feelings means honoring your Self. And you must love your neighbor as you love yourself. How can you ever expect to understand and honor the feelings of another if you cannot honor the feelings within your Self?

The first question in any interactive process with another is: now Who Am I, and Who Do I Want to Be, in relationship to that?

Often you do not remember Who You Are, and do not know Who You Want to Be until you *try out* a few ways of being. That is why honoring your truest feelings is so important.

If your first feeling is a negative feeling, simply *having the feeling* is frequently all that is needed to step away from it. It is when you *have* the anger, *have* the upset, *have* the disgust, *have* the rage, *own* the feeling of wanting to "hurt back," that you can disown these first feelings as "not Who You Want to Be."

The Master is one who has lived through enough such experiences to know in advance what her final choices are. She does not need to "try out" anything.

She's worn these clothes before and knows they *do not fit;* they are not "her." And since a Master's life is devoted to the constant realization of Self as one *knows oneself to be,* such ill-fitting feelings would never be entertained.

That is why Masters are imperturbable in the face of what others might call calamity. A Master blesses calamity, for the Master knows that from the seeds of disaster (and all experience) comes the growth of Self. And the Master's second life purpose is always *growth.* For once one has fully Self realized, there is *nothing left to do* except *be more of that.*

It is at this stage that one moves from soul work to God work, for this is what *I* am up to!

I will assume for the purposes of this discussion that you are still up to soul work. You are still seeking to realize (make "real") Who You Truly Are. Life (I) will give you bountiful opportunities to create that (remember, life is not a process of discovery, life is a process of creation).

You can create Who You Are over and over again. Indeed, you do—every day. As things now stand, you do not always come up with the same answer, however. Given an identical outer experience, on day one you may choose to be patient, loving, and kind in relationship to it. On day two you may choose to be angry, ugly, and sad.

The Master is one who *always comes up with the same answer*—and that answer is always the *highest choice.*

In this the Master is imminently predictable. Conversely, the student is completely unpredictable. One can tell how one is doing on the road to mastery by simply noticing how predictably one makes the highest choice in responding or reacting to any situation.

Of course, this throws open the question, *what choice is highest?*

That is a question around which have revolved the philosophies and theologies of man since the beginning of time. If the question truly engages you, *you are already on your way to mastery.* For it is still true that most people continue to be engaged by another question altogether. Not, what is the highest choice, but, what is the most profitable? Or, how can I lose the least?

When life is lived from a standpoint of damage control or optimum advantage, the *true* benefit of life is forfeited. The opportunity is lost. The chance is missed. For a life lived thusly is a life lived from fear—and that life speaks a lie about you.

For you are not fear, you are love. Love that needs no protection, love that cannot be lost. Yet you will never know this in your *experience* if you continually answer the second question and not the first. For only a person who thinks there is something *to gain or to lose* asks the second question. And only a person who sees life in a different way; who sees Self as a higher being; who understands that winning or losing is *not* the test, but only loving or failing to love—only that person asks the first.

He who asks the second question says, "I am my body." She who asks the first says, "I am my soul."

Yea, let all those who have ears to hear, listen. For I tell you this: at the critical juncture in all human relationships, there is only one question:

What would love do now?

No other question is relevant, no other question is meaningful, no other question has any importance to your soul.

Now we come upon a very delicate point of interpretation, for this principle of love-sponsored action has been widely misunderstood—and it is this misunderstanding which has led to the resentments and angers of life—which, in turn, have caused so many to stray from the path.

For centuries you have been taught that love-sponsored action arises out of the choice to be, do, and have whatever produces the highest good for another.

Yet I tell you this: the highest choice is that which produces the highest good *for you.*

As with all profound spiritual truth, this statement opens itself to immediate misinterpretation. The mystery clears a bit the moment one decides what *is* the highest "good" one could do for oneself. And when the absolute highest choice is made, the mystery dissolves, the circle completes itself, and the highest good for you becomes the highest good for another.

It may take lifetimes to understand this—and even more lifetimes to implement—for this truth revolves around an even greater one: What you do for your Self, you do for another. What you do for another, you do for the Self.

This is because you and the other are one.

And *this* is because . . .

There is naught but You.

All the Masters who have walked your planet have taught this. ("Verily, verily, I say unto you, inasmuch as ye have done it unto one of the least of these my brethren, ye have done it unto Me.") Yet this has remained for most people merely a grand esoteric truth, with *little practical application.* In fact, it is the most practically applicable "esoteric" truth of all time.

It is important in relationships to remember this truth, for without it relationships will be very difficult.

Let's go back to the practical applications of this wisdom and step away from the purely spiritual, esoteric aspect of it for now.

So often, under the old understandings, people—well-meaning and well-intentioned and many very religious—did what they thought would be best for the other person in their relationships. Sadly, all this produced in many cases (in *most* cases) was continued abuse by the other. Continued mistreatment. Continued dysfunction in the relationship.

Ultimately, the person trying to "do what is right" by the other— to be quick to forgive, to show compassion, to continually look past certain problems and behaviors—becomes resentful, angry, and mistrusting, even of God. For how can a just God demand such unending suffering, joylessness, and sacrifice, even in the name of love?

The answer is, God does not. God asks only that you *include yourself* among those you love.

God goes further. God suggests—*recommends*—that you put yourself first.

I do this knowing full well that some of you will call this blasphemy, and therefore not My word, and that others of you will do what might be even worse: *accept* it as My word and misinterpret or distort it to suit your own purposes; to justify unGodly acts.

I tell you this—putting yourself first in the highest sense *never* leads to an unGodly act.

If, therefore, you have caught yourself in an unGodly act as a result of doing what is best for you, the confusion is not in having put yourself first, but rather in misunderstanding what is best for you.

Of course, determining what is best for you will require you to also determine what it is you are trying to do. This is an important step that many people ignore. What are you "up to"? What is your purpose in life? Without answers to these questions, the matter of what is "best" in any given circumstances will remain a mystery.

As a practical matter—again leaving esoterics aside—if you look to what is best for you in these situations where you are being abused, at the very least what you will do is stop the abuse. And that will be good for both you *and* your abuser. *For even an abuser is abused when his abuse is allowed to continue.*

This is not healing to the abuser, but damaging. For if the abuser finds that his abuse is acceptable, what has he learned? Yet if the abuser finds that his abuse will be accepted no more, what has he been allowed to discover?

Therefore, treating others with love does not necessarily mean allowing others to do as they wish.

Parents learn this early with children. Adults are not so quick to learn it with other adults, nor nation with nation.

Yet despots cannot be allowed to flourish, but must be stopped in their despotism. Love of Self, and *love of the despot*, demands it.

This is the answer to your question, "If love is all there is, how can man ever justify war?"

Sometimes man must go to war to make the grandest statement about who man truly is: he who abhors war.

There are times when you may have to *give up* Who You Are in order to *be* Who You Are.

There are Masters who have taught: you cannot *have* it all until you are willing to *give it all up*.

Thus, in order to "have" yourself as a man of peace, you may have to give up the idea of yourself as a man who never goes to war. History has called upon men for such decisions.

The same is true in the most individual and the most personal relationships. Life may more than once call upon you to prove Who You Are by demonstrating an aspect of Who You Are Not.

This is not so difficult to understand if you have lived a few years, though for the idealistically young it may seem the ultimate contradiction. In more mature retrospection it seems more divine dichotomy.

This does not mean in human relationships that if you are being hurt, you have to "hurt back." (Nor does it mean so in relationships between nations.) It simply means that to *allow* another to continually inflict damage may not be the most loving thing to do—for your Self or the other.

This should put to rest some pacifist theories that highest love requires no forceful response to what you consider evil.

The discussion here turns esoteric once more, because no serious exploration of this statement can ignore the word "evil," and the value judgments it invites. In truth, there is nothing evil, only objective phenomena and experience. Yet your very purpose in life requires you to select from the growing collection of endless phenomena a scattered few which you call evil—for unless you do, you cannot call yourself, nor anything else, good—and thus cannot know, or create, your Self.

By that which you call evil do you define yourself—and by that which you call good.

The biggest evil would therefore be to declare nothing evil at all.

You exist in this life in the world of the relative, where one thing can exist only insofar as it relates to another. This is at one and the same time both the function and the purpose of relationship: to provide a field of experience within which you find yourself, define yourself, and—if you choose—constantly recreate Who You Are.

Choosing to be God-like does not mean you choose to be a martyr. And it certainly does not mean you choose to be a victim.

On your way to mastery—when all possibility of hurt, damage, and loss is eliminated—it would be well to recognize hurt, damage, and loss as part of your experience, and decide Who You Are in relationship to it.

Yes, the things that others think, say, or do *will* sometimes hurt you—until they do not anymore. What will get you from here to there most quickly is total honesty—being willing to assert, acknowledge, and declare exactly how you feel about a thing. Say your truth—kindly, but fully and completely. Live your truth, gently, but totally and consistently. Change your truth easily and quickly when your experience brings you new clarity.

No one in right mind, least of all God, would tell you, when you are hurt in a relationship, to "stand aside from it, cause it to mean nothing." If you are *now hurting,* it is too late to cause it to mean nothing. Your task now is to decide what it *does* mean—and to demonstrate that. For in so doing, you choose and become Who You Seek to Be.

So I *don't* have to be the long-suffering wife or the belittled husband or the victim of my relationships in order to render them holy, or to make me pleasing in the eyes of God.

Good grief, of course not.

And I *don't* have to put up with attacks on my dignity, assaults on my pride, damage to my psyche, and wounds to my heart in order to say that I "gave it my best" in a relationship; "did my duty" or "met my obligation" in the eyes of God and man.

Not for one minute.

Then, pray God, tell me—what promises should I make in relationship; what agreements must I keep? What obligations do relationships carry? What guidelines should I seek?

The answer is the answer you cannot hear—for it leaves you without guidelines and renders null and void every agreement in the moment you make it. The answer is: you have *no* obligation. Neither in relationship, nor in all of life.

No obligation?

No obligation. Nor any restriction or limitation, nor any guidelines or rules. Nor are you bound by any circumstances or situations, nor constrained by any Code or law. Nor are you punishable for any offense, nor *capable* of any—for there is no such thing as being "offensive" in the eyes of God.

I've heard this before—this "there are no rules" kind of religion. That's spiritual anarchy. I don't see how that can work.

There is no way it *cannot* work—if you are about the business of creating your Self. If, on the other hand, you imagine yourself to be about the task of trying to be what someone *else* wants you to be, the absence of rules or guidelines might indeed make things difficult.

Yet the thinking mind begs to ask: if God has a way She wants me to be, why didn't She simply *create me that way to begin with?* Why all this struggle for me to "overcome" who I am in order for me to become what God wants me to be? This the probing mind demands to know—and rightly so, for it is a proper inquiry.

The religionists would have you believe that I created you as less than Who I Am so that you could have the chance to *become* as Who I Am, working against all odds—and, I might add, against *every natural tendency I am supposed to have given you.*

Among these so-called natural tendencies is the tendency to sin. You are taught that you were *born* in sin, that you will *die* in sin, and that to sin is your *nature.*

One of your religions even teaches you that you *can do nothing about this.* Your own actions are irrelevant and meaningless. It is arrogant to think that by some action of *yours* you can "get to heaven." There is only *one* way to heaven (salvation) and that is through no undertaking of your own, but through the grace granted you by God through acceptance of His Son as your intermediary.

Once this is done you are "saved." Until it is done, nothing that you do—not the life you live, not the choices you make, not anything you undertake of your own will in an effort to improve yourself or render you worthy—has any effect, bears any influence. You are *incapable* of rendering yourself worthy, because you are inherently unworthy. You were *created* that way.

Why? God only knows. Perhaps He made a mistake. Perhaps He didn't get it right. Maybe He wishes He could have it all to do over again. But there it is. What to do. . . .

You're making mock of me.

No. You are making mock of *Me*. You are saying that I, God, made inherently imperfect beings, then have demanded of them to be perfect, or face damnation.

You are saying then that, somewhere several thousand years into the world's experience, I relented, saying that from then on you didn't necessarily *have* to be good, you simply had to feel bad when you were not being good, and accept as your savior the One Being who could *always* be perfect, thus satisfying My hunger for perfection. You are saying that My Son—who you call the One Perfect One—has saved you from your own imperfection—the imperfection *I gave you.*

In other words, God's Son has saved you from *what His Father did.*

This is how you—many of you—say I've set it up.

Now *who is mocking whom?*

That is the second time in this book you seem to have launched a frontal attack on fundamentalist Christianity. I am surprised.

You have chosen the word "attack." I am simply engaging the issue. And the issue, by the way, is not "fundamentalist Christianity," as you put it. It is the entire nature of God, and of God's relationship to man.

The question comes up here because we were discussing the matter of obligations—in relationships and in life itself.

You cannot believe in an obligation-less relationship because you cannot accept who and what you really are. You call a life of complete freedom "spiritual anarchy." I call it God's great promise.

It is only within the context of this promise that God's great plan can be completed.

You have *no* obligation in relationship. You have only opportunity.

Opportunity, not obligation, is the cornerstone of religion, the basis of all spirituality. So long as you see it the other way around, you will have missed the point.

Relationship—your relationship to all things—was created as your perfect tool in the work of the soul. That is why all human relationships are sacred ground. It is why every personal relationship is holy.

In this, many churches have it right. Marriage *is* a sacrament. But not because of its sacred obligations. Rather, because of its unequalled opportunity.

Never do anything in relationship out of a sense of obligation. Do whatever you do out of a sense of the glorious opportunity your relationship affords you to decide, and to be, Who You Really Are.

I can hear that—yet over and over in my relationships I have given up when the going gets tough. The result is that I've had a string of relationships where I thought, as a kid, that I'd have only one. I don't seem to know what it's like to hold onto a relationship. Do you think I will ever learn? What do I have to do to make it happen?

You make it sound as if holding onto a relationship means it's been a success. Try not to confuse longevity with a job well done. Remember, your job on the planet is not to see how long you can stay in relationship, it's to decide, and experience, Who You Really Are.

This is not an argument for *short*-term relationships—yet neither is there a requirement for long-term ones.

Still, while there is no such requirement, this much should be said: long-term relationships do hold remarkable opportunities for *mutual* growth, *mutual* expression, and *mutual* fulfillment—and that has its own reward.

I know, I know! I mean, I've always suspected that. So how do I get there?

First, make sure you get into a relationship for the right reasons. (I'm using the word "right" here as a relative term. I mean "right" relative to the larger purpose you hold in your life.)

As I have indicated before, most people still enter relationships for the "wrong" reasons—to end loneliness, fill a gap, bring themselves love, or someone to love—and those are some of the *better* reasons. Others do so to salve their ego, end their depressions, improve their sex life, recover from a previous relationship, or, believe it or not, to relieve boredom.

None of these reasons will work, and unless something dramatic changes along the way, neither will the relationship.

I didn't enter into my relationships for any of those reasons.

I would challenge that. I don't think you know why you entered your relationships. I don't think you thought about it in this way. I don't think you entered your relationships purposefully. I think you entered your relationships because you "fell in love."

That's exactly right.

And I don't think you stopped to look at why you "fell in love." What was it to which you were responding? What need, or set of needs, was being fulfilled?

For most people, love is a response to need fulfillment.

Everyone has needs. You need this, another needs that. You both see in each other a chance for *need fulfillment.* So you agree—tacitly—to a trade. I'll trade you what I've got if you'll give me what you've got.

It's a transaction. But you don't tell the truth about it. You don't say, "I trade you very much." You say, "I love you very much," and then the disappointment begins.

You've made this point before.

Yes, and you've *done* this thing before—not once, but several times.

Sometimes this book seems to be going in circles, making the same points over and over again.

Sort of like life.

Touché.

The process here is that you're asking the questions and I'm merely answering them. If you ask the same question three different ways, I'm obliged to continue answering it.

Maybe I keep hoping You'll come up with a different answer. You take a lot of the romance out of it when I ask You about relationships. What's *wrong* with falling head over heels in love without having to *think* about it?

Nothing. Fall in love with as many people as you like that way. But if you're going to form a lifelong relationship with them, you may want to add a little thought.

On the other hand, if you enjoy going through relationships like water—or, worse yet, staying in one because you think you "have to," then living a life of quiet desperation—if you enjoy repeating these patterns from your past, keep right on doing what you've been doing.

Okay, okay. I get it. Boy, You're relentless, aren't You?

That's the problem with truth. The *truth* is relentless. It won't leave you alone. It keeps creeping up on you from every side, showing you what's really so. That can be annoying.

Okay. So I want to find the tools for a long-term relationship—and you say entering relationships purposefully is one of them.

Yes. Be sure you and your mate agree on purpose.
If you both agree at a conscious level that the purpose of your relationship is to create an opportunity, not an obligation—an opportunity for growth, for full Self expression, for lifting your lives to their highest potential, for healing every false thought or small idea you ever had about you, and for ultimate reunion with God through the communion of your two souls—if you take that vow instead of the vows you've been taking—the relationship has begun on a very good note. It's gotten off on the right foot. That's a very good beginning.

Still, it's no guarantee of success.

If you want guarantees in life, then you don't want *life*. You want rehearsals for a script that's already been written.
Life by its nature *cannot* have guarantees, or its whole purpose is thwarted.

Okay. Got it. So now I've got my relationship off to this "very good start." Now, how do I keep it going?

Know and understand that there will be challenges and difficult times.
Don't try to avoid them. Welcome them. Gratefully. See them as grand gifts from God; glorious opportunities to do what you came into the relationship—and *life*—to do.
Try very hard not to see your partner as the enemy, or the opposition, during these times.
In fact, seek to see no one, and nothing, as the enemy—or even the problem. Cultivate the technique of seeing all problems as opportunities. Opportunities to . . .

. . . I know, I know—"be, and decide, Who You Really Are."

Right! You're getting it! You are getting it!

Sounds like a pretty dull life to me.

Then you're setting your sights too low. Broaden the scope of your horizons. Extend the depth of your vision. See more in you than you think there is to be seen. See more in your partner, too.

You will never disserve your relationship—nor anyone—by seeing more in another than they are showing you. For there is more there. Much more. It is only their fear that stops them from showing you. If others notice that you see them as more, they will feel safe to show you what you obviously already see.

People tend to live up to our expectations of them.

Something like that. I don't like the word "expectations" here. Expectations *ruin* relationships. Let's say that people tend to see in themselves what we see in them. The grander our vision, the grander their willingness to access and display the part of them *we have shown them*.

Isn't that how all truly blessed relationships work? Isn't that part of the healing process—the process by which we give people permission to "let go" of every false thought they've ever had about themselves?

Isn't that what I am doing *here*, in this book, for *you*?

Yes.

And that is the work of God. The work of the soul is to wake yourself up. The work of God is to wake everybody *else* up.

We do this by seeing others as Who They Are—by reminding them of Who They Are.

This you can do in two ways—by reminding them of Who They Are (very difficult, because they will not believe you), and by remembering Who You Are (much easier, because you do not need *their* belief, only your own). Demonstrating this constantly ultimately reminds others of Who They Are, for they will see themselves in you.

Many Masters have been sent to the Earth to demonstrate Eternal Truth. Others, such as John the Baptist, have been sent as messengers, telling of the Truth in glowing terms, speaking of God with unmistakable clarity.

These special messengers have been gifted with extraordinary insight, and the very special power to see and receive Eternal Truth, plus the ability to communicate complex concepts in ways that can and will be understood by the masses.

You are such a messenger.

I am?

Yes. Do you believe this?

It is such a difficult thing to accept. I mean, all of us want to be special . . .

. . . all of you *are* special . . .

. . . and the ego gets in there—at least with *me* it does, and tries to make us feel somehow "chosen" for an amazing assignment. I have to fight that ego all the time, seek to purify and re-purify my every thought, word, and deed so as to keep personal aggrandizement out of it. So it's very difficult to hear what you're saying, because I'm aware that it plays to my ego, and I've spent all my life fighting my ego.

I know you have.
And sometimes not too successfully.

I am chagrined to have to agree.

Yet always when it has come to God, you have let the ego drop. Many is the night you have begged and pleaded for clarity, beseeched the heavens for insight, not so that you could enrich yourself, or heap honor upon yourself, but out of the deep purity of a simple yearning to *know*.

Yes.

And you have promised Me, over and over again, that should you be caused to know, you would spend the rest of your life— every waking moment—sharing Eternal Truth with others . . . not out of a need to gain glory, but out of your heart's deepest desire to end the pain and suffering of others; to bring joy and gladness, and help and healing; to reconnect others with the sense of partnership with God you have always experienced.

Yes. Yes.

And so I have chosen you to be My messenger. You, and many others. For now, during these times immediately ahead, the world will need many trumpets to sound the clarion call. The world will need many voices to speak the words of truth and healing for which millions long. The world will need many hearts joined together in the work of the soul, and prepared to do the work of God.

Can you honestly claim that you are not aware of this?

No.

Can you honestly deny that this is why you came?

No.

Are you ready then, with this book, to decide and to declare your own Eternal Truth, and to announce and articulate the glory of Mine?

Must I include these last few exchanges in the book?

You don't *have* to do anything. Remember, in *our* relationship you have no obligation. Only opportunity. Is this not the opportunity for which you have waited all your life? Have you not devoted your Self to this mission—and the proper preparation for it—from the *earliest moments of youth?*

Yes.

Then do not what you are obliged to do, but what you have an opportunity to do.

As to placing all this in our book, why would you not? Think you that I want you to be a messenger in secret?

No, I suppose not.

It takes great courage to announce oneself as a man of God. You understand, the world will much more readily accept you as virtually anything else—but a man of God? An actual *messenger?*

Every one of My messengers has been defiled. Far from gaining glory, they have gained nothing but heartache.

Are you willing? Does your heart *ache* to tell the truth about Me? Are you willing to endure the ridicule of your fellow human beings? Are you prepared to give *up* glory on Earth for the greater glory of the soul fully realized?

You're making this all sound suddenly pretty heavy, God.

You want I should kid you about it?

Well, we could just lighten up a little here.

Hey, I'm all for *enlightenment!* Why don't we end this chapter with a joke?

Good idea. You got one?

No, but you do. Tell the one about the little girl drawing a picture. . . .

Oh, yes, that one. Okay. Well, a Mommy came into the kitchen one day to find her little girl at the table, crayons everywhere, deeply concentrating on a freehand picture she was creating.

"My, what are you so busy drawing?" the Mommy asked.

"It's a picture of God, Mommy," the beautiful girl replied, eyes shining.

"Oh honey, that's so sweet," the Mommy said, trying to be helpful. "But you know, no one really knows what God looks like."

"Well," chirped the little girl, "if you'll just let me *finish*. . . ."

That's a beautiful little joke. Do you know what's most beautiful? The little girl *never doubted* that she knew *exactly* how to draw Me!

Yes.

Now I'll tell you a story, and with that we can end this chapter.

Alright.

There once was a man who suddenly found himself spending hours each week writing a book. Day after day he would race to pad and pen—sometimes in the middle of the night—to capture each new inspiration. Finally, someone asked him what he was up to.

"Oh," he replied, "I'm writing down a very long conversation I'm having with God."

"That's very sweet," his friend indulged him, "but you know, no one really knows for sure what God would say."

"Well," the man grinned, "if you'll just *let me finish*."

9

You may think this is easy, this "be Who You Really Are" business, but it's the most challenging thing you'll ever do in your life. In fact, you may never get there. Few people do. Not in one lifetime. Not in many.

So why try? Why enter the fray? Who needs it? Why not simply play life as if it were what it apparently is anyway—a simple exercise in meaninglessness leading to nowhere in particular, a game you can't lose no matter how you play; a process that leads to the same result, ultimately, for everyone? You say there is no hell, there is no punishment, there is no way to lose, so why bother trying to win? What is the incentive, given how difficult it is to get where You say we're trying to go? Why not take our good-natured time and just relax about all this God-stuff, and "being Who You Really Are."

My, we *are* frustrated aren't we. . . .

Well, I get tired of trying, trying, trying, only to have You come here and tell me how hard it's all going to be, and how only one in a million makes it anyway.

Yes, I see that you do. Let Me see if I can help. First, I would like to point out that you already *have* taken your "good-natured time" about it. Do you think this is your first attempt at this?

I have no idea.

It doesn't seem as if you've been here before?

Sometimes.

Well, you have. Many times.

How many times?

Many times.

That's supposed to encourage me?

It's supposed to inspire you.

How so?

First, it takes the worry out of it. It brings in the "can't fail" element you just talked about. It assures you that the intention is for you *not* to fail. That you'll get *as many chances as you want and need.* You can come back again and again and again. If you do get to the next step, if you evolve to the next level, it's because you *want* to, not because you *have* to.

You don't *have* to do anything! If you enjoy life at this level, if you feel this is the ultimate for you, you can have this experience over and over and over again! In fact, you *have* had it over and over again—for exactly that reason! You *love* the drama. You *love* the pain. You love the "not knowing," the mystery, the suspense! You love it all! That's why you're *here!*

Are You kidding me?

Would I kid you about a thing like that?

I don't know. I don't know what God kids about.

Not about this. This is too close to the Truth; too close to Ultimate Knowing. I never kid about "how it is." Too many people have played with your mind about that. I'm not here to get you more mixed up. I'm here to help you get things clarified.

So clarify. You're telling me I'm here because I *want* to be?

Of course. Yes.

I *chose* to be?

Yes.

And I've made that choice many times?

Many.

How many?

Here we go again. You want an exact count?

Just give me a ballpark estimate. I mean are we talking about handfuls here, or dozens?

Hundreds.

Hundreds? I've lived *hundreds of lives?*

Yes.

And this is as far as I've gotten?

This is quite some distance, actually.

Oh, it *is*, is it?

Absolutely. Why, in past lives you've actually killed people.

What's wrong with that? You said yourself that sometimes war is necessary to end evil.

We're going to have to elaborate on that, because I can see that statement being used and misused—just as you're doing now—to try to make all sorts of points, or rationalize all sorts of insanity.

By the highest standards I have observed humans devise, killing can never be justified as a means of expressing anger, releasing hostility, "righting a wrong," or punishing an offender. The statement that war is sometimes necessary to end evil stands true—for you have made it so. You have determined, in the creation of Self, that respect for all human life is, and must be, a high prime value. I am pleased with your decision, because I did not create life that it may be destroyed.

It is respect for *life* which sometimes makes war necessary, for it is through war against immediate impending evil, it is through defense against immediate threat to *another* life, that you make a statement of Who You Are in relationship to that.

You have a right under highest moral law—indeed, you have an obligation under that law—to stop aggression on the person of another, or yourself.

This does not mean that killing as a punishment is appropriate, nor as retribution, nor as a means of settling petty differences.

In your past, you have killed in personal duels over the affection of a *woman*, for heaven's sake, and called this *protecting your
honor*, when it was all honor you were losing. It is absurd to use
deadly force as an *argument solver*. Many humans are *still* using
force—killing force—to solve ridiculous arguments even today.

Reaching to the height of hypocrisy, some humans even kill *in
the name of God*—and that is the highest blasphemy, for it does not
speak of Who You Are.

Oh, then there *is* something wrong with killing?

Let's back up. There's nothing "wrong" with *anything*. "Wrong"
is a relative term, indicating the opposite of that which you call
"right."

Yet, what is "right"? Can you be truly objective in these matters?
Or are "right" and "wrong" simply descriptions overlaid on events
and circumstances by you, out of your decision about them?

And what, pray tell, forms the *basis* of your decision? Your own
experience? No. In most cases, you've chosen to accept someone
else's decision. Someone who came before you and, presumably,
knows better. Very few of your daily decisions about what is "right"
and "wrong" are being made by *you*, based on *your* understanding.

*This is especially true on important matters. In fact, the more
important the matter, the less likely are you to listen to your own
experience, and the more ready you seem to be to make someone
else's ideas your own.*

This explains why you've given up virtually total control over
certain areas of your life, and certain questions that arise within the
human experience.

These areas and questions very often include the subjects most
vital to your soul: the nature of God; the nature of true morality;
the question of ultimate reality; the issues of life and death surrounding war, medicine, abortion, euthanasia, the whole sum and
substance of personal values, structures, judgments. These most of
you have abrogated, assigned to others. You don't want to make
your own decisions about them.

"Someone else decide! I'll go along, I'll go along!" you shout.
"Someone else just tell me what's right and wrong!"

This is why, by the way, human religions are so popular. It
almost doesn't matter what the belief system is, as long as it's firm,

consistent, clear in its expectation of the follower, and rigid. Given those characteristics, you can find people who believe in almost anything. The strangest behavior and belief can be—has been—attributed to God. It's God's way, they say. God's word.

And there are those who will *accept* that. *Gladly.*

Because, you see, *it eliminates the need to think.*

Now, let's think about killing. Can there ever be a justifiable reason for killing anything? Think about it. You'll find you need no outside authority to give you direction, no higher source to supply you with answers. If you think about it, if you look to see what you feel about it, the answers will be obvious to you, and you will act accordingly. This is called acting on your own authority.

It is when you act on the authority of others that you get yourself into trouble. Should states and nations use killing to achieve their political objectives? Should religions use killing to enforce their theological imperatives? Should societies use killing as a response to those who violate behavioral Codes?

Is killing an appropriate political remedy, spiritual convincer, or societal problem solver?

Now, is killing something you can do if someone is trying to kill *you*? Would you use killing force to defend the life of a loved one? Someone you didn't even know?

Is killing a proper form of *defense* against those who would kill if they are not in some other way stopped?

Is there a difference between killing and murder?

The state would have you believe that killing to complete a purely political agenda is perfectly defensible. In fact, the state *needs* you to take its word on this in order to exist as an entity of power.

Religions would have you believe that killing to spread and maintain knowledge of, and adherence to, their particular truth is perfectly defensible. In fact, religions *require* you to take their word on this in order to exist as an entity of power.

Society would have you believe that killing to punish those who commit certain offenses (these have changed through the years) is perfectly defensible. In fact, society must have you take its word for it in order to exist as an entity of power.

Do you believe these positions are correct? Have you taken another's word for it? What does your Self have to say?

There is no "right" or "wrong" in these matters.

But by your decisions you paint a portrait of Who You Are.

Indeed, by their decisions your states and nations have already painted such pictures.

By their decisions your religions have created lasting, indelible impressions. By their decisions your societies have produced their self-portraits, too.

Are you pleased with these pictures? Are these the impressions you wish to make? Do these portraits represent Who You Are?

Be careful of these questions. They may require you to think.

Thinking is hard. Making value judgments is difficult. It places you at pure creation, because there are so many times you II have to say, "I don't *know*. I just don't *know*." Yet still you'll have to decide. And so you'll have to choose. You'll have to make an arbitrary choice.

Such a choice—a decision coming from *no previous personal knowledge*—is called *pure creation*. And the individual is aware, deeply aware, that in the making of such decisions is the *Self* created.

Most of you are not interested in such important work. Most of you would rather leave that to others. And so most of you are not self-created, but creatures of habit—other-created creatures.

Then, when others have told you how you should feel, and it runs directly counter to how you do feel—you experience a deep inner conflict. Something deep inside you tells you that what others have told you is *not Who You Are*. Now where to go with that? What to do?

The first place you go is to your religionists—the people who put you there in the first place. You go to your priests and your rabbis and your ministers and your teachers, and they tell you to *stop listening* to your Self. The worst of them will try to scare you away from it; scare you away from what you intuitively *know*.

They'll tell you about the devil, about Satan, about demons and evil spirits and hell and damnation and every frightening thing *they* can think of to get *you* to see how what you were intuitively knowing and feeling was *wrong*, and how the only place you'll find any comfort is in *their* thought, *their* idea, *their* theology, *their* definitions of right and wrong, and *their* concept of Who You Are.

The seduction here is that all you have to do to get instant approval is to *agree*. Agree and you have instant approval. Some will even sing and shout and dance and wave their arms in hallelujah!

That's hard to resist. Such approval, such rejoicing that you have seen the light; that you've been *saved!*

Approvals and demonstrations seldom accompany inner decisions. Celebrations rarely surround choices to follow personal truth. In fact, quite the contrary. Not only may others fail to celebrate, they may actually subject you to ridicule. What? You're thinking for *yourself?* You're deciding on *your own?* You're applying your own yardsticks, your own judgments, your own values? *Who do you think you are, anyway?*

And, indeed, *that is precisely the question you are answering.*

But the work must be done very much alone. Very much without reward, without approval, perhaps without even any notice.

And so you ask a very good question. Why go on? Why even start off on such a path? What is to be gained from embarking on such a journey? Where *is* the incentive? What *is* the reason?

The reason is ridiculously simple.

THERE IS NOTHING ELSE TO DO.

What do You mean?

I mean this is the only game in town. There is nothing else to do. In fact, there is nothing else you *can* do. You are going to be doing what you are doing for the rest of your life—just as you have been doing it since birth. The only question is whether you'll be doing it consciously, or unconsciously.

You see, you cannot *disembark* from the journey. You embarked before you were born. Your birth is simply a sign that the journey has begun.

So the question is not: Why start off on such a path? You have *already* started off. You did so with the first beat of your heart. The question is: Do I wish to walk this path consciously, or unconsciously? With awareness or lack of awareness? As the cause of my experience, or at the effect of it?

For most of your life you've lived at the effect of your experiences. Now, you're invited to be the cause of them. That is what is known as conscious living. That is what is called *walking in awareness.*

Now, many of you have walked quite some distance, as I've said. You have made no small progress. So you should not feel that after all these lives you've "only" come to this. Some of you are highly evolved creatures, with a very sure sense of Self. You know Who You Are and you know what you'd like to become. Furthermore, you even know the way to get from here to there.

That's a great sign. That's a sure indication.

Of what?

Of the fact that you now have very few lives left.

Is that good?

It is, now—for you. And that is so because you say it is so. Not long ago all you wanted to do was stay here. Now, all you want to do is leave. That's a very good sign.

Not long ago you killed things—bugs, plants, trees, animals, *people*—now you cannot kill a thing without knowing exactly what you're doing, and why. That's a very good sign.

Not long ago you lived life as though it had no purpose. Now you *know* it has no purpose, save the one *you give it. That's* a very good sign.

Not long ago you begged the universe to bring you Truth. Now you *tell* the universe *your* truth. And that's a *very* good sign.

Not long ago you sought to be rich and famous. Now you seek to be simply, and wonderfully, your *Self*.

And not so very long ago you *feared* Me. Now you *love* Me, enough to call Me your equal.

All of these are very, *very* good signs.

Well, gosh. . . . You make me feel good.

You *should* feel good. Anybody who uses "gosh" in a sentence can't be all bad.

You really *do* have a sense of humor, don't You. . . .

I *invented* humor!

Yes, You've made that point. Okay, so the reason for going on is that there's nothing else to do. This is what's happening here.

Precisely.

Then may I ask You—does it at least get any easier?

Oh, my darling friend—it is so much easier for you *now* than it was three lifetimes ago, I can't even tell you.

Yes, yes—it does get easier. The more you remember, the more you are able to experience, the more you know, so to speak. And the more you know, the more you remember. It is a circle. So yes, it gets easier, it gets better, it becomes even more joyful.

But remember, *none* of it has been exactly a drudge. I mean, you've loved *all* of it! Every last minute! Oh, it's delicious, this thing called life! It's a scrumptious experience, no?

Well, yes, I suppose.

You *suppose*? How much more scrumptious could I have made it? Are you not being allowed to experience *everything*? The tears, the joy, the pain, the gladness, the exaltation, the massive depression, the win, the lose, the draw? What more *is* there?

A little less pain, perhaps.

Less pain without more wisdom defeats your purpose; does not allow you to experience infinite joy—which is What I Am.

Be patient. You *are* gaining wisdom. And your joys are now increasingly available *without* pain. That, too, is a very good sign.

You are learning (remembering how) to love without pain; to let go without pain; to create without pain; to even cry without pain. Yes, you're even able to *have your pain* without pain, if you know what I mean.

I think I do. I'm enjoying even my own life dramas more. I can stand back and see them for what they are. Even laugh.

Exactly. And you don't call this growth?

I suppose I do.

And so then, keep on growing, My son. Keep on becoming. And keep on deciding what you want to become in the next highest version of your Self. Keep on working toward that. Keep on! Keep on! This is God Work we're up to, you and I. So keep on!

10

I love You, You know that?

I know you do. And I love you.

11

I'd like to get back to my list of questions. There's so much more detail I want to go into on every one of these. We could do a whole book on relationships alone, and I know that. But then I'd never get to my other questions.

> There'll be other times, other places. Even other books. I'm with you. Let's move on. We'll come back to it here if we have time.

Okay. My next question, then: Why can't I ever seem to attract enough money in my life? Am I destined to be forever scrimping and scraping? What is blocking me from realizing my full potential regarding money?

> The condition is manifested not just by you, but by a great many people.

Everyone tells me it's a problem of self-worth; a lack of self-worth. I've had a dozen New Age teachers tell me that lack of anything is always traceable to lack of self-worth.

> That is a convenient simplification. In this case your teachers are wrong. You do not suffer from a lack of self-worth. Indeed, your greatest challenge all your life has been to control your ego. Some have said it's been a case of too *much* self-worth!

Well, here I am, embarrassed and chagrined again, but You are right.

> You keep saying you're embarrassed and chagrined every time I simply tell the truth about you. *Embarrassment is the response of a person who still has an ego investment in how others see him.* Invite yourself to move past that. Try a new response. Try laughter.

Okay.

Self-worth is not your problem. You are blessed with an abundance of it. Most people are. You all think very highly of yourself, as rightly you should. So self-worth, for the great mass of the people, is not the problem.

What is?

The problem is lack of understanding of the principles of abundance together, usually, with a massive misjudgment about what is "good" and what is "evil."

Let Me give you an example.

Please do.

You carry a thought around that money is bad. You also carry a thought around that God is good. Bless you! Therefore, in your thought system, God and money do not mix.

Well, in a sense, I guess, that's true. That *is* how I think.

This makes things interesting, because this then makes it difficult for you to take money for any good thing.

I mean, if a thing is judged very "good" by you, you value it *less* in terms of money. So the "better" something is (i.e., the more worthwhile), the less *money* it's worth.

You are not alone in this. Your whole society believes this. So your teachers make a pittance and your stripteasers, a fortune. Your leaders make so little compared to sports figures that they feel they have to steal to make up the difference. Your priests and your rabbis live on bread and water while you *throw* coins at entertainers.

Think about it. Everything on which you place a high *intrinsic* value, you insist must come cheaply. The lonely research scientist seeking a cure for AIDS goes begging for money, while the woman who writes a book on a hundred new ways to have sex and creates tapes and weekend seminars to go with it . . . makes a fortune.

This having-it-all-backwards is a propensity with you, and it stems from wrong thought.

The wrong thought is your idea about money. You love it, and yet you say it is the root of all evil. You adore it, and yet you call it "filthy lucre." You say that a person is "filthy rich." And if a person *does* become wealthy doing "good" things, you immediately become suspect. You make that "wrong."

So, a doctor had better not make *too* much money, or had better learn to be discreet about it. And a *minister*—whoa! She'd *really* better not make lots of money (assuming you'll even let a "she" *be* a minister), or there'll surely be trouble.

You see, in *your mind, a person who chooses the highest calling should get the lowest pay. . . .*

Hmmm.

Yes, "hmmm" is right. You *should* think about that. Because it is such wrong thought.

I thought there was no such thing as wrong or right.

There isn't. There is only what serves you, and what does not. The terms "right" and "wrong" are relative terms, and I use them that way when I use them at all. In this case, relative to what serves you—relative to what you *say you want*—your money thoughts are wrong thoughts.

Remember, thoughts are creative. So if you think money is bad, yet think yourself good . . . well, you can see the conflict.

Now you, in particular, My son, act out this race consciousness in a very big way. For most people the conflict is not nearly so enormous as for you. Most people do what they hate for a living, so they don't mind taking money for it. "Bad" for the "bad," so to speak. But you love what you do with the days and times of your life. You adore the activities with which you cram them.

For you, therefore, to receive large amounts of money for what you do would be, in your thought system, taking "bad" for the "good" and that is unacceptable to you. You'd rather starve than take "filthy lucre" for pure service . . . as if somehow the service loses its purity if you take money for it.

So here we have this real ambivalence about money. Part of you rejects it, and part of you resents not having it. Now, the universe doesn't know what to do about that, because the universe has received two different thoughts from you. So your life with regard to money is going to go in fits and starts, because you keep going in fits and starts about money.

You don't have a clear focus; you're not really sure what's true for you. And the universe is just a big Xerox machine. It simply produces multiple copies of your thoughts.

Now there's only one way to change all that. You have to change your *thought* about it.

How can I change the way I *think*? The way I think about something is the way I think about something. My thoughts, my attitudes, my ideas were not created in a minute. I have to guess they are the result of years of experience, a lifetime of encounters. You are right about the way I think about money, but how do I change that?

This could be the most interesting question in the book. The usual method of creation for most human beings is a three-step process involving thought, word, and deed, or action.

First comes thought; the formative idea; the initial concept. Then comes the word. Most thoughts ultimately form themselves into words, which are often then written or spoken. This gives added energy to the thought, pushing it out into the world, where it can be noticed by others.

Finally, in some cases words are put into action, and you have what you call a result; a physical world manifestation of what all started with a thought.

Everything around you in your man-made world came into being in this way—or some variation of it. All three creation centers were used.

But now comes the question: how to change a Sponsoring Thought?

Yes, that is a very good question. And a very important one. For if humans do not change some of their Sponsoring Thoughts, humankind could doom itself to extinction.

The most rapid way to change a root thought, or sponsoring idea, is *to reverse the thought-word-deed process.*

Explain that.

Do the deed that you want to have the new thought about. Then say the words that you want to have your new thought about. Do this often enough and you'll train the mind to *think a new way.*

Train the mind? Isn't that like mind control? Isn't that just mental manipulation?

Do you have any idea how your mind came up with the thoughts it *now* has? Do you not know that your world has manipulated your mind to think as you do? *Wouldn't it be better for you to manipulate your mind than for the world to?*

Would you not be better off to think the thoughts you want to think, than those of others? Are you not better armed with creative thoughts than with reactive thoughts?

Yet your mind is filled with reactive thought—thought that springs from the experience of others. Very few of your thoughts spring from self-produced data, much less self-produced preferences.

Your own root thought about money is a prime example. Your thought about money (it is bad) runs directly counter to your experience (it's great to have money!). So you have to run around and lie to yourself about your experience in order to justify your root thought.

You are so *rooted* in this thought, it never occurs to you that your *idea* about money *may be inaccurate.*

So now what we are up to is coming up with some self-produced data. And *that* is how we change a root thought, and cause it to be *your* root thought, not another's.

You have one more root thought about money, by the way, which I've yet to mention.

What's that?

That there's not enough. In fact you have this root thought about just about everything. There's not enough money, there's not enough time, there's not enough love, there's not enough food, water, compassion in the world. . . . Whatever there is that's good, there's just *not enough.*

This race consciousness of "not-enough-ness" creates and recreates the world as you see it.

Okay, so I have two root thoughts—Sponsoring Thoughts—to change about money.

Oh, at least two. Probably many more. Let's see. money is bad . . . money is scarce . . . money may not be received for doing God's work (that's a big one with you) . . . money is never given freely . . . money doesn't grow on trees (when, in fact, it does) . . . money corrupts.

I see I've got a lot of work to do.

Yes, you do, if you're not happy with your present money situation. On the other hand, it's important to understand that you're unhappy with your present money situation *because* you're unhappy with your present money situation.

Sometimes You're hard to follow.

Sometimes you're hard to lead.

Say, listen, You're the God here. Why don't You make it easy to understand?

I *have* made it easy to understand.

Then why don't You just *cause* me to understand, if that's what You truly want?

I truly want what you truly want—nothing different and nothing more. Don't you see that is My greatest gift to you? If I wanted for you something other than what you want for you, and then went so far as to *cause you to have it*, where is your free choice? How can you be a creative being if I am dictating what you shall be, do, and have? *My joy is in your freedom, not your compliance.*

Okay, what did You mean, I'm unhappy with my money situation because I'm unhappy with my money situation?

You are what you think you are. It's a vicious circle when the thought is a negative one. You've got to find a way to break out of the circle.

So much of your present experience is based on your previous thought. Thought leads to experience, which leads to thought, which leads to experience. This can produce constant joy when the Sponsoring Thought is joyous. It can, and does, produce continual hell when the Sponsoring Thought is hellatious.

The trick is to change Sponsoring Thought. I was about to illustrate how to do that.

Go.

Thank you.

The first thing to do is reverse the thought-word-deed paradigm. Do you remember the old adage, "Think before you act"?

Yes.

Well, forget it. If you want to change a root thought, you have to act *before you think.*

Example: you're walking down the street and come across an old lady begging for quarters. You realize she's a bag lady and is living day-to-day. You instantly know that as little money as you have, you surely have enough to share with her. Your first impulse is to give her some change. There's even a part of you that's ready to reach in your pocket for a little folding money—a one, or even a five. What the heck, make it a grand moment for her. Light her up.

Then, thought comes in. What, are you crazy? We've only got seven dollars to get *us* through the day! You want to give her a five? So you start fumbling around for that one.

Thought again: Hey, hey, c'mon. You don't have that many of these that you can just *give them away!* Give her some coins, for heaven's sake, and let's get out of here.

Quickly you reach into the other pocket to try to come up with some quarters. Your fingers feel only nickels and dimes. You're embarrassed. Here you are, fully clothed, fully fed, and you're going to nickel-and-dime this poor woman who has nothing.

You try in vain to find a quarter or two. Oh, there's one, deep in the fold of your pocket. But by now you've walked past her, smiling wanly, and it's too late to go back. She gets nothing. You get nothing, either. Instead of the joy of knowing your abundance and sharing, you now feel as poor as the woman.

Why didn't you *just give her the paper money!* It was your first impulse, but your thought got in the way.

Next time, decide to act before you think. Give the money. Go ahead! You've got it, and there's more where that came from. That's the only thought which separates you from the bag lady. You're clear there's more where that came from, and she doesn't know that.

When you want to change a root thought, act in accordance with the new idea you have. But you must act quickly, or your mind will kill the idea before you know it. I mean that literally. The idea, the new truth, will be dead in you *before you've had a chance to know it.*

So act quickly when the opportunity arises, and, if you do this often enough, your mind will soon *get the idea.* It will be your new thought.

Oh, I just got something! Is that what's meant by the New Thought Movement?

If not, it should be. New thought is your only chance. It's your only real opportunity to evolve, to grow, to truly become Who You Really Are.

Your mind is right now filled with old thoughts. Not only old thoughts, but mostly someone else's old thoughts. It's important now, it's time now, to *change your mind* about some things. This is what evolution is all about.

12

Why can't I do what I really want to do with my life and still make a living?

What? You mean you actually want to have *fun* in your life, and still earn your keep? Brother, are *you* dreaming!

What?—

Only kidding—just doing a little mind reading, that's all. You see, that's been *your* thought about it.

It's been my experience.

Yes. Well, we've been all through this now a number of times. The people who make a living doing what they love are the people who insist on doing so. They don't give up. They never give in. They dare life *not* to let them do what they love.

But there's another element that must be brought up, because this is the missing element in most people's understanding when it comes to life work.

What's that?

There's a difference between being and doing, and most people have placed their emphasis on the latter.

Shouldn't they?

There's no "should" or "should not" involved. There's only what you choose, and how you can have it. If you choose peace and joy and love, you won't get much of it through what you're doing. If you choose happiness and contentment, you'll find little of that on the path of doingness. If you choose reunion with God, supreme knowing, deep understanding, endless compassion, total awareness, absolute fulfillment, you won't achieve much of that out of what you're doing.

In other words, if you choose *evolution*—the evolution of your soul—you won't produce that by the worldly activities of your body.

Doing is a function of the body. *Being* is a function of the soul. The body is always doing *something*. Every minute of every day it's up to *something*. It never stops, it never rests, it's constantly *doing* something.

It's either doing what it's doing at the behest of the soul—or in spite of the soul. The quality of your life hangs in the balance.

The soul is forever *being*. It is being what it is being, regardless of what the body is doing, not *because* of what it's doing.

If you think your life is about doingness, you do not understand what you are about.

Your soul doesn't care *what* you do for a living—and when your life is over, neither will you. Your soul cares only about what you're *being* while you're doing *whatever* you're doing.

It is a state of beingness the soul is after, not a state of doing-ness.

What is the soul seeking to be?

Me. You.

Yes, Me. Your soul *is* Me, and it knows it. What it is doing, is trying to *experience that*. And what it is remembering is that the best way to have this experience is by *not doing anything*. There is nothing to do but to be.

Be what?

Whatever you want to be. Happy. Sad. Weak. Strong. Joyful. Vengeful. Insightful. Blind. Good. Bad. Male. Female. You name it.

I mean that literally. *You name it.*

This is all very profound, but what does it have to do with my career? I'm trying to find a way to stay alive, to survive, to support myself and my family, doing what I like to do.

Try being what you like to be.

What do you mean?

Some people make lots of money doing what they do, others can't make a go of it—and they're *doing the same thing.* What makes the difference?

Some people have more skill than others.

That's the first cut. But now we get to the second cut. Now we're down to two people with relatively equal skills. Both graduated from college, both were at the top of their class, both understand the nature of what they're doing, both know how to use their tools with great facility—yet one still does better than the other; one flourishes while the other struggles. What's that about?

Location.

Location?

Somebody once told me there are only three things to consider when starting a new business—location, location, and location.

In other words, not "What are you going to do?" but "Where are you going to be?"

Exactly.

That sounds like the answer to my question as well. The soul is concerned only with where you are going to be.

Are you going to be in a place called fear, or in a place called love? Where *are* you—and where are you coming *from*—as you encounter life?

Now, in the example of the two equally qualified workers, one is successful and the other is not, not because of anything either is doing, but because of what both are being.

One person is being open, friendly, caring, helpful, considerate, cheerful, confident, even joyful in her work, while the other is being closed, distant, uncaring, inconsiderate, grumpy, even resentful of what she is doing.

Now suppose you were to select even loftier states of being-ness? Suppose you were to select goodness, mercy, compassion, understanding, forgiveness, love? What if you were to select Godliness? What *then* would be your experience?

I tell you this:

Beingness attracts beingness, and produces experience.

You are not on this planet to produce anything with your body. You are on this planet to produce something with your soul. Your body is simply and merely the tool of your soul. Your mind is the power that makes the body go. So what you have here is a power tool, used in the creation of the soul's desire.

What *is* the soul's desire?

Indeed, what is it?

I don't know. I'm asking You.

I don't know. I'm asking you.

This could go on forever.

It has.

Wait a minute! A moment ago You said the soul is seeking to be *You*.

So it is. Then *that* is the soul's desire.

In the broadest sense, yes. But this Me it is seeking to be is very complex, very multi-dimensional, multi-sensual, multi-faceted. There are a million aspects to Me. A billion. A trillion. You see? There is the profane and the profound, the lesser and the larger, the hollow and the holy, the ghastly and the Godly. You see?

Yes, yes, I see . . . the up and the down, the left and the right, the here and the there, the before and the after, the good and the bad. . . .

Precisely. I *am* the Alpha and the Omega. That was not just a pretty saying, or a nifty concept. That was Truth expressed.

So, in seeking to be Me, the soul has a grand job ahead of it; an enormous menu of *beingness* from which to choose. And that is what it is doing in this moment now.

Choosing states of being.

Yes—and then producing the right and perfect *conditions* within which to create the experience of that. It is therefore true that nothing happens to you or through you that is not for your own highest good.

You mean my soul is creating all of my experience, including not only the things I am doing, but the things that are happening to me?

Let us say that the soul leads you to the right and perfect *opportunities* for you to experience exactly what you had planned to experience. What you actually experience is up to you. It could be what you planned to experience, or it could be something else, depending upon what you choose.

Why would I choose something I don't wish to experience?

I don't know. Why would you?

Do You mean that sometimes the soul wishes one thing, and the body or the mind wishes another?

What do you think?

But how can the body, or the mind, overrule the soul? Doesn't the soul always get what it wants?

The spirit of you seeks, in the largest sense, that grand moment when you have conscious awareness of its wishes, and join in joyful oneness with them. But the spirit will never, ever, force its desire on the present, conscious, physical part of you.

The Father will not force His will upon the Son. It is a violation of His very nature to do so, and thus, quite literally, impossible.

The Son will not force His will upon the Holy Spirit. It is against His very nature to do so, and thus, quite literally, impossible.

The Holy Spirit will not force His will upon your soul.

It is outside of the nature of the spirit to do so, and thus, quite literally, impossible.

Here is where the impossibilities end. The mind very often *does* seek to exert its will on the body—and does so. Similarly, the body seeks often to control the mind—and frequently succeeds.

Yet the body and the mind together do not have to do anything to control the soul—for the soul is completely without need (unlike the body and the mind, which are shackled with it), and so allows the body and the mind to have their way all the time.

Indeed, the soul would have it no other way—for if the entity which is you is to create, and thus know, who it really is, it must be through an act of conscious volition, not an act of unconscious obedience.

Obedience is not creation, and thus can never produce salvation.

Obedience is a response, while creation is pure choice, undictated, unrequired.

Pure choice produces salvation through the pure creation of highest idea in this moment now.

The function of the soul is to *indicate* its desire, not *impose* it.

The function of the mind is to *choose* from its alternatives.

The function of the body is to *act out* that choice.

When body, mind, and soul create together, in harmony and in unity, God is made flesh.

Then does the soul know itself in its own experience.

Then do the heavens rejoice.

Right now, in this moment, your soul has again created opportunity for you to be, do, and have what it takes to know Who You Really Are.

Your soul has *brought* you to the words you are reading right now—as it has brought you to words of wisdom and truth before.

What will you do now? What will you choose to be?

Your soul waits, and watches with interest, as it has many times before.

Do I understand You to say that it is out of the state of beingness I select that my worldly success (I am still trying to talk about my career here) will be determined?

I am not concerned about your worldly success, only you are.

It is true that when you achieve certain states of being over a long period of time, success in what you are doing in the world is very difficult to avoid. Yet you are not to worry about "making a living." *True Masters are those who have chosen to make a life, rather than a living.*

From certain states of being will spring a life so rich, so full, so magnificent, and so rewarding that worldly goods and worldly success will be of no concern to you.

Life's irony is that as soon as worldly goods and worldly success are of no concern to you, the way is open for them to flow to you.

Remember, you cannot have what you want, but you may experience whatever you have.

I cannot have what I want?

No.

You said this before, very early in our dialogue. Still, I don't understand. I thought you've been telling me I could have *whatever* I want. "As you think, as you believe, so shall it be done unto you," and all that.

The two statements are not inconsistent with each other.

They aren't? They sure feel inconsistent to me.

That is because you lack understanding.

Well, I admit that. That's why I'm talking with You.

I will then explain. You cannot have *anything* you want. The very act of wanting something pushes it away from you, as I said earlier, in Chapter One.

Well, You may have said it earlier, but You're losing me—fast.

Fight to keep up. I'll go over it again in greater detail. Try to stay with it. Let's go back to a point you do understand: *thought is creative.* Okay?

Okay.

Word is creative. Got it?

Got it.

Action is creative. Thought, word, and deed are the three levels of creation. Still with Me?

Right there.

Good. Now let's take "worldly success" as our subject for the moment, since that's what you've been talking about, asking about.

Terrific.

Now, do you have a thought, "I want worldly success"?

Sometimes, yes.

And do you also sometimes have the thought, "I want more money"?

Yes.

You can therefore neither have worldly success *nor* more money.

Why *not?*

Because the universe has no choice but to bring you *the direct manifestation of your thought about it.*

Your thought is, "I want worldly success." You understand, the creative power is like a genie in a bottle. Your words are its command. You understand?

Then why don't I have more success?

I said, your words are its command. Now your *words* were, "I want success." And the universe says, "Okay, you do."

I'm still not sure I follow.

Think of it this way. The word "I" is the key that starts the engine of creation. The words "I am" are extremely powerful. They are statements to the universe. Commands.

Now, whatever follows the word "I" (which calls forth the Great I Am) tends to manifest in physical reality.

Therefore "I" + "want success" produces you *wanting success.* "I" + "want money" must produce you *wanting money.* It can produce no other thing, because thoughts, words are creative. Actions are, too. And if you act in a way which says that you want success and money, then your thoughts, words, *and* actions are in accord, and you are *sure* to have the experience of this wantingness.

You see?

Yes! My God—does it really work that way?

Of course! You are a *very powerful creator.* Now granted, if you had a thought, or made a statement, just once—as in anger, for instance, or frustration, it's not very likely that you'll convert those thoughts or words into reality. So you don't have to worry about "Drop dead!" or "Go to hell," or all the other less-than-nice things you sometimes think or say.

Thank God.

You're welcome. But, if you repeat a thought, or say a word, over and over again—not once, not twice, but dozens, hundreds, thousands of times—do you have any idea of the creative power of that?

A thought or a word expressed and expressed and expressed becomes just that—expressed. *That is,* pushed out. *It becomes outwardly realized. It becomes your physical reality.*

Good grief.

That's exactly what it produces very often—*good grief.* You love the grief, you love the drama. That is, until you don't anymore. There comes a certain point in your evolution when you cease to love the drama, cease to love the "story" as you've been living it. That's when you decide—actively choose—to change it. Only most don't know how. You now do. To change your reality, simply *stop thinking like that.*

In this case, instead of thinking "I want success," think "I have success."

That feels like a lie to me. I'd be kidding myself if I said that. My mind would shout, "The hell you say!"

Then think a thought you *can* accept. "My success is coming to me now," or "all things lead to my success."

So this is the trick behind the New Age practice of affirmations.

Affirmations do not work if they are merely statements of what you want to be true. Affirmations work only when they are statements of something you already know *to be true.*

The best so-called affirmation is a statement of gratitude and appreciation. "Thank you, God, for bringing me success in my life." Now, *that* idea, thought, spoken, and acted upon, produces wonderful results—when it comes from true knowing; not from an attempt to *produce* results, but from an awareness that results have *already* been produced.

Jesus had such clarity. Before every miracle, He thanked Me in advance for its deliverance. It never occurred to Him not to be grateful, because it never occurred to Him that what He declared would not happen. The thought *never entered His mind.*

So sure was He of Who He Was and of His relationship to Me that His every thought, word, and deed reflected his awareness—just as your thoughts, words, and deeds reflect yours. . . .

If, now, there is something you choose to experience in your life, do not "want" it—choose *it.*

Do you choose success in worldly terms? Do you choose more money? *Good.* Then *choose* it. Really. Fully. Not half-heartedly.

Yet at your stage of development do not be surprised if "worldly success" no longer concerns you.

What is that supposed to mean?

There comes a time in the evolution of every soul when the chief concern is no longer the survival of the physical body, but the growth of the spirit; no longer the attainment of worldly success, but the realization of Self.

In a sense, this is a very dangerous time, particularly at the outset, because the entity housed in the body now knows it is just that: a being in a body—not a body-being.

At this stage, before the growing entity matures in this point of view, there is often a sense of no longer caring about affairs of the body in any way. The soul is so excited about being "discovered" at last!

The mind abandons the body, and all matters of the body. Everything is ignored. Relationships are set aside. Families are disappeared. Jobs are made secondary. Bills go unpaid. The body itself is not even fed for long periods. The entire focus and attention of the entity are now on the soul, and matters of the soul.

This can lead to a major personal crisis in the day-to-day life of the being, although the mind perceives no trauma. It is hanging out in bliss. Other people say you have lost your mind—and in a sense you may have.

Discovery of the truth that life has nothing to do with the body can create an imbalance the *other* way. Whereas at first the entity acted as if the body were all there is, now it acts as if the body matters not at all. This, of course, is not true—as the entity soon (and sometimes painfully) remembers.

You are a tri-part being, made of body, mind, and spirit. You will *always* be a tri-part being, not just while you are living on the Earth.

There are those who hypothesize that upon death the body and the mind are dropped. The body and the mind are *not* dropped. The body changes form, leaving its most dense part behind, but retaining always its outer shell. The mind (not to be confused with the brain) goes with you, too, joining with the spirit and the body as the one energy mass of three dimensions, or facets.

Should you choose to return to this experiencing opportunity that you call life on Earth, your divine self will once again separate its true dimensions into what you call body, mind, and spirit. In truth you are all one energy, yet with three distinct characteristics.

As you undertake to inhabit a new physical body here on Earth, your ethereal body (as some of you have termed it) lowers its vibrations—slows itself from a vibration so rapid that it cannot even be seen, to a speed that produces mass and matter. This actual matter is the creation of pure thought—the work of your mind, the higher mind aspect of your three-part being.

This matter is a coagulation of a million billion trillion different energy units into one enormous mass—controllable by the mind . . . you really are a master mind!

As these tiny energy units have expended their energy, they are discarded by the body, while the mind creates new ones. This the mind creates out of its continuing thought about Who You Are! The ethereal body "catches" the thought, so to speak, and lowers the vibration of more energy units (in a sense "crystallizes" them), and they become matter—the new matter of you. In this way, every cell of your body changes every several years. You are—quite literally—*not the same person* you were a few years ago.

If you think thoughts of illness or disease (or continuing anger, hatred, and negativity), your body will translate these thoughts into physical form. People will see this negative, sick form and they will say, "What's the matter?" They will not know how accurate their question is.

The soul watches this whole drama play out, year after year, month after month, day after day, moment after moment, and always holds the Truth about you. It never forgets the blueprint; the original plan; the first idea; the creative thought. Its job is to remind you—that is, to literally *re-mind* you—so that you may remember once again Who You Are—and then choose Who You now Wish to Be.

In this way the cycle of creation and experience, imaging and fulfilling, knowing and growing into the unknown, continues, both now and even forever more.

Whew!

Yes, exactly. Oh, and there's much more to explain. So much more. But never, ever in one book—nor probably even in one lifetime. Yet you have begun, and that is good. Just remember this. It is as your grand teacher William Shakespeare said: "There are more things in Heaven and Earth, Horatio, than are dreamt of in your philosophy."

May I ask you some questions about this? Like, when you say the mind goes with me after death, does that mean my "personality" goes with me? Will I know in the afterlife who I was?

Yes . . . and who you have *ever* been. It will *all* be opened onto you—because then it will profit you to know. Now, in this moment, it will not.

And, with regard to this life, will there be an "accounting"—a review—a tally taking?

There is no judgment in what you call the afterlife. You will not even be allowed to judge yourself (for you would surely give yourself a low score, given how judgmental and unforgiving you are with yourself in *this* life).

No, there is no accounting, no one giving "thumbs-up" or "thumbs-down." Only humans are judgmental, and because you are, you assume that I must be. Yet I am not—and that is a great truth you cannot accept.

Nonetheless, while there will be no judgment in the afterlife, there will be opportunity to look again at all you have thought, said, and done here, and to decide if that is what you would choose again, based on Who You say You Are, and Who You Want to Be.

There is an Eastern mystical teaching surrounding a doctrine called Kama Loca—according to this teaching, at the time of our death each person is given the opportunity to relive every thought ever entertained, every word ever spoken, every action ever taken, not from our standpoint, but from the standpoint of every other person affected. In other words, we've *already* experienced what *we* felt thinking, saying, and doing what we did—now we're given the experience of feeling what the *other* person felt in each of these moments—and it is by *this* measure that we'll decide whether we'll think, say, or do those things again. Any comment?

What occurs in your life after this is far too extraordinary to describe here in terms you could comprehend—because the experience is other-dimensional and literally defies description using tools as severely limited as words. It is enough to say that you will have the opportunity to review again this, your present life, without pain or fear or judgment, for the purpose of deciding how you feel about your experience here, and where you want to go from there.

Many of you will decide to come back here; to return to this world of density and relativity for another chance to experience out the decisions and choices you make about your Self at this level.

Others of you—a select few—will return with a different mission. You will return to density and matter for the soul purpose of bringing others *out* of density and matter. Always there are on the Earth those among you who have made such a choice. You can tell them apart at once. Their work is finished. They have returned to Earth simply and merely to help others. This is their joy. This is their exaltation. They seek naught but to be of service.

You cannot miss these people. They are everywhere. There are more of them than you think. Chances are you know one, or know of one.

Am I one?

No. If you have to ask, you know you are not one. One such as this asks questions of no one. There is nothing to ask.

You, My son, in this lifetime are a messenger. A harbinger. A bringer of news; a seeker and frequently a speaker of Truth. That is enough for one lifetime. Be happy.

Oh, I *am*. But I can always hope for more!

Yes! And you will! Always you will hope for more. It is in your nature. It is divine nature to seek always to be more.

So seek, yes, by all means *seek*.

Now I want to answer definitively the question with which you started this segment of our ongoing conversation.

Go ahead and *do* what you really love to do! Do nothing else! You have so little time. How can you think of wasting a moment doing something for a *living* you don't like to do? What kind of a living is *that?* That is not a living, that is a *dying!*

If you say, "But, but . . . I have others who depend on me . . . little mouths to feed . . . a spouse who is looking to me. . . ." I will answer: If you insist that your life is about what your body is doing, you do not understand why you came here. At least do something that pleases you—that speaks of Who You Are.

Then at least you can stay out of resentment and anger toward those you imagine are keeping you from your joy.

What your body is doing is not to be discounted. It is important. But not in the way that you think. The actions of the body were meant to be reflections of a state of being, not attempts to attain a state of being.

In the true order of things one does not *do* something in order to *be* happy—one *is* happy and, hence, *does* something. One does not *do* some things in order to *be* compassionate, one *is* compassionate and, hence, acts in a certain way. The soul's decision precedes the body's action in a highly conscious person. Only an unconscious person attempts to produce a state of the soul through something the body is doing.

This is what is meant by the statement, "Your life is not about what your body is doing." Yet it *is* true that what your body is doing is a reflection of what your life is about.

It is another divine dichotomy.

Yet, know this if you understand nothing else:

You have a *right* to your joy; children or no children; spouse or no spouse. Seek it! Find it! And you will have a joyful family, no matter how much money you make or don't make. And if they aren't joyful, and they get up and leave you, then release them with love to seek *their* joy.

If, on the other hand, you have evolved to the point where things of the body are not of concern to you, then you are even more free to seek your joy—on Earth as it is in heaven. God says it's *okay to be happy*—yes, even happy in your *work.*

Your life work is a statement of Who You Are. If it is not, then why are you doing it?

Do you imagine that you *have* to?

You don't have to do anything.

If "man who supports his family, at all costs, even his own happiness" is Who You Are, then *love* your work, because it is *facilitating* your creation of a *living statement of Self.*

If "woman who works at job she hates in order to meet responsibilities as she sees them" is Who You Are, then love, love, *love* your job, for it totally supports your Self image, your Self concept.

Everyone can love everything the moment they understand what they are doing, and why.

No one does anything he doesn't want to do.

13

How can I solve some of the health problems I face? I have been the victim of enough chronic problems to last three lifetimes. Why am I having them all now—in *this* lifetime?

First, let's get one thing straight. You love them. Most of them, anyway. You've used them admirably to feel sorry for yourself and to get attention for yourself.

On the few occasions when you haven't loved them, it's only because they've gone too far. Farther than you thought they ever would when you created them.

Now let's understand what you probably already know: all illness is self-created. Even conventional medical doctors are now seeing how people *make themselves sick.*

Most people do so quite unconsciously. (They don't even know what they're doing.) So when they *get* sick, they don't know what hit them. It feels as though something has *befallen* them, rather than that they did something to themselves.

This occurs because most people move through life—not simply health issues and consequences—unconsciously.

People smoke and wonder why they get cancer.

People ingest animals and fat and wonder why they get blocked arteries.

People stay angry all their lives and wonder why they get heart attacks.

People compete with other people—mercilessly and under incredible stress—and wonder why they have strokes.

The not-so-obvious truth is that most people *worry themselves to death.*

Worry is just about the worst form of mental activity there is—next to hate, which is deeply self destructive. Worry is pointless. It is wasted mental energy. It also creates bio-chemical reactions which harm the body, producing everything from indigestion to coronary arrest, and a multitude of things in between.

Health will improve almost at once when *worrying ends*.

Worry is the activity of a mind which does not understand its connection with Me.

Hatred is the most severely damaging mental condition. It poisons the body, and its effects are virtually irreversible.

Fear is the opposite of everything you are, and so has an effect of opposition to your mental and physical health. *Fear is worry magnified.*

Worry, hate, fear—together with their offshoots: anxiety, bitterness, impatience, avarice, unkindness, judgmentalness, and condemnation—all attack the body at the cellular level. It is impossible to have a healthy body under these conditions.

Similarly—although to a somewhat lesser degree—conceit, self-indulgence, and greed lead to physical illness, or lack of well-*being*.

All illness is created first in the mind.

How can that be? What of conditions contracted from another? Colds—or, for that matter, AIDS?

Nothing occurs in your life—nothing—which is not first a thought. Thoughts are like magnets, drawing effects to you. The thought may not always be obvious, and thus clearly causative, as in, "I'm going to contract a terrible disease." The thought may be (and usually is) far more subtle than that. ("I am not worthy to live.") ("My life is always a mess.") ("I am a loser.") ("God is going to punish me.") ("I am sick and tired of my life!")

Thoughts are a very subtle, yet extremely powerful, form of energy. Words are less subtle, more dense. Actions are the most dense of all. Action is energy in heavy physical form, in heavy motion. When you think, say, *and* act out a negative concept such as "I am a loser," you place tremendous creative energy into motion. Small wonder you come down with a cold. That would be the least of it.

It is very difficult to reverse the effects of negative thinking once they have taken physical form. Not impossible—but very difficult. It takes an act of extreme faith. It requires an extraordinary belief in the positive force of the universe—whether you call that God, Goddess, the Unmoved Mover, Prime Force, First Cause, or whatever.

Healers have just such faith. It is a faith that crosses over into Absolute Knowing. They *know* that you are meant to be whole, complete, and perfect in *this moment now*. This knowingness is also a thought—and a very powerful one. It has the power to move mountains—to say nothing of molecules in your body. That is why healers can heal, often even at a distance.

Thought knows no distance. Thought travels around the world and traverses the universe faster than you can say the word.

"Say but the word and my servant shall be healed." And it was so, in that selfsame hour, even before his sentence was finished. Such was the faith of the centurion.

Yet *you* are all mental lepers. Your mind is eaten away with negative thoughts. Some of these are thrust upon you. Many of these you actually make up—conjure up—yourselves, and then harbor and entertain for hours, days, weeks, months—even years.

. . . and you wonder why you are sick.

You can "solve some of the health problems," as you put it, by solving the problems in your thinking. Yes, you can heal some of the conditions you have already acquired (given yourself), as well as prevent major new problems from developing. And you can do this all by changing your thinking.

Also—and I hate to suggest this because it sounds so mundane coming, as it were, from God, but—for God's sake, *take better care of yourself.*

You take rotten care of your body, paying it little attention at all until you suspect something's going wrong with it. You do virtually nothing in the way of preventive maintenance. You take better care of your car than you do of your body—and that's not saying much.

Not only do you fail to prevent breakdowns with regular check-ups, once-a-year physicals, and use of the therapies and medicines you've been given (why do you go to the doctor, get her help, then not use the remedies she suggests? Can you answer Me that one?)—you also mistreat your body terribly between these visits about which you do nothing!

You do not exercise it, so it grows *flabby* and, worse yet, weak from non-use.

You do not nourish it properly, thereby weakening it further.

Then you fill it with toxins and poisons and the most absurd substances posing as food. And still it runs for you, this marvelous engine; still it chugs along, bravely pushing on in the face of this onslaught.

It's horrible. The conditions under which you ask your body to survive are horrible. But you will do little or nothing about them. You will read this, nod your head in regretful agreement, and go right back to the mistreatment. And do you know why?

I'm afraid to ask.

Because you have *no will to live.*

That seems a harsh indictment.

It's not meant to be harsh, nor is it meant as an indictment. "Harsh" is a relative term; a judgment you have laid on the words. "Indictment" connotes guilt, and "guilt" connotes wrongdoing. There is no wrongdoing involved here, hence no guilt and no indictment.

I have made a simple statement of truth. Like all statements of truth, it has the quality of waking you up. Some people don't like to be awakened. Most do not. Most would rather sleep.

The world is in the condition that it's in because the world is full of sleepwalkers.

With regard to my statement, what about it seems untrue? You *have* no will to live. At least you have had none until now.

If you tell me you've had an "instant conversion," I will reassess my prediction of what you will now do. I acknowledge that my prediction is based on past experience.

. . . it was also meant to wake you up. Sometimes, when a person is really deeply asleep, you have to shake him a little.

I have seen in the past that you have had little will to live. Now you may deny that, but in this case your actions speak louder than your words.

If you ever lit a cigarette in your life—much less smoked a pack a day for 20 years as you have—you have very little will to live. You don't care *what* you do to your body.

But I *stopped* smoking over 10 years ago!

Only after 20 years of grueling physical punishment. And if you've ever taken alcohol into your body, you have very little will to live.

I drink very moderately.

The body was not meant to intake alcohol. It impairs the mind.

But *Jesus* took alcohol! He went to the wedding and turned water into wine!

So who said Jesus was perfect?

Oh, for God's sake.

Say, are you becoming annoyed with Me?

Well, far be it from me to become *annoyed with God.* I mean, that would be a bit presumptuous, wouldn't it? But I do think we can carry all this a bit too far. My father taught me, "all things in moderation." I think I've stuck to that where alcohol is concerned.

The body can more easily recover from only moderate abuse. The saying is therefore useful. Nevertheless, I'll stick to my original statement: the body was not meant to intake alcohol.

But even some medicines contain alcohol!

I have no control over what you call medicine. I'll stay with my statement.

You really are rigid, aren't You?

Look, truth is truth. Now if someone said "A little alcohol won't hurt you," and placed that statement in the context of life as you now live it, I would have to agree with them. That does not change the truth of what I've said. It simply allows you to ignore it.

Yet consider this. Currently, you humans wear your bodies out, typically, within 50 to 80 years. Some last longer, but not many. Some stop functioning sooner, but not the majority. Can we agree on that?

Yes, okay.

Alright, so we have a good starting point for discussion. Now, when I said I could agree with the statement "A little alcohol won't hurt you," I qualified that by adding "in the context of life *as you now live it.*" You see, you people seem *satisfied* with life as you now live it. But life, it may surprise you to learn, was meant to be

lived a whole different way. And your body was designed to last a
great deal longer.

It was?

Yes.

How much longer?

Infinitely longer.

What does that mean?

It means, My son, your body was designed to last forever.

Forever?

Yes. Read that: "for ever more."

You mean we were—are—never supposed to die?

You never *do* die. Life is eternal. You are immortal. You never
do die. You simply change form. You didn't even have to do that.
You decided to do that, *I* didn't. I made you bodies that would last
forever. Do you really think the best God could do, the best I could
come up with, was a body that could make it 60, 70, maybe 80
years before falling apart? Is that, do you imagine, the limit of My
ability?

I never thought of putting it that way, exactly. . . .

I designed your magnificent body to last *forever!* And the earliest of you *did* live in the body virtually pain-free, and without fear
of what you now call death.

In your religious mythology, you symbolize your cellular memory of these first-version humans by calling them Adam and Eve.
Actually, of course, there were more than two.

At the outset, the idea was for you wonderful souls to have a
chance to know your Selves as Who You Really Are through experiences gained in the physical body, in the relative world—as I have
explained repeatedly here.

This was done through the slowing down of the unfathomable
speed of all vibration (thought form) to produce matter—including
that matter you call the physical body.

Life evolved through a series of steps in the blink of an eye that you now call billions of years. And in this holy instant came you, out of the sea, the water of life, onto the land and into the form you now hold.

Then the evolutionists are *right!*

I find it amusing—a source of continual amusement, actually—that you humans have such a need to break everything down into right and wrong. It never occurs to you that you've *made those labels up* to help you define the material—and your Self.

It never occurs to you (except to the finest minds among you) that a thing could be both right *and* wrong; that only in the relative world are things one or the other. In the world of the absolute, of time-no time, *all things are everything.*

There is no male and female, there is no before and after, there is no fast and slow, here and there, up and down, left and right—and no right and wrong.

Your astronauts and cosmonauts have gained a sense of this. They imagined themselves to be rocketing *upward* to get to outer space, only to find when they got there that they were looking *up* *at the Earth.* Or *were* they? Maybe they were looking *down* at the Earth! But then, where was the sun? Up? Down? No! Over there, to the *left.* So now, suddenly, a thing was neither up *nor* down—it was *sideways* . . . and all definitions thus *disappeared.*

So it is in My world—*our* world—our real realm. All definitions disappear, rendering it difficult to even talk about this realm in definitive terms.

Religion is your attempt to speak of the unspeakable. It does not do a very good job.

No, My son, the evolutionists are *not* right. I created all of this—all of this—in the blink of an eye; in one holy instant—just as the creationists have said. And . . . it came about through a process of evolution taking billions and billions of what *you* call years, just as the evolutionists claim.

They are both "right." As the cosmonauts discovered, *it all depends on how you look at it.*

But the real question is: one holy instant/billions of years—what's the difference? Can you simply agree that on some of the questions of life the mystery is too great for even you to solve? Why not hold the mystery as sacred? And why not allow the sacred to be sacred, and leave it alone?

I suppose we all have an insatiable need to know.

But you *already* know! I've just *told* you! Yet you don't want to know the Truth, you want to know the truth *as you understand it.* This is the greatest barrier to your enlightenment. You think you already *know* the truth! You think you already *understand* how it is. So you agree with everything you see or hear or read that falls into the paradigm of your understanding, and reject everything which does not. And this you call learning.

This you call being open to the teachings. *Alas, you can never be open to the teachings so long as you are closed to everything save your own truth.*

Thus will this very book be called blasphemy—the work of the devil—by some.

Yet those who have ears to hear, let them listen. I tell you this: *You were not meant to ever die.* Your physical form was created as a magnificent convenience; a wonderful tool; a glorious vehicle allowing you to experience the reality you have created with your mind, that you may know the Self you have created in your soul.

The soul conceives, the mind creates, the body experiences. The circle is complete. The soul then knows itself in its own experience. If it does not like what it is experiencing (feeling), or wishes a different experience for any reason, it simply conceives of a *new* experience of Self, and, quite literally, *changes its mind.*

Soon the body finds itself in a new experience. ("I am the resurrection and the Life" was a magnificent example of this. How do you think Jesus *did* it anyway? Or do you not believe it ever happened? *Believe* it. It *happened!*)

Yet this much is so: the soul will never override the body or the mind. I made you as a three-in-one being. You are three beings in one, made in the image and likeness of Me.

The three aspects of Self are in no wise unequal to each other. Each has a function, but no function is greater than another, nor does any function actually *precede* another. All are interrelated in an exactly equal way.

Conceive—create—experience. What you conceive you create, what you create you experience, what you experience you conceive.

That is why it is said, if you can cause your body to experience something (take abundance, for example), you will soon have the feeling of it in your soul, which will conceive of itself in a new way (namely, abundant), thus presenting your mind with a new thought about that. From the new thought springs more experience, and the body begins living a new reality as a permanent state of being.

Your body, your mind, and your soul (spirit) are one. In this, you are a microcosm of Me—the Divine All, the Holy Everything, the Sum and Substance. You see now how I am the beginning and the end of everything, the Alpha and the Omega.

Now I will explain to you the ultimate mystery: your exact and true relationship to Me.

YOU ARE MY BODY.

As *your* body is to *your* mind and soul, so, too, are *you* to *My* mind and soul. Therefore:

Everything I experience, I experience through you.

Just as your body, mind, and spirit are one, so, too, are Mine.

So it is that Jesus of Nazareth, among the many who understood this mystery, spoke immutable truth when he said, *"I and the Father are One."*

Now I will tell you, there are even larger truths than this to which you will one day become privy. For even as you are the body of Me, I am the body of another.

You mean, You are *not* God'?

Yes, I am God, as you now understand Him. I am Goddess as you now comprehend Her. I am the Conceiver and the Creator of Everything you now know and experience, and you are My children . . . even as I am the child of another.

Are You trying to tell me that even God has a God?

I am telling you that your perception of ultimate reality is more limited than you thought, and that Truth is more *un*limited than you can imagine.

I am giving you ever-so-small a glimpse of infinity—and infinite love. (A much larger glimpse and you could not hold it in your reality. You can barely hold *this*.)

Wait a minute! You mean I'm really *not* talking with God here?

I have told you—if you conceive of God as your creator and master—even as you are the creator and master of your own body—I am the God of your understanding. And you are talking with Me, yes. It has been a delicious conversation, no?

Delicious or not, I thought I was talking with the real God. The God of Gods. You know—the top guy, the chief honcho.

You are. Believe Me. You are.

And yet You say that there is someone above You in this hierarchal scheme of things.

We are now trying to do the impossible, which is to speak of the unspeakable. As I said, that is what religion seeks to do. Let Me see if I can find a way to summarize this.

Forever is longer than you know. Eternal is longer than Forever. God is more than you imagine. God *is* the energy you call imagination. God *is* creation. God *is* first thought. And God *is* last experience. And God is everything in between.

Have you ever looked down a high-powered microscope, or seen pictures or movies of molecular action, and said, "Good heavens, there's a *whole universe* down there. And to that universe, I, the now-present observer, must feel like God!" Have you ever said that, or had that kind of experience?

Yes, I should imagine every thinking person has.

Indeed. You have given yourself your own glimpse of what I am showing you here.

And what would you do if I told you that this reality of which you have given yourself a glimpse *never ends?*

Explain that. I'd ask You to explain that.

Take the smallest part of the universe you can imagine. Imagine this tiny, tiny particle of matter.

Okay.

Now cut it in half.

Okay.

What have you got?

Two smaller halves.

Precisely. Now cut those in half. What now?

Two *smaller* halves,

Right. Now again, and *again!* What's left?

Smaller and smaller particles.

Yes, but when does it *stop?* How many times can you divide matter until it ceases to exist?

I don't know. I guess it never ceases to exist.

You mean you can never *completely destroy* it? All you can do is change its form?

It would seem so.

I tell you this: you have just learned the secret of all of life, and seen into infinity.
Now I have a question to ask you.

Okay. . . .

What makes you think infinity goes only one way?

So . . . there is no end going up, any more than there is going down.

There *is* no up or down, but I understand your meaning.

But if there is no end to smallness, that means there is no end to bigness.

Correct.

But if there is no end to bigness, then there is no *biggest*. That means, in the largest sense, there *is no God!*￼

Or, perhaps—*all of it is God*, and *there is nothing else.*

I tell you this: I AM THAT I AM.

And YOU ARE THAT YOU ARE. You cannot *not* be. You can change form all you wish, but you cannot fail to be. Yet you *can* fail to know Who You Are—and in this failing, experience *only the half of it*.

That would be hell.

Exactly. Yet you are not condemned to it. You are not relegated to it forevermore. All that it takes to get out of hell—to get out of not knowing—is to know again.

There are many ways and many places (dimensions) in which you can do this.

You are in one of those dimensions now. It is called, in your understanding, the third dimension.

And there are many more?

Have I not told you that in My Kingdom there are many mansions? I would not have told it to you were it not so.

Then there *is* no hell—not really. I mean, there *is* no place or dimension to which we are everlastingly condemned!

What would be the purpose of that?

Yet you are always limited by your know-ingness—for you—we—are a self-created being.

You cannot be what you do not know your Self to be.

That is why you have been given this life—so that you might know yourself in your own experience. Then you can conceive of yourself as Who You Really Are, and create yourself as that in your experience—and the circle is again complete . . . only bigger.

And so, you are in the process of growing—or, as I have put it throughout this book, of *becoming*.

There is *no limit* to what you can become.

You mean, I can even become—dare I say it?—a God . . . just like You?

What do *you* think?

I don't know.

Until you do, you cannot. Remember the triangle—the Holy Trinity: spirit-mind-body. Conceive-create-experience. Remember, using your symbology:

HOLY SPIRIT = INSPIRATION = CONCEIVE
FATHER = PARENTING = CREATE
SON = OFFSPRING = EXPERIENCE

The Son experiences the creation of the fathering thought, which is conceived of by the Holy Ghost.

Can you conceive of yourself as one day being a God?

In my wildest moments.

Good, for I tell you this: You are *already* a God. *You simply do not know it.*

Have I not said, "Ye are Gods"?

14

There now. I have explained it all for you. Life. How it works. Its very reason and purpose. How else can I serve you?

There's nothing more I could ask. I am filled with thanks for this incredible dialogue. It's been so far-reaching, so encompassing. And, as I look at my original questions, I see we've covered the first five—having to do with life and relationships, money and careers, and health. I had more questions on that original list, as you know, but somehow these discussions make those questions seem irrelevant.

Yes. Still, you've asked them. Let's just quickly answer the remainder of them, one by one. Now that we're moving this rapidly through the material—

—What material?—

The material I brought you here to expose you to—now that we're moving this rapidly though the material, let's just take those remaining questions and deal with them quickly.

6. What is the karmic lesson I'm supposed to be learning here? What am I trying to master?

You are learning nothing here. You have nothing to learn. You have only to remember. That is, re-member Me.
What are you trying to master? You are trying to master *mastering itself.*

7. Is there such a thing as reincarnation? How many past lives have I had? What was I in them? Is "karmic debt" a reality?

It is difficult to believe there is still a question about this. I find it hard to imagine. There have been so many reports from thoroughly reliable sources of past life experiences. Some of these people have brought back strikingly detailed descriptions of events, and such completely verifiable data as to eliminate any possibility that they were making it up or had contrived to somehow deceive researchers and loved ones.

You have had 647 past lives, since you insist on being exact. This is your 648th. You were *everything* in them. A king, a queen, a serf. A teacher, a student, a master. A male, a female. A warrior, a pacifist. A hero, a coward. A killer, a savior. A sage, a fool. You have been *all* of it!

No, there is no such thing as karmic debt—not in the sense that you mean in this question. A debt is something that must or should be repaid. *You are not obligated to do anything.*

Still, there are certain things that you want to do; choose to experience. And some of these choices hinge on—the desire for them has been created by—what you have experienced before.

That is as close as words can come to this thing you call karma.

If karma is the innate desire to be better, to be bigger, to evolve and to grow, and to look at past events and experiences as a measure of that, then, yes, karma does exist.

But it does not require anything. Nothing is ever required. You are, as always you have ever been, a being of free choice.

8. I sometimes feel very psychic. Is there such a thing as being psychic? Am I that? Are people who claim to be psychic "trafficking with the devil"?

Yes, there is such a thing as being psychic. You are that. *Everyone* is that. There is not a person who does not have what you call psychic ability, there are only people who do not use it.

Using psychic ability is nothing more than using your sixth sense.

Obviously, this is not "trafficking with the devil," or I would not have *given* this sense to you. And, of course, there *is* no devil with whom to traffic.

Someday—perhaps in Book Two—I'll explain to you exactly how psychic energy and psychic ability works.

There is going to be a Book Two?

Yes. But let's finish this one first.

9. Is it okay to take money for doing good? If I choose to do healing work in the world—God's work—can I do that and become financially abundant, too? Or are the two mutually exclusive?

I've already covered this.

10. Is sex okay? C'mon—what is the real story behind this human experience? Is sex purely for procreation, as some religions say? Is true holiness and enlightenment achieved through denial—or transmutation—of the sexual energy? Is it okay to have sex without love? Is just the physical sensation of it okay enough as a reason?

Of course sex is "okay." Again, if I didn't want you to play certain games, I wouldn't have given you the toys. Do you give your children things you don't want them to play with?

Play with sex. *Play* with it! It's *wonderful* fun. Why, it's just about the most fun you can *have* with your body, if you're talking of strictly physical experiences alone.

But for goodness sake, don't destroy sexual innocence and pleasure and the purity of the fun, the joy, by misusing sex. Don't use it for power, or hidden purpose; for ego gratification or domination; for any purpose other than the purest joy and the highest ecstasy, given and shared—which is *love*, and love *recreated*—which is new life! Have I not chosen a delicious way to *make more of you*?

With regard to denial, I have dealt with that before. Nothing holy has ever been achieved through denial. Yet *desires* change as even larger realities are glimpsed. It is not unusual, therefore, for people to simply *desire* less, or even no, sexual activity—or, for that matter, any of a number of activities of the body. For some, the activities of the soul become foremost—and by far the more pleasurable.

Each to his own, without judgment—that is the motto.

The end of your question is answered this way: You don't need to have a reason for anything. Just *be cause*.

Be the cause of your experience.

Remember, experience produces concept of Self, conception produces creation, creation produces experience.

You want to experience yourself as a person who has sex without love? Go ahead! You'll do that until you don't want to anymore. And the only thing that will—that could ever—cause you to stop this, or *any*, behavior, is your newly emerging thought about Who You Are.

It's as simple—and as complex—as that.

11. Why did You make sex so good, so spectacular, so powerful a human experience if all we are to do is stay away from it as much as we can? What gives? For that matter, why are all fun things either "immoral, illegal, or fattening"?

I've answered the end of this question too, with what I've just said. All fun things are *not* immoral, illegal, or fattening. Your life is, however, an interesting exercise in defining what fun is.

To some, "fun" means sensations of the body. To others, "fun" may be something entirely different. It all depends on who you think you are, and what you are doing here.

There is much more to be said about sex than is being said here—but nothing more essential than this: sex is *joy*, and many of you have made sex everything else but.

Sex is sacred, too—yes. But joy and sacredness *do* mix (they are, in fact, the same thing), and many of you think they do not.

Your attitudes about sex form a microcosm of your attitudes about life. Life should be a joy, a celebration, and it has become an experience of fear, anxiety, "not enough-ness," envy, rage, and tragedy. The same can be said about sex.

You have repressed sex, even as you have repressed life, rather than fully Self expressing, with abandon and joy.

You have shamed sex, even as you have shamed life, calling it evil and wicked, rather than the highest gift and the greatest pleasure.

Before you protest that you have not shamed life, look at your collective attitudes about it. Four-fifths of the world's people consider life a trial, a tribulation, a time of testing, a karmic debt that must be paid, a school with harsh lessons that must be learned, and, in general, an experience to be endured while awaiting the *real* joy, which is *after death*.

It *is* a shame that so many of you *think* this way. Small wonder you have applied shame to the very act which creates life.

The energy which underscores sex is the energy which underscores life; which *is* life! The feeling of attraction and the intense and often urgent desire to move *toward* each other, to become one, is the essential dynamic of all that lives. I have built it into everything. It is inbred, inherent, *inside* All That Is.

The moral Codes, religious constrictions, social taboos, and emotional conventions you have placed around sex (and, by the way, around love—and all of life) have made it virtually impossible for you to *celebrate your being.*

From the beginning of time all man has ever wanted is to love and be loved. And from the beginning of time man has done everything in his power to make it impossible to do that. Sex is an extraordinary expression of love—love of another, love of Self, love of *life.* You ought to therefore *love* it! (And you *do*—you just can't *tell* anyone you do; you don't dare *show* how *much* you love it, or you'll be called a pervert. Yet *this* is the idea that is *perverted.*)

In our next book, we shall look at sex much more closely; explore its dynamics in greater detail, for this is an experience and an issue of sweeping implications on a global scale.

For now—and for you, personally—simply know this: *I have given you nothing shameful, least of all your very body, and its functions. There is no need to hide your body or its functions—nor your love of them, and of each other.*

Your television programs think nothing of showing naked violence, but shrink from showing naked love. Your whole society reflects that priority.

12. Is there life on other planets? Have we been visited by it? Are we being observed now? Will we see evidence—irrevocable and indisputable—of extraterrestrial life in our lifetime? Does each form of life have its own God? Are You the God of it all?

Yes to the first part. Yes to the second. Yes to the third. I cannot answer the fourth part, since that would require Me to predict the future—something I am not going to do.

We will, however, talk a great deal more about this thing called the future in Book Two—and we'll talk about extraterrestrial life and the nature(s) of God in Book Three.

Ohmigosh. There's going to be a Book *Three?*

Let me outline the plan here.

Book One is to contain basic truths, primary understandings, and address essential personal matters and issues.

Book Two is to contain more far-reaching truths, grander under-standings, and address global matters and issues.

Book Three is to contain the largest truths you are now capable of understanding, and address universal matters and issues—matters being dealt with by all the beings of the universe.

I see. This is an order?

No. If you can ask that question you have understood nothing in this book.

You have *chosen* to do this work—and you have *been* chosen. The circle is complete.

Do you understand?

Yes.

13. **Will Utopia ever come to the planet Earth? Will God ever show Himself to Earth's people, as promised? Is there such a thing as the Second Coming? Will there ever be an end of the world—or an apoca-lypse, as prophesied in the Bible? Is there a one true religion? If so, which one?**

That's a book in itself, and will comprise much of Volume Three. I've kept this opening volume limited to more personal matters, more practical issues. I'll move to larger questions and matters of global and universal implication in succeeding installments.

Is that it? Is that all for now? Are we to speak no more here?

You miss me already?

I do! This has been fun! Are we quitting now?

You need a little rest. And your readers need a rest, too. There's a lot here to absorb. A lot to wrestle with. A lot to ponder. Take some time off. Reflect on this. Ponder it.

Do not feel abandoned. I am always with you. If you have questions—day-to-day questions—as I know you do even now, and will continue to—know that you can call on Me to answer them. You do not need the form of this book.

This is not the only way I speak to you. Listen to Me in the truth of your soul. Listen to Me in the feelings of your heart. Listen to Me in the quiet of your mind.

Hear Me, everywhere. Whenever you have a question, simply *know* that I have answered it *already*. Then open your eyes to your world. My response could be in an article already published. In the sermon already written and about to be delivered. In the movie now being made. In the song just yesterday composed. In the words about to be said by a loved one. In the heart of a new friend about to be made.

My Truth is in the whisper of the wind, the babble of the brook, the crack of the thunder, the tap of the rain.

It is the feel of the earth, the fragrance of the lily, the warmth of the sun, the pull of the moon.

My Truth—and your surest help in time of need—is as awesome as the night sky, and as simply, incontrovertibly, trustful as a baby's gurgle.

It is as loud as a pounding heartbeat—and as quiet as a breath taken in unity with Me.

I will not leave you, I *cannot* leave you, for you are My creation and My product, My daughter and My son, My purpose and My . . . Self.

Call on Me, therefore, wherever and whenever you are separate from the peace that I am.

I will be there. With Truth. And Light. And Love.

Book 2

for

Samantha
Tara-Jenelle
Nicholas
Travis
Karus
Tristan
Devon
Dustin
Dylan

*You have gifted me far more
than I ever gifted you.
I have not been the father I had hoped to be.
But wait. We are not through with each other.
This is a work in progress.*

Acknowledgments

Always I want to place at the top of my list of acknowledgments That Which Is All Things, and which is the Source of all things, including this book. Some of you choose to call that God, as do I, yet it matters not what name you give The Source. It was, is, and always will be The Source Forever, and even forever more.

Second, I want to acknowledge that I had wonderful parents, through whom God's sourcing of life itself, and so many of my life's most important rememberings, flowed. Taken together, my Mom and Dad were a terrific team. Not everybody who looked on from the sidelines may have agreed, but the two of them were very clear about that. They called each other "Pest" and "Poison." Mom said Dad was a "pest," and Dad said Mom was a "poison" he could not resist.

My mother, Anne, was an extraordinary person; a woman of endless compassion, of deep understanding, of quiet and unending forgiveness, of seemingly limitless giving, of ongoing patience, of soft wisdom, and of an abiding faith in God so strong that, moments before her death, the new, young priest who had administered to her the final rites of the Roman Catholic Church (and who was clearly nervous) came to me from her bedside trembling with admiration. "My God," he whispered, "she was comforting me."

It is the highest tribute to Mom to say that I wasn't surprised by that.

My father, Alex, had few of the graces of gentler beings. He was blustery, gruff, he could be embarrassingly abrasive, and there are those who say he was often cruel, particularly to my mother. I am not willing to judge him for that (or anything else). My mother refused to judge or condemn him (quite to the contrary, praising him even with her last words), and I cannot imagine how it serves me to ignore her clear example by sinking beneath it.

Besides, Dad had a huge pile of enormously positive traits, traits of which my Mother never lost sight. These included an unwavering belief in the indomitability of the human spirit, and a deep clarity that conditions which needed to be changed were not changed by complaining about them, but by leadership. He taught me that I could do anything I set my mind to. He was a man upon whom his wife and family could, and did, depend until the very end. He was the absolute embodiment of loyalty, of never being a fence-sitter, but always taking a stand, of refusing to take no for an answer from a world which defeated so many others. His mantra in the face of even the most overwhelming odds was, "Ah, there's nothing to it." I used that mantra in every challenging time of my life. It worked every time.

It is the highest tribute to Dad to say that I wasn't surprised by that.

Between the two of them, I felt challenged and called to a place of supreme confidence in myself, and unconditional love for everyone else. What a combo!

In my previous book I acknowledged some other members of my family and circle of friends who've made an enormous contribution to my life—and still do. I want to include now two special people who have come into my life since the first book was written, and have made an extraordinary impact on me:

Dr. Leo and Mrs. Letha Bush . . . who have demonstrated to me with their daily lives that in moments of selfless caring for family and loved ones, of concern for friends, of kindness to those in need, of hospitality to all, and of abiding faith and love in and for each other, will be found life's richest rewards. I am instructed by them, and deeply inspired.

Also in this space I wish to acknowledge some of my other teachers, special angels sent to me by God to bring me a particular message which I am now clear it was important for me to hear. Some of them touched me personally, some from a distance, and some from a point on the Matrix so far away that they don't even know (at a conscious level) I exist. Still, their energy has been received here, in my soul. By these beings, in this particular lifetime, I have been gifted and benefited:

Dolly Parton . . . whose music and smile and whole personhood has blessed a nation, and gladdened my heart so often—even when it was broken and I was sure it couldn't be gladdened anymore. Now there's a special magic.

Terry Cole-Whittaker . . . whose wit and wisdom and insight and joy in life and absolute honesty have stood for me as both an example and a measurement since the day I met her. Thousands have been enlarged, enhanced and enlivened by her.

Neil Diamond . . . who has reached into the depth of his soul for his artistry, and so has reached into the depth of mine, and touched the soul of a generation. His talent, and the emotional generosity with which he has shared it, is monumental.

Thea Alexander . . . who has dared through her writing to shake me awake to the possibility of expressing human affection without limitation, without hurtfulness, without hidden agendas, without bitter jealousies, and without needfulness or expectations. She has reignited in the world the restless spirit of boundless love and our most natural desire for sexual celebration, making it wondrous and beautiful and innocently pure again.

Robert Rimmer . . . who has done exactly the same.

Warren Spahn . . . who taught me that reaching excellence in any area of life means setting the highest standards, and refusing to fall back from them; asking the most of oneself, even when accepting the least would hardly be noticed (perhaps, especially then). A sports hero of the first magnitude, a hero on the battlefield under fire, and a life hero who has never wavered in his commitment to excel, no matter how much work it took to do that.

Jimmy Carter . . . who courageously insists on playing international politics by not playing politics, but coming from his heart, and from what he knows under the Highest Law is right. A breath of air so fresh, this stale world has hardly known what to do with it.

Shirley MacLaine . . . who has demonstrated that intellect and entertainment are not mutually exclusive; that we can rise above the base and the banal and the lowest common denominator. She insists that we can talk about larger things as well as small; heavier things as well as light; deeper things as well as shallow. She's struggling to raise the level of our discourse, and so, of our consciousness; to use constructively her enormous influence on the marketplace of ideas.

Oprah Winfrey . . . who is doing exactly the same.

Steven Spielberg . . . who is doing exactly the same.

George Lucas . . . who is doing exactly the same.

Ron Howard . . . who is doing exactly the same.

Hugh Downs . . . who is doing exactly the same.

And Gene Roddenberry . . . whose Spirit can hear this now, and is smiling . . . because he led the way in so much of this; took the gamble; stepped to the edge; went, in truth, where no one had gone before.

These people are treasures, as are we all. Unlike some of us, however, they have chosen to give from their treasury of Self on a massive scale; to put themselves out there in a huge way; to risk all of it, to lose their privacy and throw their personal world into upheaval forever, in order to give of who they truly are. They have not even known whether the gift they had to give would be received. Still, they gave it.

I acknowledge them for that. Thank you all. My life has been made richer by you.

Introduction

We are living in a different world today. Things are not the way they were when this book was originally published. Yet, not a word in it is outdated. In fact, *the exact opposite is true.* The book may well have been ahead of its time. What is certain is that the words here are more relevant than ever.

The hundreds of thousands who have already read this book and who made it a *New York Times* best-seller have called it easily the most controversial in the original *Conversations with God* trilogy. Whereas *CWG-1* looked at individual life and addressed many questions related to it, this book explores the collectively created reality on this planet, touching on global issues and diving deeply into subjects related to the group experience of the larger human community. It comes not a moment too soon.

The events of the past several years—including the rise and fall of the terribly oppressive Taliban regime in Afghanistan, the continuing and seemingly unending conflict between Israelis and Palestinians in the Middle East, the terrorist activities throughout the world and the 9/11 attacks in the United States, the military intervention in Iraq and its aftermath—make it clear that our species has approached the furthest edge of sustainable possibility. In short, we can't keep going on like this.

We can't keep creating our collective experience in a "power over\rdblquote rather than a "power with\rdblquote paradigm, and we can't keep trying to solve the problems and end the conflicts which such a paradigm inevitably produces using violence and killing as our chief means. We can't keep doing this because, of course, we are not solving the problems or ending the conflicts at all, but merely prolonging them, or, at best, postponing them.

Sooner or later we must ask a fundamental question: What keeps us coming back to this place? Why is it that after all these years—nay, after all these *millennia*—the human race has still not found the key to living together in peace and harmony?

This extraordinary book provides some striking possible answers. It offers some daring options. It presents sweeping and belief-shaking statements that could lead the whole of humanity out of its nightmare and into its dream at last.

What is needed here, in the reading of this book, is an open mind. I understand that this is not always easy to come by. To have an open mind, we have to agree with ourselves not to dismiss out of hand that which appears to violate every sense of things that we have previously had, every idea about life that we have previously held to be true. We have to be willing to pass over individual statements that annoy or confound us, to see if, in the aggregate, the sum of the argument here at least holds sufficient value to justify our reexamining prior assumptions.

Let me tell you something. We are *already* being forced to reexamine every prior assumption we have had about God and about Life. And we are being forced to do so not by something as benign as a book, but by the horror of human events and the disruptive, angry, and violent people who are causing them.

The human race *will* change course, that much I can promise you. The only question is whether that course change will come about as a result of coercion or cooperative and open-minded exploration. We need to seek alternative ways of being and living together. Clearly, the way we are now doing it isn't working. It is non-functional. This book offers a basis for opening discussion. If it is startling in some of its conclusions, that can serve to shake us loose from our malaise. Indeed, it is the intention of this dialogue to do so.

So, this book will be anything but boring. No exploration of the *Conversations with God* message can be complete without it. You may find yourself agreeing with it or disagreeing with it strongly, or agreeing with it strongly in one place and disagreeing with it strongly in another. That's good. That makes for a good read. It also makes for a good conversation. It is a conversation that I hope *you* will have with God—and with each other.

Read what is here, then check in with God in the best way that you know how, and converse about this material. Talk about our world, too—the world that is discussed here. Ask God what you can do to help change our world, to help humanity move away from the intolerance and the selfishness, the anger and the violence that seems to permeate our everyday life. If my conversation with God as related here does nothing more than stimulate you to have your own conversation with God, it will have done everything it was meant to do.

There have been those, and there will more, who say (many with some anger) that I have never had a conversation with God, and that to claim that I have is to be a blasphemer and an apostate. Because those who say this so fervently believe it, they condemn this book. Yet condemnation of every thought or idea that challenges those currently held leads not to expanded awareness and growth, but to shrinking vistas and reduced possibilities and ever more limited options in the face of wildly increasing challenges and problems.

Perhaps the way to meet tomorrow's challenges is not to use yesterday's solutions, but to dare to think the previously unthinkable, to speak the previously unspeakable, and to try that which was previously out of the question.

From its first word to its last, this book invites us to do that. To do *just* that. And now, ten years after it was written, more hangs on our willingness to be that courageous than ever.

Neale Donald Walsch
Ashland, Oregon
April 2003

1

Thank you for coming. Thank you for being here.

You are here by appointment, true; but still, you could have failed to show up. You could have decided not to. You chose instead to be here, at the appointed hour, at the appointed place, for this book to come into your hands. So thank you.

Now if you have done all this subconsciously, without even knowing what you were doing or why, some of this may be a mystery to you, and a little explaining may be in order.

Let's start by causing you to notice that this book has arrived in your life at the right and perfect time. You may not know that now, but when you finish with the experience that is in store for you, you will know it absolutely. Everything happens in perfect order, and the arrival of this book in your life is no exception.

What you have here is that for which you have been looking, that for which you have been yearning, for a very long time. What you have here is your latest—and for some of you perhaps your first—very real contact with God.

This *is* a contact, and it is very real.

God is going to have an actual conversation with you now, through me. I wouldn't have said this a few years ago; I'm saying it now because I've already had such a dialogue and I therefore know that such a thing is possible. Not only is it possible, it is happening all the time. Just as this is happening, right here, right now.

What is important for you to understand is that you, in part, have caused this to happen, just as you have caused this book to be in your hands at this moment. We are all at cause in creating the events of our lives, and we are all co-creators with the One Great Creator in producing each of the circumstances leading up to those events.

My first experience of talking to God on your behalf occurred in 1992-93. I had written an angry letter to God, asking why my life had become such a monument to struggle and failure. In everything from my romantic relationships to my life work to my interactions with my children to my health—*in everything*—I was experiencing nothing but struggle and failure. My letter to God demanded to know why—and what it took to make life work.

To my astonishment, that letter was answered.

How it was answered, and what those answers were, became a book, published in May 1995 under the title *Conversations with God, Book 1*. Perhaps you've heard of it or maybe have even read it. If so, you do not need any further preamble to this book.

If you are not familiar with the first book, I hope you soon will be, because *Book 1* outlines in much greater detail how all of this began and answers many questions about our personal lives—questions about money, love, sex, God, health and sickness, eating, relationships, "right work," and many other aspects of our day-to-day experience—which are not addressed here.

If there is one gift I would ask God to give to the world at this time, it would be the information in *Book 1*. True to form *("Even before you ask, I will have answered.")*, God has already done so.

So I hope that, after reading this book (or maybe even before you finish it), you will choose to read the first. It's all a matter of choice, just as Pure Choice brought you to these words right now. Just as Pure Choice has created every experience you ever had. (A concept that is explained in that first book.)

These first paragraphs of *Book 2* were written in March 1996, to provide a brief introduction to the information which follows. As in *Book 1*, the process by which this information "arrived" was exquisitely simple. On a blank sheet of paper, I would merely write a question—any question . . . usually, the first question that came to my head—and no sooner was the question written than the answer would form in my head, as if Someone were whispering in my ear. I was taking dictation!

With the exception of these few opening lines, all the material in this book was placed on paper between Spring 1993 and a little over one year later. I'd like to present it to you now, just as it came from me and was given to me. . . .

* * *

It is Easter Sunday 1993, and—as instructed—I am here. I am here, pencil in hand, writing pad before me, ready to begin.

I suppose I should tell you God asked me to be here. We had a date. We're to begin—today—*Book 2*, the second in a trilogy which God and I and you are experiencing together.

I have no idea yet what this book is going to say, or even the specific subjects that we'll touch upon. That's because there is no plan for this book in my head. There can't be. I'm not the one deciding what's going to go into it. God is.

On Easter Sunday 1992—one year ago today—God began a dialogue with me. I know that sounds ridiculous, but it's what happened. Not long ago, that dialogue ended. I was given instructions to take a rest . . . but told also that I had a "date" to return to this conversation this day.

You have a date, too. You're keeping it right now. I am clear that this book is being written not only to me, but to you *through* me. Apparently you've been looking for God—and for Word *from* God—for a very long time. So have I.

Today we shall find God together. That is always the best way to find God. Together. We shall never find God apart. I mean that two ways. I mean we shall never find God so long as *we* are apart. For the first step in finding that we are not apart from God is finding that we are not apart from each other, and until we know and realize that all of *us* are One, we cannot know and realize that we and God are One.

God is not apart from us, ever, and we only *think* we are apart from God.

It's a common error. We also think we're apart from each other. And so the fastest way to "find God," I've discovered, is to find each other. To stop hiding out from each other. And, of course, to stop hiding out from ourselves.

The fastest way to stop hiding out is to tell the truth. To everyone. All the time.

Start telling the truth now, and never stop. Begin by telling the truth to yourself about yourself. Then tell the truth to yourself about another. Then tell the truth about yourself to another. Then tell the truth about another to that other. Finally, tell the truth to everyone about everything.

These are the *Five Levels of Truth Telling*. This is the five-fold path to freedom. The truth *shall* set you free.

This book is about truth. Not my truth, God's truth.

Our initial dialogue—God's and mine—was concluded just a month ago. I assume this one will go just like the first. That is, I ask questions and God answers. I guess I'll stop, and ask God right now.

God—is this how it's going to go?

> Yes.

I thought so.

> Except that in this book I'll bring some subjects up Myself, without you asking. I didn't do much of that in the first book, as you know.

Yes. Why are You adding that twist here?

> Because this book is being written at My request. I asked you here—as you've pointed out. The first book was a project you started by yourself.
>
> With the first book you had an agenda. With this book you have no agenda, except to do My Will.

Yes. That's correct.

> That, Neale, is a very good place to be. I hope you—and others—will go to that place often.

But I thought Your Will was my will. How can I *not* do Your Will if it's the same as mine?

> That is an intricate question—and not a bad place to start; not a bad place at all for us to begin this dialogue.
>
> Let's go back a few paces. I have never said that My Will was your will.

Yes, You have! In the last book, You said to me very clearly: "Your will is My Will."

> Indeed—but that is not the same thing.

It's not? You could have fooled me.

> When I say "Your will is My Will," that is not the same thing as saying My Will is your will.

If you did My Will all the time, there would be nothing more for you to do to achieve Enlightenment. The process would be over. You would be already there.

One *day* of doing nothing but My Will would bring you Enlightenment. If you had been doing My Will all the years you've been alive, you'd hardly need to be involved in this book right now.

So it's clear you have not been doing My Will. In fact, most of the time you don't even *know* My Will.

I don't?

No, you don't.

Then why don't You tell me what it is?

I do. You just don't listen. And when you do listen, you don't really hear. And when you do hear, you don't believe what you're hearing. And when you do believe what you're hearing, you don't follow instructions anyway.

So to say that My Will is your will is demonstrably inaccurate.

On the other hand, your will *is* My Will. First, because I know it. Second, because I accept it. Third, because I praise it. Fourth, because I love it. Fifth, because I own it and *call it My Own.*

This means *you* have *free* will to do as you wish—and that I *make* your will Mine, through unconditional love.

Now for My Will to be yours, you would have to do the same.

First, you would have to know it. Second, you would have to accept it. Third, you would have to praise it. Fourth, you would have to love it. Finally, you would have to *call it your own.*

In the whole history of your race, only a few of you have ever done this consistently. A handful of others have done it nearly always. Many have done it a great deal. A whole slew of people have done it from time to time. And virtually everyone has done it on rare occasion—although some have never done it at all.

Which category am I in?

Does it matter? Which category do you want to be in *from now on*? Isn't that the pertinent question?

Yes.

And your answer?

I'd like to be in the first category. I'd like to know and do Your Will all the time.

That's laudable, commendable, and probably impossible.

Why?

Because you have far too much growing to do before you can claim that. Yet I tell you this: You *could* claim that, you could move to Godhood, this *instant* if you chose to. Your growth need not take so much time.

Then why *has* it taken so much time?

Indeed. Why has it? What are you waiting for? Surely you don't believe it is I holding you back?

No. I'm clear that I'm holding myself back.

Good. Clarity is the first step to mastery.

I'd like to get to mastery. How can I do that?

Keep reading this book. That's exactly where I'm taking you.

2

I'm not sure I know where this book is going. I'm not sure where to begin.

Let's take time.

How much time do we need to take? It's already taken me *five months* to get from the first chapter to this. I know that people read this and think it's all put down in one even, uninterrupted flow. They don't realize that 20 *weeks* separated the 32nd and 33rd paragraph of this book. They don't understand that sometimes the moments of inspiration are half a *year apart*. How much time do we have to take?

That's not what I meant. I mean, let's take "Time" as our first subject, as a place to begin.

Oh. Okay. But while we're on the subject, why *does* it take months sometimes to complete a simple paragraph? Why are You so long between visits?

My dear and wonderful son, I am not long between "visits." I am never *not* with you. You are simply not always *aware*.

Why? Why am I not aware of You if You're always here?

Because your life gets caught up in other things. Let's face it; you've had a pretty busy five months.

I have. Yes, I have. A lot's been going on.

And you've made these things more important than Me.

That doesn't feel like my truth.

I invite you to look at your actions. You've been deeply involved in your physical life. You've paid very little attention to your soul.

It's been a challenging period.

Yes. All the more reason to have included your soul in the process. These past months would have all gone much more smoothly with My help. So may I suggest that you don't lose contact?

I try to stay close, but I seem to get lost—caught up, as You put it—in my own drama. And then, somehow, I don't find time for You. I don't meditate. I don't pray. And I certainly don't write.

I know. It's an irony of life that when you need our connection the most, you step away from it.

How can I stop doing that?

Stop doing that.

That's what I just said. But how?

You stop doing that by stopping doing that.

It's not that simple.

It is that simple.

I wish it were.

Then it *really* will be, because what you wish is My command. Remember, My cherished one, your desires are My desires. Your will is My Will.

All right. Okay. Then I wish for this book to be finished by March. It's October now. I wish for no more five-month gaps in the material coming.

So will it be.

Good.

Unless it's not.

Oh, man. Do we have to play these games?

No. But so far that's how you've decided to live your Life. You keep changing your mind. Remember, life is an ongoing process of creation. You are creating your reality every minute. The decision you make today is often not the choice you make tomorrow. Yet here is a secret of all Masters: *keep choosing the same thing.*

Over and over again? Once is not enough?

Over and over until your will is made manifest in your reality.

For some that could take years. For some, months. For others, weeks. For those approaching mastery, days, hours, or even minutes. For *Masters,* creation is *instantaneous.*

You can tell you are on your way to mastery when you see the gap closing between Willing and Experiencing.

You said, "The decision you make today is often not the choice you make tomorrow." So what? Are You saying we should never indulge in a change of mind?

Change your mind all you want. Yet remember that with each change of mind comes a change in the direction of the whole universe.

When you "make up your mind" about something, you set the universe into motion. Forces beyond your ability to comprehend—far more subtle and complex than you could imagine—are engaged in a process, the intricate dynamics of which you are only just now beginning to understand.

These forces and this process are all part of the extraordinary web of interactive energies which comprise the entirety of existence which you call life itself.

They are, in essence, *Me.*

So when I change my mind I'm making it difficult for You, is that it?

Nothing is difficult for Me—but you might be making things very difficult for yourself. Therefore, be of one mind and of single purpose about a thing. And don't take your mind off of it until you have produced it in reality. Keep focused. Stay centered.

This is what is meant by being single-minded. If you choose something, choose it with all your might, with all your heart. Don't be faint-hearted. Keep going! Keep moving toward it. Be determined.

Don't take *no* for an answer.

Exactly.

But what if *no is* the right answer? What if what we want is not for us—not for our own good, not in our best interests? Then you won't give it to us, right?

Wrong. I will "give" you whatever you call forth, whether it's "good" for you or "bad" for you. Have you looked at your life lately?

But I've been taught that we can't always have what we desire—that God won't give it to us if it's not for our highest good.

That's something people tell you when they want you not to be disappointed with a particular outcome.

First of all, let's move back to clarity about our relationship. I don't "give" you anything—you call it forth. *Book 1* explains exactly how you do this, in considerable detail.

Secondly, I don't make a judgment about what you call forth. I don't call a thing "good" or "bad." (You, too, would do well to not do so.)

You are a creative being—made in the image and likeness of God. You may have whatever you choose. But you may not have anything you want. In fact, you'll never get *anything* you want if you want it badly enough.

I know. You explained that in *Book 1* as well. You said that the act of wanting a thing pushes it away from us.

Yes, and do you remember why?

Because thoughts are creative, and the thought of wanting a thing is a statement to the universe—a declaration of a truth—which the universe then produces in my reality.

Precisely! Exactly! You *have* learned. You *do* understand. That's great.

Yes, that's how it works. The moment you say "I want" something, the universe says "Indeed you do" and gives you that precise experience—*the experience of "wanting" it!*

Whatever you put after the word "I" becomes your creative command. The genie in the bottle—which I Am—exists but to obey.

I produce what you call forth! You call forth precisely what you think, feel, and say. It's as simple as that.

So tell me again—why does it take so much time for me to create the reality I choose?

For a number of reasons. Because you do not believe you can have what you choose. Because you do not know *what* to choose. Because you keep trying to figure out what's "best" for you. Because you want guarantees ahead of time that all your choices will be "good." And because you keep changing your mind!

Let me see if I understand. I shouldn't try to figure out what's best for me?

"Best" is a relative term, depending on a hundred variables. That makes choices very difficult. There should be only one consideration when making any decision—Is this a statement of Who I Am? Is this an announcement of Who I Choose to Be?

All of life should be such an announcement. In fact, all of life *is*. You can allow that announcement to be made by *chance* or by *choice*.

A life lived by choice is a life of conscious action. A life lived by chance is a life of unconscious reaction.

Reaction is just that—an action you have taken before. When you "re-act," what you do is assess the incoming data, search your memory bank for the same or nearly the same experience, and *act the way you did before*. This is all the work of the mind, not of your soul.

Your soul would have you search *its* "memory" to see how you might create a truly *genuine experience* of You in the Now Moment. This is the experience of "soul searching" of which you have so often heard, but you have to be literally "out of your mind" to do it.

When you spend your time trying to figure out what's "best" for you, you are doing just that: *spending your time*. Better to *save* your time than to spend it wastefully.

It is a great time-saver to be out of your mind. Decisions are reached quickly, choices are activated rapidly, because your soul creates out of present experience only, without review, analysis, and criticism of past encounters.

Remember this: the soul creates, the mind reacts.

The soul knows in Its wisdom that the experience you are having in This Moment is an experience sent to you by God before you had any conscious awareness of it. This is what is meant by a "pre-sent" experience. It's already on the way to you even as you are seeking it—for even before you ask, I shall have answered you. Every Now Moment is a glorious gift from God. That's why it is called the *present.*

The soul intuitively seeks the perfect circumstance and situation now needed to heal wrong thought and bring you the rightful experience of Who You Really Are.

It is the soul's desire to bring you back to God—to bring you home to Me.

It is the soul's intention to know itself *experientially*—and thus to know Me. For the soul understands that You and I are One, even as the mind denies this truth and the body acts out this denial.

Therefore, in moments of great decision, be out of your mind, and do some soul searching instead.

The soul understands what the mind cannot conceive.

If you spend your time trying to figure out what's "best" for you, your choices will be cautious, your decisions will take forever, and your journey will be launched on a sea of expectations.

If you are not careful, you will *drown* in your expectations.

Whew! That's quite an answer! But how do I listen to my soul? How do I know what I'm hearing?

The soul speaks to you in feelings. Listen to your feelings. Follow your feelings. Honor your feelings.

Why does it seem to me that honoring my feelings is precisely what has caused me to get into trouble in the first place?

Because you have labeled growth "trouble," and standing still "safe."

I tell you this: Your feelings will *never* get you into "trouble," because your feelings are your *truth.*

If you want to live a life where you never follow your feelings, but where every feeling is filtered through the machinery of your Mind, go right ahead. Make your decisions based on your Mind's analysis of the situation. But don't look for joy in such machinations, nor for celebration of Who You Truly Are.

Remember this: True celebration is mindless.

If you listen to your soul you will know what is "best" for you, because what is best for you is what is true for you.

When you act only out of what is true for you, you speed your way down the path. When you *create* an experience based on your "now truth" rather than *react* to an experience based on a "past truth," you produce a "new you."

Why does it take so much time to create the reality you choose? This is why: because you have not been living your truth.

Know the truth, and the truth shall set you free.

Yet once you come to know your truth, don't keep *changing your mind about it*. This is your mind trying to figure out what's "best." Stop it! Get out of your mind. Get back to your *senses!*

That is what is *meant* by "getting back to your senses." It is a returning to how you *feel*, not how you *think*. Your thoughts are just that—thoughts. Mental constructions. "Made up" creations of your mind. But your *feelings*—now *they* are *real*.

Feelings are the language of the soul. And your soul is your truth.

There. Now does that tie it all together for you?

Does this mean we are to express any feeling—no matter how negative or destructive?

Feelings are neither negative nor destructive. They are simply truths. How you express your truth is what matters.

When you express your truth with love, negative and damaging results rarely occur, and, when they do, it is usually because someone else has chosen to experience your truth in a negative or damaging way. In such a case, there is probably nothing you can do to avoid the outcome.

Certainly, *failing* to express your truth would hardly be appropriate. Yet people do this all the time. So afraid are they to cause or to face possible unpleasantness that they hide their truth altogether.

Remember this: It is not nearly so important how well a message is received as how well it is sent.

You cannot take responsibility for how well another accepts your truth; you can only ensure how well it is communicated. And by how well, I don't mean merely how clearly; I mean how lovingly, how compassionately, how sensitively, how courageously, and how completely.

This leaves no room for half truths, the "brutal truth," or even the "plain truth." It does mean the truth, the whole truth, and nothing but the truth, so help you God.

It's the "so help you God" part that brings in the Godly qualities of love and compassion—for I will help you communicate in this way always, if you will ask Me.

So yes, express what you call your most "negative" feelings, but not destructively.

Failure to express (i.e. push out) negative feelings does not make them go away; it *keeps them in.* Negativity "kept in" harms the body and burdens the soul.

But if another person hears every negative thought you have about that person, it would have to affect the relationship, no matter how lovingly those thoughts were delivered.

I said to express (push out, get rid of) your negative feelings—I did not say how, or to whom.

All negativity need not be shared with the person about whom it is felt. It is only necessary to communicate these feelings to the other when failure to do so would compromise your integrity or cause another to believe an untruth.

Negativity is never a sign of ultimate truth, even if it seems like your truth at the moment. It may arise out of an unhealed part of you. In fact, *always it does.*

That is why it is so important to get these negativities out, to release them. Only by letting go of them—putting them out there, placing them in front of you—can you see them clearly enough to know whether you really believe them.

You have all said things—ugly things—only to discover that, once having been said, they no longer feel "true."

You have all expressed feelings—from fear to anger to rage—only to discover that, once having been expressed, they no longer reveal how you *really* feel.

In this way, feelings can be tricky. Feelings *are* the language of the soul, but you must make sure you are listening to your *true feelings* and not some counterfeit model constructed in your mind.

Oh, man, so now I can't even trust my *feelings*. Great! I thought that was the way to truth! I thought that was what You were *teaching* me.

It *is*. I *am*. But listen, because it is more complex than you now understand. Some feelings are *true feelings*—that is, feelings born in the soul—and some feelings are counterfeit feelings. These are constructed in your mind.

In other words, they are not "feelings" at all—they are *thoughts*. Thoughts *masquerading* as feelings.

These thoughts are based on your previous experience and on the observed experience of others. You see someone grimace when having a tooth pulled, *you* grimace when having *your* tooth pulled. It may not even *hurt*, but you grimace anyway. Your reaction has nothing to do with reality, only how you *perceive* reality, based on the experience of others or on something that's happened to *you* in the *past*.

The greatest challenge as human beings is to Be Here Now, to stop making things up! Stop creating thoughts about a pre-sent moment (a moment you "sent" yourself *before* you had a thought about it). Be *in the moment*. Remember, you *sent* your Self this moment as a gift. The moment contained the seed of a tremendous truth. It is a truth you wished to remember. Yet when the moment arrived, you immediately began constructing thoughts about it. Instead of being *in* the moment, you stood *outside* the moment and judged it. Then you re-acted. That is, you acted as you *did once before*.

Now look at these two words:

REACTIVE

CREATIVE

Notice they are the *same word*. Only the "C" has been moved! When you "C" things correctly, you become Creative, rather than Reactive.

That's very clever.

Well, God is like that.

But, you see, the point I am trying to make is that when you come to each moment cleanly, *without a previous thought about it*, you can *create* who you are, rather than *re-enact* who you *once were*.

Life is a process of creation, and you keep living it as if it were a process of re-enactment!

But how can any rational human being ignore one's previous experience in the moment something occurs? Isn't it normal to call up everything you know on the subject and respond from that?

It may be normal, but it is not *natural*. "Normal" means something usually done. "Natural" is how you are when you're not trying to be "normal"!

Natural and normal are not the same thing. In any given moment you can do what you normally do, or you can do what comes naturally.

I tell you this: *Nothing is more natural than love.*

If you act lovingly, you will be acting naturally. If you react fearfully, resentfully, angrily, you may be acting *normally*, but you will never be acting *naturally*.

How can I act with love when all my previous experience is screaming at me that a particular "moment" is likely to be painful?

Ignore your previous experience and *go into the moment*. Be Here Now. See what there is to work with *right now* in *creating yourself anew*.

Remember, *this is what you are doing here*.

You have come to this world in this way, at this time, in this place, to Know Who You Are—and to create Who You Wish to Be.

This is the purpose of all of life. Life is an ongoing, never-ending process of re-creation. You keep recreating your selves in the image of your next highest idea about yourselves.

But isn't that rather like the man who jumped off the highest building, sure that he could fly? He ignored his "previous experience" *and* the "observed experience of others" and jumped off the building, all the while declaring, "I am God!" That doesn't seem very smart.

And I tell you this: Men have achieved results much greater than flying. Men have healed sickness. Men have raised the dead.

One man has.

You think only one man has been granted such powers over the physical universe?

Only one man has demonstrated them.

Not so. Who parted the Red Sea?

God.

Indeed, but who called upon God to do that?

Moses.

Exactly. And who called upon Me to heal the sick, and raise the dead?

Jesus.

Yes. Now, do you think that what Moses and Jesus did, you _cannot_ do?

But they didn't _do_ it! They asked _You_ to! That's a different thing.

Okay. We'll go with your construction for now. And do you think that _you_ cannot ask Me these same miraculous things?

I suppose I could.

And would I grant them?

I don't know.

That's the difference between you and Moses! That's what separates you from Jesus!

Many people believe if they ask in Jesus' name, You _will_ grant their request.

Yes, many people do believe that. They believe they have no power, but they have _seen_ (or believe others who had seen) the power of Jesus, so they ask in his name. Even though he said, "Why are you so amazed? These things, and more, shall you also do." Yet the people could not believe it. Many do not to this day.

You all imagine you are unworthy. So you ask in the name of Jesus. Or the Blessed Virgin Mary. Or the "patron saint" of this or that. Or the Sun God. Or the spirit of the East. You'll use anybody's name—_anybody's_—but your own!

Yet I tell you this—_Ask and you shall receive. Seek and you shall find. Knock and it shall be opened unto you._

Jump off the building and you shall fly.

There have been people who have levitated. Do you believe this?

Well, I've heard of it.

And people who have walked through walls. And even left their bodies.

Yes, yes. But I've never *seen* anybody walk through walls—and I don't suggest anyone try it. Nor do I think we should jump off buildings. That's probably not good for your health.

That man fell to his death not because he could not have flown if he were coming from the right state of Being but because he could *never* have demonstrated Godliness by trying to show himself as separate from you.

Please explain.

The man on the building lived in a world of self-delusion in which he imagined himself to be *other than the rest of you.* By declaring "I am God," he *began* his demonstration with a lie. He hoped to make himself separate. Larger. More powerful.

It was an act of the ego.

Ego—that which is separate, individual—can never duplicate or demonstrate that which is One.

By seeking to demonstrate that he was God, the man on the building demonstrated only his separateness, not his unity, with all things. Thus, he sought to demonstrate Godliness by demonstrating Ungodliness, and failed.

Jesus, on the other hand, demonstrated Godliness by demonstrating Unity—and seeing Unity and Wholeness wherever (and upon whomever) he looked. In this his consciousness and My consciousness were One, and, in such a state, whatever he called forth was made manifest in his Divine Reality in that Holy Moment.

I see. So all it takes is "Christ Consciousness" to perform miracles! Well, that should make things simple. . . .

Actually, it does. More simple than you think. And many have achieved such consciousness. Many have been Christed, not just Jesus of Nazareth.

You can be Christed, too.

How—?

By seeking to be. By choosing to be. But it is a choice you must make every day, every minute. It must become the very *purpose of your life.*

It *is* the purpose of your life—you simply do not know it. And even if you know it, even if you remember the exquisite reason for your very existence, you do not seem to know how to *get* there from where you are.

Yes, that is the case. So how *can* I get from where I am to where I want to be?

I tell you this—again: *Seek and ye shall find. Knock and it shall be opened unto you.*

I've been "seeking" and "knocking" for 35 years. You'll pardon me if I'm a little bored with that line.

If not to say, disillusioned, yes? But really, while I have to give you good grades for trying—an "A for effort," so to speak—I can't say, I can't agree with you, that you've been seeking and knocking for 35 years.

Let's agree that you've been seeking and knocking *on and off* for 35 years—mostly off.

In the past, when you were very young, you came to Me only when you were in trouble, when you needed something. As you grew older and matured, you realized that was probably not a *right relationship* with God, and sought to create something more meaningful. Even then, I was hardly more than a *sometimes thing.*

Still later, as you came to understand that *union* with God can be achieved only through *communion* with God, you undertook the practices and behaviors that could *achieve* communion, yet even these you engaged sporadically, inconsistently.

You meditated, you held ritual, you called Me forth in prayer and chant, you evoked the Spirit of Me in you, but only when it suited you, only when you felt inspired to.

And, glorious as your experience of Me was even on these occasions, still you've spent 95 percent of your life caught up in the illusion of *separateness*, and only flickering moments here and there in the realization of *ultimate reality*.

You still think your life is about car repairs and telephone bills and what you want out of relationships, that it's about the *dramas* you've created, rather than the *creator* of those dramas.

You have yet to learn *why* you keep creating your dramas. You're too busy playing them out.

You say you understand the meaning of life, but you do not live your understandings. You say you know the way toward communion with God, but you do not take that way. You claim you are on the *path*, but you do not walk it.

Then you come to Me and say you've been seeking and knocking for 35 years.

I hate to be the one to disillusion you, but. . . .

It's time you stopped being disillusioned in Me and started seeing *you* as you really are.

Now—I tell you this: You want to be "Christed"? *Act* like Christ, *every minute of every day.* (It's not that you don't know how. He has shown you the way.) Be like Christ in every circumstance. (It's not that you can't. He has left you *instructions*.)

You are not without help in this, should you seek it. I am giving you guidance every minute of every day. I Am the still small voice within which knows which way to turn, which path to take, which answer to give, which action to implement, which word to say—which *reality to create* if you truly seek communion and unity with Me.

Just *listen* to Me.

I guess I don't know how to do that.

Oh, nonsense! *You're doing it right now!* Simply do it *all the time.*

I can't walk around with a yellow legal pad every minute of the day. I can't stop everything and start writing notes to You, hoping You'll be there with one of Your brilliant answers.

Thank you. They *are* brilliant! And here's another one: *Yes, you can!*

I mean, if someone told you that you could have a direct Connection with God—a direct link, a direct line—and all you had to do was make sure you had paper and pen handy at all times, would you do it?

Well, yes, of *course.*

Yet you just said you *wouldn't.* Or "can't." So what's the matter with you? What are you saying? What *is* your truth?

Now the Good News is that you don't even *need* a pad and pen. *I am with you always.* I don't live in the pen. *I live in you.*

That *is* true, isn't it. . . . I mean, I can really believe that, can't I?

Of course you can believe it. It's what I've been *asking* you to believe from the beginning. It's what every Master, including Jesus, has said to you. It is the central teaching. It is the ultimate truth.

I am with you always, even unto the end of time.

Do you believe this?

Yes, now I do. More than ever, I mean.

Good. Then *use* Me. If it works for you to take out a pad and a pen (and, I must say, that seems to work pretty well for you), then *take out a pad and a pen.* More *often.* Every day. Every hour, if you have to.

Get close to Me. *Get close to Me!* Do what you can. Do what you have to. Do what it takes.

Say a rosary. Kiss a stone. Bow to the East. Chant a chant. Swing a pendulum. Test a muscle.

Or write a book.

Do what it takes.

Each of you has your own construction. Each of you has understood Me—created Me—in your own way.

To some of you I am a man. To some of you I am a woman. To some, I am both. To some, I am neither.

To some of you I am pure energy. To some, the ultimate feeling, which you call love. And some of you have no idea what I am. You simply know that I AM.

And so it is.

I AM.

I am the wind which rustles your hair. I am the sun which warms your body. I am the rain which dances on your face. I am the smell of flowers in the air, and I am the flowers which send their fragrance upward. I am the air which *carries* the fragrance.

I am the beginning of your first thought. I am the end of your last. I am the idea which sparked your most brilliant moment. I am the glory of its fulfillment. I am the feeling which fueled the most loving thing you ever did. I am the part of you which yearns for that feeling again and again.

Whatever works for you, whatever makes it happen—*whatever* ritual, ceremony, demonstration, meditation, thought, song, word, or action it *takes* for you to "reconnect"—*do this.*

Do this in remembrance of Me.

3

So, going back and summarizing what you are telling me, I seem to come up with these main points.

- Life is an ongoing process of creation.
- A secret of all Masters is to stop changing one's mind; keep choosing the same thing.
- Don't take *no* for an answer.
- We "call forth" what we think, feel, and say.
- Life can be a process of creation or reaction.
- The soul *creates*, the mind *reacts*.
- The soul understands what the mind cannot conceive.
- Stop trying to figure out what is "best" for you (how you can win the most, lose the least, get what you want) and start going with what feels like Who You Are.
- Your feelings are your truth. What is best for you is what is true for you.
- Thoughts are *not* feelings; rather, they are ideas of how you "should" feel. When thoughts and feelings get confused, truth becomes clouded, lost.
- To get back to your feelings, be *out of your mind* and *get back to your senses*.
- Once you know your truth, *live* it.
- Negative feelings are not true feelings at all; rather, they are your thoughts about something, based always on the previous experience of yourself and others.
- Previous experience is no indicator of truth, since Pure Truth is created here and now, not reenacted.
- To change your response to anything, be in the present (that is, the "pre-sent") moment—the moment that was sent to you and was what it was before you had a thought about it. . . . In other words, Be Here Now, not in the past or the future.

- The past and the future can exist only in thought. The Pre-sent Moment is the Only Reality. *Stay* there!
- Seek and you shall find.
- Do whatever it takes to stay connected with God/Goddess/Truth. Don't stop the practices, the prayers, the rituals, the meditations, the readings, the writings, the *"whatever works" for you* to stay in touch with All That Is.

How's that so far?

Great! So far, so good. You've got it. Now, can you live it?

I'm going to try.

Good.

Yes. Now, can we go to where we left off? Tell me about Time.

There *is* no Time like the pre-sent!

You've heard that before, I'm sure. But you didn't understand it. Now you do.

There is no time but *this* time. There is no moment but this moment. "Now" is all there is.

What about "yesterday" and "tomorrow"?

Figments of your imagination. Constructions of your mind. Nonexistent in Ultimate Reality.

Everything that ever happened, is happening, and ever will happen, is happening right *now.*

I don't understand.

And you can't. Not completely. But you can *begin* to. And a beginning grasp is all that is needed here.

So . . . just listen.

"Time" is not a continuum. It is an element of relativity that exists vertically, not horizontally.

Don't think of it as a "left to right" thing—a so-called time line that runs from birth to death for each individual, and *from* some finite point *to* some finite point for the universe.

"Time" is an "up and down" thing! Think of it as a spindle, representing the Eternal Moment of Now.

Now picture leafs of paper on the spindle, one atop the other. These are the elements of time. Each element separate and distinct, yet each existing *simultaneously with the other.* All the paper on the spindle at once! As much as there will ever *be*—as much as there ever *was.* . . .

There is only One Moment—*this* moment—the Eternal Moment of Now.

It is *right now* that everything is happening —and I am glorified. There is no waiting for the glory of God. I made it this way because *I just couldn't wait!* I was so *happy* to Be Who I Am that I just couldn't wait to make that manifest in My reality. So BOOM, here it is—right here, right now—ALL OF IT!

There is no Beginning to this, and there is no End. It—the All of Everything—just IS.

Within the Isness is where your experience—and your greatest secret—lies. You can move in consciousness within the Isness to any "time" or "place" you choose.

You mean we can time travel?

Indeed—and many of you have. *All* of you have, in fact—and you do it routinely, usually in what you call your dream state. Most of you are not aware of it. You cannot retain the awareness. But the energy sticks to you like glue, and sometimes there's enough residue that others—sensitive to this energy—can pick up things about your "past" or your "future." They feel or "read" this residue, and you call them seers and psychics. Sometimes there is enough residue that even you, in your limited consciousness, are aware you've "been here before." Your whole being is suddenly jarred by the realization that you've "done this all before"!

Déjà vu!

Yes. Or that wonderful feeling when you meet someone that you've *known them all your life*—known them for all *eternity!*

That's a spectacular feeling. That's a marvelous feeling. And that's a *true* feeling. You *have* known that soul *forever!*

Forever is a right now thing!

So you have *often* looked up, or looked down, from your "piece of paper" on the spindle, and seen all the other pieces! And you've seen yourself there—because *a part of You is on every piece!*

How is that possible?

I tell you this: You have always been, are now, and always will be. There has *never* been a time when you were not—nor will there ever *be* such a time.

But wait! What about the concept of *old souls*! Aren't some souls "older" than others?

Nothing is "older" than *anything*. I created it ALL AT ONCE, and All Of It exists *right now*.

The experience of "older" and "younger" to which you refer has to do with the *levels of awareness* of a particular soul, or Aspect of Being. You are all Aspects of Being, simply parts of What Is. Each part has the consciousness of the Whole imbedded within it. Every element carries the imprint.

"Awareness" is the experience of that consciousness being awakened. The individual aspect of the ALL becomes aware of Itself. It becomes, quite literally, *self conscious*.

Then, gradually, it becomes conscious of all others, and then, of the fact that there *are* no others—that All is One.

Then, ultimately, of Me. Magnificent Me!

Boy, You really *like* You, don't You?

Don't you—?

Yes, yes! I think You're great!

I agree. And I think *you're* great! That's the only place where You and I disagree. *You don't think you're great!*

How can I see myself as great when I see all my foibles, all my mistakes—all my evil?

I tell you this: There *is* no evil!

I wish that could be true.

You are perfect, just as you are.

I wish that could be true, too.

It *is* true! A tree is no less perfect because it is a seedling. A tiny infant is no less perfect than a grown-up. It is *perfection itself.* Because it cannot *do* a thing, does not *know* a thing, that does not make it somehow less perfect.

A child makes mistakes. She stands. She toddles. She falls. She stands again, a bit wobbly, hanging on to her mommy's leg. Does that make the child imperfect?

I tell you it is just the opposite! That child is *perfection itself,* wholly and completely adorable.

So, too, are *you.*

But the child hasn't done anything wrong! The child hasn't consciously disobeyed, hurt another, damaged herself.

The child doesn't *know* right from wrong.

Precisely.

Neither do you.

But I *do.* I know that it is wrong to kill people, and that it is right to love them. I know that it is wrong to hurt and right to heal, to make things better. I know that it is wrong to take what is not mine, to use another, to be dishonest.

I could show you instances where each of those "wrongs" would be *right.*

You're playing with me now.

Not at all. Merely being factual.

If you are saying there are exceptions to every rule, then I agree.

If there are *exceptions* to a rule, then it is not a *rule.*

Are you telling me that it is *not* wrong to kill, to hurt, to take from another?

That depends on what you are trying to *do.*

Okay, okay, I get it. But that doesn't make these things *good.* Sometimes one has to do bad things to achieve a good end.

Which doesn't make them "bad things" at all, then, does it? They are just means to an end.

Are you saying the end justifies the means?

What do you think?

No. Absolutely not.

So be it.

Don't you see what you're doing here? You're *making up the rules as you go along!*

And don't you see something else? *That's perfectly okay.*

It's what you're *supposed* to be doing!

All of life is a process of deciding Who You Are, and then experiencing that.

As you keep expanding your vision, you make up new rules to cover that! As you keep enlarging your idea about your Self, you create new do's and don'ts, yeses and nos to encircle that. These are the boundaries that "hold in" something which *cannot* be held in.

You cannot hold in "you," because you are as boundless as the Universe. Yet you can create a *concept* about your boundless self by imagining, and then accepting, *boundaries*.

In a sense, this is the only way you can *know* yourself as anything in particular.

That which is boundless is boundless. That which is limitless is limitless. It cannot exist anywhere, because it is everywhere. If it is *everywhere*, it is *nowhere in particular*.

God is everywhere. Therefore, God is nowhere in particular, because to be somewhere in particular, God would have to *not be somewhere else*—which is *not possible for God*.

There is only one thing that is "not possible" for God, and that is for God to *not be God*. God cannot "not be." Nor can God not be like Itself. God cannot "un-God" Itself.

I am everywhere, and that's all there is to it. And since I am everywhere, I am nowhere. And if I am NOWHERE, where am I?

NOW HERE.

I love it! You made this point in the first book, but I love it, so I let You go on.

That's very kind of you. And do you understand it better now? Do you see how you have created your ideas of "right" and "wrong" simply to *define Who You Are?*

Do you see that without these definitions—boundaries—you are nothing?

And do you see that, like Me, you keep changing the boundaries as you change your Ideas of Who You Are?

Well, I get what You are saying, but it does not seem that I have changed the boundaries—my own personal boundaries—very much. To me it has always been wrong to kill. It has always been wrong to steal. It has always been wrong to hurt another. The largest concepts by which we govern ourselves have been in place since the beginning of time, and most human beings agree on them.

Then why do you have war?

Because there will always be some who break the rules. There's a rotten apple in every barrel.

What I'm going to tell you now, and in the passages which follow, may be very difficult for some people to understand and accept. It is going to violate much of what is held as truth in your present thought system. Yet I cannot let you go on living with these constructions if this dialogue is to serve you. So we must, now, in this second book, meet some of these concepts head on. But it's going to be bumpy going here for a while. Are you ready?

I think so, yes. Thanks for the warning. What is it that's so dramatic or difficult to understand or accept that You're going to tell me?

I am going to tell you this: there are *no* "rotten apples." There are only people who *disagree with your point of view on things,* people who construct a different model of the world. I am going to tell you this: No persons do anything inappropriate, given their model of the world.

Then their "model" is all messed up. *I* know what's right and wrong, and because some other people don't, that doesn't make *me* crazy because I *do. They're* the ones who are crazy!

I'm sorry to say that's exactly the attitude which starts wars.

I know, I know. I was doing that on purpose. I was just repeating here what I've heard many other people say. But how *can* I answer people like that? What *could* I say?

You could tell them that people's ideas of "right" and "wrong" change—and have changed—over and over again from culture to culture, time period to time period, religion to religion, place to place . . . even from family to family and person to person. You could point out to them that what many people considered "right" at one time—burning people at the stake for what was considered witchcraft, as an example—is considered "wrong" today.

You could tell them that a definition of "right" and "wrong" is a definition established not only by time, but also by simple geography. You could allow them to notice that some activities on your planet (prostitution, for instance) are illegal in one place, and, just a few miles down the road, legal in another. And so, whether a person is judged as having done something "wrong" is not a matter of what that person has actually *done*, but of *where he has done it*.

Now I am going to repeat something I said in *Book 1*, and I know that it was very, very difficult for some to grasp, to understand.

Hitler went to heaven.

I'm not sure people are ready for this.

The purpose of this book, and of all the books in the trilogy we are creating, is to create readiness—readiness for a new paradigm, a new understanding; a larger view, a grander idea.

Well, I'm going to have to ask the questions here that I know so many people are thinking and wanting to ask. How could a man like Hitler have gone to heaven? Every religion in the world . . . I would think *every* one, has declared him condemned and sent straight to hell.

First, he could not have gone to hell because hell does not exist. Therefore, there is only one place left to which he *could* have gone. But that begs the question. The real issue is whether Hitler's actions where "wrong." Yet I have said over and over again that there is no "right" or "wrong" in the universe. A thing is not intrinsically right or wrong. A thing simply *is*.

Now your thought that Hitler was a monster is based on the fact that he ordered the killing of millions of people, correct?

Obviously, yes.

> Yet what if I told you that what you call "death" is *the greatest thing that could happen to anyone*—what then?

I'd find that hard to accept.

> You think that life on Earth is better than life in heaven? I tell you this, at the moment of your death you will realize the greatest freedom, the greatest peace, the greatest joy, and the greatest love you have ever known. Shall we therefore punish Bre'r Fox for throwing Bre'r Rabbit into the briar patch?

You are ignoring the fact that, however wonderful life after death may be, our lives here should not be ended against our will. We came here to achieve something, to experience something, to learn something, and it is not right that our lives be cut short by some maniacal hoodlum with insane ideas.

> First of all, you are not here to *learn anything.* (Reread *Book 1*!) Life is not a school, and your purpose here is not to learn; it is to re-member. And on your larger point, life is often "cut short" by many things . . . a hurricane, an earthquake. . . .

That's different. You're talking about an Act of God.

> *Every* event is an Act of God.
> Do you imagine that an event could take place if I did not want it to? Do you think that you could so much as lift your little finger if I chose for you not to? You can do *nothing* if I am against it.
> Yet let us continue to explore this idea of "wrongful" death together. Is it "wrong" for a life to be cut short by disease?

"Wrong" isn't a word that applies here. Those are natural causes. That's not the same as a human being like Hitler murdering people.

> What about an accident? A stupid accident—?

Same thing. It's unfortunate, tragic, but that's the Will of God. We can't peer into God's mind and find out why these things happen. We ought not try, because God's Will is immutable and incomprehensible. To seek to unravel Divine Mystery is to lust for knowledge beyond our ken. It is sinful.

How do you know?

Because if God wanted us to understand all of this, we *would*. The fact that we *don't—can't—*is evidence that it is God's *will* that we don't.

I see. The fact that you don't *understand* it is evidence of God's Will. The fact that it *happens* is *not* evidence of God's Will. Hmmmm. . . .

I guess I'm not very good at explaining some of this, but I know what I believe.

Do you believe in God's Will, that God is All Powerful?

Yes.

Except where Hitler was concerned. What happened there was *not* God's Will.

No.

How can that be?

Hitler violated the Will of God.

Now how do you think he could do that if My Will is all powerful?

You allowed him to.

If I *allowed* him to, then it was My *Will* that he should.

It would seem that way . . . but what possible *reason* could You have? No. It was Your Will that he have Free Choice. It was *his* will that he do what he did.

You're so close on this. So close.

You're right, of course. It was My Will that Hitler—that *all* of you—have Free Choice. But it is *not* My Will that you be punished unceasingly, unendingly, if you do not make the choice I want you to make. If that were the case, how "free" have I made *your* choice? Are you really free to do what you want if you know you'll be made to suffer unspeakably if you do not do what *I* want? What kind of choice is that?

It isn't a question of punishment. It's just Natural Law. It's simply a question of consequences.

> I see you've been schooled well in all the theological construc-tions that allow you to hold Me as a vengeful God—without making Me responsible for it.
>
> But who *made* these Natural Laws? And if we can agree that *I* must have put them into place, why would I put into place such laws—then give you the power to overcome them?
>
> If I didn't want you affected by them—if it was My Will that My wonderful beings never should suffer—why would I create the *pos-sibility* that you could?
>
> And then, why would I continue to tempt you, day and night, to break the laws I've set down?

You don't tempt us. The devil does.

> There you go again, making Me not responsible.
>
> Don't you see that the only way you can rationalize your theol-ogy is to render Me powerless? Do you understand that the only way your constructions make sense is if Mine *don't?*
>
> Are you really comfortable with the idea of a God who creates a being whose actions it cannot control?

I didn't say You can't control the devil. You can control *everything.* You're *God!* It's just that You *choose not to.* You *allow* the devil to tempt us, to try to win our souls.

> But *why?* Why would I *do* that if I don't *want* to have you not return to Me?

Because You want us to come to You out of choice, not because there is no choice. You set up Heaven and Hell so there could be a choice. So we could act out of choosing, and not out of simply following a path because there is no other.

> I can see how you've come to this idea. That's how I've set it up in your world, and so you think that's how it must be in *Mine.*
>
> In your reality, Good cannot exist without Bad. So you believe it must be the same in Mine.

Yet I tell you this: There *is* no "bad" where I Am. And there is no Evil. There is only the All of Everything. The Oneness. And the Awareness, the Experience, of that.

Mine is the Realm of the Absolute, where One Thing does not exist in relationship to Another, but quite independent of anything.

Mine is the place where All There Is is Love.

And there are no consequences to anything we think, say or do on Earth?

Oh, but there *are* consequences. Look around you.

I mean after death.

There is no "death." Life goes on forever and ever. Life Is. You simply change form.

All right, have it Your way—after we "change form."

After you change form, consequences cease to exist. There is just Knowing.

Consequences are an element of relativity. They have no place in the Absolute because they depend on linear "time" and sequential events. These do not exist in the Realm of the Absolute.

In that realm there is naught but peace and joy and love.

In that realm you will know at last the Good News: that your "devil" does not exist, that you are who you always thought you were—goodness and love. Your idea that you might be something else has come from an insane outer world, causing you to act insanely. An outer world of judgment and condemnation. Others have judged you, and from their judgments you have judged yourself.

Now you want God to judge you, and I will not do it.

And because you cannot understand a God who will not act as humans would, you are lost.

Your theology is your attempt to find yourself again.

You call our theologies insane—but how can any theology work without a system of Reward and Punishment?

Everything depends on what you perceive to be the purpose of life—and therefore the basis of the theology.

If you believe life exists as a test, a trial, a period of putting you through your paces to see if you are "worthy," your theologies begin to make sense.

If you believe that life exists as an *opportunity*, a process through which you discover—remember—that you *are* worthy (and have *always* been), then your theologies seem insane.

If you believe God is an ego-filled God who requires attention, adoration, appreciation, and affection—*and will kill to get it*—your theologies start to hold together.

If you believe that God is without ego or need, but the *source* of all things, and the seat of all wisdom and love, then your theologies fall apart.

If you believe that God is a vengeful God, jealous in His love and wrathful in His anger, then your theologies are perfect.

If you believe God is a peaceful God, joyous in Her love and passionate in Her ecstasy, then your theologies are useless.

I tell you this: the purpose of life is not to please God. The purpose of life is to know, and to recreate, Who You Are.

In so doing you *do* please God, and glorify *Her* as well.

Why do you keep saying "Her"? Are you a She?

I am neither a "he" *nor* a "she." I occasionally use the feminine pronoun to jar you out of your parochial thinking.

If you think God is one thing, then you will think God is not another. And that would be a large mistake.

Hitler went to heaven for these reasons:

There is no hell, so there is no place else for him to go.

His actions were what you would call mistakes—the actions of an unevolved being—and mistakes are not punishable by condemnation, but dealt with by providing the chance for correction, for evolution.

The mistakes Hitler made did no harm or damage to those whose deaths he caused. Those souls were released from their earthly bondage, like butterflies emerging from a cocoon.

The people who were left behind mourn those deaths only because they do not know of the joy into which those souls entered. No one who has experienced death *ever mourns the death of anyone.*

Your statement that their deaths were nevertheless untimely, and therefore somehow "wrong," suggests that something could happen in the universe *when it is not supposed to.* Yet given Who and What I Am, that is impossible.

Everything occurring in the universe is occurring perfectly. God hasn't made a mistake in a very long time.

When you see the utter perfection in everything—not just those things with which you agree, but (and perhaps especially) those things with which you disagree—you achieve mastery.

I know all of this, of course. We've been through all of this in *Book 1*. But for those who have not read *Book 1*, I thought it important to have a basis of understanding early in this book. That's why I've led into this series of questions and answers. But now, before we go on, I'd like to talk just a bit more about some of the very complex theologies we human beings have created. For instance, I was taught as a child that I was a sinner, that all human beings are sinners, that we can't help it; we're born that way. We're born *into sin.*

Quite an interesting concept. How did anyone get you to believe that?

They told us the story of Adam and Eve. They told us in 4th, 5th, and 6th grade catechism that, well, *we* may not have sinned, and certainly *babies* haven't—but Adam and Eve *did*—and we are their descendants and have thus inherited their guilt, as well as their sinful natures.

You see, Adam and Eve ate of the forbidden fruit—partook of the knowledge of Good and Evil—and thus sentenced all of their heirs and descendants to separation from God at birth. All of us are born with this "Original Sin" on our souls. Each of us shares in the guilt. So we are given Free Choice to see, I guess, if we will do the same stuff as Adam and Eve and disobey God, or if we can overcome our natural, inherited tendency to "do bad," and do the right things instead, in spite of the world's temptations.

And if you do "bad"?

Then You send us to hell.

I do?

Yes. Unless we repent.

I see.

If we say we're sorry—make a Perfect Act of Contrition—You'll save us from Hell—but not from *all* suffering. We'll still have to go to Purgatory for a while, to cleanse us of our sins.

How long will you have to dwell in "Purgatory"?

Depends. We have to have our sins burned away. It's not too pleasant, I can tell you. And the more sins we've got, the longer it takes to burn them out—the longer we stay. That's what I've been told.

I understand.

But at least we won't go to hell, which is forever. On the other hand, if we die in mortal sin, we go *straight* to hell.

Mortal sin?

As opposed to venial sin. If we die with a venial sin on our soul, we only go to Purgatory. Mortal sin sends us right to hell.

Can you give me an example of these various categories of sin you were told about?

Sure. Mortal sins are serious. Kind of like Major Crimes. Theological Felonies. Things like murder, rape, stealing. Venial sins are rather minor. Theological Misdemeanors. A venial sin would be like missing church on Sunday. Or, in the old days, eating meat on Friday.

Wait a minute! This God of yours sent you to Purgatory if you ate meat on Friday?

Yes. But not any more. Not since the early sixties. But if we ate meat on Fridays *before* the early sixties, woe be unto us.

Really?

Absolutely.

Well, what happened in the early sixties to make this "sin" no longer a sin?

The Pope said it was no longer a sin.

I see. And this God of yours—He *forces* you to worship Him, to go to church on Sundays? Under pain of punishment?

Failure to attend Mass is a sin, yes. And if not confessed—if you die with that sin on your soul—you'll have to go to Purgatory.

But—what about a child? What about an innocent little child who doesn't know all these "rules" by which God loves?

Well, if a child dies before it is baptized into the faith, that child goes to Limbo.

Goes to *where?*

Limbo. It's not a place of punishment, but it's not heaven, either. It's . . . well . . . *limbo.* You can't be with God, but at least you don't have to "go to the devil."

But why couldn't that beautiful, innocent child be with God? The child did nothing *wrong.* . . .

That's true, but the child was not baptized. No matter how faultless or innocent babies are—or any persons, for that matter—they have to be baptized to get into heaven. Otherwise God can't accept them. That's why it's important to have your children baptized quickly, soon after birth.

Who told you all this?

God. Through His church.

Which church?

The Holy Roman Catholic Church, of course. That *is* God's church. In fact, if you are a Catholic and you should happen to attend *another* church, that's also a sin.

I thought it was a sin *not* to go to church!

It is. It's also a sin to go to the *wrong* church.

What's a "wrong" church?

Any church that is not Roman Catholic. You can't be baptized in the wrong church, you can't get married in the wrong church—you can't even *attend* a wrong church. I know this for a fact because as a young man I wanted to go with my parents to the wedding of a friend—I was actually asked to be *in* the wedding as an usher—but the nuns told me I should not accept the invitation because it was in the *wrong church.*

Did you obey them?

The nuns? No. I figured God—You—would show up at the other church just as willingly as You showed up at mine, so I went. I stood in the sanctuary in my tuxedo and I felt fine.

Good. Well, let's see now, we have heaven, we have hell, we have purgatory, we have limbo, we have mortal sin, we have venial sin—is there anything else?

Well, there's confirmation and communion and confession—there's exorcism and Extreme Unction. There's—

Hold it—

—there's Patron Saints and Holy Days of Obligation—

Every day is sanctified. Every *minute* is holy. *This, now,* is the *Holy Instant.*

Well, yes, but some days are *really* holy—the Holy Days of Obligation—and on those days we also have to go to church.

Here we go with the "have tos" again. And what happens if you don't?

It's a sin.

So you go to hell.

Well, you go to Purgatory if you die with that sin on your soul. That's why it's good to go to Confession. Really, as often as you can. Some people go every week. Some people every *day*. That way they can wipe the slate clean—keep it clean so if they should happen to die. . . .

Wow—talk about living in constant fear.

Yes, you see, that's the purpose of religion—to put the fear of God into us. Then we do right and resist temptation.

Uh-huh. But now, what if you do commit a "sin" between confessions, and then get into an accident or something, and die?

It's okay. No panic. Just make a Perfect Act of Contrition. "Oh, my God, I am heartily sorry for having offended Thee . . ."

Okay, okay—enough.

But wait. That's just one of the world's religions. Don't You want to look at some others?

No, I get the picture.

Well, I hope that people don't think I'm simply ridiculing their beliefs.

You're really ridiculing no one, just saying it like it is. It's as your American President Harry Truman used to say. "Give 'em hell, Harry!" people would shout, and Harry'd say, "I don't give 'em hell. I just quote 'em directly, and it *feels* like hell."

4

Boy, we really got sidetracked there. We started out talking about Time and ended up talking about organized religion.

> Yes, well, that's what it's like talking with God. It's hard to keep the dialogue limited.

Let me see if I can summarize the points You make in Chapter 3.

- There is no time but *this* time; there is no moment but *this* moment.
- Time is not a continuum. It is an aspect of Relativity that exists in an "up and down" paradigm, with "moments" or "events" stacked on top of each other, happening or occurring at the same "time."
- We are constantly traveling between realities in this realm of time–no time–all time, usually in our sleep. *"Déjà vu"* is one way we are made aware of this.
- There has never been a time when we were "not"—nor will there ever be.
- The concept of "Age" as it relates to souls really has to do with levels of awareness, not length of "time."
- There is no evil.
- We are Perfect, just as we are.
- "Wrong" is a conceptualization of the mind, based in Relative Experience.
- We are making up the rules as we go along, changing them to fit our Present Reality, and that's perfectly all right. It's as it should be, *must* be, if we are to be evolving beings.
- Hitler went to heaven(!)
- Everything that happens is God's Will—*everything*. That includes not just hurricanes, tornadoes, and earthquakes, but Hitler as well. The secret of understanding is knowing the *Purpose* behind all events.
- There are no "punishments" after death, and all consequences exist only in Relative Experience, not in the Realm of the Absolute.
- Human theologies are mankind's insane attempt to explain an insane God who does not exist.

• The only way human theologies make sense is if we accept a God who makes no sense at all.

How's that? Another good summary?

Excellent.

Good. Because now I've got a million questions. Statements 10 and 11, for instance, beg for further clarification. Why *did* Hitler go to heaven? (I know You just tried to explain this, but somehow I need more.) And what *is* the purpose behind all events? And how does this Larger Purpose relate to Hitler and other despots?

Let's go to Purpose first.

All events, all experiences, have as their purpose the creating of *opportunity*. Events and experiences are Opportunities. Nothing more, nothing less.

It would be a mistake to judge them as "works of the devil," "punishments from God," "rewards from Heaven," or anything in between. They are simply Events and Experiences—things that happen.

It is what we *think* of them, *do* about them, *be* in response to them, that gives them meaning.

Events and experiences are opportunities drawn to you—created *by* you individually or collectively, through consciousness. Consciousness creates experience. You are attempting to raise your consciousness. You have drawn these opportunities to you in order that you might use them as tools in the creation and experiencing of Who You Are. Who You Are is a being of higher consciousness than you are now exhibiting.

Because it is My Will that you should know, and experience, Who You Are, I allow you to draw to yourself whatever event or experience you choose to create in order to do that.

Other Players in the Universal Game join you from time to time—either as Brief Encounters, Peripheral Participants, Temporary Teammates, Long-Term Interactors, Relatives and Family, Dearly Loved Ones, or Life Path Partners.

These souls are drawn to you *by* you. You are drawn to them *by* them. It is a mutually creative experience, expressing the choices and desires of both.

No one comes to you by accident.

There is no such thing as coincidence.

Nothing occurs at random.

Life is not a product of chance.

Events, like people, are drawn to you, by you, for your own purposes. Larger planetary experiences and developments are the result of group consciousness. They are drawn to your group as a whole as a result of the choices and desires of the group as a whole.

What do You mean by the term "your group"?

Group consciousness is something that is not widely understood—yet it is extremely powerful and can, if you are not careful, often overcome individual consciousness. You must always, therefore, endeavor to create group consciousness wherever you go, and with whatever you do, if you wish your larger life experience on the planet to be harmonious.

If you are in a group whose consciousness does not reflect your own, and you are unable at this time to effectively alter the group consciousness, it is wise to leave the group, or the group could lead *you*. It will go where *it* wants to go, regardless of where you want to go.

If you cannot find a group whose consciousness matches your own, be the *source* of one. Others of like consciousness will be drawn to you.

Individuals and smaller groups must affect larger groups—and, ultimately, the largest group of all, which is ALL humankind—for there to be permanent and significant change on your planet.

Your world, and the condition it is in, is a reflection of the total, combined consciousness of everyone living there.

As you can see by looking around you, much work is left to be done. Unless of course, you are satisfied with your world as it is.

Surprisingly, *most people are.* That is why the world does not change.

Most people *are* satisfied with a world in which differences, not similarities, are honored, and disagreements are settled by conflict and war.

Most people are satisfied with a world in which survival is for the fittest, "might is right," competition is required, and winning is called the highest good.

If such a system happens also to produce "losers"—so be it—so long as you are not among them.

Most people *are* satisfied, even though such a model produces people who are often killed when they are judged "wrong," starved and rendered homeless when they are "losers," oppressed and exploited when they are not "strong."

Most people define "wrong" as that which is different from them. Religious differences, in particular, are not tolerated, nor are many social, economic, or cultural differences.

Exploitation of the underclass is justified by the self-congratulatory pronouncements from the upper class of how much better off their victims are now than they were before these exploitations. By this measure the upper class can ignore the issue of how all people *ought* to be treated if one were being truly *fair,* rather than merely making a horrible situation a tiny bit better—and profiting obscenely in the bargain.

Most people *laugh* when one suggests any kind of system other than the one currently in place, saying that behaviors such as competing and killing and the "victor taking the spoils" are what makes their civilization *great!* Most people even think there is no other natural way to *be*, that it is the *nature* of humans to behave in this manner, and that to act any other way would kill the inner spirit that drives man to succeed. (No one asks the question, "Succeed at *what?*")

Difficult as it is for truly enlightened beings to understand, most people on your planet believe in this philosophy, and that is why most people don't *care* about the suffering masses, the oppression of minorities, the anger of the underclass, or the *survival* needs of anyone but themselves and their immediate families.

Most people do not see that they are destroying their Earth—the very planet which gives them *Life*—because their actions seek only to enhance their quality of life. Amazingly, they are not far-sighted enough to observe that short-term gains can produce long-term losses, and often do—and will.

Most people are *threatened* by group consciousness, a concept such as the collective good, a one-world overview, or a God who exists in unity with all creation, rather than separate from it.

This fear of anything leading to unification and your planet's glorification of All That Separates produces division, disharmony, discord—yet you do not seem to have the ability even to learn from your own experience, and so you continue your behaviors, with the same results.

The inability to experience the suffering of another as one's own is what allows such suffering to continue.

Separation breeds indifference, false superiority. Unity produces compassion, genuine equality.

The events which occur on your planet—which have occurred regularly for 3,000 years—are, as I've said, a reflection of the Collective Consciousness of "your group"—the whole group on your planet.

That level of consciousness could best be described as primitive.

Hmmm. Yes. But we seem to have digressed here from the original question.

Not really. You asked about Hitler. The Hitler Experience was made possible as a result of group consciousness. Many people want to say that Hitler manipulated a group—in this case, his countrymen—through the cunning and the mastery of his rhetoric. But this conveniently lays all the blame at Hitler's feet—which is exactly where the mass of the people want it.

But Hitler could do nothing without the cooperation and support and willing submission of millions of people. The subgroup which called itself Germans must assume an enormous burden of responsibility for the Holocaust. As must, to some degree, the larger group called Humans, which, if it did nothing else, allowed itself to remain indifferent and apathetic to the suffering in Germany until it reached so massive a scale that even the most cold-hearted isolationists could no longer ignore it.

You see, it was *collective consciousness* which provided fertile soil for the growth of the Nazi movement. Hitler seized the moment, but he did not create it.

It's important to understand the *lesson* here. A group consciousness which speaks constantly of separation and superiority produces loss of compassion on a massive scale, and loss of compassion is inevitably followed by loss of conscience.

A collective concept rooted in strict nationalism ignores the plights of others, yet makes everyone else responsible for *yours*, thus justifying retaliation, "rectification," and war.

Auschwitz was the Nazi solution to—an attempt to "rectify"—the "Jewish Problem."

The horror of the Hitler Experience was not that he perpetrated it on the human race, but that *the human race allowed him to*.

The astonishment is not only that a Hitler came along, but also that so many others *went* along.

The shame is not only that Hitler killed millions of Jews, but also that millions of Jews *had* to be killed before Hitler was stopped.

The purpose of the Hitler Experience was to show humanity to itself.

Throughout history you have had remarkable teachers, each presenting extraordinary opportunities to remember Who You Really Are. These teachers have shown you the highest and the lowest of the human potential.

They have presented vivid, breathtaking examples of what it can mean to be human—of where one can go with the experience, of where the *lot* of you can and *will* go, *given your consciousness.*

The thing to remember: Consciousness is everything, and creates your experience. *Group* consciousness is powerful and produces outcomes of unspeakable beauty or ugliness. The choice is always yours.

If you are not satisfied with the consciousness of your group, seek to change it.

The best way to change the consciousness of others is by your example.

If your example is not enough, form your own group—*you* be the *source* of the consciousness you wish others to experience. They *will*—when you do.

It begins with *you*. Everything. All things.

You want the world to change? Change things in your own world.

Hitler gave you a golden opportunity to do that. The Hitler Experience—like the Christ Experience—is profound in its implications and the truths it revealed to you *about* you. Yet those larger awarenesses live—in the case of Hitler *or* Buddha, Genghis Kahn *or* Hare Krishna, Attila the Hun or Jesus the Christ—only so long as your memories of them live.

That is why Jews build monuments to the Holocaust and ask you never to forget it. For there is a little bit of Hitler in all of you— and it is only a matter of degree. Wiping out a people is wiping out a people, whether at Auschwitz or Wounded Knee.

So Hitler was sent to us to provide us a lesson about the horrors man can commit, the levels to which man can sink?

Hitler was not sent to you. Hitler was created *by* you. He arose out of your Collective Consciousness, and could not have existed without it. *That* is the lesson.

The consciousness of separation, segregation, superiority—of "we" versus "they," of "us" and "them"—is what creates the Hitler Experience.

The consciousness of Divine Brotherhood, of unity, of Oneness, of "ours" rather than "yours"/"mine," is what creates the Christ Experience.

When the pain is "ours," not just "yours," when the joy is "ours," not just "mine," when the *whole life experience* is Ours, then it is at last truly that—a Whole Life experience.

Why did Hitler go to heaven?

Because Hitler did nothing "wrong." Hitler simply did what he did. I remind you again that for many years millions thought he was "right." How, then, could he help but think so?

If you float out a crazy idea, and ten million people agree with you, you might not think you're so crazy.

The world decided—finally—that Hitler was "wrong." That is to say, the world's people made a new assessment of Who They Are, and Who They Chose To Be, in relationship to the Hitler Experience.

He held up a yardstick! He set a parameter, a border against which we could measure and limit our ideas about ourselves. Christ did the same thing, at the other end of the spectrum.

There have been other Christs, and other Hitlers. And there will be again. Be ever vigilant, then. For people of both high and low consciousness walk among you—even as *you* walk among others. Which consciousness do you take with you?

I still don't understand how Hitler could have gone to heaven; how he could have been *rewarded* for what he did?

First, understand that death is not an end, but a beginning; not a horror, but a joy. It is not a closing down, but an opening up.

The happiest moment of your life will be the moment it ends.

That's because it *doesn't* end but only goes on in ways so magnificent, so full of peace and wisdom and joy, as to make it difficult to describe and impossible for you to comprehend.

So the first thing you have to understand—as I've already explained to you—is that Hitler didn't *hurt* anyone. In a sense, he didn't *inflict* suffering, he *ended* it.

It was the Buddha who said "Life is suffering." The Buddha was right.

But even if I accept that—Hitler didn't *know* he was actually doing *good*. He thought he was doing *bad!*

No, he didn't think he was doing something "bad." He actually thought he was helping his people. And that's what you don't understand.

No one does *anything* that is "wrong," given their model of the world. If you think Hitler acted insanely and all the while *knew* that he was insane, then you understand nothing of the complexity of human experience.

Hitler thought he was doing *good* for his people. And his people thought so, too! *That was the insanity of it!* The largest part of the nation *agreed with him!*

You have declared that Hitler was "wrong." Good. By this measure you have come to define yourself, know more about yourself. Good. But don't condemn Hitler for *showing you that*.

Someone had to.

You cannot know cold unless there is hot, up unless there is down, left unless there is right. Do not condemn the one and bless the other. To do so is to fail to understand.

For centuries people have been condemning Adam and Eve. They are said to have committed Original Sin. I tell you this: It was the Original Blessing. For without this event, the partaking of the knowledge of good and evil, *you* would not even know the two possibilities existed! Indeed, before the so-called Fall of Adam, these two possibilities *did not* exist. There *was* no "evil." Everyone and everything existed in a state of constant perfection. It was, literally, paradise. Yet you didn't *know* it was paradise—could not *experience* it as perfection—because you *knew nothing else*.

Shall you then condemn Adam and Eve, or thank them?

And what, say you, shall I do with Hitler?

I tell you this: God's love and God's compassion, God's wisdom and God's forgiveness, God's intention and God's *purpose*, are large enough to include the most heinous crime and the most heinous criminal.

You may not agree with this, but it does not matter. You have just learned what you came here to discover.

5

You promised in the first book to explain in *Book 2* a long list of larger things—such as time and space, love and war, good and evil, and planetary geopolitical considerations of the highest order. You also promised to further explain—in some detail—the human experience of sex.

Yes, I promised all those things.

Book 1 had to do with more personal inquiries; with one's life as an individual. *Book 2* deals with your collective life on the planet. *Book 3* concludes the Trilogy with the largest truths: the cosmology, the whole picture, the journey of the soul. Taken together, My best current advice and information on everything from tying your shoe to understanding your universe.

Have You said all You're going to say about time?

I've said all you need to know.

There is no time. All things exist simultaneously. All events occur at once.

This Book is being written, and as it's being written it's *already* written; it already exists. In fact, that's where you're getting all this information—from the book that already exists. You're merely bringing it into form.

This is what is meant by: "Even before you ask, I will have answered."

This information about Time all seems . . . well, interesting, but rather esoteric. Does it have any application to real life?

A true understanding of time allows you to live much more peacefully within your reality of relativity, where time is experienced as a movement, a flow, rather than a constant.

It is *you* who are moving, not time. Time *has* no movement. There is only One Moment.

At some level you deeply understand this. That is why, when something really magnificent or significant occurs in your life, you often say it is as if "time stands still."

It *does*. And when *you do also*, you often experience one of those life-defining moments.

I find this hard to believe. How can this be possible?

Your science has already *proven* this mathematically. Formulas have been written showing that if you get into a spaceship and fly far enough *fast* enough, you could swing back around toward the Earth and *watch yourself taking off*.

This demonstrates that Time is not a *movement* but a field through which *you* move—in this case on Spaceship Earth.

You say it takes 365 "days" to make a year. Yet what is a "day"? You've decided—quite arbitrarily, I might add—that a "day" is the "time" it takes your Spaceship to make one complete revolution on its axis.

How do you know it's made such a spin? (You can't *feel* it moving!) You've chosen a reference point in the heavens—the Sun. You say it takes a full "day" for the portion of the Spaceship you are on to face the Sun, turn away from the Sun, then face the Sun again.

You've divided this "day" into 24 "hours"—again quite arbitrarily. You could just as easily have said "10" or "73"!

Then you divided each "hour" into "minutes." You said each hourly unit contained 60 smaller units, called "minutes"—and that each of *those* contained 60 tiny units, called "seconds."

One day you noticed that the Earth was not only spinning, it was also *flying!* You saw that it was moving through space *around the sun.*

You carefully calculated that it took 365 revolutions of the Earth for the Earth itself to revolve around the sun. This number of Earth spins you called a "year."

Things got kind of messy when you decided that you wanted to divide up a "year" into units smaller than a "year" but larger than a "day."

You created the "week" and the "month," and you managed to get the same number of months in every year, but not the same number of *days in every month.*

You couldn't find a way to divide an odd number of days (365) by an even number of months (12), so you just decided that *some months contained more days than others!*

You felt you had to stay with twelve as the yearly sub-divider because that was the number of Lunar Cycles you observed your moon moving through during a "year." In order to reconcile these three spatial events—revolutions around the sun, spins of the Earth on its axis, and moon cycles—you simply adjusted the number of "days" in each "month."

Even this device didn't solve all the problems because your earlier inventions kept creating a "build up" of "time" which you didn't know what to do with. So you also decided that every so often one year would have to have a *whole day more!* You called this Leap Year, and joked about it, but you actually *live* by such a construction—and then you call *My* explanation of time "unbelievable"!

You've just as arbitrarily created "decades" and "centuries" (based, interestingly, on 10's, *not* 12's) to further measure the passage of "time"—but all along what you've really been doing is merely devising a way to measure *movements through space.*

Thus we see that it is not time which "passes," but *objects* which pass *through,* and move around *in,* a static field which you call *space.* "Time" is simply your way of *counting movements!*

Scientists deeply understand this connection and therefore speak in terms of the "Space-Time Continuum."

Your Dr. Einstein and others realized that time was a mental construction, a *relational concept.* "Time" was what it was *relative to the space* that existed between objects! (If the universe is expanding—which it is—then it takes "longer" for the Earth to revolve around the sun today than it did a billion years ago. There's more "space" to cover.)

Thus, it took more minutes, hours, days, weeks, months, years, decades, and centuries for all these cyclical events to occur recently than it did in 1492! (When is a "day" not a day? When is a "year" not a year?)

Your new, highly sophisticated timing instruments now record this "time" discrepancy, and every year clocks around the world are adjusted to accommodate a universe that won't sit still! This is called Greenwich Mean Time . . . and it is "mean" because it makes a liar out of the universe!

Einstein theorized that if it wasn't "time" which was moving, but *he* who was moving through space at a given rate, all he had to do was change the amount of space between objects—or change the rate of *speed* with which he moved through space from one object to another—to "alter" time.

It was his General Theory of Relativity which expanded your modern day understanding of the co-relation between time and space.

You now may begin to understand why, if you make a long journey through space and return, you may have aged only ten years—while your friends on Earth will have aged thirty! The farther you go, the more you will warp the Space-Time Continuum, and the less your chances when you land of finding alive on the Earth anyone who was there when you left!

However, if scientists on Earth in some "future" time developed a way to propel themselves *faster,* they could "cheat" the universe and stay in sync with "real time" on Earth, returning to find that the same time had passed on Earth as had passed on the Spaceship.

Obviously, if even more propulsion were available, one could return to the Earth before one took off! That is to say, time on Earth would pass *more slowly* than time on the spaceship. You could come back in ten of your "years" and the Earth would have "aged" only four! Increase the speed, and ten years in space might mean ten minutes on Earth.

Now, come across a "fold" in the fabric of space (Einstein and others believed such "folds" exist—and they were correct!) and you are suddenly propelled across "space" in one infinitesimal "moment." Could such a time-space phenomenon literally "fling" you back into "time"?

It should not be quite as difficult to now see that "time" does not exist except as a construction of your mentality. Everything that's ever happened—and is ever *going* to happen—is happening *now*. The ability to observe it merely depends on your point of view—your "place in space."

If you were in *My* place, you could see it All—*right now!*

Comprehend?

Wow! I'm *beginning* to—on a theoretical level—*yes!*

Good. I've explained it to you here very simply, so that a child could understand it. It may not make good science, but it produces good comprehension.

Right now physical objects are limited in terms of their speed—but *nonphysical objects*—**my thoughts . . . my soul . . . could theoretically move through the ether at incredible speeds.**

Exactly! *Precisely!* And that is what happens often in dreams and other out-of-body and psychic experiences.

You now understand *Déjà vu*. You probably *have* been there before!

But . . . if everything has already *happened*, **then it follows that I am powerless to change my future. Is this predestination?**

No! Don't buy into that! That is not true. In fact, this "set up" should *serve* you, not *disserve* you!

You are always at a place of free will and total choice. Being able to see into the "future" (or get others to do it for you) should enhance your ability to live the life you want, not limit it.

How? I need help here.

If you "see" a future event or experience you do not like, don't *choose* it! Choose again! Select another!

Change or alter your behavior so as to *avoid the undesired outcome*.

But how can I avoid that which has already happened?

It has not happened to you—yet! You are at a place in the Space-Time Continuum where you are not *consciously aware* of the occurrence. You do not "know" it has "happened." You have not "remembered" your future!

(This forgetfulness is the *secret of all time*. It is what makes it possible for you to "play" the great game of life! I'll explain later!)

What you do not "know" is not "so." Since "you" do not "remember" your future, it has not "happened" to "you" yet! A thing "happens" only when it is "experienced." A thing is "experienced" only when it is "known."

Now let's say you've been blessed with a brief glimpse, a split-second "knowing," of your "future." What's happened is that your

Spirit—the nonphysical part of you—has simply sped to another place on the Space-Time Continuum and brought back some residual energy—some images or impressions—of that moment or event.

These you can "feel"—or sometimes another who has developed a metaphysical gift can "feel" or "see" these images and energies that are swirling about you.

If you don't like what you "sense" about your "future," step away from that! Just step away from it! In that instant you change your experience—and everyone of You breathes a sigh of relief!

Wait a minute! Whoaaaa—?

You must know—you are now ready to be told—that you exist at every level of the Space-Time Continuum *simultaneously.*

That is, your soul Always Was, Always Is, and Always Will Be— world without end—amen.

I "exist" more places than one?

Of course! You exist *every*where—and at all times!

There is a "me" in the future and a "me" in the past?

Well, "future" and "past" do not exist, as we've just taken pains to understand—but, using those words as you have been using them, yes.

There is more than one of me?

There is *only* one of you, but you are much *larger* than you think!

So when the "me" that exists "now" changes something he doesn't like about his "future," the "me" that exists in the "future" no longer has that as part of his experience?

Essentially yes. The whole mosaic changes. But he never loses the experience he's given himself. He's just relieved and happy that "you" don't have to go through that.

But the "me" in the "past" has yet to "experience" this, so he walks right into it?

In a sense, yes. But, of course, "you" can help "him."

I *can?*

Sure. First, by changing what the "you" in *front* of you experienced, the "you" *behind* you may never *have* to experience it! It is by this device that your soul evolves.

In the same way, the *future you* got help from his *own* future self, thus helping *you* avoid what *he* did not.

Did you follow that?

Yes. And it's intriguing. But now I have another question. What about past lives? If I have always been "me"—in the "past" and in the "future"—how could I have been someone *else*, another person, in a past life?

You are a Divine Being, capable of more than one experience at the same "time"—and able to divide your Self into as many different "selves" as you choose.

You can live the "same life" over and over again, in different ways—as I've just explained. And you can also live different lives at different "times" on the Continuum.

Thus, all the while you're being you, here, now—you can also be, and have been—other "selves" in other "times" and "places."

Good grief—this gets "complicateder" and "complicateder"!

Yes—and we've really only just scratched the surface here.

Just know this: You are a being of Divine Proportion, knowing no limitation. A part of you is choosing to know yourself as your presently-experienced Identity. Yet this is by far not the limit of your Being, although you *think that it is.*

Why?

You *must* think that it is, or you cannot do what you've given yourself this life to do.

And what is that? You've told me before, but tell me again, "here" and "now."

You are using all of Life—all of *many* lives—to *be* and *decide* Who You Really Are; to choose and to create Who You Really Are; to experience and to fulfill your current idea about yourself.

You are in an Eternal Moment of Self creation and Self fulfillment through the process of Self expression.

You have drawn the people, events, and circumstances of your life to you as tools with which to fashion the Grandest Version of the Greatest Vision you ever had about yourself.

This process of creation and recreation is ongoing, never ending, and multi-layered. It is all happening "right now" and on many levels.

In your linear reality you see the experience as one of Past, Present, and Future. You imagine yourself to have one life, or perhaps many, but surely only one *at a time.*

But what if there *were* no "time"? Then you'd be having *all your "lives"* at once!

You *are!*

You are living *this* life, your presently realized life, in your Past, your Present, your Future, all at once! Have you ever had a "strange foreboding" about some future event—so powerful that it made you turn away from it?

In your language you call that premonition. From My viewpoint it is simply an awareness you suddenly have of something you've just experienced in your "future."

Your "future you" is saying, "Hey, this was no fun. Don't *do* this!"

You are also living other lives—what you call "past lives"—right now as well—although you experience them as having been in your "past" (if you experience them at all), and that is just as well. It would be very difficult for you to play this wonderful game of life if you had *full awareness* of what is going on. Even this description offered here cannot give you that. If it did, the "game" would be over! The Process *depends* on the Process being complete, as it is—including your lack of total awareness at this stage.

So bless the Process, and accept it as the greatest gift of the Kindest Creator. Embrace the Process, and move through it with peace and wisdom and joy. Use the Process, and transform it from something you *endure* to something you *engage* as a tool in the creation of the most magnificent experience of All Time: the fulfillment of your Divine Self.

How? How can I best do that?

Do not waste the precious moments of this, your present reality, seeking to unveil all of life's secrets.

Those secrets are secrets for a *reason*. Grant your God the benefit of the doubt. Use your Now Moment for the Highest Purpose—the creation and the expression of Who You Really Are.

Decide Who You Are—Who you *want* to be—and then do everything in your power to *be* that.

Use what I have told you about time as a framework, within your limited understanding, upon which to place the constructions of your Grandest Idea.

If an impression comes to you about the "future," *honor* it. If an idea comes to you about a "past life," see if it has any use for you—don't simply ignore it. Most of all, if a way is made known to you to create, display, express, and experience your Divine Self in ever more glory right here, right now, *follow* that way.

And a way *will* be made known to you, because you have asked. Producing this book is a sign of your asking, for you could not be producing it, right now before your very eyes, without an open mind, an open heart, and a soul which is ready to know.

The same is true of those who are now *reading* it. For *they have created it, too.* How *else* could they now be *experiencing it?*

Everyone is creating everything now being experienced—which is another way of saying that *I* am creating everything now being experienced, for *I* am everyone.

Are you getting the symmetry here? Are you seeing the Perfection?

It is all contained in a single truth:

THERE IS ONLY ONE OF US.

6

Tell me about space.

Space is time . . . demonstrated.

In truth there is no such thing as space—pure, "empty" space, with nothing in it. Everything is *something*. Even the "emptiest" space is filled with vapors so thin, so stretched out over infinite areas, that they seem to not be there.

Then, after the vapors are gone, there is energy. Pure energy. This manifests as vibration. Oscillations. Movements of the All at a particular frequency.

Invisible "energy" is the "space" which holds "matter together."

Once—using your linear time as a model—all the matter in the universe was condensed into a tiny speck. You cannot imagine the denseness of this—but that is because you think that matter as it *now* exists is dense.

Actually, what you now call matter is mostly space. All "solid" objects are 2 percent solid "matter" and 98 percent "air"! The space between the tiniest particles of matter in all objects is enormous. It is something like the distance between heavenly bodies in your night sky. Yet these objects you call *solid*.

At one point the entire universe actually *was* "solid." There was virtually *no space* between the particles of matter. All the matter had the "space" taken out of it—and with the enormous "space" gone, that matter filled an area smaller than the head of a pin.

There was actually a "time" before that "time" when there was no matter at all—just the purest form of Highest Vibration Energy, which you would call *anti-matter*.

This was the time "before" time—before the physical universe as you know it existed. *Nothing* existed as matter. Some people conceive of this as paradise, or "heaven," because "nothing was the matter"!

(It is no accident that today in your language, when you suspect something is wrong, you say, "What's the matter?")

In the beginning, pure energy—*Me!*—vibrated, oscillated, so fast as to form matter—*all the matter of the universe!*

You, too, can perform the same feat. In fact, you *do*, every day. Your *thoughts* are pure vibration—and they can and *do* create physical matter! If enough of you hold the same thought, you can impact, and even create, portions of your physical universe. This was explained to you in detail in *Book 1*.

Is the universe now expanding?

At a rate of speed you cannot imagine!

Will it expand forever?

No. There will come a time when the energies driving the expansion will dissipate, and the energies holding things together will take over—pulling everything "back together" again.

You mean the universe will contract?

Yes. Everything will, quite literally, "fall into place"! And you'll have paradise again. No matter. Pure energy.

In other words—*Me!*

In the end, it'll all come back to Me. That is the origin of your phrase: "It all comes down to this."

That means that we will no longer exist!

Not in physical form. But you will *always exist*. You cannot *not* exist. You *are* that which *Is*.

What will happen after the universe "collapses"?

The whole process will start over again! There will be another so-called Big Bang, and another universe will be born.

It will expand and contract. And then it will do the same thing all over again. And again. And again. Forever and ever. World without end.

This is the breathing in and breathing out of God.

Well, this is all, again, very interesting—but it has very little to do with my everyday life.

As I said before, spending an inordinate amount of time trying to unravel the deepest mysteries of the universe is probably not the most efficient use of your life. Yet there are benefits to be gained from these simple layman's allegories and descriptions of the Larger Process.

Like what?

Like understanding that all things are cyclical—including life itself.

Understanding about the life of the universe will help you to understand about the life of the universe inside *you*.

Life moves in cycles. Everything is cyclical. Everything. When you understand this, you become more able to enjoy the Process—not merely endure it.

All things move cyclically. There is a natural rhythm to life, and everything moves to that rhythm; everything goes with that flow. Thus it is written: "For everything there is a season; and a time for every Purpose under Heaven."

Wise is the one who understands this. Clever is the one who uses it.

Few people understand the rhythms of life more than women. Women live their whole lives by rhythm. They are *in* rhythm with life itself.

Women are more able to "go with the flow" than men. Men want to push, pull, resist, *direct* the flow. Women *experience* it—then mold with it to produce harmony.

A woman hears the melody of flowers in the wind. She sees the beauty of the Unseen. She feels the tugs and pulls and urges of life. She *knows* when it is time to run, and time to rest; time to laugh and time to cry; time to hold on and time to let go.

Most women leave their bodies gracefully. Most men fight the departure. Women treat their bodies more gracefully when they are *in* them, too. Men treat their bodies horribly. That is the same way they treat life.

Of course, there are exceptions to every rule. I'm speaking here in generalities. I'm speaking of how things have been until now. I'm speaking in the broadest terms. But if you look at life, if you admit to yourself what you are seeing, have seen, if you acknowledge what is so, you may find truth in this generality.

Yet that makes me feel sad. That makes me feel as though women are somehow superior beings. That they have more of the "right stuff" than men.

Part of the glorious rhythm of life is the yin and the yang. One Aspect of "Being" is not "more perfect" or "better" than another. Both aspects are simply—and wonderfully—that: aspects.

Men, obviously, embody other reflections of Divinity, which women eye with equal envy.

Yet it has been said that being a man is your testing ground, or your probation. When you have been a man long enough—when you have suffered enough through your own foolishness; when you have inflicted enough pain through the calamities of your own creation; when you have hurt others enough to stop your own behaviors—to replace aggression with reason, contempt with compassion, always-winning with no-one-losing—then you may become a woman.

When you have learned that might is *not* "right"; that strength is *not* power *over*, but power *with*; that absolute power demands of others absolutely nothing; when you understand these things, then you may deserve to wear a woman's body—for you will at last have understood her Essence.

Then a woman *is* better than a man.

No! Not "better"—different! It is *you* making that judgment. There is no such thing as "better" or "worse" in objective reality. There is only what Is—and what you wish to Be.

Hot is no better than cold, up no better than down—a point I have made before. Hence, female is no "better" than male. It just *is* what it Is. Just as you are what you are.

Yet none of you are restricted, more limited. You can Be what you wish to Be, choose what you wish to experience. In this lifetime or the next, or the next after that—just as you did in the lifetime before. Each of you is always at choice. Each of you is made up of All of It. There is male and female in each of you. Express and experience that aspect of you which it pleases you to express and experience. Yet know that it is *all* open to each of you.

I don't want to get off onto other topics. I want to stay with this male-female paradigm for a while longer. You promised at the end of the last book to discuss in much more detail the whole sexual aspect of this duality.

Yes—I think it is time that we talked, you and I, about Sex.

7

Why did you create two sexes? Was this the only way you could figure for us to recreate? How should we deal with this incredible experience called sexuality?

Not with shame, that's for sure. And not with guilt, and not with fear.

For shame is not virtue, and guilt is not goodness, and fear is not honor.

And not with lust, for lust is not passion; and not with abandon, for abandon is not freedom; and not with aggressiveness, for aggressiveness is not eagerness.

And, obviously, not with ideas of control or power or domination, for these have nothing to do with Love.

But . . . may sex be used for purposes of simple personal gratification? The surprising answer is yes—because "personal gratification" is just another word for Self Love.

Personal gratification has gotten a bad rap through the years, which is the main reason so much guilt is attached to sex.

You are told you are not to use for personal gratification something which is *intensely personally gratifying!* This obvious contradiction is apparent to you, but you don't know where to go with the conclusion! So you decide that if you feel *guilty* about how good you feel during and after sex, that will at least make it all right.

It's not unlike the famous singer you all know, whom I will not name here, who receives millions of dollars for singing her songs. Asked to comment on her incredible success and the riches it has brought her, she said, "I feel almost *guilty* because I love doing this so much."

The implication is clear. If it's something you love doing, you should not also be rewarded additionally with money. Most people earn money by *doing something they hate*—or something that is at least *hard work,* not *endless joy!*

So the world's message is: If you feel negatively about it, *then you can enjoy it!*

Guilt is often used by you in your attempt to feel *bad* about something you feel *good* about—and thus reconcile yourself with God . . . who you think does not want you to feel good about *anything!*

You are especially not to feel good about joys of the body. And *absolutely* not about (as your grandmother used to whisper) "S-E-X . . ."

Well, the good news is *it's all right to love sex!*

It's also all right to *love your Self!*

In fact, it's mandatory.

What does *not* serve you is to become *addicted* to sex (or anything else). But it *is* "okay" to fall in love with it!

Practice saying this ten times each day:

I LOVE SEX

Practice saying *this* ten times:

I LOVE MONEY

Now, you want a really tough one? Try saying *this* ten times:

I LOVE *ME!*

Here are some other things you are not supposed to love. Practice loving them:

POWER
GLORY
FAME
SUCCESS
WINNING

Want some more? Try *these.* You should *really* feel guilty if you love *these:*

THE ADULATION OF OTHERS
BEING BETTER
HAVING MORE
KNOWING HOW
KNOWING *WHY*

Had enough? Wait! Here's the *ultimate guilt.* You should feel the ultimate guilt if you feel that you:

KNOW GOD

Isn't this interesting? All through your life you have been made to feel guilty about

THE THINGS YOU WANT MOST.

Yet I tell you this: love, love, *love* the things you desire—for your love of them *draws them to you.*

These things are the stuff of life. When you love them, you *love life!* When you declare that you desire them, you announce that you choose all the good that life has to offer!

So choose *sex*—all the sex you can get! And choose *power*—all the power you can muster! And choose *fame*—all the fame you can attain! And choose *success*—all the success you can achieve! And choose *winning*—all the winning you can experience!

Yet do not choose sex instead of love, *but as a celebration of it.* And do not choose power over, *but power with.* And do not choose fame as an end in itself, *but as a means to a larger end.* And do not choose success at the expense of others, *but as a tool with which to assist others.* And do not choose winning at any cost, *but winning that costs others nothing,* and even brings *them gain as well.*

Go ahead and choose the adulation of others—but see all others as beings upon which *you* can shower adulation, and *do* it!

Go ahead and choose being better—but not better than others; rather, better than *you were before.*

Go ahead and choose having more, but only so that you have *more to give.*

And yes, *choose "knowing how" and "knowing why"*—so that you can share all knowledge with others.

And by all means choose to KNOW GOD. In fact, CHOOSE THIS FIRST, and all else will follow.

All of your life you have been taught that it is better to give than to receive. *Yet you cannot give what you do not have.*

This is why self-gratification is so important—and why it is so unfortunate that it has come to sound so ugly.

Obviously, self-gratification at the expense of others is not what we're talking about here. This is not about ignoring the needs of others. Yet life should also not have to be about *ignoring your own needs.*

Give yourself abundant pleasure, and you will have abundant pleasure to give others.

The masters of Tantric sex know this. That's why they encourage masturbation, which some of you actually call a sin.

Masturbation? Oh, boy—You have really stretched the limit here. How can You bring up something like that—how can You even *say* it—in a message that's supposed to be coming from God?

I see. You have a judgment about masturbation.

Well, *I* don't, but a lot of readers might. And I thought You said we were producing this book for others to read.

We are.

Then why are You deliberately offending them?

I am not "deliberately offending" anyone. People are free to be "offended" or not, as they choose. Yet do you really think it is going to be possible for us to candidly and openly talk about human sexuality without *someone* choosing to be "offended"?

No, but there's such a thing as going too far. I don't think most people are ready to hear God talk about masturbation.

If this book is to be limited to what "most people" are ready to hear God talk about, it's going to be a very small book. Most people are never ready to hear what God talks about when God is talking about it. They usually wait 2,000 years.

All right, go ahead. We've all gotten over our initial shock.

Good. I was merely using this life experience (in which you've all engaged, by the way, but of which no one wants to speak) to illustrate a larger point.
The larger point, restated: *Give yourself abundant pleasure, and you will have abundant pleasure to give to others.*
Teachers of what you call Tantric sex—which is a very high form of sexual expression, incidentally—know that if you come to sex with *hunger* for sex, your ability to pleasure your partner and to experience a prolonged and joyful union of souls and bodies—which is a very high reason to experience sexuality, by the way—is greatly diminished.

Tantric lovers, therefore, often self-pleasure before they pleasure each other. This is frequently done in the presence of each other, and usually with the encouragement and help and loving guidance of each other. Then, when initial hungers have been satisfied, the deeper thirst of the two—the thirst for ecstasy through prolonged union—can be gloriously satisfied.

The mutual self-pleasuring is all part of the joyfulness, the playfulness, the lovingness of sexuality fully expressed. It is one of *several* parts. The experience you call coitus, or intercourse, might come at the end of a 2-hour encounter of love. Or it might not. For most of you it is very nearly the *only point* of a 20-minute exercise. That is, 20 minutes if you're lucky!

I had no idea this was going to turn into a sex manual.

It's not. But it wouldn't be so bad if it did. Most people have a lot to learn about sexuality, and its most wondrous, beneficial expression.

I was nevertheless still seeking to illustrate the larger point. The more pleasure you give yourself, the more pleasure you can give to another. Likewise, if you give yourself the pleasure of power, you have more power to share with others. The same is true of fame, wealth, glory, success, or anything else which makes you feel good.

And by the way, I think it's time we looked at why a certain thing *does* make you "feel good."

Okay—I give up. Why?

"Feeling good" is the soul's way of shouting "This is who I am!"

Have you ever been in a classroom where the teacher was taking attendance—calling the roll—and when your name was called you had to say "here"?

Yes.

Well, "feeling good" is the soul's way of saying "here!"

Now a lot of people are ridiculing this whole idea of "doing what feels good." They say this is the road to hell. Yet *I* say it is the road to *heaven!*

Much depends, of course, on what you say "feels good." In other words, what kinds of experiences feel good to you? Yet I tell you this—no kind of evolution ever took place through *denial*. If you are to evolve, it will not be because you've been able to successfully *deny* yourself the things that you *know* "feel good," but because you've *granted* yourself these pleasures—and found something even greater. For how can you know that something is "greater" if you've never tasted the "lesser"?

Religion would have you take its word for it. That is why all religions ultimately fail.

Spirituality, on the other hand, will always succeed.

Religion asks you to learn from the experience of others. Spirituality urges you to seek your own.

Religion cannot stand Spirituality. It cannot abide it. For Spirituality may bring you to a *different conclusion* than a particular religion—and this no known religion can tolerate.

Religion encourages you to explore the thoughts of others and accept them as your own. Spirituality invites you to toss *away* the thoughts of others and come *up* with your own.

"Feeling good" is your way of telling yourself that your last thought was *truth*, that your last word was *wisdom*, that your last action was *love*.

To notice how far you have progressed, to measure how highly you have evolved, simply look to see what makes you "feel good."

Yet don't seek to *force* your evolution—to evolve further, faster—by *denying* what feels good, or stepping away from it.

Self-denial is self-destruction.

Yet also know this—self-regulation is not self-denial. Regulating one's behavior is an *active choice* to do or not do something based on one's decision regarding who they are. If you declare that you are a person who respects the rights of others, a decision not to steal or rob from them, not to rape and plunder, is hardly "self-denial." It is self-*declaration*. That is why it is said that the measure of how far one has evolved is what makes one feel good.

If acting irresponsibly, if behaving in a way which you know might damage others or cause hardship or pain, is what makes you "feel good," then you have not evolved very far.

Awareness is the key here. And it is the task of the elders in your families and communities to create and spread this awareness among the young. It is likewise the job of God's messengers to increase awareness among *all* peoples, so that they may understand that what is done to or for one is done to or for all—because we are all One.

When you come from "we are all One," it is virtually impossible to find that hurting another "feels good." So-called "irresponsible behavior" vanishes. It is within these parameters that evolving beings seek to experience life. It is within these parameters that I say *grant yourself permission* to have *all* that life has to offer—and you will discover it has *more to offer than you've ever imagined.*

You are what you experience. You experience what you express. You express what you have to express. You have what you grant yourself.

I love this—but can we get back to the original question?

Yes. I created two sexes for the same reason I put the "yin" and "yang" in everything—in the whole universe! They are *part* of the yin and the yang, this male and this female. They are the highest living expression of it in your world.

They are the yin and the yang . . . *in form.* In one of *many physical forms.*

The yin and yang, the here and the there . . . the this and the that . . . the up and the down, the hot and the cold, the big and the small, the fast and the slow—the matter and the anti-matter . . .

All of it is necessary for you to experience life as you know it.

How may we best express this thing called sexual energy?

Lovingly. Openly.
Playfully. Joyfully.
Outrageously. Passionately. Sacredly. Romantically.
Humorously. Spontaneously. Touchingly. Creatively. Unabashedly. Sensually.
And, of course, Frequently.

There are those who say that the only legitimate purpose of human sexuality is procreation.

Rubbish. Procreation is the happy aftereffect, not the logical forethought, of most human sexual experience. The idea that sex is only to make babies is naive, and the corollary thought that sex should therefore stop when the last child is conceived is worse than naive. It violates human nature—and that is the nature I *gave* you.

Sexual expression is the inevitable result of an eternal process of attraction and rhythmic energy flow which fuels all of life.

I have built into all things an energy that transmits its signal throughout the universe. Every person, animal, plant, rock, tree—*every* physical thing—sends out energy, like a radio transmitter.

You are sending off energy—emitting energy—right now, from the center of your being in all directions. This energy—which is *you*—moves outward in wave patterns. The energy leaves you, moves through walls, over mountains, past the moon, and into Forever. It *never, ever stops.*

Every thought you've ever had colors this energy. (When you think of someone, if that person is sensitive enough, he or she can *feel* it.) Every word you've ever spoken shapes it. Everything you've ever done affects it.

The vibration, the rate of speed, the wavelength, the frequency of your emanations shift and change constantly with your thoughts, moods, feelings, words, and actions.

You've heard the saying "sending off good vibes," and it's true. That's very accurate!

Now, every other person is, naturally, doing the same thing. And so the ether—the "air" between you—is *filled with energy;* a Matrix of intertwining, interwoven personal "vibes" that form a tapestry more complex than you could ever imagine.

This weave is the combined energy field within which you live. It is *powerful*, and affects *everything*. Including *you*.

You then send out newly created "vibes," impacted as you are by the *incoming* vibes to which you are being subjected, and these, in turn, add to and shift the Matrix—which in turn affects the energy field of everybody else, which impacts the *vibes they* send off, which impacts the Matrix—which impacts *you* . . . and so forth.

Now you may think this is all just fanciful illusion—but have you ever walked into a room where the "air was so thick you could cut it with a knife"?

Or have you ever heard of two scientists working on the same problem at the same time—on opposite sides of the globe—each working on the problem without the other's knowledge, and each suddenly coming up with the same solution simultaneously—and *independently?*

These are common occurrences, and some of the more obvious manifestations of The Matrix.

The Matrix—the combined current energy field within any given parameter—is a powerful vibe. It can directly impact, affect, and *create* physical objects and events.

("Wherever two or more are gathered in My name. . . .")

Your popular psychology has termed this energy Matrix the "Collective Consciousness." It can, and does, affect *everything on your planet:* the prospects of war and the chances for peace; geophysical upheaval or a planet becalmed; widespread illness or worldwide wellness.

All is the result of consciousness.

So, too, the more specific events and conditions in your personal life.

That's fascinating, but what does it have to do with sex?

Patience. I'm getting to that.

All the world is exchanging energy all the time.

Your energy is pushing out, touching everything else. Everything and everyone else is touching you. But now an interesting thing happens. At some point midway between you and everything else—those energies *meet.*

To make a more vivid description, let's imagine two people in a room. They are on the far sides of the room from each other. We'll call them Tom and Mary.

Now Tom's personal energy is transmitting signals about Tom in a 360-degree circle out in the universe. Some of that energy wave hits Mary.

Mary, meanwhile, is emitting her own energy—some of which hits Tom.

But these energies meet each other in a way you may not have thought of. They meet *midway between* Tom and Mary.

Here, the energies unite (remember now, these energies are *physical phenomena;* they can be *measured, felt*) and combine to form a new energy unit we'll call "Tomary." It is the energy of Tom and Mary combined.

Tom and Mary could very well call this energy The Body Between Us—for it is just that: a body of energy to which both are connected, which both are feeding the continuing energies which flow to it, and which is *sending energies back* to its two "sponsors" along the thread, or cord, or pipeline that always exists within the Matrix. (Indeed, this "pipeline" *is* the Matrix.)

It is *this experience* of "Tomary" which is the *truth* of Tom and Mary. It is *to* this Holy Communion that both are drawn. For they feel, along the pipeline, the sublime joy of the Body Between, of the Joined One, of the Blessed Union.

Tom and Mary, standing off at a distance, can *feel*—in a *physical way*—what is going on in the Matrix. Both are urgently *drawn* toward this experience. They want to move toward each other! At once!

Now their "training" sets in. The world has trained them to slow down, to mistrust the feeling, to guard against "hurt," to hold back.

But the soul . . . wants to know *"Tomary"*—now!

If the two are lucky, they will be free enough to set aside their fears and trust that love is all there is.

They are irrevocably drawn now, these two, to the Body Between Them. TOMARY is *already* being experienced *metaphysically*, and Tom and Mary will want to experience it *physically*. So they'll move closer together. Not to get to each *other*. It looks that way to the casual observer. But they are each trying to get to TOMARY. They are trying to reach that place of Divine Union which *already exists* between them. The place where they already know they are One—and what it is like to *Be* One.

So they move toward this "feeling" they are experiencing, and, as they close the gap between them, as they "shorten the cord," the energy they are both sending to TOMARY travels a shorter distance and is thus more intense.

They move closer still. The shorter the distance, the greater the intensity. They move closer still. Once more the intensity increases.

Now they stand just a few feet apart. The Body Between them is glowing hot. Vibrating with terrific speed. The "connection" to and from TOMARY is thicker, wider, brighter, burning with the transfer of incredible energy. The two are said to be "burning with desire." They *are!*

They move closer still.

Now, they touch.

The sensation is almost unbearable. Exquisite. They feel, at the point of their touch, all the energy of TOMARY—all the compacted, intensely unified substance of their Combined Being.

If you open yourself to your greatest sensitivity, you'll be able to feel this subtle, sublime energy as a tingling when you touch—sometimes the "tingling" will run right *through* you—or as heat at the point of your touch—heat which you may also suddenly feel throughout your body—but concentrated deeply within your lower chakra, or energy center.

It will "burn" there especially intensely—and Tom and Mary will now be said to have the "hots" for each other!

Now the two embrace, and they close the gap even further, with Tom, Mary, and Tomary all filling nearly the same space. Tom and Mary can *feel* Tomary between them—and they want to get even *closer*—to literally *meld* with Tomary. To *become* Tomary in *physical form*.

I have created in the male and female bodies a way to do that. At this moment, Tom and Mary's bodies are ready to do that. Tom's body is now ready to literally *enter* Mary. Mary's body is ready to literally *receive Tom within her*.

The tingling, the burning, is now *beyond* intense. It is . . . indescribable. The two physical bodies join. Tom, Mary, *and* Tomary become *One*. In the *flesh*.

Still the energies flow between them. Urgently. Passionately.

They heave. They move. They can't get enough of each other, can't get close enough together. They strive to get *close*. *Close*. *CLOSER*.

They explode—literally—and their entire physical bodies convulse. The vibration sends ripples to their fingertips. In the explosion of their oneness they have known the God and the Goddess, the Alpha and the Omega, the All and the Nothing—the Essence of life—the Experience of That Which Is.

There are physical chemistries as well. The two *have* become One—and a *third* entity often *is* created of the two, in *physical form*.

Thus, an *outpicturing* of TOMARY is created. Flesh of their flesh. Blood of their blood.

They have literally *created life!*

Have I not said that *ye are Gods?*

That is the most beautiful description of human sexuality I have ever heard.

You see beauty where you desire to see it. You see ugliness where you are afraid to see beauty.

It would amaze you to know how many people see what I've just said as ugly.

No, it wouldn't. I've already seen how much fear, *and* ugliness, the world has placed around sex. But You do leave a lot of questions.

I am here to answer them. But allow Me to go on with My narrative just a bit further before you start throwing them at Me.

Yes, *please.*

This . . . *dance* that I've just described, this energy interaction I've explained, is occurring all the time—in and with *everything.*

Your energy—beamed from you like a Golden Light—is interacting constantly with everything and everyone else. The closer you are, the more intense the energy. The further away, the more subtle. Yet you are never totally disconnected from *anything.*

There is a point between You and every other person, place, or thing which exists. It is here that two energies meet, forming a third, much less dense, but no less real, energy unit.

Every*one* and every*thing* on the planet—and in the universe— is emitting energy in every direction. This energy mixes with all other energies, criss-crossing in patterns of complexity beyond the ability of your most powerful computers to analyze.

The criss-crossing, intermingling, intertwining energies racing between everything that you can call physical is what *holds physicality together.*

This is the Matrix, of which I have spoken. It is along this Matrix that you send signals to each other—messages, meanings, healings, and other physical effects—created sometimes by individuals but mostly by mass consciousness.

These innumerable energies are, as I have explained, attracted to each other. This is called the Law of Attraction. In this Law, Like attracts Like.

Like Thoughts attract Like Thoughts along the Matrix—and when enough of these similar energies "clump together," so to speak, their vibrations become heavier, they slow down—and some become Matter.

Thoughts *do* create physical form—and when many people are thinking the *same* thing, there is a very high likelihood their thoughts will form a Reality.

(That is why "We'll pray for you" is such a powerful statement. There are enough testimonies to the effectiveness of unified prayer to fill a book.)

It is also true that un-prayerlike thoughts can create "effects." A worldwide consciousness of fear, for instance, or anger, or lack, or insufficiency, can create that experience—across the globe or within a given locale where those collective ideas are strongest.

The Earth nation you call the United States, for example, has long thought itself to be a nation "under God, indivisible, with liberty and justice for all." It is not a coincidence that this nation rose to become the most prosperous on Earth. It is also not surprising that this nation is gradually losing all that it has worked so hard to create—for this nation seems to have lost its vision.

The terms "under God, indivisible," meant just that—they expressed the Universal Truth of Unity; Oneness: a Matrix very difficult to destroy. But the Matrix has been weakened. Religious freedom has become religious righteousness bordering on religious intolerance. Individual freedom has all but vanished as individual responsibility has disappeared.

The notion of *individual responsibility* has been distorted to mean "every man for himself." This is the new philosophy that imagines itself to be harkening back to the Early American tradition of rugged individualism.

But the original sense of individual responsibility upon which the American vision and the American dream was based found its deepest meaning and its highest expression in the concept of *Brotherly Love.*

What made America great was not that every man struggled for his *own* survival, but that every man accepted individual responsibility for the survival of *all.*

America was a nation that would not turn its back on the hungry, would never say no to the needy, would open its arms to the weary and the homeless, and would share its abundance with the world.

Yet as America became great, Americans became greedy. Not all, but many. And, as time went on, more and more.

As Americans saw how good it was *possible* to have it, they sought to have it even better. Yet there was only one way to have more and more and *more.* Someone else had to have less and less and less.

As greed replaced greatness in the American character, there was less room for compassion for the least among the people. The less fortunate were told it was their "own damned fault" if they didn't have more. After all, America was the Land of Opportunity, was it not? No one *except* the less fortunate found it possible to admit that America's opportunity was limited, *institutionally,* to those already on the inside track. In general, these have not included many minorities, such as those of certain skin color or gender.

Americans became arrogant internationally as well. As millions starved across the globe, Americans threw away enough food each day to feed entire nations. America was generous with some, yes—but increasingly her foreign policy came to be an extension of her own vested interests. America helped others when it served America to do so. (That is, when it served America's power structure, America's richest elite, or the military machine that protected those elite—and their collective assets.)

America's founding ideal—Brotherly Love—had been eroded. Now, any talk of being "your brother's keeper" is met with a new brand of Americanism—a sharp mind toward what it takes to hold on to one's own, and a sharp word to any among the less fortunate who would dare ask for their fair share, for their grievances to be redressed.

Each person *must* take responsibility for herself or himself—that is undeniably true. But America—and your world—can truly work only when every person is willing to stand responsible for *all* of you as a *Whole*.

So Collective Consciousness produces collective results.

Exactly—and this has been demonstrated time and time again throughout all of your recorded history.

The Matrix draws itself into itself—exactly as your scientists describe the so-called Black Hole phenomenon. It pulls like-energy to like-energy, even drawing physical objects toward each other.

Those objects must then repel each other—move *away*—or they will merge forever—in effect, disappearing in their present form and taking on a new form.

All beings of consciousness intuitively know this, so all beings of consciousness *move away* from the Permanent Melding in order to maintain their relationship to all other beings. If they did not, they would meld *into* all other beings, and experience the Oneness Forever.

This is the state from which we have come.

Having moved away from this state, we are constantly re-attracted *to* it.

This ebb and flow, "to and fro" movement is the basic rhythm of the universe, *and everything in it.* This is sex—the Synergistic Energy Exchange.

You are constantly being attracted, compelled toward union with one another (and with all that is in the Matrix), then, at the Moment of Unity, being repelled by conscious choice away from that Unity. Your choice is to remain free of It, so that you can *experience* it. For once you become part of that Unity and *remain* there, you cannot *know* it as Unity, since you no longer know Separation.

Put another way: for God to *know* Itself as the All of It, God must know Itself as *not* the All of It.

In you—and in every other energy unit of the universe—God knows Itself as the *Parts* of *All*—and thus gives Itself the possibility of knowing Itself as the *All in All* in Its Own Experience.

I can only experience what I am by experiencing what I am not. Yet I *am* what I am not—and so you see the Divine Dichotomy. Hence, the statement: I Am that I Am.

Now as I said, this natural ebb and flow, this natural *rhythm* of the universe, typifies all of life—including the very movements that *create* life in your reality.

Toward each other you are compelled, as if by some urgent force, only to pull away and separate, only to urgently push toward each other again, once more to separate, and again to hungrily, passionately, urgently seek total union.

Together-apart, together-apart, together-apart your bodies dance, in a movement so basic, so *instinctual*, that you have very little conscious awareness of deliberate action. At some point you shift into automatic. No one needs to tell your bodies what to do. They simply *do it*—with the urgency of *all of life.*

This is life itself, expressing itself as life itself.

And this is life itself producing *new* life in the bosom of its own experience.

All of life works on such a rhythm; all of life IS the rhythm.

And so, all of life is imbued with the gentle rhythm of God— what you call the cycles of life.

Food grows in such cycles. Seasons come and go. Planets spin and circle. Suns explode and implode, and explode again. Universes breathe in and breathe out. All of it happens, *all* of it, in cycles, in rhythms, in vibrations matching the frequencies of God/Goddess—the All.

For God *is* the All, and the Goddess is *everything,* and there is nothing else that is; and all that *ever* was, is *now*, and ever *shall* be, is your world without end.

Amen.

8

The interesting thing about talking with You is that You always leave me with more questions than answers. Now I have questions about politics as well as sex!

> Some say they're the same thing, that in politics all you ever do is get—

Wait a minute! You're not going to use an *obscenity*, are You?

> Well, yes, I thought I would shock you a little.

Hey, HEY! Cut it *out!* God isn't supposed to talk like that!

> Then why do *you?*

Most of us *don't.*

> The hell you don't.

Those people who are *God fearing* don't!

> Oh, I see, you have to *fear* God in order not to offend Him. And who says I am *offended*, anyway, by a simple word?
> And, finally, don't you find it interesting that a word some of you use in the height of passion to describe great sex, you also use as your highest insult? Does that tell you anything about the way you feel about sexuality?

I think You've gotten confused. I don't think people use that term to describe a glorious, truly romantic sexual moment.

> Oh, really? Have you been in any bedrooms lately?

No. Have You?

> I am in *all* of them—all the time.

Well, that should make us all feel comfortable.

What? Are you saying that you do things in your bedroom that you wouldn't do in front of God—?

Most people aren't comfortable with *anyone* watching, much less *God*.

Yet in some cultures—Aboriginal, some Polynesian—lovemaking is done quite openly.

Yes, well, most people haven't progressed to that level of freedom. In fact, they would consider such behavior regression—to a primitive, pagan state.

These people you call "pagans" have an enormous respect for life. They know nothing of rape, and there are virtually no killings in their societies. Your society puts sex—a very natural, normal human function—under cover, then turns around and kills people right out in the open. *That* is the obscenity!

You've made sex so dirty, shameful, taboo, that you're embarrassed to do it!

Nonsense. Most people simply have a different—they might even say a higher—sense of propriety about sex. They consider it a private interacting; for some, a sacred part of their relationship.

Lack of privacy does not equal lack of sanctity. Most of humanity's most sacred rites are performed in public.

Do not confuse privacy with sanctity. Most of your *worst* actions are taken in private, and you save only your best behavior for public display.

This is not an argument for public sex; it is merely a noting that privacy does not necessarily equal sanctity—nor does publicity rob you of it.

As for propriety, that single word and the behavioral concept behind it have done more to inhibit men's and women's greatest joys than any other human construction—except the idea that God is punitive—which *finished* the job.

Apparently, you don't believe in propriety.

The trouble with "propriety" is that someone has to set the standards. This means, automatically, that your behaviors are being limited, directed, *dictated* by someone *else's* idea of what should bring you joy.

In matters of sexuality—as in all other matters—this can be more than "limiting"; it can be devastating.

I can think of nothing more sad than a man or woman feeling they'd *like* to experience some things, then holding back because they think that what they've dreamt of, fantasized about, would violate the "Standards of Propriety"!

Mind you, it's not something that *they* wouldn't do—it's just something that violates "propriety."

Not just in matters of sexuality, but in all of life, never, ever, *ever,* fail to do something simply because it might violate someone *else's* standards of propriety.

If I had one bumper sticker on my car, it would read:

VIOLATE PROPRIETY

I would certainly put such a sign in every bedroom.

But our sense of what's "right" and "wrong" is what holds society together. How can we cohabitate if we have no agreement on that?

"Propriety" has nothing to do with your relative values of "rightness" or "wrongness." You might all agree that it's "wrong" to kill a man, but is it "wrong" to run naked in the rain? You might all agree that it's "wrong" to take a neighbor's wife, but is it "wrong" to "take" your own wife—or have your wife "take" you—in a particularly delicious way?

"Propriety" seldom refers to legalistic limitations, but more often to simpler matters of what is deemed "appropriate."

"Appropriate" behavior is not always the behavior that's in what you call your "best interests." It is rarely the behavior that brings you the most joy.

Getting back to sexuality, You're saying, then, that any behavior is acceptable behavior so long as there is mutual consent among all those involved and affected?

Shouldn't that be true of all of life?

But sometimes we don't know who will be affected, or how—

You must be sensitive to that. You must be keenly aware. And where you truly cannot know, and cannot guess, you must err on the side of Love.

The central question in ANY decision is, "What would love do now?"

Love for *yourself*, and love for *all others* who are *affected or involved.*

If you love another, you will not do anything that you believe could or would hurt that person. If there is any question or doubt, you will wait until you can get to clarity on the matter.

But that means others can hold you "hostage." All they have to say is that such and such a thing would "hurt" them, and your actions are restricted.

Only by your Self. Wouldn't you *want* to restrict your own actions to those which do not damage the ones you love?

But what if *you* feel damaged by *not* doing something?

Then you must tell your loved one your truth—that you are feeling hurt, frustrated, reduced by not doing a certain thing; that you would like to do this thing; that you would like your loved one's agreement that you may do it.

You must strive to seek such an agreement. Work to strike a compromise; seek a course of action in which everybody can win.

And if such a course cannot be found?

Then I'll repeat what I have said before:

> *Betrayal*
> *of yourself*
> *in order not to betray*
> *another*
> *is*
> *Betrayal*
> *nonetheless.*
> *It is the*
> *Highest Betrayal.*

Your Shakespeare put this another way:

To thine own Self be true,
and it must follow, as the night the day,
Thou canst not then be false
to any man.

But the man who always "goes with" what he wants becomes a very selfish man. I can't believe You are advocating this.

You assume that man will always make what you call the "selfish choice." I tell you this: Man *is* capable of making the *highest* choice.

Yet I also tell you this:

The Highest Choice is not *always* the choice which seems to serve another.

In other words, sometimes we must put ourselves first.

Oh, *always* you must put yourselves first! Then, depending upon what you are trying to do—or what you are seeking to experience—you will make your choice.

When your purpose—your *life* purpose—is very high, so will your choices also be.

Putting yourself first does not mean being what you term "selfish"—it means being self *aware*.

You lay a pretty broad basis for the conduct of human affairs.

It is only through the exercise of the greatest freedom that the greatest growth is achieved—or even possible.

If all you are doing is following someone *else's* rules, then you have not grown, you have obeyed.

Contrary to your constructions, obedience is not what I want from you. Obedience is not growth, and growth is what I desire.

And if we do not "grow," you throw us in hell, right?

Wrong. But I have discussed that in *Book 1*, and we'll do so at length in *Book 3*.

Okay. So, within these broad parameters you've laid out, may I ask you some final questions about sex before we leave the subject?

Shoot.

If sex is so wonderful a part of the human experience, why do so many spiritual teachers preach abstinence? And why were so many masters apparently celibate?

For the same reason most of them have been depicted as living simply. Those who evolve to a high level of understanding bring their bodily desires into balance with their minds and souls.

You are three-part beings, and most people experience themselves as a body. Even the mind is forgotten after age 30. No one reads anymore. No one writes. No one teaches. No one learns. The mind is forgotten. It is not nourished. It is not expanded. No new input. The minimum output required. The mind is not fed. It is not awakened. It is lulled, dulled. You do everything you can to disengage it. Television, movies, pulp paperbacks. Whatever you do, don't think, don't think, *don't think!*

So most people live life on a body level. Feed the body, clothe the body, give the body "stuff." Most people haven't read a good book—I mean a book from which they can *learn* something—in years. But they can tell you the entire television schedule for the week. There's something extraordinarily sad in that.

The truth is, most people don't want to have to *think*. They elect leaders, they support governments, they adopt religions requiring *no independent thought.*

"Make it easy for me. Tell me what to do."

Most people want that. Where do I sit? When do I stand? How should I salute? When do I pay? What do you wish me to do?

What are the rules? Where are my boundaries? Tell me, tell me, *tell* me. I'll do it—somebody just *tell* me!

Then they get disgusted, disillusioned. They followed all the rules, they did as they were told. What went wrong? When did it turn sour? Why did it fall apart?

It fell apart the moment you abandoned your mind—the greatest creative tool you ever had.

It's time to make friends with your mind again. Be a companion to it—it's felt so alone. Be a nourisher of it—it's been so starved.

Some of you—a small minority—have understood that you have a body *and* a mind. You've treated your mind well. Still, even among those of you who honor your mind—and things of the mind—few have learned to *use* the mind at more than one-tenth its capacity. If you knew of what your mind is capable, you would never cease to partake of its wonders—and its powers.

And if you think the number of you who balance your life between your body and your mind is small, the number who see yourselves as *three*-part beings—Body, Mind, and Spirit—is minuscule.

Yet you *are* three-part beings. You are more than your body, and more than a body with a mind.

Are you nurturing your soul? Are you even *noticing* it? Are you healing it or hurting it? Are you growing or withering? Are you expanding or contracting?

Is your soul as lonely as your mind? Is it even more neglected? And when was the last time you felt your soul being *expressed*? When was the last time you cried with joy? Wrote poetry? Made music? Danced in the rain? Baked a pie? Painted *anything*? Fixed something that was broken? Kissed a baby? Held a cat to your face? Hiked up a hill? Swam naked? Walked at sunrise? Played the harmonica? Talked 'til dawn? Made love for hours . . . on a beach, in the woods? Communed with nature? Searched for God?

When was the last time you sat alone with the silence, traveling to the deepest part of your being? When was the last time you said hello to your soul?

When you live as a single-faceted creature, you become deeply mired in matters of the body: Money. Sex. Power. Possessions. Physical stimulations and satisfactions. Security. Fame. Financial gain.

When you live as a dual-faceted creature, you broaden your concerns to include matters of the mind. Companionship; creativity; stimulation of new thoughts, new ideas; creation of new goals, new challenges; personal growth.

When you live as a three-part being, you come at last into balance with yourself. Your concerns include matters of the soul: spiritual identity; life purpose; relationship to God; path of evolution; spiritual growth; ultimate destiny.

As you evolve into higher and higher states of consciousness, you bring into full realization every aspect of your being.

Yet evolution does not mean *dropping* some aspects of Self in favor of others. It simply means expanding focus; turning away from almost exclusive involvement with one aspect, toward genuine love and appreciation for *all* aspects.

Then why do so many teachers espouse complete abstinence from sex?

Because they do not believe that humans can achieve a balance. They believe the sexual energy—and the energies surrounding other worldly experiences—is too powerful to simply moderate; to bring into balance. They believe abstinence is *the only way* to spiritual evolution, rather than merely one possible *result* of it.

Yet isn't it true that some beings who are highly evolved *have* "given up sex"?

Not in the classic sense of the words "to give up." It is not a forced letting go of something you still want but know is "no good to have." It's more of a simple releasing, a movement away from—as one pushes oneself away from the second helping of dessert. Not because the dessert is no good. Not even because it's no good *for* you. But simply because, wonderful as it was, you've had enough.

When you can drop your involvement with sex for that reason, you may want to do so. Then again, you may not. You may never decide that you've "had enough" and may always want this experience, in balance with the other experiences of your Beingness.

That's okay. That's all right. The sexually active are no less qualified for enlightenment, no less spiritually evolved, than the sexually inactive.

What enlightenment and evolution *do* cause you to drop is your *addiction* to sex, your deep *need* to have the experience, your compulsive behaviors.

So, too, your *preoccupation* with money, power, security, possessions, and other experiences of the body will vanish. Yet your genuine *appreciation* for them will not and *should* not. Appreciation for *all* of life is what honors the Process I have created. Disdain for life or any of its joys—even the most basic, physical ones—is disdain for *Me*, the Creator.

For when you call My creation unholy, what do you call Me? Yet when you call My creation sacred, you sanctify your experience of it, and Me as well.

I tell you this: I have created *nothing* disdainful—and, as your Shakespeare said, *nothing* is "evil" lest thinking make it so.

This leads me to some other, final, questions about sex. Is any kind of sex between consenting adults okay?

Yes.

I mean even "kinky" sex? Even loveless sex? Even gay sex?

First, let's be once again clear that nothing is disapproved of by God.

I do not sit here in judgment, calling one action *Good* and another *Evil*.

(As you know, I have discussed this at some length in *Book 1*.)

Now—within the context of what serves you, or disserves you, on your Path of Evolution, only *you* can decide that.

There is a broad-based guideline, however, upon which most evolved souls have agreed.

No action which causes hurt to another leads to rapid evolution.

There is a second guideline as well.

No action involving another may be taken without the other's agreement and permission.

Now let us consider the questions you've just asked within the context of these guidelines.

"Kinky" sex? Well, if it hurts no one, and is done with everyone's permission, what reason would anyone have to call it "wrong"?

Loveless sex? Sex for the "sake of sex" has been debated from the beginning of time. I often think whenever I hear this question that I'd like to go into a roomful of people someday and say, "Everybody here who's never had sex outside of a relationship of deep, lasting, committed, abiding love, raise your hand."

Let me just say this: Loveless *anything* is not the fastest way to the Goddess.

Whether it's loveless sex or loveless spaghetti and meat balls, if you've prepared the feast and are consuming it without love, you're missing the most extraordinary part of the experience.

Is it wrong to miss that? Here again, "wrong" may not be the operative word. "Disadvantageous" would be closer, given that you desire to evolve into a higher spiritual being as rapidly as you can.

Gay sex? So many people want to say that I am against gay sexuality—or the acting out of it. Yet I make no judgment, on this or any other choice you make.

People want to make all kinds of value judgments—about *everything*—and I kind of spoil the party. I won't join them in those judgments, which is especially disconcerting to those who say that *I originated them.*

I do observe this: There was once a time when people thought that marriage between people of differing *races* was not only inadvisable, but *against the law of God.* (Amazingly, some people *still* think this.) They pointed to their Bible as their authority—even as they do for their authority on questions surrounding homosexuality.

You mean it is okay for people of differing races to join together in marriage?

The question is absurd, but not nearly as absurd as some people's certainty that the answer is "no."

Are the questions on homosexuality equally absurd?

You decide. I have no judgment about that, or *anything.* I know you wish that I did. That would make your lives a lot easier. No decisions to make. No tough calls. Everything decided for you. Nothing to do but obey. Not much of a life, at least in terms of creativity or self-empowerment, but what the heck . . . no stress, either.

Let me ask You some questions about sex and children. At what age is it appropriate to allow children to become aware of sexuality as a life experience?

Children are aware of themselves as sexual beings—which is to say, as *human* beings—from the outset of their lives. What many parents on your planet now do is try to discourage them from noticing that. If a baby's hand goes to the "wrong place," you move it away. If a tiny child begins to find moments of self-pleasure in its innocent delight with its own body, you react in horror, and pass that sense of horror on to your child. The child wonders, what did I do, what did I do? Mommy's mad; what did I do?

With your race of beings, it has not been a question of when you introduce your offspring to sex, it has been a question of when you stop demanding that they deny their own identity as sexual beings. Somewhere between the ages of 12 and 17 most of you give up the fight already and say, essentially (although naturally not with words—you don't speak of these things), "Okay, now you can notice that you have sexual parts and sexual things to do with them."

Yet by this time the damage has been done. Your children have been shown for ten years or more that they are to be *ashamed* of those body parts. Some are not even told the proper *name* for them. They hear everything from "wee wee" to "your bottom" to words some of you must strain mightily to invent—all to avoid simply saying "penis" or "vagina."

Having thus gotten very clear that all things having to do with *those* parts of the body are to be hidden, not spoken of, denied, your offspring then explode into puberty not knowing at all what to make of what's going on with them. They've had no preparation at all. Of course, they then act miserable, responding to their newest and most urgent urges awkwardly, if not inappropriately.

This is not necessary, nor do I observe it as serving your offspring, far too many of whom enter their adult lives with sexual taboos, inhibitions, and "hang ups" to beat the band.

Now in enlightened societies offspring are never discouraged, reprimanded, or "corrected" when they begin to find early delight in the nature of their very being. Nor is the sexuality of their parents— that is, the *identity* of their parents as sexual beings—particularly avoided or necessarily hidden. Naked bodies, whether of the parents or the children or their siblings, are seen and treated as being totally natural, totally wonderful, and totally okay—not as things of which to be ashamed.

Sexual functions are also seen and treated as totally natural, totally wonderful, and totally okay.

In some societies, parents couple in full view of their offspring— and what could give children a greater sense of the beauty and the wonder and the pure joy and the total okayness of the sexual expression of love than this? For parents are constantly modeling the "rightness" and "wrongness" of *all* behaviors, and children pick up subtle and not-so-subtle signals from their parents about *everything* through what they see their parents thinking, saying, and doing.

As noted earlier, you may call such societies "pagan" or "primitive," yet it is observable that in such societies rape and crimes of passion are virtually nonexistent, prostitution is laughed at as being absurd, and sexual inhibitions and dysfunctions are unheard of.

While such openness is not recommended just now for your own society (in all but the most extraordinary of settings it would no doubt be far too culturally stigmatizing), it *is* time that the so-called modern civilizations on your planet do something to end the repression, guilt, and shame which too often surrounds and characterizes the totality of your society's sexual expression and experience.

Suggestions? Ideas?

Stop teaching children from the very beginning of their lives that things having to do with the very natural functioning of their bodies are shameful and wrong. Discontinue demonstrating to your offspring that anything sexual is to be hidden. Allow your children to see and observe the romantic side of *you*. Let them see you hugging, touching, gently fondling—let them see that their parents *love each other* and that *showing their love physically* is something that is very natural and very wonderful. (It would surprise you to know in how many families such a simple lesson has never been taught.)

When your children begin to embrace their own sexual feelings, curiosities and urges, cause them to connect this new and expanding experience of themselves with an inner sense of joy and celebration, not guilt and shame.

And for heaven sake, stop hiding your *bodies* from your children. It's okay if they see you swimming in the nude in a country water hole on a camping trip or in the backyard pool; don't go into apoplexy should they catch a glimpse of you moving from the bedroom to the bathroom without a robe; end this frantic need to cover up, close off, shut down any opportunity, however innocent, for your child to be introduced to you as a being with your own sexual identity. Children think their parents are asexual because their parents have *portrayed themselves that way.* They then imagine that *they* must be this way, because *all children emulate their parents.* (Therapists will tell you that some grown-up offspring have, to this very day, the most difficult time imagining their parents actually "doing it," which, of course, fills these offspring—now patients in the therapist's office—with rage or guilt or shame, because they, naturally, *desire* to "do it," and they can't figure out *what's wrong with them.*)

So talk about sex with your children, laugh about sex with your children, teach them and allow them and remind them and *show them how* to *celebrate* their sexuality. *That* is what you can do for your children. And you do this from the day they are born, with the first kiss, the first hug, the first touch they receive from you, and that they see you receiving from each other.

Thank You. *Thank You.* I was so hoping that You'd bring some *sanity* to this subject. But one final question. When is it appropriate to specifically introduce or discuss or describe sexuality with your children?

They will tell you when that time has come. Each child will make it clear, unmistakably, if you are really watching and listening. It comes in increments, actually. It arrives incrementally. And you will know the age-appropriate way of dealing with the incremental arrival of your child's sexuality if *you* are clear, if you are finished with your own "unfinished business" about all of this.

How do we get to *that* place?

Do what it takes. Enroll in a seminar. See a therapist. Join a group. Read a book. Meditate on it. Discover each other—most of all, discover *each other* as male and female again; discover, revisit, regain, reclaim your *own* sexuality. Celebrate *that*. Enjoy *that*. Own *that*.

Own your own joyful sexuality, and then you can allow and encourage your children to own theirs.

Again, thank You. Now, getting away from the consideration of children and moving back to the larger subject of human sexuality, I have to ask You one more question. And it may seem impertinent and it may seem flippant even, but I can't let this dialogue end without asking it.

Well, stop apologizing and just ask it.

Fine. Is there such a thing as "too much" sex?

No. Of course not. But there is such a thing as too much of a need for sex.

I suggest this:

Enjoy everything.
Need nothing.

Including people?

Including people. *Especially* people. Needing someone is the fastest way to kill a relationship.

But we all like to feel needed.

Then stop it. Like to feel unneeded instead—for the greatest gift you can give someone is the strength and the power *not to need you*, to need you for nothing.

9

Okay, I'm ready to move on. You promised to talk about some of the larger aspects of life on Earth, and ever since your comments about life in the United States I've wanted to talk more about all of this.

Yes, good. I want *Book 2* to address some of the larger issues facing your planet. And there is no larger issue than the education of your offspring.

We are not doing this well, are we. . . . I can tell by the way You brought that up.

Well, of course, everything is relative. Relative to what you say you are trying to do, no, you are not doing it well.

Everything I say here, everything I have included in this discussion so far and have caused to be placed in this document, must be put into that context. I am not making judgments of "rightness" or "wrongness," "goodness" or "badness." I simply make observations of your *effectiveness* relative to what you *say you are trying to do.*

I understand that.

I know you say that you do, but the time may come—even before this dialogue is finished—when you will accuse Me of being judgmental.

I would never accuse You of that. I know better.

"Knowing better" has not stopped the human race from calling Me a judgmental God in the past.

Well, it will stop me.

We shall see.

You wanted to talk about education.

Indeed. I observe that most of you have misunderstood the meaning, the purpose, and the function of education, to say nothing of the process by which it is best undertaken.

That's a huge statement, and I need some help with it.

Most of the human race has decided that the meaning and the purpose and the function of education is to pass on knowledge; that to educate someone is to give them knowledge—generally, the accumulated knowledge of one's particular family, clan, tribe, society, nation, and world.

Yet education has very little to do with knowledge.

Oh? You could have fooled me.

Clearly.

What does it have to do with then?

Wisdom.

Wisdom.

Yes.

Okay, I give up. What is the difference?

Wisdom is knowledge applied.

So we aren't supposed to try to give our offspring knowledge. We are supposed to try to give our offspring wisdom.

First of all, don't "try" to do anything. *Do it.* Secondly, don't ignore knowledge in favor of wisdom. That would be fatal. On the other hand, don't ignore wisdom in favor of knowledge. That would also be fatal. It would kill education. On your planet, it *is* killing it.

We are ignoring wisdom in favor of knowledge?

In most cases, yes.

How are we doing this?

You are teaching your children what to think instead of how to think.

Explain, please.

Certainly. When you give your children knowledge, you are telling them what to think. That is, you are telling them what they are supposed to know, what you want them to understand is true.

When you give your children wisdom, you do not tell them what to know, or what is true, but, rather, *how to get to their own truth.*

But without knowledge there can be no wisdom.

Agreed. That is why I have said, you cannot ignore knowledge in favor of wisdom. A certain amount of knowledge must be passed on from one generation to the next. Obviously. But as little knowledge as possible. The smaller amount, the better.

Let the child discover for itself. Know this: Knowledge is lost. Wisdom is never forgotten.

So our schools should teach as little as possible?

Your schools should turn their emphasis around. Right now they are focused highly on knowledge, and paying precious little attention to wisdom. Classes in critical thinking, problem solving, and logic are considered by many parents to be threatening. They want such classes out of the curriculum. As well they might, if they want to protect their way of life. Because children who are allowed to develop their own critical thinking processes are very much likely to *abandon* their parents' morals, standards, and entire way of life.

In order to protect your way of life, you have built an education system based upon the development in the child of memories, not abilities. Children are taught to *remember* facts and fictions—the fictions each society has set up about itself—rather than given the ability to discover and create their own truths.

Programs calling for children to develop *abilities* and *skills* rather than *memories* are soundly ridiculed by those who imagine that they know what a child needs to learn. Yet what you have been teaching your children has led your world *toward* ignorance, not away from it.

Our schools don't teach fictions, they teach facts.

Now you are lying to yourself, just as you lie to your children.

We lie to our children?

Of course you do. Pick up any history book and see. Your histories are written by people who want their children to see the world from a particular point of view. Any attempt to expand historical accounts with a larger view of the facts is sneered at, and called "revisionist." You will not tell the truth about your past to your children, lest they see you for what you really are.

Most history is written from the point of view of that segment of your society you would call white Anglo Saxon Protestant males. When females, or blacks, or others in the minority, say, "Hey, wait a minute. This isn't how it happened. You've left out a huge part here," you cringe and holler and demand that the "revisionists" stop trying to change your textbooks. You don't *want* your children to know how it *really* happened. You want them to know how you *justified* what happened, from your point of view. Shall I give you an example of this?

Please.

In the United States, you do not teach your children everything there is to know about your country's decision to drop atom bombs on two Japanese cities, killing or maiming hundreds of thousands of people. Rather, you give them the facts as you see them—and as you want them to see them.

When an attempt is made to balance this point of view with the point of view of another—in this case, the Japanese—you scream and rage and rant and rave and jump up and down and demand that schools don't *dare* even *think* about presenting such data in their historical review of this important event. Thus you have not taught history at all, but politics.

History is supposed to be an accurate, and full, account of what actually happened. Politics is never about what actually happened. Politics is always one's *point of view* about what happened.

History reveals, politics justifies. History uncovers; tells all. Politics covers; tells only one side.

Politicians hate history truly written. And history, truly written, speaks not so well of politicians, either.

Yet you are wearing the Emperor's New Clothes, for your children ultimately see right through you. Children taught to critically think look at your history and say, "My, how my parents and elders have deluded themselves." This you cannot tolerate, so you drum it out of them. You do not want your children to have the most basic facts. You want them to have *your* take on the facts.

I think you are exaggerating here. I think you've taken this argument a little far.

Really? Most people in your society do not even want their children to know the most basic facts of *life*. People went bananas when schools simply started teaching children how the human body functions. Now you are not supposed to tell children how AIDS is transmitted, or how to *stop it* from being transmitted. Unless, of course, you tell them from a particular *point of view* how to avoid AIDS. Then it is all right. But simply give them the facts, and let them decide for themselves? Not on your life.

Children are not ready to decide these things for themselves. They have to be properly guided.

Have you looked at your world lately?

What about it?

That's how you've guided your children in the past.

No, it's how we *mis*guided them. If the world is in rotten shape today—and in many ways, it is—it is not because we've tried to teach our children the *old* values, but because we've allowed them to be taught all this "new fangled" stuff!

You really believe that, don't you?

You're damned right, I really believe it! If we'd just kept our children limited to the 3 R's instead of feeding them all this "critical thinking" garbage, we'd be a lot better off today. If we'd kept so-called "sex education" out of the classroom and in the home where it belonged, we wouldn't be seeing teenagers having babies, and single mothers at 17 applying for welfare, and a world run amok. If we'd insisted our young ones live by *our* moral standards, rather than letting them go off and create their own, we wouldn't have turned our once strong, vibrant nation into a pitiable imitation of its former self.

I see.

And one more thing. Don't stand there and tell me how we are supposed to suddenly see ourselves as "wrong" for what we did at Hiroshima and Nagasaki. We *ended the war,* for God's sake. We saved thousands of lives. On *both* sides. It was the price of war. Nobody liked the decision, but it had to be made.

I see.

Yeah, you see. You're just like all the rest of those el pinko liberal Commies. You want us to revise our history, all right. You want us to revise ourselves right out of existence. Then you liberals can have your way at last; take over the world; create your decadent societies; redistribute the wealth. *Power to the people,* and all that crap. Except that's never gotten us anywhere. What we need is a return to the past; to the values of our forefathers. That's what we need!

Done now?

Yeah, I'm done. How did I do?

Pretty good. That was really good.

Well, when you've been around talk radio for a few years, it comes pretty easily.

That is how people on your planet think, isn't it?

You bet it is. And not just in America. I mean, you could change the name of the country, and change the name of the war; insert any offensive military action by any nation at any time in history. Doesn't matter. Everybody thinks they're right. Everyone knows its the *other* person who is wrong. Forget about Hiroshima. Insert Berlin instead. Or Bosnia.

Everybody knows the old values are the ones which worked, too. Everybody knows the world is going to hell. Not just in America. All over. There is a hue and cry for a return to old values, and for a return to nationalism, everywhere on the planet.

I know that there is.

And what I've done here is try to articulate that feeling, that concern, that outrage.

You did a good job. Almost had Me convinced.

Well? What do you say to those who really do think like this?

I say, do you really think things were better 30 years ago, 40 years ago, 50 years ago? I say memory has poor vision. You remember the good of it, and not the worst of it. It's natural, it's normal. But don't be deceived. Do some *critical thinking*, and not just *memorizing* what others want you to think.

To stay with our example, do you really imagine it was absolutely necessary to drop the atom bomb on Hiroshima? What do your American historians say about the many reports, by those who claim to know more about what really happened, that the Japanese Empire had privately revealed to the United States its willingness to end the war *before* the bomb was dropped? How much of a part did revenge for the horror of Pearl Harbor play in the bombing decision? And, if you accept that dropping the Hiroshima bomb was necessary, why was it necessary to drop a second bomb?

It could be, of course, that your own account of all this is correct. It could be that the American point of view on all this is the way it actually happened. That is not the point of this discussion. The point here is that your educational system does not allow for critical thinking on these issues—or very many other issues, for that matter.

Can you imagine what would happen to a social studies or history teacher in Iowa who asked a class the above questions, inviting and encouraging the students to examine and explore the issues in depth and draw their own conclusions?

That is the point! You don't *want* your young ones drawing their own conclusions. You want them to *come to the same conclusions you came to*. Thus, you doom them to repeat the mistakes to which your conclusions led *you*.

But what about these statements made by so many people about old values and the disintegration of our society today? What about the incredible rise in teen births, or welfare mothers, or our world run amok?

Your world has run amok. On this I will agree. But your world has not run amok because of what you have allowed your schools to teach your children. It has run amok because of what you have not allowed them to teach.

You have not allowed your schools to teach that love is all there is. You have not allowed your schools to speak of a love which is unconditional.

Hell, we won't even allow our *religions* to speak of that.

That's right. And you will not allow your offspring to be taught to celebrate themselves and their bodies, their humanness and their wondrous sexual selves. And you will not allow your children to know that they are, first and foremost, spiritual beings inhabiting a body. Nor do you treat your children as spirits coming into bodies.

In societies where sexuality is openly spoken of, freely discussed, joyously explained and experienced, there is virtually no sexual crime, only a tiny number of births which occur when they are not expected, and no "illegitimate" or unwanted births. In highly evolved societies, *all* births are blessings, and all mothers and all children have their welfare looked after. Indeed, the society would have it no other way.

In societies where history is not bent to the views of the strongest and most powerful, the mistakes of the past are openly acknowledged and never repeated, and *once is enough* for behaviors which are clearly self destructive.

In societies where critical thinking and problem solving and skills for living are taught, rather than facts simply memorized, even so-called "justifiable" actions of the past are held up to intense scrutiny. Nothing is accepted on face value.

How would that work? Let's use our example from World War II. How would a school system teaching life skills, rather than merely facts, approach the historical episode at Hiroshima?

Your teachers would describe to their class exactly what happened there. They would include all the facts—*all* the facts—which led up to that event. They would seek the views of historians from *both* sides of the encounter, realizing that there is more than one point of view on *everything*. They would then not ask the class to memorize the facts of the matter. Instead, they would challenge the class. They would say: "Now, you've heard all about this event. You know all that came before, and all that happened after. We've given you as much of the 'knowledge' of this event as we could get our hands on. Now, from this 'knowledge,' what 'wisdom' comes to you? If you were chosen to solve the problems which were being faced in those days, and which were solved by the dropping of the bomb, how would you solve them? Can you think of a better way?"

Oh, *sure*. That's easy. Anybody can come up with answers *that way*—with the benefit of *hindsight*. Anybody can look over their shoulder and say, "I would have done it differently."

Then why don't you?

I beg your pardon?

I said, then why don't you? Why have you not looked over your shoulder, *learned* from your past, and done it differently? I'll tell you why. Because to allow your children to look at your past and analyze it critically—indeed, to *require* them to do so as a part of their education—would be to run the risk of them *disagreeing* with *how you did things*.

They will disagree anyway, of course. You just won't allow too much of it in your classrooms. So they have to take to the streets. Wave signs. Tear up draft cards. Burn bras and flags. Do whatever they can do to get your attention, to get you to see. Your young people have been screaming at you, "There must be a better way!" Yet you do not hear them. You do not *want* to hear them. And you certainly don't want to encourage them in the *classroom* to start critically thinking about the facts you are giving them.

Just *get it*, you say to them. Don't come in here and tell us we've been doing it wrong. Just *get* that we've been doing it *right*.

That's how you educate your children. That's what you've been calling education.

But there are those who would say it's the young people and their crazy, wacko, liberal ideas, who have taken this country and this world down the tubes. Sent it to hell. Pushed it to the edge of oblivion. Destroyed our values-oriented culture, and replaced it with a do-what-ever-you-want-to-do, whatever "feels good," morality which threatens to end our very way of life.

The young people *are* destroying your way of life. The young people have *always* done that. Your job is to encourage it, not discourage it.

It is not your young people who are destroying the rain forests. They are asking you to *stop it.* It is not your young people who are depleting your ozone layer. They are asking you to *stop it.* It is not your young people who are exploiting the poor in sweat shops all over the world. They are asking you to *stop it.* It is not your young people who are taxing you to death, then using the money for war and machines of war. They are asking you to *stop* it. It is not your young people who are ignoring the problems of the weak and the downtrodden, letting hundreds of people die of starvation every day on a planet with more than enough to feed everybody. They are asking you to *stop it.*

It is not your young people who are engaging in the politics of deception and manipulation. They are asking you to *stop it.* It is not your young people who are sexually repressed, ashamed and embarrassed about their own bodies and passing on this shame and embarrassment to their offspring. They are asking you to *stop it.* It is not your young people who have set up a value system which says that "might is right" and a world which solves problems with violence. They are asking you to *stop it.*

Nay, they are not asking you . . . they are *begging you.*

Yet it is young people who are violent! Young people who join gangs and kill each other! Young people who thumb their nose at law and order—at *any* kind of order. Young people who are driving us *crazy!*

When the cries and pleas of young people to change the world are not heard and never heeded; when they see that their cause is lost—that you will have it your way no matter what—young people, who are not stupid, will do the next best thing. If they can't beat you, they will join you.

Your young people have joined you in your behaviors. If they are violent, it is because you are violent. If they are materialistic, it is because you are materialistic. If they are acting crazy, it is because you are acting crazy. If they are using sex manipulatively, irresponsibly, shamefully, it is because they see you doing the same. The only difference between young people and older people is that young people do what they do out in the open.

Older people hide their behaviors. Older people think that young people cannot see. Yet young people see everything. Nothing is hidden from them. They see the hypocrisy of their elders, and they try desperately to change it. Yet having tried and failed, they see no choice but to imitate it. In this they are wrong, yet they have *never been taught differently.* They have not been allowed to critically analyze what their elders have been doing. They have only been allowed to memorize it.

What you memorize, you memorialize.

How, then, should we educate our young?

First, treat them as spirits. They are spirits, entering a physical body. That is not an easy thing for a spirit to do; not an easy thing for a spirit to get used to. It is very confining, very limiting. So the child will cry out at suddenly being so limited. Hear this cry. Understand it. And give your children as much of a sense of "unlimitedness" as you possibly can.

Next, introduce them to the world you have created with gentleness and care. Be full of care—that is to say, be careful—of what you put into their memory storage units. Children remember everything they see, everything they experience. Why do you spank your children the moment they exit the womb? Do you really imagine this is the only way to get their engines going? Why do you take your babies away from their mothers minutes after they have been separated from the only life-form they have known in all of their present existence? Will not the measuring and the weighing and the prodding and the poking wait for just a moment while the newly born experience the safety and the comfort of that *which has given it life?*

Why do you allow some of the earliest images to which your child is exposed to be images of violence? Who told you this was good for your children? And why do you hide images of love?

Why do you teach your children to be ashamed and embarrassed of their own bodies and their functions by shielding your own body from them, and telling them not to ever touch themselves in ways which pleasure them? What message do you send them about pleasure? And what lessons about the body?

Why do you place your children in schools where competition is allowed and encouraged, where being the "best" and learning the "most" is rewarded, where "performance" is graded, and moving at one's own pace is barely tolerated? What does your child understand from this?

Why do you not teach your children of movement and music and the joy of art and the mystery of fairy tales and the wonder of life? Why do you not bring out what is naturally found *in* the child, rather than seek to put in what is unnatural to the child?

And why do you not allow your young ones to learn logic and critical thinking and problem solving and creation, using the tools of their own intuition and their deepest inner knowing, rather than the rules and the memorized systems and conclusions of a society which has already proven itself to be wholly unable to evolve by these methods, yet continues to use them?

Finally, teach *concepts*, not *subjects*.

Devise a new curriculum, and build it around three Core Concepts:

Awareness

Honesty

Responsibility

Teach your children these concepts from the earliest age. Have them run through the curriculum until the final day. Base your entire educational model upon them. Birth all instruction deep within them.

I don't understand what that would mean.

It means everything you teach would come from within these concepts.

Can you explain that? How would we teach the three R's?

From the earliest primers to your more sophisticated readers, all tales, stories, and subject matter would revolve around the core concepts. That is, they would be stories of awareness, stories dealing with honesty, stories about responsibility. Your children would be introduced to the concepts, injected into the concepts, immersed in the concepts.

Writing tasks likewise would revolve around these Core Concepts, and others which are attendant to them as the child grows in the ability to self express.

Even computation skills would be taught within this framework. Arithmetic and mathematics are not abstractions, but are the most basic tools in the universe for living life. The teaching of all computation skills would be contextualized within the larger life experience in a way which draws attention to, and places focus upon, the Core Concepts and their derivatives.

What are these "derivatives?"

To use a phrase which your media people have made popular, they are the spin-offs. The entire educational model can be based on these spin-offs, replacing the subjects in your present curriculum, which teach, basically, facts.

For instance?

Well, let's use our imagination. What are some of the concepts which are important to you in life?

Uh . . . well, I would say . . . honesty, as you have said.

Yes, go ahead. That's a Core Concept.

And, um . . . fairness. That's an important concept to me.

Good. Any others?

Treating others nicely. That's one. I don't know how to put that into a concept.

Go on. Just let the thoughts flow.

Getting along. Being tolerant. Not hurting others. Seeing others as equal. Those are all things I would hope I could teach my children.

Good. Excellent! Keep going.

Uh . . . believing in yourself. That's a good one. And, uh . . . wait, wait . . . there's one coming. Uh . . . yeah, that's it: walking in dignity. I guess I would call it *walking in dignity*. I don't know how to put that into a better concept, either, but it has to do with the way one carries oneself in one's life, and the way one honors others, and the path others are taking.

This is good stuff. This is all good stuff. You're getting down to it now. And there are many other such concepts which all children must deeply understand if they are to evolve and grow into complete human beings. Yet you do not teach these things in your schools. These are the most important things in life, these things we are now talking of, but you do not teach them in school. You do not teach what it means to be honest. You do not teach what it means to be responsible. You do not teach what it means to be aware of other people's feelings and respectful of other people's paths.

You say it is up to parents to teach these things. Yet parents can only pass on what has been passed on to them. And the sins of the father have been visited upon the son. So you are teaching in your homes the same stuff your parents taught you in their homes.

So? What's wrong with that?

As I keep saying repeatedly here, taken a look at the world lately?

You keep bringing us back to that. You keep making us look at that. But all that isn't our fault. We can't be blamed for the way the rest of the world is.

It is not a question of blame, it is a question of choice. And if you are not responsible for the choices humankind has been making, and *keeps* making, who is?

Well, we can't make ourselves responsible for *all* of it!

I tell you this: Until you are willing to take responsibility for all of it, *you cannot change any of it.*

You cannot keep saying *they* did it, and *they* are doing it, and if only *they* would get it right! Remember the wonderful line from Walt Kelly's comic strip character, Pogo, and never forget it:

"*We have met the enemy, and they is us.*"

We've been repeating the same mistakes for hundreds of years, haven't we. . . .

For thousands of years, my son. You've been making the same mistakes for thousands of years. Humankind has not evolved in its most basic instincts much beyond the caveman era. Yet every attempt to change that is met with scorn. Every challenge to look at your values, and maybe even restructure them, is greeted with fear, and then anger. Now along comes an idea from Me to actually teach higher concepts in *schools.* Oh, boy, now we're really treading on thin ice.

Still, in highly evolved societies, that is exactly what is done.

But the problem is, not all people agree on these concepts, on what they mean. That's why we can't teach them in our schools. Parents go nuts when you try to introduce these things into the curriculum. They say you are teaching "values," and that the school has no place in such instruction.

They are wrong! Again, based on what you say as a race of people that you are trying to do—which is build a better world—they are *wrong*. Schools are *exactly* the place for such instruction. Precisely *because* schools are detached from parents' prejudices. Precisely *because* schools are separated from parents' preconceived notions. You've *seen* what has resulted on your planet from the passing down of values from parent to child. Your planet is a *mess*.

You don't understand the most basic concepts of civilized societies.

You don't know how to solve conflict without violence.

You don't know how to live without fear.

You don't know how to act without self interest.

You don't know how to love without condition.

These are basic—*basic*—understandings, and you have not even begun to approach a full comprehension of them, much less implement them . . . after *thousands and thousands of years.*

Is there any way out of this mess?

Yes! It is in your schools! It is in the education of your young! Your hope is in the next generation, and the next! But you must stop immersing them in the ways of the *past*. Those ways have not worked. They have not taken you where you say you want to go. Yet if you are not careful, you are going to get exactly where you are headed!

So *stop!* Turn around! Sit down together and collect your thoughts. Create the grandest version of the greatest vision you ever had about yourselves as a human race. Then, take the values and concepts which undergird such a vision and *teach them in your schools.*

Why not courses such as . . .

• Understanding Power
• Peaceful Conflict Resolution
• Elements of Loving Relationships
• Personhood and Self Creation

- Body, Mind and Spirit: How They Function
- Engaging Creativity
- Celebrating Self, Valuing Others
- Joyous Sexual Expression
- Fairness
- Tolerance
- Diversities and Similarities
- Ethical Economics
- Creative Consciousness and Mind Power
- Awareness and Wakefulness
- Honesty and Responsibility
- Visibility and Transparency
- Science and Spirituality

Much of this *is* taught right now. We call it Social Studies.

I am not talking about a 2-day unit in a semester-long course. I am talking about *separate courses* on each of these things. I am talking about a complete revision of your schools' curricula. I am speaking of a values-based curriculum. You are now teaching what is largely a facts-based curriculum.

I am talking about focusing your children's attention as much on understanding the core concepts and the theoretical structures around which their value system may be constructed as you now do on dates and facts and statistics.

In the highly evolved societies of your galaxy and your universe (which societies we will be talking about much more specifically in *Book 3*), concepts for living are taught to offspring beginning at a very early age. What you call "facts," which in those societies are considered far less important, are taught at a much later age.

On your planet you have created a society in which little Johnnie has learned how to read before getting out of pre-school, but still hasn't learned how to stop biting his brother. And Susie has perfected her multiplication tables, using flash cards and rote memory, in ever earlier and earlier grades, but has not learned that there is nothing shameful or embarrassing about her body.

Right now your schools exist primarily to provide answers. It would be far more beneficial if their primary function was to ask questions. What does it mean to be honest, or responsible, or "fair"? What are the implications? For that matter, what does it mean that $2+2=4$? What are the implications? Highly evolved societies encourage all children to *discover and create those answers for themselves.*

But . . . but, that would lead to *chaos!*

As opposed to the non-chaotic conditions under which you now live your life. . . .

Okay, okay . . . so it would lead to *more* chaos.

I am not suggesting that your schools never share with your offspring any of the things which you have learned or decided about these things. Quite to the contrary. Schools serve their students when they share with Young Ones what Elders have learned and discovered, decided and chosen in the past. Students may then observe how all this has worked. In your schools, however, you present these data to the student as That Which Is Right, when the data really should be offered as simply that: data.

Past Data should not be the basis of Present Truth. Data from a prior time or experience should always and only be the basis for new questions. Always the treasure should be in the question, not in the answer.

And always the questions are the same. With regard to this past data which we have shown you, do you agree, or do you disagree? What do you think? Always, this is the key question. Always this is the focus. What do you think? What do *you* think? *What do you think?*

Now obviously children will bring to this question the values of their parents. Parents will continue to have a strong role—obviously the primary role—in creating the child's system of values. The school's intention and purpose would be to encourage offspring, from the earliest age until the end of formal education, to explore those values, and to learn how to use them, apply them, functionalize them—and yes, even to question them. For parents who do not want children questioning their values are not parents who love their children, but rather, who love themselves *through* their children.

I wish—oh, how I wish—that there were schools such as the ones you describe!

There are some which seek to approach this model.

There are?

Yes. Read the writings of the man called Rudolph Steiner. Explore the methods of The Waldorf School, which he developed.

Well, of course, I know about those schools. Is this a commercial?

This is an observation.

Because you knew I was familiar with the Waldorf Schools. You knew that.

Of course I knew that. Everything in your life has served you, brought you to this moment. I have not just started talking with you at the beginning of this book. I have been talking with you for years, through all of your associations and experiences.

You're saying the Waldorf School is the best?

No. I am saying it is a model which works, given where you say as a human race you want to go; given what you claim you want to do; given what you say you want to be. I am saying it is an example—one of several I could cite, although on your planet and in your society they are rare—of how education may be accomplished in a way which focuses on "wisdom" more than simply "knowledge."

Well, it is a model I very much approve of. There are many differences between a Waldorf School and other schools. Let me give an example. It is a simple one, but it dramatically illustrates the point.

In the Waldorf School, the teacher moves with the children through all levels of the primary and elementary learning experience. For all those years the children have the same teacher, rather than moving from one person to another. Can you imagine the bond which is formed here? Can you see the value?

The teacher comes to know the child as if it were his or her own. The child moves to a level of trust and love with the teacher which opens doors many traditionally oriented schools never dreamed existed. At the end of those years, the teacher reverts to the first grade, starting over again with another group of children and moving through all the years of the curriculum. A dedicated Waldorf teacher may wind up working with only four or five groups of children in an entire career. But he or she has meant something to those children beyond anything that is possible in a traditional school setting.

This educational model recognizes and announces that the *human relationship*, the *bonding* and the *love* which is shared in such a paradigm is just as important as any *facts* the teacher may impart to the child. It is like home schooling, outside the home.

Yes, it is a good model.

There are other good models?

Yes. You are making some progress on your planet with regard to education, but it is very slow. Even the attempt to place a goals oriented, skill-development-focused curriculum in public schools has met with enormous resistance. People see it as threatening, or ineffective. They want children to learn *facts*. Still, there are some inroads. Yet there is much to be done.

And that is only one area of the human experience which could use some overhauling, given what you say as human beings that you are seeking to be.

Yes, I should imagine the political arena could use some changes, too.

To be sure.

10

I've been waiting for this. This is more of what I assumed You were promising me when You told me that *Book 2* would deal with planetary issues on a global scale. So, can we begin our look at our human politics by my asking you what may seem like an elementary question?

> No questions are undeserving or unworthy. Questions are like people.

Ah, good one. Okay then, let me ask: is it wrong to undertake a foreign policy based on your country's own vested interests?

> No. First, from My standpoint, *nothing* is "wrong." But I understand how you use the term, so I will speak within the context of your vocabulary. I'll use the term "wrong" to mean "that which is not serving you, given who and what you choose to be." This is how I've always used the terms "right" and "wrong" with you; it is always within this context, for, in truth, there is no Right and Wrong.
>
> So, within that context, no, it is not wrong to base foreign policy decisions on vested interest considerations. What is wrong is to pretend that you're not doing so.
>
> This most countries do, of course. They take action—or *fail* to take action—for one set of reasons, then give as a rationale another set of reasons.

Why? Why do countries do that?

> Because governments know that if people understood the real reasons for most foreign policy decisions, the people would not support them.
>
> This is true of governments everywhere. There are very few governments which do not deliberately mislead their people. Deception is part of government, for few people would choose to be governed the way they are governed—few would choose to be

306

governed at all—unless government convinced them that its decisions were for their own good.

This is a hard convincing, for most people plainly see the foolishness in government. So government must lie to at least try to hold the people's loyalty. Government is the perfect portrayer of the accuracy of the axiom that if you lie big enough, long enough, the lie becomes the "truth."

People in power must never let the public know how they came to power—nor all that they've done and are willing to do to stay there.

Truth and politics do not and *cannot* mix because politics is the *art* of saying only what needs to be said—and saying it in just the right way—in order to achieve a desired end.

Not all politics are bad, but the art of politics is a *practical* art. It recognizes with great candor the psychology of most people. It simply notices that most people operate out of self-interest. So politics is the way that people of power seek to convince you that *their* self-interest is *your own*.

Governments understand self-interest. That is why governments are very good at designing programs which *give* things to people.

Originally, governments had very limited functions. Their purpose was simply to "preserve and protect." Then someone added "provide." When governments began to be the people's *provider* as well as the people's protector, governments started *creating* society, rather than preserving it.

But aren't governments simply doing what the people want? Don't governments merely provide the mechanism through which the people provide for themselves on a societal scale? For instance, in America we place a very high value on the dignity of human life, individual freedom, the importance of opportunity, the sanctity of children. So we've made laws and asked government to create programs to provide income for the elderly, so they can retain their dignity past their earning years; to ensure equal employment and housing opportunities for all people— even those who are different from us, or with whose lifestyle we don't agree; to guarantee, through child labor laws, that a nation's children don't become a nation's slaves, and that no family with children goes without the basics of a life with dignity—food, clothing, shelter.

Such laws reflect well upon your society. Yet, in providing for people's needs, you must be careful not to rob them of their greatest dignity: the exercise of personal power, individual creativity, and the single-minded ingenuity which allows people to notice that they can provide for themselves. It is a delicate balance which must be struck. You people seem to know only how to go from one extreme to the other. Either you want government to "do it all" for the people, or you want to kill all government programs and erase all government laws tomorrow.

Yes, and the problem is that there are so many who *can't* provide for themselves in a society which gives the best life opportunities routinely to those holding the "right" credentials (or, perhaps, not holding the "wrong" ones); who *can't* provide for themselves in a nation where landlords won't rent to large families, companies won't promote women, justice is too often a product of status, access to preventive health care is limited to those with sufficient income, and where many other discriminations and inequalities exist on a massive scale.

Governments, then, must replace the conscience of the people?

No. Governments *are* the people's conscience, outspoken. It is through governments that people seek, hope, and determine to correct the ills of society.

That is well said. Yet, I repeat, you must take care not to smother yourself in laws trying to guarantee people a chance to breathe! You cannot legislate morality. You cannot mandate equality.

What is needed is a *shift* of collective consciousness, not an *enforcer* of collective conscience.

Behavior (and all laws, and all government programs) must spring from Beingness, must be a true reflection of Who You *Are*.

The laws of our society *do* reflect who we are! They say to everyone, "This is how it *is* here in America. This is who Americans *are*."

In the best of cases, perhaps. But more often than not, your laws are the announcements of what those in *power* think you *should* be but are not.

The "elitist few" instruct the "ignorant many" through the law.

Precisely.

What's wrong with that? If there are a few of the brightest and best among us willing to look at the problems of society, of the world, and propose solutions, does that not serve the many?

> It depends on the motives of those few. And on their clarity. Generally, nothing serves "the many" more than letting them govern themselves.

Anarchy. It's never worked.

> You cannot grow and become great when you are constantly being told what to do by government.

It could be argued that government—by that I mean the law by which we've chosen to govern ourselves—is a reflection of society's greatness (or lack thereof), that great societies pass great laws.

> And very few of them. For in great societies, very few laws are *necessary*.

Still, truly lawless societies are primitive societies, where "might is right." Laws are man's attempt to level the playing field; to ensure that what is truly right will prevail, weakness or strength notwithstanding. Without codes of behavior upon which we mutually agree, how could we coexist?

> I am not suggesting a world with no codes of behavior, no agreements. I am suggesting that your agreements and codes be based on a higher understanding and a grander definition of self-interest.
>
> What most laws actually *do* say is what the most powerful among you have as their vested interest.
>
> Let's just look at one example. Smoking.
>
> Now the law says you cannot grow and use a certain kind of plant, hemp, because, so government tells you, it is not good for you.
>
> Yet the same government says it is all right to grow and use *another* kind of plant, tobacco, not because *it* is good for you (indeed, the government itself says it is *bad*), but, presumably, because you've always done so.
>
> The real reason that the first plant is outlawed and the second is not has nothing to do with health. It has to do with economics. And that is to say, *power*.

Your laws, therefore, do *not* reflect what your society thinks of itself, and wishes to be—your laws reflect *where the power is.*

No fair. You picked a situation where the contradictions are apparent. Most situations are not like that.

On the contrary. Most *are.*

Then what is the solution?

To have as few laws—which are really limits—as possible.

The reason the first weed is outlawed is only *ostensibly* about health. The *truth* is, the first weed is no more addictive and no more a health risk than cigarettes or alcohol, both of which are *protected* by the law. Why is it then not allowed? Because if it were grown, half the cotton growers, nylon and rayon manufacturers, and timber products people in the world would go out of business.

Hemp happens to be one of the most useful, strongest, toughest, longest-lasting materials on your planet. You cannot produce a better fiber for clothes, a stronger substance for ropes, an easier-to-grow-and-harvest source for pulp. You cut down hundreds of thousands of trees per year to give yourself Sunday papers, so that you can read about the decimation of the world's forests. Hemp could provide you with millions of Sunday papers without cutting down one tree. Indeed, it could substitute for so many resource materials, at one-tenth the cost.

And *that is the catch.* Somebody *loses money* if this miraculous plant—which also has extraordinary medicinal properties, incidentally—is allowed to be grown. And *that* is why marijuana is illegal in your country.

It is the same reason you have taken so long to mass produce electric cars, provide affordable, sensible health care, or use solar heat and solar power in every home.

You've had the wherewithal and the technology to produce *all* of these things for *years.* Why, then, do you not have them? *Look to see who would lose money if you did.* There you will find your answer.

This is the Great Society of which you are so proud? Your "great society" has to be dragged, kicking and screaming, to consider the common good. Whenever common good or collective good is mentioned, everyone yells "communism!" In your society, if providing

for the good of the many does not produce a huge profit for someone, the *good of the many is more often than not ignored.*

This is true not only in your country, but also around the world.
The basic question facing humankind, therefore, is: Can self-interest ever be replaced by the best interests, the *common* interest, of
humankind? If so, how?

In the United States you have tried to provide for the common
interest, the best interest, through laws. You have failed miserably.
Your nation is the richest, most powerful on the Earth, and it has
one of the highest infant mortality rates. Why? Because *poor people* cannot *afford* quality pre-natal and post-natal care—and your
society is *profit driven.* I cite this as just one example of your miserable failure. The fact that your babies are dying at a higher rate
than most other industrialized nations in the world should bother
you. It does not. That says volumes about where your priorities are
as a society. Other countries provide for the sick and needy, the
elderly and infirm. You provide for the rich and wealthy, the influential and the well-placed. Eighty-five percent of retired Americans
live in poverty. Many of these older Americans, and most people
on low income, use the local hospital emergency room as their
"family doctor," seeking medical treatment under only the most
dire of circumstances, and receiving virtually no preventive health
maintenance care at all.

There's no profit, you see, in people who have little to spend
. . . they've worn out their *usefulness* . . .

And this is your *great society—*

**You make things sound pretty bad. Yet America has done more for the
underprivileged and the unfortunate—both here and abroad—then any
other nation on Earth.**

America has done much, that is observably true. Yet do you
know that as a percentage of its gross national product, the United
States provides proportionately less for foreign aid than many much
smaller countries? The point is that, before you allow yourself to
become too self-congratulatory, perhaps you should look at the
world around you. For if this is the best your world can do for the
less fortunate, you all have much to learn.

You live in a wasteful, decadent society. You've built into virtually everything you make what your engineers call "planned
obsolescence." Cars cost three times as much and last a third as

long. Clothes fall apart after the tenth wearing. You put chemicals in your food so they can stay on the shelf longer, even if it means your stay on the planet is shorter. You support, encourage, and enable sports teams to pay obscene salaries for ridiculous efforts, while teachers, ministers, and researchers fighting to find a cure for the diseases which kill you go begging for money. You throw away more food each day in your nation's supermarkets, restaurants, and homes than it would take to feed half the world.

Yet this is not an indictment, merely an observation. And not of the United States alone, for the attitudes that sicken the heart are epidemic around the world.

The underprivileged everywhere must grovel and scrimp to merely stay alive, while the few in power protect *and* increase great hoards of cash, lie on sheets of silk, and each morning twist bathroom fixtures made of gold. And as emaciated children of ribs and skin die in the arms of weeping mothers, their country's "leaders" engage in political corruptions which keep donated food stuffs from reaching the starving masses.

No one seems to have the power to alter these conditions, yet the truth is, power is not the problem. No one seems to have the *will.*

And thus it will always be, so long as no one sees another's plight as his own.

Well, why *don't* we? How can we see these atrocities daily and allow them to continue?

Because you do not *care.* It is a lack of *caring.* The entire planet faces a crisis of consciousness. You must decide whether you simply *care for each other.*

It seems such a pathetic question to have to ask. Why can't we love the members of our own family?

You *do* love the members of your own family. You simply have a very limited view of who your family members *are.*

You do not consider yourself part of the human family, and so the problems of the human family are not your own.

How can the peoples of the Earth change their world view?

That depends on what you want to change it *to.*

How can we eliminate more of the pain, more of the suffering?

By eliminating all separations between you. By constructing a new model of the world. By holding it within the framework of a *new idea*.

Which is?

Which is going to be a radical departure from the present world view.

Presently, you see the world—we're speaking geopolitically now—as a collection of nation states, each sovereign, separate and independent of each other.

The internal problems of these independent nation states are, by and large, not considered the problems of the group as a whole—unless and until they *affect* the group as a whole (or the most powerful members of that group).

The group as a whole reacts to the conditions and problems of individual states based on the vested interests of the larger group. If no one in the larger group has anything to *lose*, conditions in an individual state could go to hell, and no one would much care.

Thousands can starve to death each year, hundreds can die in civil war, despots can pillage the countryside, dictators and their armed thugs can rape, plunder, and murder, regimes can strip the people of basic human rights—and the rest of you will do nothing. It is, you say, an "internal problem."

But, when *your* interests are threatened there, when *your* investments, *your* security, *your* quality of life is on the line, you rally your nation, and try to rally your world behind you, and rush in where angels fear to tread.

You then tell the Big Lie—claiming you are doing what you are doing for humanitarian reasons, to help the oppressed peoples of the world, when the truth is, you are simply protecting your own interests.

The proof of this is that where you do not *have* interests, you do not have concern.

The world's political machinery operates on self-interest. What else is new?

Something will have to be new if you wish your world to change. You must begin to see someone else's interests as your own. This will happen only when you reconstruct your global reality and govern yourselves accordingly.

Are you talking about a one-world government?

I am.

11

You promised that in *Book 2* You would get into larger geopolitical issues facing the planet (as opposed to the basically personal issues addressed in *Book 1*), but I didn't think You would enter into *this* debate!

> It is time for the world to stop kidding itself, to wake up, to realize that the *only problem of humanity* is lack of love.
>
> Love breeds tolerance, tolerance breeds peace. Intolerance produces war and looks indifferently upon intolerable conditions.
>
> Love cannot be indifferent. It does not know how.
>
> The fastest way to get to a place of love and concern for all humankind is to see all humankind as your *family*.
>
> The fastest way to see all humankind as your family is to *stop separating yourself*. Each of the nation states now making up your world must *unite*.

We do have the United Nations.

> Which has been powerless and impotent. In order for that body to work, it would have to be completely restructured. Not impossible, but perhaps difficult and cumbersome.

Okay—what do You propose?

> I don't have a "proposal." I merely offer observations. In this dialogue, you tell me what your new choices are, and I offer observations on ways to manifest that. What is it you now *choose* with regard to the current relationship between people and nations on your planet?

I'll use Your words. If I had my way, I would choose for us "to get to a place of love and concern for all humankind."

> Given that choice, I observe that what would work would be the formation of a new world political community, with each

315

nation state having an equal say in the world's affairs, and an equal proportionate share of the world's resources.

It'll never work. The "haves" will never surrender their sovereignty, wealth, and resources to the "have-nots." And, argumentatively, why should they?

Because it is *in their best interest.*

They don't see that—and I'm not sure I do.

If you could add billions of dollars a year to your nation's economy—dollars which could be spent to feed the hungry, clothe the needy, house the poor, bring security to the elderly, provide better health, and produce a dignified standard of living for all—wouldn't that be in your nation's best interest?

Well, in America there are those who would argue that it would help the poor at the expense of the rich and of the middle-income taxpayer. Meanwhile, the country continues to go to hell, crime ravages the nation, inflation robs the people of their life savings, unemployment skyrockets, the government grows bigger and fatter, and in school they're handing out condoms.

You sound like a radio talk show.

Well, these *are* the concerns of many Americans.

Then they are short-sighted. Do you not see that if billions of dollars a year—that's millions a month, hundreds and hundreds of thousands a week, unheard of amounts each *day*—could be sunk back into your system . . . that if you *could* use these monies to feed your hungry, clothe your needy, house your poor, bring security to your elderly, and provide health care and dignity to all . . . the *causes* of *crime* would be lost forever? Do you not see that new jobs would mushroom as dollars were pumped back into your economy? That your own government could even be reduced *because it would have less to do?*

I suppose some of that could happen—I can't imagine government *ever* getting smaller!—but just where are these millions and billions going to come from? Taxes imposed by Your new world government? More taking from those who've "worked to get it" to give to those who won't "stand upon their own two feet" and go after it?

> Is that how you frame it?

No, but it is how a great *many* people see it, and I wanted to fairly state their view.

> Well, I'd like to talk about that later. Right now I don't want to get off track—but I want to come back to that later.

Great.

> But you've asked where these new dollars would come from. Well, they would not have to come from any new taxes imposed by the new world community (although members of the community—individual citizens—would *want*, under an enlightened governance, to send 10 percent of their income to provide for society's needs as a whole). Nor would they come from new taxes imposed by any local government. In fact, some local governments would surely be able to reduce taxes.
>
> All of this—all of these benefits—would result from the simple restructuring of your world view, the simpler reordering of your world political configuration.

How?

> The money you save from building defense systems and attack weapons.

Oh, *I* get it! You want us to *close down the military!*

> Not just *you. Everybody* in the *world.*
>
> But not close *down* your military, simply reduce it—drastically. Internal order would be your only need. You could strengthen local police—something you say you want to do, but cry each year at budget time that you cannot do—at the same time dramatically reducing your spending on weapons of war and preparations for war; that is, offensive and defensive weapons of mass destruction.

First, I think Your figures exaggerate how much could be saved by doing that. Second, I don't think You'll ever convince people they should give up their ability to defend themselves.

Let's look at the numbers. Presently (it is March 25, 1994, as we write this) the world's governments spend about one trillion dollars a year for military purposes. That's a *million dollars a minute* worldwide.

The nations that are *spending* the most could *redirect* the most to the other priorities mentioned. So larger, richer nations *would* see it in their best interests to do so—*if* they thought it was possible. But larger, richer nations cannot imagine going defenseless, for they fear aggression and attack from the nations which envy them and *want what they have.*

There are two ways to eliminate this threat.

1. Share enough of the world's total wealth and resources with all of the world's people so that no one will want and need what someone else has, and everyone may live in dignity and remove themselves from fear.

2. Create a system for the resolution of differences that eliminates the need for war—and even the possibility *of* it.

The people of the world would probably never do this.

They already have.

They have?

Yes. There is a great experiment now going on in your world in just this sort of political order. That experiment is called the United States of America.

Which You said was failing miserably.

It is. It has very far to go before it could be called a success. (As I promised earlier, I'll talk about this—and the attitudes which are now preventing it—later.) Still, it is the best experiment going.

It is as Winston Churchill said. "Democracy is the worst system," he announced, "except all others."

Your nation was the first to take a loose confederation of individual states and successfully unite them into a cohesive group, each submitting to one central authority.

At the time, none of the states wanted to do this, and each resisted mightily, fearing the loss of its individual greatness and claiming that such a union would not serve its best interests.

It may be instructive to understand just what was going on with these individual states at that time.

While they had joined together in a loose confederation, there was no real U.S. Government, and hence no power to enforce the Articles of Confederation to which the states had agreed.

States were conducting their own foreign affairs, several reaching private agreements on trade and other matters with France, Spain, England, and other countries. States traded with each other as well, and although their Articles of Confederation forbade it, some states added tariffs to the goods shipped in from other states—just as they did for goods from across the ocean! Merchants had no choice but to pay at the harbor if they wanted to buy or sell their goods, there being no central *authority*—although there was a written *agreement* to prohibit such taxing.

The individual states also fought wars with each other. Each state considered its militia a standing army, nine states had their own navies, and "Don't tread on me" could have been the official motto of every state in the Confederation.

Over half of the states were even printing their own money. (Although the Confederation had agreed that doing so would also be illegal!)

In short, your original states, though joined together under the *Articles* of Confederation, were acting *exactly as independent nations do today.*

Although they could see that the agreements of their Confederation (such as the granting to Congress the sole authority to coin money) were not working, they staunchly resisted creating and submitting to a central authority that could *enforce* these agreements and put some teeth into them.

Yet, in time, a few progressive leaders began to prevail. They convinced the rank and file that there was more to be *gained* by creating such a new Federation than they would ever lose.

Merchants would save money and increase profits because individual states could no longer tax each other's goods.

Governments would save money and have more to put into programs and services that truly helped *people* because resources would not have to be used to protect individual states from each other.

The people would have greater security and safety, and greater prosperity, too, by cooperating with, rather than fighting with, each other.

Far from losing their greatness, each state could become greater still.

And that, of course, is exactly what has happened.

The same could be made to happen with the 160 nation states in the world today if *they* were to join together in a United Federation. It could mean an end to war.

How so? There would still be disagreements.

So long as humans remain attached to outer things, that is true. There is a way to truly eliminate war—and *all* experience of unrest and lack of peace—but that is a spiritual solution. We are here exploring a geopolitical one.

Actually, the trick is to *combine the two*. Spiritual truth must be lived in practical life to change everyday experience.

Until this change occurs, there *would* still be disagreements. You are right. Yet there need not be wars. There need not be killing.

Are there wars between California and Oregon over water rights? Between Maryland and Virginia over fishing? Between Wisconsin and Illinois, Ohio and Massachusetts?

No.

And why not? Have not various disputes and differences arisen between them?

Through the years, I suppose so.

You can bet on it. But these individual states have voluntarily agreed—it was a simple, *voluntary agreement*—to abide by certain laws and abide by certain compromises on matters common to them, while retaining the right to pass separate statutes on matters relating to each individually.

And when disputes between states *do* arise, due to differing interpretations of the federal law—or someone simply breaking that law—the matter is taken to a court . . . which has been *granted the authority* (that is, *given the authority by the states*) to resolve the dispute.

And, if the current body of law does not provide a precedent or a means by which the matter can be brought through the courts to a *satisfactory* resolution, the states and the people in them send their representatives to a central government to try to create agreement on *new* laws that *will* produce a satisfactory circumstance— or, at the very least, a reasonable compromise.

This is how your federation *works*. A system of laws, a system of courts *empowered* by you to interpret those laws, and a Justice system—backed by armed might, if needed—to enforce the decisions of those courts.

Although no one could argue that the system doesn't need improving, this political concoction has worked for more than 200 years!

There is no reason to doubt that *the same recipe will work between nation states as well.*

If this is so simple, why hasn't it been tried?

It *has*. Your League of Nations was an early attempt. The United Nations is the latest.

Yet one failed and the other has been only minimally effective because—like the 13 States of America's original Confederation—the member nation states (particularly the most powerful) are afraid they have *more to lose than to gain* from the reconfiguration.

That is because the "people of power" are more concerned with holding on to their power than with improving the quality of life for *all* people. The "Haves" *know* that such a World Federation would inevitably produce more for the "have-nots"—but the "haves" believe this would come at *their expense* . . . and they're giving up nothing.

Isn't their fear justified—and is wanting to hold on to what you have so long struggled for unreasonable?

First, it is *not* necessarily true that, to give more to those who now hunger and thirst and live without shelter, others must give up their abundance.

As I have pointed out, all you would have to do is take the $1,000,000,000,000 a year spent annually worldwide for military purposes and shift that to humanitarian purposes, and you will have solved the problem without spending an additional penny or shifting *any* of the wealth from where it now resides to where it does not.

(Of course, it could be argued that those international conglomerates whose profits come from war and tools for war would be "losers"—as would their employees and *all* those whose abundance is derived from the world's conflict consciousness—but perhaps your source of abundance is misplaced. If one has to *depend* on the world living in strife in order for one to survive, perhaps this dependence explains why your world resists *any* attempt to create a structure for lasting peace.)

As for the second part of your question, wanting to hold on to what you have struggled so long to acquire, as an individual or as a nation, is not unreasonable, if you come from an Outside World consciousness.

A what?

If you derive your life's greatest happiness from experiences obtainable only in the Outside World—the physical world outside of yourself—you will *never* want to give up an *ounce* of all that you've piled up, as a person and a nation, to make you happy.

And as long as those who "have not" see their *un*happiness tied to the *lack* of material things, they, too, will get caught in the trap. They will constantly want what you have got, and you will constantly refuse to share it.

That is why I said earlier that there is a way to truly eliminate war—and *all* experience of unrest and lack of peace. But this is a *spiritual* solution.

Ultimately, every geopolitical problem, just as every personal problem, breaks down to a spiritual problem.

All of *life* is spiritual, and therefore all of life's problems are spiritually based—and *spiritually solved.*

Wars are created on your planet because somebody has something that somebody else wants. This is what *causes* someone to *do* something that somebody *else* does not want them to do.

All conflict arises from misplaced desire.

The only peace in all the world that is sustaining is Internal Peace.

Let each person find peace within. When you find peace within, you also find that you can do without.

This means simply that you no longer need the things of your outside world. "Not needing" is a great freedom. It frees you, first, from fear: fear that there is something you won't have; fear that there is something you have that you will lose; and fear that without a certain thing, you won't be happy.

Secondly, "not needing" frees you from anger. *Anger is fear announced.* When you have nothing to fear, you have nothing over which to be angry.

You are not angry when you don't get what you want, because your wanting it was simply a preference, not a necessity. You therefore have no fear associated with the possibility of not getting it. Hence, no anger.

You are not angry when you see others doing what you don't want them to do, because you don't *need* them to do or not do *any* particular thing. Hence, no anger.

You are not angry when someone is unkind, because you have no *need* for them to be kind. You have no anger when someone is unloving, because you have no *need* for them to love you. You have no anger when someone is cruel, or hurtful, or seeks to damage you, for you have no *need* for them to behave any other way, and you are clear that you cannot be damaged.

You do not even have anger should someone seek to take your life, because you do not fear death.

When fear is taken from you, all else can be taken from you and you will not be angry.

You know inwardly, intuitively, that everything you've created can be created again, or—more importantly—that it doesn't matter.

When you find Inner Peace, neither the presence nor the absence of any person, place or thing, condition, circumstance, or situation can be the Creator of your state of mind or the cause of your experience of being.

This does not mean that you reject all things of the body. Far from it. You experience being fully in your body and the *delights* of that, as you never have before.

Yet your involvement with things of the body will be voluntary, not mandatory. You will experience bodily sensations because you *choose* to, not because your are *required* to in order to feel happy or to justify sadness.

This one simple change—seeking and finding peace within—could, were it undertaken by everyone, end all wars, eliminate conflict, prevent injustice, and bring the world to everlasting peace.

There is no other formula necessary, or *possible*. World peace is a personal thing!

What is needed is not a change of circumstance, but a change of consciousness.

How can we find inner peace when we are hungry? Be at a place of serenity when we thirst? Remain calm when we are wet and cold and without shelter? Or avoid anger when our loved ones are dying without cause?

You speak so poetically, but is poetry practical? Does it have anything to say to the mother in Ethiopia who watches her emaciated child die for lack of one slice of bread? The man in Central America who feels a bullet rip his body because he tried to stop an army from taking over his village? And what does your poetry say to the woman in Brooklyn raped eight times by a gang? Or the family of six in Ireland blown away by a terrorist bomb planted in a church on a Sunday morning?

This is difficult to hear, but I tell you this: There is perfection in everything. Strive to see the perfection. This is the change of consciousness of which I speak.

Need nothing. Desire everything. Choose what shows up.

Feel your feelings. Cry your cries. Laugh your laughs. Honor your truth. Yet when all the emotion is done, be still and know that I am God.

In other words, in the midst of the greatest tragedy, see the glory of the process. Even as you die with a bullet through your chest, even as you are being gang-raped.

Now this sounds like such an impossible thing to do. Yet when you move to God consciousness, you can do it.

You don't *have* to do it, of course. It depends on how you wish to experience the moment.

In a moment of great tragedy, the challenge always is to quiet the mind and move deep within the soul.

You automatically do this when you have no control over it.

Have you ever talked with a person who accidentally ran a car off a bridge? Or found himself facing a gun? Or nearly drowned? Often they will tell you that time slowed way down, that they were overcome by a curious calm, that there was no fear at all.

"Fear not, for I am with you." That is what poetry has to say to the person facing tragedy. In your darkest hour, I will be your light. In your blackest moment, I will be your consolation. In your most difficult and trying time, I will be your strength. Therefore, have faith! For I am your shepherd; you shall not want. I will cause you to lie down in green pastures; I will lead you beside still waters.

I will restore your soul, and lead you in the paths of righteousness for My Name's sake.

And yea, though you walk through the valley of the Shadow of Death, you will fear *no* evil; for I am with you. My rod and My staff *will* comfort you.

I am preparing a table before you in the presence of your enemies. I shall anoint your head with oil. Your cup will run over.

Surely, goodness and mercy will follow you all the days of your
life, and you will dwell in My house—and in My heart—forever.

12

That's wonderful. What You said there is just wonderful. I wish the world could get that. I wish the world could understand, could believe.

> This book will help that. You are helping that. So you are playing a role, you are doing your part, in raising the Collective Consciousness. That is what all must do.

Yes.

Can we move to a new subject now? I think it's important that we talk about this attitude—this idea of things—which You said a while back that You wanted to fairly present.

The attitude to which I am referring is this attitude, held by many people, that the poor have been given enough; that we must stop taxing the rich—penalizing them, in effect, for working hard and "making it"—to provide even more for the poor.

These people believe that the poor are poor basically because they want to be. Many don't even attempt to pull themselves up. They would rather suckle at the government teat than assume responsibility for themselves.

There are many people who believe that redistribution of the wealth—sharing—is a socialistic evil. They cite the Communist Manifesto—"from each according to his ability, to each according to his need"—as evidence of the satanic origin of the idea of ensuring the basic human dignity of all through the efforts of everyone.

These people believe in "every man for himself." If they are told that this concept is cold and heartless, they take refuge in the statement that opportunity knocks at the door of everyone equally; they claim that no man operates under an inherent disadvantage; that if *they* could "make it," *everybody can*—and if someone doesn't, "it's his own damn fault."

> You feel that is an arrogant thought, rooted in ungratefulness.

Yes. But what do You feel?

I have no judgment in the matter. It is simply a thought. There is only one question of any relevance regarding this or any other thought. Does it serve you to hold that? In terms of Who You Are and Who You seek to Be, does that thought serve you?

Looking at the world, that is the question people have to ask. Does it serve us to hold this thought?

I observe this: There *are* people—indeed, entire *groups* of people—who have been *born into* what you call disadvantage. This is observably true.

It is also true that at a very high metaphysical level, no one is "disadvantaged," for each soul creates for itself the exact people, events, and circumstances needed to accomplish what It wishes to accomplish.

You choose everything. Your parents. Your country of birth. All the circumstances surrounding your re-entry.

Similarly, throughout the days and times of your life you continue to choose and to create people, events, and circumstances designed to bring you the exact, right, and perfect opportunities you now desire in order to know yourself as you *truly are*.

In other words, no one is "disadvantaged," given what the *soul* wishes to accomplish. For example, the soul may *wish* to work with a handicapped body or in a repressive society or under enormous political or economic constraints, in order to produce the conditions needed to accomplish what it has set out to do.

So we see that people *do* face "disadvantages" in the *physical* sense, but that these are actually the right and perfect conditions *metaphysically*.

As a practical matter, what does that mean to us? Should we offer help to the "disadvantaged," or simply see that, in truth, they are just where they *want* to be and thus allow them to "work out their own Karma"?

That's a very good—and a very important—question.

Remember first that everything you think, say, and do is a reflection of what you've decided about yourself; a statement of Who You Are; an act of *creation* in your deciding who you want to be. I keep returning to that, because that is the only thing you are doing here; that is what you are up to. There is nothing else going on, no other agenda for the soul. You are seeking to be and to experience Who You Really Are—and to create that. You are creating yourself anew in every moment of Now.

Now, within that context, when you come across a person who appears, in relative terms as observed within your world, to be disadvantaged, the first question you have to ask is: Who am I and who do I choose to *be*, in relationship to that?

In other words, the first question when you encounter another in *any* circumstance should always be: What do I want here?

Did you hear that? Your first question, always, must be: What do I want here?—not: What does the other person want here?

That's the most fascinating insight I have ever received about the way to proceed in human relationships. It also runs against everything I've ever been taught.

I know. But the reason your relationships are in such a mess is that you're always trying to figure out what the other person wants and what other *people* want—instead of what *you* truly want. Then you have to decide whether to *give* it to them. And here is how you decide: You decide by taking a look at what you may want from *them*. If there's nothing you think you'll want from them, your first reason for giving them what they want disappears, and so you very seldom do. If, on the other hand, you see that there is something you want or may want from them, then your self-survival mode kicks in, and you try to give them what they want.

Then you resent it—especially if the other person doesn't eventually give you what *you* want.

In this game of *I'll Trade You,* you set up a very delicate balance. You meet my needs and I'll meet yours.

Yet the purpose of all human relationships—relationships between nations as well as relationships between individuals—has nothing to do with any of this. The purpose of your Holy Relationship with every other person, place, or thing is not to figure out what *they* want or need, but what *you* require or desire now in order to *grow,* in order to be Who you *want* to Be.

That is why I *created* Relationship to other things. If it weren't for this, you could have continued to live in a *vacuum,* a void, the Eternal Allness whence you came.

Yet in the Allness you simply *are* and cannot *experience* your "awareness" as *anything in particular* because, in the Allness, there is *nothing you are not.*

So I devised a way for you to create anew, and *Know,* Who You Are *in your experience.* I did this by providing you with:

1. Relativity—a system wherein you could exist as a thing in relationship to something else.

2. Forgetfulness—a process by which you willingly submit to total amnesia, so that you can *not know* that relativity is merely a trick, and that you are All of It.

3. Consciousness—a state of Being in which you grow until you reach full awareness, then becoming a True and Living God, creating and experiencing your own reality, expanding and exploring that reality, changing and *re*-creating that reality as you stretch your consciousness to new limits—or shall we say, to *no limit*.

In this paradigm, *Consciousness is everything*.

Consciousness—that of which you are truly aware—is the basis of all truth and thus of all true spirituality.

But what is the point of it all? First You make us *forget* Who We Are, so that we can remember Who We Are?

Not quite. So that you can *create* Who You Are and Who You *Want to Be*.

This is the act of God being God. It is Me being Me—through *you!*

This is the point of all life.

Through you, I *experience* being Who and What I Am.

Without you, I could know it, but not experience it.

Knowing and experiencing are two different things. I'll choose experiencing every time.

Indeed, I *do*. Through *you*.

I seem to have lost the original question here.

Well, it's hard to keep God on one subject. I'm kind of expansive.

Let's see if we can get back.

Oh, yes—what to do about the less fortunate.

First, decide Who and What You Are in Relationship to them.

Second, if you decide you wish to experience yourself as being Succor, as being Help, as being Love and Compassion and Caring, then look to see how you can *best be those things*.

And notice that your ability to be those things *has nothing to do with what others are being or doing*.

Sometimes the best way to love someone, and the most help you can give, is to *leave them alone* or empower them to help themselves.

It is like a feast. Life is a smorgasbord, and you can give them a *big helping* of *themselves*.

Remember that the greatest help you can give a person is to *wake them up*, to remind them of Who They Really Are. There are many ways to do this. Sometimes with a little bit of help; a push, a shove, a nudge . . . and sometimes with a decision to let them run their course, follow their path, walk their walk, without any inter- ference or intervention from you. (All parents know about this choice and agonize over it daily.)

What you have the opportunity to do for the less fortunate is to re-*mind* them. That is, cause them to be of a New Mind about themselves.

And you, too, have to be of a New Mind about them, for if *you* see them as unfortunate, *they* will.

Jesus' great gift was that he saw everyone as who they truly are. He refused to accept appearances; he refused to believe what oth- ers believed of themselves. He always had a higher thought, and he always invited others *to* it.

Yet he also honored where others chose to be. He did not require them to accept his higher idea, merely held it out as an invitation.

He dealt, too, with compassion—and if others chose to see themselves as Beings needing assistance, he did not reject them for their faulty assessment, but allowed them to love their Reality— and lovingly assisted them in playing out their choice.

For Jesus knew that for some the fastest path to Who They Are was the path *through* Who They Are Not.

He did not call this an imperfect path and thus condemn it. Rather he saw this, *too*, as "perfect"—and thus supported everyone in being just who they wanted to be.

Anyone, therefore, who asked Jesus for help received it.

He denied no one—but was always careful to see that the help he gave supported a person's full and honest desire.

If others genuinely sought enlightenment, honestly expressing readiness to move to the next level, Jesus gave them the strength, the courage, the wisdom to do so. He held himself out—and right- ly so—as an example and encouraged people, if they could do nothing else, to have faith in *him*. He would not, he said, lead them astray.

Many did put their faith in him—and to this day he helps those who call upon his name. For his soul is committed to waking up those who seek to be fully awake and fully alive in Me.

Yet Christ had *mercy* on those who did not. He therefore rejected self-righteousness and—as does his Father in heaven—made no judgments, ever.

Jesus' idea of Perfect Love was to grant all persons exactly the help they requested, after telling them the kind of help they could *get*.

He never refused to help anyone, and least of all would he do so out of a thought that "you made your bed, now lie in it."

Jesus knew that if he gave people the help they asked for, rather than merely the help he wanted to give, that he was empowering them *at the level at which they were ready to receive empowerment.*

This is the way of all great masters. Those who have walked your planet in the past, and those who are walking it now.

Now I am confused. When is it *dis*empowering to offer help? When does it work against, rather than for, another's growth?

When your help is offered in such a way that it creates continued dependence, rather than rapid independence.

When you allow another, in the name of compassion, to begin to rely on you rather than rely on themselves.

That is not compassion, that is compulsion. You have a power compulsion. Because that sort of helping is really power-tripping. Now this distinction can be very subtle here, and sometimes you don't even know you are power-tripping. You really believe you are simply doing your best to help another . . . yet be careful that you are not simply seeking to create your own self-worth. For to the extent that you allow other persons to make you responsible for them, to that extent you have allowed them to make you powerful. And that, of course, makes you feel worthy.

Yet this kind of help *is an aphrodisiac which seduces the weak.*

The goal is to help the weak grow strong, not to let the weak become weaker.

This is the problem with many government assistance programs, for they often do the latter, rather than the former. Government programs can be self-perpetuating. Their objective can be every bit as much to justify their existence as to help those they are meant to assist.

If there were a limit to all government assistance, people would be helped when they genuinely need help but could not become addicted to that help, substituting *it* for their own self-reliance.

Governments understand that help is power. That is why governments offer as much help to as many people as they can get away with—for the more people government helps, the more people help the government.

Whom the government supports, supports the government.

Then there *should* be no redistribution of wealth. The Communist Manifesto *is* satanic.

Of course, there *is* no Satan, but I understand your meaning.

The idea behind the statement "From each according to his ability, to each according to his need" is not evil, it is beautiful. It is simply another way of saying you are your brother's keeper. It is the implementation of this beautiful idea that can become ugly.

Sharing must be a way of life, not an edict imposed by government. Sharing should be voluntary, not forced.

But—here we go again!—at its best, government *is the people*, and its programs are simply mechanisms by which the people share with many others, as a "way of life." And I would argue that people, collectively through their political systems, have chosen to do so because people have observed, and history has shown, that the "haves" do *not* share with the "have-nots."

The Russian peasant could have waited until hell froze over for the Russian nobility to share its wealth—which was usually gained and enlarged through the hard work of peasants. The peasants were given just enough to subsist on, as the "incentive" to keep working the land—and make the land barons richer. Talk about a *dependency relationship!* This was an I'll-help-you-only-if-you-help-me arrangement more exploitive and more obscene than anything *ever* invented by government!

It was this obscenity against which the Russian peasants revolted. A government which ensured that all people were treated equally was born out of the people's frustration that the "haves" would *not* give to the "have-nots" *of their own accord.*

It was as Marie Antoinette said of the starving masses clamoring beneath her window in rags, while she lounged in a gold inlaid tub on a bejeweled pedestal, munching imported grapes: "Let them eat cake!"

This is the attitude against which the downtrodden have railed. This is the condition causing revolution and creating governments of so-called oppression.

Governments which take from the rich and give to the poor are called oppressive, while governments which do nothing while the rich *exploit* the poor are repressive.

Ask the peasants of Mexico even today. It is said that twenty or thirty families—the rich and powerful elite—literally *run* Mexico (principally because they *own* it!), while twenty or thirty *million* live in utter deprivation. So the peasants in 1993-94 undertook a revolt, seeking to force the elitist government to recognize its duty to help the people provide the means for a life of at least meager dignity. There is a difference between elistist governments and governments "of, by, and for the people."

Are not people's governments created by angry people frustrated over the basic selfishness of human nature? Are not government programs created as a remedy for man's unwillingness to provide a remedy himself?

Is this not the genesis of fair housing laws, child labor statutes, support programs for mothers with dependent children?

Wasn't Social Security government's attempt to provide for older people something that their own families would not or could not provide?

How do we reconcile our hatred of government control with our lack of willingness to do anything we don't *have* to do when there *are* no controls?

It is said that some coal miners worked under *horrible* conditions before governments required the filthy rich mine owners to clean up their filthy mines. Why didn't the owners do so themselves? Because it would have cut into their *profits!* And the rich didn't care how many of the poor *died* in unsafe mines to keep the profits flowing—and growing.

Businesses paid *slave* wages to beginning workers before governments imposed minimum wage requirements. Those who favor going back to the "good old days" say, "So what? They provided *jobs*, didn't they? And who's taking the *risk*, anyway? The worker? No! The *investor*, the *owner*, takes all the risks! So to him should go the biggest reward!"

Anyone who thinks that the workers on whose labors the owners depend should be treated with dignity is called a *communist*.

Anyone who thinks that a person should not be denied housing because of skin color is called a *socialist*.

Anyone who thinks that a woman should not be denied employment opportunities or promotion simply because she's the wrong sex is called a *radical feminist.*

And when governments, through their elected representatives, move to solve these problems that people of power in society steadfastly refuse to solve themselves, those governments are called oppressive! (Never by the people they help, incidentally. Only by the people who refuse to provide the help *themselves.*)

Nowhere is this more evident than in health care. In 1992 an American President and his wife decided it was unfair and inappropriate for millions of Americans to have no access to preventative health care; that notion started a health care debate which catapulted even the medical profession and the insurance industry into the fray.

The real question is not whose solution was better: the plan proposed by the Administration or the plan proposed by private industry. The real question is: *Why didn't private industry propose its own solution long ago?*

I'll *tell* you why. Because it didn't *have to.* No one was complaining. And the industry was driven by profits.

Profits, profits, *profits.*

My point, therefore, is this. We can rail and cry and complain all we want. The plain truth is, governments provide solutions when the private sector won't.

We can also claim that governments are doing what they are doing against the wishes of the people, but so long as people control the government—as they do to a large extent in the United States—the government will continue to produce and require solutions to social ills because the *majority of the people* are *not* rich and powerful, and therefore *legislate for themselves what society will not give them voluntarily.*

Only in countries where the majority of the people do *not* control the government does government do little or nothing about inequities.

So, then, the problem: How much government is too much government? And how much is too little? And where and how do we strike the balance?

> Whew! I've never seen you go *on* like this! That's as long as you've held the floor in either of our two books.

Well, you said this book was going to address some of the larger, global problems facing the family of man. I think I've laid out a big one.

Eloquently, yes. Everyone from Toynbee to Jefferson to Marx has been trying to solve it for hundreds of years.

Okay—What's *Your* solution?

We are going to have to go backwards here; we are going to have to go over some old ground.

Go ahead. Maybe I need to hear it twice.

Then we'll start with the fact that I *have* no "solution." And that is because I see none of this as problematical. It just is what it is, and I have no preferences regarding that. I am merely describing here what is observable; what anyone can plainly see.

Okay, You have no solution and You have no preference. Can You offer me an observation?

I observe that the world has yet to come up with a system of government which provides a total solution—although the government in the United States has come the closest so far.

The difficulty is that goodness and fairness are moral issues, not political ones.

Government is the human attempt to mandate goodness and ensure fairness. Yet there is only one place where goodness is born, and that is in the human heart. There is only one place where fairness can be conceptualized, and that is in the human mind. There is only one place where love can be experienced truly, and that is in the human soul. Because the human soul *is love*.

You cannot legislate morality. You cannot pass a law saying "love each other."

We are now going around in circles, as we have covered all of this before. Still, the discussion is good, so keep plugging away at it. Even if we cover the same ground twice or three times, that is okay. The attempt here is to get to the bottom of it; see how you want to create it now.

Well then, I'll ask the same question I asked before. Aren't all laws simply man's attempt to codify moral concepts? Is not "legislation" simply our combined agreement as to what is "right" and "wrong"?

Yes. And certain civil laws—rules and regulations—are required in your primitive society. (You understand that in nonprimitive societies such laws are unnecessary. All beings regulate themselves.) In your society, you are still confronted with some very elementary questions. Shall you stop at the street corner before proceeding? Shall you buy and sell according to certain terms? Will there be any restrictions on how you behave with one another?

But truly, even these basic laws—prohibitions against murdering, damaging, cheating, or even running a red light—shouldn't be needed and *wouldn't* be needed if all people everywhere simply followed the *Laws of Love*.

That is, God's Law.

What is needed is a growth in consciousness, not a growth of government.

You mean if we just followed the Ten Commandments we'd be all right!

There's no such thing as the Ten Commandments. (See *Book 1* for a complete discussion of this.) God's Law is No Law. This is something you cannot understand.

I require nothing.

Many people cannot believe Your last statement.

Have them read *Book 1*. It completely explains this.

Is that what You are suggesting for this world? Complete anarchy?

I am suggesting nothing. I am merely observing what works. I am telling you what is observably so. And no, I do not observe that anarchy—the absence of governance, rules, regulations, or limitations of any kind—would work. Such an arrangement is only practical with advanced beings, which I do not observe human beings to be.

So some level of governance is going to be required until your race evolves to the point where you *naturally do* what is *naturally right.*

You are very wise to govern yourselves in the interim. The points you made a moment ago are salient, unassailable. People often do *not* do what is "right" when left to their own devices.

The real question is not why do governments impose so many rules and regulations on the people, but why do governments *have* to?

The answer has to do with your Separation Consciousness.

The fact that we see ourselves as separate from each other.

Yes.

But if we aren't separate, then we *are* One. And doesn't that mean we *are* responsible for each other?

Yes.

But doesn't that disempower us from achieving individual greatness? If I am responsible for all others, then the Communist Manifesto was right! "From each according to his ability, to each according to his need."

That is, as I've already said, a very noble idea. But it is robbed of its nobility when it is ruthlessly enforced. That was the difficulty with communism. Not the concept, but its implementation.

There are those who say that the concept *had* to be forced because the concept violates the basic nature of man.

You've hit the nail on the head. What needs to be changed is the basic nature of man. That's where the work must be done.

To create the consciousness shift of which You've spoken.

Yes.

But we're going around in circles again. Would not a group consciousness cause individuals to be disempowered?

Let's look at it. If every person on the planet had basic needs met—if the mass of the people could live in dignity and escape the struggle of simple survival—would this not open the way for all of humankind to engage in more noble pursuits?

Would individual greatness really be suppressed if individual survival were guaranteed?

Must universal dignity be sacrificed to individual glory?

What kind of glory is obtained when it is achieved at the expense of another?

I have placed more than sufficient resources on your planet to ensure adequate supplies for all. How can it be that thousands starve to death each year? That hundreds go homeless? That millions cry out for simple dignity?

The kind of help that would end *this* is not the kind of help which disempowers.

If your well-off say they do not want to help the starving and the homeless because they do not want to disempower them, then your well-off are hypocrites. For no one is truly "well off" if they are well off while others are dying.

The evolution of a society is measured by how well it treats the least among its members. As I have said, the challenge is to find the balance between helping people and hurting them.

Any guidelines You can offer?

An overall guideline might be this: When in doubt, always err on the side of compassion.

The test of whether you are helping or hurting: Are your fellow humans enlarged or reduced as a result of your help? Have you made them bigger or smaller? More able or less able?

It has been said that if you give everything to individuals, they will be less willing to work for it themselves.

Yet why should they have to work for the simplest dignity? Is there not enough for all? Why should "working for it" have to do with anything?

Isn't basic human dignity the birthright of every-one? *Oughtn't* it be?

If one seeks *more* than minimum levels—more food, bigger shelters, finer coverings for the body—one can seek to achieve those goals. But ought one have to struggle to even *survive*—on a planet where there is more than enough for everyone?

That is the central question facing humankind.

The challenge is not to make everyone equal, but to give every-one at least the assurance of basic survival with dignity, so that each may then have the chance to choose what more they want from there.

There are those who argue that some don't take that chance even when it is given them.

And they observe correctly. This raises yet another question: to those who don't take the opportunities presented to them, do you owe another chance, and another?

No.

If I took that attitude, you would be lost to hell forever.

I tell you this: Compassion never ends, love never stops, patience never runs out in God's World. Only in the world of man is goodness limited.

In My World, goodness is endless.

Even if we don't deserve it.

You *always* deserve it!

Even if we throw Your goodness back in Your face?

Especially if you do ("If a man slaps you on the right cheek, turn and offer him your left. And if a man asks you to go one mile with him, go with him twain.") When you throw My goodness back in My face (which, by the way, the human race has done to God for millennia), I see that you are merely *mistaken.* You do not know what is in your best interest. I have compassion because your mistake is based not in evil, but in ignorance.

But some people are *basically evil.* Some people are intrinsically bad.

Who told you that?

It is my own observation.

Then you cannot see straight. I have said it to you before: No one does anything evil, given his model of the world.

Put another way, all are doing the best they can at any given moment.

All actions of everyone depend on the data at hand.

I have said before—consciousness is everything. Of what are you aware? What do you know?

But when people attack us, hurt us, damage us, even kill us for their own ends, is that not evil?

I have told you before: *all attack is a call for help.*

No one truly desires to hurt another. Those who do it—including your own governments, by the way—do it out of a misplaced idea that it is the only way to get something they want.

I've already outlined in this book the *higher solution* to this problem. Simply *want nothing*. Have preferences, but no *needs*.

Yet this is a very high state of being; it is the place of Masters.

In terms of geopolitics, why not work together as a world to meet the most basic needs of everyone?

We're doing that—or trying.

After all these thousands of years of human history, that's the most you can say?

The fact is, you have barely evolved at all. You still operate in a primitive "every man for himself" mentality.

You plunder the Earth, rape her of her resources, exploit her people, and systematically disenfranchise those who disagree with you for doing all of this, calling *them* the "radicals."

You do all this for your own selfish purposes, because you've developed a lifestyle that you *cannot maintain any other way.*

You *must* cut down millions of acres of trees each year or you won't be able to have your Sunday paper. You *must* destroy miles of the protective ozone which covers your planet, or you cannot have your hairspray. You *must* pollute your rivers and streams beyond repair or you cannot have your industries to give you Bigger, Better, and More. And you *must* exploit the least among you—the least advantaged, the least educated, the least aware—or you cannot live at the top of the human scale in unheard-of (and unnecessary) luxury. Finally, you must *deny that you are doing this,* or you cannot live with yourself.

You cannot find it in your heart to "live simply, so that others may simply live." That bumper sticker wisdom is too simple for you. It is too much to ask. Too much to give. After all, you've worked so *hard* for what you've got! *You ain't giving up none of it!* And if the rest of the human race—to say nothing of your own children's children—have to suffer for it, tough bananas, right? You did what *you* had to do to survive, to "make it"—they can do the same! After all, it *is* every man for himself, is it not?

Is there any way out of this mess?

Yes. Shall I say it again? A *shift of consciousness.*

You cannot solve the problems which plague humankind through governmental action or by political means. You have been trying that for thousands of years.

The change that must be made can be made only in the hearts of men.

Can You put the change that must be made into one sentence?

I already have several times.

You must stop seeing God as separate from you, and you as separate from each other.

The *only* solution is the Ultimate Truth: nothing exists in the universe that is separate from anything else. *Everything* is intrinsically connected, irrevocably interdependent, interactive, interwoven into the fabric of all of life.

All government, all politics, must be based on this truth. All laws must be rooted in it.

This is the future hope of your race; the only hope for your planet.

How does the Law of Love You spoke of earlier work?

Love gives all and requires nothing.

How can we require nothing?

If everyone in your race gave all, what would you require? The only reason you require *anything* is because someone else is holding back. *Stop holding back!*

This could not work unless we all did it at once.

Indeed, a global consciousness is what is required.

Yet, how will that come about? *Somebody has to start.*

The opportunity is here for you.

You can be the source of this New Consciousness.

You can be the inspiration.

Indeed, you *must* be.

I must?

Who else is there?

13

How can I begin?

Be a light unto the world, and hurt it not. Seek to build, not to destroy.

Bring My people home.

How?

By your shining example. Seek only Godliness. Speak only in truthfulness. Act only in love.

Live the Law of Love now and forevermore. Give everything, require nothing.

Avoid the mundane.

Do not accept the unacceptable.

Teach all who seek to learn of Me.

Make every moment of your life an outpouring of love.

Use every moment to think the highest thought, say the highest word, do the highest deed. In this, glorify your Holy Self, and thus, too, glorify Me.

Bring peace to the Earth by bringing peace to all those whose lives you touch.

Be peace.

Feel and express in every moment your Divine Connection with the All, and with every person, place, and thing.

Embrace every circumstance, own every fault, share every joy, contemplate every mystery, walk in every man's shoes, forgive every offense (including your own), heal every heart, honor every person's truth, adore every person's God, protect every person's rights, preserve every person's dignity, promote every person's interests, provide every person's needs, presume every person's holiness, present every person's greatest gifts, produce every person's blessing, and pronounce every person's future secure in the assured love of God.

Be a living, breathing example of the Highest Truth that resides within you.

Speak humbly of yourself, lest someone mistake your Highest Truth for a boast.

Speak softly, lest someone think you are merely calling for attention.

Speak gently, that all might know of Love.

Speak openly, lest anyone think you have something to hide.

Speak candidly, so you cannot be mistaken.

Speak often, so that your word may truly go forth.

Speak respectfully, that no one be dishonored.

Speak lovingly, that every syllable may heal.

Speak of Me with every utterance.

Make of your life a gift. Remember always, you *are* the gift!

Be a gift to everyone who enters your life, and to everyone whose life you enter. Be careful *not to enter* another's life if you cannot be a gift.

(You can always be a gift, because you always are the gift—yet sometimes you don't let yourself know that.)

When someone enters your life unexpectedly, *look for the gift that person has come to receive from you.*

What an extraordinary way of putting it.

Why else do you think a person has come to you?

I tell you this: *every* person who has ever come to you has come to receive a gift from you. In so doing, he gives a gift *to* you—the gift of your experiencing and fulfilling Who You Are.

When you see this simple truth, when you understand it, you see the greatest truth of all:

I HAVE SENT YOU
NOTHING BUT ANGELS.

14

I am confused. Can we go back just a bit? There seems to be some contradictory data. I felt that You were saying that sometimes the best help we can give people is to leave them alone. Then I felt You were saying, never fail to help someone if you see that person needs help. These two statements seem to be at odds.

Let Me clarify your thinking on this.

Never offer the kind of help that disempowers. Never insist on offering the help you think is needed. Let the person or people in need know all that you have to give—then listen to what they want; see what they are ready to receive.

Offer the help that is wanted. Often, the person or people will say, or exhibit by their behavior, that they just want to be left alone. Despite what *you* think you'd like to give, leaving them alone might be the Highest Gift you can then offer.

If, at a later time, something else is wanted or desired, you will be caused to notice if it is yours to give. If it is, then give it.

Yet strive to give nothing which disempowers. That which disempowers is that which promotes or produces dependency.

In truth, there is *always* some way you can help others which also empowers them.

Completely *ignoring* the plight of another who is truly seeking your help is not the answer, for doing too little no more empowers the other than doing too much. To be of higher consciousness, you may not deliberately ignore the genuine plight of brothers or sisters, claiming that to let them "stew in their own juice" is the highest gift you can give them. That attitude is righteousness and arrogance at the highest level. It merely allows you to justify your noninvolvement.

I refer you again to the life of Jesus and to his teachings.

For it was Jesus who told you that I would say to those on My right, Come, you blessed of My children, inherit the kingdom which I have had prepared for you.

For I was hungry and you gave Me to eat; I was thirsty and you gave Me to drink; I was homeless, and you found Me shelter.

I was naked and you clothed Me; I was ill and you visited Me; I was in prison and you brought Me comfort.

And they will say to Me, Lord, when did we see You hungry, and feed You? Or thirsty, and give You drink? And when did we see You homeless and find You shelter? Or naked, and clothe You? And when did we see You ill, or in prison, and comfort You?

And I will answer them, replying:

Verily, verily, I say unto you—inasmuch as you have done it to the least of these, My brethren, so have you done it to Me.

This is My truth, and it still stands for all the ages.

15

I love You, You know that?

I know you do. And I love you.

16

Since we are discussing larger aspects of life on a planetary scale, as well as reviewing some of the elements of our individual lives which were explored initially in *Book 1*, I would like to ask You about the environment.

What do you want to know?

Is it really being destroyed, as some environmentalists claim, or are these people simply wild-eyed radicals, el-pinko liberal Commies, all of whom graduated from Berkeley and smoke dope?

Yes to both questions.

Whaaa—???

Just kidding. Okay, yes to the first question, no to the second.

The ozone layer *is* depleted? The rain forests *are* being decimated?

Yes. But it is not just about such obvious things. There are matters less obvious about which you should be concerned.

Help me out here.

Well, for instance, there is rapidly developing a soil shortage on your planet. That is, you are running out of good soil in which to grow your food. This is because soil needs time to reconstitute itself, and your corporate farmers *have* no time. They want land that is producing, producing, producing. So the age-old practice of alternating growing fields from season to season is being abandoned or shortened. To make up for the loss of time, chemicals are being dumped into the land in order to render it fertile faster. Yet in this, as with all things, you cannot develop an artificial substitute for Mother Nature which comes even close to providing what She provides.

The result is that you are eroding, down to a few inches really, in some places, the available nutritive topsoil reserve. In other words, you are growing more and more food in soil which has less and less nutritional content. No irons. No minerals. Nothing which you count on the soil to provide. Worse yet, you are eating foods filled with chemicals which have been poured into the soil in a desperate attempt to reconstitute it. While causing no apparent damage to the body in the short term, you will discover to your sadness that in the long run these trace chemicals, which remain in the body, are not health producing.

This problem of soil erosion through rapid growing-field turnover is not something of which most of your people may be aware, nor is the dwindling growable soil reserve a fantasy made up by yuppie environmentalists looking for their next fashionable cause. Ask any Earth scientist about it and you will hear plenty. It is a problem of epidemic proportions; it is worldwide, and it is serious.

This is just one example of the many ways you are damaging and depleting your Mother, the Earth, the giver of all life, out of a complete disregard for her needs and natural processes.

You are concerned about little on your planet except the satisfying of your own passions, the meeting of your own immediate (and mostly bloated) needs, and quenching the endless human desire for Bigger, Better, More. Yet you might do well as a species to ask, when is enough enough?

Why do we not listen to our environmentalists? Why do we not heed their warnings?

In this, as in all really important matters affecting the quality and style of life on your planet, there is a pattern which is easily discernable. You have coined a phrase in your world which answers the question perfectly. "Follow the money trail."

How can we ever begin to hope to solve these problems when fighting something as massive and insidious as that?

Simple. Eliminate money.

Eliminate money?

Yes. Or at the very least, eliminate its invisibility.

I don't understand.

Most people hide the things they are ashamed of or don't want other people to know about. That is why the largest number of you hide your sexuality, and that is why nearly all of you hide your money. That is to say, you are not open about it. You consider your money to be a very private matter. And therein lies the problem.

If every*one* knew every*thing* about every*body's* money situation, there would be an uprising in your country and on your planet, the likes of which you have never seen. And in the aftermath of that there would be fairness and equity, honesty and true for-the-good-of-all priority in the conduct of human affairs.

It is now not possible to bring fairness or equity, honesty, or the common good to the marketplace because money is so easy to hide. You can actually, physically, take it and *hide it*. There are also all manner of means by which creative accountants can cause corporate money to be "hidden" or to "disappear."

Since money can be hidden, there is no way for anyone to know exactly how much anyone else has or what they are doing with it. This makes it possible for a plethora of inequity, if not to say double-dealing, to exist. Corporations can pay two people vastly different wages for doing the same job, for instance. They can pay one person $57,000 a year while paying the other $42,000 a year, for performing the exactly identical function, giving one employee more than the other simply because the first employee has something the second employee does not.

What's that?

A penis.

Oh.

Yes. Oh, indeed.

But You don't understand. Having a penis makes the first employee more valuable than the second; quicker witted, smarter by half, and, obviously, more capable.

Hmmm. I don't remember constructing you that way. I mean, so unequal in abilities.

Well, You did, and I'm surprised You don't know it. Everyone on this planet knows it.

> We'd better stop this now, or people will think we're really serious.

You mean You're not? Well, *we* are! The people on this planet are. That's why women can't be Roman Catholic or Mormon priests, or show up on the wrong side of the Wailing Wall in Jerusalem, or climb to the top job in Fortune 500 companies, or pilot airliners, or—

> Yes, we get the point. And *My* point is that pay discrimination, at least, would be much more difficult to get away with if all money transactions were made visible, instead of hidden. Can you imagine what would happen in every workplace on the globe if all companies were forced to publish all the salaries of all the employees? Not the salary *ranges* for particular job classifications, but the *actual compensation awarded* to each individual.

Well, there goes "playing two ends against the middle," right out the window.

> Yup.

And there goes, "What he doesn't know won't hurt him."

> Yup.

And there goes, "Hey, if we can get her for a third less, why should we pay more?"

> Uh-huh.

And there goes apple polishing, and kissing up to the boss, and the "inside track," and company politics, and—

> And much, much more would disappear from the workplace, and from the world, through the simple expedient of uncovering the money trail.
>
> Think of it. If you knew exactly how much money each of you holds and the real earnings of all of your industries and corporations and each of their executives—as well as how each person and corporation is *using* the money it has—don't you think that would change things?

Think about this. In what ways do you think things would change?

The plain fact is that people would never put up with 90 percent of what is going on in the world if they *knew* what was going on. Society would never sanction the extraordinarily disproportionate distribution of wealth, much less the means by which it is gained, or the manner in which it is used to gain more, were these facts known, specifically and immediately, by all people everywhere.

Nothing breeds appropriate behavior faster than exposure to the light of public scrutiny. That is why your so-called Sunshine Laws have done so much good in clearing away some of the awful mess of your political and governance system. Public hearings and public accountability has gone far toward eliminating the kinds of backroom antics that went on in the twenties, thirties, forties, and fifties in your town halls and school boards and political precincts—and national government as well.

Now it is time to bring some "sunshine" to the way you deal with compensation for goods and services on your planet.

What are You suggesting?

This is not a suggestion, it is a dare. I dare you to throw out all your money, all your papers and coins and individual national currencies, and start over. Develop an international monetary system that is wide open, totally visible, immediately traceable, completely accountable. Establish a Worldwide Compensation System by which people would be given Credits for services rendered and products produced, and Debits for services used and products consumed.

Everything would be on the system of Credits and Debits. Returns on investments, inheritances, winnings of wagers, salaries and wages, tips and gratuities, everything. And nothing could be purchased without Credits. There would be no other negotiable currency. And everyone's records would be open to everyone else.

It has been said, show me a man's bank account, and I'll show you the man. This system comes close to that scenario. People would, or at least could, know a great deal more about you than they know now. But not only would you know more about each other; you would know more about *everything*. More about what corporations are paying and spending—and what their cost is on an item, as well as their price. (Can you imagine what corporations would do if they had to put *two* figures on every price tag—the price and *their* cost? Would that bring prices down, or what! Would that increase competition, and boost fair trade? You can't even imagine the consequences of such a thing.)

Under the new Worldwide Compensation System, WCS, the transfer of Debits and Credits would be immediate and totally visible. That is, anybody and everybody could inspect the account of any other person or organization at any time. Nothing would be kept secret, nothing would be "private."

The WCS would deduct 10 percent of all earnings each year from the incomes of those *voluntarily requesting* such a deduction. There would be no income tax, no forms to file, no deductions to figure, no "escape hatch" to construct or obfuscation to manufacture! Since all records would be open, everyone in the society would be able to observe who was choosing to offer the 10 percent for the general good of all, and who was not. This voluntary deduction would go toward support of all the programs and services of the government, as voted on by the people.

The whole system would be all very simple, all very visible.

The world would never agree to such a thing.

Of course not. And do you know why? Because such a system would make it impossible for anyone *to do anything they didn't want someone else to know about*. Yet why would you want to do something like that anyway? I'll tell you why. Because currently you live within an interactive social system based on "taking advantage," "getting the edge," "making the most," and "the survival of the so-called fittest."

When the chief aim and goal of your society (as it is in all truly enlightened societies) is the survival of *all;* the benefit, equally, of *all;* the providing of a good life for *all,* then your need for secrecy and quiet dealings and under the table maneuverings and money which can be hidden will disappear.

Do you realize how much good old-fashioned *corruption,* to say nothing of lesser unfairnesses and inequities, would be eliminated through the implementation of such a system?

The secret here, the watchword here, is *visibility.*

Wow. What a concept. What an idea. Absolute visibility in the conduct of our monetary affairs. I keep trying to find a reason why that would be "wrong," why that would not be "okay," but I can't find one.

Of course you can't, *because you've got nothing to hide.* But can you imagine what the people of money and power in the world would do, and how they would scream, if they thought that every move, every purchase, every sale, every dealing, every corporate action and pricing choice and wage negotiation, every decision whatsoever could be reviewed by *anyone* simply looking at the bottom line?

I tell you this: *nothing* breeds fairness faster than *visibility.*

Visibility is simply another word for *truth.*

Know the truth, and the truth shall set you free.

Governments, corporations, people of power know that, which is why they will never allow the truth—the plain and simple truth— to be the basis of any political, social, or economic system they would devise.

In enlightened societies there *are no secrets.* Everyone knows what everyone else has, what everyone else earns, what everyone else pays in wages and taxes and benefits, what every other corporation charges and buys and sells and for how much and for what profit and *everything. EVERYTHING.*

Do you know why this is possible only in enlightened societies? Because no one in enlightened societies is willing to get *anything,* or *have* anything, at *someone else's expense.*

That is a radical way to live.

It seems radical in primitive societies, yes. In enlightened societies it seems obviously appropriate.

I am intrigued by this concept of "visibility." Could it extend beyond monetary affairs? Might it be a watchword for our personal relationships as well?

One would hope so.

And yet it isn't.

As a rule, no. Not yet on your planet. Most people still have too much to hide.

Why? What's that about?

In personal relationships (and in all relationships, really) it's about *loss*. It's about being afraid of what one might lose or fail to gain. Yet the best personal relationships, and certainly the best romantic ones, are relationships in which everyone knows everything; in which *visibility* is not only the watchword, but the *only word;* in which there simply are no secrets. In these relationships nothing is withheld, nothing is shaded or colored or hidden or disguised. Nothing is left out or unspoken. There is no guesswork, there is no game playing; no one is "doing a dance," "running a number," or "shining you on."

But if everyone knew everything we were thinking—

Hold it. This isn't about having no mental privacy, no safe space in which to move through your personal process. That's not what I'm talking about here.

This is about simply being open and honest in your dealings with another. This is about simply telling the truth when you speak, and about withholding no truth when you know it should be spoken. This is about never again lying, or shading, or verbally or mentally manipulating, or twisting your truth into the hundred and one other contortions which typify the largest number of human communications.

This is about coming clean, telling it like it is, giving it to them straight. This is about ensuring that all individuals have all the data and know everything they need to know on a subject. This is about fairness and openness and, well . . . *visibility.*

Yet this does not mean that every single thought, every private fear, every darkest memory, every fleeting judgment, opinion, or reaction must be placed on the table for discussion and examination. That is not visibility, that is insanity, and it will make you crazy.

We are talking here about simple, direct, straightforward, open, honest, complete communication. Yet even at that, it is a striking concept, and a little-used one.

You can say that again.

Yet even at that, it is a striking concept, and a little-used one.

You should have been in vaudeville.

Are you kidding? I am.

But seriously, this is a magnificent idea. Imagine, an entire society built around the Principle of Visibility. Are You sure it would work?

I'll tell you something. Half the world's ills would go away tomorrow. Half the world's worries, half the world's conflicts, half the world's anger, half the world's frustration . . .

Oh, there would be anger and frustration at first, make no mistake about that. When it was finally discovered just how much the average person *is* being played like a fiddle, used like a disposable commodity, manipulated, lied to, and downright cheated, there would be *plenty* of frustration and anger. But "visibility" would clean most of that up within 60 days; make it go away.

Let me invite you again—just think about it.

Do you think you could live a life like this? No more secrets? Absolute visibility?

If not, why not?

What are you keeping from others that you don't want them to know?

What are you saying to someone that isn't true?

What are you not saying to someone that is?

Has lying by omission or commission brought your world where you really want it to be? Has manipulation (of the marketplace, of a particular situation, or simply of a person) through silence and secrecy really benefited us? Is "privacy" really what makes our governmental, corporate, and individual lives work?

What would happen if everybody could see everything?

Now there is an irony here. Don't you see that this is the one thing you fear about your first meeting with God? Don't you get that what you've been afraid of is that the gig is up, the game is over, the tap dance is finished, the shadow boxing is done, and the long, long trail of deceits, big and small, has come to—quite literally—a *dead end*?

Yet the good news is that there is no reason for fear, no cause to be scared. No one is going to judge you, no one is going to make you "wrong," no one is going to throw you into the everlasting fires of hell.

(And to you Roman Catholics, no, you won't even go to purgatory.)

(And to you Mormons, no, you won't be trapped forever in the lowest heaven, unable to get to "highest heaven," nor will you be labeled Sons of Perdition and banished forever to realms unknown.)

(And to you. . . .)

Well, you get the picture. Each of you has constructed, within the framework of your own particular theology, some idea, some concept of God's Worst Punishment. And I hate to tell you this, because I see the fun you're having with the drama of it all, but, well . . . *just ain't no such thing.*

Perhaps when you lose the fear of having your life become totally visible at the moment of your death, you can get over the fear of having your life become totally visible *while you are living it.*

Wouldn't *that* be something. . . .

Yes, wouldn't it, though? So here's the formula to help you get started. Turn back to the very beginning of this book and review again the *Five Levels of Truth Telling.* Determine to memorize this model and implement it. Seek the truth, say the truth, live the truth every day. Do this with yourself and with every person whose life you touch.

Then get ready to be naked. Stand by for *visibility.*

This feels scary. This feels real scary.

Look to see what you are afraid of.

I'm afraid everyone will leave the room. I'm afraid no one will like me any more.

I see. You feel you have to lie to get people to like you?

Not lie, exactly. Just not tell them *everything.*

Remember what I said before. This is not about blurting out every little feeling, thought, idea, fear, memory, confession, or whatever. This is simply about always speaking the truth, showing yourself completely. With your dearest loved one you can be physically naked, can you not?

Yes.

Then why not be emotionally naked as well?

The second is much harder than the first.

I understand that. That does not fail to recommend it, however, for the rewards are great.

Well, You've certainly brought up some interesting ideas. Abolish hidden agendas, build a society on visibility, tell the truth all the time to everyone about everything. Whew!

On these few concepts entire societies have been constructed. Enlightened societies.

I haven't found any.

I wasn't speaking of your planet.

Oh.

Or even your solar system.

OH.

But you don't have to leave the planet or even leave your house to begin experiencing what such a New Thought system would be like. Start in your own family, in your own home. If you own a business, start in your own company. Tell everyone in your firm exactly what you make, what the company is making and spending, and what each and every employee makes. You will shock the hell out of them. I mean that quite literally. You will shock the hell *right out of them.* If everyone who owned a company did this, work would no longer be a living hell for so many because a greater sense of equity, fair play, and appropriate compensation would automatically come to the workplace.

Tell your customers exactly what a product or service costs you to provide. Put those two numbers on your price tag: your cost and your price. Can you still be proud of what you are asking? Do you encounter any fear that someone will think you are "ripping them off" should they know your cost/price ratio? If so, look to see what kind of adjustment you want to make in your pricing to bring it back down into the realm of basic fairness, rather than "get what you can while the gettin's good."

I dare you to do this. I dare you.

It will require a complete change in your thinking. You will have to be just as concerned with your customers or clients as you are with yourself.

Yes, you can begin to build this New Society right now, right here, today. The choice is yours. You can continue to support the old system, the present paradigm, or you can blaze the trail and show your world a new way.

You can *be* that new way. In everything. Not just in business, not just in your personal relationships, not just in politics or economics or religion or this aspect or that of the overall life experience, but in *everything*.

Be the new way. Be the higher way. Be the grandest way. Then you can truly say, *I am the way and the life. Follow me.*

If the whole world followed you, would you be pleased with where you took it?

Let that be your question for the day.

17

I hear Your challenge. I hear it. Please tell me more now about life on this planet on a grander scale. Tell me how nation can get along with nation so there will be "war no more."

There will always be disagreements between nations, for disagreement is merely a sign—and a healthy one—of individuality. *Violent resolution* of disagreements, however, is a sign of extraordinary immaturity.

There is no reason in the world why violent resolution cannot be avoided, given the willingness of nations to avoid it.

One would think that the massive toll in death and destroyed lives would be enough to produce such willingness, but among primitive cultures such as yours, that is not so.

As long as you think you can win an argument, you will have it. As long as you think you can win a war, you will fight it.

What is the answer to all of this?

I do not have an answer, I only have—

I know, I know! An observation.

Yes. I observe now what I observed before. A short-term answer could be to establish what some have called a one-world government, with a world court to settle disputes (one whose verdicts may not be ignored, as happens with the present World Court) and a world peacekeeping force to guarantee that no one nation—no matter how powerful or how influential—can ever again aggress upon another.

Yet understand that there may still be violence upon the Earth. The peacekeeping force may *have* to use violence to get someone to *stop* doing so. As I noted in *Book 1*, failure to stop a despot empowers a despot. Sometimes the only way to *avoid* a war is to *have* a war. Sometimes you have to do what you don't *want* to do in order to ensure that you won't *have to keep on doing it!* This apparent contradiction is part of the Divine Dichotomy, which says that sometimes the only way to ultimately *Be* a thing—in this case, "peaceful"—may be, at first, to *not* be it!

In other words, often the only way to know yourself as That Which You Are is to experience yourself as That Which You Are *Not*.

It is an observable truth that power in your world can no longer rest disproportionately with any individual nation, but must rest in the hands of the total group of nations existing on this planet. Only in this way can the world finally be at peace, resting in the secure knowledge that no despot—no matter how big or powerful his individual nation—can or will ever again infringe upon the territories of another nation, nor threaten her freedoms.

No longer need the smallest nations depend upon the goodwill of the largest nations, often having to bargain away their own resources and offer their prime lands for foreign military bases in order to earn it. Under this new system, the security of the smallest nations will be guaranteed not by whose back they scratch, but by who is backing *them*.

All 160 nations would rise up should one nation be invaded. All 160 nations would say *No!* should one nation be violated or threatened in any way.

Similarly, nations would no longer be threatened economically, blackmailed into certain courses of action by their bigger trading partners, required to meet certain "guidelines" in order to receive foreign aid, or mandated to perform in certain ways in order to qualify for simple humanitarian assistance.

Yet there are those among you who would argue that such a system of global governance would erode the independence and the greatness of individual nations. The truth is, it would *increase* it—and that is precisely what the largest nations, whose independence is assured by power, not by law or justice, are afraid of. For then no longer would only the largest nation always get its way automatically, but the considerations of all nations would have to be heard equally. And no longer would the largest nations be able to control and hoard the mass of the world's resources, but would be required to share them more equally, render them accessible more readily, provide their benefits more uniformly to *all* the world's people.

A worldwide government would level the playing field—and this idea, while driving to the core of the debate regarding basic human dignity, is anathema to the world's "haves," who want the "have-nots" to go seek their *own* fortunes—ignoring, of course, the fact that the "haves" *control* all that others would seek.

Yet it feels as though we are talking about redistribution of wealth here. How can we maintain the incentive of those who *do* want more, and are willing to work for it, if they know they must share with those who do not care to work that hard?

First, it is not merely a question of those who *want* to "work hard" and those who don't. That is a simplistic way to cast the argument (usually constructed in that way by the "haves"). It is more often a question of opportunity than willingness. So the real job, and the first job in restructuring the social order, is to make sure each person and each nation has equal *opportunity*.

That can never happen so long as those who currently possess and control the mass of the world's wealth and resources hold tightly to that control.

Yes. I mentioned Mexico, and without wanting to get into "nation bashing," I think this country provides an excellent example of that. A handful of rich and powerful families control the wealth and resources of that entire nation—and have for 40 years. "Elections" in this so-called Western Democracy are a farce because the same families have controlled the same political party for decades, assuring virtually no serious opposition. Result? "The rich get richer and the poor get poorer."

If wages should jump from $1.75 to a whopping $3.15 an hour, the rich point to how much they've done for the poor in providing jobs and opportunity for economic advancement. Yet the only ones making quantum advances are the *rich*—the industrialists and business owners who sell their commodities on the national and world market at huge profits, given the low cost of their labor.

America's rich know this is true—which is why many of America's rich and powerful are rebuilding their plants and factories in Mexico and other foreign countries where slave-labor wages are considered a grand opportunity for the peasants. Meanwhile, these workers toil in unhealthy and wholly unsafe conditions, but the local government—controlled by the same few reaping the profits from these ventures—imposes few regulations. Health and safety standards and environmental protections are virtually nonexistent in the workplace.

The people are not being cared for, nor is the Earth, on which they are being asked to live in their paper shacks next to streams in which they do their laundry and into which they sometimes defecate—for indoor plumbing is also often not one of their dignities.

What is created by such crass disregard for the masses is a population which cannot afford the very products it is manufacturing. But the rich factory owners don't care. They can ship their goods to other nations where there are people who can.

Yet I believe that sooner or later this spiral will turn in upon itself—with devastating consequences. Not just in Mexico, but wherever humans are exploited.

> Revolutions and civil war are inevitable, as are wars between nations, so long as the "haves" continue seeking to exploit the "have-nots" under the guise of providing *opportunity*.

Holding on to the wealth and the resources has become so *institutionalized* that it almost now appears *acceptable* even to some fair-minded people, who see it as simply open market economics.

> Yet only the *power* held by the world's wealthy individuals and nations makes that illusion of fairness possible. The truth is, it is *not* fair to the largest percentage of the world's people and nations, who are held down from even attempting to achieve what the Powerful have achieved.
>
> The system of governance described here would drastically shift the balance of power away from the resource-rich to the resource-poor, forcing the resources themselves to be fairly shared.

This is what the powerful fear.

> Yes. So the short-term solution to the world's foment may be a new social structure—a new, worldwide, government.
>
> There have been those leaders among you who have been insightful enough and brave enough to propose the beginnings of such a new world order. Your George Bush, whom history will judge to be a man of far greater wisdom, vision, compassion, and courage than contemporary society was willing or able to acknowledge, was such a leader. So was Soviet President Mikhail Gorbachev, the first communist head of state ever to win the Nobel Peace Prize and a man who proposed enormous political changes, virtually ending what you've called the Cold War. And so was your

President Carter, who brought your Mr. Begin and Mr. Sadat to come to agreements no one else ever had dreamt of, and who, long after his presidency, pulled the world back from violent confrontation time and time again through the simple assertion of a simple truth: No one's point of view is less worthy of being heard than another's; No one human being has less dignity than another.

It is interesting that these courageous leaders, each of whom brought the world from the brink of war in their own time, and each of whom espoused and proposed massive movements away from the prevailing political structure, each served only one term, removed from office as they were by the very people they were seeking to elevate. Incredibly popular worldwide, they were soundly rejected at home. It is said that a man is without honor in his own home. In the case of these men, it is because their vision was miles ahead of their people, who could see only limited, parochial concerns, and imagined nothing but loss proceeding from these larger visions.

So, too, has every leader who has dared to step out and call for the end of oppression by the powerful been discouraged and defiled.

Thus it will always be until a *long*-term solution, *which is not a political one*, is put into place. That long-term solution—and the only real one—is a New Awareness, and a New Consciousness. An awareness of Oneness and a consciousness of Love.

The incentive to succeed, to make the most of one's life, should not be economic or materialistic reward. It is misplaced there. This misplaced priority is what has created all of the problems we have discussed here.

When the incentive for greatness is not economic—when economic security and basic materialistic needs are guaranteed to all—then incentive will not disappear, but be of a different sort, *increasing* in strength and determination, producing *true* greatness, not the kind of transparent, transient "greatness" which present incentives produce.

But why isn't living a better life, creating a better life for our children, a good incentive?

"Living a better life" *is* a proper incentive. Creating a "better life" for your children *is* a good incentive. But the question is, what makes for a "better life"?

How do you define "better"? How do you define "life"?

If you define "better" as *bigger, better, more* money, power, sex, and *stuff* (houses, cars, clothes, CD collections—whatever) . . . and if you define "life" as the period elapsing between birth and death in this your present existence, then you're doing nothing to get out of the trap that has *created* your planet's predicament.

Yet if you define "better" as a larger experience and a greater expression of your grandest State of Being, and "life" as an eternal, ongoing, never-ending process of *Being*, you may yet find your way.

A "better life" is not created by the accumulation of things. Most of you know this, all of you say you understand it, yet your lives—and the decisions you make which drive your lives—have as much to do with "things" as anything else, and usually more.

You strive for things, you work for things, and when you get some of the things you want, you never let them go.

The incentive of most of humankind is to achieve, acquire, obtain *things*. Those who do not care about things let them go easily.

Because your present incentive for greatness has to do with accumulation of all the world has to offer, all of the world is in various stages of struggle. Enormous *portions* of the population are still struggling for simple physical survival. Each day is filled with anxious moments, desperate measures. The mind is concerned with basic, vital questions. Will there be enough food? Is shelter available? Will we be warm? *Enormous* numbers of people are still concerned with these matters daily. Thousands *die* each month for lack of food alone.

Smaller numbers of people are able to reasonably rely on the basics of survival appearing in their lives, but struggle to provide something more—a modicum of security, a modest but decent home, a better tomorrow. They work hard, they fret about how and whether they'll ever "get ahead." The mind is concerned with urgent, worrisome questions.

By far the smallest number of people have all they could ever ask for—indeed, everything the other two groups *are* asking for—but, interestingly, many in this last group are still *asking for more*.

Their minds are concerned with *holding on to* all that they have acquired and increasing their holdings.

Now, in addition to these three groups, there is a fourth. It is the smallest group of all. In fact, it is tiny.

This group has detached itself from the need for material things. It is concerned with spiritual truth, spiritual reality, and spiritual experience.

The people in this group see life as a spiritual encounter—a journey of the soul. They respond to all human events within that context. They hold all human experience within that paradigm. Their struggle has to do with the search for God, the fulfillment of Self, the expression of truth.

As they evolve, this struggle becomes not a struggle at all, but a process. It is a process of Self-definition (not self-discovery), of Growth (not learning), of Being (not doing).

The *reason* for seeking, striving, searching, stretching, and *succeeding* becomes completely different. The reason for doing *anything* is changed, and with it the doer is likewise changed. The reason becomes the process, and the doer becomes a be-er.

Whereas, before, the reason for reaching, for striving, for working hard all of one's life was to provide worldly things, now the reason is to experience heavenly things.

Whereas, before, the concerns were largely the concerns of the body, now the concerns are largely the concerns of the soul.

Everything has moved, everything has shifted. The purpose of life has changed, and so has life itself.

The "incentive for greatness" has shifted, and with it the need for coveting, acquiring, protecting, and increasing worldly possessions has disappeared.

Greatness will no longer be measured by how much one has accumulated. The world's resources will rightly be seen as belonging to all the world's people. In a world blessed with sufficient abundance to meet the basic needs of all, the basic needs of all *will be met.*

Everyone will *want* it that way. There will no longer be a need to subject anyone to an involuntary tax. You will all *volunteer* to send 10 percent of your harvest and your abundance to programs supporting those whose harvest is less. It will no longer be possible for thousands to stand by watching thousands of others starve—not for lack of food, but for lack of sufficient human *will* to create a simple political mechanism by which people can get the food.

Such moral obscenities—now commonplace among your primitive society—will be erased forever the day you change your incentive for greatness and your definition of it.

Your new incentive: to become what I created you to be—the physical out-picturing of Deity Itself.

When you choose to be Who You Really Are—God made manifest—you will never again act in an ungodly manner. No longer will you have to display bumper stickers which read:

GOD SAVE ME
FROM YOUR FOLLOWERS

18

Let me see if I'm tracking this. What seems to be emerging here is a world view of equality and equanimity, where all nations submit to one world government, and all people share in the world's riches.

Remember when you talk about equality that we're meaning equal *opportunity,* not equality *in fact.*

Actual "equality" will never be achieved, and be grateful that is so.

Why?

Because equality is sameness—and the last thing the world needs is sameness.

No—I am not arguing here for a world of automatons, each receiving identical allotments from a Big Brother Central Government.

I am speaking of a world in which two things are guaranteed:

1. The meeting of basic needs.
2. The opportunity to go higher.

With all your world's resources, with all your abundance, you have not yet managed those two simple things. Instead, you have trapped millions on the lowest end of the socioeconomic scale and devised a world view that systematically keeps them there. You are allowing thousands to die each year for lack of simple basics.

For all the world's magnificence, you have not found a way to be magnificent enough to stop people from starving to death, much less stop killing each other. You actually let *children* starve to death right in front of you. You actually kill people because they disagree with you.

You are primitive.

And we think we are so advanced.

The first mark of a primitive society is that it thinks itself advanced. The first mark of a primitive consciousness is that it thinks itself enlightened.

So let's summarize it. The way we'll get to the first step on the ladder, where these two fundamental guarantees are accorded everyone. . . .

Is through two shifts, two changes—one in your political paradigm, one in your spiritual.

The movement to a unified world government would include a greatly empowered world court to resolve international disputes and a peacekeeping force to give power to the laws by which you choose to govern yourselves.

The world government would include a Congress of Nations— two representatives from every nation on Earth—and a People's Assembly—with representation in direct proportion to a nation's population.

Exactly the way the U.S. Government is set up—with two houses, one providing proportional representation and one providing equal voice to all of the states.

Yes. Your U.S. Constitution was God inspired.

The same balance of powers should be built in to the new world constitution.

There would be, likewise, an executive branch, legislative branch, and a judicial branch.

Each nation would keep its internal peacekeeping police, but all national armies would be disbanded—exactly as each of your individual states disbanded their armies and navies in favor of a federal peacekeeping force serving the entire group of states you now call a nation.

Nations would reserve the right to form and call up their own militia on a moment's notice, just as your states each have the constitutional right to keep and activate a state militia.

And—just as your states do now—each of the 160 Nation States in the union of nations would have the right to secede from the union based upon a vote of the people (though why it would want to do so is beyond Me, given that its people would be more secure and more abundant than ever before).

And—once more for those of us who are slow—such a unified world federation would produce—?

1. An end to wars between nations and the settling of disputes by killing.

2. An end to abject poverty, death by starvation, and mass exploitation of people and resources by those of power.

3. An end to the systematic environmental destruction of the Earth.

4. An escape from the endless struggle for bigger, better, more.

5. An opportunity—*truly* equal—for *all* people to rise to the highest expression of Self.

6. An end to all limitations and discriminations holding people back—whether in housing, in the workplace, or in the political system, or in personal sexual relationships.

Would your new world order require a redistribution of wealth?

It would require nothing. It would *produce*, voluntarily and quite automatically, a redistribution of *resources*.

All people would be offered a proper education, for instance. *All* people would be offered open opportunity to use that education in the workplace—to follow careers which bring them *joy*.

All people would be guaranteed access to health care whenever and however needed.

All people would be guaranteed they won't starve to death or have to live without sufficient clothing or adequate shelter.

All people would be granted the basic dignities of life so that *survival* would never again be the issue, so that simple comforts and basic dignities were provided *all* human beings.

Even if they did nothing to earn it?

Your thought that these things need to be *earned* is the basis for your thought that you have to *earn your way to heaven*. Yet you cannot earn your way into God's good graces, and you do not have to, because you are already there. This is something you cannot accept, because it is something you cannot *give*. When you learn to *give* unconditionally (which is to say, *love* unconditionally), then will you learn to *receive* unconditionally.

This life was created as a vehicle through which you might be allowed to experience that.

Try to wrap yourself around this thought: People have a right to basic survival. Even if they do *nothing*. Even if they contribute *nothing*. Survival with dignity is one of the basic rights of life. I have given you enough resources to be able to guarantee that to everyone. All you have to do is share.

But then what would stop people from simply wasting their lives, lollygagging around, collecting "benefits"?

First of all, it is not yours to judge what is a life wasted. Is a life wasted if a person does nothing but lie around thinking of poetry for 70 years, then comes up with a single sonnet which opens a door of understanding and insight for thousands of people? Is a life wasted if a person lies, cheats, schemes, damages, manipulates, and hurts others all his life, but then remembers something of his true nature as a result of it—remembers, perhaps, something he has been spending lifetimes trying to remember—and thus evolves, at last, to the Next Level? Is that life "wasted"?

It is not for you to judge the journey of another's soul. It is for you to decide who YOU are, not who another has been or has failed to be.

So, you ask what would stop people from simply wasting their lives, lollygagging around, collecting "benefits," and the answer is: nothing.

But do You really think this would work? You don't think those who *are* contributing wouldn't begin to resent those who are not?

Yes, they would, if they are not enlightened. Yet enlightened ones would look upon the noncontributors with great compassion, not resentment.

Compassion?

Yes, because the contributors would realize that noncontributors are missing the greatest opportunity and the grandest glory: the opportunity to create and the glory of experiencing the *highest idea* of Who They Really Are. And the contributors would know that this was punishment enough for their laziness, if, indeed, punishment were required—which it is not.

But wouldn't those who are really contributing be angry at having the fruits of their labor taken from them and given to the lazy ones?

You are not listening. *All* would be given minimal survival portions. Those who have more would be given an opportunity to contribute 10 percent of their earnings in order to make this possible.

As to how income would be decided, the open marketplace would determine the value of one's contribution, just as it does today in your country.

But then we would *still* have the "rich" and the "poor," just as we do today! That is not *equality*.

But it is equal *opportunity*. For everyone would have the *opportunity* to live a basic existence without worries of survival. And everyone would be given an equal opportunity to acquire knowledge, develop skills, and use his or her natural talents in the Joy Place.

The Joy Place?

That's what the "work place" will then be called.

But won't there still be envy?

Envy, yes. Jealousy, no. Envy is a natural emotion urging you to strive to be more. It is the two-year-old child yearning and urging herself to reach that doorknob which her big brother can reach. There is nothing wrong with that. There is nothing wrong with envy. It is a motivator. It is pure desire. It gives birth to greatness.

Jealousy, on the other hand, is a fear-driven emotion making one willing for the other to have less. It is an emotion often based in bitterness. It proceeds from anger and leads to anger. And it kills. Jealousy can kill. Anyone who's been in a jealous triangle knows that.

Jealousy kills, envy gives birth.

Those who are envious will be given every opportunity to succeed in *their* own way. No one will be held back economically, politically, socially. Not by reason of race, gender or sexual orientation. Not by reason of birth, class status or age. Nor for any reason at all. Discrimination for *any* reason will simply no longer be tolerated.

And yes, there may still be the "rich" and the "poor," but there will no longer be the "starving" and the "destitute."

You see, the incentive *won't* be taken out of life . . . *merely the desperation*.

But what will guarantee that we'll have enough contributors to "carry" the noncontributors?

The greatness of the human spirit.

Oh?

Contrary to your apparent dire belief, the average person will *not* be satisfied with subsistence levels and nothing more. In addition, the whole incentive for greatness will change when the second paradigm shift—the spiritual shift—takes place.

What would cause such a shift? It hasn't occurred yet in the 2000-year history—

Try two-*billion*-year history—

—of the planet. Why should it occur now?

Because with the shift away from material survival—with the elimination of the need to succeed mightily in order to acquire a modicum of security—there will be no other reason to achieve, to stand out, to become magnificent, save *the experience of magnificence itself!*

And that will be sufficient motivation?

The human spirit rises; it does not fall in the face of true opportunity. The soul seeks a higher experience of itself, not a lower. Anyone who has experienced *true magnificence*, if only for a moment, knows this.

How about power? In this special reordering, there would still be those with inordinate wealth and power.

Financial earnings would be limited.

Oh, boy—here we go. You want to explain how that would work before I explain why it won't?

Yes. Just as there would be lower limits on income, so would there be upper limits. First, nearly everyone will tithe 10 percent of their income to the world government. This is the voluntary 10 percent deduction I mentioned before.

Yes . . . the old "equal tax" proposal.

In your present society at this present time it would have to take the form of a tax because you are not sufficiently enlightened to see that voluntary deduction for the general good of all is in your best interest. Yet when the shift in consciousness I have been describing occurs, such an open, caring, freely offered deduction from your harvest will be seen by you as obviously appropriate.

I have to tell You something. Do You mind if I interrupt You here to tell You something?

No, go right ahead.

This conversation is seeming very strange to me. I never thought I'd have a conversation with God in which God would start recommending political courses of action. I mean, really. How do I convince people that *God is for the flat tax!*

Well, I see you keep insisting on seeing it as a "tax," but I understand that, because the concept of simply offering to share 10 percent of your abundance seems so foreign to you. Nevertheless, why do you find it difficult to believe I would have an idea about this?

I thought God was nonjudgmental, had no opinion, didn't care about such things.

Wait, let me get this straight. In our last conversation—which you called *Book 1*—I answered all sorts of questions. Questions about what makes relationships work, questions about right livelihood, questions about diet, even. How does that differ from this?

I don't know. It just *seems* different. I mean, do You really have a political point of view? Are You a card-carrying Republican? What a truth to come out of this book! God is a *Republican.*

You'd rather I be a Democrat? Good God!

Cute. No, I'd rather you be *apolitical.*

I am apolitical. I have no political point of view whatsoever.

Sort of like Bill Clinton.

Hey, good! Now *you're* being cute! I like humor, don't you?

I guess I didn't expect God to be humorous *or* political.

Or anything human, eh?

Okay, let Me place this book and *Book 1,* for that matter, into context for you once again.

I have no preference in the matter of how you conduct your life. My only desire is that you experience yourself fully as a creative being, so that you might know Who You Really Are.

Good. I understand that. So far, so good.

Every question I have answered here and every inquiry to which I responded in *Book 1* has been heard and responded to within the context of what you, as a creative being, say you are attempting to be and do. For instance, in *Book 1* you asked Me many questions about how you could finally make relationships work. Do you remember?

Yes, of course.

Did you find My answers so problematic? Did you find it difficult to believe that I would have a point of view on this?

I never thought about it. I just read the answers.

Yet, you see, I was placing My answers within the context of your questions. That is, given that you desire to be or do so-and-so, what is a way to go about that? And I showed you a way.

Yes, You did.

I am doing the same thing here.

It's just . . . I don't know . . . more difficult to believe that God would say these things than it was to believe that God would say those things.

Are you finding it more difficult to *agree with* some of the things said here?

Well . . .

Because if you are, that's very okay.

It is?

Of course.

It's okay to disagree with God?

Certainly. What do you think I'm going to do, squash you like an insect?

I hadn't gotten that far in my thinking, actually.

Look, the world has been disagreeing with Me since this whole thing started. Hardly anyone has been doing it My Way since it began.

That's true, I guess.

You can be sure it's true. Had people been following My instructions—left with you through hundreds of teachers over thousands of years—the world would be a much different place. So if you wish to disagree with Me now, go right ahead. Besides, I could be wrong.

What?

I said, besides, I could be wrong. Oh, my goodness . . . you're not taking this all as *gospel,* are you?

You mean I'm not supposed to put any stock in this dialogue?

Oops, hold it. I think you've missed a big part of all this. Let's go back to Square One: *You're making this all up.*

Oh, well, that's a relief. For a while there I thought I was actually getting some real guidance.

The guidance you are getting is to *follow your heart.* Listen to your *soul.* Hear your *self.* Even when I present you with an option, an idea, a point of view, you are under no obligation to accept that as your own. If you disagree, then *disagree*. That is *the whole point of this exercise*. The idea wasn't for you to substitute your dependency on everything and everyone else *with a dependency on this book*. The idea was to cause you to *think*. To think for your *self*. And that is who I Am right now. I am you, *thinking*. I am you, thinking out loud.

You mean this material is not coming from the Highest Source?

Of course it is! Yet here is the one thing you still cannot believe: *you are the Highest Source*. And here is the one thing you still apparently do not grasp: *you are creating it all—all of your life—right here, right now*. You . . . YOU . . . are creating it. Not Me. YOU.

So . . . are there some answers to these purely political questions that you do not like? *Then change them*. Do it. Now. Before you start hearing them as *gospel*. Before you start making them *real*. Before you start calling your last thought about something more important, more valid, more true than your *next* thought.

Remember, it's always your *new thought* that creates your reality. Always.

Now, do you find anything in this political discussion of ours that you want to change?

Well, not really. I'm sort of agreeing with You, as it happens. I just did-n't know what to make of all of this.

Make of it what you wish. Don't you get it? *That's what you're doing with all of life!*

Okay, all right . . . I think I've got it. I would like to continue with this conversation, if only to see where it's going.

Fine, then let's do that.

You were about to say . . .

I was about to say that in other societies—enlightened societies—the putting aside of a set amount of what one receives (what you call "income") to be used for the general good of the society itself is a rather common practice. Under the new system we have been exploring for your society, everyone would earn as much each year as they could—and they would retain what they earn, up to a certain limit.

What limit?

An arbitrary limit, agreed to by everyone.

And anything above that limit?

Would be contributed to the world charitable trust *in the name of the contributor*, so all the world would know its benefactors.

Benefactors would have the option of direct control over the disbursement of 60 percent of their contribution, providing them the satisfaction of putting most of their money exactly where they want it.

The other 40 percent would be allocated to programs legislated by the world federation and administered by it.

If people knew that after a certain income limit everything would be taken from them, what would be their incentive to keep working? What would cause them not to stop in midstream, once they reached their income "limit"?

Some would. So what? Let them stop. Mandatory work above the income limit, with contributions to the world charitable trust, would not be required. The money saved from the elimination of mass production of weapons of war would be sufficient to supply everyone's basic need. The 10 percent tithe of all that is earned worldwide on top of those savings would elevate all of society, not just the chosen few, to a new level of dignity and abundance. And the contribution of earnings above the agreed-upon limit would produce such widespread opportunity and satisfaction for everyone that jealousy and social angers would virtually disintegrate.

So some *would* stop working—especially those who *saw* their life activity as *real work*. Yet those who saw their activity as *absolute joy* would *never* stop.

Not everyone can have a job like that.

Untrue. Everyone can.

Joy at the work place has nothing to do with function, and every-thing to do with purpose.

The mother who wakes up at 4 o'clock in the morning to change her baby's diaper understands this perfectly. She hums and coos to the baby, and for all the world it doesn't look like what she is doing is any work at all. Yet it is her attitude about what she is doing, it is her intention with regard to it, it is her *purpose* in under-taking this activity, which make the activity a true joy.

I have used this example of motherhood before, because the love of a mother for her child is as close as you may be able to come to understanding some of the concepts of which I am speak-ing in this book and in this trilogy.

Still, what would be the purpose of eliminating "limitless earning potential"? Wouldn't that rob the human experience of one of its great-est opportunities, one of its most glorious adventures?

You would still have the opportunity and the adventure of earn-ing a ridiculous amount of money. The upper limit on retainable income would be very high—more than the average person . . . the average ten people . . . would ever need. And the amount of income you could *earn* would not be limited—simply the amount you would choose to retain for personal use. The remainder—everything, say, over $25 million a year (I use a strictly arbitrary figure to make a point)—would be spent for programs and servic-es benefitting all humankind.

As to the reason—the *why* of it . . .

The upper retainable income limit would be a reflection of a consciousness shift on the planet; an awareness that the highest purpose of life is not the accumulation of the greatest wealth, but the doing of the greatest good—and a corollary awareness that, indeed, the *concentration of wealth*, not the sharing of it, is the largest single factor in the creation of the world's most persistent and striking social and political dilemmas.

The opportunity to amass wealth—unlimited wealth—is the corner-stone of the capitalistic system, a system of free enterprise and open competition that has produced the greatest society the world has ever known.

The problem is, you really believe that.

No, I don't. But I've mouthed it here on behalf of those who *do* believe it.

Those who do believe it are terribly deluded and see nothing of the current reality on your planet.

In the United States, the top one and a half percent hold more wealth than the bottom 90 percent. The net worth of the richest 834,000 people is nearly a trillion dollars greater than the poorest *84 million people combined.*

So? They've worked for it.

You Americans tend to see class status as a function of individual effort. Some have "made good," so you assume that anybody can. That view is simplistic and naive. It assumes that everyone has equal opportunity, when in fact, in America just as in Mexico, the rich and powerful strive and contrive to hold on to their money and their power *and to increase it.*

So? What's wrong with that?

They *do* so by systematically *eliminating* competition, by institutionally *minimizing* true opportunity, and by collectively *controlling* the flow and the growth of wealth.

This they accomplish through all manner of devices, from unfair labor practices which exploit the masses of the world's poor to good-old-boy network competitive practices which minimize (and all but destroy) a newcomer's chances of entering the Inner Circle of the successful.

They then seek to control public policy and governmental programs around the world to *further* ensure that the masses of people remain regulated, controlled, and subservient.

I don't believe that the rich do this. Not the largest number of them. There may be a handful of conspirators, I suppose. . . .

In most cases it isn't rich *individuals* who do it; it's the social systems and institutions they represent. Those systems and institutions were *created* by the rich and powerful—and it is the rich and powerful who continue to support them.

By standing behind such social systems and institutions, individuals can wash their hands of any personal responsibility for the conditions which oppress the masses while favoring the rich and powerful.

For example, let's go back to health care in America. Millions of America's poor have no access to preventive medical care. One cannot point to any *individual doctor* and say, "this is your doing, it is your fault" that, in the richest nation on earth, millions cannot get in to see a doctor unless they're in dire straits in an emergency room.

No *individual* doctor is to blame for that, yet *all doctors benefit.* The entire medical profession—and every allied industry—enjoys unprecedented profits from a delivery system which has *institutionalized* discrimination against the working poor and the unemployed.

And that's just one example of how the "system" keeps the rich rich and the poor poor.

The point is that it is the rich and powerful who support such social structures and *staunchly resist any real effort to change them.* They stand against any political or economic approach which seeks to provide true opportunity and genuine dignity to all people.

Most of the rich and powerful, taken individually, are certainly nice enough people, with as much compassion and sympathy as anyone. But mention a concept as threatening to *them* as yearly income limits (even ridiculously high limits, such as $25 million annually), and they start whining about usurpation of individual rights, erosion of the "American way," and "lost incentives."

Yet what about the right of *all* people to live in minimally decent surroundings, with enough food to keep from starving, enough clothing to stay warm? What about the right of people *everywhere* to have adequate health care—the right not to have to *suffer* or *die* from relatively minor medical complications which those with money overcome with the snap of a finger?

The resources of your planet—*including* the *fruits of the labors* of the masses of the indescribably poor who are continually and systematically exploited—belong to all the world's people, not just those who are rich and powerful enough to do the exploiting.

And here is how the exploitation works: Your rich industrialists go into a country or an area where there is no work at all, where the people are destitute, where there is abject poverty. The rich set up a factory there, offering those poor people jobs—sometimes 10-, 12-, and 14-hour-a-day jobs—at substandard, if not to say *subhuman,* wages. Not enough, mind you, to allow those workers to escape their rat-infested villages, but just enough to let them live *that* way, as opposed to having *no food or shelter at all.*

And when they are called on it, these capitalists say, *"Hey, they've* got it better than *before,* don't they? We've *improved their lot!* The people are *taking* the jobs, aren't they? Why, we've brought them *opportunity!* And *we're* taking all the *risk!"*

Yet how much risk is there in paying people 75 cents an hour to manufacture sneakers which are going to sell for $125 a pair?

Is this risk-taking or exploitation, pure and simple?

Such a system of rank obscenity could exist only *in a world motivated by greed, where profit margin, not human dignity, is the first consideration.*

Those who say that "relative to the standards in their society, those peasants are doing *wonderfully!"* are hypocrites of the first order. They would throw a drowning man a rope, but *refuse to pull him to shore.* Then they would brag that a *rope is better than a rock.*

Rather than raising the people to true dignity, these "haves" give the world's "have-nots" just enough to make them dependent— but not enough to ever make them truly powerful. For people of true economic power have the ability to then *impact,* and not merely be subject to, "the system." And that's the last thing the creators of the system want!

So the conspiracy continues. And for most of the rich and powerful it is not a conspiracy of action, but a *conspiracy of silence.*

So go now—go your way—and by all means say *nothing* about the obscenity of a socioeconomic system which rewards a corporate executive with a 70-million-dollar bonus for increasing sales of a soft drink, while 70 million *people* can't afford the luxury of drinking the stuff—much less eating enough to stay healthy.

Don't see the obscenity of it. Call this the world's Free Market Economy, and tell everyone how *proud* you are of it.

Yet it is written:

If thou wilt be perfect,

go and sell what thou hast, and give to the poor,

and thou shalt have treasure in heaven.

But when the young man heard this, he went away, sorrowful,

for he had great possessions.

19

I've rarely seen You so indignant. God doesn't become indignant. This proves You are not God.

> God is *everything,* and God *becomes* everything. There is nothing which God is not, and all that God is experiencing of Itself, God is experiencing in, as, and through *you.* It is *your* indignation which you are feeling.

You're right. Because I agree with everything You've said.

> Know that every thought I am sending you, you are receiving through the filter of your own experience, of your own truth, of your own understandings, and of your own decisions, choices, and declarations about Who You Are and Who You Choose to Be. There's no other way you can receive it. There's no other way you should.

Well, here we go again. Are You saying that none of these ideas and feelings are *Yours,* that this *whole book* could be wrong? Are You telling me that this entire experience of my conversation with You could be nothing more than a compilation of *my* thoughts and feelings on a thing?

> Consider the possibility that *I am giving you* your thoughts and feelings on a thing (where do you suppose these are coming from?); that I am co-creating with you your experiences; that I am part of your decisions, choices, and declarations. Consider the possibility that I have chosen you, along with many others, to be My messenger long before this book came to be.

That's hard for me to believe.

> Yes, we went over all of that in *Book 1.* Yet I will speak to this world, and I will do it, among other ways, through my teachers and my messengers. And in this book I will tell your world that its

economic, political, social, and religious systems are primitive. I observe that you have the collective arrogance to think they are the best. I see the largest number of you resisting any change or improvement which takes anything away from you—never mind who it might help.

I say again, what is needed on your planet is a massive shift in consciousness. A change in your awareness. A renewed respect for all of life, and a deepened understanding of the inter-relatedness of everything.

Well, You're God. If You don't want things the way they are, why don't You change them?

As I have explained to you before, My decision from the beginning has been to give you the freedom to create your life—and hence, your Self—as you wish to *be*. You cannot know your Self as the Creator if I tell you what to create, how to create, and then force, require, or cause you to do so. If I do that, My purpose is lost.

But now, let us just notice what *has* been created on your planet, and see if it doesn't make *you* a bit indignant.

Let's look at just four inside pages of one of your major daily newspapers on a typical day.

Pick up today's paper.

Okay. It's Saturday, April 9, 1994, and I am looking at the *San Francisco Chronicle*.

Good. Open it to any page.

All right. Here's page A-7.

Fine. What do you see there?

The headline says DEVELOPING NATIONS TO DISCUSS LABOR RIGHTS.

Excellent. Go on.

The story reports on what it calls an "old schism" between industrialized nations and developing countries over labor rights. Leaders of some developing nations are said to be "fearful that a campaign to expand

labor rights could create a back door means of barring their low-wage products from the rich nation's consumer markets."

It goes on to say that negotiators for Brazil, Malaysia, India, Singapore and other developing nations have refused to establish a permanent committee of the World Trade Organization which would be charged with drafting a labor rights policy.

> What rights is the story talking about?

It says, "basic rights for workers," such as prohibitions on forced labor, establishment of workplace safety standards, and a guarantee of the opportunity to bargain collectively.

> And why do developing nations not want such rights as part of an international agreement? I'll *tell* you why. But first, let's get clear that it's not the *workers* in those countries who resist such rights. Those "negotiators" for the developing nations are the same people, or are closely allied with the same people, *who own and run the factories.* In other words—the rich and powerful.
>
> As in the days before the labor movement in America, those are the people now benefitting from the mass exploitation of workers.
>
> You can be sure that they are being quietly assisted by big money in the U.S. and other rich nations, where industrialists—no longer able to unfairly exploit workers in their own nations—are subcontracting to factory owners in these developing countries (or building their own plants there) in order to exploit foreign workers who are still unprotected from being used by others to increase their already-obscene profits.

But the story says it's our government—the present administration— which is pushing for workers' rights to be part of a worldwide trade agreement.

> Your current leader, Bill Clinton, is a man who believes in basic workers' rights, even if your powerful industrialists do not. He is courageously fighting big money's vested interests. Other American presidents and leaders throughout the world have been killed for less.

Are you saying President Clinton is going to be murdered?

> Let's just say there are going to be tremendous powers attempting to remove him from office. They've got to get him *out* of there—just as they had to remove John Kennedy 30 years earlier.

Like Kennedy before him, Bill Clinton is doing everything big money hates. Not only pressing for workers' rights worldwide, but siding with the "little person" over the entrenched establishment on virtually every social question.

He believes it's the right of every person, for instance, to have access to adequate health care—whether or not he or she can afford to pay the exorbitant prices and fees that America's medical community has come to enjoy. He has said these costs have got to come down. That has not made him very popular with another very large segment of America's rich and powerful—from pharmaceutical manufacturers to insurance conglomerates, from medical corporations to business owners having to provide decent coverage for their workers—a great many people who are now making a lot of money are going to have to make a little bit less if America's poor are to be given universal health care.

This is not making Mr. Clinton the most popular man in town. At least not among certain elements—who have already proven in this century that they have the ability to remove a president from office.

Are you saying—?

I am saying that the struggle between the "haves" and the "have-nots" has been going on forever and is epidemic on your planet. It will ever be thus so long as economic interests, rather than humanitarian interests, run the world—so long as man's body, and not man's soul, is man's highest concern.

Well, I guess you're right. On page A-14 of the same paper there's a headline: RECESSION SPAWNS ANGER IN GERMANY. The lower headline reads, "With joblessness at postwar high, rich and poor grow further apart."

Yes. And what does this story say?

It says there is great foment among the country's laid-off engineers, professors, scientists, factory workers, carpenters, and cooks. It says the nation has encountered some economic setbacks, and there are "widespread feelings this hardship has not been fairly distributed."

That is correct. It has not been. Does the story say what has caused so many layoffs?

Yes. It says the angry employees are "workers whose employers have moved to countries where labor is cheaper."

Aha. I wonder whether many people reading your *San Francisco Chronicle* on this day saw the connection between the stories on pages A-7 and A-14.

The story also points out that when layoffs come, female workers are the first to go. It says "women comprise more than half of the jobless nationwide, and nearly two-thirds in the east."

Of course. Well, I continue to point out—though most of you do not want to see it or admit it—that your socioeconomic mechanism *systematically* discriminates against classes of people. You are *not* providing equal opportunity all the while you are loudly protesting that you *are*. You need to believe your fiction about this, though, in order to keep feeling good about yourself, and you generally resent anyone who shows you the truth. You will all deny the evidence even as it is being presented to you.

Yours is a society of ostriches.

Well—what *else* is in the newspaper on this day?

On page A-4 is a story announcing NEW FEDERAL PRESSURE TO END HOUSING BIAS. It says "Federal housing officials are putting together a plan that would force . . . the most serious efforts ever to eliminate racial discrimination in housing."

What you must ask yourself is, why must such efforts be forced?

We have a Fair Housing Act which bars discrimination in housing on the basis of race, color, religion, sex, national origin, disability, or family composition. Yet many local communities have done little to eliminate such bias. Many people in this country still feel that a person ought to be able to do what he wants to with his private property—including rent to or *not* rent to whomever he chooses.

Yet if everyone who owned rental property were allowed to make such choices, and if those choices tended to reflect a group consciousness and a generalized attitude toward certain categories and classes of people, then entire segments of the population could be systematically eliminated from any opportunity to find decent places in which to live. And, in the absence of decent *affordable housing*, land barons and slumlords would be able to charge exorbitant prices for terrible dwellings, providing little or no upkeep. And once again the rich and powerful exploit the masses, this time under the guise of "property rights."

Well, property owners should have *some* rights.

Yet when do the rights of the few infringe upon the rights of the many?

That is, and has always been, the question facing every civilized society.

Does there come a time when the higher good of all supersedes individual rights? Does society have a responsibility to itself?

Your fair housing laws are your way of saying yes.

All the failures to follow and enforce those laws are the rich and powerful's way of saying "No—all that counts are *our* rights."

Once again, your current president and his administration is forcing the issue. Not all American presidents have been so willing to confront the rich and powerful on yet another front.

I see that. The newspaper article says that Clinton Administration housing officials have initiated more investigations of housing discrimination in the brief time they've been in office *than were investigated in the prior ten years*. A spokesperson for the Fair Housing Alliance, a national advisory group in Washington, said the Clinton Administration's insistence that fair housing statutes be obeyed was something they had tried to get other administrations to do for years.

And so this current president makes even more enemies among the rich and powerful: manufacturers and industrialists, drug companies and insurance firms, doctors and medical conglomerates, and investment property owners. All people with money and influence.

As observed earlier, look for Clinton to have a tough time staying in office.

Even as this is being written—April 1994—the pressure is mounting against him.

Does your April 9, 1994, edition of the newspaper tell you anything else about the human race?

Well, back on page A-14 there's a picture of a Russian political leader brandishing his fists. Underneath the photograph is a news story headlined

ZHIRINOVSKY ASSAULTS COLLEAGUES IN PARLIAMENT. The article notes that Vladimir Zhirinovsky "got into another fist fight yesterday, beating up" a political opponent and screaming in his face, "I'll have you rot in jail! I'll tear your beard out hair by hair!"

And you wonder why *nations* go to war? Here is a major leader of a massive political movement, and in the halls of Parliament he has to prove his manhood by *beating up his opponents*.

Yours is a very primitive race, where strength is all you understand. There is no true law on your planet. True Law is Natural Law—inexplicable and not *needed* to be explained or taught. It is *observable*.

True law is that law by which the people freely agree to be governed because they are governed by it, naturally. Their agreement is therefore not so much an agreement as it is a mutual recognition of what is So.

Those laws don't have to be enforced. They already *are* enforced, by the simple expedient of undeniable consequence.

Let Me give you an example. Highly evolved beings do not hit themselves on the head with a hammer, because it hurts. They also don't hit anyone *else* on the head with a hammer, for the same reason.

Evolved beings have noticed that if you hit someone else with a hammer, that person gets hurt. If you keep doing it, that person gets angry. If you keep getting him angry, he finds a hammer of his own and eventually hits you back. Evolved beings therefore know that if you hit someone else with a hammer, you are hitting yourself with a hammer. It makes no difference if you have more hammers, or a bigger hammer. Sooner or later you're going to get hurt.

This result is observable.

Now nonevolved beings—*primitive* beings—observe the same thing. They simply don't care.

Evolved beings are not willing to play "The One With The Biggest Hammer Wins." Primitive beings play nothing else.

Incidentally, this is largely a male game. Among your species, very few women are willing to play Hammers Hurt. They play a new game. They say, "If I had a hammer, I'd hammer out justice, I'd hammer out freedom, I'd hammer out love between my brothers and my sisters, all over this land."

Are you saying women are more evolved than men?

I'm making no judgment one way or the other on that. I simply observe.

You see, truth—like natural law—is observable.

Now, any law that is not natural law is not observable, and so has to be explained to you. You have to be *told* why it's for your own good. It has to be shown to you. This is not an easy task because if a thing is for your own good, *it is self-evident.*

Only that which is not self-evident has to be explained to you.

It takes a very unusual and determined person to convince people of something which is not self-evident. For this purpose you have invented politicians.

And clergy.

Scientists don't say much. They're usually not very talkative. They don't have to be. If they conduct an experiment, and it succeeds, they simply show you what they've done. The results speak for themselves. So scientists are usually quiet types, not given to verbosity. It is not necessary. The reason for their work is self-evident. Furthermore, if they try something and fail, they have nothing to say.

Not so with politicians. Even if they've *failed*, they talk. In fact, sometimes the more they fail, the more they talk.

The same is true of religions. The more they fail, the more they talk.

Yet I tell you this.

Truth and God are found in the same place: in the silence.

When you have found God, and when you have found truth, it is not necessary to talk about it. It is self-evident.

If you are *talking* a lot about God, it is probably because you are still searching. That's okay. That's all right. Just know where you are.

But teachers talk about God all the time. That's all *we* talk about in this book.

You teach what you choose to learn. And yes, this book does speak about Me, as well as about life, which makes this book a very good case in point. You have engaged yourself in writing this book *because you are still searching.*

Yes.

Indeed. And the same is true of those who are reading it.

But we were on the subject of creation. You asked Me at the beginning of this chapter why, if I didn't like what I was seeing on Earth, I didn't change it.

I have no judgment about what you do. I merely observe it and from time to time, as I have done in this book, describe it.

But now I must ask you—forget My observations and forget My descriptions—how do *you* feel about what you have observed of your planet's creations? You've taken just one day's stories out of the newspaper, and so far you've uncovered:

- Nations refusing to grant basic rights to workers.

- The rich getting richer and the poor getting poorer in the face of a depression in Germany.

- The government having to force property owners to obey fair housing laws in the United States.

- A powerful leader telling political opponents, "I'll have you rot in jail! I'll tear your beard out hair by hair!" while punching them in the face on the floor of the national legislature in Russia.

Anything else this newspaper has to show Me about your "civilized" society?

Well, there's a story on page A-13 headlined CIVILIANS SUFFER MOST IN ANGOLAN CIVIL WAR. The drop head says: "In rebel areas, top guns live in luxury while many thousands starve."

Enough. I'm getting the picture. And this is just one day's paper?

One *section* of one day's paper. I haven't gotten out of Section A.

And so I say again—your world's economic, political, social, and religious systems are *primitive*. I will do nothing to change that, for the reasons I've given. You must have *free choice* and *free will* in these matters in order for you to experience My highest goal for you—which is to know yourself as the Creator.

And so far, after all these thousands of years, this is how far you have evolved—this is what you have created.

Does it not make you indignant?

Yet you have done one good thing. You have come to Me for advice.

Repeatedly your "civilization" has turned to God, asking: "Where did we go wrong?" "How can we do better?" The fact that you have systematically ignored My advice on every other occasion does not stop Me from offering it again. Like a good parent, I'm always willing to offer a helpful observation when asked. Also like a good parent, I'm willing to keep loving you if I'm ignored.

So I'm describing things as they really are. And I'm telling you how you can do better. I'm doing so in a way which causes you to feel some indignation because I want to get your attention. I see that I have done so.

What could *cause* the kind of massive consciousness shift of which You've spoken now repeatedly in this book?

There is a slow chipping away happening. We are gradually stripping the block of granite which is the human experience of its unwanted excess, as a sculptor chips away to create and reveal the true beauty of the final carving.

"We?"

You and I, through our work on these books, and a great many others, messengers all. The writers, the artists, the television and movie producers. The musicians, the singers, the actors, the dancers, the teachers, the shamans, the gurus. The politicians, the leaders (yes, there are some very good ones, some very sincere ones), the doctors, the lawyers (yes, there are some very good ones, some very sincere ones!), the moms and dads and grandmas and grandpas in living rooms and kitchens and backyards all over America, and all around the world.

You are the forbearers, the harbingers.

And the consciousness of many people is shifting.

Because of you.

Will it take a worldwide calamity, a disaster of gargantuan proportions, as some have suggested? Must the Earth tilt on its axis, be hit by a meteor, swallow its continents whole, before its people will listen? Must we be visited by beings from outer space and scared out of our minds before having sufficient sight to realize that we are all One? Is it required that we all face the threat of death before we can be galvanized to find a new way to live?

Such drastic events are not necessary—but could occur.

Will they occur?

Do you imagine that the future is predictable—even by God? I tell you this: Your future is creatable. Create it as you want it.

But earlier You said that in the true nature of time there *is* no "future"; that all things are happening in the Instant Moment—the Forever Moment of Now.

That is true.

Well, are there earthquakes and floods and meteors hitting the planet "right now" or aren't there? Don't tell me that as God You don't *know*.

Do you want these things to happen?

Of course not. But *You* said everything that's *going* to happen already *has* happened—*is* happening *now*.

That is true. But the Eternal Moment of Now is also *forever changing*. It is like a mosaic—one that is always there, but constantly shifting. You can't blink, because it will be different when you open your eyes again. Watch! Look! *See?* There it goes again!
I AM CONSTANTLY CHANGING.

What makes You change?

Your idea about Me! Your *thought* about *all* of it is what makes It change—*instantly*.
Sometimes the change in the All is subtle, virtually indiscernible, depending upon the power of the thought. But when there is an intense thought—or a *collective thought*—then there is *tremendous* impact, incredible effect.
Everything changes.

So—*will* there be the kind of major, Earth-wide calamity You speak of?

I don't know. Will there?
You decide. Remember, you are choosing your reality *now*.

I choose for it not to happen.

Then it will not happen. Unless it does.

Here we go again.

Yes. You must learn to live within the contradiction. And you must understand the greatest truth: Nothing Matters.

Nothing matters?

I'll explain that in *Book 3*.

Well . . . okay, but I don't like to have to wait on these things.

There is so much here for you to absorb already. Give yourself some time. Give yourself some space.

Can we not leave yet? I sense You are leaving. You always start talking like that when You are getting ready to leave. I'd like to talk about a few other things . . . such as, for instance, beings from outer space—*are* there such things?

Actually, we were going to cover that, too, in *Book 3*.

Oh, come on, give me a glimpse, a peek.

You want to know if there is intelligent life elsewhere in the universe?
Yes. Of course.

Is it as primitive as ours?

Some of the life forms are more primitive, some less so. And some are far more advanced.

Have we been visited by such extraterrestrial beings?

Yes. Many times.

For what purpose?

To inquire. In some cases to gently assist.

How do they assist?

Oh, they give a boost now and then. For instance, surely you're aware that you've made more technological progress in the past 75 years than in *all of human history before that*.

Yes, I suppose so.

Do you imagine that everything from CAT scans to supersonic flight to computer chips you imbed in your body to regulate your heart all came from the mind of man?

Well . . . yes!

Then why didn't man think them up thousands of years before now?

I don't know. The technology wasn't available, I guess. I mean, one thing leads to another. But the beginning technology wasn't there, until it was. It's all a process of evolution.

You don't find it strange that in this billion-year process of evolution, somewhere around 75 to 100 years ago there was a huge "comprehension explosion"?

You don't see it as *outside the pattern* that many people now on the planet have seen the development of everything from radio to radar to radionics *in their lifetime?*

You don't get that what has happened here represents a quantum leap? A step forward of such magnitude and such proportion as to defy any progression of logic?

What are You saying?

I am saying, consider the possibility you've been helped.

If we're being "helped" technologically, why aren't we being helped spiritually? Why aren't we being given some assistance with this "consciousness shift"?

You are.

I am?

What do you think this book is?

Hmmm.

In addition, every day, new ideas, new thoughts, new concepts are being placed in front of you.

The process of shifting the consciousness, increasing the spiritual awareness, of an entire planet, is a slow process. It takes time and great patience. Lifetimes. Generations.

Yet slowly you are coming around. Gently you are shifting. Quietly, there is change.

And You're telling me that beings from outer space are helping us with that?

Indeed. They are among you now, many of them. They have been helping for years.

Why don't they then make themselves known? Reveal themselves? Wouldn't that render their impact twice as great?

Their purpose is to assist in the change they see that most of you desire, not create it; to foster, not force.

Were they to reveal themselves, you would be forced, by the sheer power of their presence, to accord them great honor and give their words great weight. It is preferred that the mass of people come to their own wisdom. Wisdom which comes from within is not nearly so easily discarded as wisdom which comes from another. You tend to hang on a lot longer to that which you've created than to that which you've been told.

Will we ever see them; ever come to know these extraterrestrial visitors as who they really are?

Oh, yes. The time will come when your consciousness will rise and your fear will subside, and then they will reveal themselves to you.

Some of them have already done so—with a handful of people.

What about the theory, now becoming more and more popular, that these beings are actually malevolent? Are there some who mean us harm?

Are there some human beings who mean you harm?

Yes, of course.

Some of these beings—the lesser evolved—may be judged by you in the same way. Yet remember My injunction. Judge not. No one does anything inappropriate, given one's model of the universe.

Some beings have advanced in their technology, but not in their thinking. Your race is rather like that.

But if these malevolent beings are so technologically advanced, surely they could destroy us. What's to stop them?

You are being protected.

We are?

Yes. You are being given the opportunity to live out your own destiny. Your own consciousness will create the result.

Which means?

Which means that in this, as in all things, what you think is what you get.

What you fear is what you will draw to you.

What you resist, persists.

What you look at disappears—giving you a chance to recreate it all over again, if you wish, or banish it forever from your experience.

What you choose, you experience.

Hmmm. Somehow it doesn't seem that way in my life.

Because you doubt the power. You doubt *Me*.

Probably not a good idea.

Definitely not.

20

Why do people doubt You?

Because they doubt themselves.

Why do they doubt themselves?

Because they have been told to; taught to.

By whom?

People who claimed to be representing Me.

I don't get it. Why?

Because it was a way, is the only way, to control people. You *must* doubt yourself, you see, or you would claim all your power. That would not do. That would not do at all. Not for the people who currently hold the power. They are holding the power which is yours—and they know it. And the only way to hold on to it is to stave off the world's movement toward seeing, and then solving, the two biggest problems in the human experience.

Which are?

Well, I've discussed them over and over again in this book. To summarize, then . . .

Most, if not all, of the world's problems and conflicts, and of your problems and conflicts as individuals, would be solved and resolved if you would, as a society:

1. Abandon the concept of Separation.
2. Adopt the concept of Visibility.

Never see yourself again as separate from one another, and never see yourself as separate from Me. Never tell anything but the whole truth to anyone, and never again accept anything less than *your* grandest truth about Me.

The first choice will produce the second, for when you see and understand that you are One with Everyone, you can *not* tell an untruth or withhold important data or be anything but totally visible with all others *because you will be clear that it is in your own best interests to do so.*

But this paradigm shift will take great wisdom, great courage, and massive determination. For Fear will strike at the heart of these concepts and call them false. Fear will eat at the core of these magnificent truths and make them appear hollow. Fear will distort, disdain, destroy. And so Fear will be your greatest enemy.

Yet you will not have, cannot produce, the society for which you have always yearned and of which you have always dreamed unless and until you see with wisdom and clarity the ultimate truth: that what you do to others, you do to yourself; what you fail to do for others, you fail to do for yourself; that the pain of others is your pain, and the joy of others your joy, and that when you disclaim any part of it, you disclaim a part of yourself. Now is the time to *reclaim yourself.* Now is the time to see yourself again as Who You Really Are, and thus render yourself visible again. For when you and your true relationship with God become visible, then We are *indivisible.* And nothing will ever divide Us again.

And although you will live again in the illusion of separation, using it as a tool to create your Self anew, you will henceforth move through your incarnations with enlightenment, seeing the illusion for what it is, using it playfully and joyfully to experience any aspect of Who We Are which it pleases you to experience, yet nevermore accepting it as reality. You will nevermore have to use the device of forgetfulness in order to recreate your Self anew, but will use Separation *knowingly,* simply *choosing* to manifest as That Which Is Separate for a particular reason and a particular purpose.

And when you are thus totally enlightened—that is, once more filled with the light—you may even choose, as your particular reason for returning to physical life, the re-minding of others. You may select to return to this physical life not to create and experience any new aspect of your Self, but to bring the light of truth to this place of illusion, that others may see. Then will you be a "bringer of the light." Then will you be part of The Awakening. There are others who have already done this.

They have come here to help us to know Who We Are.

Yes. They are enlightened souls, souls which have evolved. They no longer seek the next higher experience of themselves. They have already had the highest experience. They desire now only to bring news of that experience to you. They bring you the "good news." They will show you the way, and the life, of God. They will *say* "I am the way and the life. Follow me." Then they will model for you what it is like to live in the everlasting glory of conscious union with God—which is called God Consciousness.

We are always united, you and I. We cannot *not* be. It is simply impossible. Yet you live now in the unconscious experience of that unification. It is also possible to live in the physical body in conscious union with All That Is; in conscious awareness of *ultimate truth*; in conscious expression of Who You Really Are. When you do this, you serve as a model for all others, others who are living in forgetfulness. You become a living re-minder. And in this you save others from becoming permanently lost in their forgetfulness.

That *is* hell, to become lost permanently in forgetfulness. Yet I will not allow it. I will not allow a single sheep to be lost, but will send . . . a shepherd.

Indeed, many shepherds will I send, and you may choose to be one of them. And when souls are awakened by you from their slumber, re-minded once again of Who They Are, all the angels in heaven rejoice for these souls. For once they were lost, and now they are found.

There are people, holy beings, like this right now on our planet, is that not right? Not just in the past, but right now?

Yes. Always there have been. Always there will be. I will not leave you without teachers; I will not abandon the flock, but always send after it My shepherds. And there are many on your planet right now, and in other parts of the universe as well. And in some parts of the universe these beings live together in constant communion and in constant expression of the highest truth. These are the enlightened societies of which I have spoken. They exist, they are real, and they have sent you their emissaries.

You mean the Buddha, Krishna, Jesus were *spacemen?*

You said that, I didn't.

Is it true?

Is this the first time you ever heard that thought?

No, but is it *true?*

Do you believe these masters existed somewhere before they came to Earth and returned to that place after their so-called death?

Yes, I do.

And where do you suppose that place is?

I'd always thought it was what we call "heaven." I thought they came from heaven.

And where do you suppose this heaven is?

I don't know. In another realm, I guess.

Another world?

Yes . . . Oh, I see. But I would have called it *the spirit world*, not another world as we know it, not another *planet.*

It *is* the spirit world. Yet what makes you think those spirits— those Holy Spirits—cannot, or would not choose to, live elsewhere in the universe, *just as they did when they came to your world?*

I suppose I just never thought of it that way. It has not been part of my ideas about all of this.

"There are more things in heaven and earth, Horatio, than are dreamt of in your philosophy."
Your wonderful metaphysician, William Shakespeare, wrote that.

Then Jesus *was* a spaceman!

I didn't say that.

Well, was he or wasn't he?

Patience, My child. You jump ahead too much. There is more. So much more. We have another whole book to write.

You mean I have to wait for *Book 3?*

I told you, I promised you from the beginning. There will be three books, I said. The first would deal with individual life truths and challenges. The second would discuss truths of life as a family on this planet. And the third, I said, would cover the largest truths, having to do with the eternal questions. In this will be revealed the secrets of the universe.

Unless they are not.

Oh, man. I don't know how much more of this I can take. I mean, I'm really tired of "living in the contradiction," as You always put it. I want what's so *to be so.*

Then *so shall it be.*

Unless it's not.

That's it! That's it! You've GOT it! Now you understand the Divine Dichotomy. Now you see the whole picture. Now you comprehend *the plan.*

Everything—*everything*—*that ever was, is now, and ever will be exists right now.* And so, all that is . . . *IS.* Yet all that IS is constantly *changing,* for life is an *ongoing process of creation.* Therefore, in a very real sense, That Which IS . . . IS NOT.

This ISNESS is NEVER THE SAME. Which means that the ISNESS is NOT.

Well, excuse me Charlie Brown, but *good grief.* How can anything then mean anything?

It doesn't. But you are jumping ahead again! All of this in good time, My son. All of this in good time. These and other larger mysteries will all be understood after reading *Book 3.* Unless . . . all together now . . .

UNLESS THEY ARE NOT.

Precisely.

Okay, okay . . . fair enough. But between now and then—or, for that matter, for the people who may never get to read these books—what avenues can be used right here, right now, to get back to wisdom, to get back to clarity, to get back to God? Do we need to return to religion? Is that the missing link?

Return to spirituality. Forget about religion.

That statement is going to anger a lot of people.

People will react to this entire book with anger . . . unless they do not.

Why do You say, forget religion?

Because it is not good for you. Understand that in order for organized religion to succeed, it has to make people believe they *need* it. In order for people to put faith in something else, they must first lose faith in themselves. So the first task of organized religion is to make you lose faith in yourself. The second task is to make you see that *it* has the answers you do not. And the third and most important task is to make you accept its answers without question.

If you question, you start to think! If you think, you start to go back to that Source Within. Religion can't have you do that, because you're liable to come up with an answer different from what it has contrived. So religion must make you doubt your Self; must make you doubt your own ability to think straight.

The problem for religion is that very often this backfires—for if you cannot accept without doubt your own thoughts, how can you not doubt the new ideas about God which religion has given you?

Pretty soon, you even doubt My *existence*—which, ironically, you never doubted before. When you were living by your *intuitive knowing*, you may not have had Me all figured out, but you definitely knew I was there!

It is religion which has created agnostics.

Any clear thinker who looks at what religion has done must assume religion has no God! For it is religion which has filled the hearts of men with fear of God, where once man loved That Which Is in all its splendor.

It is religion which has ordered men to bow down before God, where once man rose up in joyful outreach.

It is religion which has burdened man with worries about God's wrath, where once man sought God to *lighten* his burden!

It is religion which told man to be ashamed of his body and its most natural functions, where once man *celebrated* those functions as the greatest gifts of life!

It is religion which taught you that you must have an *intermediary* in order to reach God, where once you thought yourself to be reaching God by the simple living of your life in goodness and in truth.

And it is religion which *commanded* humans to adore God, where once humans adored God because it was impossible *not* to!

Everywhere religion has gone it has created disunity—which is the *opposite* of God.

Religion has separated man from God, man from man, man from woman—some religions actually *telling* man that he is *above* woman, even as it claims God is above man—thus setting the stage for the greatest travesties ever foisted upon half the human race.

I tell you this: God is *not* above man, and man is *not* above woman—that is *not* the "natural order of things"—but it *is* the way everyone who had power (namely, men) *wished* it was when they formed their male-worship religions, systematically editing out half the material from their final version of the "holy scriptures" and twisting the rest to fit the mold of their male model of the world.

It is religion which insists *to this very day* that women are somehow less, somehow second-class spiritual citizens, somehow not "suited" to teach the Word of God, preach the Word of God, or minister to the people.

Like children, you are still arguing over which gender is ordained by Me to be My priests!

I tell you this: You are *all* priests. *Every single one of you.*

There is no one person or class of people more "suited" to do My work than any other.

But so many of your men are just like your nations. Power hungry. They do not like to share power, merely exercise it. And they have constructed the same kind of God. A power hungry God. A God who does not like to share power but merely exercise it. Yet I tell you this: God's greatest gift is the sharing of God's power.

I would have you be like Me.

But we cannot be like You! That would be blasphemy.

The blasphemy is that you have been taught such things. I tell you this: *You have been made in the Image and Likeness of God—it is that destiny you came to fulfill.*

You did not come here to strive and to struggle and to never "get there." Nor did I send you on a mission impossible to complete.

Believe in the goodness of God, and believe in the goodness of God's creation—namely, your holy Selves.

You said something earlier in this book which intrigued me. I'd like to go back as we come to the end of this volume. You said: "Absolute Power demands absolutely nothing." Is this the nature of *God?*

You have now understood.

I have said, "God is everything, and God *becomes* everything. There is nothing which God is not, and all that God is experiencing of Itself, God is experiencing in, as, and through you." In My purest form, I am the Absolute. I am Absolutely Everything, and therefore, I need, want, and demand absolutely nothing.

From this absolutely pure form, I am as you make Me. It is as if you were finally to see God and say, "Well, what do you make of that?" Yet, no matter what you make of Me, I cannot forget, and will always return to, My Purest Form. All the rest is a fiction. It is something you are *making up.*

There are those who would make Me a jealous God; but who could be jealous when one has, and is, Everything?

There are those who would make Me a wrathful God; but what could cause Me to be angry when I can not be hurt or damaged in any way?

There are those who would make Me a vengeful God; but on whom would I take vengeance, since all that exists is Me?

And why would I punish Myself for simply creating? Or, if you must think of us as separate, why would I create you, give *you* the power to create, give you the freedom of choice to create what you wish to experience, then punish you forever for making the "wrong" choice?

I tell you this: I would not do such a thing—and in that truth lies your freedom from the tyranny of God.

In truth, there *is* no tyranny—except in your imagination.

You may come home whenever you wish. We can be together again whenever you want. The ecstasy of your union with Me is yours to know again. At the drop of a hat. At the feel of the wind on your face. At the sound of a cricket under diamond skies on a summer night.

At the first sight of a rainbow and the first cry of a newborn babe. At the last ray of a spectacular sunset and the last breath in a spectacular life.

I am with you always, even unto the end of time. Your union with Me is complete—it always was, always is, and always will be.

You and I *are* One—both now and even forevermore.

Go now, and make of your life a statement of this truth.

Cause your days and nights to be reflections of the highest idea within you. Allow your moments of Now to be filled with the spectacular ecstasy of God made manifest through you. Do it through the expression of your Love, eternal and unconditional, for all those whose lives you touch. Be a light unto the darkness, and curse it not.

Be a bringer of the light.

You *are* that.

So be it.

Book 3

for

NANCY FLEMING-WALSCH

Best friend, dear companion,
passionate lover, and wonderful wife,
who has brought me and taught me
more than any human being
on Earth.

I am blessed in Thee
beyond my highest dream.
You have made my soul sing again.
You have shown me love
in miracle form.
And you have given me
back to myself.

I humbly dedicate this book to you,
my greatest teacher.

Acknowledgments

As always, I wish first to thank my best friend, God. I hope one day that everyone can have a friendship with God.

Next, I acknowledge and thank my wonderful life partner, Nancy, to whom this book is dedicated. When I think of Nancy, my words of gratitude seem feeble next to her deeds, and I feel stuck with not being able to find a way to express how really extraordinary she is. This much I know. My work would not have been possible without her.

Then, I wish to acknowledge Robert S. Friedman, publisher at Hampton Roads Publishing Company, for his courage in first placing this material before the public in 1995, and in publishing all volumes of the *CWG* trilogy. His decision to accept a manuscript that was rejected by four other publishers has changed the lives of millions.

And I can't let the moment of this last installment in the *CWG* trilogy pass without acknowledging the extraordinary contribution to its publication made by Jonathan Friedman, whose clarity of vision, intensity of purpose, depth of spiritual understanding, endless well of enthusiasm, and monumental gift of creativity is in large measure the reason *Conversations with God* made its way to bookshelves when it did, how it did. It was Jonathan Friedman who recognized the enormity of this message and its importance, predicting that it would be read by millions, foreseeing that it would become a classic of spiritual literature. It was his determination which produced the timing and design of *CWG*, and his unwavering dedication which had much to do with the efffectiveness of its initial distribution. All lovers of *CWG* are forever indebted to Jonathan, as am I.

I wish to thank Matthew Friedman also, for his tireless work on this project from the beginning. The value of his co-creative efforts in design and production cannot be overstated.

Finally, I want to acknowledge some of the authors and teachers whose work has so altered the philosophical and spiritual landscape of

America and the world, and who inspire me daily with their commitment to telling a larger truth regardless of the pressures and personal complications that such a decision creates.

To Joan Borysenko, Deepak Chopra, Dr. Larry Dossey, Dr. Wayne Dyer, Dr. Elisabeth Kübler-Ross, Barbara Marx Hubbard, Stephen Levine, Dr. Raymond Moody, James Redfield, Dr. Bernie Siegel, Dr. Brian Weiss, Marianne Williamson, and Gary Zukav—all of whom I have come to personally know and deeply respect—I pass on the thanks of a grateful public, and my personal appreciation and admiration.

These are some of our modern day way-show-ers, these are the pathfinders, and if I have been able to embark on a personal journey as a public declarer of eternal truth, it is because they, and others like them whom I have not met, have made it possible. Their life work stands as testimony to the extraordinary brilliance of the light in all our souls. They have *demonstrated* what I have merely talked about.

Introduction

There has been no time before in the history of our civilization in which humans yearned more deeply for answers to life's largest questions than they do right now.

Everything in life seems topsy-turvy right now. Everything seems upside-down. And the funny thing is, we understand perfectly well that things are not the way they "should be," that our life is not being lived the way it was meant to be, but we don't seem to know how to "set things to right." And so, we search. We search for answers, we search for solutions, we search for each other, we search for ourselves, and we search for God.

All of this is what makes the gift of the *Conversations with God* series of books so profound. For in this one body of work, covering eight extraordinary volumes, our questions are answered. Now, these answers are not the only answers, nor is it the claim that they are the best answers, but they do provide a breathtaking overview of the New Spirituality and a marvelous beginning point for deeper exploration of life's largest questions. Also, by the very nature of the dialogue itself, they encourage further inquiry, which is what spirituality must do—and what too many religions do not do.

This book closes out the original *CwG* trilogy, providing enormous stimulation of that process of inquiry with its extraordinary commentary on all aspects of life. One will be hard pressed to leave this book unchallenged. And that's good, because what the world could use right now is a direct challenge to its current beliefs.

I am convinced that if we continue believing what most of the human race presently believes about God and about life, the human species will alter the course of its history in nightmarish ways, perhaps ultimately producing its own self-destruction. That is because our current beliefs about God and about life *are not life-sustaining.*

That which is life-sustaining automatically produces peace, joy, and harmony. Humanity's beliefs obviously do not. What is striking here is that, while all of us can see this, only a few of us seem willing to do anything about it. I am presuming that you are among them, or you would not be looking at this book right now. The fact that you have even glanced at it suggests to me that your mind is open to possibilities that most of the human race will not consider.

This book is for the brave, not for the timid. It is for the courageous, not the overly cautious. It is for the visionary, not the shortsighted. For it envisions a world in which love is the answer to every question, in which fear of God has been abandoned forever as the basis of theology, and in which fear of each other has been rejected utterly as a rationale for economic, political, and social conventions.

On these pages are descriptions of Highly Evolved Beings and Highly Evolved Societies—wonderful beginning suggestions for how our own human cultures might reorganize themselves, so to achieve humanity's highest goals and live humanity's grandest dream, at last.

So take this book and read it thoroughly. Then read it again, and one more time still. Absorb its contents. Ponder deeply its wisdom. Hold closely its sacred secret—that the truth lies within you—as does all the power you will ever need to change the direction of your life and the course of human history.

If ever human history could use a course correction, it is now. Where are we headed? Into more of that from which we have just emerged? Into more strife and anger and violence and killing? Into more suffering and squalor for the masses while the few live lives of obscene wastefulness? Into more dysfunction and chaos, as the systems we've created continue to break down, one by one?

Let these be our questions for the day. Then, allow the answers to come through you, as you. And use all the resources at your command, all the tools at your disposal, all the insight you can muster, and all the wisdom you can draw to you (as you have done with this book) to recreate yourself and your world anew in the next grandest version of the greatest vision ever you held about Who You Are.

Be the miracle for which you pray, be the strength for which you call out, be the love for which you yearn, and be the change you wish to see.

Be it.

Be *all* that you seek for this world and end your search at last, knowing that everything for which you looked, you always possessed, but simply could not experience until you gave it away.

Embark now, here, on the journey of *Conversations with God, Book 3*—a book that *you called to you* at this exact moment—as a means of remembering all of this, and more. Travel back in time with me now, to the moment when this present book was first given to humanity, and savor the fact that its wisdom has been gifted to you *by* you at *this* moment, for its wisdom is more applicable now than ever before.

Neale Donald Walsch
Ashland, Oregon
July 2003

_1_

It is Easter Sunday, 1994, and I am here, pen in hand, as instructed. I am waiting for God. He's promised to show up, as She has the past two Easters, to begin another yearlong conversation. The third and last—for now.

This process—this extraordinary communication—began in 1992. It will be complete on Easter, 1995. Three years, three books. The first dealt with largely personal matters—romantic relationships, finding one's right work, dealing with the powerful energies of money, love, sex, and God; and how to integrate them into our daily lives. The second expanded on those themes, moving outward to major geopolitical considerations—the nature of governments, creating a world without war, the basis for a unified, international society. This third and final part of the trilogy will focus, I am told, on the largest questions facing man. Concepts dealing with other realms, other dimensions, and how the whole intricate weave fits together.

The progression has been

Individual Truths
Global Truths
Universal Truths

As with the first two manuscripts, I have no idea where this is going. The process is simple. I put pen to paper, ask a question—and see what thoughts come to my mind. If nothing is there, if no words are given to me, I put everything away until another day. The whole process took about a year for the first book, over a year for the second. (That book is still in process as this is begun.)

I expect this will be the most important book of all.

For the first time since starting this process, I am feeling very self-conscious about it. Two months have passed since I wrote those first four or five paragraphs. Two months since Easter, and nothing has come—nothing but self-consciousness.

I have spent weeks reviewing and correcting errors in the typeset manuscript of the first book in this trilogy—and just this week received the
final, corrected version of *Book 1*, only to have to send it back to type-
setting again, with 43 separate errors to correct. The second book,
meanwhile, still in handwritten form, was completed only last week—
two months behind "schedule." (It was supposed to be done by Easter
'94.) This book, begun on Easter Sunday in spite of the fact that *Book 2*
was unfinished, has languished in its folder ever since—and, now that
Book 2 is complete—cries out for attention.

Yet for the first time since 1992, when this all began, I seem to be
resisting this process, if not almost resenting it. I am feeling trapped by
the assignment, and I've never liked to do anything I *have* to do. Further,
having distributed to a few people uncorrected copies of the first manuscript and heard their reactions to it, I am now convinced that all three
of these books will be widely read, thoroughly examined, analyzed for
theological relevance, and passionately debated for dozens of years.

That has made it very difficult to come to this page; very difficult to
consider this pen my friend—for while I know this material must be
brought through, I know that I am opening myself up to the most scur-
rilous attacks, the ridicule, and perhaps even the hatred of many people
for daring to put forth this information—much less for daring to
announce that it is coming to me directly from God.

I think my greatest fear is that I will prove to be an inadequate, inappropriate "spokesperson" for God, given the seemingly endless series of
mistakes and misdeeds which have marked my life and characterized my
behavior.

Those who have known me from my past—including former wives
and my own children—would have every right to step forward and
denounce these writings, based on my lackluster performance as a
human being in the simple, rudimentary functions of husband and
father. I have failed miserably at this, and at other aspects of life having
to do with friendship and integrity, industry and responsibility.

I am, in short, keenly aware that I am not worthy to represent myself
as a man of God or a messenger of truth. I should be the last person to
assume such a role, or to even presume to. I do an injustice to the truth
by presuming to speak it, when my whole life has been a testimony to
my weaknesses.

For these reasons, God, I ask that You relieve me of my duties as Your
scribe, and that You find someone whose life renders them worthy of
such an honor.

I should like to finish what we started here—though you are under no obligation to do so. You have no "duties," to Me or to anyone else, though I see that your thought that you do has led you to much guilt.

I have let people down, including my own children.

Everything that has happened in your life has happened perfectly in order for you—and all the souls involved with you—to grow in exactly the way you've needed and wanted to grow.

That is the perfect "out" constructed by everyone in the New Age who wishes to escape responsibility for their actions and avoid any unpleasant outcomes.

I feel that I've been selfish—incredibly selfish—most of my life, doing what pleases me regardless of its impact on others.

There is nothing wrong in doing what pleases you. . . .

But, so many people have been hurt, let down—

There is only the question of what pleases you most. You seem to be saying that what now pleases you most are behaviors which do little or no damage to others.

That's putting it mildly.

On purpose. You must learn to be gentle with yourself. And stop judging yourself.

That's hard—particularly when others are so ready to judge. I feel I am going to be an embarrassment to You, to the truth; that if I insist on completing and publishing this trilogy, I will be such a poor ambassador for Your message as to discredit it.

You cannot discredit truth. Truth is truth, and it can neither be proven nor disproven. It simply is.

The wonder and the beauty of My message cannot and will not be affected by what people think of you.

Indeed, you are one of the best ambassadors, because you have lived your life in a way that you call less than perfect.

People can relate to you—even as they judge you. And if they see that you are truly sincere, they can even forgive you your "sordid past."

Yet I tell you this: So long as you are still worried about what others think of you, you are owned by them.

Only when you require no approval from outside yourself can you own yourself.

My concern was more for the message than for me. I was concerned that the message would get besmirched.

If you are concerned about the message, then get the message out. Do not worry about besmirching it. The message will speak for itself.

Remember what I have taught you. It is not nearly so important how well a message is received as how well it is sent.

Remember this also: You teach what you have to learn.

It is not necessary to have achieved perfection to speak of perfection.

It is not necessary to have achieved mastery to speak of mastery.

It is not necessary to have achieved the highest level of evolution to speak of the highest level of evolution.

Seek only to be genuine. Strive to be sincere. If you wish to undo all the "damage" you imagine yourself to have done, demonstrate that in your actions. Do what you can do. Then let it rest.

That's easier said than done. Sometimes I feel so guilty.

Guilt and fear are the only enemies of man.

Guilt is important. It tells us when we've done wrong.

There is no such thing as "wrong." There is only that which does not serve you; does not speak the truth about Who You Are, and Who You Choose to Be.

Guilt is the feeling that keeps you stuck in who you are not.

But guilt is the feeling that at least lets us notice we've gone astray.

Awareness is what you are talking about, not guilt.

I tell you this: Guilt is a blight upon the land—the poison that kills the plant.

You will not grow through guilt, but only shrivel and die.

Awareness is what you seek. But awareness is not guilt, and love is not fear.

Fear and guilt, I say again, are your only enemies. Love and awareness are your true friends. Yet do not confuse the one with the other, for one will kill you, while the other gives you life.

Then I should not feel "guilty" about anything?

Never, ever. What good is there in that? It only allows you to not love yourself—and that kills any chance that you could love another.

And I should fear nothing?

Fear and caution are two different things. Be cautious—be conscious—but do not be fearful. For fear only paralyzes, while consciousness mobilizes.

Be mobilized, not paralyzed.

I was always taught to fear God.

I know. And you have been paralyzed in your relationships with Me ever since.

It was only when you stopped fearing Me that you could create any kind of meaningful relationship with Me.

If I could give you any gift, any special grace, that would allow you to find Me, it would be fearlessness.

Blessed are the fearless, for they shall know God.

That means you must be fearless enough to drop what you think you know about God.

You must be fearless enough to step away from what others have told you about God.

You must be so fearless that you can dare to enter into your *own experience* of God.

And then you must not feel guilty about it. When your own experience is violating what you thought you knew, and what everyone else has told you, about God, you must not feel guilty.

Fear and guilt are the only enemies of man.

Yet there are those who say that to do as You suggest is trafficking with the devil; that only the devil would suggest such a thing.

There is no devil.

That's something else the devil would say.

The devil would say everything that God says, is that it?

Only more cleverly.

The devil is more clever than God?

Let's say, more cunning.

And so the devil "connives" by saying what God would say?

With just a little "twist"—just enough to get one off the path; to lead one astray.

I think we have to have a little talk about the "devil."

Well, we talked a lot about this in *Book 1*.

Not enough, apparently. Besides, there may be those who haven't read *Book 1*. Or *Book 2*, for that matter. So I think a good place for us to begin would be to summarize some of the truths found in those books. That will set the stage for the larger, universal truths in this third book. And we'll get to the devil again, too, early on. I want you to know how, and why, such an entity was "invented."

Okay. All right. You win. I'm already into the dialogue, so apparently it's going to continue. But there's one thing people should know as I enter this third conversation: Half a *year* has passed since I wrote the first words presented here. It's now November 25, 1994—the day after Thanksgiving. It's taken 25 weeks to get this far; 25 weeks since your last words above, to my words in this paragraph. A lot has happened in those 25 weeks. But one thing that has not happened is that this book has not moved one inch forward. *Why is this taking so long?*

Do you see how you can block yourself? Do you see how you can sabotage yourself? Do you see how you can stop yourself in your tracks just when you are on to something good? You've been doing this all your life.

Hey, wait a minute! *I'm* not the one who has been stalling on this project. I can't do *anything*—can't write a single word—unless I feel moved to, unless I feel . . . I hate to use the word, but I guess I have to . . . *inspired* to come to this yellow legal pad and continue. And inspiration is *Your* department, not mine!

I see. So you think I've been stalling, not you.

Something like that, yes.

My wonderful friend, this is so much like you—and other humans. You sit on your hands for half a year, doing nothing about your highest good, actually pushing it from you, then blame someone or something outside of yourself for you not getting anywhere. Do you not see a pattern here?

Well . . .

I tell you this: There is never a time when I am not with you; never a moment when I am not "ready."
Have I not told you this before?

Well, yes, but . . .

I am always with you, even unto the end of time.
Yet I will not impose My will on you—ever.
I choose your highest good for you, but above that, I choose your will for you. And this is the surest measure of love.
When I want for you what *you* want for you, then I truly love you. When I want for you what *I* want for you, then I am loving Me, *through* you.
So, too, by the same measure, can you determine whether others love you, and whether you truly love others. For love chooses naught for itself, but only seeks to make possible the choices of the beloved other.

That seems to directly contradict what You put in *Book 1* about love being not at all concerned with what the other is being, doing, and having, but only with what the *Self* is being, doing, and having.

It brings up other questions as well, like . . . what of the parent who shouts at the child, "Get out of the street!" Or, better yet, risks his own life to run out into swirling traffic and snatch the child up? What of that parent? Is she not loving her child? Yet she has imposed her own will. Remember, the child was in the street because it *wanted to be.*

How do You explain these contradictions?

There is no contradiction. Yet you cannot see the harmony. And you will not understand this divine doctrine about love until you understand that My highest choice for Me is the same as your highest choice for you. And that is because you and I are one.

You see, the Divine Doctrine is also a Divine Dichotomy, and that is because life itself is a dichotomy—an experience within which two apparently contradictory truths can exist in the same space at the same time.

In this case, the apparently contradictory truths are that you and I are separate, and you and I are one. The same apparent contradiction appears in the relationship between you and everyone else.

I stand by what I said in *Book 1:* The biggest mistake people make in human relationships is to be concerned for what the other is wanting, being, doing, or having. Be concerned only for the Self. What is the Self being, doing, or having? What is the Self wanting, needing, choosing? What is the highest choice for the Self?

I also stand by another statement I made in that book: The highest choice for the Self becomes the highest choice for another when the Self realizes that there is no one else.

The mistake, therefore, is not in *choosing* what is best for you, but rather, in not *knowing* what is best. This stems from not knowing Who You Really Are, much less who you are seeking to be.

I don't understand.

Well, let me give you an illustration. If you are seeking to win the Indianapolis 500, driving 150 miles per hour might be what is best for you. If you are seeking to get to the grocery store safely, it might not.

You're saying it's all contextual.

Yes. All of *life* is. What is "best" depends on who you are, and who you seek to be. You cannot intelligently choose what is best for you until you intelligently decide who and what you are.

Now I, as God, *know* what I am seeking to be. I therefore know what is "best" for Me.

And what is that? Tell me, what is "best" for God? This ought to be interesting . . .

What is best for Me is *giving you what you decide is best for you*. Because what I am trying to be is My Self, expressed. And I am being this *through you*.

Are you following this?

Yes, believe it or not, I actually am.

Good. Now I will tell you something you may find difficult to believe.

I am always giving you what is best for you . . . though I admit that you may not always know it.

This mystery clears up a bit now that you have begun to understand what I am up to.

I am God.

I am the Goddess.

I am the Supreme Being. The All of Everything. The Beginning and The End. The Alpha and Omega.

I am the Sum and the Substance. The Question and the Answer. The Up and the Down of it. The Left and the Right, the Here and the Now, the Before and the After.

I am the Light, and I am the Darkness that creates the Light, and makes it possible. I am the Goodness Without End, and the "Badness" which makes the "Goodness" good. I am all of these things—the All of Everything—and I cannot experience any part of My Self without experiencing All of My Self.

And this is what you do not understand about Me. You want to make Me the one, and not the other. The high and not the low. The good, and not the bad. Yet in denying half of Me, you deny half of your Self. And in so doing, you can never be Who You Really Are.

I am the Magnificent Everything—and what I am seeking is to know Myself experientially. I am doing this through you, and through everything else that exists. And I am experiencing My Self as magnificent through the choices I make. For each choice is self creative. Each choice is definitive. Each choice represents Me— that is, re-presents Me—as Who I Choose to Be Right Now.

Yet I cannot choose to be magnificent *unless there is something to choose from*. Some part of Me must be *less* than magnificent for Me to choose the part of Me which *is* magnificent.

So, too, is it with you.

I am God, in the act of creating My Self.

And so, too, are you.

This is what your soul longs to do. This is that for which your spirit hungers.

Were I to stop you from having what you choose, I would stop My Self from having what I choose. For My greatest desire is to experience My Self as What I Am. And, as I carefully and painstakingly explained in *Book 1*, I can only do that in the space of What I Am Not.

And so, I have carefully created What I Am Not, in order that I might experience What I Am.

Yet I Am *everything* I create—therefore I Am, in a sense, What I Am *Not*.

How can someone be what they are not?

Easy. You do it all the time. Just watch your behaviors.

Seek to understand this. There is *nothing* that I am not. Therefore, I Am what I Am, and I Am What I Am Not.

THIS IS THE DIVINE DICHOTOMY.

This is the Divine Mystery which, until now, only the most sublime minds could understand. I have revealed it for you here in a way that more can understand.

This was the message of *Book 1*, and this basic truth you must understand—you must deeply know—if you are to understand and know the even more sublime truths to come, here, in *Book 3*.

Yet let Me now get to one of those more sublime truths—for it is contained in the answer to the second part of your question.

I was hoping we were going to get back to that part of my question. How is the parent loving the child if he says or does what is best for the child, even if he has to *thwart the child's own will* to do it? Or does the parent demonstrate the truest love by letting the child play in traffic?

This is a wonderful question. And it's the question asked by every parent, in some form or another, since parenting began. The answer is the same for you as a parent as it is for Me as God.

So *what is the answer?*

Patience, My son, patience. "All good things come to those who wait." Have you never heard of that?

Yeah, my father used to say it and I hated it.

I can understand that. But do have patience with your Self, especially if your choices are not bringing you what you think you want. The answer to the second part of your question, for example.

You say that you want the answer, but you are not choosing it. You know you are not choosing it, because you do not experience having it. In truth, you have the answer, and have had it all along. You simply are not choosing it. You are choosing to believe you do not know the answer—and so you do not.

Yes, You went over this, too, in *Book 1*. I have everything I choose to have right now—including a complete understanding of God—yet I will not *experience* that I have it until I *know* that I do.

Precisely! You've put it perfectly.

But how can I *know* that I do until I *experience* that I do? How can I know something I haven't experienced? Wasn't there a great mind who said, "All knowing is experience"?

He was wrong.
Knowing does not follow experience—it precedes it.
In this, half the world has it backwards.

So You mean that I have the answer to the second part of my question, I just don't *know* that I do?

Exactly.

Yet if I don't *know* that I do, then I *don't*.

That's the paradox, yes.

I don't get it . . . except I do.

Indeed.

So how can I get to this place of "knowing that I know" something if I don't "know that I know"?

To "know that you know, act as if you do."

You mentioned something about that in *Book 1* also.

Yes. A good place to start here would be to recap what's gone before in the previous teaching. And you "just happen" to be asking the right questions, allowing Me to summarize in short form at the beginning of this book the information we discussed in prior material in some detail.

Now in *Book 1*, we talked about the Be-Do-Have paradigm, and how most people have it reversed.

Most people believe if they "have" a thing (more time, money, love—whatever), then they can finally "do" a thing (write a book, take up a hobby, go on vacation, buy a home, undertake a relationship), which will allow them to "be" a thing (happy, peaceful, content, or in love).

In actuality, they are reversing the Be-Do-Have paradigm. In the universe as it really is (as opposed to how you think it is), "havingness" does not produce "beingness," but the other way around.

First you "be" the thing called "happy" (or "knowing," or "wise," or "compassionate," or whatever), then you start "doing" things from this place of beingness—and soon you discover that what you are doing winds up bringing you the things you've always wanted to "have."

The way to set this creative process (and that's what this is . . . the process of creation) into motion is to look at what it is you want to "have," ask yourself what you think you would "be" if you "had" that, then go right straight to *being*.

In this way you reverse the way you've been using the Be-Do-Have paradigm—in actuality, set it right—and work with, rather than against, the creative power of the universe.

Here is a short way of stating this principle:

In life, you do not have to *do anything*.

It is all a question of what you are *being*.

This is one of the three messages I will touch on again at the end of our dialogue. I will close the book with it.

For now, and to illustrate this, think of a person who just knows that if he could only have a little more time, a little more money, or a little more love, he'd be truly happy.

He does not get the connection between his "not being very happy" right now and his not having the time, money, or love he wants.

That's right. On the other hand, the person who is "being" happy seems to have time to do everything that's really important, all the money that's needed, and enough love to last a lifetime.

He finds he has everything he needs to "be happy" . . . by "being happy" to begin with!

Exactly. Deciding *ahead of time* what you choose to be *produces that in your experience.*

"To be, or not to be. That is the question."

Precisely. Happiness is a state of mind. And like all states of mind, it reproduces itself in physical form.
There's a statement for a refrigerator magnet:
"All states of mind reproduce themselves."

But how can you "be" happy to begin with, or "be" *anything* you are seeking to be—more prosperous, for instance, or more loved—if you are not having what you think you need in order to "be" that?

Act as if you are, and you will draw it to you.
What you act as if you are, you become.

In other words, "Fake it until you make it."

Something like that, yes. Only you can't really be "faking." Your actions have to be sincere.
Everything you do, do out of sincerity, or the benefit of the action is lost.
This is not because I won't "reward you." God does not "reward" and "punish," as you know. But Natural Law requires the body, mind, and spirit to be united in thought, word, and action for the process of creation to work.
You cannot fool your mind. If you are insincere, your mind knows it, and that's that. You've just ended any chance that your mind can help you in the creative process.
You can, of course, create without your mind—it's just a great deal more difficult. You can ask your body to do something your mind doesn't believe, and if your body does it long enough, your

mind will begin to let go of its former thought about that, and create a New Thought. Once you have a New Thought about a thing, you're well on your way to creating it as a permanent aspect of your being, rather than something you're just acting out.

This is doing things the hard way, and even in such instances, the action must be sincere. Unlike what you can do with people, you cannot manipulate the universe.

So here we have a very delicate balance. The body does something in which the mind does not believe, yet the mind must add the ingredient of sincerity to the body's action for it to work.

How can the mind add sincerity when it does not "believe in" what the body is doing?

By taking out the selfish element of personal gain.

How?

The mind may not be able to sincerely agree that the actions of the body can bring you that which you choose, but the mind seems very clear that God will bring good things through you to another.

Therefore, whatever you choose for yourself, give to another.

Would You say that again, please?

Of course.

Whatever you choose for yourself, give to another.

If you choose to be happy, cause another to be happy.

If you choose to be prosperous, cause another to prosper.

If you choose more love in your life, cause another to have more love in theirs.

Do this sincerely—not because you seek personal gain, but because you really want the other person to have that—and all the things you give away will come to you.

Why is that so? How does that work?

The very act of your giving something away causes you to experience that you *have* it to give away. Since you cannot give to another something you do not now have, your mind comes to a new conclusion, a New Thought, about you—namely, that you must have this, *or you could not be giving it away.*

This New Thought then becomes your experience. You start "being" that. And once you start "being" a thing, you've engaged the gears of the most powerful creation machine in the universe—your Divine Self.

Whatever you are being, you are creating.

The circle is complete, and you will create more and more of that in your life. It will be made manifest in your physical experience.

This is the greatest secret of life. It is what *Book 1* and *Book 2* were written to tell you. It was all there, in far greater detail.

Explain to me, please, why sincerity is so important in giving to another what you choose for yourself.

If you give to another as a contrivance, a manipulation meant to get something to come to *you,* your mind knows this. You've just given it a signal that *you do not now have this.* And since the universe is nothing but a big copying machine, reproducing your thoughts in physical form, *that will be your experience.* That is, you will continue to experience "not having it"—no matter *what* you do!

Furthermore, that will be the experience of the person to whom you're trying to give it. They will see that you are merely seeking to get something, that you have nothing, really, to offer, and your giving will be an empty gesture, seen for all the self-serving shallowness from which it springs.

The very thing you sought to attract, you will thus push away.

Yet when you give something to another with purity of heart—because you see that they want it, need it, and should have it—then you will discover that you have it to give. And that is a grand discovery.

This is true! It really *works* this way! I can remember once, when things were not going so well in my life, holding my head and thinking that I had no more money, and very little food, and that I didn't know when I was going to eat my next square meal, or how I could pay my rent. That very evening I met a young couple at the bus station. I'd gone down to pick up a package, and there these kids were, huddled on a bench, using their coats for a blanket.

I saw them and my heart went out to them. I remembered when I was young, how it was when we were kids, just skimming by, and on the move like that. I walked over to them and asked them if they'd like to come over to my place and sit by a hot fire, have a little hot chocolate, maybe open up the day bed and get a good night's rest. They looked up at me with eyes wide, like children on Christmas morning.

Well, we got to the house, and I made 'em a meal. We all ate better that night than any of us had for quite a while. The food had always been there. The refrigerator was loaded. I just had to reach back, and grab all the stuff I'd shoved back there. I made an "everything-in-the-fridge" stir fry, and *it was terrific!* I remember thinking, where did all this food come from?

The next morning I even gave the kids breakfast, and sent them on their way. I reached into my pocket as I dropped them off back at the bus station and gave them a twenty-dollar bill. "Maybe this will help," I said, gave 'em a hug and sent them on their way. I felt better about my own situation all day. Heck, all *week*. And that experience, which I have never forgotten, produced a profound change in my outlook and my understandings about life.

Things got better from there, and as I looked at myself in the mirror this morning, I noticed something very important. *I'm still here.*

> That's a beautiful story. And you're right. *That's exactly how it works.* So when you want something, give it away. You will then no longer be "wanting" it. You will immediately experience "having" it. From there on, it is only a question of degree. Psychologically, you will find it much easier to "add onto," than to create out of thin air.

I feel I have just heard something very profound here. Can You relate this now to the second part of my question? Is there a connection?

> What I'm proposing, you see, is that you already *have* the answer to that question. Right now you are living the thought that you do not have the answer; that if you had the answer, you would have wisdom. So you come to Me for wisdom. Yet I say to you, *be* wisdom, and you will have it.
>
> And what is the fastest way to "be" wisdom? Cause *another* to be wise.
>
> Do you choose to have the answer to this question? *Give the answer to another.*
>
> So, now, I'll ask *you* the question. I'll pretend that I "don't know," and you give Me the answer.

*How can the parent who pulls a child out of traffic be truly lov-
ing the child, if love means that you want for the other what they
want for themselves?*

I don't know.

*I know you don't. But if you thought you did, what would your
answer be?*

Well, I'd say that the parent *did* want for the child what the child wanted—which was to *stay alive*. I'd say that the child did not want to die,
but simply did not know that wandering around in traffic could cause
that. So that in running out there to get the child, the parent wasn't
depriving the child of the opportunity to exercise its will at all—but simply getting in touch with the child's true choice, its deepest desire.

That would be a very good answer.

If that's true, then You, as God, should be doing nothing but *stopping
us from hurting ourselves,* for it can't be our deepest desire to do damage to ourselves. Yet we do damage to ourselves all the time, and You just
sit around and watch us.

*I am always in touch with your deepest desire, and always I give
you that.
Even when you do something that would cause you to die—if
that is your deepest desire, that is what you get: the experience of
"dying."
I never, ever interfere with your deepest desire.*

Do You mean that when we do damage to ourselves, that is what we
wanted to do? That is our *deepest desire?*

*You cannot "do damage" to yourselves. You are incapable of
being damaged. "Damage" is a subjective reaction, not an objective phenomenon. You can choose to experience "damage" to
yourself out of any encounter or phenomenon, but that is entirely
your decision.
Given that truth, the answer to your question is, Yes—when you
have "damaged" yourself, it is because you wanted to. But I'm
speaking on a very high, esoteric level, and that is not really where
your question is "coming from."*

In the sense that you mean it, as a matter of conscious choice, I would say that no, every time you do something that damages yourself, it is not because you "wanted to."

The child who gets hit by a car because he wandered into the street did not "want" (desire, seek, consciously choose) to get hit by a car.

The man who keeps marrying the same kind of woman—one who is all wrong for him—packaged in different forms, does not "want" (desire, seek, consciously choose) to keep creating bad marriages.

The person who hits a thumb with a hammer could not be said to have "wanted" the experience. It was not desired, sought, consciously chosen.

Yet all objective phenomena are drawn to you subconsciously; all events are created by you unconsciously; every person, place, or thing in your life was drawn to you by you—was Self-created, if you will—to provide you with the exact and perfect conditions, the perfect opportunity, to experience what you next wish to experience as you go about the business of evolving.

Nothing can happen—I say to you, nothing can occur—in your life which is not a precisely perfect opportunity for you to heal something, create something, or experience something that you wish to heal, create, or experience in order to be Who You Really Are.

And who, really, am I?

Whomever you choose to be. Whatever aspect of Divinity you wish to be—that's Who You Are. That can change at any given moment. Indeed, it often does, from moment to moment. Yet if you want your life to settle down, to stop bringing you such a wide variety of experiences, there's a way to do that. Simply stop changing your mind so often about Who You Are, and Who You Choose to Be.

That may be easier said than done!

What I see is that you are making these decisions at many different levels. The child who decides to go out into the street to play in traffic is not making a choice to die. She may be making a number of other choices, but dying is not one of them. The mother knows that.

The problem here is not that the child has chosen to die, but that the child has made choices that could lead to more than one outcome, including her dying. That fact is not clear to her; it is unknown to her. It is the missing data—which stops the child from making a clear choice, a better choice.

So you see, you have analyzed it perfectly.

Now, I, as God, will never interfere with your choices—but I will always know what they are.

Therefore, you may assume that if a thing happens to you, it is perfect that it did so—for nothing escapes perfection in God's world.

The design of your life—the people, places, and events in it—have all been perfectly created by the perfect creator of perfection itself: you. And Me . . . in, as, and through you.

Now We can work together in this co-creative process consciously or unconsciously. You can move through life aware, or unaware. You can walk your path asleep, or awake.

You choose.

Wait, go back to that comment about making decisions at many different levels. You said that if I wanted life to settle down, I should stop changing my mind about who I am and who I wish to be. When I said that may not be easy, You made the observation that all of us are making our choices at many different levels. Can You elaborate on that? What does that mean? What are the implications?

If all you desired is what your soul desired, everything would be very simple. If you listened to the part of you which is pure spirit, all of your decisions would be easy, and all the outcomes joyous. That is because . . .

. . . the choices of spirit are always the highest choices.

They don't need to be second-guessed. They don't need to be analyzed or evaluated. They simply need to be followed, acted on.

Yet you are not only a spirit. You are a Triune Being made up of body, mind, and spirit. That is both the glory and the wonder of you. For you often make decisions and choices at all three levels simultaneously—and *they by no means always coincide.*

It is not uncommon for your body to want one thing, while your mind seeks another, and your spirit desires yet a third. This can be especially true of children, who are often not yet mature enough to make distinctions between what sounds like "fun" to the body, and what makes sense to the mind—much less what resonates with the soul. So the child waddles into the street.

Now, as God, I am aware of all your choices—even those you make subconsciously. I will never interfere with them, but rather, just the opposite. It is My job to ensure that your choices are granted. (In truth, you grant them to your Self. What I have done is put a system into place that allows you to do that. This system is called the process of creation, and is explained in detail in *Book 1*.)

When your choices conflict—when body, mind, and spirit are not acting as one—the process of creation works at all levels, producing mixed results. If, on the other hand, your being is in harmony, and your choices are unified, astonishing things can occur.

Your young people have a phrase—"having it all together"—which could be used to describe this unified state of being.

There are also levels within levels in your decision making. This is particularly true at the level of the mind.

Your mind can, and does, make decisions and choices from one of at least three interior levels: logic, intuition, emotion—and sometimes from all three—producing the potential for even more inner conflict.

And within one of those levels—emotion—there are five more levels. These are the *five natural emotions*: grief, anger, envy, fear, and love.

And within these, also, there are two final levels: love and fear.

The five natural emotions include love and fear, yet love and fear are the basis of all emotions. The other three of the five natural emotions are outgrowths of these two.

Ultimately, all thoughts are sponsored by love or fear. This is the great polarity. This is the primal duality. Everything, ultimately, breaks down to one of these. All thoughts, ideas, concepts, understandings, decisions, choices, and actions are based in one of these.

And, in the end, there is really only one.

Love.

In truth, love is all there is. Even fear is an outgrowth of love, and when used effectively, expresses love.

Fear expresses *love*?

In its highest form, yes. Everything expresses love, when the expression is in its highest form.

Does the parent who saves the child from being killed in traffic express fear, or love?

Well, both, I suppose. Fear for the child's life, and love—enough to risk one's own life to save the child.

Precisely. And so here we see that fear in its highest form becomes love . . . *is love* . . . expressed as fear.

Similarly, moving up the scale of natural emotions, grief, anger, and envy are all some form of fear, which, in turn, is some form of love.

One things leads to another. Do you see?

The problem comes in when any of the five natural emotions become distorted. Then they become grotesque, and not recognizable at all as outgrowths of love, much less as God, which is what Absolute Love is.

I've heard of the five natural emotions before—from my wonderful association with Dr. Elisabeth Kübler-Ross. She taught me about them.

Indeed. And it was I who inspired her to teach about this.

So I see that when I make choices, much depends on "where I'm coming from," and that where I'm "coming from" could be several layers deep.

Yes, that is what is so.

Please tell me—I would like to hear it again, because I've forgotten much of what Elisabeth taught me—all about the five natural emotions.

Grief is a natural emotion. It's that part of you which allows you to say goodbye when you don't want to say goodbye; to express—push out, propel—the sadness within you at the experience of any kind of loss. It could be the loss of a loved one, or the loss of a contact lens.

When you are allowed to express your grief, you get rid of it. Children who are allowed to be sad when they are sad feel very healthy about sadness when they are adults, and therefore usually move through their sadness very quickly.

Children who are told, "There, there, don't cry," have a hard time crying as adults. After all, they've been told all their life not to do that. So they repress their grief.

Grief that is continually repressed becomes chronic depression, a very unnatural emotion.

People have killed because of chronic depression. Wars have started, nations have fallen.

Anger is a natural emotion. It is the tool you have which allows you to say, "No, thank you." It does not have to be abusive, and it never has to be damaging to another.

When children are allowed to express their anger, they bring a very healthy attitude about it to their adult years, and therefore usually move through their anger very quickly.

Children who are made to feel that their anger is not okay—that it is wrong to express it, and, in fact, that they shouldn't even experience it—will have a difficult time appropriately dealing with their anger as adults.

Anger that is continually repressed becomes rage, a very unnatural emotion.

People have killed because of rage. Wars have started, nations have fallen.

Envy is a natural emotion. It is the emotion that makes a five-year-old wish he could reach the doorknob the way his sister can—or ride that bike. Envy is the natural emotion that makes you want to do it again; to try harder; to continue striving until you succeed. It is very healthy to be envious, very natural. When children are allowed to express their envy, they bring a very healthy attitude about it to their adult years, and therefore usually move through their envy very quickly.

Children who are made to feel that envy is not okay—that it is wrong to express it, and, in fact, that they shouldn't even experience it—will have a difficult time appropriately dealing with their envy as adults.

Envy that is continually repressed becomes jealousy, a very unnatural emotion.

People have killed because of jealousy. Wars have started, nations have fallen.

Fear is a natural emotion. All babies are born with only two fears: the fear of falling, and the fear of loud noises. All other fears are learned responses, brought to the child by its environment, taught to the child by its parents. The purpose of natural fear is to build in a bit of caution. Caution is a tool that helps keep the body alive. It is an outgrowth of love. Love of Self.

Children who are made to feel that fear is not okay—that it is wrong to express it, and, in fact, that they shouldn't even experience it—will have a difficult time appropriately dealing with their fear as adults.

Fear that is continually repressed becomes panic, a very unnatural emotion.

People have killed because of panic. Wars have started, nations have fallen.

Love is a natural emotion. When it is allowed to be expressed, and received, by a child, normally and naturally, without limitation or condition, inhibition or embarrassment, it does not require anything more. For the joy of love expressed and received in this way is sufficient unto itself. Yet love which has been conditioned, limited, warped by rules and regulations, rituals and restrictions, controlled, manipulated, and withheld, becomes unnatural.

Children who are made to feel that their natural love is not okay—that it is wrong to express it, and, in fact, that they shouldn't even experience it—will have a difficult time appropriately dealing with love as adults.

Love that is continually repressed becomes possessiveness, a very unnatural emotion.

People have killed because of possessiveness. Wars have started, nations have fallen.

And so it is that the natural emotions, when repressed, produce unnatural reactions and responses. And most natural emotions are repressed in most people. Yet these are your friends. These are your gifts. These are your divine tools, with which to craft your experience.

You are given these tools at birth. They are to help you negotiate life.

Why are these emotions repressed in most people?

They have been taught to repress them. They have been told to.

By whom?

Their parents. Those who have raised them.

Why? Why would they do that?

Because they were taught by their parents, and their parents were told by theirs.

Yes, yes. But *why?* What is going *on?*

What is going on is that you have the wrong people doing the parenting.

What do you mean? Who are the "wrong people"?

The mother and the father.

The mother and the father are the wrong people to raise the children?

When the parents are young, yes. In most cases, yes. In fact, it's a miracle that so many of them do as good a job as they do.

No one is more ill-equipped to raise children than young parents. And no one knows this, by the way, better than young parents.

Most parents come to the job of parenting with very little life experience. They're hardly finished being parented themselves. They're still looking for answers, still searching for clues.

They haven't even discovered themselves yet, and they're trying to guide and nurture discovery in others even more vulnerable than they. They haven't even defined themselves, and they're thrust into the act of defining others. They are still trying to get over how badly they have been mis-defined by their parents.

They haven't even discovered yet Who They Are, and they're trying to tell you who you are. And the pressure is so great for them to get it right—yet they can't even get their own lives "right." So they get the whole thing wrong—their lives, and the lives of their children.

If they're lucky, the damage to their children won't be too great. The offspring will overcome it—but not, probably, before passing some on to their offspring.

Most of you gain the wisdom, the patience, the understanding, and the love to be wonderful parents *after your parenting years are over.*

Why is this? I don't understand this. I see that Your observation is in many cases correct, but why is this?

Because young child-makers were never intended to be child-raisers. Your child-raising years should really begin when they are now over.

I'm still a little lost here.

Human beings are biologically capable of creating children while they are children themselves—which, it may surprise most of you to know, they are for 40 or 50 years.

Human beings are "children themselves" *for 40 or 50 years?*

From a certain perspective, yes. I know this is difficult to hold as your truth, but look around you. Perhaps the behaviors of your race might help prove My point.

The difficulty is that in your society, you are said to be "all grown up" and ready for the world at 21. Add to this the fact that many of you were raised by mothers and fathers *who were not much older than 21 themselves* when they began raising you, and you can begin to see the problem.

If child-bearers were *meant* to be child-raisers, child bearing would not have been made possible until you were fifty!

Child *bearing* was meant to be an activity of the young, whose bodies are well developed and strong. Child *raising* was meant to be an activity of the elders, whose minds are well developed and strong.

In your society you have insisted on making child-bearers responsible for child raising—with the result that you've made not only the process of parenting very difficult, but distorted many of the energies surrounding the sexual act as well.

Uh . . . could You explain?

Yes.

Many humans have observed what I've observed here. Namely, that a good many humans—perhaps most —are not truly capable of raising children when they are capable of having them. However, having discovered this, humans have put in place exactly the wrong solution.

Rather than allow younger humans to enjoy sex, and if it produces children, have the elders raise them, you tell young humans not to engage in sex *until they are ready to take on the responsibility of raising children*. You have made it "wrong" for them to have sexual experiences before that time, and thus have created a taboo around what was intended to be one of life's most joyful celebrations.

Of course, this is a taboo to which offspring will pay little attention—and for good reason: *it is entirely unnatural to obey it.*

Human beings desire to couple and copulate as soon as they feel the inner signal which says they are ready. *This is human nature.*

Yet their thought about their own nature will have more to do with what you, as parents, have told them than about what they are feeling inside. Your children look to you to tell them what life is all about.

So when they have their first urges to peek at each other, to play innocently with each other, to explore each other's "differences," they will look to you for signals about this. Is this part of their human nature "good"? Is it "bad"? Is it approved of? Is it to be stifled? Held back? Discouraged?

It is observed that what many parents have told their offspring about this part of their human nature has had its origin in all manner of things: what *they* were told; what their *religion* says; what their *society* thinks—everything except the natural order of things.

In the natural order of your species, sexuality is budding at anywhere from age 9 to age 14. From age 15 onward it is very much present and expressing in most human beings. Thus begins a race against time—with children stampeding toward the fullest release of their own joyful sexual energy, and parents stampeding to stop them.

Parents have needed all the assistance and all the alliances they could find in this struggle, since, as has been noted, they are asking their offspring to *not do something* that is every bit a part of their nature.

So adults have invented all manner of familial, cultural, religious, social, and economic pressures, restrictions, and limitations to justify their unnatural demands of their offspring. Children have thus grown to accept that their own sexuality is *unnatural*. How can anything that is "natural" be so shamed, so always-stopped, so controlled, held at bay, restrained, bridled, and denied?

Well, I think You're exaggerating a bit here. Don't You think You're exaggerating?

Really? What do you think is the impact on a four- or five-year-old child when parents won't even use the correct *name* for certain of their body parts? What are you telling the child about your level of comfort with that, and what you think *theirs should be?*

Uh . . .

Yes . . . "uh . . ." indeed.

Well, "we just don't use those words," as my grammy used to say. It's just that "wee-wee" and "your bottom" *sounds* better.

Only because you have so much negative "baggage" attached to the actual names of these body parts that you can barely use the words in ordinary conversation.

At the youngest ages, of course, children don't know why parents feel this way, but merely are left with the impression, the often *indelible* impression, that certain body parts are "not okay," and that anything having to do with them is embarrassing—if not "wrong."

As children grow older and move into their teens, they may come to realize that this is not true, but then they are told in very clear terms about the connection between pregnancy and sexuality, and about how they will have to raise the children they create, and so they now have another reason for feeling that sexual expression is "wrong"—and the circle is complete.

What this has caused in your society is confusion and not a little havoc—*which is always the result of fooling around with nature.*

You have created sexual embarrassment, repression, and shame—which has led to sexual inhibition, dysfunction, and violence.

You will, as a society, always be inhibited about that over which you are embarrassed; always be dysfunctional with behaviors which have been repressed, and always act out violently in protest of being made to feel shame about that over which *you know in your heart you should never have felt shame at all.*

Then Freud was on to something when he said that a huge amount of the anger in the human species might be sexually related—deep-seated rage over having to repress basic and natural physical instincts, interests, and urges.

More than one of your psychiatrists has ventured as much. The human being is angry because it knows it should feel no shame over something that feels so good—and yet it does feel shame, and guilt.

First, the human becomes angry with the Self for feeling so good about something which is supposed to be so obviously "bad."

Then, when they finally realize they've been duped—that sexuality is supposed to be a wonderful, honorable, glorious part of the human experience—they become angry with others: parents, for repressing them, religion for shaming them, members of the opposite sex for daring them, the whole society for controlling them.

Finally, they become angry with themselves, for allowing all of this to inhibit them.

Much of this repressed anger has been channeled into the construction of distorted and misguided moral values in the society in which you now live—a society which glorifies and honors, with monuments, statues, and commemorative stamps, films, pictures, and TV programs, some of the world's ugliest acts of violence, but hides—or worse yet, cheapens—some of the world's most beautiful acts of love.

And all of this—_all of this_—has emerged from a single thought: that those who bear children, bear also the sole responsibility for raising them.

But if the people who have children aren't responsible for raising them, who is?

The whole community. With special emphasis on the elders.

The elders?

In most advanced races and societies, elders raise the offspring, nurture the offspring, train the offspring, and pass on to the offspring the wisdom, teachings, and traditions of their kind. Later, when we talk about some of these advanced civilizations, I'll touch on this again.

In any society where producing offspring at a young age is not considered "wrong"—because the tribal elders raise them and there is, therefore, no sense of overwhelming responsibility and burden—sexual repression is unheard of, and so is rape, deviance, and social-sexual dysfunction.

Are there such societies on our planet?

Yes, although they have been disappearing. You have sought to eradicate them, assimilate them, because you have thought them to be barbarian. In what you have called your nonbarbarian societies, children (and wives, and husbands, for that matter) are thought of as property, as personal possessions, and child-bearers must therefore become child-raisers, because they must take care of what they "own."

A root thought at the bottom of many of your society's problems is this idea that spouses and children are personal possessions, that they are "yours."

We'll examine this whole subject of "ownership" later, when we explore and discuss life among highly evolved beings. But for now, just think about this for a minute. Is anyone really emotionally ready to raise children at the time they're physically ready to have them?

The truth is, most humans are not equipped to raise children even in their 30s and 40s—and shouldn't be expected to be. They really haven't lived enough as adults to pass deep wisdom to their children.

I've heard that thought before. Mark Twain had a take on this. He was said to have commented, "When I was 19, my father knew nothing. But when I was 35, I was amazed at how much the Old Man had learned."

He captured it perfectly. Your younger years were never meant to be for truth-teaching, but for truth-gathering. *How can you teach children a truth you* haven't yet gathered?

You can't, of course. So you'll wind up telling them the only truth you know—the truth of others. Your father's, your mother's, your culture's, your religion's. Anything, everything, but your own truth. You are still searching for that.

And you will be searching, and experimenting, and finding, and failing, and forming and reforming your truth, your idea about yourself, until you are half a century on this planet, or near to it.

Then, you may begin at last to settle down, and settle in, with your truth. And probably the biggest truth on which you'll agree is that there is no constant truth at all; that truth, like life itself, is a changing thing, a growing thing, an evolving thing—and that just when you think that process of evolution has stopped, it has not, but only really just begun.

Yes, I've already come to that. I'm past 50, and I've arrived at that.

Good. You are now a wiser man. An elder. Now you should raise children. Or better yet, ten years from now. It is the elders who should raise the offspring—and who were intended to.

It is the elders who know of truth, and life. Of what is important and what is not. Of what is really meant by such terms as integrity, honesty, loyalty, friendship, and love.

I see the point You have been making here. It is difficult to accept, but many of us *have* barely moved from "child" to "student" when we have children of our own, and feel we have to start teaching *them*. So we figure, well, I'll teach them what my parents taught me.

Thus, the sins of the father are visited upon the son, even unto the seventh generation.

How can we change that? How can we end the cycle?

Place the raising of children in the hands of your respected Old Ones. Parents see the children whenever they wish, live with them if they choose, but are not solely responsible for their care and upbringing. The physical, social, and spiritual needs of the children are met by the entire community, with education and values offered by the elders.

Later in our dialogue, when we talk about those other cultures in the universe, we'll look at some new models for living. But these models won't work the way you've currently structured your lives.

What do You mean?

I mean it's not just parenting you're doing with an ineffective model, but your whole way of living.

Again, what do You mean?

You've moved away from each other. You've torn apart your families, disassembled your smaller communities in favor of huge cities. In these big cities there are more people, but fewer "tribes," groups, or clans whose members see their responsibility as including responsibility for the whole. So, in effect, you have no elders. None at arm's reach, in any event.

Worse than moving away from your elders, you've pushed them aside. Marginalized them. Taken their power away. And even resented them.

Yes, some members of your society are even resenting the seniors among you, claiming that they are somehow leeching on the system, demanding benefits that the young have to pay for with ever-increasing proportions of their income.

It's true. Some sociologists are now predicting a generation war, with older people being blamed for requiring more and more, while contributing less and less. There are so many more older citizens now, what with the "baby boomers" moving into their senior years, and people living longer in general.

Yet if your elders aren't contributing, it is because you have not allowed them to contribute. You have required them to retire from their jobs just when they could really do the company some good, and to retire from most active, meaningful participation in life, just when their participation could bring some sense to the proceedings.

Not just in parenting, but in politics, economics, and even in religion, where elders at least had a toehold, you have become a youth-worshipping, elder- dismissing society.

Yours has also become a singular society, rather than a plural one. That is, a society made up of individuals, rather than groups.

As you have both individualized and youthened your society, you have lost much of its richness and resource. Now you are without both, with too many of you living in emotional and psychological poverty and depletion.

I'm going to ask you again, is there any way we can end this cycle?

First, recognize and acknowledge that it's real. So many of you are living in denial. So many of you are pretending that what's so is simply not so. You are lying to yourselves, and you do not want to hear the truth, much less tell it.

This, too, we'll talk about again later, when we take that look at the civilizations of highly evolved beings, because this denial, this failure to observe and acknowledge what's so, is not an insignificant thing. And if you truly want to change things, I hope you will just allow yourself to hear Me.

The time has come for truth telling, plain and simple. Are you ready?

I am. That's why I came to You. That's how this whole conversation began.

Truth is often uncomfortable. It is only comforting to those who do not wish to ignore it. Then, truth becomes not only comforting, but inspiring.

For me, this whole three-part dialogue has been inspiring. Please, go on.

There is some good reason to be upbeat, to feel optimistic. I observe that things have begun to change. There's more emphasis among your species on creating community, and building extended families, than ever in recent years. And, more and more, you are honoring your elders, producing meaning and value in, and from, their lives. This is a big step in a wonderfully useful direction.

So things are "turning around." Your culture seems to have taken that step. Now, it's onward from there.

You cannot make these changes in one day. You cannot, for instance, change your whole way of parenting, which is how this current train of thought began, in one fell swoop. Yet you *can* change your future, step by step.

Reading this book is one of those steps. This dialogue will circle back over many important points before we are finished. That repetition will not be by accident. It is for emphasis.

Now, you have asked for ideas for the construction of your tomorrows. Let us begin by looking at your yesterdays.

2

What does the past have to do with the future?

When you know about the past, you can better know about all your possible futures. You have come to Me asking how to make your life work better. It will be useful for you to know how you got to where you are today.

I would speak to you of power, and of strength—and the difference between the two. And I would chat with you about this Satan figure you have invented, how and why you invented him, and how you decided that your God was a "He," and not a "She."

I would speak to you of Who I Really Am, rather than who you have said I am in your mythologies. I would describe to you My Beingness in such a way that you will gladly replace the mythology with the cosmology—the true cosmology of the universe, and its relationship to Me. I would have you know about life, how it works, and why it works the way it works. This chapter is about all those things.

When you know those things, then you can decide what you wish to discard of that which your race has created. For this third portion of our conversation, this third book, is about building a newer world, creating a new reality.

You have been living too long, My children, in a prison of your own devise. It is time to set yourself free.

You have imprisoned your five natural emotions, repressing them and turning them into very unnatural emotions, which have brought unhappiness, death, and destruction to your world.

The model of behavior for centuries on this planet has been: do not "indulge" your emotions. If you're feeling grief, get over it; if you're feeling angry, stuff it; if you're feeling envious, be ashamed of it; if you're feeling fear, rise above it; if you're feeling love, control it, limit it, wait with it, run from it—do whatever you have to do to stop from expressing it, full out, right here, right now.

It is time to set yourself free.

In truth, you have imprisoned your Holy Self. And it is time to set your Self free.

I'm starting to get excited here. How do we start? Where do we begin?

In our brief study of how it all got to be this way, let us go back to the time when your society reorganized itself. That is when men became the dominant species, and then decided it was inappropriate to display emotions—or in some cases to even have them.

What do You mean, "when society reorganized itself"? What are we talking about here?

In an earlier part of your history, you lived on this planet in a matriarchal society. Then there was a shift, and the patriarchy emerged. When you made that shift, you moved away from expressing your emotions. You labeled it "weak" to do so. It was during this period that males also invented the devil, and the masculine God.

Males invented the devil?

Yes. Satan was essentially a male invention. Ultimately, all of society went along with it, but the turning away from emotions, and the invention of an "Evil One," was all part of a male rebellion against the matriarchy, a period during which women ruled over everything from their emotions. They held all governmental posts, all religious positions of power, all places of influence in commerce, science, academia, healing.

What power did men have?

None. Men had to justify their existence, for they had very little importance beyond their ability to fertilize female eggs and move heavy objects. They were very much like worker ants and bees. They did the heavy physical labor, and made sure that children were produced and protected.

It took men hundreds of years to find and to create a larger place for themselves in the fabric of their society. Centuries passed before males were even allowed to participate in their clan's affairs; to have a voice or a vote in community decisions. They weren't considered by women to be intelligent enough to understand such matters.

Boy, it is difficult to imagine that any society would actually prohibit one whole class of people from even voting, based simply on gender.

> I like your sense of humor about this. I really do.
> Shall I go on?

Please.

> Centuries more passed before they could think of actually holding the positions of leadership for which they finally had the chance to vote. Other posts of influence and power within their culture were similarly denied them.

When males finally obtained positions of authority within society, when they at last rose above their former place as baby-makers and virtual physical slaves, it is to their credit that they did not ever turn the tables on women, but have always accorded females the respect, power, and influence that all humans deserve, regardless of gender.

> There's that humor again.

Oh, I'm sorry. Do I have the wrong planet?

> Let's get back to our narrative. But before we go on about the invention of "the devil," let us talk a bit about power. Because this, of course, is what the invention of Satan was all about.

You're going to make the point now that men have all the power in today's society, right? Let me jump ahead of You and tell You why I think this happened.

You said that in the matriarchal period, men were very much like worker bees serving the queen bee. You said they did the difficult physical work, and made sure that children were produced and protected. And I felt like saying, "So what's changed? That's what they do *now!*" And I'll bet that many men would probably say that not a great deal *has* changed—except that men have extracted a price for maintaining their "thankless role." They do have more power.

> Actually, most of the power.

Okay, most of the power. But the irony I see here is that both genders think they are handling the thankless tasks, while the other is having all the fun. Men resent the women who are attempting to take back some of their power, because men say they'll be damned if they'll do all that they do for the culture, and not at least have *the power it takes to do it.*

Women resent men keeping all the power, saying they'll be damned if they'll continue doing for the culture what they do, and still remain powerless.

You've analyzed it correctly. And both men and women are damned to repeat their own mistakes in an endless cycle of self-inflicted misery until one side or the other gets that life is not about power, but about strength. And until both see that it's not about separation, but unity. For it is in the *unity* that *inner strength* exists, and in the separation that it dissipates, leaving one feeling weak, and powerless—and hence, struggling for power.

I tell you this: Heal the rift between you, end the illusion of separation, and you shall be delivered back to the source of your inner strength. That is where you will find true power. The power to do anything. The power to be anything. The power to have anything. For the power to create is derived from the inner strength that is produced through unity.

This is true of the relationship between you and your God—just as it is remarkably true of the relationship between you and your fellow humans.

Stop thinking of yourself as separate, and all the true power that comes from the inner strength of unity is yours—as a worldwide society, and as an individual part of that whole—to wield as you wish.

Yet remember this:

Power comes from inner strength. Inner strength does not come from raw power. In this, most of the world has it backwards.

Power without inner strength is an illusion. Inner strength without unity is a lie. A lie that has not served the race, but that has nevertheless deeply embedded itself into your race consciousness. For you think that inner strength comes from *individuality* and from *separateness*, and that is simply not so. Separation from God and from each other is the cause of all your dysfunction and suffering. Still, separation continues to masquerade as strength, and your politics, your economics, and even your religions have perpetuated the lie.

This lie is the genesis of all wars and all the class struggles that lead to war; of all animosity between races and genders, and all the power struggles that lead to animosity; of all personal trials and tribulations, and all the internal struggles that lead to tribulations.

Still, you cling to the lie tenaciously, no matter where you've seen it lead you—even as it has led you to your own destruction.

Now I tell you this: Know the truth, and the truth shall set you free.

There is no separation. Not from each other, not from God, and not from anything that is.

This truth I will repeat over and over on these pages. This observation I will make again and again.

Act as if you were separate from nothing, and no one, and you will heal your world tomorrow.

This is *the greatest secret of all time*. It is the answer for which man has searched for millennia. It is the solution for which he has worked, the revelation for which he has prayed.

Act as if you were separate from nothing, and you heal the world.

Understand that it is about power with, not power over.

Thank You. I got that. So, getting back, first it was females who had power over males, and now it is the other way around. And males invented the devil in order to wrest this power away from the female tribal or clan leaders?

Yes. They used fear, because fear was the only tool they had.

Again, not much has changed. Men do that to this day. Sometimes even before appeals to *reason* are tried, men use fear. Particularly if they are the bigger men; the stronger men. (Or the bigger or stronger nation.) Sometimes it seems actually ingrained in men. It seems *cellular*. Might is right. Strength is power.

Yes. This has been the way since the overturn of the matriarchy.

How did it get that way?

That's what this short history is all about.

Then go on, please.

What men had to do to gain control during the matriarchal period was not to convince women that men ought to be given more power over their lives, but to convince other men.

Life was, after all, going smoothly, and there were worse ways men could have to get through the day than simply doing some physical work to make themselves valued, and then have sex. So it was not easy for men, who were powerless, to convince other powerless men to seek power. Until they discovered fear.

Fear was the one thing women hadn't counted on.

It began, this fear, with seeds of doubt, sown by the most disgruntled among the males. These were usually the least "desirable" of the men; the unmuscled, the unadorned—and hence, those to whom women paid the least attention.

And I'll bet that because this was so, their complaints were discounted as the ravings of rage born of sexual frustration.

That is correct. Still, the disgruntled men had to use the only tool they had. So they sought to grow fear from the seeds of doubt. What if the women were wrong? they asked. What if their way of running the world wasn't the best? What if it was, in fact, leading the whole society—all of the race—into sure and certain annihilation?

This is something many men could not imagine. After all, didn't women have a direct line to the Goddess? Were they not, in fact, exact physical replicas of the Goddess? And was not the Goddess good?

The teaching was so powerful, so pervasive, that men had no choice but to invent a devil, a Satan, to counteract the unlimited goodness of the Great Mother imagined and worshipped by the people of the matriarchy.

How did they manage to convince anyone that there was such a thing as an "evil one"?

The one thing all of their society understood was the theory of the "rotten apple." Even the women saw and knew from their experience that some children simply turned out "bad," no matter what they did. Especially, as everybody knew, the boy children, who just could not be controlled.

So a myth was created.

One day, the myth went, the Great Mother, the Goddess of Goddesses, brought forth a child who turned out to be *not good*. No matter what the Mother tried, the child would not be good. Finally, he struggled with his Mother for her very throne.

This was too much, even for a loving, forgiving Mother. The boy was banished forever—but continued to show up in clever disguises and clever costumes, sometimes even posing as the Great Mother herself.

This myth laid the basis for men to ask, "How do we know the Goddess we worship is a Goddess at all? It could be the bad child, now grown up and wanting to fool us."

By this device, men got other men to worry, then to be angry that women weren't taking their worries seriously, then to rebel.

The being you now call Satan was thus created. It was not difficult to create a myth about a "bad child," and not difficult, either, to convince even the women of the clan of the possibility of the existence of such a creature. It was also not difficult getting anyone to accept that the bad child was male. Weren't males the inferior gender?

This device was used to set up a mythological problem. If the "bad child" was male, if the "evil one" was masculine, who would there be to overpower him? Surely, not a feminine Goddess. For, said the men cleverly, when it came to matters of wisdom and insight, of clarity and compassion, of planning and thinking, no one doubted feminine superiority. Yet in matters of brute strength, was not a male needed?

Previously in Goddess mythology, males were merely consorts—companions to the females, who acted as servants and fulfilled their robust desire for lustful celebration of their Goddess magnificence.

But now a male was needed who could do more; a male who could also protect the Goddess and defeat the enemy. This transformation did not occur overnight, but across many years. Gradually, very gradually, societies began seeing the male consort as also the male protector in their spiritual mythologies, for now that there was someone to protect the Goddess *from,* such a protector was clearly needed.

It was not a major leap from male as protector to male as *equal partner,* now standing alongside the Goddess. The *male God* was created, and, for a while, Gods and Goddesses ruled mythology together.

Then, again gradually, Gods were given larger roles. The need for protection, for strength, began to supplant the need for wisdom and love. A new kind of love was born in these mythologies. A love which protects with brute force. But it was a love which also covets what it protects; which was jealous of its Goddesses; which now did not simply serve their feminine lusts, but fought and died for them.

Myths began to emerge of Gods of enormous power, quarreling over, fighting for, Goddesses of unspeakable beauty. And so was born the *jealous God*.

This is fascinating.

Wait. We're coming to the end, but there's just a little more.

It wasn't long before the jealousy of the Gods extended not only to the Goddesses—but to all creations in all realms. We had better love Him, these jealous Gods demanded, and no other God—*or else!*

Since males were the most powerful species, and Gods were the most powerful of the males, there seemed little room for argument with this new mythology.

Stories of those who did argue, and lost, began to emerge. The *God of wrath was born.*

Soon, the whole idea of Deity was subverted. Instead of being the source of all love, it became the source of all fear.

A model of love which was largely feminine—the endlessly tolerant love of a mother for a child, and yes, even of a woman for her not-too-bright, but, after all, useful man, was replaced by the jealous, wrathful love of a demanding, intolerant God who would brook no interference, allow no insouciance, ignore no offense.

The smile of the amused Goddess, experiencing limitless love and gently submitting to the laws of nature, was replaced by the stern countenance of the not-so-amused God, proclaiming power over the laws of nature, and forevermore limiting love.

This is the God you worship today, and that's how you got where you are now.

Amazing. Interesting and amazing. But what is the point of telling me all of this?

It's important for you to know that you've *made it all up*. The idea that "might is right," or that "power is strength," was born in your male-created theological myths.

The God of wrath and jealousy and anger was an imagining. Yet, something you imagined for so long, *it became real.* Some of you still consider it real today. Yet it has nothing to do with ultimate reality, or what's really going on here.

And what is that?

What's going on is that your soul yearns for the *highest experience of itself* it can imagine. It came here for that purpose—to realize itself (that is, make itself real) in its experience.

Then it discovered pleasures of the flesh—not just sex, but all manner of pleasures—and as it indulged in these pleasures, it gradually forgot the pleasures of the spirit.

These, too, are pleasures—greater pleasures than the body could ever give you. But the soul forgot this.

Okay, now we're getting away from all the history, and back into something You've touched on before in this dialogue. Could You go over this again?

Well, we're not actually getting away from the history. We're tying everything in together. You see, it's really quite simple. The purpose of your soul—its reason for coming to the body—is to be and express Who You Really Are. The soul yearns to do this; yearns to know itself and its own experience.

This yearning to know is life seeking to be. This is God, choosing to express. The God of your histories is not the God who really is. That is the point. Your soul is the tool through which I express and experience Myself.

Doesn't that pretty much *limit* Your experience?

It does, unless it doesn't. That's up to you. You get to be the expression and the experience of Me at whatever level you choose. There have been those who have chosen very grand expressions. There have been none higher than Jesus, the Christ—though there have been others who have been equally as high.

Christ is not the highest example? He is not God made Man?

Christ is the highest example. He is simply not the only example to reach that highest state. Christ is God made Man. He is simply not the only man made of God.

Every man is "God made Man." You are Me, expressing in your present form. Yet don't worry about limiting Me; about how limited that makes Me. For I am not limited, and never have been. Do you think that you are the only form that I have chosen? Do you think you are the only creatures whom I've imbued with the Essence of Me?

I tell you, I am in every flower, every rainbow, every star in the heavens, and everything in and on every planet rotating around every star.

I am the whisper of the wind, the warmth of your sun, the incredible individuality and the extraordinary perfection of every snowflake.

I am the majesty in the soaring flight of eagles, and the innocence of the doe in the field; the courage of lions, the wisdom of the ancient ones.

And I am not limited to the modes of expression seen on your planet alone. You do not know Who I Am, but only think you do. Yet think not that Who I Am is limited to you, or that My Divine Essence—this most Holy Spirit—was given to you and you alone. That would be an arrogant thought, and a misinformed one.

My Beingness is in everything. Everything. The All-ness is My Expression. The Wholeness is My Nature. There is nothing that I Am Not, and something I Am Not cannot be.

My purpose in creating you, My blessed creatures, was so that I might have an experience of Myself as the Creator of My Own Experience.

Some people don't understand. Help all of us to understand.

The one aspect of God that only a very special creature could create was the aspect of Myself as The Creator.

I am not the God of your mythologies, nor am I the Goddess. I am The Creator—That Which Creates. Yet I choose to Know Myself in My Own Experience.

Just as I know My perfection of design through a snowflake, My awesome beauty through a rose, so, too, do I know My creative power—through you.

To you I have given the ability to consciously create your experience, which is the ability I have.

Through you, I can know every aspect of Me. The perfection of the snowflake, the awesome beauty of the rose, the courage of lions, the majesty of eagles, all resides in you. In you I have placed all of these things—and one thing more: the consciousness to be aware of it.

Thus have you become Self-conscious. And thus have you been given the greatest gift, for you have been aware of yourself being yourself—which is exactly what I Am.

I am Myself, aware of Myself *being* Myself.

This is what is meant by the statement, I Am That I Am.

You are that Part of Me which is the awareness, experienced.

And what you are experiencing (and what I am experiencing through you) is Me, creating Me.

I am in the continual act of creating Myself.

Does that mean God is not a constant? Does that mean You do not know what *You're* going to *be* in the next moment?

How can I know? You haven't decided yet!

Let me get this straight. *I* am deciding all this?

Yes. You are Me choosing to be Me.

You are Me, choosing to be What I Am—and choosing what I am going to be.

All of you, collectively, are creating that. You are doing it on an individual basis, as each of you decides Who You Are, and experiences that, and you are doing it collectively, as the co-creative collective being that you are.

I Am the collective experience of the lot of you!

And You really don't know who You are going to be in the next moment?

I was being lighthearted a moment ago. Of course I know. I already know all of your decisions, so I know Who I Am, Who I Have Always Been, and Who I Will Always Be.

How can You know what I am going to choose to be, do, and have in the next moment, much less what the whole human race is going to choose?

Simple. You've already done the choosing. Everything you're ever going to be, do, or have, you've already done. You're doing it right now!

Do you see? There is no such thing as time.

This, too, we have discussed before.

It is worth reviewing here.

Yes. Tell me again how this works.

Past, present, and future are concepts you have constructed, realities you have invented, in order to create a context within which to frame your present experience. Otherwise, all of your (Our) experiences would be overlapping.

They actually are overlapping—that is, happening at the same "time"—you simply don't know this. You've placed yourself in a perception shell that blocks out the Total Reality.

I've explained this in detail in *Book 2*. It might be good for you to re-read that material, in order to place what's being said here into context.

The point I am making here is that everything is happening at once. Everything. So yes, I do know what I'm "going to be," what I "am," and what I "was." I know this always. That is, all ways.

And so, you see, there is no way you can surprise Me.

Your story—the whole worldly drama—was created so that you could know Who You Are in your own experience. It's also been designed to help you forget Who You Are, so that you might remember Who You Are once again, and create it.

Because I can't *create* who I am if I am already experiencing who I am. I can't create being six feet tall if I am *already* six feet tall. I'd have to be *less* than six feet tall—or at least *think that I am*.

Exactly. You understand it perfectly. And since it is the greatest desire of the soul (God) to experience Itself as The Creator, and since everything has already been created, We had no choice other than to find a way to forget all about Our creation.

I am amazed that we found a way. Trying to "forget" that we are all One, and that the One of us which we are is God, must be like trying to forget that a pink elephant is in the room. How could we be so mesmerized?

Well, you've just touched on the secret reason for all of physical life. It is life in the physical which has so mesmerized you—and rightly so, because it is, after all, an extraordinary adventure!

What We used here to help Us forget is what some of you would call the Pleasure Principle.

The highest nature of all pleasure is that aspect of pleasure which causes you to create Who You Really Are in your experience right here, right now—and to re-create, and re-create, and re-create again Who You Are at the next highest level of magnificence. That is the highest pleasure of God.

The lower nature of all pleasure is that part of pleasure which causes you to forget Who You Really Are. Do not condemn the lower nature, for without it, you could not experience the higher.

It's almost as if the pleasures of the flesh at first cause us to forget Who We Are, then become the very avenue through which we remember!

There you have it. You've just said it. And the use of physical pleasure as an avenue to remembering Who You Are is achieved by raising up, through the body, the basic energy of all life.

This is the energy which you sometimes call "sexual energy," and it is raised up along the inner column of your being, until it reaches the area you call the Third Eye. This is the area just behind the forehead between and slightly above the eyes. As you raise the energy, you cause it to course all through your body. It is like an inner orgasm.

How is this done? How do you do that?

You "think it up." I mean that, just as I said it. You literally "think it up" the inner pathway of what you have called your "chakras." Once the life energy is raised up repeatedly, one acquires a taste for this experience, just as one acquires a hunger for sex.

The experience of the energy being raised is very sublime. It quickly becomes the experience most desired. Yet you never completely lose your hunger for the lowering of the energy—for the basic passions—nor ought you try. For the higher cannot exist without the lower in your experience—as I have pointed out to you many times. Once you get to the higher, you must go back to the lower, in order to experience again the pleasure of moving to the higher.

This is the sacred rhythm of all life. You do this not only by moving the energy around inside your body. You also do this by moving around the larger energy inside the Body of God.

You incarnate as lower forms, then evolve into higher states of consciousness. You are simply raising the energy in the Body of God. You *are* that energy. And when you arrive at the highest state, you experience it fully, then you decide what next you choose to experience, and where in the Realm of Relativity you choose to go in order to experience it.

You may wish to again experience yourself becoming your Self—it is a grand experience, indeed—and so you may start all over again on the Cosmic Wheel.

Is this the same as the "karmic wheel"?

No. There is no such thing as a "karmic wheel." Not the way you have imagined it. Many of you have imagined that you are on, not a wheel, but a *treadmill*, in which you are working off the debts of past actions, and trying valiantly not to incur any new ones. This is what some of you have called "the karmic wheel." It is not so very different from a few of your Western theologies, for in both paradigms you are seen as an unworthy sinner, seeking to gain the purity to move on to the next spiritual level.

The experience which I have described here, on the other hand, I am calling the *Cosmic* Wheel, because there is nothing of unworthiness, debt-repayment, punishment, or "purification." The Cosmic Wheel simply describes the ultimate reality, or what you might call the cosmology of the universe.

It is the cycle of life, or what I sometimes term The Process. It is a picture phrase describing the no-beginning-and-no-end nature of things; the continually connected path to and from the all of everything, on which the soul joyfully journeys throughout eternity.

It is the sacred rhythm of all life, by which you move the Energy of God.

Wow, I've never had that all explained to me so simply! I don't think I've ever understood all this so clearly.

Well, clarity is what you brought yourself here to experience. That was the purpose of this dialogue. So I am glad you are achieving that.

In truth, there is no "lower" or "higher" place on the Cosmic Wheel. How can there be? It's a *wheel*, not a *ladder*.

That is excellent. That is an excellent imagery and an excellent understanding. Therefore, condemn not that which you call the lower, basic, animal instincts of man, yet bless them, honoring them as the path through which, and by which, you find your way back home.

This would relieve a lot of people of a lot of guilt around sex.

It is why I have said, play, play, *play* with sex—and with all of life!

Mix what you call the sacred with the sacrilegious, for until you see your altars as the ultimate place for love, and your bedrooms as the ultimate place for worship, you see nothing at all.

You think "sex" is separate from God? I tell you this: *I am in your bedroom every night!*

So go ahead! Mix what you call the profane and the profound—so that you can see that there is no difference, and experience All as One. Then when you continue to evolve, you will not see yourself as letting go of sex, but simply enjoying it at a higher level. For all of *life* is S.E.X.—Synergistic Energy eXchange.

And if you understand this about sex, you will understand this about everything in life. Even the end of life—what you call "death." At the moment of your death, you will not see yourself as letting go of life, but simply enjoying it at a higher level.

When at last you see that there is no separation in God's World—that is, nothing which is not God—then, at last, will you let go of this invention of man which you have called Satan.

If Satan exists, he exists as every thought you ever had of separation from Me. You cannot be separate from Me, for I Am All That Is.

Men invented the devil to scare people into doing what they wanted, under the threat of separation from God if they did not. Condemnation, being hurled into the everlasting fires of hell, was the *ultimate scare tactic*. Yet now you need be afraid no more. For nothing can, or ever will, separate you from Me.

You and I are One. We cannot be anything else if I Am What I Am: All That Is.

Why then would I condemn Myself? And how would I do it? How could I separate Myself from Myself when My Self is All There Is, and there is nothing else?

My purpose is to evolve, not to condemn; to grow, not to die; to experience, not to fail to experience. My purpose is to Be, not to cease to Be.

I have no way to separate Myself from you—or anything else. "Hell" is simply not knowing this. "Salvation" is knowing and understanding it completely. You are now saved. You needn't worry about what's going to happen to you "after death" anymore.

3

Can we talk about this death business for a minute? You said this third book was going to be about higher truths; about universal truths. Well, through all the conversation we've had, we haven't talked that much about death—and what happens after that. Let's do that now. Let's get to that.

Fine. What do you want to know?

What happens when you die?

What do you choose to have happen?

You mean that what happens is whatever we choose to have happen?

Do you think that just because you've died you stop creating?

I don't know. That's why I'm asking You.

Fair enough. (You do know, incidentally, but I see you have forgotten—which is great. Everything's gone according to plan.)

When you die, you do not stop creating. Is that definitive enough for you?

Yes.

Good.

Now the reason you do not stop creating when you die is that you don't ever die. You cannot. For you are life itself. And life cannot *not* be life. Therefore you cannot die.

So, at the moment of your death what happens is... you go on living.

This is why so many people who have "died" do not believe it—because they do not have the experience of being dead. On the contrary, they feel (because they are) very much alive. So there's confusion.

The Self may see the body lying there, all crumpled up, not moving, yet the Self is suddenly moving all over the place. It has the experience, often, of literally flying all over the room—then of being everywhere in the space, all at once. And when it desires a particular point of view, it suddenly finds itself experiencing that.

If the soul (the name we will now give to the Self) wonders, "Gee, why is my body not moving?" it will find itself right there, hovering right over the body, watching the stillness curiously.

If someone enters the room, and the soul thinks, "Who is that?"—immediately the soul is in front of, or next to, that person.

Thus, in a very short time the soul learns that it can go anywhere—with the speed of its thought.

A feeling of incredible freedom and lightness overtakes the soul, and it usually takes a little while for the entity to "get used to" all this bouncing around with every thought.

If the person had children, and should think of those children, immediately the soul is in the presence of those children, wherever they are. Thus the soul learns that not only can it be wherever it wants with the speed of its thought—it can be in two places at once. Or three places. Or five.

It can exist, observe, and conduct activities in these places simultaneously, without difficulty or confusion. Then it can "rejoin" itself, returning to one place again, simply by refocusing.

The soul remembers in the next life what it would have been well to remember in this life—that all effect is created by thought, and that manifestation is a result of intention.

What I focus on as my intention becomes my reality.

Exactly. The only difference is the speed with which you experience the result. In the physical life there might be a lapse between thought and experience. In the spirit's realm there is no lapse; results are instantaneous.

Newly departed souls therefore learn to monitor their thoughts very carefully, because whatever they think of, they experience.

I use the word "learn" here very loosely, more as a figure of speech than an actual description. The term "remember" would be more accurate.

If physicalized souls learned to control their thoughts as quickly and as efficiently as spiritualized souls, their whole lives would change.

In the creation of individual reality, thought control, or what some might call prayer—is everything.

Prayer?

Thought control is the highest form of prayer. Therefore, think only on good things, and righteous. Dwell not in negativity and darkness. And even in moments when things look bleak—especially in those moments—see only perfection, express only gratefulness, and then imagine only what manifestation of perfection you choose next.

In this formula is found tranquillity. In this process is found peace. In this awareness is found joy.

That's extraordinary. That's an extraordinary piece of information. Thanks for bringing that through me.

Thanks for letting it come through. Some times you are "cleaner" than at other times. Some moments you are more open—like a strainer which has just been rinsed. It is more "open." There are more holes open.

Good way of putting it.

I do My best.

To recap then: Souls released from the body quickly remember to monitor and control their thoughts very carefully, for whatever they think of, that is what they create and experience.

I say again, it is the same for souls still residing with a body, except the results are usually not as immediate. And it is the "time" lapse between thought and creation—which can be days, weeks, months, or even years—which creates the illusion that things are happening *to* you, not *because* of you. *This is an illusion,* causing you to *forget that you are at cause* in the matter.

As I have described now several times, this forgetting is "built into the system." It is part of the process. For you cannot create Who You Are until you forget Who You Are. So the illusion causing forgetfulness is an effect created on purpose.

When you leave the body, it will therefore be a big surprise to see the instant and obvious connection between your thoughts and your creations. It will be a shocking surprise at first, and then a very pleasant one, as you begin to remember that you are at cause in the creation of your experience, not at the effect of it.

Why is there such a delay between thought and creation *before* we die, and no delay at all after we die?

> Because you are working within the illusion of time. There is no delay between thought and creation away from the body, because you are also away from the parameter of time.

In other words, as You have said so often, time does not exist.

> Not as you understand it. The phenomenon of "time" is really a function of perspective.

Why does it exist while we are in the body?

> You have caused it to by moving into, by assuming, your present perspective. You use this perspective as a tool with which you can explore and examine your experiences much more fully, by separating them into individual pieces, rather than a single occurrence.
>
> Life is a single occurrence, an event in the cosmos that is happening *right now*. All of it is happening. Everywhere.
>
> There is no "time" but *now*. There is no "place" but *here*.
>
> Here and now is All There Is.
>
> Yet you chose to experience the magnificence of here and now in its every detail, and to experience your Divine Self as the here and now creator of that reality. There were only two ways—two fields of experience—in which you could do that. Time and space.
>
> So magnificent was this thought that you literally exploded with delight!
>
> In that explosion of delight was created space between the parts of you, and the time it took to move from one part of yourself to another.
>
> In this way you literally *tore your Self apart* to look at the pieces of you. You might say that you were so happy, you "fell to pieces."
>
> You've been picking up the pieces ever since.

That's all my life is! I'm just putting together the pieces, trying to see if they make any sense.

> And it is through the device called time that you have managed to separate the pieces, to divide the indivisible, thus to see it and experience it more fully, as you are creating it.

Even as you look at a solid object through a microscope, seeing that it is not solid at all, but actually a conglomeration of a million different effects—different things all happening at once and thus creating the larger effect—so, too, do you use time as the microscope of your soul.

Consider the Parable of the Rock.

Once there was a Rock, filled with countless atoms, protons, neutrons, and subatomic particles of matter. These particles were racing around continually, in a pattern, each particle going from "here" to "there," and taking "time" to do so, yet going so fast that the Rock itself seemed to move not at all. It just *was*. There it lay, drinking in the sun, soaking up the rain, and moving not at all.

"What is this, inside of me, that is moving?" the Rock asked.

"It is You," said a Voice from Afar.

"Me?" replied the Rock. "Why, that is impossible. I am not moving at all. Anyone can see that."

"Yes, *from a distance*," the Voice agreed. "From way over *here* you *do* look as if you are solid, still, not moving. But when I come closer—when I look very closely at what is actually happening—I see that everything that comprises What You Are is *moving*. It is moving at incredible speed through time and space in a particular pattern which *creates* You as the thing called 'Rock.' And so, you are like magic! You are moving and *not moving* at the same time."

"But," asked the Rock, "which, then, is the illusion? The oneness, the stillness, of the Rock, or the separateness and the movement of Its parts?"

To which the Voice replied, "Which, then, is the illusion? The oneness, the stillness, of God? Or the separateness and movement of Its parts?"

And I tell you this: Upon this Rock, I will build My church. For this is the Rock of Ages. This is the eternal truth that leaves no stone unturned. I have explained it all for you here, in this little story. This is The Cosmology.

Life is a series of minute, incredibly rapid movements. These movements do not affect at all the immobility and the Beingness of Everything That Is. Yet, just as with the atoms of the rock, it is the movement which is creating the stillness, right before your eyes.

From this distance, there is no separateness. There cannot be, for All That Is is All There Is, and there *is nothing else*. I am the Unmoved Mover.

From the limited perspective with which you view All That Is, you see yourself as separate and apart, not one unmovable being, but many, many beings, constantly in motion.

Both observations are accurate. Both realities are "real."

And when I "die," I don't die at all, but simply shift into awareness of the macrocosm—where there is no "time" or "space," now and then, before and after.

Precisely. You've got it.

Let me see if I can say it back to You. Let me see if *I* can describe it.

Go ahead.

From a macro perspective, there is no separateness, and from "way back there" all the particles of everything merely look like the Whole.

As you look at the rock at your feet, you see the rock, right then and there, as whole, complete, and perfect. Yet even in the fraction of a moment that you hold that rock in your awareness, there is a lot going on within that rock—there is incredible movement, at incredible speed, of the particles of that rock. And what are those particles doing? They are making that rock what it is.

As you look at this rock, you do not see this process. Even if you are conceptually aware of it, to you it is all happening "now." The rock isn't *becoming* a rock; it *is* a rock, right here—right now.

Yet if you were the consciousness of one of the submolecular particles inside that rock, you would experience yourself moving at insane speed, first "here," then "there." And if some voice outside the rock said to you, "It is all happening at once," you would call it a liar or a charlatan.

Still, from the perspective of a distance from the rock, the idea that any part of the rock is separate from any other part, and, further, is moving around at insane speed, would appear to be the lie. From that distance could be seen what could not be seen up close—that all is One, and that all the movement *hasn't moved anything*.

You have it. You have a grasp of it. What you are saying—and you are correct—is that life is all a matter of perspective. If you continue to see this truth, you will begin to understand the macro reality of God. And you will have unlocked a secret of the whole universe: *All of it is the same thing.*

The universe is a molecule in the body of God!

That's actually not so very far off.

And it is to the macro reality that we return in consciousness when we do the thing called "die"?

Yes. Yet even the macro reality to which you return is but a *micro reality* of an *even larger macro reality,* which is a smaller part of a larger reality *still*—and so on, and on, and on, forever and ever, and even forever more, world without end.

We are God—the "It that Is"—constantly in the act of creating Our Selves, constantly in the act of being what we are now . . . until we aren't that anymore, but become something else.

Even the rock will not be a rock forever, but only what "seems like forever." Before it was a rock, it was something else. It fossilized into that rock, through a process taking hundreds of thousands of years. It was once something else, and will be something else again.

The same is true of you. You were not always the "you" that you are now. You were something else. And today, as you stand there in your utter magnificence, you truly are . . . "something else again."

Wow, that's amazing. I mean, that's absolutely amazing! I've never heard anything like that. You've taken the whole cosmology of life and put it in terms I can hold in my mind. That is amazing.

Well, thank you. I appreciate that. I'm doing My best.

You're doing a damned good job.

That's probably not the phrase you should have chosen there.

Oops.

Just kidding. Lightening things up here. Having a little fun. I cannot actually be "offended." Yet your fellow human beings often allow themselves to be offended on My behalf.

So I've noticed. But, getting back, I think I've just caught hold of something.

What's that?

This whole explanation rolled out when I asked a single question: "How come 'time' exists when we're in the body, but not when the soul is released?" And what You seem to be saying is that "time" is really *perspective;* that it neither "exists" nor "ceases to exist," but that as the soul alters its perspective, we experience ultimate reality in different ways.

That's exactly what I'm saying! You've got it!

And You were making the larger point that in the *macrocosm* the soul is *aware* of the *direct relationship* between *thought and creation;* between one's ideas and one's experience.

Yes—at the macro level, it's like seeing the rock and seeing the movement within the rock. There is no "time" between the movement of the atoms and the appearance of the rock it creates. The rock "is," even as the movements occur. Indeed, *because* the movements occur. This cause and effect is instant. The movement is occurring and the rock is "being," all at the "same time."

This is what the soul realizes at the moment of what you call "death." It is simply a change in perspective. You see more, so you understand more.

After death, you are no longer limited in your understanding. You see the rock, and you see *into* the rock. You will look at what now seem to be the most complex aspects of life and say, "Of course." It will all be very clear to you.

Then there will be new mysteries for you to ponder. As you move around the Cosmic Wheel, there will be larger and larger realities—bigger and bigger truths.

Yet if you can remember this truth—your perspective creates your thoughts, and your thoughts create everything—and if you can remember it *before you leave the body,* not after, *your whole life will change.*

And the way to control your thoughts is to change your perspective.

Precisely. Assume a different perspective and you will have a different thought about everything. In this way you will have learned to control your thought, and, in the creation of your experience, controlled thought is everything.

Some people call this constant prayer.

You've said this before, but I don't think I've ever thought of prayer in this way.

Why not see what happens if you do so? If you imagined that the controlling and directing of your thoughts is the highest form of prayer, you would think only on good things, and righteous. You would dwell not in negativity and darkness, though you may be immersed in it. And in moments when things look bleak—perhaps especially in those moments—you would see only perfection.

You have come back to that, over and over again.

I am giving you tools. With these tools you can change your life. I am repeating the most important of them. Over and over again I am repeating them, for repetition will produce re-cognition— "knowing again"—when you need it most.

Everything that occurs—everything that has occurred, is occur- ring, and ever will occur—is the outward physical manifestation of your innermost thoughts, choices, ideas, and determinations regarding Who You Are and Who You Choose to Be. Condemn not, therefore, those aspects of life with which you disagree. Seek instead to change them, and the conditions that made them possi- ble.

Behold the darkness, yet curse it not. Rather, be a light unto the darkness, and so transform it. Let your light so shine before men, that those who stand in the darkness will be illumined by the light of your being, and all of you will see, at last, Who You Really Are.

Be a Bringer of the Light. For your light can do more than illu- minate your own path. Your light can be the light which truly lights the world.

Shine on, then, O Illuminati! Shine on! That the moment of your greatest darkness may yet become your grandest gift. And even as you are gifted, so, too, will you gift others, giving to them the unspeakable treasure: Themselves.

Let this be your task, let this be your greatest joy: to give peo- ple back to themselves. Even in their darkest hour. Especially in that hour.

The world waits for you. Heal it. Now. In the place where you are. There is much you can do.

For My sheep are lost and must now be found. Be ye, therefore, as good shepherds, and lead them back to Me.

4

Thank You. Thank You for that call and for that challenge. Thank You for that placement of the goal before me. Thank You. For always keeping me heading in the direction You know I really want to take. That is why I come to You. That is why I have loved, and blessed, this dialogue. For it is in conversation with You that I find the Divine within me, and begin to see it within all others.

My dearly beloved, the heavens rejoice when you say that. That is the very reason I have come to you, and will come to everyone who calls to Me. Even as I have come now to those others who are reading these words. For this conversation was never intended to be with you alone. It was intended for millions around the world. And it has been placed in each person's hands just exactly when they have needed it, sometimes in the most miraculous ways. It has brought them to the wisdom they, themselves, have called forth, perfectly suited for this moment in their lives.

This is the wonder of what has been happening here: that each of you is producing this result by yourself. It "looks as if" someone else gave you this book, brought you to this conversation, opened you to this dialogue, yet *you brought your Self here.*

So let us now explore together the remaining questions which you have held in your heart.

May we, please, speak more of life after death? You were explaining what happens to the soul after death, and I so want to know as much about that as I can.

We will speak of it, then, until your yearning has been satisfied.

I said earlier that what happens is whatever you want to have happen. I meant that. You create your own reality not only when you are with the body, but when you are away from it.

At first you may not realize this, and so you may not be consciously creating your reality. Your experience will then be created

474

by one of two other energies: your uncontrolled thoughts, or the collective consciousness.

To the degree that your uncontrolled thoughts are stronger than the collective consciousness, to that degree you will experience them as reality. To the degree that the collective consciousness is accepted, absorbed, and internalized, to that degree you will experience *it* as your reality.

This is no different from how you create what you call reality in your present life.

Always in life you have before you three choices:

1. You may allow your uncontrolled thoughts to create The Moment.

2. You may allow your creative consciousness to create The Moment.

3. You may allow the collective consciousness to create The Moment.

Here is an irony:

In your present life you find it difficult to create consciously from your individual awareness, and, indeed, often assume your individual understandings to be wrong, given all that you are seeing around you, and so, you surrender to the collective consciousness, whether it serves you to do so or not.

In the first moments of what you call the afterlife, on the other hand, you may find it *difficult* to surrender to the collective consciousness, given all that you are seeing around you (which may be unbelievable to you), and so you will be tempted to hold to your own individual understandings, whether they serve you or not.

I would tell you this: It is when you are surrounded by lower consciousness that you will benefit more from remaining with your individual understandings, and when you are surrounded by higher consciousness that you receive greater benefit from surrender.

It may, therefore, be wise to seek beings of high consciousness. I cannot overemphasize the importance of the company you keep.

In what you call the afterlife, there is nothing to worry about on this score, for you will instantly and automatically be surrounded by beings of high consciousness—and by high consciousness itself.

Still, you may not know that you are being so lovingly enveloped; you may not immediately understand. It may, therefore, seem to you as if you are having things "happen" to you; that you are at the whim of whatever fortunes are working at the moment. In truth, you experience the consciousness in which you die.

Some of you have expectations without even knowing it. All your life you've had thoughts about what occurs after death, and when you "die" those thoughts are made manifest, and you suddenly realize (make real) what you've been thinking about. And it is your strongest thoughts, the ones you've held most fervently, that, as always in life, will prevail.

Then a person *could* go to hell. If people believed all during life that hell is a place which most certainly existed, that God will judge "the quick and the dead," that He will separate the "wheat from the chaff" and the "goats from the sheep," and that they are surely "going to hell," given all that they have done to offend God, then they *would* go to hell! They would burn in the everlasting fires of damnation! How could they escape it? You've said repeatedly throughout this dialogue that hell does not exist. Yet You also say that we create our own reality, and have the power to create any reality at all, out of our thought about it. So hellfire and damnation *could* and *does* exist *for those who believe in it.*

Nothing exists in Ultimate Reality save that Which Is. You are correct in pointing out that you may create any subreality you choose—including the experience of hell as you describe it. I have never said at any point in this entire dialogue that you could not experience hell; I said that hell does not exist. *Most of what you experience does not exist, yet you experience it nonetheless.*

This is unbelievable. A friend of mine named Barnet Bain just produced a movie about this. I mean, about this *exactly*. It is August 7, 1998, as I write this sentence. I am inserting this in the dialogue, in between lines of a discussion of two years ago, and I have never done this before. But just before sending this to the publisher, I was re-reading the manuscript one last time, and I realized: Hold it! Robin Williams has just made a movie about *exactly what we're talking about here*. It's called *What Dreams May Come*, and it's a startling depiction on film of what You've just said.

I am familiar with it.

You are? *God goes to the movies?*

God makes movies.

Whoa.

Yes. You never saw *Oh, God?*

Well, sure, but . . .

What, you think God only writes books?

So, is the Robin Williams movie literally true? I mean, is that how it is?

No. No movie or book or other human explanation of the Divine is literally true.

Not even the Bible? The Bible is not literally true?

No. And I think you know that.

Well, what about *this* book? Surely *this* book is literally true!

No. I hate to tell you this, but you are bringing this through your personal filter. Now I will agree that the mesh on your filter is thinner, finer. You have become a very good filter. But you are a filter nonetheless.

I know that. I just wanted it stated again, here, because some people take books like this, and movies like *What Dreams May* Come, as literal truth. And I want to stop them from doing that.

The writers and producers of that film brought some enormous truth through an imperfect filter. The point they sought to make is that you will experience after death exactly what you expect, and choose, to experience. They made that point very effectively.

Now, shall we get back to where we were?

Yes. I'd like to know just what I wanted to know when I was watching that movie. If there is no hell, yet I am experiencing hell, *what the hell is the difference?*

There wouldn't be any, as long as you remain in your created reality. Yet you will not create such a reality forever. Some of you won't experience it for more than what you would call a "nanosecond." And therefore you will not experience, even in the private domains of your own imagination, a place of sadness or suffering.

What would stop me from creating such a place for all eternity if I believed all my life that there was such a place, and that something I'd done had caused me to deserve such a place?

> Your knowledge and understanding.
>
> Just as in this life your next moment is created out of the new understandings you've gained from your last moment, so, too, in what you call the afterlife, will you create a new moment from what you've come to know and understand in the old.
>
> And one thing you will come to know and understand very quickly is that you are at choice, always, about what you wish to experience. That is because in the afterlife results are instantaneous, and you will not be able to miss the connection between your thoughts about a thing, and the experience those thoughts create.
>
> You will understand yourself to be creating your own reality.

This would explain why some people's experience is happy, and some people's experience is frightening; why some people's experience is profound, while other people's experience is virtually nonexistent. And why so many different stories exist about what happens in the moments after death.

Some people come back from near-death experiences filled with peace and love, and with no fear, ever again, of death, while others return very frightened, certain that they have just encountered dark and evil forces.

> The soul responds to, re-creates, the mind's most powerful suggestion, producing that in its experience.
>
> Some souls remain in that experience for a time, making it very real—even as they remained in their experiences while with the body, though they were equally as unreal and impermanent. Other souls quickly adjust, see the experience for what it is, begin to think new thoughts, and move immediately to new experiences.

Do You mean that there is no one particular way things *are* in the afterlife? Are there no eternal truths that exist outside of our own mind? Do we continue to go on creating myths and legends and make-believe experiences right past our death and into the next reality? When do we get released from the bondage? When do we come to know the truth?

> When you choose to. That was the point of the Robin Williams movie. That is the point being made here. Those whose only desire

is to know the eternal truth of All That Is, to understand the great mysteries, to experience the grandest reality, do so.

Yes, there is a One Great Truth; there is a Final Reality. But you will always get what you choose, regardless of that reality—precisely because the reality is that you are a divine creature, divinely creating your reality even as you are experiencing It.

Yet should you choose to stop creating your own individual reality and begin to understand and experience the larger, unified reality, you will have an immediate opportunity to do that.

Those who "die" in a state of such choosing, of such desiring, of such willingness and such knowing, move into the experience of the Oneness at once. Others move into the experience only if, as, and when they so desire.

It is precisely the same when the soul is with the body.

It is all a matter of desire, of your choosing, of your creating, and, ultimately, of your creating the uncreateable; that is, of your experiencing that which has *already been created*.

This is The Created Creator. The Unmoved Mover. It is the alpha and the omega, the before and the after, the now-then-always aspect of everything, which you call God.

I will not forsake you, yet I will not force My Self upon you. I have never done so and I never will. You may return to Me whenever you wish. Now, while you are with the body, or after you have left it. You may return to the One and experience the loss of your individual Self whenever it pleases you. You may also re-create the experience of your individual Self whenever you choose.

You may experience any aspect of the All That Is that you wish, in its tiniest proportion, or its grandest. You may experience the microcosm or the macrocosm.

I may experience the particle or the rock.

Yes. Good. You are getting this.

When you reside with the human body, you are experiencing a smaller portion than the whole; that is, a portion of the microcosm (although by no means the smallest portion thereof). When you reside away from the body (in what some would call the "spirit world"), you have enlarged by quantum leaps your perspective. You will suddenly seem to know everything; be able to be everything. You will have a macrocosmic view of things, allowing you to understand that which you do not now understand.

One of the things you will then understand is that there is a larger macrocosm still. That is, you will suddenly become clear that All That Is is even greater than the reality you are then experiencing. This will fill you at once with awe and anticipation, wonder and excitement, joy and exhilaration, for you will then know and understand what I know and understand: that the game never ends.

Will I ever get to a place of true wisdom?

In the time after your "death" you may choose to have every question you ever had answered—and open yourself to new questions you never dreamed existed. You may choose to experience Oneness with All That Is. And you will have a chance to decide what you wish to be, do, and have next.

Do you choose to return to your most recent body? Do you choose to experience life again in human form, but of another kind?

Do you choose to remain where you are in the "spirit world," at the level you are then experiencing? Do you choose to go on, go further, in your knowing and experiencing? Do you choose to "lose your identity" altogether and now become part of the Oneness?

What do you choose? What do you choose? What do you *choose?*

Always, that is the question I will be asking you. Always, that is the inquiry of the universe. For the universe knows nothing except how to grant your fondest wish, your greatest desire. Indeed, it is doing that every moment, every day. The difference between you and Me is that you are not consciously aware of this.

I am.

Tell me . . . will my relatives, my loved ones, meet me after I die, and help me understand what is going on, as some people say they will? Will I be reunited with "those who have gone before"? Will we be able to spend eternity together?

What do you choose? Do you choose for these things to happen? Then they will.

Okay, I'm confused. Are You saying that all of us have free will, and that this free will extends even past our death?

Yes, that is what I am saying.

If that is true, then the free will of my loved ones would have to coin-cide with mine—they must have the same thought and desire that I have, when I'm having it—or they wouldn't be there for me when I die. Further, what if I wanted to spend the rest of eternity with them, and one or two of them wanted to move on? Maybe one of them wanted to move higher and higher, into this experience of Reunification with the Oneness, as You put it. Then what?

> There is no contradiction in the universe. There are things that look like contradictions, but there are none in fact. Should a situa-tion arise such as the one you describe (it is a very good question, by the way), what will happen is that you will both be able to have what you choose.

Both?

> Both.

May I ask how?

> You may.

Okay. How . . .

> What is your thought about God? Do you think that I exist in one place, and one place only?

No. I think You exist everywhere at once. I believe God is omnipresent.

> Well, you are right about that. There is nowhere that I Am Not. Do you understand this?

I think so.

> Good. So what makes you think it's any different with you?

Because You're God, and I am a mere mortal.

> I see. We're still hung up on this "mere mortal" thing. . . .

Okay, okay . . . suppose I assume for the sake of discussion that I, too, am God—or at least made up of the same stuff as God. Then are You saying that I, too, can be everywhere, all the time?

It is merely a matter of what the consciousness chooses to hold in its reality. In what you would call the "spirit world," what you can imagine, you can experience. Now, if you want to experience yourself being one soul, in one place, at one "time," you may do that. Yet if you wish to experience your spirit being larger than that, being in more than one place at one "time," *you may do that as well.* Indeed, you may experience your spirit as being *anywhere you wish*, any "time." That is because, in truth, there is only one "time" and one "place," and you are in all of it, always. You may thus experience any part, or *parts*, of it you wish, whenever you choose.

What if *I* want my relatives to be with *me*, but one of *them* wants to be a "part of the All" that is somewhere else? What then?

It is not possible for you and your relatives not to want the same thing. You and I, and your relatives and I—all of us—are one and the same.

The very act of your desiring something is the act of Me desiring something, since you are simply Me, acting out the experience called *desire*. Therefore, what you desire, I desire.

Your relatives and I are also one and the same. Therefore, what I am desiring, they are desiring. So it follows, then, that what you desire, your relatives are also desiring.

On Earth it is also true that all of you desire the same thing. You desire peace. You desire prosperity. You desire joy. You desire fulfillment. You desire satisfaction and self-expression in your work, love in your life, health in your body. You all desire the same thing.

You think this is a coincidence? It is not. *It is the way life works.* I am explaining that to you right now.

Now the only thing that's different on Earth from the way it is in what you call the spirit world is that on Earth, while you all desire the same thing, you all have different ideas about how to go about having it. So you're all going in different directions, seeking the same thing!

It is these differing ideas you have that produce your differing results. These ideas might be called your Sponsoring Thoughts. I have spoken to you of this before.

Yes, in *Book 1*.

One such thought which many of you share in common is your idea of insufficiency. Many of you believe at the core of your being that there is *simply not enough*. Not enough of *anything*.

There's not enough love, not enough money, not enough food, not enough clothing, not enough shelter, not enough time, not enough good ideas to go around, and certainly not enough of *you* to go around.

This Sponsoring Thought causes you to employ all sorts of strategies and tactics in seeking to acquire what you think there is "not enough" of. These are approaches you would abandon at once were you clear that there is enough for everybody . . . of *whatever* it is that you desire.

In what you call "heaven," your ideas of "not enough-ness" disappear, because you become aware that there is no separation between you and anything you desire.

You are aware that there is even more than enough of you. You are aware that you can be in more than one place at any given "time," so there is no reason not to want what your brother wants, not to choose what your sister chooses. If they want you in their space at the moment of their death, the very thought of you calls you to them—and you have no reason not to race to them, since your going there takes away nothing from whatever else you may be doing.

This state of having no reason to say No is the state in which I reside at all times.

You have heard it said before, and it is true: God never says No.

I will give you all exactly what you desire, always. Even as I have done from the beginning of time.

Are You really always *giving everyone exactly what they desire* at any given time?

Yes, My beloved, I am.

Your life is a reflection of what you desire, and what you believe you may have of what you desire. I cannot give you what you do not believe you may have—no matter how much you desire it—because I will not violate your own thought about it. I cannot. That is the law.

Believing that you cannot have something is the same thing as not desiring to have it, for it produces the same result.

But on Earth we cannot have what*ever* we desire. We cannot be in two places at once, for instance. And there are many other things we may desire, but cannot have, because on Earth we are all so limited.

I know that you see it that way, and so that is the way it is for you, for one thing that remains eternally true is that you will always be given the experience you believe you will be given.

Thus, if you say that you cannot be in two places at once, then you cannot be. But if you say that you can be anywhere you wish with the speed of your thought, and can even make yourself manifest in physical form in more than one place at any given time, then you may do that.

Now, You see, that's where this dialogue leaves me. I want to believe that this information is coming straight from God—but when You say things like that, I get all crazy inside, because I just can't believe that. I mean, I just don't think what You've said there is true. Nothing in the human experience has demonstrated that.

On the contrary. Saints and sages of all religions have been said to have done both of these things. Does it take a very high level of belief? An *extraordinary* level of belief? The level of belief attained by one being in a thousand years? Yes. Does that mean it is impossible? No.

How can I create that belief? How can I get to that level of belief?

You cannot get there. You can only *be* there. And I am not trying to play with words. I mean that. This kind of belief—what I would call Complete Knowing—is not something you try to acquire. In fact, if you are trying to *acquire it*, you cannot have it. It is something you simply *are*. You simply *are* this Knowing. You *are* this being.

Such beingness comes out of a state of *total awareness*. It can come out of *only* such a state. If you are seeking to *become* aware, then you cannot be.

It is like trying to "be" six feet tall when you are 4-foot-9. You cannot be six feet tall. You can only "be" what you *are*—4-foot-9. You will "be" six feet tall *when you grow into that*. When you *are* six feet tall, you will then be able to do all the things that six-foot-tall people can do. And when you *are* in a state of total awareness, then you will be able to do all the things that beings in a state of total awareness can do.

Do not, therefore, "try to believe" that you can do these things. Try, instead, to move to a state of total awareness. Then belief will no longer be necessary. Complete Knowing will work its wonders.

Once, when I was meditating, I had the experience of total oneness, total awareness. It was wonderful. It was ecstatic. Ever since then, I have been trying to have that experience again. I sit in meditation and try to have that total awareness again. And I have never been able to. This is the reason, right? You are saying to me that as long as I am seeking to have something, I cannot have it, because my very seeking is a statement that I do not now have it. The same wisdom You have been giving me throughout this dialogue.

Yes, yes. Now you understand it. It is becoming more clear to you now. That is why we keep going around in circles here. That is why we keep repeating things, revisiting things. You get it the third, the fourth, maybe the fifth time around.

Well, I'm glad I asked the question, because this could be dangerous stuff, this business about "you can be in two places at once," or "you can do anything you want to do." This is the kind of stuff that makes people run to jump off the Empire State Building shouting "I am God! Look at me! I can fly!"

You had better be in a state of total awareness before you do that. If you have to prove yourself to be God by demonstrating it to others, then you do not know yourself to be, and this "not knowing" will demonstrate itself in your reality. In short, you will fall flat on your face.

God seeks to prove Itself to no one, for God has no need to do that. God Is, and that is what is so. Those who know themselves to be One with God, or have the experience of God within, have no need, nor do they seek, to prove that to anyone, least of all themselves.

And so it was, that when they taunted him, saying, "If you are the Son of God, come down from that cross!"—the man called Jesus did nothing.

Yet three days later, quietly and unobtrusively, when there were no witnesses and no crowds and no one to whom to prove anything, he did something a great deal more astonishing—and the world has been talking about it ever since.

And in this miracle is found your salvation, for you have been shown the truth, not only of Jesus, but of Who You Are, and may thus be saved from the lie about yourself, which you have been told, and which you have accepted as your truth.

God invites you always to your highest thought about yourself.

There are those on your planet right now who have manifested many of these higher thoughts; including causing physical objects to appear and disappear, making themselves appear and disappear, even "living forever" in the body, or coming back to the body and living again—and all of this, all of this, has been made possible because of their faith. Because of their knowing. Because of their immutable clarity about how things are, and how they are meant to be.

And while, in the past, whenever people in earthly form have done these things, you have called the events miracles and have made the people saints and saviors, yet they are no more saints and saviors than you. For you are all saints and saviors. *Which is the very message they have been bringing you.*

How can I believe that? I want to believe that with all my heart, but I can't. I just can't.

No, you cannot believe it. You can only *know* it.

How can I know it? How can I come to that?

Whatever you choose for yourself, give to another. If you cannot come to that, help someone else come to that. *Tell* someone else that they already have. *Praise* them for it. *Honor* them for it.

This is the value in having a guru. That is the whole point. There has been a lot of negative energy in the West on the word "guru." It has almost become pejorative. To be a "guru" is to somehow be a charlatan. To give your allegiance to a guru is to somehow give your power away.

Honoring your guru is *not* giving your power away. It is *getting* your power. For when you honor the guru, when you praise your master teacher, what you say is, "I see you." And what you see in another, you can begin to see in yourself. It is outward evidence of your inner reality. It is outward proof of your inner truth. The truth of your being.

This is the truth which is being brought through you in the books you write.

I don't see myself as writing these books. I see You, *God*, as the author, and me as merely the scribe.

God is the author... *and so are you*. There is no difference between My writing them and you writing them. As long as you think there is, you will have missed the point of the writing itself. Yet most of humanity has missed this teaching. And so I send you new teachers, more teachers, all with the same message as the teachers of old.

I understand your reluctance to accept the teaching as your own personal truth. Were you to go around claiming to be One with God—or even a part of God—speaking or writing these words, the world would not know what to make of you.

People can make of me whatever they wish. This much I know: I do not deserve to be the recipient of the information I have been given here, and in all of these books. I do not feel worthy to be the messenger of this truth. I am working on this third book, yet I know even before its release that I, of all people, with all the mistakes I have made, all the selfish things I have done, am simply not *worthy* to be the bringer of this wonderful truth.

Yet that, perhaps, is the greatest message of this trilogy: That God stays hidden from no man, but speaks to everyone, even the least worthy among us. For if God will speak to me, God will speak directly into the heart of every man, woman, and child who seeks the truth.

There is thus hope for all of us. None of us is so horrible that God would forsake us, nor so unforgivable that God would turn away.

Is that what you believe—all of that which you have just written?

Yes.

Then so be it, and so shall it be with you.

Yet I tell you this. You *are* worthy. As is everyone else. Unworthiness is the worst indictment ever visited upon the human race. You have based your sense of worthiness on the past, while I base your sense of worthiness on the future.

The future, the future, always the future! That is where your life is, not in the past. The future. That is where your truth is, not in the past.

What you have done is unimportant compared to what you are about to do. How you have erred is insignificant compared to how you are about to create.

I forgive your mistakes. All of them. I forgive your misplaced passions. All of them. I forgive your erroneous notions, your misguided understandings, your hurtful actions, your selfish decisions. All of them.

Others may not forgive you, but I do. Others may not release you from your guilt, but I do. Others may not let you forget, allow you to go on, become something new, but I do. For I know that you are not what you were, but are, and always will be, what you are now.

A sinner can become a saint in one minute. In one second. In one breath.

In truth, there is no such thing as a "sinner," for no one can be sinned against—least of all Me. That is why I say that I "forgive" you. I use the phrase because it is one you seem to understand.

In truth, I do *not* forgive you, and will not forgive you *ever*, for *anything*. I do not have to. There is nothing to forgive. But I can release you. And I hereby do. Now. Once again. As I have done so often in the past, through the teachings of so many other teachers.

Why have we not heard them? Why have we not believed this, Your greatest promise?

Because you cannot believe in the goodness of God. Forget, then, about believing in My goodness. Believe, instead, in simple logic.

The reason I have no need to forgive you is that you cannot offend Me, nor can I be damaged or destroyed. Yet you imagine yourself capable of offending, even damaging, Me. What an illusion! What a magnificent obsession!

You cannot hurt Me, nor can I be harmed in any way. For I am the Unharmable. And that which cannot be harmed cannot, and would not, harm another.

You understand now the logic behind the truth that I do not condemn, nor shall I punish, nor have I a need to seek retribution.

I have no such need, for I have not been, and cannot be, offended or damaged or hurt in any way.

The same is true of you. And of all others—though all of you imagine that you can be, and have been, hurt and damaged and destroyed.

Because you imagine damage, you require revenge. Because you experience pain, you need another to experience pain as retribution for your own. Yet what possible justification can that be for inflicting pain upon another? Because (you imagine) someone has inflicted injury upon you, you feel it right and proper to inflict injury in return? That which you say is not okay for human beings to do to each other, is okay for *you* to do, so long as you are justified?

This is insanity. And what you do not see in this insanity is that *all* people who inflict pain on others assume themselves to be justified. Every action a person takes is *understood by that person to be the right action*, given what it is they seek and desire.

By your definition, what they seek and desire is wrong. But by their definition, it is not. You may not agree with their model of the world, with their moral and ethical constructions, with their theological understandings, nor with their decisions, choices, and actions . . . but *they* agree with them, based on their values.

You call their values "wrong." But who is to say your values are "right"? Only you. Your values are "right" because you say they are. Even this might make some sense if you kept your word about it, but you, yourself, change your mind constantly about what you consider "right" and "wrong." You do this as individuals, and you do this as societies.

What your society considered "right" just a few decades ago, you consider "wrong" today. What you considered "wrong" in the not-too-distant past, you now call "right." Who can tell what is what? How do you know the players without a scorecard?

And yet we dare to sit in judgment of one another. We dare to condemn, because some other person has failed to keep up with our own changing ideas about what is permitted and what is not. Whew. We're really something. We can't even keep our own minds made up about what's "okay" and what's not.

That isn't the problem. Changing your ideas of what's "right" and "wrong" isn't the problem. You *have* to change those ideas, or you would never grow. Changing is a product of evolution.

No, the problem is not that you have changed, or that your values have changed. The problem is that so many of you insist on thinking that the values you now have are the right and perfect ones, and that everyone else should adhere to them. Some of you have become self-justified and self-righteous.

Stick to your beliefs, if that serves you. Hold tight. Do not waiver. For your ideas about "right" and "wrong" are your definitions of Who You Are. Yet do not require that others define themselves according to your terms. And do not stay so "stuck" in your present beliefs and customs that you halt the process of evolution itself.

Actually, you could not do that if you wanted to, for life goes on, with you or without you. Nothing stays the same, nor can anything remain unchanged. To be unchanged is to not move. And to not move is to die.

All of life is motion. Even rocks are filled with motion. Everything moves. *Everything.* There is nothing that is not in motion. Therefore, by the very fact of motion, nothing is the same from one moment to the next. Nothing.

Remaining the same, or seeking to, moves against the laws of life. This is foolish, because in this struggle, life will always win.

So change! Yes, change! Change your ideas of "right" and "wrong." Change your notions of this and that. Change your structures, your constructions, your models, your theories.

Allow your deepest truths to be altered. Alter them yourself, for goodness' sake. I mean that quite literally. Alter them yourself, for *goodness' sake.* Because your new idea of Who You Are is where the growth is. Your new idea of What Is So is where evolution accelerates. Your new idea of the Who, What, Where, When, How, and Why of it is where the mystery gets solved, the plot unravels, the story ends. Then you can begin a new story, and a grander one.

Your new idea about *all of it* is where the excitement is, where the creation is, where God-in-you is made manifest and becomes fully realized.

No matter how "good" you think things have been, they can be better. No matter how wonderful you think your theologies, your ideologies, your cosmologies, they can be full of even more wonder. For there are "more things in heaven and earth than are dreamt of in your philosophy."

Be open, therefore. Be OPEN. Don't close off the possibility of new truth because you have been comfortable with an old one. Life begins at the end of your comfort zone.

Yet be not quick to judge another. Rather, seek to avoid judgment, for another person's "wrongs" were your "rights" of yestermorn; another person's mistakes are your own past actions, now corrected; another person's choices and decisions are as "hurtful" and "harmful," as "selfish" and "unforgivable," as many of your own have been.

It is when you "just can't imagine" how another person could "do such a thing" that you have forgotten where you came from, and where both you and the other person are going.

And to those of you who think yourselves to be the evil ones, who think yourselves to be unworthy and irredeemable, I tell you this: There is not a one among you who is lost forever, nor will there ever be. For you are all, *all*, in the process of becoming. You are all, *all*, moving though the experience of evolution.

That is what I am up to.

Through you.

5

I remember a prayer I was taught as a child. "Lord, I am not worthy that Thou shouldst enter under my roof. Yet say but the word, and my soul shall be healed." You have said these words, and I feel healed. I no longer feel unworthy. You have a way of making me feel worthy. If I could give one gift to all human beings, that would be it.

You have given them that gift, with this dialogue.

I would like to keep on giving it when this conversation is over.

This conversation will *never* be over.

Well, when this trilogy, then, is complete.

There will be ways for you to do that.

For that, I am very happy. Because this is the gift my soul yearns to give. All of us have a gift to give. I'd like this to be mine.

Go, then, and give it. Seek to make everyone whose life you touch feel worthy. Give everyone a sense of their own worthiness as a person, a sense of the true wonder of who they are. Give this gift, and you will heal the world.

I humbly ask Your help.

You will always have it. We are friends.

Meanwhile, I am loving this dialogue, and would like to ask a question about something You said before.

I'm here.

When You were talking about life "between lives," so to speak, You said, "You may re-create the experience of your individual Self whenever you choose." What does that mean?

It means you may emerge from The All anytime you wish, as a new "Self," or the same Self you were before.

You mean I can retain, and return to, my individual consciousness, my awareness of "me"?

Yes. You may have, at all times, whatever experience you desire.

And so I can return to this life—to the Earth—as the same person I was before I "died"?

Yes.

In the flesh?

Have you heard of Jesus?

Yes, but I am not Jesus, nor would I ever claim to be like him.

Did he not say, "These things, and more, shall you also do?"

Yes, but he wasn't talking about miracles like that, I don't think.

I am sorry you don't think so. Because Jesus was not the only one to have risen from the dead.

He wasn't? Others have risen from the dead?

Yes.

My god, that's blasphemy.

It's blasphemy that someone other than Christ has risen from the dead?

Well, some people would say that it is.

Then those people have never read the Bible.

The Bible? The *Bible* says that people other than Jesus came back to the body after death?

Ever hear of Lazarus?

Oh, no fair. It was through the Christ power that he was *raised* from the dead.

Precisely. And you think that "Christ power," as you call it, was reserved only for Lazarus? One person, in the history of the world?

I hadn't thought about it that way.

I tell you this: Many have there been who have been risen from the "dead." Many have there been who have "come back to life." It's happening every day, right now, in your hospitals.

Oh, come on. No fair again. That's medical science, not theology.

Oh, I see. God has nothing to do with today's miracles, only yesterday's.

Hmph . . . okay, I'll give You the point on technical grounds. But *no one has raised himself from the dead on their own, like Jesus did!* No one has come back from the "dead" *that* way.

Are you sure?

Well . . . pretty sure . . .

Have you ever heard of Mahavatar Babaji?

I don't think we should bring Eastern mystics into this. A lot of people don't buy that stuff.

I see. Well, of course, they must be right.

Let me get this straight. Are You saying that souls can return from the so-called "dead" in spirit form or in physical form, if that's what they desire?

You're beginning to understand now.

All right, then why haven't more people done it? Why don't we hear about it every day? This kind of thing would make international news.

Actually, a lot of people do do it, in spirit form. Not many, I'll admit, choose to return to the body.

Ha! There! I gotcha! *Why not?* If this is so easy, *why don't more souls do it?*

It's not a question of ease, it's a question of desirability.

Meaning?

Meaning it's a very rare soul who desires to return to physicality in the same form as before.

If a soul chooses to return to the body, it almost always does so with another body; a different one. In this way it begins a new agenda, experiences new rememberings, undertakes new adventures.

Generally, souls leave bodies because they are finished with them. They've completed what they joined with the body to do. They've experienced the experience they were seeking.

What about people who die by accident? Were they finished with their experience, or was it "cut off"?

Do you still imagine people die by accident?

You mean they don't?

Nothing in this universe occurs by accident. There is no such thing as an "accident," nor is there any such thing as "coincidence."

If I could convince myself that was true, I would never mourn again for those who have died.

Mourning for them is the last thing they would want you to do.

If you knew where they were, and that they were there by their own higher choice, you would *celebrate* their departure. If you experienced what you call the afterlife for one moment, having come to it with your grandest thought about yourself and God, you would smile the biggest smile at their funeral, and let joy fill your heart.

We cry at funerals for our loss. It is our sadness in knowing that we will never see them again, never hold or hug or touch or be with someone we loved.

And that is a good crying. That honors your love, and your beloved. Yet even this mourning would be short if you knew what grand realities and wondrous experiences await the joyous soul leaving the body.

What *is* it like in the afterlife? Really. Tell me all of it.

There are some things which cannot be revealed, not because I do not choose to, but because in your present condition, at your present level of understanding, you would be unable to conceive of what is being told to you. Still, there is more which can be said.

As we discussed earlier, you may do one of three things in what you call the afterlife, just as in the life you are now experiencing. You may submit to the creations of your uncontrolled thoughts, you may create your experience consciously out of choice, or you may experience the collective consciousness of All That Is. This last experience is called Reunification, or Rejoining the One.

Should you take the first path, most of you will not do so for very long (unlike the way you behave on Earth). This is because in the moment you don't like what you are experiencing, you will choose to create a new and more pleasant reality, which you will do by simply stopping your negative thoughts.

Because of this, you will never experience the "hell" of which you are so afraid, unless you choose to. Even in that case you will be "happy," in that you will be getting what you want. (More people than you know are "happy" being "miserable.") So you will keep experiencing it until you don't choose to any more.

For most of you, the moment you even begin to experience it, you will move away from it and create something new.

You can eliminate the hell in your life on Earth exactly the same way.

Should you take the second path and consciously create your experience, you will no doubt experience going "straight to heaven," because this is what anyone who is freely choosing, and who believes in heaven, would create. If you do not believe in heaven, you will experience whatever you wish to experience—and the moment you understand that, your wishes will get better and better. And then you *will* believe in heaven!

Should you take the third path and submit to the creations of the collective consciousness, you will move very quickly into total acceptance, total peace, total joy, total awareness, and total love, for that is the consciousness of the collective. Then you will become one with the Oneness, and there will be nothing else except That Which You Are—which is All There Ever Was, until you decide that there should be something else. This is nirvana, the "one with the Oneness" experience that many of you have had very briefly in meditation, and it is an indescribable ecstasy.

After you experience the Oneness for an infinite time-no time, you will cease to experience it, because you cannot experience the Oneness *as* Oneness unless and until That Which Is Not One also exists. Understanding this, you will create, once again, the idea and the thought of separation, or disunity.

Then you will keep traveling on the Cosmic Wheel, keep going, keep circling, keep on being, forever and ever, and even forever more.

You will return to the Oneness many times—an infinite number of times and for an infinite period each time—and you will know that you have the tools to return to the Oneness at any point on the Cosmic Wheel.

You may do so now, even as you are reading this.

You may do so tomorrow, in your meditation.

You may do so at any time.

And You've said that we do not have to stay at the level of consciousness we're at when we die?

No. You may move to another as quickly as you wish. Or take as much "time" as you like. If you "die" in a state of limited perspective and uncontrolled thoughts, you'll experience whatever that state brings you, until you don't want to anymore. Then you'll "wake up"—become conscious—and start experiencing yourself creating your reality.

You'll look back at the first stage and call it purgatory. The second stage, when you can have anything you want with the speed of your thought, you'll call heaven. The third stage, when you experience the bliss of the Oneness, you'll call Nirvana.

I have one more thing I'd like to explore along these lines. It's not about "after death," but it is about experiences outside of the body. Can You explain those to me? What is happening there?

The essence of Who You Are has simply left the physical body. This can happen during normal dreaming, often during meditation, and frequently in a sublime form while the body is in deep sleep.

During such an "excursion," your soul can be anywhere it wishes. Frequently, the person reporting such an experience has no after-memory of having made volitional decisions about this. They may experience it as "just something that happened to me." However, nothing which involves an activity of the soul is nonvolitional.

How can we be "shown" things, how can things be "revealed" to us, during one of these experiences, if all we are doing is creating as we go along? It seems to me that the only way things could be revealed to us would be if those things existed separate from us, not as part of our own creation. I need some help with this.

Nothing exists separate from you, and everything is your own creation. Even your apparent lack of understanding is your own creation; it is, literally, a figment of your imagination. You imagine that you do not know the answer to this question, and so you do not. Yet as soon as you imagine that you do, you do.

You allow yourself to do this sort of imagining so that The Process can go on.

The Process?

Life. The eternal Process.

In those moments during which you experience yourself being "revealed" to yourself—whether these are what you call out-of-body experiences, or dreams, or magic moments of wakefulness when you are greeted by crystal clarity—what has happened is that you have simply slipped into "remembering." You are remembering what you have already created. And these rememberings can be very powerful. They can produce a personal epiphany.

Once you've had such a magnificent experience, it can be very difficult to go back to "real life" in a way that blends well with what other people are calling "reality." That is because *your* reality has shifted. It has become something else. It has expanded, grown. And it cannot be shrunk again. It's like trying to get the genie back in the bottle. It can't be done.

Is that why many people who come back from out-of-body experiences, or so-called "near-death" experiences, sometimes seem very different?

Exactly. And they *are* different, because now they know so much more. Yet, frequently, the further they get from such experiences, the more time that passes, the more they revert to their old behaviors, because they have again forgotten what they know.

Is there any way to "keep remembering"?

Yes. Act out your knowingness in every moment. Keep acting on what you know, rather than what the world of illusion is showing you. Stay with it, no matter how deceiving appearances are.

This is what all masters have done, and do. They judge not by appearances, but act according to what they know.

And there is another way to remember.

Yes?

Cause another to remember. That which you wish for yourself, give to another.

That's what it feels I am doing with these books.

That is exactly what you are doing. And the longer you keep on doing it, the less you will have to do it. The more you send this message to another, the less you will have to send it to your Self.

Because my Self and the other are One, and what I give to another, I give to myself.

You see, now you are giving Me the answers. And that, of course, is how it works.

Wow. I just gave God an answer. That is cool. That is really cool.

You're telling Me.

That's what's *cool*—the fact that *I'm telling You.*

And I will tell *you* this: The day will come when we will speak as One. That day will come for all people.

Well, if that day is going to come for me, I'd like to make sure I understand exactly what it is You're saying. So I'd like to go back to something else, just one more time. I know You said this more than once, but I really want to make sure I really understand it.

Am I clear that, once we reach this state of Oneness which many call Nirvana—once we return to the Source—we don't stay there? The reason I am asking this again is that this seems to run counter to my understanding of many Eastern esoteric and mystical teachings.

> To remain in the state of sublime no-thing, or Oneness with the All, would make it impossible to be there. As I've just explained, That Which Is cannot be, except in the space of That Which Is Not. Even the total bliss of Oneness cannot be experienced as "total bliss" unless something less than total bliss exists. So, something less than the total bliss of total Oneness had to be—and continually has to be—created.

But when we are in total bliss, when we have merged once more with the Oneness, when we have become Everything/No-thing, how can we even *know* that we exist? Since there is nothing else that we are experiencing . . . I don't know. I don't seem to understand this. This is one I can't seem to get a handle on.

> You are describing what I call the Divine Dilemma. This is the same dilemma God has always had—and that God solved with the creation of that which was not God (or thought it was not).
>
> God gave—and gives again, in every instant—a part of Itself to the Lesser Experience of not knowing Itself, so that the Rest of Itself can know Itself as Who and What It Really Is.
>
> Thus, "God gave His only begotten son, that you might be saved." You see now from where this mythology has sprung.

I think that we are all God—and that we are constantly, every one of us, journeying from Knowing to Not Knowing to Knowing again, from being to not being to being again, from Oneness to Separation to Oneness again, in a never-ending cycle. That this *is* the cycle of life—what You call the Cosmic Wheel.

> Exactly. Precisely. That is well said.

But do we all have to go back to *ground zero?* Do we always have to start over, completely? Go back to the beginning? Return to square one? Do not pass "Go," do not collect $200?

You do not *have* to do anything. Not in this lifetime, not in any other. You will have choice—*always you will have free choice*—to go anywhere you wish to go, do anything you wish to do, in your re-creation of the experience of God. You can move to any place on the Cosmic Wheel. You may "come back" as anything you wish, or in any other dimension, reality, solar system, or civilization you choose. Some of those who have reached the place of total union with the Divine have even chosen to "come back" as enlightened masters. And, yes, some were enlightened masters when they left, and then chose to "come back" as *themselves.*

You must surely be aware of reports of gurus and masters who have returned to your world over and over again, manifesting in repeated appearances throughout the decades and centuries.

You have one entire religion based on such a report. It is called the Church of Jesus Christ of Latter Day Saints, and it is based on the report of Joseph Smith that the Being calling himself Jesus returned to Earth many centuries after his apparently "final" departure, this time appearing in the United States.

So you may return to any point on the Cosmic Wheel to which it pleases you to return.

Still, even that could be depressing. Don't we ever get to *rest?* Don't we ever get to stay in nirvana, to *remain* there? Are we doomed forever to this "coming and going"—this "now you see it, now you don't" treadmill? Are we on an eternal journey to nowhere?

Yes. That's the greatest truth. There is nowhere to go, nothing to do, and no one you have to "be" except exactly who you're being right now.

The truth is that there is no journey. You are right now what you are attempting to be. You are right now where you are attempting to go.

It is the master who knows this, and thus ends the struggle. And then does the master seek to assist you in ending *your* struggle, even as you will seek to end the struggle of others when you reach mastery.

Yet this process—this Cosmic Wheel—is not a depressing treadmill. It is a glorious and continual reaffirmation of the utter magnificence of God, and all life—and there is nothing depressing about that at all.

Still seems depressing to me.

Let Me see if I can change your mind. Do you like sex?

I love it.

Most people do, except those with really weird ideas about it. So, what if I told you that beginning tomorrow you can have sex with every single person for whom you felt attraction and love. Would that make you happy?

Would this have to be against their will?

No. I would arrange it so that every one you wish to celebrate the human experience of love with in this way also wishes to do so with you. They would feel great attraction and love for you.

Wow! Hey—okaaay!

There's just one condition: You have to stop between each one. You can't just go from one to the other without interruption.

You're telling me.

So, in order to experience the ecstasy of this kind of physical union, you have to also experience *not* being united sexually with someone, if only for a while.

I think I see where you're going.

Yes. Even the ecstasy would not be ecstasy were there not a time when there was no ecstasy. This is as true with spiritual ecstasy as it is with physical.

There is nothing depressing about the cycle of life, there is only joy. Simply joy and more joy.

True masters are never less than joyful. This staying at the level of mastery is what you may now find desirable. Then you can move in and out of the ecstasy and still be joyful always. You do not need the ecstasy to be joyful. You are joyful simply knowing that ecstasy is.

6

I'd like to change the subject now, if I could, and talk about Earth changes. But before I do, I'd like to just make an observation. It seems as though there are a lot of things being said here more than once. I sometimes feel like I'm hearing the same things, over and over again.

> That's good! Because you are! As I said earlier, this is by design.
>
> This message is like a spring. When it is coiled, it circles back onto itself. One circle covers the other, and it seems to be, literally, "going around in circles." Only when the spring is uncoiled will you see that it stretches out in a spiral, farther than you could have ever imagined.
>
> Yes, you are right. Much of what is being said has been said a number of times, in different ways. Sometimes in the *same* way. The observation is correct.
>
> When you are finished with this message, you should be able to repeat its essential points virtually verbatim. The day may come when you may wish to.

Okay, fair enough. Now, moving *forward*, a bunch of people seem to think I have a "direct line to God," and they want to know, is our planet doomed? I know I asked this before, but now I'd really like a direct answer. Will the Earth changes occur, as so many are predicting? And if not, what are all those psychics seeing? A made-up vision? Should we be praying? Changing? Is there anything we can do? Or is it all, sadly, hopeless?

> I will be happy to address those questions, but we will not be "moving forward."

We won't?

> No, because the answers have already been given you, in My several previous explanations of time.

503

You mean the part about "everything that's ever going to happen has already happened."

Yes.

But what IS the "everything that has already happened?" How did it happen? *What* happened?

All of it happened. All of it has already happened.
Every possibility exists as fact, as completed events.

How can that be? I still don't understand how that can be.

I am going to put this in terms to which you can better relate. See if this helps. Have you ever watched children use a CD-ROM to play a computerized video game?

Yes.

Have you ever asked yourself how the computer knows how to respond to every move the child makes with the joystick?

Yes, actually, I have wondered that.

It's all on the disc. The computer knows how to respond to every move the child makes because every possible move has already been placed on the disc, *along with its appropriate response.*

That's spooky. Almost surreal.

What, that every ending, and every twist and turn producing that ending, is already programmed on the disc? There's nothing "spooky" about it. It's just technology. And if you think that the technology of video games is something, wait 'til you see the technology of the *universe!*

Think of the Cosmic Wheel as that CD-ROM. All the endings already exist. The universe is just waiting to see which one you choose *this time.* And when the game is over, whether you win, lose, or draw, the universe will say, "Want to play again?"

Your computer disc doesn't care whether you win or not, and you can't "hurt its feelings." It just offers you a chance to play again. All the endings already exist, and which ending you experience depends on the choices you make.

So God is nothing more than a CD-ROM?

I wouldn't put it that way, exactly. But throughout this dialogue I have been trying to use illustrations that embody concepts everyone can hold in their understanding. So I think the CD-ROM illustration is a good one.

In many ways, life *is* like a CD-ROM. All the possibilities exist and have already occurred. Now you get to select which one you choose to experience.

This relates directly to your question about Earth changes.

What many of the psychics are saying about the Earth changes is true. They have opened a window onto the "future," and they have seen it. The question is, *which* "future" have they seen? As with the end of the game on the CD-ROM, there is *more than one version.*

In one version, the Earth will be in upheaval. In another version, it won't.

Actually, *all* of the versions have *already happened.* Remember, time—

—I know, I know. "Time does not exist"—

—that's *right.* And so?

So everything's happening at once.

Right again. All that has ever happened, is happening now, and ever will happen, exists right now. Just as all the moves in the computer game exist right now on that disc. So if you think it would be interesting for the doomsday predictions of the psychics to come true, focus all your attention on that, and you can draw that to yourself. And if you think you would like to experience a different reality, focus on that, and that is the outcome you can draw to you.

So You won't tell me whether the Earth changes will occur or not, is that it?

I am waiting for you to tell Me. You will decide, by your thoughts, words, and actions.

How about the Year 2000 computer problem? There are those who are saying now that what we are now calling the "Y2K" glitch is going to be the cause of a great upheaval in our social and economic systems. Will it be?

What do you say? What do you choose? Do you think that you have nothing to do with any of this? I tell you, that would be inaccurate.

Won't You tell us how this will all turn out?

I am not here to predict your future, and I will not do that. This much I can tell you. This much *anybody* can tell you. If you are not careful, you will get exactly where you are going. If, therefore, you don't like the way you are headed, *change direction*.

How do I do that? How can I affect such a large outcome? What *should* we do in the face of all these predictions of disaster by persons of psychic or spiritual "authority"?

Go inside. Search your place of inner wisdom. See what this calls on you to do. Then do it.

If that means write your politicians and your industrialists, asking them to take action on environmental abuses that could lead to Earth changes, do it. If that means bringing your community leaders together to work on the Y2K problem, do it. And if that means just walking your path, sending out positive energy every day, and keeping those around you from falling into a panic which *brings on* a problem, do it.

Most important of all, do not be afraid. You cannot "die" in any event, so there is nothing to be afraid of. Be aware of The Process unfolding, and quietly know that everything is going to be okay with you.

Seek to get in touch with the perfection of all things. Know that you will be exactly where you have to be in order to experience exactly what you choose as you go about creating Who You Really Are.

This is the way to peace. In all things, see the perfection.

Finally, don't try to "get out" of anything. What you resist, persists. I told you that in the first book, and it's true.

People who are sad about what they "see" in the future, or what they've been "told" about the future, are failing to "stay in the perfection."

Any other advice?

Celebrate! Celebrate life! Celebrate Self! Celebrate the predictions! Celebrate God!

Celebrate! Play the game.

Bring joy to the moment, whatever the moment seems to bring, because joy is Who You Are, and Who You Will Always Be.

God cannot create anything imperfect. If you think that God can create anything imperfect, then you know nothing of God.

So celebrate. Celebrate the perfection! Smile and celebrate and see only the perfection, and that which others call the imperfection will not touch you in any way which is imperfect for you.

You mean I can avoid the Earth shifting on its axis, or being smashed by a meteor, or being crumpled by earthquakes, or being caught in a confusing and hysterical aftermath of Y2K?

You can definitely avoid being affected negatively by any of that.

That isn't what I asked You.

But it is what I answered. Face the future fearlessly, understanding The Process and seeing the perfection of all of it.

That peace, that serenity, that calmness will lead you away from most of the experiences and outcomes others would have called "negative."

What if You are wrong about all of this? What if You are not "God" at all, but just the overworkings of my fertile imagination?

Ah, back to that question, eh?

Well, what if? So what? Can you think of a better way to live?

All I am saying here is to stay calm, stay peaceful, stay serene, in the face of these dire predictions of planet-wide calamity, and you will have the best outcome possible.

Even if I'm not God, and I'm just "you," making it all up, can you get any better advice?

No, I think not.

So, as usual, it makes no difference whether I'm "God" or not.

With this, as with the information in all three books, just live the wisdom. Or, if you can think of a better way to proceed, *do that.*

Look, even if it really is just Neale Donald Walsch doing the talking in all these books, you could hardly find better advice to follow, on any of the subjects covered. So look at it this way: Either I am God talking, or this Neale fellow is a pretty bright guy.

What's the difference?

The difference is, if I were convinced it was really God saying these things, I'd listen more closely.

Oh, bananas. I've sent you messages a thousand times in a hundred different forms, and you've ignored most of them.

Yeah, I suppose I have.

You suppose?

Okay, I have.

So this time, don't ignore. Who do you suppose brought you to this book? You did. So if you can't listen to God, listen to yourself.

Or my friendly psychic.

Or your friendly psychic.

You're kidding with me now, but this does bring up another subject I wanted to discuss.

I know.

You know?

Of course. You want to discuss psychics.

How did You know?

I'm psychic.

Hey, I'll bet You are. You're the Mother of all psychics. You're the *Chief Honcho*, the *Top Banana*, the *Big Cheese*. You're The Man, The Boss, The Unit, The Chairman of the Board.

My man, you have got . . . it . . . right.

Gimme *five*.

Cool, brother. Right on.

So what I want to know is, what is "psychic power"?

You all have what you call "psychic power." It is, truly, a sixth sense. And you all have a "sixth sense about things."

Psychic power is simply the ability to step out of your limited experience into a broader view. To step back. To feel more than what the limited individual you have imagined yourself to be would feel; to know more than he or she would know. It is the ability to tap into the *larger truth* all around you; to sense a different energy.

How does one develop this ability?

"Develop" is a good word. It's sort of like muscles. You all have them, yet some of you choose to develop them, whereas in others they remain undeveloped, and far less useful.

To develop your psychic "muscle," you must exercise it. Use it. Every day. All the time.

Right now the muscle is there, but it's small. It's weak. It's under-used. So you'll get an intuitive "hit" now and then, but you won't act on it. You'll get a "hunch" about something, but you'll ignore it. You'll have a dream, or an "inspiration," but you'll let it pass, paying it scant attention.

Thank goodness you did pay attention to the "hit" you had about this book, or you wouldn't be reading these words now.

You think you came to these words by accident? By chance?

So the first step in developing psychic "power" is to know you have it, and to use it. Pay attention to every hunch you have, every feeling you feel, every intuitive "hit" you experience. *Pay attention.*

Then, act on what you "know." Don't let your mind talk you out of it. Don't let your fear pull you away from it.

The more that you act on your intuition fearlessly, the more your intuition will serve you. It was always there, only now you're paying attention to it.

But I'm not talking about the always-finding-a-parking-space kind of psychic ability. I'm talking about real psychic power. The kind that sees into the future. The kind that lets you know things about people you'd have no way of knowing otherwise.

That's what I was talking about, too.

How does this psychic power work? Should I listen to people who have it? If a psychic makes a prediction, can I change it, or is my future set in stone? How can some psychics tell things about you the minute you walk into the room? What if—

Wait. That's four different questions there. Let's slow down a bit and try one at a time.

Okay. How does psychic power work?

There are three rules of psychic phenomena that will allow you to understand how psychic power works. Let's go over them.
1. All thought is energy.
2. All things are in motion.
3. All time is now.

Psychics are people who have opened themselves to the experiences these phenomena produce: vibrations. Sometimes formed as pictures in the mind. Sometimes a thought in the form of a word.

The psychic becomes adept at feeling these energies. This may not be easy at first, because these energies are very light, very fleeting, very subtle. Like the slightest breeze on a summer night that you think you felt rustle your hair—but maybe didn't. Like the faintest sound in the farthest distance that you think you heard, but can't be sure. Like the dimmest flicker of an image at the corner of your eye that you swore was there, but, when you look head on, is gone. Vanished. Was it there at all?

That's the question the beginning psychic is always asking. The accomplished psychic never asks, because to ask the question sends the answer away. Asking the question engages the mind, and that's the last thing a psychic wants to do. Intuition does not reside in the mind. To be psychic, you've got to be out of your mind. Because intuition resides in the psyche. In the soul.

Intuition is the ear of the soul.

The soul is the only instrument sensitive enough to "pick up" life's faintest vibrations, to "feel" these energies, to sense these waves in the field, and to interpret them.

You have six senses, not five. They are your sense of smell, taste, touch, sight, hearing, and . . . *knowing.*

So here is how "psychic power" works.

Every time you have a thought, it sends off an energy. It *is* energy. The soul of the psychic picks up that energy. The true psychic will not stop to interpret it, but will probably just blurt out what that energy feels like. That's how a psychic can tell you what you're thinking.

Every feeling you've ever had resides in your soul. Your soul is the sum total of all your feelings. It is the repository. Even though it may have been years since you've stored them there, a psychic who is truly open can "feel" these "feelings" here and now. That's because—all together now—

There's no such thing as time—

That's how a psychic can tell you about your "past."

"Tomorrow" also does not exist. All things are occurring right now. Every occurrence sends off a wave of energy, prints an indelible picture on the cosmic photographic plate. The psychic sees, or feels, the picture of "tomorrow" as if it is happening right now—*which it is*. That is how some psychics tell the "future."

How is this done, physiologically? Perhaps without actually knowing what he's doing, a psychic, through the act of intense focusing, is sending out an actual submolecular component of himself. His "thought," if you will, leaves the body, zings out into space, and goes far enough, fast enough, to be able to turn around and "see" from a distance the "now" that you have not yet experienced.

Submolecular time travel!

You could say that.

Submolecular time travel!

Ohhhh-*kay*. We've decided to turn this into a vaudeville show.

No, no, I'll be good. I promise . . . really. Go on. I really do want to hear this.

Okay. The submolecular part of the psychic, having absorbed the energy of the image gained from focusing, zings back to the psychic's body, bringing the energy with it. The psychic "gets a picture"—sometimes with a shiver—or "feels a feeling," and tries very hard not to do any "processing" of the data, but simply—and instantly—describes it. The psychic has learned not to question what he's "thinking" or suddenly "seeing" or "feeling," but merely to allow it to "come through" as untouched as possible.

Weeks later, if the event pictured or "felt" actually occurs, the psychic is called a clairvoyant—which, of course, is true!

If that's the case, how come some "predictions" are "wrong"; that is, they never "happen"?

Because the psychic has not "predicted the future," merely offered a glimpse of one of the "possible possibilities" observed in the Eternal Moment of Now. It is always the subject of the psychic reading who has made the choice. He could just as easily make another choice—a choice not in concert with the prediction.

The Eternal Moment contains all "possible possibilities." As I have explained now several times, everything has already happened, in a million different ways. All that's left is for you to make some perception choices.

It is all a question of perception. When you change your perception, you change your thought, and your thought creates your reality. Whatever outcome you could anticipate in any situation is already there for you. All you have to do is perceive it. Know it.

This is what is meant by "even before you ask, I will have answered." In truth, your prayers are "answered" before the prayer is offered.

Then how come we don't all get what we pray for?

This was covered in *Book 1*. You don't always get what you ask, but you always get what you create. Creation follows thought, which follows perception.

This is mind-boggling. Even though we've been over this before, this is still mind-boggling.

Isn't it, though? That's why it's good to keep going over it. Hearing it several times gives you a chance to wrap your mind around it. Then your mind gets "unboggled."

If everything is all happening now, what dictates which *part* of it all I'm experiencing in *my* moment of "now"?

Your choices—and your belief in your choices. That belief will be created by your thoughts on a particular subject, and those thoughts arise out of your perceptions—that is, "the way you look at it."

So the psychic sees the choice you are now making about "tomorrow," and sees that played out. But a true psychic will always tell you it doesn't have to be that way. You can "choose again," and change the outcome.

In effect, I'd be changing the experience I've already had!

Exactly! Now you're getting it. Now you're understanding how to live in the paradox.

But if it's "already happened," to whom has it "happened"? And if I change it, who is the "me" that experiences the change?

There is more than one of "you" moving down the time-line. This was all described in detail in *Book 2*. I'm going to suggest that you re-read that. Then combine what's there with what's here, for a richer understanding.

Okay. Fair enough. But I'd like to talk about this psychic stuff a while longer. A lot of people claim to be psychic. How can I tell the real from the fake?

Everyone *is* "psychic," so they're *all* "real." What you want to look for is their purpose. Are they seeking to help you, or to enrich themselves?

Psychics—so called "professional psychics"—who are seeking to enrich themselves often promise to do things with their psychic power—"return a lost lover," "bring wealth and fame," even help you lose weight!

They promise they can do all this—but only for a fee. They'll even do a "reading" on another—your boss, your lover, a friend—and tell you all about them. They'll say, "Bring me something. A scarf, a picture, a sample of their handwriting."

And they *can* tell you about the other. Often, quite a bit. Because everyone leaves a trace, a "psychic fingerprint," an energy trail. And a true sensitive can feel this.

But a sincere intuitive will never offer to cause another to come back to you, get a person to change his mind, or *create any result whatsoever with her psychic "power."* A true psychic—one who has given her life to the development and use of this gift—knows that another's free will is never to be tampered with, and that another's thoughts are never to be invaded, and that another's psychic space is never to be violated.

I thought You said there is no "right" and "wrong." What are all these "nevers" all of a sudden?

Every time I lay down an "always" or a "never," it is within the context of what I know you are seeking to accomplish; what it is you are trying to do.

I know that you are all seeking to evolve, to grow spiritually, to return to the Oneness. You are seeking to experience yourself as the grandest version of the greatest vision you ever had about Who You Are. You are seeking this individually, and as a race.

Now there are no "rights" and "wrongs," no "do's" and "don'ts" in My world—as I have said many times—and you do not burn in the everlasting fires of hell if you make a "bad" choice, because neither "bad" nor "hell" exists—unless, of course, you think that it does.

Still there are natural laws that have been built into the physical universe—and one of those is the law of cause and effect.

One of the most important laws of cause and effect is this:

All caused effect is ultimately experienced by the Self.

What does that mean?

Whatever you cause another to experience, you will one day experience.

Members of your New Age community have a more colorful way of putting it.

"What goes around, comes around."

Right. Others know this as the Jesus Injunction: *Do unto others as you would have it done unto you.*

Jesus was teaching the law of cause and effect. It is what might be called the Prime Law. Somewhat like the Prime Directive given to Kirk, Picard, and Janeway.

Hey, God is a *Trekkie*!

Are you kidding? I wrote half the episodes.

Better not let Gene hear You say that.

Come on...Gene *told* Me to say that.

You're in touch with Gene Roddenberry?

And Carl Sagan, and Bob Heinlein, and the *whole gang* up here.

You know, we shouldn't kid around like this. It takes away from the believability of the whole dialogue.

I see. A conversation with God has to be serious.

Well, at least believable.

It's not believable that I've got Gene, Carl, and Bob right here? I'll have to tell them that. Well, back to how you can tell a true psychic from a "fake" one. A true psychic knows and lives the Prime Directive. That's why, if you ask her to bring back a "long-lost love," or read the aura of another person whose handkerchief or letter you have, a true psychic will tell you:

"I'm sorry, but I won't do that. I will never interfere with, intervene in, or look in on, the path walked by another.

"I will not attempt to affect, direct, or impact their choices in any way.

"And I will not divulge to you information about any individual that is personal or private."

If a person offers to perform one of these "services" for you, that person is what you would call a shyster, using your own human weaknesses and vulnerabilities to extract money from you.

But what about psychics who help people locate a missing loved one— a child who was abducted, a teenager who ran away and has too much pride to call home, even though they desperately want to? Or how about the classic case of locating a person—dead or alive—for the police?

Of course, these questions all answer themselves. What the true psychic always avoids is imposing his will upon another. She is there only to serve.

Is it okay to ask a psychic to contact the dead? Should we attempt to reach out to those who have "gone before"?

Why would you want to?

To see if they have something they want to say to us; to tell us.

> If somebody from "the other side" has something they want you to know, they'll find a way to cause you to know it, don't worry.
>
> The aunt, the uncle, the brother, the sister, the father, the mother, the spouse, and lover who have "gone before" are continuing their own journey, experiencing complete joy, moving toward total understanding.
>
> If part of what they want to do is to come back to you—to see how you are, to bring you an awareness that they're all right, whatever—trust that they'll do that.
>
> Then, watch for the "sign" and catch it. Don't dismiss it as just your imagination, "wishful thinking," or coincidence. Watch for the message, and receive it.

I know of a lady who was nursing her dying husband, and she begged him: If he had to go, please come back to her and let her know that he was all right. He promised he would, and died two days later. Not a week went by when the lady was awakened one night by the feeling that someone had just sat down on the bed beside her. When she opened her eyes, she could have sworn she saw her husband, sitting at the foot of the bed, smiling at her. But when she blinked and looked again, he was gone. She told me the story later, saying then that she must have been hallucinating.

> Yes, that's very common. You receive signs—irrefutable, obvious signs—and you ignore them. Or dismiss them as your own mind playing tricks on you.
>
> You have the same choice now, with this book.

Why do we do that? Why do we ask for something—like the wisdom contained in these three books—then refuse to believe it when we receive it?

> Because you doubt the greater glory of God. Like Thomas, you have to see, feel, touch, before you will believe. Yet that which you wish to know cannot be seen, felt, or touched. It is of another realm. And you are not open to that; you are not ready. Yet do not fret. When the student is ready, the teacher will appear.

So are You saying, then—to get back to the original line of questioning—that we should *not* go to a psychic or a séance seeking to contact those on the other side?

I'm not saying that you should or shouldn't do anything. I'm just not sure what the point would be.

Well, supposing you had something *you* wanted to say to the other, rather than something you wanted to hear from *them?*

Do you imagine that you could say it and they not hear it? The slightest thought having to do with a being existing on what you call "the other side" brings that being's consciousness flying to you.

You cannot have a thought or an idea about a person who is what you call "deceased" without that person's Essence becoming completely aware of it. It is not necessary to use a medium to produce such communication. *Love is the best "medium" of communication.*

Ah, but how about *two-way* communication? Would a medium be helpful there? Or is such communication even possible? Is it all hogwash? Is it dangerous?

You are talking now about communication with spirits. Yes, such communication is possible. It is dangerous? Virtually everything is "dangerous" if you are afraid. What you fear, you create. Yet there is really nothing to be afraid of.

Loved ones are never far from you, never more than a thought away, and will always be there if you need them, ready with counsel or comfort or advice. If there is a high level of stress on your part about a loved one being "okay," they will send you a sign, a signal, a little "message" that will allow you to know everything's fine.

You won't even have to call on them, because souls who loved you in this life are drawn to you, pulled to you, fly to you, the moment they sense the slightest trouble or disturbance in your auric field.

One of their first opportunities, as they learn about the possibilities of their new existence, is to provide aid and comfort to those they love. And you will feel their comforting presence if you are really open to them.

So the stories we hear of people "who could have sworn" that a deceased loved one was in the room could be true.

Most assuredly. One might smell the loved one's perfume or cologne, or get a whiff of the cigar they smoked, or faintly hear a song they used to hum. Or, out of nowhere, some personal possession of theirs may suddenly appear. A handkerchief, or a wallet, or some cufflink or piece of jewelry just "shows up" for "no reason." It's "found" in a chair cushion, or under a stack of old magazines. There it is. A picture, a photograph, of a special moment—just when you were missing that person and thinking about them and feeling sad about their death. These things don't "just happen." These kinds of things don't "just appear" at "just the right moment" by chance. I tell you this: *There are no coincidences in the universe.*

This is very common. Very common.

Now, back to your question: Do you need a so-called "medium" or "channel" to communicate with beings out of the body? No. Is it sometimes helpful? Sometimes. So much depends, again, on the psychic or medium—and on their motivation.

If someone refuses to work in this way with you—or to do any kind of "channeling" or "go-between" work—without high compensation; run, don't walk, the other way. That person may be in it only for the money. Don't be surprised if you get "hooked" into returning time and time again for weeks or months, or even years, as they play on your need or desire for contact with the "spirit world."

A person who is only there—as the spirit is there—to help, asks nothing for himself except what is needed to continue to do the work they seek to do.

If a psychic or medium is coming from that place when she agrees to help you, make sure you offer all the help in return that you can. Don't take advantage of such extraordinary generosity of the spirit by giving little, or not at all, when you know you could do more.

Look to see who is truly serving the world, truly seeking to share wisdom and knowledge, insight and understanding, caring and compassion. Provide for those people, and provide grandly. Pay them the highest honor. Give them the largest amount. For these are the Bringers of the Light.

7

We've covered a lot here. Boy, we've really covered a lot. Can we make another shift? Are You ready to go on?

Are you?

Yes, I'm rolling now. I've finally gotten on a roll. And I want to ask every question I've been waiting three years to ask.

I'm okay with that. Go.

Coolness. So I would like now to talk about another of the esoteric mysteries. Will You speak to me about reincarnation?

Sure.

Many religions say that reincarnation is a false doctrine; that we get only one life here; one chance.

I know. That is not accurate.

How can they be so wrong about something so important? How can they not know the truth about something so basic?

You must understand that humans have many fear-based religions whose teachings surround a doctrine of a God who is to be worshipped and feared.

It was through fear that your entire Earth society reformed itself from the matriarchy into the patriarchy. It was through fear that the early priests got people to "mend their wicked ways" and "heed the word of the Lord." It was through fear that churches gained, and controlled, their membership.

One church even insisted that God would punish you if you did not go to church every Sunday. Not going to church was declared a sin.

And not just any church. One had to attend one particular church. If you went to a church of a different denomination, that, too, was a sin. This was an attempt at control, pure and simple, using fear. The amazing thing is, it worked. Hell, it still works.

Say, You're God. Don't swear.

Who was swearing? I was making a statement of fact. I said, "Hell—it *still works.*"

People will always believe in hell, and in a God who would send them there, as long as they believe that God is like man—ruthless, self-serving, unforgiving, and vengeful.

In days past, most people could not imagine a God who might rise above all of that. So they accepted the teaching of many churches to "fear the terrible vengeance of the Lord."

It was as if people couldn't trust themselves to be good, to act appropriately, on their own, for their own built-in reasons. So they had to create a religion that taught the doctrine of an angry, retributive God in order to keep themselves in line.

Now the idea of reincarnation threw a monkey wrench into all of that.

How so? What made that doctrine so threatening?

The church was proclaiming that you'd better be nice, or *else*—and along came the reincarnationists, saying: "You'll have another chance after this, and another chance after that. And still more chances. So don't worry. Do the best you can. Don't become so paralyzed with fear that you can't budge. Promise yourself to do better, and get on with it."

Naturally, the early church couldn't hear of such a thing. So it did two things. First, it denounced the doctrine of reincarnation as heretical. Then it created the sacrament of confession. Confession could do for the churchgoer what reincarnation promised. That is, *give him another chance.*

So then we had a setup where God would punish you for your sins, unless you *confessed them.* In that case you could feel safe, knowing that God had heard your confession and forgiven you.

Yes. But there was a catch. This absolution *could not come directly from God.* It had to flow through the church, whose priests pronounced "penances" which had to be performed. These were usually prayers which were required of the sinner. So now you had two reasons to keep up your membership.

The church found confession to be such a good drawing card that soon it declared it to be a sin *not to go to confession*. Everybody had to do it at least once a year. If they didn't, God would have *another* reason to be angry.

More and more rules—many of them arbitrary and capricious—began to be promulgated by the church, each rule having the power of God's eternal condemnation behind it, unless, of course, failure was *confessed*. Then the person was forgiven by God, and condemnation avoided.

But now there was another problem. People figured out that this must mean they could do anything, as long as they confessed it. The church was in a quandary. Fear had left the hearts of the people. Church attendance and membership dropped. People came to "confess" once a year, said their penances, were absolved of their sins, and went on with their lives.

There was no question about it. A way had to be found to strike fear into the heart again.

So purgatory was invented.

Purgatory?

Purgatory. This was described as a place something like hell, but not eternal. This new doctrine declared that God would make you suffer for your sins *even if you confessed them*.

Under the doctrine, a certain amount of suffering was decreed by God for each nonperfect soul, based on the number and type of sins committed. There were "mortal" sins and "venial" sins. Mortal sins would send you right to hell if not confessed before death.

Once more, church attendance shot up. Collections were up, too, and especially contributions—for the doctrine of purgatory also included a way one could *buy one's way out of the suffering*.

I'm sorry—?

According to the church's teaching, one could receive a special indulgence—but again, not directly from God—only from an official of the church. These special indulgences freed one from the suffering in purgatory which they had "earned" with their sins—or at least part of it.

Something like "time off for good behavior?"

Yes. But, of course, these reprieves were granted to very few. Generally, those who made a conspicuous contribution to the church.

For a really huge sum, one could obtain a *plenary* indulgence. This meant *no time in purgatory at all*. It was a nonstop ticket straight to heaven.

This special favor from God was available for even fewer. Royalty, perhaps. And the super rich. The amount of money, jewels, and land given to the church in exchange for these plenary indulgences was enormous. But the exclusivity of all this brought great frustration and resentment to the masses—no pun intended.

The poorest peasant hadn't a hope of gaining a bishop's indulgence—and so the rank and file lost faith in the system, with attendance threatening to drop once again.

Now what did they do?

They brought in the novena candles.

People could come to the church and light a novena candle for the "poor souls in purgatory," and by saying a novena (a series of prayers in a particular order that took some time to complete), they could knock years off the "sentence" of the dearly departed, extricating them from purgatory sooner than God would otherwise have allowed.

They couldn't do anything for themselves, but at least they could pray for mercy for the departed. Of course, it would be helpful if a coin or two were dropped through the slot for each candle lit.

A lot of little candles were flickering behind a lot of red glass, and a lot of pesos and pennies were being dropped into a lot of tin boxes, in an attempt to get Me to "ease up" on the suffering being inflicted on the souls in purgatory.

Whew! This is *unbelievable*. And You mean people could not see right through all that? People did not see it as the desperate attempt of a desperate church to keep its members desperate to do anything to protect themselves from this *desperado* they called God? You mean people actually bought this stuff?

Quite literally.

No wonder the church declared reincarnation to be an untruth.

Yes. Yet when I created you, I did not create you so that you could live one lifetime—an infinitesimal period, really, given the age of the universe—make the mistakes you were inevitably going to make, then hope for the best at the end. I've tried to imagine setting it up that way, but I can never figure out what My purpose would be.

You could never figure it out either. That's why you've had to keep saying things like, "The Lord works in mysterious ways, His wonders to perform." But I don't work in mysterious ways. Everything I do has a reason, and it's perfectly clear. I've explained why I created you, and the purpose of your life, many times now during this trilogy.

Reincarnation fits perfectly into that purpose, which is for Me to create and experience Who I Am through you, lifetime after lifetime, and through the millions of other creatures of consciousness I have placed in the universe.

Then there IS life on other—

Of course there is. Do you really believe that you are alone in this gigantic universe? But that's another topic we can get to later. . . .

. . . Promise?

Promise.

So, your purpose as a soul is to experience yourself as All Of It. We are evolving. We are . . . becoming.

Becoming what? We do not know! We cannot know until We get there! But for Us, the journey is the joy. And as soon as We "get there," as soon as We create the next highest idea of Who We Are, We'll create a grander thought, a higher idea, and continue the joy forever.

Are you with Me here?

Yes. By this time I almost *could* repeat this verbatim.

Good.

So . . . the point and purpose of your life is to decide and to be Who You Really Are. You're doing that every day. With every action, with every thought, with every word. That's what you're doing.

Now, to the degree that you're pleased with that—pleased with Who You Are in your experience—to that degree you'll stick, more or less, with the creation, making only minor adjustments here and there to get it closer and closer to perfect.

Paramahansa Yogananda is an example of a person who was very close to "perfect" as an out-picturing of what he thought of himself. He had a very clear idea about himself, and about his relationship to Me, and he used his life to "out-picture" that. He wanted to experience his idea about himself in his own reality; to know himself as that, experientially.

Babe Ruth did the same thing. He had a very clear idea about himself, and his relationship to Me, and he used his life to out-picture that; to know himself in his own experience.

Not many people live that level. Now granted, the Master and the Babe had two entirely different ideas about themselves, yet they both played them out magnificently.

They also both had different ideas about Me, that's for sure, and were coming from different levels of consciousness about Who I Am, and about their true relationship to Me. And those levels of consciousness were reflected in their thoughts, words, and actions.

One was in a place of peace and serenity most of his life, and brought deep peace and serenity to others. The other was in a place of anxiousness, turmoil, and occasional anger (particularly when he couldn't get his way), and brought turmoil to the lives of those around him.

Both were good-hearted, however—there was never a softer touch than the Babe—and the difference between the two is that one had virtually nothing in terms of physical acquisitions, but never wanted more than what he got, while the other "had everything," and never got what he really wanted.

If that were the end of it for George Herman, I suppose we could all feel a little sad about that, but the soul that embodied itself as Babe Ruth is far from finished with this process called evolution. It has had an opportunity to review the experiences it produced for itself, as well as the experiences it produced for others, and now gets to decide what next it would like to experience as it seeks to create and re-create itself in grander and grander versions.

We'll drop our narrative regarding these two souls here, because both have already made their next choice regarding what they want to now experience—and, in fact, both are now experiencing that.

You mean both have already reincarnated into other bodies?

It would be a mistake to assume that reincarnating—returning to another physical body—was the only option open to them.

What *are* the other options?

In truth, whatever they want them to be.

I've already explained here what occurs after what you call your death.

Some souls feel that there is a lot more they would like to know, and so they find themselves going to a "school," whereas other souls—what you call "old souls"—teach them. And what do they teach them? *That they have nothing to learn.* That they *never* had anything to learn. That all they ever had to do was remember. Remember Who and What They Really Are.

They are "taught" that the experience of Who They Are is gained in the acting out of it; in *being it*. They are reminded of this by having it gently shown to them.

Other souls have already remembered this by the time they get to—or soon after they get to—the "other side." (I'm using language now with which you are familiar, speaking in your vernacular, to keep, as much as possible, the words out of the way.) These souls may then seek the immediate joy of experiencing themselves as whatever they wish to "be." They may select from the million, kajillion aspects of Me, and choose to experience that, right then and there. Some may opt to return to physical form to do that.

Any physical form?

Any.

Then it's *true* that souls could return as animals—that God could be a cow? And that cows really are sacred? Holy cow!

(Ahem.)

Sorry.

You've had a whole lifetime to do stand-up comedy. And, by the way, looking at your life, you've done a pretty good job of it.

Cha-*boom*. That was a rim shot. If I had a cymbal here, I'd give you a cymbal crash.

Thank you, thank you.

But seriously, folks...

The answer to the question you are basically asking—can a soul return as an animal—is yes, of course. The real question is, would it? The answer is, probably not.

Do animals have souls?

Anyone who has ever stared into the eyes of an animal already knows the answer to that.

Then how do I know it is *not* my grandmother, come back as my cat?

The Process we are discussing here is evolution. Self-creation and evolution. And evolution proceeds one way. Upward. Ever upward.

The soul's greatest desire is to experience higher and higher aspects of itself. And so it seeks to move upward, not downward, on the evolutionary scale, until it experiences what has been called nirvana—total Oneness with the All. That is, with Me.

But if the soul desires higher and higher experiences of itself, why would it even bother returning as a human being? Surely that can't be a step "upward."

If the soul returns to human form, it is always in an effort to further experience, and thus, further evolve. There are many levels of evolution observable and demonstrated in humans. One could come back for many lifetimes—many hundreds of lifetimes—and continue to evolve upward. Yet upward movement, the grandest desire of the soul, is not achieved with return to a lower life form. Thus, such a return does not occur. Not until the soul reaches ultimate reunion with All That Is.

That must mean there are "new souls" coming into the system every day, taking lower life forms.

No. Every soul that was ever created was created At Once. We are all here Now. But, as I have explained before, when a soul (a part of Me) reaches ultimate realization, it has the option to "start over," to literally "forget everything," so that it can remember all over again, and re-create itself anew once more. In this way, God continues to re-experience Itself.

Souls may also choose to "recycle" through a particular life form at a particular level as often as they like.

Without reincarnation—without the ability to return to a physical form—the soul would have to accomplish everything it seeks to accomplish within one lifetime, which is one billion times shorter than the blink of an eye on the cosmic clock.

So, yes, of course, reincarnation is a fact. It's real, it's purposeful, and it's perfect.

Okay, but there's one thing I'm confused about. You said there is nothing such as time; that all things are happening right now. Is that correct?

It is.

And then You implied—and in *Book 2* You went into depth on this—that we exist "all the time" on different levels, or at various points, in the Space-Time Continuum.

That's true.

Okay, but now here's where it gets crazy. If one of the "me's" on the Space-Time Continuum "dies," then *comes back* here as *another person* . . . then . . . then, who am I? I would have to be existing as *two people at once*. And if I kept on doing this through all eternity, which You say I do, then I am being a *hundred* people at once! A thousand. A *million*. A million versions of a million people at a million points on the Space-Time Continuum.

Yes.

I don't understand that. My mind can't grasp that.

Actually, you've done well. It's a very advanced concept, and you've done pretty well with it.

But . . . but . . . if that's true, then "I"—the part of "me" that is immortal—must be evolving in a billion different ways in a billion different forms at a billion different points on the Cosmic Wheel in the eternal moment of now.

Right again. That's exactly what I'm doing.

No, no. I said that's what *I* must be doing.

Right again. That's what I just said.

No, no, I said—

I know what you said. You said just what I said you said. The confusion here is that you still think there's more than one of Us here.

There's not?

There was never more than one of Us here. Ever. Are you just finding that out?

You mean I've just been talking to *myself* here?

Something like that.

You mean You're *not God?*

That's not what I said.

You mean You *are* God?

That's what I said.

But if You're God, and You're me, and I'm You—then . . . then . . . *I'm* God!

Thou art God, yes. That is correct. You grok it in fullness.

But I'm not only God—I'm also everyone *else*.

Yes.

But—does that mean that no one, and nothing else, exists but me?

Have I not said, I and My Father are One?

Yes, but . . .

And have I not said, We are all One?

Yes. But I didn't know You meant that *literally*. I thought You meant that figuratively. I thought it was more of a philosophical statement, not a statement of *fact*.

> It's a statement of fact. We are all One. That is what is meant by "whatsoever ye do unto the least of these . . . ye do unto me."
> Do you understand now?

Yes.

> Ah, at last. At long last.

But—You'll forgive me for arguing this, but . . . when I'm with another—my spouse for instance, or my children—it feels that I am *separate* from them; that they are *other* than "me."

> Consciousness is a marvelous thing. It can be divided into a thousand pieces. A million. A million times a million.
> I have divided Myself into an infinite number of "pieces"—so that each "piece" of Me could look back on Itself and behold the wonder of Who and What I Am.

But why do I have to go through this period of forgetfulness; of disbelief? I'm *still* not totally believing! I'm *still* hanging out in forgetfulness.

> Don't be so hard on your Self. That's part of The Process. It's okay that it's happening this way.

Then why are You telling me all this now?

> Because you were starting not to have fun. Life was beginning not to be a joy anymore. You were starting to get so caught up in The Process that you forgot it *was* just a process.
> And so, you called out to Me. You asked Me to come to you; to help you understand; to show you the divine truth; to reveal to you the greatest secret. The secret you've kept from yourself. The secret of Who You Are.

Now I have done so. Now, once again, you have been caused to remember. Will it matter? Will it change how you act tomorrow? Will it cause you to see things differently tonight?

Will you now heal the hurts of the wounded, quell the anxieties of the fearful, meet the needs of the impoverished, celebrate the magnificence of the accomplished, and see the vision of Me everywhere?

Will this latest remembrance of truth change your life, and allow you to change the lives of others?

Or will you return to forgetfulness; fall back into selfishness; revisit, and reside again in, the smallness of who you imagined yourself to be before this awakening?

Which will it be?

8

Life really does go on forever and ever, doesn't it?

It most certainly does.

There is no end to it.

No end.

Reincarnation *is* a fact.

It is. You may return to mortal form—that is, a physical form which can "die"—whenever and however you wish.

Do we decide when we want to come back?

"If" and "when"—yes.

Do we also decide when we want to leave? Do we choose when we want to die?

No experience is visited upon any soul against the soul's will. That is, by definition, not possible, since the soul is creating every experience.

The soul wants nothing. The soul has everything. All wisdom, all knowing, all power, all glory. The soul is the part of You which never sleeps; never forgets.

Does the soul desire that the body dies? No. It is the soul's desire that you never die. Yet the soul will leave the body—change its bodily form, leaving most of the material body behind—at the drop of a hat when it sees no purpose in remaining in that form.

If it is the soul's desire that we never die, why *do* we?

You do not. You merely change form.

If it is the soul's desire that we never do *that*, why *do* we?

That is not the soul's desire!

You are a "shape-shifter"!

When there is no further usefulness in staying in a particular form, the soul changes form—willfully, voluntarily, joyfully—and moves on, on the Cosmic Wheel.

Joyfully?

With great joy.

No soul dies regretfully?

No soul dies—ever.

I mean, no soul has regrets that the current physical form is changing; is about to "die"?

The body never "dies," but merely changes form with the soul. Yet I understand your meaning, so for now I use the vocabulary you have established.

If you have a clear understanding of what you wish to create with regard to what you have chosen to call the afterlife, or if you have a clear set of beliefs that support an after-death experience of reuniting with God, then, no, the soul never, ever has regrets over what you call death.

Death in that instance is a glorious moment; a wonderful experience. Now the soul can return to its natural form; its normal state. There is an incredible lightness; a sense of total freedom; a limitlessness. And an awareness of Oneness that is at once blissful and sublime.

It is not possible for the soul to regret such a shift.

You're saying, then, that death is a *happy* experience?

For the soul that wishes it to be, yes, always.

Well, if the soul wants out of the body so bad, why doesn't it just leave it? Why is it hanging around?

I did not say the soul "wants out of the body," I said the soul is joyful when it is out. Those are two different things.

You can be happy doing one thing, and happy then doing another. The fact that you are joyful doing the second does not mean you were unhappy doing the first.

The soul is not unhappy being with the body. Quite to the contrary, the soul is pleased to be you in your present form. That does not preclude the possibility that the soul might be equally pleased to be disconnected from it.

There is obviously much about death I do not understand.

Yes, and that is because you do not like to think about it. Yet you must contemplate death and loss the instant you perceive any moment of life, or you will not have perceived life at all, but know only the half of it.

Each moment ends the instant it begins. If you do not see this, you will not see what is exquisite in it, and you will call the moment ordinary.

Each interaction "begins to end" the instant it "begins to begin." Only when this is truly contemplated and deeply understood does the full treasure of every moment—and of life itself— open to you.

Life cannot give itself to you if you do not understand death. You must do more than understand it. *You must love it, even as you love life.*

Your time with each person would be glorified if you thought it was your *last* time with that person. Your experience of each moment would be enhanced beyond measure if you thought it was the last such moment. Your refusal to contemplate your own death leads to your refusal to contemplate your own life.

You do not see it for what it is. You miss the *moment*, and all it holds for you. You look right past it instead of right through it.

When you look deeply at something, you see right through it. To contemplate a thing deeply is to see right through it. Then the illusion ceases to exist. Then you see a thing for what it really is. Only then can you truly enjoy it—that is, *place joy into it*. (To "enjoy" is to render something joyful.)

Even the illusion you can then enjoy. For you will *know* it is an illusion, and that is half the enjoyment! It is the fact that you think it is real that causes you all the pain.

Nothing is painful which you understand is not real. Let Me repeat that.

Nothing is painful which you understand is not real.

It is like a movie, a drama, played out on the stage of your mind. You are creating the situation and the characters. You are writing the lines.

Nothing is painful the moment you understand that nothing is real.

This is as true of death as it is of life.

When you understand that death, too, is an illusion, then you *can* say, "O death, where is thy sting?"

You can even *enjoy* death! You can even enjoy someone *else's* death.

Does that seem strange? Does that seem a strange thing to say?

Only if you do not understand death—and life.

Death is never an end, but always a beginning. A death is a door opening, not a door closing.

When you understand that life is eternal, you understand that death is your illusion, keeping you very concerned with, and therefore helping you believe that you *are*, your body. Yet you are *not* your body, and so the destruction of your body is of no concern to you.

Death should teach you that what is real is life. And life teaches you that what is unavoidable is not death, but impermanence.

Impermanence is the only truth.

Nothing is permanent. All is changing. In every instant. In every moment.

Were anything permanent, it could not *be*. For even the very concept of permanence depends upon impermanence to have any meaning. Therefore, *even permanence is impermanent*. Look at this deeply. Contemplate this truth. Comprehend it, and you comprehend God.

This is the Dharma, and this is the Buddha. This is the Buddha Dharma. This is the teaching and the teacher. This is the lesson and the master. This is the object and the observer, rolled into one.

They never have been *other* than One. It is you who have unrolled them, so that your life may unroll before you.

Yet as you watch your own life roll out before you, do not yourself become unraveled. Keep your Self together! See the illusion! Enjoy it! But do not *become* it!

You are *not* the illusion, but the *creator of it*.

You are in this world, but not of it.

So use your illusion of death. *Use* it! Allow it to be the key that opens you to more of life.

See the flower as dying and you will see the flower sadly. Yet see the flower as part of a whole tree that is changing, and will soon bear fruit, and you see the flower's true beauty. When you understand that the blossoming and the falling away of the flower is a sign that the tree is ready to bear fruit, then you understand life.

Look at this carefully and you will see that life is its own metaphor.

Always remember, you are not the flower, nor are you even the fruit. You are the tree. And your roots are deep, embedded in Me. I am the soil from which you have sprung, and both your blossoms and your fruit will return to Me, creating more rich soil. Thus, life begets life, and cannot know death, ever.

That is so beautiful. That is so, so beautiful. Thank You. Will You speak to me now of something that is troubling me ? I need to talk about suicide. Why is there such a taboo against the ending of one's life?

Indeed, why is there?

You mean it's not wrong to kill yourself?

The question cannot be answered to your satisfaction, because the question itself contains two false concepts; it is based on two false assumptions; it contains two errors.

The first false assumption is that there is such a thing as "right" and "wrong." The second false assumption is that killing is possible. Your question itself, therefore, disintegrates the moment it is dissected.

"Right" and "wrong" are philosophical polarities in a human value system which have nothing to do with ultimate reality—a point which I have made repeatedly throughout this dialogue. They are, furthermore, not even constant constructs within your own system, but rather, values which keep shifting from time to time.

You are doing the shifting, changing your mind about these values as it suits you (which rightly you should, as evolving beings), yet insisting at each step along the way that you haven't done this, and that it is your *unchanging* values which form the core of your society's integrity. You have thus built your society on a paradox. You keep changing your values, all the while proclaiming that it is unchanging values which you . . . well, *value!*

The answer to the problems presented by this paradox is not to throw cold water on the sand in an attempt to make it concrete, but to celebrate the shifting of the sand. Celebrate its beauty while it holds itself in the shape of your castle, but then also celebrate the new form and shape it takes as the tide comes in.

Celebrate the shifting sands as they form the new mountains you would climb, and atop which—and with which—you will build your new castles. Yet understand that these mountains and these castles are monuments to *change*, not to permanence.

Glorify what you are today, yet do not condemn what you were yesterday, nor preclude what you could become tomorrow.

Understand that "right" and "wrong" are figments of your imagination, and that "okay" and "not okay" are merely announcements of your latest preferences and imaginings.

For example, on the question of ending one's life, it is the current imagining of the majority of people on your planet that it is "not okay" to do that.

Similarly, many of you still insist that it is not okay to assist another who wishes to end his or her life.

In both cases you say this should be "against the law." You have come to this conclusion, presumably, because the ending of the life occurs relatively quickly. Actions which end a life over a somewhat longer period of time are not against the law, even though they achieve the same result.

Thus, if a person in your society kills himself with a gun, his family members lose insurance benefits. If he does so with cigarettes, they do not.

If a doctor assists you in your suicide, it is called manslaughter, while if a tobacco company does, it is called commerce.

With you, it seems to be merely a question of time. The legality of self-destruction—the "rightness" or "wrongness" of it—seems to have much to do with *how quickly* the deed is done, as well as who is doing it. The faster the death, the more "wrong" it seems to be. The slower the death, the more it slips into "okayness."

Interestingly, this is the exact opposite of what a truly humane society would conclude. By any reasonable definition of what you would call "humane," the shorter the death, the better. Yet your society punishes those who would seek to do the humane thing, and rewards those who would do the insane.

It is insane to think that endless suffering is what God requires, and that a quick, humane end to the suffering is "wrong."

"Punish the humane, reward the insane."

This is a motto which only a society of beings with limited understanding could embrace.

So you poison your system by inhaling carcinogens, you poison your system by eating food treated with chemicals that over the long run kill you, and you poison your system by breathing air which you have continually polluted. You poison your system in a hundred different ways over a thousand different moments, and you do this *knowing these substances are no good for you.* But because it takes a longer time for them to kill you, *you commit suicide with impunity.*

If you poison yourself with something that works faster, you are said to have done something against moral law.

Now I tell you this: *It is no more immoral to kill yourself quickly than it is to kill yourself slowly.*

So a person who ends his own life is not punished by God?

I do not punish. I love.

What of the often-heard statement that those who think they are going to "escape" their predicament, or end their condition, with suicide only find that they are facing the same predicament or condition in the afterlife, and therefore escaped and ended nothing?

Your experience in what you call the afterlife is a reflection of your consciousness at the time you enter it. Yet you are always a being of free will, and may alter your experience whenever you choose.

So loved ones who have ended their physical life are okay?

Yes. They are very okay.

There is a wonderful book on this subject called *Stephen Lives,* by Anne Puryear. It is about her son, who ended his life when he was a teenager. So many people have found it helpful.

Anne Puryear is a wonderful messenger. As is her son.

So You can recommend this book?

It is an important book. It says more on this subject than we are saying here, and those who have deep hurts or lingering issues surrounding the experience of a loved one ending their life will be opened to healing through this book.

It is sad that we even have such deep hurts or issues, but much of that, I think, is a result of what our society has "laid on us" about suicide.

In your society, you often do not see the contradictions of your own moral constructions. The contradiction between doing things that you know full well are going to shorten your life, but doing them slowly, and doing things that will shorten your life quickly is one of the most glaring in the human experience.

Yet it seems so obvious when You spell them out like this. Why can't we see such obvious truths on our own?

Because if you saw these truths, you would have to *do something about them*. This you do not wish to do. So you have no choice but to look right at something and not see it.

But why would we not want to do something about these truths if we saw them?

Because you believe that in order to do something about them, you would have to end your pleasures. And ending pleasures is something you have no desire to do.

Most of the things which cause your slow deaths are things which bring you pleasure, or result from those things. And most of the things which bring you pleasure are things which satisfy the body. Indeed, this is what marks yours as a primitive society. *Your lives are structured largely around seeking and experiencing pleasures of the body.*

Of course, all beings everywhere seek to experience pleasures. There is nothing primitive in that. In fact, it is the natural order of things. What differentiates societies, and beings within societies, is what they *define as pleasurable*. If a society is structured largely around pleasures of the *body*, it is operating at a different level from a society structured around pleasures of the soul.

And understand, too, that this does not mean that your Puritans were right, and that all pleasures of the body should be denied. It means that in elevated societies, pleasures of the physical body do not make up the largest number of pleasures which are enjoyed. They are not the prime focus.

The more elevated a society or being, the more elevated are its pleasures.

Wait a minute! That sounds like such a value judgment. I thought You—God—didn't make value judgments.

Is it a value judgment to say that Mt. Everest is higher than Mt. McKinley?

Is it a value judgment to say that Aunt Sarah is older than her nephew Tommy?

Are these value judgments or observations?

I have not said it is "better" to be elevated in one's consciousness. In fact, it is not. Any more than it is "better" to be in fourth grade than in first.

I am simply observing what fourth grade is.

And we are not in fourth grade in this planet. We are in first. Is that it?

My child, you are not yet even in kindergarten. You are in nursery school.

How can I not hear that as an insult? Why does it sound to me as if You're putting the human race down?

Because you are deeply ego invested in being something you are not—and in not being what you are.

Most people hear insults when only an observation has been made, if what is being observed is something they don't want to own.

Yet until you hold a thing, you cannot let it go. And you cannot disown that which you have never owned.

You cannot change that which you do not accept.

Precisely.

Enlightenment begins with acceptance, without judgment of "what is."

This is known as moving into the Isness. It is in the Isness where freedom will be found.

What you resist, persists. What you look at disappears. That is, it ceases to have its illusory form. You see it for what it Is. And what Is can always be changed. It is only what Is Not that cannot be changed. Therefore, to change the Isness, move into it. Do not resist it. Do not deny it.

What you deny you declare. What you declare you create.

Denial of something is re-creation of it, for the very act of denying something places it there.

Acceptance of something places you in control of it. That which you deny you cannot control, for you have said it is not there. Therefore what you deny controls you.

The majority of your race does not want to accept that you have not yet evolved to kindergarten. It does not want to accept that the human race is still in nursery school. Yet this lack of acceptance is exactly what keeps it there.

You are so deeply ego invested in being what you are not (highly evolved) that you are not being what you are (evolving). You are thus working against yourself, fighting yourself. And hence, evolving very slowly.

The fast track of evolution begins with admitting and accepting what is, not what is not.

And I will know I have accepted "what is" when I no longer feel insulted as I hear it described.

Exactly. Are you insulted if I say you have blue eyes?

So now I tell you this: The more elevated a society or being, the more elevated are its pleasures.

What you call "pleasure" is what declares your level of evolution.

Help me with this term "elevated." What do You mean by that?

Your being is the universe in microcosm. You, and your whole physical body, are composed of raw energy, clustered around seven centers, or chakras. Study the chakra centers and what they mean. There are hundreds of books written about this. This is wisdom I have given the human race before.

What is pleasurable, or stimulates, your lower chakras is not the same as what is pleasurable to your higher chakras.

The higher you raise the energy of life through your physical being, the more elevated will be your consciousness.

Well, here we go again. That seems to argue for celibacy. That seems to be the whole argument against expression of sexual passion. People

who are "elevated" in their consciousness don't "come from" their root chakra—their first, or lowest, chakra—in their interactions with other humans.

    That is true.

But I thought You've said throughout this dialogue that human sexuality was to be *celebrated,* not repressed.

    That is correct.

Well, help me out here, because we seem to have a contradiction.

    The world is full of contradictions, My son. Lack of contradictions is not a necessary ingredient in truth. Sometimes greater truth lies *within* the contradiction.
    What we have here is Divine Dichotomy.

Then help me understand the dichotomy. Because all my life I've heard about how desirable it was, how "elevated" it was, to "raise the kundalini energy" out of the root chakra. This has been the chief justification for mystics living lives of sexless ecstasy.

I realize we've gotten way off the subject of death here; and I apologize for dragging us into this unrelated territory—

    What are you apologizing for? A conversation goes where a conversation goes. The "topic" we are on in this whole dialogue is what it means to be fully human, and what life is about in this universe. That is the only topic, and this falls within that.
    Wanting to know about death is wanting to know about life—a point I made earlier. And if our exchanges lead to an expansion of our inquiry to include the very act which creates life, and celebrates it magnificently, so be it.
    Now let's get clear again about one thing. It is not a requirement of the "highly evolved" that all sexual expression be muted, and all sexual energy be elevated. If that were true, then there would be no "highly evolved" beings anywhere, because all evolution would have stopped.

A rather obvious point.

Yes. And so anyone who says that the very holiest people never have sex, and that this is a sign of their holiness, does not understand how life was meant to work.

Let Me put this in very clear terms. If you want a yardstick with which to judge whether a thing is good for the human race or not, ask yourself a simple question:

What would happen if everyone did it?

This is a very easy measure, and a very accurate one. If everyone did a thing, and the result was of ultimate benefit to the human race, then that is "evolved." If everyone did it and it brought disaster to the human race, then that is not a very "elevated" thing to recommend. Do you agree?

Of course.

Then you've just agreed that no real master will ever say that sexual celibacy is the path to mastery. Yet it is this idea that sexual abstinence is somehow the "higher way," and that sexual expression is a "lower desire," that has shamed the sexual experience, and caused all manner of guilt and dysfunction to develop around it.

Yet if the reasoning against sexual abstinence is that it would prohibit procreation, couldn't it be argued that once sex has served this function, there is no more need for it?

One does not engage in sex because one realizes one's responsibility to the human race to procreate. One engages in sex because it is *the natural thing to do.* It is built into the genes. You obey a biological imperative.

Precisely! It is a *genetic signal* that drives to the question of species survival. But once the survival of the species is assured, isn't it the "elevated" thing to do to "ignore the signal"?

You misinterpret the signal. The biological imperative is not to guarantee the survival of the species, but to *experience the Oneness* which is the true nature of your being. Creating new life is what happens when Oneness is achieved, but it is not the reason Oneness is sought.

If procreation were the only reason for sexual expression—if it were nothing more than a "delivery system"—you would no longer need to engage in it with one another. You can unite the chemical elements of life in a petri dish.

Yet this would not satisfy the most basic urges of the soul, which it turns out, are much larger than mere procreation, but have to do with re-creation of Who and What You Really Are.

The biological imperative is not to *create* more life, but to *experience* more life—and to experience that life as it really is: *a manifestation of Oneness.*

That is why You will never stop people from having sex, even though they have long ago stopped having children.

Of course.

Yet some say that sex *should* stop when people stop having children, and that those couples who continue with this activity are just caving in to base physical urges.

Yes.

And that this is not "elevated," but merely animalistic behavior, beneath the more noble nature of man.

This gets us back to the subject of chakras, or energy centers.

I said earlier that "the higher you raise the energy of life through your physical being, the more elevated will be your consciousness."

Yes! And that seems to say "no sex."

No, it does not. Not when you understand it.

Let Me go back to your previous comment and make something clear: There is nothing ignoble, or unholy, about having sex. You have got to get that idea out of your mind, and out of your culture.

There is nothing base, or gross, or "less than dignified" (much less *sanctified*), about a passionate, desire-filled sexual experience. Physical urges are not manifestations of "animalistic behavior." Those physical urges were *built into the system*—by Me.

Who do you suppose created it that way?

Yet physical urges are but *one ingredient* in a complex mixture of responses that you all have to each other. Remember, you are a three-part being, with seven chakra centers. When you respond to one another from all three parts, and all seven centers, at the same time, then you have the peak experience you are looking for—that you have been created for!

And there is nothing unholy about any of these energies—yet if you choose just one of them, that is "un-whole-y." *It is not being whole!*

When you are not being whole, you are being less than yourself. *That* is what is meant by "unholy."

Wow! I get it. I *get* it!

The admonition against sex for those who choose to be "elevated" was never an admonition from Me. It was an invitation. An invitation is not an admonition, yet you have made it so.

And the invitation was not to stop having sex, but to stop being *un-whole*.

Whatever you are doing—having sex or having breakfast, going to work or walking the beach, jumping rope or reading a good book—*whatever* you are doing, do it as a whole being; as the whole being *you are.*

If you are having sex from only your lower chakra center, you are operating from the root chakra alone, and missing by far the most glorious part of the experience. Yet if you are being loving with another person and coming from all *seven* energy centers while you are being that, now you are having a peak experience. How can this not be holy?

It can't. I'm unable to imagine such an experience not being holy.

And so the invitation to raise the life energy through your physical being to the top chakra was never meant to be a suggestion or a demand that you *disconnect from the bottom.*

If you have raised the energy to your heart chakra, or even to your crown chakra, that doesn't mean it cannot be in your root chakra as well.

Indeed, if it is not, you are disconnected.

When you have raised the life energy to your higher centers, you may or may not choose to have what you would call a sexual experience with another. But if you do not, it will not be because to do so would be to violate some cosmic law on holiness. Nor will it make you somehow more "elevated." And if you do choose to be sexual with another, it will not "lower" you to a root-chakra-only level—unless you do the opposite of disconnecting at the bottom, and *disconnect from the top.*

So here is the invitation—not an admonition, but an invitation:

Raise your energy, your life force, to the highest level possible in every moment, and you will be elevated. This has nothing to do with having sex or not having sex. It has to do with raising your consciousness no matter *what* you are doing.

I get it! I understand. Although I don't know *how* to raise my consciousness. I don't think I know *how* to raise the life energy through my chakra centers. And I'm not sure most people even know what these centers are.

Anyone who earnestly wishes to know more about the "physiology of spirituality" can find out easily enough. I have sourced this information before, in very clear terms.

You mean in other books, through other writers.

Yes. Read the writings of Deepak Chopra. He is one of the clearest enunciators right now on your planet. He understands the mystery of spirituality, and the *science* of it.

And there are other wonderful messengers as well. Their books describe not only how to raise your life force up through your body, but also how to *leave* your physical body.

You can remember through these additional readings how joyous it is letting the body go. Then you will understand how it could be that you might never again fear death. You will understand the dichotomy: how it is a joy to be with the body, and a joy to be free of it.

9

Life must be kind of like school. I can remember being excited every fall about the first day of school—and, at the end of the year, thrilled to be getting out.

Precisely! Exactly! You've hit it. That's it exactly. Only life is not a school.

Yes, I remember. You explained all that in *Book 1*. Until then, I thought that life *was* a "school," and that we had come here to "learn our lessons." You helped me tremendously in *Book 1* to see that this was a false doctrine.

I'm glad. That's what we're trying to do here with this trilogy— bring you to clarity. And now you're clear about why and how the soul can be overjoyed after "death" without necessarily *ever* regretting "life."

But you asked a larger question before, and we should revisit it.

I'm sorry?

You said, "If the soul is so unhappy in the body, why doesn't it just leave?"

Oh, yes.

Well, it *does*. And I don't mean only at "death," as I've just explained. But it does not leave because it is unhappy. Rather, it leaves because it wishes to regenerate, rejuvenate.

Does it do this often?

Every day.

The soul leaves the body *every day?* When?

When the soul yearns for its larger experience. It finds this experience rejuvenating.

It just *leaves?*

Yes. The soul leaves your body all the time. Continually. Throughout your life. This is why We invented sleep.

The soul leaves the body during sleep?

Of course. That is *what sleep is.*

Periodically throughout your life the soul seeks rejuvenation, refueling, if you will, so that it can continue lumbering along in this carrier you call your body.

You think it is easy for your soul to inhabit your body? It is not! It may be *simple*, but it is not *easy!* It is a joy, but it is not *easy*. It is the most difficult thing your soul has ever done!

The soul, which knows a lightness and a freedom which you can't imagine, yearns for that state of being again, just as a child who loves school can yearn for summer vacation. Just as an adult who yearns for company can also, while having company, yearn to be alone. The soul seeks a true state of being. The soul is lightness and freedom. It is also peace and joy. It is also limitlessness and painlessness; perfect wisdom and perfect love.

It is all these things, and more. Yet it experiences precious few of these things while it is with the body. And so it made an arrangement with itself. It told itself it would stay with the body as long as it needs to in order to create and experience itself as it now chooses—but only if it could *leave* the body whenever it wished!

It does this daily, through the experience you call sleep.

"Sleep" is the experience of the soul leaving the body?

Yes.

I thought we fell asleep because the body needed rest.

You are mistaken. It is the other way around. The *soul* seeks the rest, and so, *causes* the body to "fall asleep."

The soul literally drops the body (sometimes right where it is standing) when it is tired of the limits, tired of the heaviness and lack of freedom of being with the body.

It will just leave the body when it seeks "refueling"; when it becomes weary of all the nontruth and false reality and imagined dangers, and when it seeks, once again, reconnection, reassurance, restfulness, and reawakening for the mind.

When the soul first embraces a body, it finds the experience extremely difficult. It is very tiring, particularly for a newly arriving soul. That is why babies sleep a lot.

When the soul gets over the initial shock of being attached to a body once more, it begins to increase its tolerance for that. It stays with it more.

At the same time, the part of you called your mind moves into forgetfulness—just as it was designed to do. Even the soul's flights out of the body, taken now on a less-frequent, but still usually daily, basis do not always bring the mind back to remembrance.

Indeed, during these times the soul may be free, but the mind may be confused. Thus, the whole being may ask: "Where am I? What am I creating here?" These searchings may lead to fitful journeys; even frightening ones. You call these trips "nightmares."

Sometimes just the opposite will occur. The soul will arrive at a place of great remembering. Now the mind will have an awakening. This will fill it with peace and joy—which you will experience in your body when you return to it.

The more your whole being experiences the reassurance of these rejuvenations—and the more it remembers what it is doing, and trying to do, with the body—the less your soul will choose to stay away from the body, for now it knows that *it came to the body for a reason, and with a purpose*. Its desire is to get on with that, and to make best use of all the time with the body that it has.

The person of great wisdom needs little sleep.

Are You saying you can tell how evolved a person is by how much sleep that person needs?

Almost, yes. You could almost say that. Sometimes a soul chooses to leave the body just for the sheer joy of it, though. It may not be seeking reawakening for the mind or rejuvenation for the body. It may simply be choosing to re-create the sheer ecstasy of knowing the Oneness. So it would not always be valid to say that the more sleep a person gets, the less evolved that person is.

Still, it is not a coincidence that as beings become more and more aware of what they are doing with their bodies—and that they are *not* their bodies, but that which is *with* their bodies—they become willing and able to spend more and more time with their bodies, and thus *appear to "need less sleep."*

Now some beings even choose to experience both the forgetfulness of being with the body, and the oneness of the soul, at once. These beings can train a *part* of themselves to not identify with the body while they are still with the body, thus experiencing the ecstasy of knowing Who They Really Are, without having to lose human wakefulness in order to do it.

How do they do this? How can I do this?

It is a question of awareness, of reaching a state of total awareness, as I said before. You cannot *do* totally aware, you can only *be* totally aware.

How? *How?* There must be *some* tools You can give me.

Daily meditation is one of the best tools with which to create this experience. With it, you can raise your life energy to the highest chakra . . . and even *leave your body while you are "awake."*

In meditation you place yourself in a state of readiness to experience total awareness while your body is in a wakened state. This state of readiness is called *true wakefulness.* You do not have to be sitting in meditation to experience this. Meditation is simply a device, a "tool," as you put it. But you do not *have* to do sitting meditation in order to experience this.

You should also know that sitting meditation is not the only kind of meditation there is. There is also stopping meditation. Walking meditation. Doing meditation. Sexual meditation.

This is the state of *true wakefulness.*

When you stop in this state, simply stop in your tracks, stop going where you are going, stop doing what you are doing, just *stop* for a moment, and just "be" right where you are, you become *right*, exactly where you *are*. Stopping, even just for a moment, can be blessed. You look around, slowly, and you notice things you did not notice while you were passing them by. The deep smell of the earth just after it rains. That curl of hair over the left ear of your beloved. How truly good it feels to see a child at play.

You don't have to leave your body to experience this. This is the state of true wakefulness.

When you walk in this state, you breathe in every flower, you fly with every bird, you feel every crunch beneath your feet. You find beauty and wisdom. For wisdom is found wherever beauty is formed. And beauty is formed everywhere, out of all the stuff of life. You do not have to seek it. It will come to you.

And you don't have to leave your body to experience this. This is the state of true wakefulness.

When you "do" in this state, you turn whatever you are doing into a meditation, and thus, into a gift, an offering, from you to your soul, and from your soul to The All. Washing dishes, you enjoy the warmth of the water caressing your hands, and marvel at the wonder of both water, and warmth. Working at your computer, you see the words appear on the screen in front of you in response to the command of your fingers, and exhilarate over the power of the mind and body, when it is harnessed to do your bidding. Preparing dinner, you feel the love of the universe which brought you this nourishment, and as your return gift, pour into the making of this meal all the love of your being. It does not matter how extravagant or how simple the meal is. Soup can be loved into deliciousness.

You don't have to leave your body to experience this. This is the state of true wakefulness.

When you experience sexual energy exchange in this state, you know the highest truth of Who You Are. The heart of your lover becomes your home. The body of your lover becomes your own. Your soul no longer imagines itself separate from anything.

You don't have to leave your body to experience this. This is the state of true wakefulness.

When you are in readiness, you are in wakefulness. A smile can take you there. A simple smile. Just stop everything for one moment, and smile. At nothing. Just because it feels good. Just because your heart knows a secret. And because your soul knows what the secret is. Smile at that. Smile a lot. It will cure whatever ails you.

You are asking me for tools, and I am giving them to you.

Breathe. That is another tool. Breathe long and deep. Breathe slowly and gently. Breathe in the soft, sweet nothingness of life, so full of energy, so full of love. It is God's love you are breathing. Breathe deeply, and you can feel it. Breathe very, very deeply, and the love will make you cry.

For joy.

For you have met your God, and your God has introduced you to your soul.

Once this experience has taken place, life is never the same. People talk of having "been to the mountain top," or having slipped into sublime ecstasy. Their beingness is changed forever.

Thank You. I understand. It is the simple things. The simple acts, and the purest.

Yes. But know this. Some people meditate for years and never experience this. It has to do with how open one is, how willing. And also, how able to move away from any expectation.

Should I meditate every day?

As in all things, there are no "shoulds" or "shouldn'ts" here. It is not a question of what you should do, but what you choose to do.

Some souls seek to walk in awareness. Some recognize that in this life most people are sleepwalking; unconscious. They are going through life without consciousness. Yet souls who walk in awareness choose a different path. They choose another way.

They seek to experience all the peace and joy, limitlessness and freedom, wisdom and love that Oneness brings, not just when they have dropped the body and it has "fallen" (asleep), but when they have risen the body up.

It is said of a soul which creates such an experience, "He is risen."

Others, in the so-called "New Age," term this a process of "consciousness raising."

It doesn't matter what terms you use (words are the least reliable form of communication), it all comes down to living in awareness. And then, it becomes total awareness.

And what is it of which you eventually become totally aware? You eventually become totally aware of Who You Are.

Daily meditation is one way you may achieve this. Yet it requires commitment, dedication—a decision to seek inner experience, not outer reward.

And remember, the silences hold the secrets. And so the sweetest sound is the sound of silence. This is the song of the soul.

If you believe the noises of the world rather than the silences of your soul, you will be lost.

So daily meditation *is* a good idea.

A good idea? Yes. Yet know again what I have just said here. The song of the soul may be sung many ways. The sweet sound of silence may be heard many times.

Some hear the silence in prayer. Some sing the song in their work. Some seek the secrets in quiet contemplation, others in less contemplative surroundings.

When mastery is reached—or even intermittently experienced—the noises of the world can be muffled, the distractions quieted, even in the midst of them. All of life becomes a meditation.

All of life *is* a meditation, in which you are contemplating the Divine. This is called true wakefulness, or mindfulness.

Experienced in this way, everything in life is blessed. There is struggle and pain and worry no more. There is only experience, which you may choose to label in any way you wish. You may choose to label all of it perfection.

So use your *life* as a meditation, and all the events in it. Walk in wakefulness, not as one asleep. Move with mindfulness, not mindlessly, and do not tarry in doubt and fear, neither in guilt nor self-recrimination, yet reside in permanent splendor in the assurance that you are grandly loved. You are always One with Me. You are forever welcome. Welcome home.

For your home is in My heart, and Mine in yours. I invite you to see this in life as you will surely see it in death. Then you will know that there is no death, and that what you have called life and death are both part of the same unending experience.

We are all that is, all that ever was, and all that ever will be, world without end.

Amen.

10

I love You, do You know that?

> Yes. And I love you. Do *you* know *that?*

I'm starting to. I'm really starting to.

> Good.

11

Will You tell me some things about the soul, please?

Sure. I will try to explain, within your limited realm of understanding. But do not allow yourself to become frustrated if certain things don't "make sense" to you. Try to remember that you're bringing this information through a unique filter—a filter which has been designed by you to shield you from too much remembering.

Remind me again why I did that.

The game would be over if you remembered everything. You came here for a particular reason, and your Divine Purpose would be thwarted if you understood how everything is put together. Some things will always remain a mystery at this level of consciousness, and it is right that they should.

So do not try to solve all the mysteries. Not at one time, anyway. Give the universe a chance. It will unfold itself in due course.

Enjoy the experience of becoming.

Make haste slowly.

Exactly.

My father used to say that.

Your father was a wise and wonderful man.

Not many people would describe him that way.

Not many people knew him.

My mother did.

Yes, she did.

And she loved him.

Yes, she did.

And she forgave him.

Yes, she did.

For all of his behaviors that were hurtful.

Yes. She understood, and loved, and forgave, and in this she was, and is, a wonderful model, a blessed teacher.

Yes. So . . . will You tell me about the soul?

I will. What do you want to know?

Let's start with the first, and obvious, question: I already know the answer, but it gives us a starting point. Is there such a thing as the human soul?

Yes. It is the third aspect of your being. You are a three-part being, made up of body, mind, and spirit.

I know where my body is; I can see that. And I think I know where my mind is—it's in the part of my body called my head. But I'm not sure I have any idea where—

Wait a minute. Hold it. You're wrong about something. Your mind is not in your head.

It's not?

No. Your *brain* is in your skull. Your mind is not.

Where is it, then?

In every cell of your body.

Whoa . . .

What you call the mind is really an energy. It is . . . thought. And thought is an energy, not an object.

Your brain is an object. It is a physical, biochemical mechanism—the largest, most sophisticated, but not the only—mechanism in the human body, with which the body translates, or converts, the energy which is your thought into physical impulses. Your brain is a transformer. So is your whole body. You have little transformers in every cell. Biochemists have often remarked at how individual cells—blood cells, for instance—seem to have their own intelligence. They do, in fact.

That goes not just for cells, but for larger parts of the body. Every man on the planet knows about a particular body part that often seems to have a mind of its own. . . .

Yes, and every woman knows how absurd men become when that is the body part they allow to influence their choices and decisions.

Some women use that knowledge to control men.

Undeniable. And some men control women through choices and decisions made from that place.

Undeniable.

Want to know how to stop the circus?

Absolutely!

This is what was meant earlier by all that talk about raising the energy of life to include all seven chakra centers.

When your choices and decisions come from a place larger than the limited locale you have described, it is impossible for women to control you, and you would never seek to control them.

The only reason that women would ever resort to such means of manipulation and control is that there seems to be no other means of control—at least none nearly as effective—and without some means of control, men often become—well—uncontrollable.

Yet if men would demonstrate more of their higher nature, and if women would appeal more to that part of men, the so-called "battle of the sexes" would be over. As would most other battles of any kind on your planet.

As I have said earlier, this does not mean men and women should give up sex, or that sex is part of a human being's lower nature. It means that sexual energy alone, when not raised to higher chakras and combined with the other energies that make one a whole person, produces choices and outcomes that do not *reflect* the whole person. These are often less than magnificent.

The Whole of You is magnificence itself, yet anything less than the Whole of You is less than magnificent. So if you want to guarantee that you'll produce a less-than-magnificent choice or outcome, make a decision from your root chakra center only. Then watch the results.

They are as predictable as can be.

Hmmm. I think I knew that.

Of course, you did. The largest question facing the human race is not when will you learn, but when will you *act on what you've already learned?*

So the mind is in every cell . . .

Yes. And there are more cells in your brain than anywhere else, so it seems as though your mind is there. Yet that is just the main processing center, not the only one.

Good. I'm clear. So where is the soul?

Where do you think it is?

Behind the Third Eye?

No.

In the middle of my chest, to the right of my heart, just beneath the breastbone?

No.

Okay, I give up.

It is everywhere.

Everywhere?

Everywhere.

Like the mind.

Whoops. Wait a minute. The mind is not everywhere.

It's not? I thought You just said it was in every cell of the body.

> That is not "everywhere." There are spaces between the cells. In fact, your body is 99 percent space.

This is where the soul is?

> The soul is *everywhere* in, through, and around you. It is that which *contains* you.

Wait a minute! Now *You* wait a minute! I was always taught that the body is the container of my soul. Whatever happened to "Your body is the temple of your being"?

> A figure of speech.
> It is useful in helping people to understand that they are more than their bodies; that there is something larger that they are. There is. Literally. The soul is *larger than the body*. It is not carried within the body, but carries the body within *it*.

I'm hearing You, but still having a hard time picturing this.

> Have you ever heard of an "aura"?

Yes. *Yes.* Is *this* the soul?

> It is as close as we can come in your language, in your understanding, to giving you a picture of an enormous and complex reality. The soul is that which holds you together—just as *the Soul of God is that which contains the universe, and holds it together.*

Wow. This is a complete reversal of everything I've ever thought.

> Hang on, My son. The reversals have just begun.

But if the soul is, in a sense, the "air in and around us," and if everyone else's soul is the same, where does one soul *end*, and another begin? Uh-oh, don't tell me, don't tell me . . .

> You see? You already know the answer!

There *is* no place where another soul "ends" and ours "begins"! Just like there is no place where the air in the living room "stops" and the air in the dining room "starts." It's all *the same air*. It's all *the same soul!*

You've just discovered the secret of the universe.

And if *You* are that which contains the *universe*, just as we are that which contains our bodies, then there is no place where *You* "end" and *we* "begin"!

(Ahem)

You can clear Your throat all You want. For me this is a miraculous revelation! I mean, I knew I always understood this—but now I *understand* it!

That's great. Isn't that great?

You see, my problem with understanding in the past had to do with the fact that the body is a discrete container, making it possible to differentiate between "this" body and "that" body, and since I always thought the soul was housed in the body, I therefore differentiated between "this" soul and "that" soul.

Quite naturally, yes.

But if the soul is everywhere inside *and outside* the body—in its "aura," as You put it—then when does one aura "end" and another "begin"? And now I'm able to see, for the first time, really, in *physical terms,* how it is possible that one soul does *not* "end" and another "begin," and that it is *physically true* that We Are All One!

Yippee! That's all I can say. Yippee.

I always thought this was a *meta*physical truth. Now I see that it's a *physical* truth! Holy smoke, religion has just become science!

Don't say I didn't tell you so.

But hold on here. If there is no place where one soul ends and another begins, does that mean there is no such thing as an individual soul?

Well, yes and no.

An answer truly befitting God.

Thank you.

But, frankly, I was hoping for more clarity.

Give Me a break here. We're moving so fast, your hand is hurting from writing.

You mean, furiously scribbling.

Yes. So let's just catch our breath here. Everybody relax. I'm going to explain it all to you.

Okay. Go ahead. I'm ready.

You remember how I've talked to you many times now about what I've called Divine Dichotomy?

Yes.

Well, this is one of them. In fact, it's the biggest one.

I see.

It's important to learn about Divine Dichotomy and understand it thoroughly if you are to live in our universe with grace.

Divine Dichotomy holds that it is possible for two apparently contradictory truths to exist simultaneously in the same space.

Now on your planet people find this difficult to accept. They like to have order, and anything that does not fit into their picture is automatically rejected. For this reason, when two realities begin to assert themselves and they seem to contradict one another, the immediate assumption is that one of them must be wrong, false, untrue. It takes a great deal of maturity to see, and accept, that, in fact, they might both be true.

Yet in the realm of the absolute—as opposed to the realm of the relative, in which you live—it is very clear that the one truth which is All There Is sometimes produces an effect which, viewed in relative terms, looks like a contradiction.

This is called a Divine Dichotomy, and it is a very real part of the human experience. And as I've said, it's virtually impossible to live gracefully without accepting this. One is always grumbling, angry, thrashing about, vainly seeking "justice," or earnestly trying to reconcile opposing forces which were never meant to be reconciled, but which, *by the very nature of the tension between them,* produce exactly the desired effect.

The realm of the relative is, in fact, held together by just such tensions. As an example, the tension between good and evil. In ultimate reality there is no such thing as good and evil. In the realm of the absolute, all there is is love. Yet in the realm of the relative you have created the experience of what you "call" evil, and you have done it for a very sound reason. You wanted to *experience* love, not just "know" that love is All There Is, and you cannot experience something when there is nothing else *but* that. And so, you created in your reality (and continue to do so every day) a polarity of good and evil, thus using one so that you might experience the other.

And here we have a Divine Dichotomy—two seemingly contradictory truths existing simultaneously in the same place. Specifically:

There is such a thing as good and evil.

All there is is love.

Thank You for explaining this to me. You've touched on this before, but thank You for helping me understand Divine Dichotomy even better.

You're welcome.

Now, as I said, the greatest Divine Dichotomy is the one we are looking at now.

There is only One Being, and hence, only One Soul. *And,* there are many souls in the One Being.

Here's how the dichotomy works: You've just had it explained to you that there is no separation between souls. The soul is the energy of life that exists within and around (as the *aura* of) all physical objects. In a sense, it is that which is "holding" all physical objects in place. The "Soul of God" holds in the universe, the "soul of man" holds in each individual human body.

The body is not a container, a "housing," for the soul; the soul is a container for the body.

That's right.

Yet there is no "dividing line" between souls—there is no place where "one soul" ends and "another" begins. And so, it is really one soul holding all bodies.

Correct.

Yet the one soul "feels like" a bunch of individual souls.

Indeed it does—indeed I do—by design.

Can You explain how it works?

Yes.

While there is no actual separation between souls, it is true that the stuff of which the One Soul is made manifests in physical reality at different speeds, producing different degrees of density.

Different speeds? When did speed come in?

All of life is a vibration. That which you call life (you could just as easily call it God) is pure energy. That energy is vibrating constantly, always. It is moving in *waves*. The waves vibrate at different speeds, producing differing degrees of density, or light. This, in turn, produces what you would call different "effects" in the physical world—actually, different physical objects. Yet while the objects are different and discrete, the energy which produces them is exactly the same.

Let Me go back to the example that you used of the air between your living room and dining room. It was a good use of imagery that just popped right out of you. An inspiration.

From guess where.

Yes, I gave it to you. Now you said that there was no specific place between those two physical locations where the "air of the living room" stopped and the "air of the dining room" began. And that is true. Yet there *is* a place where the "air of the living room" becomes *less dense*. That is, it dissipates, becomes "thinner." So, too, the "air of the dining room." The further from the dining room you go, the less you smell dinner!

Now the air in the *house* is the *same air*. There is no "separate air" in the dining room. Yet the air in the dining room sure *seems* like "other air." For one thing, it smells different!

So because the air has taken on different *characteristics*, it seems as though it is *different air*. But it is not. It is all the *same air*, *seeming* different. In the living room you smell the fireplace, in the dining room you smell dinner. You might even go into one room and say, "Whew, it's stuffy. *Let's get some air in here*," as if there was no air at all. And yet, of course, there's plenty of air. What you are wanting to do is change its characteristics.

So you bring in some air from the outside. *Yet that is the same air, too.* There is only one air, moving in, around, and through *everything.*

This is cool. I totally "get" this. I love the way You explain the universe to me in ways I can totally "get."

Well, thank you. I'm trying here. So let Me go on.

Please.

Like the air in your house, the energy of life—what we'll call the "Soul of God"—takes on different characteristics as it surrounds different physical objects. Indeed, that energy coalesces in a particular way to *form* those objects.

As particles of energy join together to form physical matter, they become very concentrated. Mashed up. Pushed together. They begin to "look like," even "feel like," distinct units. That is, they begin to seem "separate," "different," from all the other energy. Yet this is all the same energy, *behaving differently.*

It is this very act of behaving differently which makes it possible for That Which Is All to manifest as That Which Is Many.

As I explain in *Book 1,* That Which Is could not experience Itself as *What* It is until It developed this *ability to differentiate.* So That Which Is All *separated* into That Which Is *This,* and That Which Is *That.* (I'm trying to make this very simple now.)

The "clumps of energy" which coalesced into discrete units that held in physical beings are what you have chosen to call "souls." The parts of Me that have become the lot of You are what We are talking about here. Thus, the Divine Dichotomy:
There is only One of us.
There are Many of us.

Whoa—this is great.

You're telling Me.
Shall I go on?

No, stop here. I'm bored.
Yes, **go on!**

Okay.

Now as energy coalesces, it becomes, as I said, very concentrated. But the further one moves from the point of this concentration, the more dissipated the energy becomes. The "air becomes thinner." The aura fades. The energy never completely disappears, because it cannot. It is the stuff of which everything is made. It's All There Is. Yet it can become very, very thin, very subtle—almost "not there."

Then, in another place (read that, another part of Itself) it can again coalesce, once more "clumping together" to form what you call matter, and what "looks like" a discrete unit. Now the two units appear separate from each other, and in truth there is no separation at all.

This is, in very, very simple and elementary terms, the explanation behind the whole physical universe.

Wow. But can it be true? How do I know I haven't just made this all up?

Your scientists are already discovering that the building blocks of all of life are the same.

They brought back rocks from the moon and found the same stuff they find in trees. They take apart a tree and find the same stuff they find in you.

I tell you this: We are all the *same stuff.*

We are all the same energy, coalesced, compressed in different ways to create different forms and different matter.

Nothing "matters" in and of itself. That is, nothing can *become matter* all by itself. Jesus said, "Without the Father, I am nothing." The Father of all is pure thought. This is the energy of life. This is what you have chosen to call Absolute Love. This is the God and the Goddess, the Alpha and the Omega, the Beginning and the End. It is the All-in-All, the Unmoved Mover, the Prime Source. It is that which you have sought to understand from the beginning of time. The Great Mystery, the Endless Enigma, the eternal truth.

There is only One of Us, and so, it is THAT WHICH YOU ARE.

12

I am filled with awe and reverence at the reading of those words. Thank You for being here with me in this way. Thank You for being here with all of us. For millions have read the words in these dialogues, and millions more will yet do so. And we are breathlessly gifted by the coming of You to our hearts.

> My dearest beings—I have always been in your hearts. I am only glad you can now actually *feel Me there*.
>
> I have always been with you. I have never left you. I am you, and you are Me, and We shall never be separated, *ever*, because that is not *possible*.

Yet on some days I feel so terribly alone. At some moments I feel that I am fighting this battle by myself.

> That's because you have left Me, My child. You have abandoned your awareness of Me. Yet where there is awareness of Me, you can never be alone.

How can I stay in my awareness?

> Bring your awareness to others. Not by proselytizing, but by example. Be the source of the love which I Am in the lives of all others. For that which you give to others, you give to yourself. Because there is only One of Us.

Thank You. Yes, You have given me that clue before. Be the source. Whatever you want to experience in yourself, You have said, be the source of it in the lives of others.

> Yes. This is the great secret. This is the sacred wisdom. *Do unto others as you would have it done unto you.*
>
> All of your problems, all of your conflicts, all of your difficulties in creating a life on your planet of peace and joy are based in your failure to understand this simple instruction, and to follow it.

I get it. Once more You have said it so plainly, so clearly, that I get it. I will try never to "lose it" again.

> You cannot "lose" that which you give away. Always remember that.

Thank You. May I ask You a few more questions now about the soul?

> I have one more general comment to make about life as you're living it.

Please.

> You just said that there are times when you feel as though you're fighting this battle by yourself.

Yes.

> What battle?

It was a figure of speech.

> I think not. I think it was a real indicator of how you (and many people) really think of life.
>
> You have it in your head that it's a "battle"—that there is some kind of struggle going on here.

Well, it's seemed that way to me sometimes.

> It is not that way inherently, and it doesn't have to seem that way, ever.

You'll forgive me, but that's hard for me to believe.

> Which is exactly why it hasn't been your reality. For you will make real what you believe is real. Yet I tell you this: Your life was never meant to be a struggle, and doesn't have to be, now or ever.
>
> I have given you the tools with which to create the grandest reality. You have simply chosen not to use them. Or, to be more accurate, you have *misused* them.
>
> The tools I am referring to here are the three tools of creation. We have talked about them much in our ongoing dialogue. Do you know what they are?

Thought, word, and action.

Good. You've remembered. I once inspired Mildred Hinckley, a spiritual teacher of Mine, to say, "You were born with the creative power of the universe at the tip of your tongue."

That is a statement of astonishing implications. As is this truth, from another of My teachers:

"As thou has believed, so be it done unto you."

These two statements have to do with thought and word. Another of My teachers had this to say, about action:

"The beginning is God. The end is action. Action is God creating—or God experienced."

***You* said that, in *Book 1*.**

Book 1 was brought through by you, My son, just as all great teachings have been inspired by Me, and brought through human forms. Those who allow such inspirations to move them, and who fearlessly share them publicly, are My greatest teachers.

I am not sure that I would put myself in that category.

The words you have been inspired to share have touched millions.

Millions, My son.

They have been translated into 24 languages. They have reached around the world.

By what measure would you grant the status of great teacher?

By the measure of one's actions, not one's words.

That is a very wise answer.

And my actions in this lifetime do not speak well of me, and certainly do not qualify me as a teacher.

You've just written off half the teachers who have ever lived.

What are You saying?

I'm saying what I said through Helen Schucman in *A Course in Miracles*: You teach what you have to learn.

Do you believe that you must be demonstrating perfection before you can teach how to reach it?

And while you have made your share of what you would call mistakes—

—more than my share—

—you have also shown great courage in bringing this conversation with Me forward.

Or great foolhardiness.

Why do you insist on putting yourself down like that? You *all* do it! Every one of you! You deny your own greatness as you deny the existence of Me *in* you.

Not me! I have *never* denied that!

What?

Well, not recently . . .

I tell you, before the cock crows, you will deny Me three times.

Every thought of your Self as smaller than you really are is a denial of Me.

Every word about your Self that puts you down is a denial of Me.

Every action flowing through your Self that plays out a role of "not-good-enough," or lack, or insufficiency of any kind, is a denial indeed. Not just in thought, not just in word, but in deed.

I really—

—Do not allow your life to represent *anything* but the grandest version of the greatest vision you *ever had* about Who You Are.

Now, what is the greatest vision you've ever had for your Self? Is it not that you would one day be a great teacher?

Well . . .

Isn't it?

Yes.

Then *so be it*. And so it *is*. Until you once again *deny it*.

I won't deny it again.

You won't?

No.

Prove it.

Prove it?

Prove it.

How?

Say, right now, "I am a great teacher."

Uh . . .

Go ahead, say it.

I am . . . you see, the problem is, all of this is going to be published. I am aware that everything I am writing on this legal pad is going to appear in print somewhere. People in Peoria are going to be reading this.

Peoria! Ha! Try *Beijing!*

Okay, China, too. That's my point. People have been asking me—bugging me—about *Book 3* since the month after *Book 2* came out! I've tried to explain why it's taken so long. I've tried to get them to understand what it's like having this dialogue when you know the *whole world* is watching, waiting. It's not like it was with *Book 1* and *Book 2*. Both of those were dialogues conducted in a void. I never even knew they *would* be books.

Yes, you did. In your heart of hearts you did.

Well, maybe I hoped they'd be. But now I *know*, and it's different writing on this legal pad.

Because now you know everyone will be reading every word you write.

Yes. And now You want me to say that I'm a great teacher. And it's difficult in front of all these people.

You want I should ask you to declare yourself in private? Is that how you think you empower yourself?

I asked you to declare Who You Are in *public* precisely because you are in public here. The whole *idea* was to get you to say it in public.

Public declaration is the highest form of visioning.

Live the grandest version of the greatest vision you ever had about Who You Are. Begin the living of it by declaring it.

Publicly.

The first step in making it so is *saying* it is so.

But what of modesty? What of decorum? Is it seemly to declare our grandest idea about ourselves to everyone we see?

Every great master has done so.

Yes, but not arrogantly.

How "arrogant" is "I am the life and the way"? Is that arrogant enough for you?

Now you said you would never deny Me again, yet you've spent the last ten minutes trying to justify doing so.

I'm not denying *You*. We are talking here about my greatest vision of *me*.

Your greatest vision of you *is* Me! *That is Who I Am!*

When you deny the greatest part of you, you deny Me. And I tell you, before the dawn tomorrow you will do this three times.

Unless I don't.

Unless you don't. That is right. And only you can decide. Only you can choose.

Now, do you know of any great teacher who was ever a great teacher *in private*? The Buddha, Jesus, Krishna—all were teachers in public, no?

Yes. But there are great teachers who are not widely known. My mother was one. You just said so earlier. It is not necessary to be widely known to be a great teacher.

Your mother was a harbinger. A messenger. A preparer of the way. She prepared *you* for the way, by *showing* you the way. Yet you, too, are a teacher.

And as good a teacher as you know your mother to be, she apparently did not teach you never to deny yourself. Yet this *you will teach others.*

Oh, I want to so badly! That is what I want to do!

Do not "want to." You may not have what you "want." You merely declare that you are in "want" of it, and that's where you will be left—you will be *left wanting.*

All right! Okay! I don't "want" to, I *choose* to!

That's better. That's much better. Now what do you choose?

I choose to teach others never to deny themselves.

Good, and what else do you choose to teach?

I choose to teach others never to deny You—God. Because to deny You is to deny themselves, and to deny themselves is to deny You.

Good. And do you choose to teach this haphazardly, almost "by chance"? Or do you choose to teach this grandly, as if on purpose?

I choose to teach it on purpose. Grandly. As my mother did. My mother *did* teach me never to deny my Self. She taught it to me every day. She was the greatest encourager I ever had. She taught me to have faith in myself, and in You. I should *be* such a teacher. I *choose* to be such a teacher of *all* the great wisdoms my Mom taught me. She made her *whole life* a teaching, not just her words. *That's what makes a great teacher.*

You are right, your mother *was* a great teacher. And you were right in your larger truth. A person does *not* have to be widely known to be a great teacher.

I was "testing" you. I wanted to see where you'd go with this.

And did I "go" where I was "supposed to go"?

You went where all great teachers go. To your own wisdom. To your own truth. That is the place to which you must always go, for it is the place you must turn around and *come from* as you teach the world.

I know. This I know.

And what is your own *deepest truth* about Who You Are?

I am . . .
. . . a great teacher.
A great teacher of eternal truth.

There you have it. Calmly said, softly spoken. There you have it. You know the truth of it in your heart, and you have only spoken your heart.

You are not boasting, and no one will hear it as boasting. You are not bragging, and no one will hear it as bragging. You are not beating your chest, you are opening your heart, and there's a big difference.

Everyone knows Who They Are in their heart. They are a great ballerina, or a great lawyer, or a great actor, or a great first baseman. They are a great detective, or a great salesperson, or a great parent, or a great architect; a great poet or a great leader, a great builder or a great healer. And they are, each and every one, a *great person*.

Everyone knows Who They Are in their heart. If they open their heart, if they share with others their heart's desire, if they live their heartfelt truth, they fill their world with magnificence.

You *are* a great teacher. And where do you suppose that gift comes from?

You.

And so, when you declare yourself to be Who You Are, you are merely declaring who I Am. Always declare Me as Source, and no one will mind you declaring yourself as great.

Yet You've always urged me to declare *myself* as Source.

You *are* the Source—of everything *I Am*. The great teacher with whom you are most familiar in your life said, "I am the life and the way."

He also said, "All these things come to Me from the Father. Without the Father, I am nothing."

And he also said, "I and the Father are One."

Do you understand?

There is only One of us.

Exactly.

Which brings us back to the human soul. Can I now ask some more questions about the soul?

Go.

Okay. How many souls are there?

One.

Yes, in the largest sense. But how many "individuations" of the One That Is All are there?

Say, I like that word there. I like the way you've used that word. The One Energy that is All Energy *individuates* Itself into many different parts. I like that.

I'm glad. So how many individuations did You create? How many souls are there?

I cannot answer that in terms you would understand.

Try me. Is it a constant number? A changing number? An infinite number? Have You created "new souls" since the "original batch"?

Yes, it is a constant number. Yes, it is a changing number. Yes, it is an infinite number. Yes, I have created new souls, and no, I have not.

I don't understand.

I know.

So help me.

Did you actually say that?

Say what?

"So help me, God?"

Ah, clever. Okay, I am going to understand this if it is the last thing I do, so help me, God.

I will. You are very determined, so I will help you—although I warn you that it is difficult to grasp or understand the infinite from a perspective that is finite. We will nevertheless give it a whirl.

Coolness!

Yes, coolness. Well, let's begin by noticing that your questions infer that a reality exists called time. In truth, there is no such reality. There is only one moment, and that is the eternal moment of Now.

All things that have ever happened, are happening Now, and ever will happen, are occurring in this moment. Nothing has happened "before," because there *is* no before. Nothing will happen "after," because there *is* no after. It is always and only Right Now.

In the Right Now of things, I am constantly changing. The number of ways in which I "individuate" (I like your word!) is therefore *always different*, and *always the same*. Given that there is only Now, the number of souls is always constant. But given that you like to think of Now in terms of now and *then*, it is always changing. We touched on this earlier when we spoke of reincarnation, and lower life forms, and how souls "come back."

Since I am always changing, the number of souls is infinite. Yet at any given "point in time" it appears to be finite.

And yes, there are "new souls" in the sense that they have allowed themselves, having reached ultimate awareness and unified with ultimate reality, to voluntarily "forget" everything and "start over"—they have decided to move to a new place on the Cosmic Wheel, and some have chosen to be "young souls" again. Yet all souls are part of the original batch, since all are being created (were created, will be created) in the Only Moment of Now.

So the number is finite and infinite, changing and unchanged, depending on how you look at it.

Because of this characteristic of ultimate reality, I am often called The Unmoved Mover. I am that which is Always Moving, and has Never Moved, is Always Changing and has Never Changed.

Okay. I get it. Nothing is absolute with You.

Except that everything is absolute.

Unless it's not.

Exactly. *Precisely.* You do "get it!" Bravo.

Well, the truth is, I think I have always understood this stuff.

Yes.

Except when I haven't.

That's right.

Unless it's not.

Exactly.

Who's on first.

No, What's on first. Who's on second.

Ta-da! So You're Abbott and I'm Costello, and it's all just a cosmic vaudeville show.

Except when it's not. There are moments and events you may want to take very seriously.

Unless I don't.

Unless you don't.

So, returning once again to the subject of souls . . .

Boy, that's a great book title there . . . *The Subject of Souls.*

Maybe we'll do that one.

Are you kidding? We already have.

Unless we haven't.

That's true.

Unless it's not.

You never know.

Except when you do.

You see? You *are* getting this. You're remembering now how it really is, and you're having fun with it! You're returning now to "living lightly." You're *lightening up*. This is what is meant by *enlightenment*.

Cool.

Very cool. Which means you're hot!

Yup. That's called "living within the contradiction." You've talked about it many times. Now, getting back to the subject of souls; what's the difference between an old soul and a young soul?

A body of energy (that is to say, a part of Me) can conceive of itself as "young" *or* "old," depending upon what it chooses after it reaches ultimate awareness.

When they return to the Cosmic Wheel, some souls choose to be old souls, and some choose to be "young."

Indeed, if the experience called "young" did not exist, neither could the experience called "old." So some souls have "volunteered" to be called "young," and some to be called "old," so that the One Soul, which is really All There Is, could know itself completely.

Similarly, some souls have chosen to be called "good," and some "bad," for exactly the same reason. And this is why no soul is ever punished. For why would the One Soul want to punish a Part of Itself for being a portion of the Whole?

This is all beautifully explained in the children's storybook *The Little Soul and The Sun,* which lays it out simply, for a child to understand.

You have a way of putting things so eloquently, of articulating terribly complex concepts so clearly, that even a child *can* understand.

Thank you.

So here comes another question about souls. Are there such things as "soul partners"?

Yes, but not the way you think of them.

What's different?

You have romanticized "soul partner" to mean the "other half of you." In truth, the human soul—the part of Me that "individuates"—is much larger than you have imagined.

In other words, what I call the soul is bigger than I think.

Much bigger. It is not the air in one room. It is the air in one entire house. And that house has many rooms. The "soul" is not limited to one identity. It is not the "air" in the dining room. Nor does the soul "split" into two individuals who are called soul partners. It is not the "air" in the living room-dining room combination. It is the "air" in the *whole mansion.*

And in My kingdom there are many mansions. And while it is the same air flowing around, in, and through every mansion, the air of the rooms in one mansion may feel "closer." You might walk into those rooms and say, "It feels 'close' in there."

So that you understand, then—there is only One Soul. Yet what you call the individuated soul is huge, hovering over, in, and through hundreds of physical forms.

At the same time?

There is no such thing as time. I can only answer this by saying, "Yes, and no." Some of the physical forms enveloped by your soul are "living now," in your understanding. Others individuated in forms that are now what you would call "dead." And some have enveloped forms that live in what you call the "future." It's all happening right now, of course, and yet, your contrivance called time serves as a tool, allowing you a greater sense of the realized experience.

So, these hundreds of physical bodies my soul has "enveloped"—that's an interesting word You've used—are all my "soul partners"?

That's closer to being accurate than the way you have been using the term, yes.

And some of my soul partners have lived before?

Yes. As you would describe it, yes.

Whoa. Hold it! I think I just *got* something here! Are these parts of me that have lived "before" what I would now describe as my "former lives"?

Good thinking! You are getting it! Yes! Some of these *are* the "other lives" you've lived "before." And some are not. And other parts of your soul are enveloping bodies that will be alive in what you call your future. And still others are embodied in different forms living on your planet right now.

When you run into one of these, you may feel an immediate sense of affinity. Sometimes you may even say, "We must have spent a 'past life' together." And you will be right. You *have* spent a "past life" *together*. Either as *the same physical form*, or as two forms in the same Space-Time Continuum.

This is fabulous! This explains everything!

Yes, it does.

Except one thing.

What's that?

How about when I just *know* that I've spent a "past life" with someone—I just *know* it; I feel it in my *bones*—and yet, when I mention this to them, they feel none of this at all? What's *that* about?

It's about your confusing the "past" with the "future."

Huh?

You *have* spent another life with them—it's just not a *past* life.

It's a "future life"?

Precisely. It's all happening in the Eternal Moment of Now, and you have an awareness of what, in a sense, has *not yet happened*.

Then why don't they "remember" the future, too?

These are very subtle vibrations, and some of you are more sensitive to them than others. Also, from person to person it is different. You may be more "sensitive" to your "past" or "future" experience with one person than another. This usually means you've spent that other time as the part of your very huge soul enveloping the *same* body, whereas when there is still that sensation of "having met before," but just not as strong of one, it may mean that you shared the same "time" together, but not the same body. Perhaps you were (or will be) husband and wife, brother and sister, parent and child, lover and beloved.

These are strong bonds, and it is natural that you would feel them when you "meet again" for the "first time" in "this" life.

If what You are saying is true, it would account for a phenomenon for which I have never before been able to account—the phenomenon of more than one person in this "lifetime" claiming to have memories of being Joan of Arc. Or Mozart. Or some other famous person from the "past." I have always thought this was proof for those who say that reincarnation is a false doctrine, for how could more than one person claim to have been the same person before? But now I see how this is possible! All that has happened is that several of the sentient beings now being enveloped by one soul are "re-membering" (becoming members once again with) the part of their single soul which was (is *now*) Joan of Arc.

Good heavens, this blows the lid off all limitations, and makes all things possible. The minute I catch myself, in the future, saying "that's impossible," I'll know that all I'm doing is demonstrating that there's a great deal I don't know.

That is a good thing to remember. A very good thing to remember.

And, if we can have more than one "soul partner," that would explain how it is possible for us to experience those intense "soul partner feelings" with more than one person a lifetime—and even more than *one person at a time*!

Indeed.

Then it *is* possible to love more than one person at a time.

Of course.

No, no. I mean, with the kind of intense, personal love that we usually reserve for one person—or, at least, one person *at a* time!

Why would you ever want to "reserve" love? Why would you want to hold it "in reserve"?

Because it's not right to love more than one person "that way." It's a betrayal.

Who told you that?

Everybody. Everybody tells me that. My parents told me that. My religion told me that. My society tells me that. Everybody tells me that!

These are some of those "sins of the father" being passed onto the son.

Your own experience teaches you one thing—that loving everyone *full out* is the most joyful thing you can do. Yet your parents, teachers, ministers tell you something else—that you may only love one person at a time "that way." And we're not just talking about sex here. If you consider one person as special as another in *any* way, you are often made to feel that you have betrayed that other.

Right! Exactly! That's how we've got it set up!

Then you are not expressing true love, but some counterfeit variety.

To what extent will true love be allowed to express itself within the framework of the human experience? What limits shall we—indeed, some would say *must* we—place on that expression? If all social and sexual energies were to be unleashed without restriction, what would be the result? Is complete social and sexual freedom the abdication of all responsibility, or the absolute height of it?

Any attempt to restrict the natural expressions of love is a denial of the experience of freedom—and thus a denial of the soul itself. For the soul *is* freedom personified. God *is* freedom, by definition—for God is limitless and without restriction of *any* kind. The soul is God, miniaturized. Therefore, the soul rebels at any imposition of limitation, and dies a new death each time it accepts boundaries from without.

In this sense, birth itself is a death, and death a birth. For in birth, the soul finds itself constricted within the awful limitations of a body, and at death escapes those constrictions again. It does the same thing during sleep.

Back to freedom the soul flies—and rejoices once again with the expression and experience of its true nature.

Yet can its true nature be expressed and experienced while *with* the body?

That is the question you ask—and it drives to the very reason and purpose of life itself. For if life with the body is nothing more than a prison or a limitation, then what good can come of it, and what can be its function, much less its justification?

Yes, I suppose that is what I am asking. And I ask it on behalf of all beings everywhere who have felt the awful constrictions of the human experience. And I am not speaking now of physical limitations—

—I know you are not—

—but emotional and psychological ones.

Yes, I know. I understand. Yet your concerns all relate to the same larger question.

Yes, all right. Still, let me finish. All my life I have been deeply frustrated by the world's inability to let me love everyone in exactly the way I've wanted to.

When I was young, it was about not talking to strangers, not saying things inappropriately. I remember once, walking down a street with my father, we came across a poor man, begging for coins. I immediately felt sorry for the man and wanted to give him some of the pennies in my pocket. My father stopped me, and brushed me past. "Trash," he said. "That's just trash." That was my father's label for all those who did not live up to his definitions of what it meant to be humans of worth.

Later, I remember an experience of my older brother, who was no longer living with us, not being allowed into the house on Christmas Eve because of some argument he'd had with my father. I loved my brother and wanted him to be with us that night, but my father stopped him on the front porch and barred him from entering the home. My mother was devastated (it was her son from a previous marriage), and I was simply mystified. How could we not love or want my brother on Christmas Eve simply because of an argument?

What kind of disagreement could be so bad that it would be allowed to ruin Christmas, when even wars were suspended for a 24-hour truce? This, my little seven-year-old heart begged to know.

As I grew older, I learned that it was not just anger that stopped the love from flowing, but also fear. This was why we oughtn't talk to strangers—but not just when we were defenseless children. Also when we were adults. I learned that it was just not okay to openly and eagerly meet and greet strangers, and that there was a certain etiquette to be followed with people to whom you've just been introduced—none of which made sense to me. I wanted to know *everything* about that new person and I wanted them to know everything about *me!* But *no.* The rules said we had to wait.

And now, in my adult life, when sexuality enters into it, I've learned that the rules are even more rigid and limiting. And I *still don't get it.*

I find that I just want to love and be loved—that I just want to love everyone in whatever way feels natural to me, in whatever way feels good. Yet society has its rules and regulations about all this—and so rigid are they that *even if the other person who is involved* agrees to an experience, if *society* doesn't agree, those two lovers are called "wrong," and are thus doomed.

What *is* that? What is that all *about?*

> Well, you've said it yourself. Fear.
> It's all about fear.

Yes, but are these fears justified? Aren't these restrictions and constrictions only appropriate, given the behaviors of our race? A man meets a younger woman, falls in love (or "in lust") with her, and leaves his wife, for instance. I use only one example. So there she is, left with the kids and no employment skills at thirty-nine or forty-three—or, worse yet, left high and dry at sixty-four by a sixty-eight-year-old man who's become enamored of a woman younger than his daughter.

> Is it your supposing that the man you describe has ceased to love his sixty-four-year-old wife?

Well, he sure acts like it.

> No. It is not his wife he does not love, and seeks to escape. It is the limitations he feels placed on him.

Oh, nonsense. It's lust, pure and simple. It's an old geezer simply trying to recapture his youth, wanting to be with a younger woman, unable to curb his childish appetites and keep his promise to the partner who has remained with him through all the tough and lean years.

Of course. You've described it perfectly. Yet nothing you have said has changed a thing that I have said. In virtually every case, this man has not stopped loving his wife. It is the limitations his wife places on him, or those placed on him by the younger woman who will have nothing to do with him if he stays with his wife, that creates the rebellion.

The point I am trying to make is that the soul will *always* rebel at limitation. Of *any* kind. That is what has sparked *every* revolution in the history of humankind, not just the revolution which causes a man to leave his wife—or a wife to suddenly leave her husband. (Which, by the way, also happens.)

Surely You are not arguing for the complete abolition of behavioral limitations of any kind! That would be behavioral anarchy. Social chaos. Surely You are not advocating people having "affairs"—or, take my breath away, *open marriage!*

I do not advocate, or fail to advocate, *anything.* I am not "for" or "against" anything. The human race keeps trying to make me a "for" or "against" kind of God, and I am not that.

I merely observe what is so. I simply watch *you* create your *own* systems of right and wrong, for and against, and I look to see whether your current ideas about that serve you, given what you say you choose and desire as a species, and as individuals.

Now, to the question of "open marriage."

I am not for or against "open marriage." Whether you are or not depends upon what you decide you want in, and out of, your marriage. And your decision about *that* creates Who You Are with regard to the experience you call "marriage." For it is as I have told you: Every act is an act of self-definition.

When making any decision, it is important to make sure the right question is being answered. The question with regard to so-called "open marriage," for instance, is not "shall we have an open marriage where sexual contact by both parties with persons outside the marriage is allowed?" The question is "Who Am I—and Who Are We—with regard to the experience called marriage?"

The answer to that question will be found in the answer to life's largest question: Who *Am* I—*period*—with regard to anything, in relationship to anything; Who Am I, and Who Do I Choose to Be?

As I have said repeatedly throughout this dialogue, the answer to that question is the answer to *every* question.

God, that frustrates me. Because the answer to that question is so broad and so general that it answers no other question at all.

Oh, really? Then what is your answer to that question?

According to these books—according to what You seem to be saying in this dialogue—I am "love." That is Who I Really Am.

Excellent! You *have* learned! That is correct. You are love. Love is all there is. So you are love, I am love, and there is nothing which is *not* love.

What about fear?

Fear is that which you are not. Fear is False Evidence Appearing Real. Fear is the opposite of love, which you have created in your reality so that you may know experientially That Which You Are.
This is what is true in the relative world of your existence: In the absence of that which you are not, that which you are . . . is *not*.

Yes, yes, we've been through this a number of times now in our dialogue. But it feels as though You have evaded my complaint. I said that the answer to the question of Who We Are (which is love) is so broad as to render it a nonanswer—it is no answer at all—to almost any other question. You say it is the answer to *every* question, and I say it is not the answer to *any*—much less to one as specific as "Should our marriage be an open marriage?"

If that is true for you, it is because you do not know what love is.

Does anybody? The human race has been trying to figure that one out since the beginning of time.

Which does not exist.

Which does not exist, yes, yes, I know. It's a figure of speech.

Let me see if I can find, using your "figures of speech," some words and some ways to explain what love is.

Super. That'd be great.

The first word that comes to mind is unlimited. That which is love is unlimited.

Well, we're right where we were when we opened this subject. We're going around in circles.

Circles are good. Don't berate them. Keep circling; keep circling around the question. Circling is okay. Repeating is okay. Revisiting, restating is okay.

I sometimes get impatient.

Sometimes? That's pretty funny.

Okay, okay, go on with what You were saying.

Love is that which is unlimited. There is no beginning and no end to it. No before and no after. Love always was, always is, and always will be.

So love is also always. It's the always reality.

Now we get back to another word we used before—freedom. For if love is unlimited, and always, then love is . . . free. Love is that which is perfectly free.

Now in the human reality, you will find that you always seek to love, and to be loved. You will find that you will always yearn for that love to be unlimited. And you will find that you will always wish you could be free to express it.

You will seek freedom, unlimitedness, and eternality in every experience of love. You may not always get it, but that is what you will seek. You will seek this because this is what love *is,* and at some deep place you *know* that, because you *are* love, and through the expression of love you are seeking to know and to experience Who and What You Are.

You are life expressing life, love expressing love, God expressing God.

All these words are therefore synonymous. Think of them as the same thing:

God
Life
Love
Unlimited
Eternal
Free

Anything which is not one of these things is *not any* of these things.

You are all of those things, and you will seek to *experience* your-self as *all of these things* sooner or later.

What does that mean, "sooner or later"?

It depends on when you get over your fear. As I've said, fear is False Evidence Appearing Real. It is that which you are not.

You will seek to experience That Which You Are when you are through experiencing that which you are not.

Who wants to experience fear?

Nobody wants to; you are taught to.

A child experiences no fear. He thinks he can do anything. Nor does a child experience lack of freedom. She thinks she can love anyone. Nor does a child experience lack of life. Children believe they will live forever—and people who act like children think nothing can hurt them. Nor does a child know any ungodly things—until that child is taught ungodly things by grownups.

And so, children run around naked and hug everyone, thinking nothing of it. If adults could only do the same thing.

Well, children do so with the beauty of innocence. Adults cannot get back to that innocence, because when adults "get naked" there is always that sex thing.

Yes. And, of course, God forbid that "that sex thing" be inno-cent and freely experienced.

Actually, God *did* forbid it. Adam and Eve were perfectly happy run-ning around naked in the Garden of Eden until Eve ate of the fruit of the tree—the Knowledge of Good and Evil. Then You condemned us to our present state, for we are all guilty of that original sin.

I did no such thing.

I know. But I had to give organized religion a shot here.

Try to avoid that if you can.

Yes, I should. Organized religionists have very little sense of humor.

There you go again.

Sorry.

I was *saying* . . . you will strive as a species to experience a love that is unlimited, eternal, and free. The institution of marriage has been your attempt at creating eternality. With it, you agreed to become partners for life. But this did little to produce a love which was "unlimited" and "free."

Why not? If the marriage is freely chosen, isn't it an expression of freedom? And to say that you are going to demonstrate your love sexually with no one else but your spouse is not a limitation, it's a choice. And a choice is not a limitation, it is the *exercise of freedom.*

So long as that continues to *be* the choice, yes.

Well, it *has* to be. That was the *promise.*

Yes—and that's where the trouble begins.

Help me here.

Look, there may come a time when you want to experience a high degree of specialness in a relationship. Not that one *person* is more special to you than another, but that the *way* you choose to demonstrate with one person the depth of love you have for all people—and for life itself—is unique to that person alone.

Indeed, the way you now demonstrate love to each person you *do* love is unique. You demonstrate your love to no two people in exactly the same way. Because you are a creature and a creator of originality, everything you create is original. It is not possible for any thought, word, or action to be duplicative. You *cannot* duplicate, you can only *originate.*

Do you know *why* no two snowflakes are alike? Because it is *impossible* for them to be. "Creation" is not "duplication," and the Creator can only create.

That is why no two snowflakes are alike, no two *people* are alike, no two thoughts are alike, no two relationships are alike, and no two of *anything* are alike.

The universe—and every thing in it—exists in singular form, and there truly is *nothing else like it.*

This is the Divine Dichotomy again. Everything is singular, yet everything is One.

Exactly. Each finger on your hand is different, yet it is all the same hand. The air in your house is the air that is everywhere, yet the air from room to room is *not* the same, but feels markedly different.

It is the same with people. All people are One, yet no two people are alike. You could not, therefore, love two people in the same way even if you tried—and you would never *want* to, because *love is a unique response to that which is unique.*

So when you demonstrate your love for one person, you are doing so in a way in which you cannot do so with another. Your thoughts, words, and actions—your responses—are literally impossible to duplicate—one of a kind . . . just as is the person for whom you have these feelings.

If the time has come when you have desired this special demonstration with one person alone, then choose it, as you say. Announce it, and declare it. Yet make your declaration an announcement moment-to-moment of your *freedom*, not your ongoing *obligation*. For true love is always free, and obligation cannot exist in the space of love.

If you see your decision to express your love in a particular way with only one particular other as a sacred *promise*, never to be broken, the day may come when you will experience that promise as an obligation—and you will resent it. Yet if you see this decision not as a promise, made only once, but as a free choice, made over and over, that day of resentment will never come.

Remember this: There is only one sacred promise—and that is to *tell and live your truth.* All other promises are forfeitures of freedom, and that can never be sacred. For freedom is Who You Are. If you forfeit freedom, you forfeit your Self. And that is not a sacrament, that is a blasphemy.

13

Whew! Those are tough words. Are You saying we should never make promises—that we should never promise anything to anyone?

As most of you are now living your life, there is a lie built into every promise. The lie is that you can know now how you will feel about a thing, and what you will want to do about that thing, on any given tomorrow. You cannot know this if you are living your life as a reactive being—which most of you are. Only if you are living life as a creative being can your promise not contain a lie.

Creative beings *can* know how they are going to feel about a thing at any time in the future, because creative beings *create* their feelings, rather than experiencing them.

Until you can *create* your future, you cannot *predict* your future. Until you can *predict* your future, you cannot promise anything truthfully about it.

Yet even one who both creates and predicts her future has the authority and the right to change. Change is a fundamental right of all creatures. Indeed, it is more than a "right," for a "right" is that which is *given*. "Change" is that which Is.

Change is.

That which is change, you are.

You cannot be *given* this. You *are* this.

Now, since you *are* "change"—and since change is *the only thing constant about you*—you cannot truthfully promise to *always be the same.*

Do You mean there are no constants in the universe? Are You saying that there is nothing which remains constant in all of creativity?

The process you call life is a process of re-creation. All of life is constantly re-creating itself anew in each moment of now. In this process identicality is impossible, since if a thing is identical, it has not changed at all. Yet while identicality is impossible, similarity is not. Similarity is the result of the process of change producing a remarkably similar version of what went before.

When creativity reaches a high level of similarity, you call that identicality. And from the gross perspective of your limited viewpoint, it is.

Therefore, in human terms, there appears to be great constancy in the universe. That is, things seem to look alike, and act alike, and *react* alike. You see consistency here.

This is good, for it provides a framework within which you may consider, and experience, your existence in the physical.

Yet I tell you this. Viewed from the perspective of all life—that which is physical and that which is nonphysical—the appearance of constancy disappears. Things are experienced as they *really are*: constantly changing.

You are saying that sometimes the changes are so delicate, so subtle, that from our less discerning viewpoint they *appear* the same—sometimes exactly the same—when, in fact, they are not.

Precisely.

There are "no such things as identical twins."

Exactly. You have captured it perfectly.

Yet we *can* re-create ourselves anew in a form sufficiently similar to produce the *effect* of constancy.

Yes.

And we can do this in human relationships, in terms of Who We Are, and how we behave.

Yes—although most of you find this very difficult.

Because true constancy (as opposed to the appearance of constancy) violates the natural law, as we have just learned, and it takes a great master to even create the *appearance* of identicality.

A master overcomes every natural tendency (remember, the natural tendency is toward change) to show up as identicality. In truth, he cannot show up identically from moment to moment. But she *can* show up as sufficiently similar to create the *appearance* of being identical.

Yet people who are *not* "masters" show up "identically" all the time. I know people whose behaviors and appearance are so predictable you can stake your life on them.

> Yet it takes great effort to do this *intentionally.*
> The master is one who creates a high level of similarity (what you call "consistency") *intentionally.* A student is one who creates consistency without necessarily intending to.
> A person who always reacts the same way to certain circumstances, for instance, will often say, "I couldn't help it."
> A master would *never* say that.
> Even if a person's reaction produces an admirable behavior—something for which they receive praise—their response will often be "Well, it was nothing. It was automatic, really. Anybody would do it."
> A master would never do that, either.
> A master, therefore, is a person who—quite literally—*knows what he is doing.*
> She also knows *why.*
> People not operating at levels of mastery often know neither.

This is why it is so difficult to keep promises?

> It is one reason. As I said, until you can predict your future, you cannot promise anything truthfully.
> A second reason people find it difficult to keep promises is that they come into conflict with authenticity.

What do You mean?

> I mean that their evolving truth about a thing differs from what they *said* their truth would always be. And so, they are deeply conflicted. What to obey—my truth, or my promise?

Advice?

> I have given you this advice before:
> *Betrayal of yourself in order not to betray another is betrayal nonetheless. It is the highest betrayal.*

But this would lead to promises being broken all over the place! Nobody's word on *anything* would matter. Nobody could be counted on for anything!

Oh, so you've been counting on others to keep their *word,* have you? No wonder you've been so miserable.

Who says I've been miserable?

You mean this is the way you look and act when you've been *happy?*

All right. Okay. So I've been miserable. Sometimes.

Oh, a great *deal* of the time. Even when you've had every *reason* to be happy, you've allowed yourself to be miserable—worrying about whether you'll be able to *hold onto* your happiness!

And the reason you've even *had* to worry about this is that "holding onto your happiness" has depended to a large degree on other people keeping their word.

You mean I don't have a right to expect—or at least *hope*—that other people will keep their word?

Why would you *want* such a right?

The only reason that another person would not keep their word to you would be because they didn't want to—or they felt they couldn't, which is the same thing.

And if a person did not want to keep his word to you, or for some reason felt he just couldn't, why on Earth would you want him to?

Do you really want someone to keep an agreement she does not want to keep? Do you really feel people should be forced to do things they don't feel they can do?

Why would you want to force anyone to do anything against his will?

Well, try this for a reason: because to let them get away with *not* doing what they said they were going to do would hurt me—or my family.

So in order to avoid injury, you're willing to inflict injury.

I don't see how it injures another simply to ask him to keep his word.

Yet *he* must see it as injurious, or he would keep it willingly.

So *I* should suffer the injury, or watch my children and family suffer the injury, rather than "injure" the one who made a promise by simply asking that it be kept?

> Do you really think that if you force another to keep a promise that you will have escaped injury?
>
> I tell you this: More damage has been done to others by persons leading lives of quiet desperation (that is, doing what they felt they "had" to do) than ever was done by persons freely doing what they wanted to do.
>
> When you give a person freedom, you *remove* danger, you don't increase it.
>
> Yes, letting someone "off the hook" on a promise or commitment made to you may *look* like it will hurt you in the short run, but it will never damage you in the long run, because when you give the other person their freedom, you give *yourself* freedom as well. And so now you are free of the agonies and the sorrows, the attacks on your dignity and your self-worth that inevitably follow when you force another person to keep a promise to you that he or she does not want to keep.
>
> The longer damage will far outweigh the shorter—as nearly everyone who has tried to hold another person to their word has discovered.

Does this same idea hold true in business as well? How could the world do business that way?

> Actually it is the only sane way *to* do business.
>
> The problem right now in your whole society is that it is based on force. Legal force (which you call the "force of law") and, too often, physical force (which you call the world's "armed forces").
>
> You have not yet learned to use the art of persuasion.

If not by legal force—the "force of law" through the courts—how would we "persuade" businesses to meet the terms of their contract and keep their agreements?

> Given your current cultural ethic, there may not be another way. Yet with a *change* of cultural ethic, the way you are now seeking to keep businesses—and individuals, for that matter—from breaking their agreements will appear very primitive.

Can You explain?

You are now using force to make sure agreements are kept. When your cultural ethic is changed to include an understanding that you are all One, you would never use force, because that would only damage your Self. You would not slap your left hand with your right.

Even if the left hand was strangling you?

That is another thing which would not happen. You would stop strangling your Self. You would stop biting your nose to spite your face. You would stop breaking your agreements. And, of course, your agreements themselves would be much different.

You would not agree to give something of value which you have to another only if they had something of value to give you in exchange. You would never hold back on giving or sharing something until you got what you call a just return.

You would give and share automatically, and so, there would be far fewer contracts to break, because a contract is about the *exchange* of goods and services, whereas your life would be about the *giving* of goods and services, *regardless* of what exchange may or may not take place.

Yet in this kind of one-way giving would your salvation be found, for you would have discovered what God has experienced: that what you give to another, you give to your Self. What goes around, comes around.

All things that proceed from you, return to you.

Sevenfold. So there is no need to worry about what you are going to "get back." There is only a need to worry about what you are going to "give out." Life is about creating the highest quality giving, not the highest quality getting.

You keep forgetting. But life is not "for getting." Life is "for giving," and in order to do that, you need to be forgiving to others—especially those who did not *give you* what you thought you were *going to get!*

This switch will entail a complete shift of your cultural story. Today, what you call "success" in your culture is measured largely by how much you "get," by how much honor and money and power and possessions you amass. In the New Culture "success" will be measured by how much you cause *others* to amass.

The irony will be that the more you cause *others* to amass, the more *you* will amass, effortlessly. With no "contracts," no "agreements," no "bargaining" or "negotiating" or lawsuits or courts which force you to give to each other what was "promised."

In the future economy, you will not do things for personal profit, but for personal growth, which will *be* your profit. Yet "profit" in material terms will come to you as you become a bigger and grander version of Who You Really Are.

In those days and times, using force to coerce someone to give you something because they "said" that they would will seem very primitive to you. If another person does not keep an agreement, you will simply allow them to walk their path, make their choices, and create their own experience of themselves. And whatever they have not given you, you will not miss, for you will know that there is "more where that came from"—and that they are not your source of that, but *you* are.

Whoa. I *got it*. But it feels like we have really gotten off the mark. This whole discussion began with my asking You about love—and if human beings would ever allow themselves to express it without limitation. And that led to a question about open marriage. And suddenly we've gotten way off the mark here.

Not really. Everything we've talked about is pertinent. And this is a perfect lead-in to your questions about so-called enlightened, or more highly evolved, societies. Because in highly evolved societies there is neither "marriage" nor "business"—nor, for that matter, any of the artificial social constructions you have created to hold your society together.

Yes, well, we'll get into that soon. Right now I just want to close down this subject. You've said some intriguing things here. What all of it breaks down to, as I get it, is that most human beings can't keep promises and so, shouldn't make them. That pretty much scuttles the institution of marriage.

I like your use of the word "institution" here. Most people experience that when they are in a marriage, they *are* in an "institution."

Yeah, it's either a mental health institution or a penal institution—or at the very least an institution of higher learning!

Exactly. Precisely. That's how most people experience it.

Well, I was kidding along with You here, but I wouldn't say "most people." There are still millions of people who love the institution of marriage, and want to protect it.

I'll stand by the statement. Most people have a very difficult time with marriage, and do *not* like what it does to them.

Your worldwide divorce statistics prove this.

So are You saying that marriage should go?

I have no preference in the matter, only—

—I know, I know. Observations.

Bravo! You keep wanting to make me a God of preferences, which I am not. Thank you for trying to stop that.

Well, we've not only just scuttled marriage, we've also just scuttled religion!

It is true that religions could not exist if the whole human race understood that God doesn't have preferences, because a religion purports to be a *statement* of God's preferences.

And if You *have* no preferences, then religion must be a lie.

Well, that's a harsh word. I would call it a fiction. It's just something you made up.

Like we made up the fiction that God prefers us to be married?

Yes. I don't prefer anything of the sort. But I notice *you* do.

Why? Why do we prefer marriage if we know that it is so difficult?

Because marriage was the only way you could figure out to bring "foreverness," or eternality, into your experience of love.

It was the only way a female could guarantee her support and survival, and the only way a male could guarantee the constant availability of sex, and companionship.

So a social convention was created. A bargain was struck. You give me this and I'll give you that. In this it *was* very much like a business. A contract was made. And since both parties needed to enforce the contract, it was said to be a "sacred pact" with God—who would punish those who broke it.

Later, when that didn't work, you created man-made laws to enforce it.

But even that hasn't worked.

Neither the so-called laws of God nor the laws of man have been able to keep people from breaking their marriage vows.

How come?

Because those vows as you have them normally constructed run counter to the only law that matters.

Which is?

Natural law.

But it is the nature of things for life to express unity, Oneness. Isn't that what I'm getting from all of this? And marriage is our most beautiful expression of that. You know, "What God has joined together, let no man put asunder," and all that.

Marriage, as most of you have practiced it, is not particularly beautiful. For it violates two of the three aspects of what is true about each human being by nature.

Will You go over it again? I think I'm just starting to pull this together.

Okay. Once more from the top.

Who You Are is love.

What love is, is unlimited, eternal, and free.

Therefore, that is what *you* are. That is the *nature* of Who You Are. You are unlimited, eternal, and free, by nature.

Now, any artificial social, moral, religious, philosophical, economic, or political construction which violates or subordinates your nature is an impingement upon your very Self—and you will rail against it.

What do you suppose gave birth to your own country? Was it not "Give me liberty, or give me death"?

Well, you've given up that liberty in your country, and you've given it up in your lives. And all for the same thing. Security.

You are so afraid to *live*—so afraid of *life itself*—that you've given up *the very nature of your being* in trade for security.

The institution you call marriage is your attempt to create security, as is the institution called government. Actually, they are both forms of the same thing—artificial social constructions designed to *govern each other's behavior.*

Good grief, I never looked at it like that. I always thought that marriage was the ultimate announcement of love.

As you have imagined it, yes, but not as you have constructed it. As you have constructed it, it is the ultimate announcement of fear.

If marriage allowed you to be unlimited, eternal, and free in your love, *then* it would be the ultimate announcement of love.

As things are now, you become married in an effort to lower your love to the level of a *promise* or a *guarantee.*

Marriage is an effort to guarantee that "what is so" now will *always be so.* If you didn't need this guarantee, you would not need marriage. And how do you use this guarantee? First, as a means of creating security (instead of creating security from that which is inside of you), and second, if that security is not forever forthcoming, as a means of punishing each other, for the marriage promise which has been broken can now form the basis of the lawsuit which has been opened.

You have thus found marriage very useful—even if it is for all the wrong reasons.

Marriage is also your attempt to guarantee that the feelings you have for each other, you will never have for another. Or, at least, that you will never *express* them with another in the same way.

Namely, sexually.

Namely, sexually.

Finally, marriage as you have constructed it is a way of saying: "This relationship is special. I hold this relationship above all others."

What's wrong with that?

Nothing. It's not a question of "right" or "wrong." Right and wrong do not exist. It's a question of what serves you. Of what re-creates you in the next grandest image of Who You Really Are.

If Who You Really Are is a being who says, "This one relationship—this single one, right over here—is more special than any other," then your construction of marriage allows you to do that perfectly. Yet you might find it interesting to notice that almost no one who is, or has been, recognized as a spiritual master is married.

Yeah, because masters are celibate. They don't have sex.

No. It's because masters cannot truthfully make the statement that your present construction of marriage seeks to make: that one person is more special to them than another.

This is not a statement that a master makes, and it is *not a statement that God makes.*

The fact is that your marriage vows, as you presently construct them, have you making a very un-Godly statement. It is the height of irony that you feel this is the holiest of holy promises, for it is a promise that God would never make.

Yet, in order to justify your human fears, you have imagined a God who *acts just like you.* Therefore, you speak of God's "promise" to his "Chosen People," and of covenants between God and those God loves, in a special way.

You cannot stand the thought of a God who loves *no one* in a way which is more special than any other, and so you create fictions about a God who only loves certain people for certain reasons. And you call these fictions Religions. I call them blasphemies. For any thought that God loves one more than another is false—and any ritual which asks *you* to make the *same statement* is not a sacrament, but a sacrilege.

Oh, my God, stop it. *Stop it!* You're killing every good thought I ever had about marriage! This can't be God writing this. God would never say such things about religion and marriage!

Religion and marriage *the way you have constructed them* is what we are talking about here. You think that this talk is tough? I tell you this: You have bastardized the Word of God in order to justify your fears and rationalize your insane treatment of each other.

You will make God say whatever you need God to say in order to continue limiting each other, hurting each other, and *killing each other* in My name.

Yea, you have invoked My name, and waved My flag, and carried crosses on your battlefields for centuries, all as proof that I love one people more than another, and would *ask you to kill to prove it.*

Yet I tell you this: My love is unlimited and unconditional.

That is the one thing you cannot hear, the one truth you cannot abide, the one statement you cannot accept, for its all-inclusiveness destroys not only the institution of marriage (as you have constructed it), but every one of your religions and governmental institutions as well.

For you have created a culture based on exclusion, and supported it with a cultural myth of a God who excludes.

Yet the culture of God is based on inclusion. In God's love, everyone is included. Into God's Kingdom *everyone* is invited.

And this truth is what *you* call a blasphemy.

And you *must*. Because if it is true, then everything you have created in your life is false. All human conventions and all human constructions are faulty to the degree that they are not unlimited, eternal, and free.

How can anything be "faulty" if there's no such thing as "right" and "wrong"?

A thing is only faulty to the degree that it does not function to suit its purpose. If a door does not open and close, you would not call the door "wrong." You would merely say its installation or operation is faulty—because it does not serve its purpose.

Whatever you construct in your life, in your human society, which does not serve your purpose in becoming human is faulty. It is a faulty construction.

And—just for review—my purpose in becoming human is?

To decide and to declare, to create and to express, to experience and to fulfill, Who You Really Are.

To re-create yourself anew in every moment in the grandest version of the greatest vision ever you had about Who You Really Are.

That is your purpose in becoming human, and that is the purpose of all of life.

So—where does that leave us? We've destroyed religion, we've dissed marriage, we've denounced governments. Where are we, then?

First of all, we've destroyed, dissed, and denounced nothing. If a construction you have created is not working and not producing what you wanted it to produce, to *describe* that condition is not to destroy, diss, or denounce the construction.

Try to remember the difference between judgment and observation.

Well, I'm not going to argue with You here, but a lot of what has just been said has sounded pretty judgmental to *me*.

We are constricted here by the awful limitation of words. There are really so few of them, and so we have to use the same ones over and over again, even when they don't always convey the same meaning, or the same kinds of thoughts.

You say that you "love" banana splits, but you surely don't mean the same thing as when you say you love each other. So you see, you have very few words, really, to describe how you're feeling.

In communicating with you in this way—in the way of words— I've allowed Myself to experience those limitations. And I will concede that, because some of this language has also been used by *you* when *you are being judgmental*, it would be easy to conclude that *I'm* being judgmental when *I* use them.

Let Me assure you here that I am not. Throughout this whole dialogue I have simply been trying to tell you how to get where you say you want to go, and to describe as impactfully as possible what is blocking your way; what is stopping you from going there.

Now, with regard to *religion*, you say where you want to go is to a place where you can truly know God and love God. I am simply observing that your religions do not take you there.

Your religions have made God the Great Mystery, and caused you not to love God, but to fear God.

Religion has done little, as well, to cause you to change your behaviors. You are still killing each other, condemning each other, making each other "wrong." And, in fact, it is your *religions* which have been encouraging you to do so.

So with regard to religion, I merely observe that you say you want it to take you to one place, and it is taking you to another.

Now you say you want *marriage* to take you to the land of eternal bliss, or at least to some reasonable level of peace, security, and happiness. As with religion, your invention called marriage does well with this in the early going, when you are first experiencing it.

Yet, as with religion, the longer you reside in the experience, the more it takes you where you say you don't want to go.

Nearly half of the people who become married dissolve their marriage through divorce, and of those who stay married, many are desperately unhappy.

Your "unions of bliss" lead you to bitterness, anger, and regret. Some—and not a small number—take you to a place of outright tragedy.

You say you want your *governments* to ensure peace, freedom, and domestic tranquillity, and I observe that, as you have devised them, they do none of this. Rather, your governments lead you to war, increasing *lack* of freedom, and domestic violence and upheaval.

You haven't been able to solve the basic problems of simply feeding and keeping people healthy and alive, much less meet the challenge of providing them equal opportunity.

Hundreds of you die every day of starvation on a planet where thousands of you throw away each day enough food to feed nations.

You can't handle the simplest task of getting the leftovers from the "Have's" to the "Have Not's"—much less resolve the issue of whether you even *want* to share your resources more equitably.

Now *these are not judgments*. These are things which are *observably* true about your society.

Why? Why is it *like* this? Why have we made so little progress in conducting our own affairs these past many years?

Years? Try *centuries*.

Okay, centuries.

It has to do with the First Human Cultural Myth, and with all the other myths which necessarily follow. Until they change, nothing else will change. For your cultural myths inform your ethics, and your ethics create your behaviors. Yet the problem is that your cultural myth is at variance with your basic instinct.

What do You mean?

Your First Cultural Myth is that human beings are inherently evil. This is the myth of original sin. The myth holds that not only is your basic nature evil, you were *born* that way.

The Second Cultural Myth, arising necessarily out of the first, is that it is the "fittest" who survive.

This second myth holds that some of you are strong and some of you are weak, and that to survive, you have to be one of the strong. You will do all that you can to help your fellow man, but if and when it comes down to your own survival, you will take care of yourself first. You will even let others die. Indeed, you will go further than that. If you think you have to, in order for you and yours to survive, you will actually kill others—presumably, the "weak"—thereby defining you as the "fittest."

Some of you say that this is your *basic instinct*. It is called the "survival instinct," and it is this cultural myth that has formed much of your societal ethic, creating many of your group behaviors.

Yet your "basic instinct" is *not* survival, but rather, fairness, oneness, and love. This is the basic instinct of all sentient beings everywhere. It is your cellular memory. It is your *inherent nature*. Thus is exploded your first cultural myth. You are *not* basically evil, you were *not* born in "original sin."

If your "basic instinct" was "survival," and if your basic nature was "evil," you would never move *instinctively* to save a child from falling, a man from drowning, or anyone from anything. And yet, when you act on your basic instincts and display your basic nature, and don't *think about* what you are doing, this is exactly how you behave, *even at your own peril*.

Thus, your "basic" instinct cannot be "survival," and your basic nature is clearly not "evil." Your instinct and your nature is to reflect the essence of Who You Are, which is fairness, oneness, and love.

Looking at the social implications of this, it is important to understand the difference between "fairness" and "equality." It is not a basic instinct of all sentient beings to seek *equality*, or to be *equal*. Indeed, exactly the opposite is true.

The basic instinct of all living things is to express uniqueness, not sameness. Creating a society in which two beings are truly equal is not only impossible, but undesirable. Societal mechanisms seeking to produce true equality—in other words, economic, political, and social "sameness"—work against, not for, the grandest idea and the highest purpose—which is that each being will have the opportunity to produce the outcome of its grandest desire, and thus truly re-create itself anew.

Equality of *opportunity* is what is required for this, not equality *in fact*. This is called *fairness*. Equality in *fact*, produced by exterior forces and laws, would *eliminate*, not *produce*, fairness. It would eliminate the opportunity for true self-re-creation, which is the highest goal of enlightened beings everywhere.

And what would *create* freedom of opportunity? Systems that would allow society to meet the basic survival needs of every individual, freeing all beings to pursue self-development and self-creation, rather than self-survival. In other words, systems that imitate the true system, called life, in which *survival is guaranteed*.

Now, because self-survival is not an issue in *enlightened* societies, these societies would never allow one of its members to suffer if there were enough for all. In these societies self-interest and mutual best interest are identical.

No society created around a myth of "inherent evilness" or "survival of the fittest" could possibly achieve such understanding.

Yes, I see this. And this "cultural myth" question is something I want to explore, along with the behaviors and ethics of more advanced civilizations, later in greater detail. But I'd like to double back one last time and resolve the questions I started out with here.

One of the challenges of talking with You is that Your answers lead us in such interesting directions that I sometimes forget where I began. But in this case I have not. We were discussing marriage. We were discussing love, and its requirements.

Love *has* no requirements. That's what makes it love.

If your love for another carries requirements, then it is not love at all, but some counterfeit version.

That is what I have been trying to tell you here. It is what I have been saying, in a dozen different ways, with every question you've asked here.

Within the context of marriage, for example, there is an exchange of vows that love does not require. Yet *you* require them, because you do not know what love *is*. And so you make each other promise *what love would never ask*.

Then You *are* against marriage!

I am "against" nothing. I am simply describing what I see.

Now you can *change* what I see. You can redesign your social construction called "marriage" so that it does *not* ask what Love would never ask, but rather, declares *what only love could declare*.

In other words, change the marriage vows.

More than that. Change the *expectations* on which the vows are based. These expectations are going to be difficult to change, because they are your cultural heritage. They arise, in turn, from your cultural myths.

Here we go again with the cultural myths routine: What's up with You about this?

I am hoping to point you in the right direction here. I see where you say you want to go with your society, and I am hoping to find human words and human terms that can direct you there.

May I give you an example?

Please.

One of your cultural myths about love is that it's about giving rather than receiving. This has become a cultural imperative. And yet it is driving you crazy, and causing more damage than you could ever imagine.

It gets, and keeps, people in bad marriages, it causes relationships of all kinds to be dysfunctional, yet no one—not your parents, to whom you look for guidance; not your clergy, to whom you look for inspiration; not your psychologists and psychiatrists, to whom you look for clarity; not even your writers and artists, to whom you look for intellectual leadership, will dare to challenge the prevailing cultural myth.

And so, songs are written, stories are told, movies are made, guidance is given, prayers are offered, and parenting is done which perpetuates The Myth. Then you are all *left to live up to it.*

And you can't.

Yet it is not *you* that is the problem, it is The Myth.

Love is *not* about giving rather than receiving?

No.

It *isn't?*

No. It never has been.

But You said Yourself just a moment ago that "Love has no requirements." You said, *that's what makes it love.*

And so it is.

Well, that sure sounds like "giving rather than receiving" to me!

Then you need to reread Chapter Eight of *Book 1.* Everything
I'm alluding to here I've explained to you there. This dialogue was
meant to be read in sequence, and to be considered as a whole.

I know. But for those who nevertheless came to these words now without having read *Book 1*; could You explain, please, what You're getting
at here? Because, frankly, even I could use the review, and I think I now
understand this stuff!

Okay. Here goes.
Everything you do, you do for yourself.
This is true because you and all others are One.
What you do for another, you therefore do for you. What you
fail to do for another, you fail to do for you. What is good for another is good for you, and what is bad for another is bad for you.
This is the most basic truth. Yet it is the truth you most frequently ignore.
Now when you are in a relationship with another, that relationship has only one purpose. It exists as a vehicle for you to decide
and to declare, to create and to express, to experience and to fulfill your highest notion of Who You Really Are.
Now if Who You Really Are is a person who is kind and considerate, caring and sharing, compassionate and loving—then, when
you are *being* these things with others, you are giving your *Self* the
grandest experience for which you came into the body.
This is why you took a body. Because only in the physical realm
of the relative could you know yourself as these things. In the realm
of the absolute from which you have come, this experience of
knowing is impossible.
All these things I've explained to you in far greater detail in
Book 1.
Now if Who You Really Are is a being who does not love the
Self, and who allows the Self to be abused, damaged, and
destroyed by others, then you will continue behaviors which allow
you to experience that.

Yet if you really *are* a person who is kind and considerate, caring and sharing, compassionate and loving, you will include your *Self* among the people with whom you are *being* these things.

Indeed, you will *start* with yourself. You will *put yourself first* in these matters.

Everything in life depends on what you are seeking to be. If, for instance, you are seeking to be One with all others (that is, if you are seeking to *experience* a conceptualization you already know to be true), you will find yourself behaving in a very specific way—a way which allows you to experience and demonstrate your Oneness. And when you do certain things as a result of this, you will not experience that you are doing something for *someone else,* but rather, that you are doing it *for your Self.*

The same will be true no matter what you are seeking to be. If you are seeking to be love, you will do loving things with others. Not *for* others, but *with* others.

Notice the difference. Catch the nuance. You will be doing loving things *with* others, *for* your *Self*—so that you can actualize and experience your grandest idea about your Self and Who You Really Are.

In this sense, it is impossible to do *anything* for another, for every act of your own volition is literally *just that:* an "act." You are *acting.* That is, creating and playing a role. Except, you are not *pretending.* You are actually *being* it.

You are a human *being.* And what you are being is decided and chosen by you.

Your Shakespeare said it: All the world's a stage, and the people, the players.

He also said, "To be or not to be, that is the question."

And he *also* said: "To thine own Self be true, and it must follow, as the night the day, thou canst not then be false to any man."

When you are true to your Self, when you do not *betray your Self,* then when it "looks like" you are "giving," you will know you are actually "receiving." You are literally giving yourself back to your Self.

You cannot truly "give" to another, for the simple reason that there *is* no "other." If We are all One, then there is only You.

This sometimes seems like a semantic "trick," a way to change the words around to alter their meaning.

It is not a trick, but it *is magic!* And it is not about changing words to alter meaning, but changing perceptions to alter experience.

Your experience of everything is based on your perceptions, and your perception is based on your understanding. And your understanding is based on your myths. That is, *on what you have been told.*

Now I tell you this: Your present cultural myths have not served you. They have not taken you where you say you want to go.

Either you are lying to yourself about where you say you want to go, or you are blind to the fact that you are not getting there. Not as an individual, not as a country, not as a species or a race.

Are there others species which are?

Oh yes, decidedly.

Okay, I've waited long enough. Tell me about them.

Soon. Very soon. But first I want to tell you about how you can alter your invention called "marriage," so that it takes you closer to where you say you want to go.

Do not destroy it, do not do away with it—*alter it.*

Yes, well, I do want to know about that. I do want to know whether there is *any* way that human beings will ever be allowed to express true love. So I end this section of our dialogue where I began it. What limits shall we—indeed, some would say *must* we—place on that expression?

None. No limits at all. And that is what *your marriage vows should state.*

That's amazing, because that's exactly what my marriage vows with Nancy *did* state!

I know.

When Nancy and I decided to get married, I suddenly felt inspired to write a whole new set of marriage vows.

I know.

And Nancy joined me. She agreed that we couldn't possibly exchange the vows that had become "traditional" at weddings.

I know.

We sat down and created *new* marriage vows that, well, that "defied the cultural imperative," as You might put it.

Yes, you did. I was very proud.

And as we were writing them, as we put the vows down on paper for the minister to read, I truly believe we were both inspired.

Of course you were!

Do you mean—?

What do you think, I only come to you when you're writing books?

Wow.

Yes, wow.
So why don't you put those marriage vows here?

Huh?

Go ahead. You've got a copy of them. Put them right here.

Well, we didn't create them to share with the world.

When this dialogue began, you didn't think *any* of it would be shared with the world.
Go ahead. Put them in.

It's just that I don't want people to think that I'm saying, "We've written the Perfect Marriage Vows!"

All of a sudden you're worried about what people will think?

C'mon. You know what I mean.

Look, no one says these are the "Perfect Marriage Vows."

Well, okay.

They're just the best anyone on your planet's come up with so far.

Hey—!

Just *kidding.* Let's lighten up here.

Go ahead. Put the vows in. I'll take responsibility for them. And people will love them. It'll give them an idea of what we're talking about here. Why, you may even want to invite others to take these vows—which are not really "vows" at all, but Marriage Statements.

Well, okay. Here's what Nancy and I said to each other when we got married . . . thanks to the "inspiration" we received:

Minister:

Neale and Nancy have not come here tonight to make a solemn promise or to exchange a sacred vow.

Nancy and Neale have come here to make *public* their love for each other; to give noticement to their truth; to declare their choice to live and partner and grow together—out loud and in your presence, out of their desire that we will all come to feel a very real and intimate part of their decision, and thus make it even more powerful.

They've also come here tonight in the further hope that their ritual of bonding will help bring us *all* closer together. If you are here tonight with a spouse or a partner, let this ceremony be a reminder—a rededication of your own loving bond.

We'll begin by asking the question: Why get married? Neale and Nancy have answered this question for themselves, and they've told me their answer. Now I want to ask them one more time, so they can be sure of their answer, certain of their understanding, and firm in their commitment to the truth they share.

(Minister gets two red roses from table . . .)

This is the Ceremony of Roses, in which Nancy and Neale share their understandings, and commemorate that sharing.

Now Nancy and Neale, you have told me it is your firm understanding that you are not entering into this marriage for reasons of security . . .

. . . that the only real security is not in owning or possessing, nor in being owned or possessed . . .

. . . not in demanding or expecting, and not even in hoping, that what you think you need in life will be supplied by the other . . .

. . . but rather, in knowing that everything you need in life . . . all the love, all the wisdom, all the insight, all the power, all the knowledge, all the understanding, all the nurturing, all the compassion, and all the strength . . . resides *within* you . . .

. . . and that you are not each marrying the other in hopes of *getting* these things, but in hopes of *giving* these gifts, that the other might have them in even greater abundance.

Is that your firm understanding tonight?

(*They say, "It is."*)

And Neale and Nancy, you have told me it is your firm understanding you are not entering into this marriage as a means of in any way limiting, controlling, hindering, or restricting each other from any true expression and honest celebration of that which is the highest and best within you—including your love of God, your love of life, your love of people, your love of creativity, your love of work, or *any* aspect of your being which genuinely represents you, and brings you joy. Is that still your firm understanding tonight?

(*They say, "It is."*)

Finally, Nancy and Neale, you have said to me that you do not see marriage as producing *obligations,* but rather as providing *opportunities* . . .

. . . opportunities for growth, for full Self-expression, for lifting your lives to their highest potential, for healing every false thought or small idea you ever had about yourself, and for ultimate reunion with God through the communion of your two souls . . .

. . . that this is truly a Holy Communion . . . a journey through life with one you love as an equal partner, sharing equally both the authority and the responsibilities inherent in any partnership, bearing equally what burdens there be, basking equally in the glories.

Is that the vision you wish to enter into now?

(*They say, "It is."*)

I now give you these red roses, symbolizing your individual understandings of these Earthly things; that you both know and agree how life will be with you in bodily form, and within the physical structure called marriage. Give these roses now to each other as a symbol of your *sharing* of these agreements and understandings with love.

Now, please each of you take this white rose. It is a symbol of your larger understandings, of your spiritual nature and your spiritual truth. It stands for the purity of your Real and Highest Self, and of the purity of God's love, which shines upon you now, and always.

(*She gives Nancy the rose with* Neale's *ring on the stem, and Neale the rose with* Nancy's *ring on it.*)

What symbols do you bring as a reminder of the promises given and received today?

(*They each remove the rings from the stems, giving them to the minister, who holds them in her hand as she says . . .*)

A circle is the symbol of the Sun, and the Earth, and the universe. It is a symbol of holiness, and of perfection and peace. It is also the symbol of the eternality of spiritual truth, love, and life . . . that which has no beginning and no end. And in this moment, Neale and Nancy choose for it to also be a symbol of unity, but not of possession; of joining, but not of restricting; of encirclement, but not of entrapment. For love cannot be possessed, nor can it be restricted. And the soul can never be entrapped.

Now Neale and Nancy, please take these rings you wish to give, one to the other.

(*They take each other's rings.*)

Neale, please repeat after me.

I, Neale . . . ask you, Nancy . . . to be my partner, my lover, my friend, and my wife . . . I announce and declare my intention to give you my deepest friendship and love . . . not only when your moments are high . . . but when they are low . . . not only when you remember clearly Who You Are . . . but when you forget . . . not only when you are acting with love . . . but when you are not . . . I further announce . . . before God and those here present . . . that I will seek always to see the Light of Divinity within you . . . and seek always to share . . . the Light of Divinity within me . . . even, and *especially* . . . in whatever moments of darkness may come.

It is my intention to be with you forever . . . in a Holy Partnership of the Soul . . . that we may do together God's work . . . sharing all that is good within us . . . with all those whose lives we touch.

(*The minister turns to Nancy.*)

Nancy, do you choose to grant Neale's request that you be his wife?

(She answers, "I do.")

Now Nancy, please repeat after me.
I, Nancy . . . ask you, Neale . . . *(She makes the same vow)*.
(Minister turns to Neale.)

Neale, do you choose to grant Nancy's request that you be her husband?
(He answers, "I do.")

Please then, both of you, take hold of the rings you would give each other, and repeat after me: With this ring . . . I thee wed . . . . I take now the ring you give to me . . . *(they exchange rings)* . . . and give it place upon my hand . . . *(they place the rings on their hands)* . . . that all may see and know . . . of my love for you.
(The Minister closes . . .)

We recognize with full awareness that only a couple can administer the sacrament of marriage to each other, and only a couple can sanctify it. Neither my church, nor any power vested in me by the State, can grant me the authority to declare what only two hearts can declare, and what only two souls can make real.

And so now, inasmuch as *you*, Nancy, and *you*, Neale, have announced the truths that are already written in your hearts, and have witnessed the same in the presence of these, your friends, and the One Living Spirit—we observe joyfully that *you* have declared yourself to be . . . husband and wife.

Let us now join in prayer.

Spirit of Love and Life: out of this whole world, two souls have found each other. Their destinies shall now be woven into one design, and their perils and their joys shall not be known apart.

Neale and Nancy, may your home be a place of happiness for all who enter it; a place where the old and the young are renewed in each other's company, a place for growing and a place for sharing, a place for music and a place for laughter, a place for prayer and a place for love.

May those who are nearest to you be constantly enriched by the beauty and the bounty of your love for one another, may your work be a joy of your life that serves the world, and may your days be good and long upon the Earth.

Amen, and amen.

I am so touched by that. I am so honored, so blessed, to have found someone in my life who could say those words with me, and mean them. Dear God, thank You for sending me Nancy.

You are a gift to her, too, you know.

I hope so.

Trust Me.

Do You know what I wish?

No. What?

I wish that all people could make those Marriage Statements. I wish people would cut them out, or copy them, and use them for *their* wedding. I bet we'd see the divorce rate plummet.

Some people would have a very hard time saying those things—and many would have a hard time staying true to them.

I just hope that *we* can stay true to them! I mean, the problem with putting those words in here is that now we have to live up to them.

You were not planning on living up to them?

Of course we were. But we're human, just like everybody else. Yet now if we fail, if we falter, if anything should happen to our relationship, or, good grief, we should ever choose to *end* it in its present form, all kinds of people are going to be disillusioned.

Nonsense. They'll know that you are being true to yourself; they'll know that you have made a later choice, a new choice. Remember what I told you in *Book 1*. Do not confuse the length of your relationship with its quality. You are not an icon, and neither is Nancy, and no one should put you there—and you should not put yourself there. Just be human. Just be fully human. If at some later point you and Nancy feel you wish to reform your relationship in a different way, you have a perfect right to do that. *That is the point of this whole dialogue.*

And it was the point of the statements we made!

Exactly. I'm glad that you see that.

Yes, I *like* those Marriage Statements, and I'm glad that we put them in! It's a wonderful new way to begin a life together. No more asking the woman to promise "to love, honor, and obey." It was self-righteous, self-inflated, self-serving men who demanded that.

You're right, of course.

And it was even more self-righteous and self-serving for men to claim that such male preeminence was *God-ordained.*

Again, you are right. I never ordained any such thing.

At last, marriage words which really are inspired by God. Words which make a chattel, personal property, out of *no one.* Words which speak the truth about love. Words which place no limitations, but promise only freedom! Words to which all hearts can *remain true.*

There are those who will say, "Of *course* anyone can keep vows which ask nothing of you!" What will you say to that?

I will say: "It is much more difficult to free someone than to control them. When you control someone, you get what *you* want. When you free someone, they get what *they* want."

You will have spoken wisely.

I have a wonderful idea! I think we should make a little booklet of those Marriage Statements, kind of a little prayer book for people to use on their wedding day.

It could be a small little book, and it would contain not only those words, but a whole ceremony, and key observations about love and relationship from all three books in this dialogue, as well as some special prayers and meditations on marriage—which, it turns out, You're *not* against!

I'm so happy, because it started to sound for a minute as if You were "anti-marriage."

How could I be against marriage? We are *all* married. We are married to *each other*—now, and forevermore. We are united. We are One. Ours is the biggest marriage ceremony ever held. My vow to you is the grandest vow ever made. I will love you forever, and free you for everything. My love will never bind you in any way, and because of this you are "bound" to eventually love Me—for freedom to Be Who You Are is your greatest desire, and My greatest gift.

Do you take Me now to be your lawfully wedded partner and co-creator, according to the highest laws of the universe?

I do.
And do *You* take *me* now as Your partner, and co-creator?

I do, and I always have. Now and through all eternity we are One. Amen.

And amen.

14

I am filled with awe and reverence at the reading of those words. Thank You for being here with me in this way. Thank You for being here with all of us. For millions have read the words in these dialogues, and millions more will yet do so. And we are breathlessly gifted by the coming of You to our hearts.

> My dearest beings—I have always been in your hearts. I am only glad you can now actually feel Me there.
> I have always been with you. I have never left you. I *am* you, and you are Me, and We shall *never* be separated, *ever,* because that is not *possible.*

Hey, wait a minute! This feels like *déjà vu.* Didn't we just say all of these words before?

> Of course! Read the beginning of Chapter 12. Only now they mean even more than they meant the first time.

Wouldn't it be neat if *déjà vu* was real, and that we really *are* sometimes experiencing something "over again" so that we can get more meaning out of it?

> What do you think?

I think that's *exactly* what's sometimes happening!

> Unless it's not.

Unless it's not!

> Good. Bravo again. You are moving so rapidly, so quickly, to massive new understandings that it is getting scary.

Yes, *isn't* it—? Now, I have something serious I need to discuss with You.

Yes, I know. Go ahead.

When does the soul join the body?

When do you think?

When it chooses to.

Good.

But people want a more definitive answer. They want to know when life begins. Life as they know it.

I understand.

So what is the signal? Is it the emergence of the body from the womb—the physical birth? Is it the moment of conception, the physical joining of the elements of physical life?

Life has no beginning, because life has no end. Life merely extends; creates new forms.

It must be like that gloppy material in those heated lava lamps that were so popular in the Sixties. The globs would lay in big, soft, round balls at the bottom, then rise from the heat, separating and forming new globs, shaping themselves as they rose, rejoining each other at the top, cascading together to form even larger globs of the all, and starting all over again. There were never any "new" globs in the tube. It was all the *same stuff,* reforming itself into what "looked like" *new* and *different stuff.* The varieties were endless, and it was fascinating to watch the process unfold over and over again.

That's a great metaphor. That's how it is with souls. The One Soul—which is really All There Is—reforms Itself into smaller and smaller parts of Itself. All the "parts" were there at the beginning. There are no "new" parts, merely portions of the All That Always Was, reforming Itself into what "looks like" new and different parts.

There's a brilliant pop song written and performed by Joan Osborne that asks, "What if God was one of us? Just a slob like one of us?" I'm going to have to ask her to change the lyric line to: "What if God was one of us? Just a glob like one of us?"

Ha! That's very good. And you know, her song *was* a brilliant song. It pushed people's buttons all over the place. People couldn't stand the thought that I am no better than one of them.

That reaction is an interesting comment, not so much on God, but on the human race. If we consider it a blasphemy for God to be compared to one of us, what does that say about us?

What, indeed?

Yet You *are* "one of us." That's exactly what You're saying here. So Joan was right.

She certainly was. Profoundly right.

I want to get back to my question. Can You tell us anything about when life as we know it starts? At what point does the soul enter the body?

The soul doesn't enter the body. The body is enveloped by the soul. Remember what I said before? The body does not house the soul. It is the other way around.

Everything is always alive. There is no such thing as "dead." There is no such state of being.

That Which Is Always Alive simply shapes itself into a new form—a new physical form. That form is charged with living energy, the energy of life, always.

Life—if you are calling life the energy that I Am—is always there. It is never *not* there. Life never *ends,* so how can there be a point when life *begins?*

C'mon, help me out here. You know what I'm trying to get at.

Yes, I do. You want Me to enter the abortion debate.

Yes, I do! I admit it! I mean, I've got God here, and I have a chance to ask the monumental question. When does life begin?

And the answer is so monumental, you can't hear it.

Try me again.

It *never* begins. Life *never* "begins," because life never *ends.* You want to get into biological technicalities so that you can make up a "rule" based on what you want to call "God's law" about how people should behave—then punish them if they do not behave that way.

What's wrong with that? That would allow us to kill doctors in the parking lots of clinics with impunity.

Yes, I understand. You have used Me, and what *you* have declared to be *My laws*, as justification for all sorts of things through the years.

Oh, come on! Why won't You just say that terminating a pregnancy is murder!

You cannot kill anyone or anything.

No. But you can end its "individuation"! And in our language, that's *killing*.

You cannot stop the process wherein which a part of Me individually expresses in a certain way without the part of Me that is expressing in that way agreeing.

What? What are You saying?

I am saying that nothing happens against the will of God.

Life, and all that is occurring, is an expression of God's will—read that, *your* will—made manifest.

I have said in this dialogue, your will is My will. That is because there is only One of Us.

Life is God's will, *expressing perfectly.* If something was happening *against* God's will, it couldn't happen. By definition of Who and What God Is, it *couldn't happen.* Do you believe that one soul can somehow *decide something* for another? Do you believe that, as individuals, you can affect each other in ways in which the other does not want to be affected? Such a belief would have to be based on the idea that you are separate from each other.

Do you believe that you can somehow affect life in a way in which God does not want life to be affected? Such a belief would have to be based on an idea that you are separate from Me.

Both ideas are false.

It is arrogant beyond measure for you to believe that you can affect the universe in a way with which the universe does not agree.

You are dealing with mighty forces here, and some of you believe that you are mightier than the mightiest force. Yet you are not. Nor are you *less* mighty than the mightiest force.

You *are* the mightiest force. No more, no less. So let the force be with you!

Are You saying that I can't kill anybody without his or her permission? Are You telling me that, at some higher level, everyone who has ever been killed has *agreed* to be killed?

You are looking at things in earthly terms and thinking of things in earthly terms, and none of this is going to make sense to you.

I can't *help* thinking in "earthly terms." I am *here*, right *now*, on the Earth!

I tell you this: You are "in this world, but not of it."

So my earthly reality is not reality at all?

Did you really think it was?

I don't know.

You've never thought, "There's something larger going on here"?

Well, yes, sure I have.

Well *this is what's going on. I'm explaining it to you.*

Okay. I got it. So I guess I can just go out now and kill anybody, because I couldn't have done it anyway if they hadn't agreed!

In fact, the human race acts that way. It's interesting that you're having such a hard time with this, yet you're going around acting as if it were true anyway.

Or, worse yet, you are killing people *against* their will, as if it didn't matter!

Well, of *course* it matters! It's just that what we want matters *more*. Don't You get it? In the moment we humans kill somebody, we are not saying that the fact that we've done that doesn't matter. Why, it would be flippant to think that. It's just that what *we* want matters *more*.

> I see. So it's easier for you to accept that it's okay to kill others *against* their will. This you can do with impunity. It's doing it because *it is* their will that you feel is wrong.

I never said that. That's not how humans think.

> It isn't? Let Me show you how hypocritical some of you are. You say it is okay to kill somebody *against* their will so long as *you* have a good and sufficient *reason* for wanting them dead, as in war, for instance, or an execution—or a doctor in the parking lot of an abortion clinic. Yet if the other person feels *they* have a good and sufficient reason for wanting *themselves* dead, you may not help them die. That would be "assisted suicide," and that would be wrong!

You are making mock of me.

> No, *you* are making mock of *Me*. You are saying that I would *condone* your killing someone *against* his will, and that I would *condemn* your killing someone in *accordance* with his will.
> *This is insane.*
> Still, you not only fail to see the insanity, you actually claim that those who *point out the insanity* are the ones who are crazy. *You* are the ones who have your head on straight, and they are just troublemakers.
> And this is the kind of tortured logic with which you construct *entire lives* and *complete theologies*.

I've never looked at it quite that way.

> I tell you this: The time has come for you to look at things a new way. This is the moment of your rebirth, as an individual and as a society. You must re-create your world now, before you destroy it with your insanities.
> Now *listen to Me*.
> We are All One.
> There is only One of Us.

You are not separate from Me, and you are not separate from each other.

Everything We are doing, We are doing in concert with each other. Our reality is a co-created reality. If you terminate a pregnancy, We terminate a pregnancy. Your will is My will.

No individual aspect of Divinity has power over any other aspect of Divinity. It is not possible for one soul to affect another against its will. There are no victims and there are no villains.

You cannot understand this from your limited perspective; but I am telling you it is so.

There is only one reason to be, do, or have anything—as a direct statement of Who You Are. If Who You Are, as an individual and as a society, is who you choose and desire to be, there is no reason to change anything. If, on the other hand, you believe there is a grander experience waiting to be had—an even greater expression of Divinity than the one currently manifesting—then move into that truth.

Since all of Us are co-creating, it may serve Us to do what we can to show others the way that some parts of Us wish to go. You can be a way-show-er, demonstrating the life that you'd like to create, and inviting others to follow your example. You might even say, "I am the life and the way. Follow me." But be careful. Some people have been crucified for making such statements.

Thank You. I'll heed the warning. I'll keep a low profile.

I can see that you're doing a real good job of that.

Well, when you say you're having a conversation with God, it's not easy to keep a low profile.

As others have discovered.

Which might be a good reason to keep my mouth shut.

It's a little late for that.

Well, whose fault is that?

I see what you mean.

It's okay. I forgive You.

You do?

Yes.

How can you forgive Me?

Because I can understand why You did it. I understand why You came to me, and started this dialogue. And when I understand why something was done, I can forgive all the complications that it may have caused or created.

Hmmm. Now that's interesting. Would that you could think of God as being so magnificent as you.

Touché.

You have an unusual relationship with Me. In some ways you think you could never be as magnificent as Me, and in other ways you think I cannot be as magnificent as you.
Don't you find that interesting?

Fascinating.

It's because you think We are separated. These imaginings would leave you if you thought that We were One.
This is the main difference between your culture—which is a "baby" culture, really; a primitive culture—and the highly evolved cultures of the universe. The most significant difference is that in highly evolved cultures, all sentient beings are clear that there is no separation between themselves and what you call "God."
They are also clear that there is no separation between themselves and others. They know that they are each having an individual experience of the whole.

Oh, good. Now You're going to get into the highly evolved societies of the universe. I've been waiting for this.

Yes, I think it's time we explored that.

But before we do, I simply must return one last time to the abortion issue. You're not saying here that, because nothing can happen to the human soul against its will, it's okay to kill people, are You? You're not condoning abortion, or giving us a "way out" on this issue, are You?

I am neither condoning nor condemning abortion, any more than I condone or condemn war.

The people of every country think I condone the war they are fighting, and condemn the war that their opponent is fighting. The people of every nation believe they have "God on their side." Every cause assumes the same thing. Indeed, every *person* feels the same thing—or at least *hopes* it is true whenever any decision or choice is made.

And do you know *why* all creatures believe God is on their side? *Because I am.* And all creatures have an intuitive knowing of this.

This is just another way of saying, "Your will for you is My will for you." And *that* is just another way of saying, I have given you all *free will*.

There is no free will if to exercise it in certain ways produces punishment. That makes a mockery of free will and renders it counterfeit.

So with regard to abortion or war, buying that car or marrying that person, having sex or not having sex, "doing your duty" or not "doing your duty," there is no such thing as right and wrong, and I have no preference in the matter.

You are all in the process of defining yourselves. Every act is an act of self-definition.

If you are pleased with how you have created yourself, if it serves you, you will continue doing so in that way. If you are not, you will stop. This is called evolution.

The process is slow because, as you evolve, you keep changing your ideas about what really serves you; you keep changing your concepts of "pleasure."

Remember what I said earlier. You can tell how highly a person or society has evolved by what that being or society calls "pleasure." And I will add here, by what it declares to serve it.

If it serves you to go to war and kill other beings, you will do so. If it serves you to terminate a pregnancy, you will do so. The only thing that changes as you evolve is your idea of what serves you. And that is based on what you think you are trying to do.

If you are trying to get to Seattle, it will not serve you to head toward San Jose. It is not "morally wrong" to go to San Jose—it simply doesn't serve you.

The question of what you are trying to do, then, becomes a question of *prime importance*. Not just in your life in general, but in every *moment* of your life specifically. Because it is in the *moments* of life that a life itself is created.

All of this was covered in great detail in the beginning of our holy dialogue, which you have come to call *Book 1*. I am repeating it here because you seem to need a reminder, or you would never have asked Me your question on abortion.

When you are preparing to have your abortion, therefore, or when you are preparing to smoke that cigarette, or when you are preparing to fry and eat that animal, and when you are preparing to cut that man off in traffic—whether the matter is large or small, whether the choice is major or minor, there is only one question to consider: Is this Who I Really Am? Is this who I now choose to be?

And understand this: *No matter is inconsequential.* There is a consequence to everything. The consequence is who and what you are.

You are in the act of defining your Self right now.

That is your answer to the abortion question. That is your answer to the war question. That is your answer to the smoking question and the meat-eating question and to *every question about behavior you've ever had.*

Every act is an act of self-definition. Everything you think, say, and do declares, "This is Who I Am."

15

I want to tell you, My dearest children, that this matter of Who You Are, and Who You Choose To Be, is of great importance. Not only because it sets the tone of your experience, but because it creates the nature of Mine.

All of your life you have been told that God created you. I come now to tell you this: You are creating God.

That is a massive rearrangement of your understanding, I know. And yet it is a necessary one if you are to go about the true work for which you came.

This is holy work We are up to, you and I. This is sacred ground We walk.

This is The Path.

In every moment God expresses Himself in, as, and through you. You are always at choice as to how God will be created now, and She will never take that choice from you, nor will She punish you for making the "wrong" choice. Yet you are not without guidance in these matters, nor will you ever be. Built into you is an internal guidance system that shows you the way home. This is the voice that speaks to you always of your highest choice, that places before you your grandest vision. All you need do is heed that voice, and not abandon the vision.

Throughout your history I have sent you teachers. During every day and time have My messengers brought you glad tidings of great joy.

Holy scriptures have been written, and holy lives have been lived, that you might know of this eternal truth: You and I are One.

Now again I send you scriptures—you are holding one of them in your hands. Now again I send you messengers, seeking to bring you the Word of God.

Will you listen to these words? Will you hear these messengers? Will you become one of them?

That is the great question. That is the grand invitation. That is the glorious decision. The world awaits your announcement. And you make that announcement with your life, lived.

The human race has no chance to lift itself from its own lowest thoughts until you lift yourself to your own highest ideas.

Those ideas, expressed through you, as you, create the template, set the stage, serve as a model for the next level of human experience.

You are the life and the way. The world will follow you. You are not at choice in this matter. It is the only matter in which you have no free choice. It is simply The Way It Is. Your world will follow your idea about yourself. Ever it has been, ever it will be. First comes your thought about yourself, then follows the outer world of physical manifestation.

What you think, you create. What you create, you become. What you become, you express. What you express, you experience. What you experience, you are. What you are, you think.

The circle is complete.

The holy work in which you are engaged has really just begun, for now, at last, you understand what you are doing.

It is you who have caused yourself to know this, you who have caused yourself to care. And you do care now, more than ever before, about Who You Really Are. For now, at last, you see the whole picture.

Who you are, I am.

You are defining God.

I have sent you—a blessed part of Me—into physical form that I might know Myself experientially as all that I know Myself to be conceptually. Life exists as a tool for God to turn concept into experience. It exists for you to do the same. For you are God, doing this.

I choose to re-create Myself anew in every single moment. I choose to experience the grandest version of the greatest vision ever I had about Who I Am. I have created you, so that you might re-create Me. This is Our holy work. This is Our greatest joy. This is Our very reason for being.

16

I am filled with awe and reverence at the reading of those words. Thank You for being here with me in this way. Thank You for being here with all of us.

> You are welcome. Thank *you* for being here for *Me*.

I have just a few remaining questions, some having to do with those "evolved beings," and then I will allow myself to finish this dialogue.

> My Beloved, you will *never* finish this dialogue, nor will you ever have to. Your conversation with God will go on forever. And, now that you are actively engaged in it, that conversation will soon lead to friendship. All good conversations eventually lead to friendship, and soon your conversation with God will produce a *Friendship with God*.

I feel that. I feel that we've actually become *friends*.

> And, as happens in all relationships, that friendship, if it is nurtured, kindled, and allowed to grow, will produce, at last, a sense of communion. You will feel and experience your Self as being in *Communion with God*.
>
> This will be a Holy Communion, for then We will speak as One.

And so this dialogue will continue?

> Yes, always.

And I won't have to say goodbye at the end of this book?

> You never have to say goodbye. You only have to say hello.

You're marvelous, do You know that? You're simply marvelous.

> And so are you, My son. And so are you.

As are all My children, everywhere.

Do You have children "everywhere"?

Of course.

No, I mean literally, *everywhere.* Is there life on other planets? Are Your children elsewhere in the universe?

Again, of course.

Are these civilizations more advanced?

Some of them, yes.

In what way?

In every way. Technologically. Politically. Socially. Spiritually. Physically. And psychologically.

For instance, your penchant for, your insistence upon, comparisons, and your constant need to characterize something as "better" or "worse," "higher" or "lower," "good" or "bad" demonstrates how far into duality you have fallen; how deeply into separatism you have submerged.

In more advanced civilizations You do not observe these characteristics? And what do You mean by duality?

The level of a society's advancement is reflected, inevitably, in the degree of its duality thinking. Social evolution is demonstrated by movement towards unity, not separatism.

Why? Why is unity such a yardstick?

Because unity is the truth. Separatism is the illusion. As long as a society sees itself as separate—a series or collection of separate units—it lives in the illusion.

All of life on your planet is built on separatism; based in duality.

You imagine yourselves to be separate families or clans, gathered in separate neighborhoods or states, collected in separate nations or countries, comprising a separate world, or planet.

You imagine your world to be the only inhabited world in the universe. You imagine your nation to be the finest nation on earth.

You imagine your state to be the best state in the nation, and your family the most wonderful in the state.

Finally, you think that *you* are better than anyone else in your family.

Oh, you claim you *don't* think any of this, but *you act as if you do.*

Your true thoughts are reflected every day in your social decisions, your political conclusions, your religious determinations, your economic choices, and your individual selections of everything from friends to belief systems to your very relationship with God. That is, Me.

You feel so separate from Me that you imagine I won't even talk to you. And so you are required to deny the veracity of your own experience. You *experience* that you and I are One, but you refuse to *believe* it. Thus you are separate not only from each other, but from your own truth.

How can a person be separate from his or her own truth?

By ignoring it. By seeing it and denying it. Or by changing it, twisting it, contorting it to fit a preconceived notion you have about what must be so.

Take the question with which you started off here. You asked, is there life on other planets? I answered, "Of course." I said, "Of *course*" because the evidence is so obvious. It is so obvious that I'm surprised you even asked the question.

Yet this is how a person can be "separate from his own truth": by looking truth in the eye so squarely he can't miss it—and then denying what he sees.

Denial is the mechanism here. And nowhere is denial more insidious than in self-denial.

You've spent a lifetime denying Who and What You Really Are.

It would be sad enough if you limited your denials to less personal things, such as your depletion of the ozone layer, your rape of old-growth forests, your horrible treatment of your young. But you are not content with denying all that you see around you. You won't rest until you deny all that you see *within* you as well.

You see goodness and compassion within you, but you deny it. You see wisdom within you, but you deny it. You see infinite possibility within you, but you deny it. And you see and experience God within you, yet you deny it.

You deny that I am within you—that I *am* you—and in this you deny Me My rightful and obvious place.

I have not, and do not, deny You.

You admit that You are God?

Well, I wouldn't say *that*...

Exactly. And I tell you this: *"Before the cock crows, you will deny Me three times."*

By your very thoughts will you deny Me.

By your very words will you deny Me.

By your very actions will you deny Me.

You *know in your heart* that I am with you, in you; that We are One. Yet you deny Me.

Oh, some of you say I exist all right. But away from you. Way out *there* somewhere. And the further away you imagine Me to be, the further away you step from your own truth.

As with so much else in life—from depletion of your planet's natural resources to the abuse of children in so many of your homes—you see it, but you don't believe it.

But why? *Why?* Why do we see, and yet not believe?

Because you are so caught up in the illusion, you are so deep in the illusion, that you cannot see past it. Indeed, you *must* not for the illusion to continue. This is the Divine Dichotomy.

You *must* deny Me if you are to continue seeking to *become* Me. And that is what you are wanting to do. Yet you cannot become what you already are. So denial is important. It is a useful tool.

Until it is not anymore.

The master knows that denial is for those who are choosing to have the illusion continue. Acceptance is for those who choose now for the illusion to end.

Acceptance, proclamation, demonstration. Those are the *three steps* to God. Acceptance of Who and What You Really Are. Proclamation of it for all the world to hear. And demonstration in every way.

Self-proclamation is *always* followed by demonstration. You will *demonstrate* your Self to be God—even as you now demonstrate what you think of your Self. Your whole life is a demonstration of that.

Yet with this demonstration will come your greatest challenge. For the moment you stop denying your Self, others will deny *you*.

The moment you proclaim your Oneness with God, others will proclaim your partnership with Satan.

The moment you speak the highest truth, others will say you speak the lowest blasphemy.

And, as happens with all masters who gently demonstrate their mastery, you will be both worshipped and reviled, elevated and denigrated, honored and crucified. Because while for you the cycle will be over, those who are still living in the illusion will not know what to make of you.

Yet what will happen to me? I don't understand. I'm confused. I thought You've said, over and over again, that the illusion must go on, that the "game" must continue, in order for there to be any "game" at all?

Yes, I have said that. And it does. The game does go on. Because one or two of you end the cycle of illusion, that does not end the game—not for you, and not for the other players.

The game is not ended until All-in-All becomes One again. Even then it is not ended. For in the moment of divine reunion, All with All, will the bliss be so magnificent, so intense, that I-We-You will literally burst wide open with gladness, exploding with joy—and the cycle will begin all over again.

It will *never* end, My child. The game will *never* end. For the game is life itself, and life is Who We Are.

But what happens to the individual element, or "Part of All," as You call it, which rises to mastery, which achieves all-knowing?

That master knows that only his part of the cycle is complete. She knows that only her experience of the illusion has ended.

Now the master laughs, because the master sees the master plan. The master sees that even with her completion of the cycle, the game goes on; the experience continues. The master then also sees the role he may now play in the experience. The master's role is to lead others to mastery. And so the master continues to play, but in a new way, and with new tools. For seeing the illusion allows the master to step outside of it. This the master will do from time to time when it suits his purpose and pleasure. Thus she proclaims and demonstrates her mastery, and he is called God/Goddess by others.

When all in your race are led to mastery and achieve it, then your race as a whole (for your race *is* a whole) will move easily through time and space (you will have mastered the laws of physics as you understood them) and you will seek to assist those belonging to other races and other civilizations in coming to mastery as well.

Even as those of other races and other civilizations are doing so now, with us?

Exactly. Precisely.

And only when all the races of all the universe have achieved mastery—

—or, as I would put it, only when All of Me has known the Oneness—

—will this part of the cycle end.

You have put it wisely. For the cycle itself will *never* end.

Because the very ending of this part of the cycle is the cycle itself!

Bravo! *Magnifico!*
You have understood!
So yes, there is life on other planets. And yes, much of it is more advanced than your own.

In what way? You never really did answer that question.

Yes I did. I said, in every way. Technologically. Politically. Socially. Spiritually. Physically. Psychologically.

Yes, but give me some examples. Those are statements so broad that they are meaningless to me.

You know, I love your truth. It's not everyone who would look God in the eye and announce that what He is saying is meaningless.

So? What are you going to do about it?

Exactly. You have exactly the right attitude. Because, of course, you're right. You can challenge Me, confront Me, and call Me into question as much as you want, and I'm not going to do a damned thing.

I may, however, do a blessed thing, such as I'm doing here, with this dialogue. Is this not a blessed event?

Yes, this is. And many people have been helped by this. Millions of people have been, are being, touched by this.

I know that. It's all part of the "master plan." The plan for how you become masters.

You knew from the beginning that this trilogy would be a massive success, didn't You?

Of course I did. Who do you suppose has made it such a success? Who do you imagine has caused those people who are reading this to have found their way to it?

I tell you this: I know every person who will come to this material. And I know the reason each has been brought.

And so do they.

Now the only question is, will they deny Me again?

Does it matter to You?

Not in the least. All My children will one day come back to Me. It is not a question of whether, but of *when.* And so, it may matter to them. Therefore, let those who have ears to hear, listen.

Yes, well—we were talking about life on other planets, and You were about to give me some examples of how it is so much more advanced than life on Earth.

Technologically, most other civilizations are far ahead of you. There are those which are behind you, so to speak, but not many. Most are far ahead of you.

In what way? *Give me an example.*

Okay, the weather. You don't seem able to control it. (You can't even accurately predict it!) You are, therefore, subject to its whims.

Most worlds are not. The beings on most planets can control the local temperature, for example.

They can? I thought temperature on a planet was a product of its distance from its sun, its atmosphere, etc.

Those things establish the parameters. Within those parameters much can be done.

How so? In what way?

By controlling the environment. By creating, or failing to create, certain conditions in the atmosphere.

You see, it is not only a matter of where you are in relationship to a sun, but what you place *between* yourself and that sun.

You have placed the most dangerous things in your atmosphere—and taken out some of the most important. Yet you are in denial about this. That is, most of you will not admit it. Even when the finest minds among you prove beyond doubt the damage you are doing, you will not acknowledge it. You call the finest minds among you crazed, and say that you know better.

Or you say that these wise people only have an ax to grind, a point of view to validate, and their own interests to protect. Yet it is *you* who are grinding an ax. It is *you* who are seeking to validate a point of view. And it is *you* who are protecting your special interests.

And your chief interest is yourself. Every evidence, no matter how scientific, no matter how demonstrable or compelling, will be denied if it violates your self-interest.

That's a rather harsh statement, and I'm not sure it's true.

Really? Now you're calling God a liar?

Well, I wouldn't put it that way, exactly. . . .

Do you know how long it has taken your nations to agree to simply stop poisoning the atmosphere with fluorocarbons?

Yes . . . Well . . .

Well, nothing. Why do you suppose it took so long? Never mind. I'll tell you. It took so long because to stop the poisoning would cost many major companies a great deal of money. It took

so long because it would cost many individual people their con-
veniences.

It took so long because for years many people and nations
chose to deny—*needed* to deny—the evidence in order to protect
their interest in the status quo; in keeping things the way they are.

Only when the rate of skin cancers increased alarmingly, only
when the temperatures began rising and the glaciers and snows
began melting, and the oceans got warmer and the lakes and rivers
began flooding, did more of you begin paying attention.

Only when *your own self-interest* demanded it, did you see the
truth that your finest minds had been placing before you for years.

What's wrong with self-interest? I thought You said in *Book 1* that self-interest was the place to start.

I did, and it is. Yet in other cultures and other societies on different planets, the definition of "self-interest" is much larger than it
is on your world. It is very clear to enlightened creatures that what
hurts one hurts the many, and that what benefits the few *must* benefit the many, or, ultimately, it benefits no one.

On your planet it is just the opposite. What hurts one is ignored
by the many, and what benefits the few is denied the many.

This is because your definition of self-interest is very narrow,
barely reaching past the individual being to his loved ones—and to
those only when they do his bidding.

Yes, I said in *Book 1* that in all relationships, do what is in the
best interests of the Self. But I also said that when you see what is
in your highest self-interest, you will see that it is that which is also
in the highest interest of the other—for you and the other are One.

You and all others are One—and this is a level of knowingness
that you have not attained.

You're asking about advanced technologies, and I tell you this:
You cannot have advanced technologies in any beneficial way
without advanced thinking.

*Advanced technology without advanced thought creates not
advancement, but demise.*

You have already experienced that on your planet, and you are
very nearly about to experience it again.

What do You mean? What are You talking about?

I am saying that once before on your planet you had reached the heights—beyond the heights, really—to which you now are slowly climbing. You had a civilization on Earth more advanced than the one now existing. And it destroyed itself.

Not only did it destroy itself, it nearly destroyed everything else as well.

It did this because it did not know how to deal with the very technologies it had developed. Its technological evolution was so far ahead of its spiritual evolution that it wound up making technology its God. The people worshipped technology, and all that it could create and bring. And so they got all that their unbridled technology brought—which was unbridled disaster.

They literally brought their world to an end.

This all happened here, on this Earth?

Yes.

Are You talking about the Lost City of Atlantis?

Some of you have called it that.

And Lemuria? The land of Mu?

That is also part of your mythology.

So then it *is* true! We did get to that place before!

Oh, beyond it, My friend. Way beyond it.

And we *did* destroy ourselves!

Why are you surprised? You're doing the same thing now.

I know we are. Will You tell us how we can stop?

There are many other books devoted to this subject. Most people ignore them.

Give us one title, I promise we won't ignore it.

Read *The Last Hours of Ancient Sunlight*.

By a man named Thom Hartmann. Yes! I love that book!

Good. This messenger is inspired. Bring this book to the attention of the world.

I will. I will.

It says everything that I would say here, in answer to your last
question. There is no need for Me to rewrite that book through
you.

It contains a summary of many of the ways in which your Earth
home is being damaged, and ways that you can stop the ruination.

**So far what the human race has been doing on this planet is not very
smart. In fact, throughout this dialogue You have described our species
as "primitive." Ever since You first made that remark I've been wonder-
ing what it must be like living in a *non*-primitive culture. You say there
are many such societies or cultures in the universe.**

Yes.

How many?

A great many.

Dozens? Hundreds?

Thousands.

Thousands? There are *thousands* of advanced civilizations?

Yes. And there are other cultures more primitive than yours.

What else marks a society as either "primitive" or "advanced"?

The degree to which it implements its own highest understandings.

This is different from what you believe. You believe that a society should be called primitive or advanced based on how high its
understandings *are*. But what good are the highest understandings
if you do not implement them?

The answer is, they are no good at all. Indeed, they are dangerous.

It is the mark of a primitive society to call regression progress.
Your society has moved backward, not forward. Much of your

world demonstrated more compassion seventy years ago than it does today.

Some people are going to have a hard time hearing this. You say You are a nonjudgmental God, yet some people may feel judged and made wrong all over the place here.

> We've been over this before. If you say you want to go to Seattle and you're actually driving to San Jose, is the person of whom you're asking directions being judgmental if you're told you're heading in a direction that won't get you where you say you want to go?

Calling us "primitive" is not simply giving us directions. The word *primitive* is pejorative.

> Really? And yet you say you so admire "primitive" art. And certain music is often savored, for its "primitive" qualities—to say nothing of certain women.

You're using word play now to change things around.

> Not at all. I'm merely showing you that "primitive" is not necessarily pejorative. It is your judgment that makes it so. "Primitive" is merely descriptive. It simply says what is true: A certain thing is in the very early stages of development. It says nothing more than that. It says nothing about "right" or "wrong." *You* add those meanings.
>
> I have not "made you wrong" here. I have merely described your culture as primitive. That would only "sound" wrong to you if you have a judgment about being primitive.
>
> I have no such judgment.
>
> Understand this: An assessment is not a judgment. It is merely an observation of What Is.
>
> I want you to know that I love you. I have no judgments about you. I look at you and see only beauty and wonder.

Like that primitive art.

> Precisely. I hear your melody and I feel only excitement.

As with primitive music.

You are understanding now. I feel the energy of your race as you would the energy of a man or woman of "primitive sensuality." And, like you, I am aroused.

Now *that* is what is true about you and Me. You do not disgust Me, you do not disturb Me, you do not even disappoint Me.

You *arouse* Me!

I am aroused to new possibilities, to new experiences yet to come. In you I am awakened to new adventures, and to the excitement of movement to new levels of magnificence.

Far from disappointing Me, you *thrill* Me! I am *thrilled* at the wonder of you. You think you are at the pinnacle of human development, and I tell you, *you are just beginning.* You have only just *begun* to experience your splendor!

Your grandest ideas are as yet unexpressed, and your grandest vision unlived.

But wait! Look! Notice! The days of your blossoming are at hand. The stalk has grown strong, and the petals are soon to open. And I tell you this: The beauty and the fragrance of your flowering shall fill the land, and you shall yet have your place in the Garden of the Gods.

17

Now *that's* what I want to hear! *That's* what I came here to experience! *Inspiration,* not degradation.

> You are never degraded unless you think you are. You are never judged or "made wrong" by God.

A lot of people don't "get" this idea of a God Who says, "There's no such thing as right and wrong," and Who proclaims that we will never be judged.

> Well, make up your mind! First you say I'm judging you, then you're upset because I'm *not.*

I know, I know. It's all very confusing. We're all very . . . complex. We don't want Your judgments, but we do. We don't want Your punishments, yet we feel lost without them. And when You say, as You did in the other two books, "I will never punish you," we cannot believe that—and some of us almost get mad about that. Because if You're not going to judge, and punish us, what will keep us walking the straight and narrow? And if there's no "justice" in heaven, who will undo all the injustice on Earth?

> Why are you counting on heaven to correct what you call "injustice"? Do not the rains fall from the heavens?

Yes.

> And I tell you this: The rain falls on the just and the unjust alike.

But what about, "Vengeance is Mine, sayeth the Lord"?

> I never said that. One of you made that up, and the rest of you believed it.

642

"Justice" is not something you experience *after* you act a certain way, but *because* you act a certain way. Justice is an *act,* not punishment *for* an act.

I see that the problem with our society is that we seek "justice" after an "injustice" has occurred, rather than "doing justice" in the first place.

Right on the head! You've hit the nail right on the head!

Justice is an action, not a *reaction.*

Do not, therefore, look to Me to somehow "fix everything in the end" by imposing some form of celestial justice in the "afterlife." I tell you this: There *is* no *"afterlife,"* but *only* life. Death does not exist. And the way you experience and create your life, as individuals and as a society, is your demonstration of what you think is just.

And in this You do not see the human race as very evolved, do You? I mean, if the whole of evolution were placed on a football field, where would we be?

On the 12-yard line.

You're kidding.

No.

We're on the *12-yard line* of evolution?

Hey, you've moved from the 6 to the 12 in the past century alone.

Any chance of ever scoring a touchdown?

Of course. If you don't fumble the ball again.

Again?

As I've said, this isn't the first time your civilization has been at this brink. I want to repeat this, because *it is vital that you hear this.*

Once before on your planet the technology you'd developed was far greater than your ability to use it responsibly. You're approaching the same point in human history again.

It's vitally important that you understand this.

Your present technology is threatening to outstrip your ability to use it wisely. Your society is on the verge of becoming a product of your technology, rather than your technology being a product of your society.

When a society becomes a product of its own technology, it destroys itself.

Why is that? Can You explain that?

Yes. The crucial issue is the balance between technology and cosmology—the cosmology of all life.

What do You mean by "the cosmology of all life"?

Simply put, it is the way things work. The System. The Process. There is a "method to My madness," you know.

I was hoping there was.

And the irony is that once you figure out that method, once you begin to understand more and more of how the universe works, you run a greater risk of causing a breakdown. In this way, ignorance can be bliss.

The universe is itself a technology. It is the *greatest* technology. It works perfectly. On its own. But once you get in there and start messing around with universal principles and universal laws, you run the risk of breaking those laws. And that's a 40-yard penalty.

A major setback for the home team.

Yes.

So, are we out of our league here?

You're getting close. Only you can determine whether you're out of your league. You'll determine that with your actions. For instance, you know enough about atomic energy now to blow yourselves to kingdom come.

Yes, but we're not going to do that. We're smarter than that. We'll stop ourselves.

Really? You keep proliferating your weapons of mass destruction the way you've been doing, and pretty soon they'll get into the hands of somebody who will hold the world hostage to them—or destroy the world trying.

You are giving matches to children, then hoping they won't burn the place down, and you've yet to learn how to *use the matches yourselves.*

The solution to all this is obvious. *Take the matches away from the children.* Then, *throw your own matches away.*

But it's too much to expect a primitive society to disarm itself. And so, nuclear disarmament—our only lasting solution—appears out of the question.

We can't even agree on a halt to nuclear testing. We are a race of beings singularly unable to control ourselves.

And if you don't kill yourselves with your nuclear madness, you'll destroy your world with your environmental suicide. You are dismantling your home planet's ecosystem and you continue to say that you're not.

As if that weren't enough, you're tinkering with the biochemistry of life itself. Cloning and genetically engineering, and not doing so with sufficient care to have this be a boon to your species, but threatening instead to make it the greatest disaster of all time. If you are not careful, you will make the nuclear and environmental threats look like child's play.

By developing medicines to do the work that your bodies were intended to do, you've created viruses so resistant to attack that they stand poised to knock out your entire species.

You're getting me a little scared here. Is all lost, then? Is the game over?

No, but it is fourth-and-ten. It's time to throw a Hail Mary, and the quarterback is looking around for receivers in the clear.

Are you clear? Are you able to receive this?

I'm the quarterback and the last time I looked, you and I were wearing the same color jersey. Are we still on the same team?

I thought there was only one team! Who is on the *other* team?

Every thought which ignores our oneness, every idea which separates us, every action which announces that we are not united. The "other team" is not real, yet it is a part of your reality, for you have made it so.

If you are not careful, your own technology—that which was created to serve you—will kill you.

Right now I can hear some people saying, "But what can one person do?"

They can start by dropping that "what can one person do?" stuff.

I've already told you, there are hundreds of books on this subject. *Stop ignoring them.* Read them. Act on them. Awaken others to them. Start a revolution. Make it an evolution revolution.

Isn't that what has been going on for a long time?

Yes, and no. The process of evolution has been ongoing forever, of course. But now that process is taking a new twist. There's a new turn here. Now you have become *aware* that you are evolving. And not only *that* you are evolving, but *how*. Now you know the *process by which evolution occurs*—and through which *your reality is created*.

Before, you were simply an observer of how your species was evolving. Now you are a conscious participant.

More people than ever before are aware of the power of the mind, their interconnectedness with all things, and their real identity as a spiritual being.

More people than ever before are living from that space, practicing principles that invoke and produce specific results, desired outcomes, and intended experiences.

This truly *is* an evolution revolution, for now larger and larger numbers of you are creating *consciously* the quality of your experience, the direct expression of Who You Really Are, and the rapid manifestation of Who You Choose to Be.

That's what makes this such a critical period. That's why this is the crucial moment. For the first time in your presently recorded history (although not for the first time in human experience), you have both the technology, and the understanding of how to use it, to destroy your entire world. You can actually render yourselves extinct.

These are the exact points made in a book by Barbara Marx Hubbard called *Conscious Evolution*.

Yes, that is so.

It's a document of breathtaking sweep, with wondrous visions of how we can avoid the dire outcomes of previous civilizations, and truly produce heaven on Earth. You probably inspired it!

I think Barbara might say that I had a hand in it. . . .

You said before that You've inspired hundreds of writers—many messengers. Are there other books we should be aware of?

Way too many to list here. Why not conduct your own search? Then, make a list of the ones that have particularly appealed to you, and share that with others.

I have been speaking through authors, poets, and playwrights from the beginning of time. I have placed my truth in the lyrics of songs, and on the faces of paintings, in the shapes of sculptures, and in every beat of the human heart for ages past. And I will for ages to come.

Each person comes to wisdom in a way that is most understandable, along a path that is most familiar. Each messenger of God derives truth from the simplest moments, and shares it with equal simplicity.

You are such a messenger. Go now and tell your people to live together in their highest truth. Share together their wisdom. Experience together their love. For they *can* exist in peace and harmony.

Then will yours, too, be an elevated society, such as those we have been discussing.

So the main difference between our society and more highly evolved civilizations elsewhere in the universe is this idea we have of separation.

Yes. The first guiding principle of advanced civilization is unity. Acknowledgment of the Oneness, and the sacredness of all life. And so what we find in all elevated societies is that under no circumstances would one being willfully take the life of another of its own species against its will.

No circumstances?

None.

Even if it were being attacked?

Such a circumstance would not occur within that society or species.

Perhaps not within the species, but what about from without?

If a highly evolved species were attacked by another, it is a guarantee that the attacker would be the lesser evolved. Indeed, the attacker would be, essentially, a primitive being. For no evolved being would attack anyone.

I see.

The only reason a species under attack would kill another would be that the attacked being forgot Who It Really Is.

If the first being thought it was its corporal body—its physical *form*—then it might kill its attacker, for it would fear the "end of its own life."

If, on the other hand, the first being understood full well that it was *not* its body, it would never end the corporal existence of another—for it would never have a reason to. It would simply lay down its own corporal body and move into the experience of its noncorporal self.

Like Obi-Wan Kenobi!

Well, exactly. The writers of what you call your "science fiction" are often leading you to greater truth.

I've got to stop here. This seems directly at variance with what was said in *Book 1.*

What was that?

Book 1 said that when someone is abusing you, it does no good to allow the abuse to continue. *Book 1* said that, when acting with love, include *yourself* among those you love. And the book seemed to say, do whatever it takes to stop the attack on you. It even said that *war* was okay as a response to attack—that, and this is a direct quote: ". . . despots cannot be allowed to flourish, but must be stopped in their despotism."

It also says that "choosing to be God-like does not mean you choose to be a martyr. And it certainly does not mean you choose to be a victim."

Now You are saying that highly *evolved* beings would *never* end the corporal life of another. How can these statements stand side by side?

Read the material in *Book 1* again. Closely.

My responses there were all given, and must all be considered, within the context you created; the context of your question.

Read your statement on the bottom of page 127 in *Book 1*. In that statement you allow as to how you are not now operating at a level of mastery. You say that other people's words and actions sometimes hurt you. Given that this is so, you asked how best to respond to these experiences of hurt or damage.

My responses are all to be taken within that context.

I first of all said that the day will come when the words and actions of others will *not* hurt you. Like Obi-Wan Kenobi, you will experience no damage, even when someone is "killing" you.

This is the level of mastery that has been reached by the members of the societies I am now describing. The beings in these societies are very clear Who They Are and who they are not. It is very difficult to cause one of them to experience being "damaged," or "hurt," least of all by placing their corporal *body* in danger. They would simply *exit* their body and leave it for you, if you felt the need to hurt it so much.

The next point I made in My response to you in *Book 1* is that you react the way *you* do to the words and actions of others because you have forgotten Who You Are. But, I say there, that is all right. That is part of the growth process. It is part of evolution.

Then I make a very important statement. All during your growth process "you must work at the level at which you are. The level of understanding, the level of willingness, the level of remembrance."

Everything else I have said there is to be taken within that context.

I have even said, on page 129, "I assume for the purpose of this discussion that you are still . . . seeking to realize (make 'real') Who You Truly Are."

Within the context of a society of beings who do not remember Who They Really Are, the responses I gave you in *Book 1* stand as given. But you didn't ask Me those questions here. You asked Me here to describe the *highly evolved societies of the universe.*

Not only with regard to the subject at hand, but with regard to all the other topics we will cover here, it will be beneficial if you do not see these descriptions of other cultures as criticisms of your own.

There are no judgments here. Nor will there be any condemnation if you do things differently—react differently—than beings who are more evolved.

And so what I have said here is that the highly evolved beings of the universe would never "kill" another sentient being in anger. First they would not *experience* anger. Second, they would not end the corporal experience of any other being without that being's permission. And third—to answer specifically your specific inquiry—they would never feel "attacked," even from outside their own society or species, because to feel "attacked" you have to feel that someone is taking something from you—your life, your loved ones, your freedom, your property, or possessions—*something*. And a highly evolved being would never experience that, because a highly evolved being would simply *give you* whatever you thought you needed so badly that you were prepared to take it by force—even if it cost the evolved being its corporal life—because the evolved being knows she can *create everything all over again*. She would quite naturally give it all away to a lesser being who did not know this.

Highly evolved beings are therefore not martyrs, nor are they victims of anyone's "despotism."

Yet it goes beyond this. Not only is the highly evolved being clear that he can create everything all over again, he is also clear that he *doesn't have to*. He is clear that he needed none of it to be happy, or to survive. He understands that he requires nothing exterior to himself, and that the "himself" which he *is* has nothing to do with anything physical.

Lesser evolved beings and races are not always clear about this.

Finally, the highly evolved being understands that she and her attackers are One. She sees the attackers as a wounded part of her Self. Her function in that circumstance is to heal all wounds, so that the All In One can again know itself as it really is.

Giving away all that she has would be like giving yourself an aspirin.

Whoa. What a concept. What an understanding! But I need to go back to something You said earlier. You said that highly evolved beings—

—Let's abbreviate that as "HEBs" from here on. It's a long name to have to use over and over again.

Good. Well, You said that "HEBs" would never end the corporal experience of another being without the being's permission.

>That's right.

But why would one being give another being permission to end its physical life?

>There could be any number of reasons. It might offer itself as food, for instance. Or to serve some other necessity—like stopping a war.

This must be why, even in our own cultures, there are those who would not kill any animal for food or hides without asking the spirit of that being for permission.

>Yes. This is the way of your Native Americans, who would not even pick a flower, an herb, or a plant without having this communication. All of your indigenous cultures do the same. Interestingly, those are the tribes and cultures that *you* call "primitive."

Oh, man, are You telling me I can't even pick a radish without asking if it's okay?

>You can do anything you choose to do. You asked Me what "HEBs" would do.

So Native Americans are highly evolved beings?

>As with all races and species, some are, and some are not. It is an individual thing. As a culture, though, they have reached a very high level. The cultural myths which inform much of their experience are very elevated. But, you have forced them to mix their cultural myths with your own.

Wait a minute! What are You *saying*? The Red Man was a savage! That's why we had to kill them by the thousands, and put the rest in land-prisons we call reservations! Why, even now we take their sacred sites and put golf courses on them. We *have* to. Otherwise they might *honor* their sacred sites, and *remember* their cultural stories, and *perform* their sacred rituals, and we can't have that.

>I get the picture.

No, really. Why, if we hadn't taken over and tried to erase their culture, they might have impacted *ours!* Then how would we have wound up?

We'd be respecting the land and the air, refusing to poison our rivers, and then where would our industry be!

The whole population would probably still be walking around naked, with *no shame,* bathing in the river, living off the land, instead of crowding into high-rises and condominiums and bungalows and going to work in the asphalt jungle.

Why, we'd probably still be listening to ancient wisdom teachings around a campfire instead of watching TV! We would have made *no progress at all.*

Well, fortunately, you know what's good for you.

18

Tell me more about highly evolved civilizations and highly evolved beings. Outside of the fact that they don't kill each other for any reason, what else makes them different from us?

They share.

Hey, *we* share!

No, they share *everything*. With *everyone*. Not a being goes without. All the natural resources of their world, of their environment, are divided equally, and distributed to everyone.

A nation or a group or a culture isn't thought to "own" a natural resource simply because it happens to occupy the physical location where that resource is found.

The planet (or planets) which a group of species calls "home" is understood to belong to everyone—to all the species in that system. Indeed, the planet or group of planets *itself* is understood to be a "system." It is viewed as a whole system, not as a bunch of little parts or elements, any one of which can be eliminated, decimated, or eradicated without damage to the system itself.

The *ecosystem*, as we call it.

Well, it's larger than that. It's not just the ecology—which is the relationship of the planet's natural resources to the planet's inhabitants. It's also the relationship of the *inhabitants* to themselves, to each other, and to the environment.

It's the *interrelationship* of *all the species of life*.

The "speciesystem"!

Yes! I like that word! It's a good word! Because what we're talking about is larger than the ecosystem. It's truly the *speciesystem*. Or what your Buckminster Fuller called the *noosphere*.

I like *speciesystem* better. It's easier to understand. I always wondered what in blazes the *noosphere* was!

"Bucky" likes your word, too. He's not attached. He always liked whatever made things simpler or easier.

You're talking to Buckminster Fuller now? You've turned this dialogue into a séance?

Let's just say I have reason to know that the essence which identified itself as Buckminster Fuller is delighted with your new word.

Wow, that's great. I mean, that's so cool—to just be able to know that.

It is "cool." I agree.

So in highly evolved cultures it's the *speciesystem* that matters.

Yes, but it isn't that individual beings *don't* matter. Quite to the contrary. The fact that individual beings *do* matter is reflected in the fact that effect on the *speciesystem* is uppermost when considering any decision.

It is understood that the *speciesystem* supports all life, and *every being*, at the optimum level. Doing nothing that would harm the speciesystem is therefore *a statement that each individual being is important.*

Not only the individual beings with status or influence or money. Not only the individual beings with power or size or the presumption of greater self-awareness. *All* beings, and all species, in the system.

How can that work? How can that be possible? On our planet, the wants and needs of some species *have* to be subordinated to the wants and needs of others, or we couldn't experience life as we know it.

You are moving dangerously close to the time when you will *not* be able to experience "life as you know it" precisely *because* you have insisted on subordinating the needs of most species to the desires of only one.

The human species.

Yes—and not even all *members* of that species, but only a few. Not even the largest number (which might have some logic to it), but by far the *smallest*.

The richest and the most powerful.

You've called it.

Here we go. Another tirade against the rich and the accomplished.

Far from it. Your civilization does not deserve a tirade; any more than a roomful of small children deserves one. Human beings will do what they are doing—to themselves and to each other—until they realize that it is no longer in their best interests. No amount of tirades will change that.

If tirades changed things, your religions would have been far more effective long before now.

Whoa! Zip! Zing! You're getting everyone today, aren't You?

I'm doing nothing of the sort. Are these simple observations stinging you? Look, then, to see why. This much we both know. The truth is often uncomfortable. Yet this book has come to bring the truth. As have others which I have inspired. And movies. And television programs.

I'm not sure I want to encourage people to watch television.

For better or worse, television is now the campfire of your society. It is not the *medium* that is taking you in directions you say you do not wish to go, it is the messages you allow to be placed there. Do not denounce the medium. You may use it one day yourself, to send a different message. . . .

Let me get back, if I can . . . can I get back to my original question here? I'm still wanting to know how a *speciesystem* can work with the needs of all species in the system treated equally.

The needs are all treated equally, but the needs themselves are not all equal. It is a question of proportion, and of balance.

Highly evolved beings deeply understand that all living things within what we have chosen here to call the *speciesystem* have needs which must be met if the physical forms that both create and sustain the system are to survive. They also understand that not all these needs are the same, or equal, in terms of the demands they place on the system itself.

Let's use your own *speciesystem* as an example.

Okay. . . .

Let's use the two living species you call "trees" and "humans."

I'm with You.

Obviously, trees do not require as much daily "maintenance" as humans. So their needs are not equal. Yet they *are* interrelated. That is, one species depends on the other. You must pay as much attention to the needs of trees as to the needs of humans, but the needs themselves are not as great. Yet if you ignore the needs of one species of living thing, you do so at your peril.

The book I mentioned earlier as being of critical importance—*The Last Hours of Ancient Sunlight*—describes all of this magnificently. It says that trees take carbon dioxide out of your atmosphere, using the carbon portion of this atmospheric gas to make *carbohydrates*—that is, to *grow*.

(Nearly everything of which a plant is made, including roots, stems, leaves—even the nuts and fruits which the tree bears—are carbohydrates.)

Meanwhile, the oxygen portion of this gas is released by the tree. It is the tree's "waste matter."

Human beings, on the other hand, need oxygen to survive. Without trees to convert the carbon dioxide, which is plentiful in your atmosphere, into oxygen—which is *not*—you as a species cannot survive.

You, in turn release (breathe *out*) carbon dioxide, which the *tree* needs to survive.

Do you see the balance?

Of course. It is ingenious.

Thank you. Now please quit destroying it.

Oh, come on. We plant two trees for every one we cut down.

Yes, and it will take only 300 years for those trees to grow to the strength and size which will allow them to produce as much oxygen as many of the old-growth trees you are chopping down.

The oxygen manufacturing plant which you call the Amazon rain forest can be replaced in its capacity to balance your planet's atmosphere in, say, two or three thousand years. Not to worry. You're clearing thousands of acres every year, but not to worry.

Why? Why are we doing that?

You clear the land so that you can raise cattle to slaughter and eat. Raising cattle is said to provide more income for the indigenous peoples of the rain forest country. So all this is proclaimed to be about making the land *productive.*

In highly evolved civilizations, however, eroding the *speciesystem* is not looked at as *productive,* but rather, *destructive.* So HEBs have found a way to balance the *total* needs of the *speciesystem.* They choose to do this, rather than serve the desires of one small portion of the system, for they realize that no species *within* the system *can survive* if the *system itself is destroyed.*

Man, that seems so obvious. That seems so painfully obvious.

The "obviousness" of it may be even more painful on Earth in the years ahead if your so-called dominant species doesn't wake up.

I get that. I get it big. And I want to do something about it. But I feel so helpless. I sometimes feel so helpless. What can I do to bring about change?

There's nothing you have to do, but there's a great deal you can be.

Help me with that.

Human beings have been trying to solve problems at the "doingness" level for a long time, without much success. That's because true change is always made at the level of "being," not "doing."

Oh, you've made certain discoveries, all right, and you've advanced your technologies, and so, in some ways, you've made your lives easier—but it's not clear whether you've made them *better.* And on the larger issues of principle, you have made very slow progress. You are facing many of the same problems of principle that you've faced for centuries on your planet.

Your idea that Earth exists for the exploitation of the dominant species is a good example.

You clearly will not change what you are *doing* around that until you change how you are *being*.

You have to change your idea about who you *are* in relationship to your environment and everything in it before you will ever *act* differently.

It is a matter of consciousness. *And you have to raise consciousness before you can change consciousness.*

How can we do that?

Stop being quiet about all this. Speak up. Raise a ruckus. Raise the issues. You might even raise some collective consciousness.

On just one issue, for instance. Why not grow hemp and use it to make paper? Do you have any idea how many trees it takes just to supply your world with daily newspapers? To say nothing of paper cups, carry-out cartons, and paper towels?

Hemp can be grown inexpensively, and harvested easily, and used not only for making paper, but the strongest rope, and the longest-lasting clothing, and even some of the most effective medicines your planet can provide. In fact, cannabis can be planted *so* inexpensively, and harvested *so* easily, and has *so* many wonderful uses, that there is a huge lobby working against it.

Too many would lose too much to allow the world to turn to this simple plant which can be grown almost anywhere.

This is just one example of how greed replaces common sense in the conduct of human affairs.

So give this book to everyone you know. Not only so that they get *this,* but so that they get everything *else* the book has to say. And there's still a *great deal more.*

Just turn the page. . . .

Yeah, but I'm starting to feel depressed, like a lot of people said they felt after *Book 2.* Is this going to be more and more talk about how we're destroying things here, and really blowing it? 'Cause I'm not sure I'm up for this. . . .

Are you up for being inspired? Are you up for being excited? Because learning about and exploring what other civilizations—advanced civilizations—are doing should both inspire and excite you!

Think of the possibilities! Think of the opportunities! Think of the golden tomorrows just around the corner!

If we *wake up*.

You *will* wake up! You *are* waking up! The paradigm *is* shifting. The world *is* changing. It's happening right in front of your eyes.

This book is part of it. You are part of it. Remember, you are in the room to heal the room. You are in the space to heal the space. There is no other reason for you to be here.

Don't give up! Don't give up! The grandest adventure has just begun!

All right. I choose to be inspired by the example and wisdom of highly evolved beings, not discouraged by it.

Good. That is a wise choice, given where you say you want to go as a species. You have much you can remember from observing these beings.

HEBs live in unity, and with a deep sense of interrelatedness. Their behaviors are created by their Sponsoring Thoughts—what you might call the basic guiding principles of their society. Your behaviors, too, are created by your Sponsoring Thoughts—or, the basic guiding principles of *your* society.

What are the basic guiding principles of a HEB Society?

Their First Guiding Principle is: We Are All One.

Every decision, every choice, all of what you would call "morals" and "ethics," is based upon this principle.

The Second Guiding Principle is: Everything in the One Interrelates.

Under this principle, no one member of a species could, or would, keep something from another simply because "he had it first," or it's his "possession," or it's in "short supply." The mutual dependency of all living things in the *speciesystem* is recognized and honored. The relative needs of every species of living organism within the system are always kept in balance—because they are always kept in *mind*.

Does this Second Guiding Principle mean there is no such thing as personal ownership?

Not as you understand it.

A HEB experiences "personal ownership" in the sense of holding *personal responsibility* for every good thing in his care. The closest word in your language to describe what a highly evolved being feels about what you would call a "prized possession" is *stewardship*. A HEB is a *steward,* not an *owner.*

The word "own," and your concept behind it, are not part of the culture of HEBs. There is no such thing as "possession" in the sense of something being a "personal belonging." HEBs do not *possess,* HEBs *caress.* That is, they hold, embrace, love, and care for things, but they do not own them.

Humans possess, HEBs caress. In your language, this is how the difference could be described.

Earlier in your history humans felt they had the right to personally possess *everything they laid their hands on.* This included wives and children, land, and the riches of the land. "Stuff," and whatever other "stuff" their "stuff" could get them, was also theirs. Much of this belief is still held as truth today in human society.

Humans became obsessed with this concept of "ownership." HEBs who watched this from a distance called this your "possession obsession."

Now, as you have evolved, you understand more and more that you can really, truly, possess nothing—least of all your spouses and children. Many of you, though, still cling to the notion that you can possess land, and everything on it, under it, and over it. (Yes, you even talk about *"air rights"*!)

The HEBs of the universe, by contrast, deeply understand that the physical planet beneath their feet is not something that can be possessed by any single one of them—although an individual HEB may be granted, through the mechanisms of his or her society, a parcel of land for which to care. If she is a good steward of the land, she may be allowed (asked) to pass stewardship on to her offspring, and they to theirs. Yet if at any time either he or his offspring prove to be poor stewards of the land, the land is no longer kept in their care.

Wow! If that were the guiding principle here, half the industries in the world would have to give up their property!

And the world's ecosystem would dramatically improve overnight.

You see, in a highly evolved culture, a "corporation," as you call it, would never be allowed to despoil the land in order to make a profit, for it would be clearly seen that the quality of the lives of the very people who own or work for the corporation are being irrevocably damaged. What profit is there in that?

Well, the damage might not be felt for many years, whereas the benefits are realized right here, right now. So that would be called Short-Term Profit/Long-Term Loss. But who cares about Long-Term Loss if you're not going to be there to experience it?

Highly evolved beings do. But then, they live a lot longer.

How much longer?

Many times longer. In some HEB societies, beings live forever— or as long as they choose to remain in corporal form. So in HEB societies, individual beings are usually around to experience the long-term consequences of their actions.

How do they manage to stay alive so long?

Of course they are never *not* alive, any more than you are, but I know what you mean. You mean "with the body."

Yes. How do they manage to stay with their bodies for so long? Why is this possible?

Well first, *because* they don't pollute their air, their water, and their land. They do not put chemicals into the ground, for instance, which are then taken up by plants and animals, and brought into the body upon consumption of those plants and animals.

A HEB, in fact, would never consume an animal, much less fill the ground, and the plants which the *animal* eats, with chemicals, then fill the animal *itself* with chemicals, and *then* consume it. A HEB would correctly assess such a practice to be suicidal.

So HEBs do not pollute their environment, their atmosphere, and their own corporal bodies, as humans do. Your bodies are magnificent creations, made to "last" infinitely longer than you allow them to.

HEBs also exhibit different psychological behaviors that equally prolong life.

Such as?

A HEB never worries—and wouldn't even understand the human concept of "worry" or "stress." Neither would a HEB "hate," or feel "rage," or "jealousy," or panic. Therefore, the HEB does not produce biochemical reactions within her own body that eat away at it and destroy it. A HEB would call this "eating itself," and a HEB would no sooner consume itself than it would consume another corporal being.

How does a HEB manage this? Are humans capable of such control over emotions?

First, a HEB understands that all things are perfect, that there is a process in the universe that is working itself out, and that all they have to do is not interfere with it. So a HEB never worries, because a HEB understands the process.

And, to answer your second question: Yes, humans have this control, although some don't believe they have it, and others simply don't choose to exercise it. The few who do make an effort live a great deal longer—assuming chemicals and atmospheric poisons haven't killed them, and also assuming they haven't voluntarily poisoned themselves in other ways.

Wait a minute. We "voluntarily poison ourselves"?

Some of you do, yes.

How?

As I said, you eat poisons. Some of you drink poisons. Some of you even smoke poisons.

A highly evolved being finds such behaviors incomprehensible. He can't imagine why you would deliberately take into your bodies substances that you know can't be doing you any good.

Well, we find eating, drinking, and smoking certain things *enjoyable*.

A HEB finds *life* in the *body* enjoyable, and can't imagine doing anything that she *knows ahead of time* could limit or terminate that, or make it painful.

Some of us don't believe that eating red meat plentifully, drinking alcohol, or smoking plants *will* limit or terminate our lives, or make them painful.

Then your observational skills are very dull. They need sharpening. A HEB would suggest that you simply look around you.

Yes, well . . . what else can You tell me about what life is like in the highly evolved societies of the universe?

There is no shame.

No shame?

Nor any such thing as guilt.

How about when a being proves to be a bad "steward" of the land? You just said they take the land away from him! Doesn't that mean he's been judged and found guilty?

No. It means he's been observed and found unable.

In highly evolved cultures, beings would never be asked to do something they've demonstrated an inability to do.

What if they still *wanted* to do it?

They would not "want" to.

Why not?

Their own demonstrated inability would eliminate their desire. This is a natural outcome of their understanding that their inability to do a particular thing could potentially damage another. This they would never do, for to damage the Other is to damage the Self, *and they know this.*

So it is still "self-preservation" that drives the experience! Just like on Earth!

Certainly! The only thing that's different is their *definition of "Self."* A human defines Self very narrowly. You speak of *your* Self, *your* family, *your* community. A HEB defines Self quite differently. She speaks of *the* Self, *the* family, *the* community.

As if there were only one.

There *is* only one. That's the whole point.

I understand.

And so, in a highly evolved culture, a being would never, for instance, insist on raising offspring if that being consistently demonstrated to itself *its own inability to do so.*

This is why, in highly evolved cultures, children don't raise children. Offspring are given to elders to raise. This doesn't mean that new offspring are torn from those who gave them life, taken from their arms and given to virtual strangers to raise. It is nothing like that.

In these cultures, elders live closely with the young ones. They are not shuffled off to live by themselves. They are not ignored, and left to work out their own final destinies. They are honored, revered, and held close, as part of a loving, caring, vibrant community.

When a new offspring arrives, the elders are right there, deep within the heart of that community and that family, and their raising of the offspring is as organically correct as it feels in your society to have the parents do this.

The difference is that, though they always know who their "parents" are—the closest term in their language would be "life-givers"— these offspring are not asked to learn about the basics of life from beings who are *still learning about the basics of life themselves.*

In HEB societies, the elders organize and supervise the learning process, as well as housing, feeding, and caring for the children. Offspring are raised in an environment of wisdom and love, great, great patience, and deep understanding.

The young ones who gave them life are usually off somewhere, meeting the challenges and experiencing the joys of their own young lives. They may spend as much time with their offspring as they choose. They may even live in the Dwelling of the Elders with the children, to be right there with them in a "home" environment, and to be experienced by them as part of it.

It is all a very unified, integrated experience. But it is the elders who do the raising, who take the responsibility. And it is an honor, for upon the elders is placed the responsibility for the future of the entire species. And in HEB societies, it is recognized that this is more than should be asked of young ones.

I touched on this earlier, when we talked about how you raise offspring on your planet, and how you might change that.

Yes. And thank You for further explaining this, and how it could work. So, getting back, a HEB does not feel guilt or shame, no matter what he does?

No. Because guilt and shame is something which is imposed on a being from outside of itself. It can then be internalized, no question about that, but it is initially imposed from the outside. *Always.* No divine being (and all beings are divine) *ever* knows itself or anything it is doing to be "shameful" or "guilty" until someone outside of Itself labels it that way.

In your culture, is a baby ashamed of its "bathroom habits"? Of course not. Not until you *tell* it to be. Does a child feel "guilty" for pleasuring itself with its genitals? Of course not. Not until you *tell* it to feel guilty.

The degree to which a culture is evolved is demonstrated by the degree to which it labels a being or an action "shameful" or "guilty."

Are *no* actions to be called shameful? Is a person *never* guilty, no matter what he does?

As I have already told you, there is no such thing as right and wrong.

There are some people who still don't understand that.

To understand what is being said here, this dialogue must be read *in its entirety*. Taking any statement out of context could make it not understandable. *Books 1* and *2* contain detailed explanations of the wisdom above. You are asking Me here to describe the highly evolved cultures of the universe. They already understand this wisdom.

Okay. How else are these cultures different from our own?

In many other ways. They do not compete.

They realize that when one loses, everyone loses. They therefore do not create sports and games which teach children (and perpetuate in adults) the extraordinary thought that someone "winning" while another is "losing" is *entertainment*.

Also, as I said, they share everything. When another is in need, they would never dream of keeping or hoarding something they had, simply because it was in scarce supply. On the contrary, that would be *their very reason for sharing it*.

In your society, the price goes up for that which is rare, if you share it at all. In this way you ensure that, if you *are* going to share something which you "possess," at least you'll *be enriched doing it*.

Highly evolved beings are also enriched by sharing rare things. The only thing that is different between HEBs and humans is how HEBs define "being enriched." A HEB feels "enriched" by sharing everything freely, without needing to "profit." Indeed, this feeling *is* the profit.

There are several guiding principles of your culture, which produce your behaviors. As I said earlier, one of your most basic ones is: *Survival of the Fittest.*

This might be called your Second Guiding Principle. It underlies everything your society has created. Its economics. Its politics. Its religions. Its education. Its social structures.

Yet, to a highly evolved being, the principle itself is an oxymoron. It is self-contradicting. Since the First Guiding Principle of a HEB is We Are All One, the "One" is not "fit" until the "All" is "fit." Survival of the "fittest" is, therefore, impossible—or the *only* thing that is possible (therefore a contradiction)—since the "fittest" is *not* "fit" until it *is*.

Are you following this?

Yes. We call it communism.

On your planet you have rejected out-of-hand any system which does not allow for the advancement of one being at the expense of another.

If a system of governance or economics requires an attempt at equitable distribution, to "all," of the benefits *created* by "all," with the resources *belonging* to "all," you have said that system of governance violates the natural order. Yet in highly evolved cultures, the natural order IS *equitable sharing.*

Even if a person or group has done nothing to deserve it? Even if there has been no contribution to the common good? Even if they are evil?

The common good is *life*. If you are alive, you are contributing to the common good. It is very difficult for a spirit to be in physical form. To agree to take such a form is, in one sense, a great sacrifice—yet one that is necessary, and even enjoyed, if the All is to know itself experientially, and to re-create Itself anew in the next grandest version of the greatest vision it ever held about Who It Is.

It is important to understand why we came here.

We?

The souls which make up the collective.

You're losing me.

As I have already explained, there is only One Soul, One Being, One Essence. Some of you call this "God." This Single Essence "individuates" Itself as Everything In The Universe—in other words, All That Is. This includes all the sentient beings, or what you have chosen to call souls.

So "God" is every soul that "is"?

Every soul that is now, ever was, and ever will be.

So God is a "collective?"

That's the word I chose, because it comes closest in your language to describing how things are.

Not a single awesome being, but a collective?

It doesn't have to be one or the other. Think "outside the box"!

God is *both?* A single Awesome Being which is a collective of individualized parts?

Good! Very good!

And why did the collective come to Earth?

To express itself in physicality. To know itself in its own experience. To be God. As I've already explained in detail in *Book 1.*

You created us to be You?

We did, indeed. That is *exactly* why you were created.

And humans were created by a collective?

Your own Bible said, "Let *Us* create man in *Our image*, and after *Our likeness*" before the translation was changed.

Life is the process through which God creates Itself, and then experiences the creation. This process of creation is ongoing and eternal. It is happening all the "time." Relativity and physi-cality are the tools with which God works. Pure energy (what you call spirit) is What God Is. This Essence is truly the Holy Spirit.

By a process through which energy becomes matter, spirit is embodied in physicality. This is done by the energy literally slow-ing itself down—changing its oscillation, or what you would call vibration.

That Which Is All does this in parts. That is, parts of the whole do this. These individuations of spirit are what you have chosen to call souls.

In truth, there is only One Soul, reshaping and reforming Itself. This might be called The Reformation. You are all Gods In Formation. (God's *information!*)

That is your contribution, and it is sufficient unto itself.

To put this simply, by taking physical form *you have already done enough.* I want, I need, nothing more. You *have* con-tributed to the common good. You have made it possible for that which is common—the One Common Element—to experience that which is good. Even you have written that God created the heavens and the Earth, and the animals who walk upon the land, and the birds of the air, and the fishes of the sea, *and it was very good.*

"Good" does not—cannot—exist experientially without its opposite. Therefore have you also created evil, which is the back-ward motion, or opposite direction, of good. It is the opposite of life—and so have you created what you call death.

Yet death does not exist in ultimate reality, but is merely a con-coction, an invention, an imagined experience, through which life becomes more valued by you. Thus, "evil" is "live" spelled back-ward! So clever you are with language. You fold into it secret wisdoms that you do not even know are there.

Now when you understand this entire cosmology, you compre-hend the great truth. You could then never demand of another being that it give you something in return for your sharing the resources and necessities of physical life.

As beautiful as that is, there are still some people who would call it communism.

If they wish to do so, then so be it. Yet I tell you this: Until your *community of beings* knows about *being in community,* you will never experience Holy Communion, and cannot know Who I Am.

The highly evolved cultures of the universe understand deeply all that I have explained here. In those cultures it would not be possible to fail to share. Nor would it be possible to think of "charging" increasingly exorbitant "prices" the more rare a necessity became. Only extremely primitive societies would do this. Only very primitive beings would see scarcity of that which is commonly needed as an opportunity for greater profits. "Supply and demand" does not drive the HEB system.

This is part of a system that humans claim contributes to their quality of life and to the common good. Yet, from the vantage point of a highly evolved being, your system *violates* the common good, for it does not allow that which is *good* to be experienced *in common.*

Another distinguishing and fascinating feature of highly evolved cultures is that within them there is no word or sound for, nor any way to communicate the meaning of, the concept of "yours" and "mine." Personal possessives do not exist in their language, and, if one were to speak in earthly tongues, one could only use articles to describe things. Employing that convention, "my car" becomes "the car I am now with." "My partner" or "my children" becomes "the partner" or "the children I am now with."

The term "now with," or "in the presence of," is as close as your languages can come to describing what you would call "ownership," or "possession."

That which you are "in the presence of" becomes the Gift. These are the true "presents" of life.

Thus, in the language of highly evolved cultures, one could not even speak in terms of "my life," but could only communicate "the life I am in the presence of."

This is something akin to your speaking of being "in the presence of God."

When you are in the presence of God (which you are, any time you are in the presence of each other), you would never think of keeping from God that which is God's—meaning, any part of That Which Is. You would naturally share, and share equally, that which is God's with any *part* of that which is God.

This is the spiritual understanding which undergirds the entire social, political, economic, and religious structures of all highly evolved cultures. This is the cosmology of all of life, and it is merely failure to observe this cosmology, to understand it and to live within it, which creates all of the discord of your experience on Earth.

19

What are the beings like on other planets, physically?

Take your pick. There are as many varieties of beings as there are species of life on your planet.

Actually, more.

Are there beings who look very much like us?

Of course, some look exactly like you—given minor variations.

How do they live? What do they eat? How are they dressed? In what way do they communicate? I want to learn all about E.T.s here. C'mon, out with it!

I understand your curiosity, yet these books are not being given to you to satisfy curiosity. The purpose of our conversation is to bring a message to your world.

Just a few questions. And they're more than curiosities. We may have something to learn here. Or, more accurately, to remember.

That really is more accurate. For you have nothing to learn, but merely to remember Who You Really Are.

You made that wonderfully clear in *Book 1*. Do these beings on other planets remember Who They Are?

As you might expect, all beings elsewhere are in various stages of evolution. But in what you have here termed highly evolved cultures, yes, the beings have remembered.

How do they live? Work? Travel? Communicate?

Travel as you know it in your culture does not exist in highly evolved societies. Technology has advanced far beyond the necessity of using fossil fuels to drive engines embedded in huge machines that move bodies around.

In addition to what has been provided by new physical technologies, understandings of the mind, and of the very nature of physicality itself, have also advanced.

As a result of the combination of these two types of evolutionary advances, it has become possible for HEBs to disassemble and reassemble their bodies at will, allowing most beings in most highly evolved cultures to "be" *wherever* they choose—whenever they choose.

Including light-years across the universe?

Yes. In most cases, yes. Such "long distance" travel across galaxies is done like a stone skipping across water. No attempt is made to go *through* The Matrix which is the universe, but rather, to "skip around" *on* it. That is the best imagery which can be found in your language to explain the physics of it.

As for what you call, in your society, "work"—such a concept does not exist in most HEB cultures. Tasks are performed, and activities are undertaken, based purely on what a being loves to do, and sees as the highest expression of Self.

That's super if one can do it, but how does the menial labor get done?

The concept of "menial labor" does not exist. What you would label as "menial" in your society is often the most highly honored in the world of highly evolved beings. HEBs who do the daily tasks that "must" be done for a society to exist and to function are the most highly rewarded, highly decorated "workers" in the service of All. I put the word "workers" in quotes here because to a HEB this is not considered "work" at all, but the highest form of self-fulfillment.

The ideas and experiences that humans have created around self-expression—which you've called work—are simply not part of the HEB culture. "Drudgery," "overtime," "pressure," and similar self-created experiences are not chosen by highly evolved beings, who, among other things, are not attempting to "get ahead," "rise to the top," or "be successful."

The very concept of "success" as you have defined it is foreign to a HEB, precisely because its opposite—*failure*—does not exist.

Then how do HEBs ever have an experience of accomplishment or achievement?

> Not through the construction of an elaborate value system surrounding "competition," "winning," and "losing," as is done in most human societies and activities—even (and especially) in your schools—but rather, through a deep understanding of what real value is in a society, and a true appreciation for it.
>
> Achieving is defined as "doing what brings value," not "doing what brings 'fame' and 'fortune,' whether it is of value or not."

Then HEBs *do* have a "value system"!

> Oh, yes. Of course. But one very unlike most humans. HEBs value that which produces benefit to All.

So do we!

> Yes, but you define "benefit" so differently. You see greater benefit in throwing a little white sphere at a man with a bat, or taking one's clothes off on a big silver screen, than in leading offspring to remember life's greatest truths, or sourcing a society's spiritual sustenance. So you honor, and pay, ballplayers and movie stars more than you do teachers and ministers. In this you have everything backward, given where you say that you want to go as a society.
>
> You have not developed very keen powers of observation. HEBs always see "what's so," and do "what works." Humans very often do not.
>
> HEBs do not honor those who teach or minister because it is "morally right." They do so because it is "what *works*," given where they choose for their society to go.

Still, where there is a value structure, there must be "haves" and "have-nots." So in HEB societies it's the teachers who are rich and famous, and the ballplayers who are poor.

> There are *no* "have-nots" in a HEB society. No one lives in the depths of degradation to which you have allowed many humans to fall. And no one dies of starvation, as 400 children an hour, and 30,000 people a day, do on your planet. And there is no such thing as a life of "quiet desperation" as there is in human work cultures.
>
> No. In HEB society there is no such thing as "the destitute" and "the poor."

How have they avoided that? *How?*

By applying two basic principles—

We are all One.

There's enough.

HEBs have an awareness of sufficiency, and a consciousness that creates it. Through the HEB consciousness of the interrelatedness of all things, nothing is wasted or destroyed of the natural resources on a HEB's home planet. This leaves plenty for everyone—hence, "there's enough."

The human consciousness of insufficiency—of "not enoughness"—is the root cause of all worry, all pressure, all competition, all jealousy, all anger, all conflict, and, ultimately, all killing on your planet.

This, plus the human insistence on believing in the separation, rather than the unity, of all things is what has created 90 percent of the misery in your lives, the sadness in your history, and the impotence of your previous efforts to make things better for everyone.

If you would change these two elements of your consciousness, everything would shift.

How? I want to do that, but I don't know *how.* Give me a tool, not just platitudes.

Good. That's fair. So here's a tool.
"Act as if."
Act as if you *were* all One. Just start acting that way tomorrow. See everyone as "you," just having a difficult time. See everyone as "you," just wanting a fair chance. See everyone as "you," just having a different experience.

Try it. Just go around tomorrow and try it. See everyone through new eyes.

Then, start acting as if "there's enough." If you had "enough" money, "enough" love, "enough" time, what would you do differently? Would you share more openly, freely, equitably?

That's interesting, because we're doing exactly that with our natural resources, and being criticized by ecologists for it: I mean, we're acting as if "there's enough."

What's really interesting is that you act as if the things which you think *benefit you* are in *short* supply, so you watch your supply of that very carefully—often even hoarding those things. Yet you play fast and loose with your environment, natural resources, and ecology. So it can only be assumed that you do not think the environment, natural resources, and your ecology benefits you.

Or that we're "acting as if" *there's enough.*

But you aren't. If you were, you would share these resources more equitably. Yet right now one-fifth of the world's people are using four-fifths of the world's resources. And you show no signs of changing that equation.

There *is* enough for everybody if you would stop thoughtlessly squandering all of it on the privileged few. If all people used resources wisely, you would use less than you do with a few people using them unwisely.

Use the resources, but don't *abuse* the resources. That's all the ecologists are saying.

Well, I'm depressed again. You keep making me depressed.

You're something, you know that? You're driving down a lonely road, lost and having forgotten how to get where you say you want to go. Someone comes along and *gives you directions.* Eureka! You're ecstatic, right? No. You're depressed.

Amazing.

I'm depressed because *I don't see us taking these directions.* I don't see us even wanting to. I see us marching right into a wall, and *yes,* it depresses me.

You are not using your powers of observation. I see hundreds of thousands of people cheering as they read this. I see millions recognizing the simple truths here. And I see a new force for change growing in intensity on your planet. Entire thought systems are being discarded. Ways of governing yourselves are being abandoned. Economic policies are being revised. Spiritual truths are being reexamined.

Yours is *a race awakening*.

The noticements and observations on these pages need not be a source of discouragement. That you *recognize them as truth* can be tremendously encouraging if you allow this to be *the fuel that drives the engine of change.*

You are the change-agent. You are the one who can *make a difference* in how humans create and experience their lives.

How? What can I do?

Be the difference. *Be* the change. *Embody* the consciousness of "We Are All One," and "There's Enough."

Change your Self, change the world.

You have given your Self this book, and all the *Conversations with God* material, so that you might remember once again how it was to live as highly evolved beings.

We lived this way once before, didn't we? You mentioned earlier that we had lived like this once before.

Yes. In what you would call ancient times and ancient civilizations. Most of what I have been describing here has been experienced by your race before.

Now a part of me wants to be even *more* depressed! You mean we got there and then lost it all? What's the point of all this "going around in circles" that we're doing?

Evolution! Evolution is *not a straight line.*

You have a chance now to re-create the best experiences of your ancient civilizations, while avoiding the worst. You don't have to let personal egos and advanced technology destroy your society this time. You can do it differently. You—*you*—can *make a difference.*

That could be very exciting to you, if you allow it to be.

Okay. I get it. And when I allow myself to think of it that way, I *am* excited! And I *will* make a difference! Tell me more! I want to remember as much as I can about how it was with us in our advanced, ancient civilizations, and how it is today with all highly evolved beings. How do they live?

They live in clusters, or what your world would call communities, but for the most part they have abandoned their version of what you call "cities," or "nations."

Why?

Because "cities" became too big, and no longer supported the purpose of clustering, but worked against that purpose. They produced "crowded individuals" instead of a clustered community.

It's the same on this planet! There is more of a sense of "community" in our small towns and villages—even in our wide open rural areas—than there is in most of our big cities.

Yes. There's only one difference, on that score, between your world and the other planets we are now discussing.

Which is?

The inhabitants of those other planets have learned this. They have observed more closely "what works."

We, on the other hand, keep creating larger and larger cities, even though we see that they are destroying our very way of life.

Yes.

We even take *pride* in our rankings! A metropolitan area moves up from number 12 to number 10 on our list of biggest cities and everyone thinks that's a cause for celebration! Chambers of Commerce actually *advertise it!*

It is the mark of a primitive society to view regression as progress.

You have said that before. You're getting me depressed again!

More and more of you are no longer doing this. More and more of you are re-creating small "intended" communities.

So, do You think we should abandon our megacities and return to our towns and villages?

I don't have a preference about it one way or the other. I am simply making an observation.

As always. So what is Your observation regarding why we continue to migrate to bigger and bigger cities, even though we see that it is not good for us?

Because many of you do *not* see that is not good for you. You believe that grouping together in large cities *solves* problems, when it only creates them.

It is true that in large cities there are services, there are jobs, there are entertainments which are not, and cannot be, found in smaller towns and villages. But your mistake is in calling these things valuable, when, in fact, they are detrimental.

Aha! You *do* have a point of view on this! You just gave yourself away! You said we made a "mistake."

If you're headed toward San Jose—

Here we go again—

Well, you insist on calling observations "judgments," and statements of fact, "preferences," and I know you are seeking greater accuracy in your communications and in your perceptions, so I'm going to call you on this every time.

If you are headed toward San Jose, all the while saying you wish to go to Seattle, is it wrong for the bystander of whom you are asking directions to say that you have "made a mistake"? Is the bystander expressing a "preference"?

I guess not.

You *guess not?*

Okay, he's not.

Then what *is* he doing?

He's merely saying "what's so," given where we say we want to go.

Excellent. You've got it.

But You've made this point before. Repeatedly. Why do I keep reverting to an idea about You as having preferences and judgments?

Because that's the God who's supported by your mythology, and you will throw Me into that category any time you can. Besides, if I *did* have a preference, that would make everything easier for you. Then you wouldn't have to figure things out and come to your *own* conclusions. You'd just have to do as *I* say.

Of course, you'd have no way of knowing *what* it is that I say, since you don't believe I've said anything for thousands of years, so you have no choice but to rely on those who claim to be teaching what I *used* to say during the days when I was actually communicating. But even this is a problem, because there are as many different teachers and teachings as there are hairs on your head. So, you're right back where you started from, having to come to your *own* conclusions.

Is there a way out of this maze—and the cycle of misery it has created for the human race? Will we ever "get it right"?

There *is* a "way out," and you *will* "get it right." You merely have to *increase your observational skills*. You have to better see what serves you. This is called "evolution." Actually, you cannot "not get it right." You cannot fail. It is merely a question of when, not of whether.

But aren't we running out of time on this planet?

Oh, if *that's* your parameter—if you want to "get it right" on *this planet*, that is, while *this particular planet still supports you*—then, within *that* context, you'd better hurry.

How can we go faster? Help us!

I am helping you. What do you suppose this dialogue is about?

Okay, so give us some more help. You said a little bit ago that in highly evolved cultures on other planets, beings also abandoned the concept of "nations." Why did they do that?

Because they saw that a concept such as what you would call "nationalism" works against their First Guiding Principle: WE ARE ALL ONE.

On the other hand, nationalism *supports* our Second Guiding Principle: SURVIVAL OF THE FITTEST.

> Exactly.
> You separate yourself into nations for reasons of survival and security—and produce just the opposite.
> Highly evolved beings refuse to join together in nations. They believe in simply one nation. You might even say they have formed "one nation, under God."

Ah, clever. But do they have "liberty and justice for all"?

> Do you?

Touché.

> The point is that all races and species are evolving, and evolution—the purpose of observing what serves you, and making behavioral adaptions—seems to keep moving in one direction, and away from another. It keeps moving towards unity, and away from separation.
> This is not surprising, since unity is the Ultimate Truth, and "evolution" is just another word for "movement toward truth."

I also notice that "observing what serves you, and making behavioral adaptations" sounds suspiciously like "survival of the fittest"—one of our Guiding Principles!

> It does, doesn't it?
> So now it's time to "observe" that "survival of the fittest" (that is, evolution of the species) is not achieved, but, indeed, entire species have been doomed—have actually *self-destructed*—by calling a "process" a "principle."

Oops. You lost me.

> The *process* is called "evolution." The "principle" which *guides* the process is what directs the course of your evolution.
> You are right. Evolution *is* "survival of the fittest." That is the *process*. Yet do not confuse "process" and "principle."
> If "evolution" and "survival of the fittest" are synonymous, and if you are claiming "survival of the fittest" as a Guiding Principle, then you are saying, "A Guiding Principle of Evolution *is evolution*."

Yet that is the statement of a race which does not know that it can *control the course of its own evolution.* That is the statement of a species which thinks itself to be relegated to the status of observer of its own evolution. Because most people think that "evolution" is a process which is simply "going on"—not a process which they are *directing,* according to certain *principles.*

And so the species is announcing, "We *evolve* by the principle of . . . well, *evolution."* But they never say what that principle IS, because they have confused the process and the principle.

The species, on the other hand, which has become clear that evolution is a process—but a process *over which the species has control*—has not confused "process" with "principle," but consciously *chooses* a principle which it *uses to guide and direct its process.*

This is called *conscious evolution,* and your species has just arrived there.

Wow, that's an incredible insight. *That's* why You gave Barbara Marx Hubbard that book! As I said, she actually called it *Conscious Evolution.*

Of course she did. I told her to.

Ah, I love it! So . . . I'd like to get back to our "conversation" about E.T.s. How do these highly evolved beings organize themselves, if not in nations? How do they govern themselves?

They do not use "evolution" as their First Guiding Principle of Evolution, but, rather, they have *created* a principle, based on pure observation. They have simply observed that they are all One, and they have devised political, social, economic, and spiritual mechanisms which *undergird,* rather than *undermine,* that First Principle.

What does that "look like"? In government, for instance?

When there is only one of You, how do you govern yourself?

Come again?

When you are the only one there is, how do you govern your behavior? Who governs your behavior? Who, outside of yourself?

No one. When I am all alone—if I were on a deserted island someplace, for instance—no one "outside of myself" would govern or control my behaviors. I would eat, dress, do exactly as I want. I would probably not dress at all. I would eat whenever I was hungry, and whatever felt good and made me feel healthy. I would "do" whatever I felt like doing, and some of that would be determined by what I thought I needed to do to survive.

> Well, as usual, you have all the wisdom within you. I've told you before, you have nothing to learn, you have only to remember.

This is how it is in advanced civilizations? They run around naked, picking berries, and carving canoes? Those sound like barbarians!

> Who do you think is happier—and closer to God?

We've been through this before.

> Yes, we have. It is the mark of a primitive culture to imagine that simplicity is barbarian, and complexity is highly advanced.
>
> Interestingly, those who are highly advanced see it as being just the other way around.

Yet the movement of all cultures—indeed, the process of evolution itself—is toward higher and higher degrees of complexity.

> In one sense, yes. Yet here is the greatest Divine Dichotomy:
> *The greatest complexity is the greatest simplicity.*
> The more "complex" a system is, the more simple is its design. Indeed, it is utterly elegant in its Simplicity.
> The master understands this. That is why a highly evolved being lives in utter simplicity. It is why all highly evolved systems are also utterly simple. Highly evolved systems of governance, highly evolved systems of education, highly evolved systems of economics or religion—all are utterly, elegantly simple.
> Highly evolved systems of governance, for instance, involve virtually *no governance at all,* save self-governance.

As if there was only one being participating. As if there was only one being affected.

> Which is all there is.

Which highly evolved cultures understand.

Precisely.

I'm starting to put it all together now.

Good. We have not much time left.

You have to go?

This book is getting very long.

20

Wait! Hold it! You can't quit now! I have more questions about E.T.s! Are they someday going to appear on Earth to "save us"? Will they rescue us from our own madness by bringing us new technologies to control the planet's polarities, clean our atmosphere, harness our sun's energy, regulate our weather, cure all disease, and bring us a better quality of life in our own little nirvana?

> You may not want that to happen. "HEBs" know this. They know that such an intervention would only subjugate you to *them,* making *them* your gods, rather than the gods to whom you now claim to be subjugated.
>
> The truth is, you are subjugated to *no one,* and this is what the beings from highly advanced cultures would have you understand. If, therefore, they would share with you some technologies, these would be given in a way, and at a rate, which would allow you to recognize your *own* powers and potentials, not those of another.
>
> Similarly, if HEBs were to share with you some teachings, these, too, would be shared in a way, and at a rate, that would allow you to see greater truths, and your *own* powers and potentials, and *not make gods of your teachers.*

Too late. We've already done that.

> Yes, I've noticed.

Which brings us to one of our greatest teachers, the man called Jesus. Even those who did *not* make him a god have recognized the greatness of his teachings.

> Teachings which have been largely distorted.

Was Jesus one of these "HEBs"—highly evolved beings?

> Do *you* think he was highly evolved?

Yes. As was the Buddha, Lord Krishna, Moses, Babaji, Sai Baba, and Paramahansa Yogananda, for that matter.

Indeed. And many others you have not mentioned.

Well, in *Book 2* You "hinted" that Jesus and these other teachers may have come from "outer space," that they may have been visitors here, sharing with us the teachings and wisdoms of highly evolved beings. So it's time to let the other shoe fall. Was Jesus a "spaceman"?

You are all "spacemen."

What does that mean?

You are not natives of this planet you now call home.

We aren't?

No. The "genetic stuff" of which you are made was *placed* on your planet, deliberately. It didn't just "show up" there by accident. The elements that have formed your life didn't combine themselves through some process of *biological serendipity*. There was a plan involved. There is something much larger going on here. Do you imagine that the billion and one biochemical reactions it has taken to cause life as you know it to appear on your planet all occurred haphazardly? Do you see this outcome as simply a fortuitous chain of random events, producing a happy result *by chance?*

No, of course not. I agree that there was a plan. *God's* plan.

Good. Because you are right. It was all My idea, and it was all My plan, and My process.

So what, then—are You saying that You are a "spaceman"?

Where have you traditionally looked when you've imagined yourself to be talking to Me?

Up. I've looked up.

Why not down?

I don't know. Everybody always looks up—to the "heavens."

From where I come?

I guess—yes.

Does that make Me a spaceman?

I don't know, does it?

And if I am a spaceman, would that make Me any less a God?

Based on what most of us say You can do, no. I guess not.

And if I am a God, does that make Me any less a spaceman?

It would all depend on our definitions, I guess.

What if I am not a "man" at all, but rather, a Force, an "Energy" in the universe, that IS the universe, and that is, in fact, All That Is. What if I am The Collective?

Well, that is, in fact, what You've said that You are. In this dialogue, You've *said* that.

Indeed, I have. And do you believe it?

Yes, I think I do. At least in the sense that I think God is All That Is.

Good. Now, do you think there are such things as what you call "spacemen"?

You mean, beings from outer space?

Yes.

Yes, I do. I think I've always believed that, and now, here, You've *told me* there are, so I surely believe it.

And are these "beings from outer space" part of "All That Is"?

Well, yes, of course.

And if I am All That Is, wouldn't that make Me a *spaceman*?

Well yes . . . but by that definition, You are also *me*.

Bingo.

Yes, but You've danced away from my question. I asked You if Jesus was a spaceman. And I think You know what I mean. I mean, was he a being from outer space, or was he born here, on Earth?

Your question once again assumes "either/or." Think *outside the box.* Reject "either/or" and consider "both/and."

Are you saying Jesus was born on Earth, but has "spaceman blood," so to speak?

Who was Jesus' father?

Joseph.

Yes, but who is said to have *conceived him?*

Some people believe that it was an immaculate conception. They say that the Virgin Mary was visited by an archangel. Jesus was "conceived by the Holy Ghost, born of the Virgin Mary."

Do you believe this?

I don't know what to believe about that.

Well, if Mary was visited by an archangel, from where do you imagine the angel would have come?

From heaven.

Did you say "from the heavens"?

I said, from *heaven.* From another realm. From God.

I see. And did we not just agree that God is a spaceman?

Not exactly. We agreed that God is *everything,* and that since spacemen are *part* of "everything," God is a spaceman, in the same sense that God is us. All of us. God is Everything. God is the collective.

Good. So this archangel who visited Mary came from another realm. A heavenly realm.

Yes.

A realm deep within your Self, because heaven is within you.

I didn't say that.

Well, then, a realm within the inner space of the universe.

No, I wouldn't say that either, because I don't know what that means.

Then from where? A realm in *outer* space?

(Long pause)

You're playing with words now.

I'm doing the best I can. I'm *using* words, in spite of their awful limitations, to get as close as I can to an idea, a concept of things, which, in truth, cannot be described in the limited vocabulary of your language, or understood within the limitations of your present level of perception.

I am seeking to open you to new perceptions by using your language in a new way.

Okay. So, You're saying that Jesus was fathered by a highly evolved being from some other realm, and thus he was a human, but also a HEB?

There have been many highly evolved beings walking your planet—and there are many today.

You mean there are "aliens among us"?

I can see that your work in newspapers, radio talk shows, and television has served you well.

How do You mean?

You can find a way to sensationalize anything. I didn't call highly evolved beings "aliens," and I didn't call Jesus an "alien."

There is nothing "alien" about God. There are no "aliens" on Earth.

We Are All One. If We Are All One, no individuation of Us is alien to itself.

Some individuation of Us—that is, some individual beings—remember more than others. The process of remembering (re-uniting with God, or becoming, once again, One with the All, with the collective) is a process you call evolution. You are all evolving beings. Some of you are highly evolved. That is, you *re-member* more. You know Who You Really Are. Jesus knew it, and declared it.

Okay, so I get that we're going to do a word dance on the Jesus thing.

Not at all. I will tell you outright. The spirit of that human you call Jesus was not of this Earth. That spirit simply filled a human body, allowed itself to learn as a child, become a man, and self-realized. He was not the only one to have done this. *All spirits* are "not of this Earth." *All souls* come from another realm, then enter the body. Yet not all souls self-realize in a particular "lifetime." Jesus did. He was a highly evolved being. (What some of you have called a god), and he came to you for a purpose, on a mission.

To save our souls.

In a sense, yes. But not from everlasting damnation. There *is* no such thing as you have conceived it. His mission was—is—to save you from not knowing and never experiencing Who You Really Are. His intention was to demonstrate that by showing you what you can become. Indeed, what you *are*—if you will only accept it.

Jesus sought to lead by example. That is why he said, "I am the way and the life. Follow me." He didn't mean "follow me" in the sense that you would all become his "followers," but in the sense that you would all *follow his example* and *become one with God.* He said, "I and the Father are One, and ye are my brethren." He couldn't have put it more plainly.

So, Jesus did not come from God, he came from outer space.

Your mistake is in separating the two. You keep insisting on making a distinction, just as you insist on making a separation and a distinction between humans and God. And I tell you, *there is no distinction.*

Hmmm. Okay. Can You tell me a few final things about beings from other worlds before we end? What do they wear? How do they communicate? And please don't say this is still all about idle curiosity. I think I have demonstrated that there may be something we can learn here.

All right. Briefly, then.

In highly evolved cultures, beings see no need to be clothed, except when some kind of covering is required to protect them from elements or conditions over which they have no control, or when ornaments are used to indicate some "rank" or honor.

A HEB would not understand why you wear total body coverings when you do not have to—she certainly wouldn't understand the concept of "shame" or "modesty"—and could never relate to the idea of coverings to make oneself "prettier." To a HEB, there could be nothing more beautiful than the naked body itself, and so the concept of wearing something on top of it to somehow render it more pleasing or attractive would be utterly incomprehensible.

Equally incomprehensible would be the idea of living—spending most of one's time—in boxes . . . which you call "buildings" and "houses." HEBs live in the natural environment, and would only stay inside a box if their environment became inhospitable—which it rarely does, since highly evolved civilizations create, control, and care for their environments.

HEBs also understand that they are One with their environment, that they share more than space with their environments, but also share a mutually dependent relationship. A HEB could never understand why you would damage or destroy that which is supporting you, and so can only conclude that you do not understand that it is your environment which supports you; that you are beings of very limited observational skills.

As for communication, a HEB uses as his first level of communication the aspect of his being which you would call feelings. HEBs are aware of their feelings and the feelings of others, and no attempt is ever made by anyone to *hide* feelings. HEBs would find it self-defeating, and therefore incomprehensible, to hide feelings, and then complain that no one understands how they feel.

Feelings are the language of the soul, and highly evolved beings understand this. It is the purpose of communication in a society of HEBs to know each other in truth. A HEB, therefore, cannot, and could never, understand your human concept called "lying."

To be successful in getting one's way by communicating an untruth would be for a HEB a victory so hollow as to render it not a victory at all, but a staggering defeat.

HEBs do not "tell" the truth, HEBs *are* the truth. Their whole beingness comes from "what is so," and "what works," and HEBs learned long ago, in a time beyond memory when communication was still accomplished through guttural utterances, that untruth does not work. You have not yet learned this in your society.

On your planet, much of society is based on secrecy. Many of you believe it is what you keep *from* each other, not what you tell *to* each other, that makes life work. Secrecy has thus become your social code, your code of ethics. It is truly your Secret Code.

This is not true of all of you. Your ancient cultures, for instance, and your indigenous people do not live by such a code. And many individuals in your present society have refused to adopt these behaviors.

Yet your government runs by this code, your businesses adopt it, and many of your relationships reflect it. Lying—about things large and small—has become so accepted by so many that they even lie about lying. Thus, you have developed a secret code about your Secret Code. Like the fact that the emperor is wearing no clothes, everybody knows it, but nobody's talking about it. You even try to pretend its not so—and in this you are lying to yourself.

You've made this point before.

I am repeating in this dialogue the essential points, the main points, you must "get" if you truly are to change things, as you say you wish to do.

And so I will say it again: The differences between human cultures and highly evolved cultures is that highly evolved beings:

1. Observe fully
2. Communicate truthfully

They see "what works" and say "what's so." This is another tiny, but profound, change which would immeasurably improve life on your planet.

And this is not, by the way, a question of morals. There are no "moral imperatives" in a HEB society, and that would be a concept equally as puzzling as lying. It is simply a matter of what is functional, of what brings benefit.

HEBs have no morals?

Not as you understand them. The idea of some group devising a set of values by which individual HEBs are called upon to live would violate their understanding of "what works," which is that each individual is the sole and final arbiter of what is, and is not, appropriate behavior for them.

The discussion is always around what *works* for a HEB society—what is functional and produces benefit for all—not around what humans would call "right" and "wrong."

But isn't that the same thing? Haven't we simply called what works "right," and what doesn't work for us, "wrong"?

You have attached guilt and shame to those labels—concepts equally foreign to HEBs—and you have labeled an astonishing number of things "wrong," not because they "don't work," but simply because you imagine them to be "inappropriate"—sometimes not even in your eyes, but in the "eyes of God." You have thus constructed artificial definitions of "what works" and what doesn't—definitions having nothing to do with "what's really so."

Honestly expressing one's feelings, for example, is often deemed by human society as "wrong." Such a conclusion could never be arrived at by a HEB, since precise awareness of feelings facilitates *life* in any community or cluster. So, as I said, a HEB would never hide feelings, or find it "socially correct" to do so.

It would be impossible in any event, because a HEB receives "vibes"—actual *vibrations*—from other beings, which make their feelings plain enough. Just as you can sometimes "feel the air" when you walk into a room, a HEB can feel what another HEB is thinking and experiencing.

Actual utterances—what you would call "words"—are rarely, if ever, used. This "telepathic communication" occurs between all highly evolved sentient beings. Indeed, it could be said that the degree to which a species—or a relationship between members of the same species—has evolved is demonstrated by the degree to which beings require the use of "words" to convey feelings, desires, or information.

And before you ask the question, yes, human beings can develop, and some *have* developed, the same capacity. Thousands of years ago, in fact, it was normal. You have since regressed to the use of primal utterances—"noises," actually—to communicate. But many of you are returning to a cleaner form of communication, more accurate and more elegant. This is especially true between loved ones—emphasizing a major truth: *Caring creates communication.*

Where there is deep love, words are virtually unnecessary. The reverse of this axiom is also true: The more words you *have* to use with each other, the less time you must be taking to *care* for each other, because caring creates communication.

Ultimately, all real communication is about truth. And ultimately, the only real truth is love. That is why, when love is present, so is communication. And when communication is difficult, it is a sign that love is not fully present.

That is beautifully put. I might say, beautifully *communicated.*

Thank you. To summarize, then, the model for life in a highly evolved society:

Beings live in clusters, or what you would call small intentional communities. These clusters are not further organized into cities, states, or nations, but each interacts with the others on a co-equal basis.

There are no governments as you would understand them, and no laws. There are councils, or conclaves. Usually of elders. And there are what could best be translated into your language as "mutual agreements." These have been reduced to a Triangular Code: Awareness, Honesty, Responsibility.

Highly evolved beings have decided long ago that this is how they choose to live together. They've made this choice based not on a moral structure or spiritual revelation that some other being or group has brought forth, but, rather, on a simple observation of *what is so,* and *what works.*

And there truly are no wars and/or conflicts?

No, mainly because a highly evolved being shares everything he has, and would give you anything you sought to take by force. He does this out of his awareness that everything belongs to everyone anyway, and that he can always create more of what he "gave away" if he really desires it.

There is no concept of "ownership" or "loss" in a society of HEBs, who understand that they are not physical beings, but beings being physical. They also understand that all beings proceed from the same source, and thus, We Are All One.

I know You said this before . . . but even if someone was threatening a HEB with his life, there would still be no conflict?

There would be no argument. He would simply lay down his body—literally leaving the body there for you. He would then create another body if he chose to, by coming into physicality again as a fully formed being, or by returning as the newly conceived offspring of a loving pair of other beings.

This is by far the preferred method of reentry into physicality, because no one is more honored in highly evolved societies than newly created offspring, and the opportunities for growth are unparalleled.

HEBs have no fear of what your culture calls "death," because HEBs know that they live forever, and it is just a matter of what *form* they are going to take. HEBs can live in a physical body usually indefinitely, because a HEB has learned to take care of the body, and the environment. If for some reason having to do with the physical laws a HEB's body is no longer functional, the HEB simply leaves it, joyfully returning its physical matter to the All of Everything for "recycling." (What you understand as "dust into dust.")

Let me go back a bit. I know You said there are no "laws," as such. But what if someone does not behave according to the "Triangular Code"? Then what? *Ka-boom?*

No. No "ka-boom." There is no "trial" or "punishment," just a simple observation of "what's so," and "what works."

It is carefully explained that "what's so"—what the being has done—is now at variance with "what works," and that when something does not work for the group, it ultimately will not work for the individual, because the individual *is* the group, and the group is the individual. All HEBs "get" this very quickly, usually early in what you would call *youth,* and so it is extremely rare that a mature HEB is found to act in a way which produces a "what's so" that is *not* "what works."

But when one does?

He is simply allowed to correct his mistake. Using the Triangular Code, he is first made aware of all the outcomes related to something he has thought or said or done. Then he is allowed to assess and declare his role in producing those outcomes. Finally, he is given an opportunity to take responsibility for those outcomes by putting corrective or remedial or healing measures into place.

What if he refuses to do so?

A highly evolved being would never refuse to do so. It is inconceivable. He would then not be a highly evolved being, and you are now talking about a different level of sentient being altogether.

Where does a HEB learn all this stuff? In school?

There is no "school system" in a HEB society, merely a *process* of education by which offspring are reminded of "what's so," and "what works." Offspring are raised by elders, not by those who conceive them, though they are not necessarily separated from their "parents" during the process, who may be with them whenever they wish, and spend as much time with them as they choose.

In what you would call "school" (actually, best translated as "learning time"), offspring set their own "curriculum," choosing which skills *they* would like to acquire, rather than being *told* what they are going to *have* to learn. Motivation is thus at its highest level, and life skills are acquired quickly, easily, and joyfully.

The Triangular Code (these are not really codified "rules," but this is the best term one can find in your languages) is not something which is "pounded into" the young HEB, but something which is *acquired*—almost by osmosis—through the behaviors *modeled* for the "child" by "adults."

Unlike your society, in which adults model behaviors *opposite* to those which they want their children to learn, in highly evolved cultures adults understand that children do what they see others doing.

It would never occur to HEBs to place their offspring for many hours in front of a device that shows pictures of behaviors they'd like their offspring to avoid. Such a decision would be, to a HEB, incomprehensible.

It would be equally incomprehensible, if a HEB *did* do this, to then deny that the pictures had anything to do with their offsprings' suddenly aberrant behaviors.

I will say again that the difference between HEB society and human society breaks down to one really very simple element, which we shall call truthful observation.

In HEB societies, beings acknowledge everything they see. In human societies, many deny what they see.

They see television ruining their children, and they ignore it. They see violence and "losing" used as "entertainment," and deny the contradiction. They observe that tobacco harms the body, and pretend it does not. They see a father who is drunken and abusive, and the whole family denies it, letting no one say a word about it.

They observe that over thousands of years their religions have failed utterly to change mass behaviors, and deny this, too. They see clearly that their governments do more to oppress than to assist, and they ignore it.

They see a health-care system that is really a disease-care system, spending one-tenth of its resources on preventing disease, and nine-tenths on managing it, and deny that *profit motive* is what stops any real progress on educating people in how to act and eat and live in a way which promotes good health.

They see that eating the flesh of animals that have been slaughtered after having been force-fed chemical-laden foods is not doing their health any good, yet they deny what they see.

They do more than that. They try to sue talk show hosts who dare even discuss the subject. You know, there's a wonderful book that explores this whole food topic with exquisite insight. It's called *Diet for a New America*, by John Robbins.

People will read that book and deny, deny, *deny* that it makes any sense. And that is the point. Much of your race lives in denial. They deny not just the painfully obvious observations of everyone around them, but the observations of their own eyes. They deny their personal feelings, and, eventually, their own truth.

Highly evolved beings—which some of you are becoming—deny *nothing*. They observe "what's so." They see clearly "what works." Using these simple tools, life becomes simple. "The Process" is honored.

Yes, but how does "The Process" work?

To answer that I have to make a point that I have made before—repeatedly, in fact—in this dialogue. *Everything depends on who you think you are, and what you are trying to do.*

If your objective is to live a life of peace, joy, and love, *violence does not work.* This has already been demonstrated.

If your objective is to live a life of good health and great longevity, consuming dead flesh, smoking known carcinogens, and drinking volumes of nerve-deadening, brain-frying liquids *does not work.* This has already been demonstrated.

If your objective is to raise offspring free of violence and rage, putting them directly in front of vivid depictions of violence and rage for years *does not work.* This has *already been demonstrated.*

If your objective is to care for Earth, and wisely husband her resources, acting as if those resources are limitless *does not work.* This has *already been* demonstrated.

If your objective is to discover and cultivate a relationship with a loving God, so that religion *can* make a difference in the affairs of humans, then teaching of a god of punishment and terrible retribution *does not work.* This, *too,* has *already been demonstrated.*

Motive is everything. Objectives determine outcomes. Life proceeds out of your intention. Your true intention is revealed in your actions, and your actions are determined by your true intention. As with everything in life (and life *itself*), it is a circle.

HEBs *see the circle.* Humans do not.

HEBs respond to what is so; humans ignore it.

HEBs tell the truth, *always.* Humans too often lie, to themselves as well as others.

HEBs say one thing, and do what they say. Humans say one thing and do another.

Deep down you *know* that something is wrong—that you intended to "go to Seattle," but you are in "San Jose." You see the contradictions in your behaviors, and you are truly ready now to abandon them. You see clearly both what is *so,* and what *works,* and you are becoming unwilling any further to support divisions between the two.

Yours is *a race awakening.* Your time of fulfillment is at hand.

You need *not* be discouraged by what you have heard here, for the groundwork has been laid for a new experience, a larger reality, and all this was merely preparation for it. You are ready now to step through the door.

This dialogue, in particular, has been intended to throw open that door. First, to point to it. *See? There it is!* For the light of truth will forever show the way. And the light of truth is what you have been given here.

Take this truth now, and live it. Hold this truth now, and share it. Embrace this truth now, and treasure it forever more.

For in these three books—the *Conversations with God* trilogy— have I spoken to you again of *what is so.*

There is no need to go further. There is no need to ask more questions or hear more answers or satisfy more curiosities or provide more examples or offer more observations. All you need in order to create the life you desire, you have found here, in this trilogy as presented so far. There is no need to go further.

Yes, you have more questions. Yes, you have more "but-what-ifs." Yes, you are not "done" yet with this exploration we have enjoyed. Because you are *never done with any exploration.*

It is clear then that this book could go on forever. And it will not. Your *conversation* with God *will,* but this book will not. For the answer to any other question you could ask will be found here, in this now complete trilogy. All we can do now is repeat, re-amplify, return to the same wisdom over and over again. Even this trilogy was an exercise in that. There is nothing new here, but simply ancient wisdom revisited.

It is good to revisit. It is good to become familiar once again. This is the process of remembrance of which I have so often spoken. You have nothing to learn. You have only to remember. . . .

So revisit this trilogy often; turn to its pages time and time again.

When you have a question that you feel has not been answered here, read the pages over again. You will find that your question has been answered. Yet if you really feel it has not, then seek your *own* answers. Have your *own* conversation. Create your *own truth.*

In this will you experience Who You Really Are.

21

I don't want You to go!

I'm not going anywhere. I am always with you. *All ways.*

Please, before we stop, just a few more questions. Some final, closing inquiries.

You do understand, don't you, that you may *go within* at any time, return to the Seat of Eternal Wisdom, and find your answers there?

Yes, I understand that, and I am grateful to the bottom of my heart that it is this way, that life has been created this way, that I have that resource always. But this has been working for me. This dialogue has been a great gift. Can't I just ask a few last questions?

Of course.

Is our world really in danger? Is our species flirting with self-destruction—with actual extinction?

Yes. And unless you consider the very real possibility of that, you cannot avoid it. For what you resist, persists. Only what you hold can disappear.

Remember, also, what I told you about time and events. All the events you could possibly imagine—indeed, have imagined—are taking place right now, in the Eternal Moment. This is the Holy Instant. This is the Moment that precedes your awareness. It is what is happening before the Light gets to you. This is the pre-sent moment, sent to you, created by you, before you even know it! You call this the "present." And it IS a "present." It is the greatest gift given to you by God.

You have the ability to choose which, of all the experiences you've ever imagined, you choose to experience *now.*

You've said it, and I am now beginning, even in my limited perception, to understand it. None of this is really "real," is it?

> No. You are living an illusion. This is a big magic show. And you are pretending that you don't know the tricks—even though *you are the magician.*
>
> It is important to remember this, otherwise you will make everything very real.

But what I see, feel, smell, touch, *does* seem very real. If that isn't "reality," what is?

> Keep in mind that what you are looking at, you are not really "seeing."
>
> Your brain is not the source of your intelligence. It is simply a data processor. It takes in data through receptors called your senses. It interprets this energy in formation according to its *previous data on the subject.* It tells you what it *perceives,* not what *really is.* Based on these perceptions, you *think you know the truth* about something, when, actually, you do not know the half of it. In reality, you are creating the truth that you know.

Including this entire dialogue with You.

> Most assuredly.

I'm afraid that will only give fuel to those who are saying, "He's not talking to God. He's making it all up."

> Tell them gently that they might try thinking "outside the box." They are thinking "either/or." They might try thinking "both/and."
>
> You cannot comprehend God if you are thinking inside your current values, concepts, and understandings. If you wish to comprehend God, you must be willing to accept that you currently have *limited data,* rather than asserting that you know all there is to know on this subject.
>
> I draw your attention to the words of Werner Erhard, who declared that true clarity can come only when someone is willing to notice:
>
> *There is something I do not know, the knowing of which could change everything.*
>
> It is just possible that you are both "talking to God" *and* "making it all up."

Indeed, here is the grandest truth: You are making *everything* up.

Life is The Process by which everything is being created. God is the energy—the pure, raw energy—which you call life. By this awareness we come to a new truth.

God is a Process.

I thought You said God was a Collective, that God is The ALL.

I did. And God is. God is also The Process by which All is created, and experiences Itself.

I have revealed this to you before.

Yes. *Yes.* You gave me that wisdom when I was writing a booklet called *Re-creating Yourself.*

Indeed. And now I say it here, for a much larger audience to receive.

God is a Process.

God is not a person, place, or thing. God is exactly what you have always thought—but not understood.

Again?

You have always thought that God is the Supreme Being.

Yes.

And you have been right about that. I am exactly that. A BEING. Notice that "being" is not a thing, it is a process.

I am the *Supreme* Being. That is, the Supreme, comma, *being.*

I am not the *result* of a process; I *am* The Process Itself. I am the Creator, and I am The Process *by which I am created.*

Everything you see in the heavens and the earth is Me, *being created.* The Process of Creation is never over. It is never complete. I am never "done." This is another way of saying everything is forever changing. Nothing stands still. Nothing—*nothing*—is without motion. Everything is energy, in motion. In your earthly shorthand, you have called this "E-motion!"

You are God's highest emotion!

When you look at a thing, you are not looking at a static "something" that is "standing there" in time and space. No! You are *witnessing an event.* Because everything is moving, changing, evolving. *Everything.*

It was Buckminster Fuller who said, "I seem to be a verb." *He was right.*

God is an *event.* You have called that event *life.* Life is a Process. That Process is observable, knowable, predictable. The more you observe, the more you know, and the more you can predict.

That's a tough one for me. I always thought that God is the Unchangeable. The One Constant. The Unmoved Mover. It was within this inscrutable absolute truth about God that I found my security.

But that IS the truth! The One Unchanging Truth is that God is always changing. That is the *truth*—and you *can't do anything to change it.* The one thing that *never* changes is that everything is always changing.

Life is change. God is *life.*

Therefore, God is change.

But I want to believe that the one thing that never changes is God's love for us.

My love for you is *always* changing, because *you* are always changing, and I love you *just the way you are.* For Me to love you just the way you are, My idea of what is "lovable" must change as your idea of Who You Are changes.

You mean You find me lovable even if I decide that Who I Am is a murderer?

We've been through this all before.

I know, but I just can't *get it!*

Nobody does anything inappropriate, given their model of the world. I love you always—all *ways.* There is no "way" you can be that could cause Me not to love you.

But You will punish us, right? You will lovingly punish us. You will send us to everlasting torment, with love in Your heart, and sadness that You had to do it.

No. I have no sadness, *ever,* because there is *nothing* I "have to do." Who would make Me "have to do it"?

I will never punish you, although you may choose to punish yourself in this life or another, until you don't anymore. I will not punish you because I have not been hurt or damaged—nor can you hurt or damage any Part of Me, which *all of you are.*

One of you may choose to *feel* hurt or damaged, yet when you return to the eternal realm, you will see that you have not been damaged in any way. In this moment will you forgive those you imagined to have damaged you, for you will have understood the larger plan.

What is the larger plan?

Do you remember the parable of *The Little Soul and the Sun* that I gave you in *Book 1?*

Yes.

There is a second half to that parable. Here it is:

"You may choose to be any Part of God you wish to be," I said to the Little Soul. "You are Absolute Divinity, experiencing Itself. What Aspect of Divinity do you now wish to experience as You?"

"You mean I have a choice?" asked the Little Soul. And I answered, "Yes. You may choose to experience any Aspect of Divinity in, as, and through you."

"Okay," said the Little Soul, "then I choose Forgiveness. I want to experience my Self as that Aspect of God called Complete Forgiveness."

Well, this created a little challenge, as you can imagine.

There was *no one to forgive.* All I have created is Perfection and Love.

"No one to forgive?" asked the Little Soul, somewhat incredulously.

"No one," I repeated. "Look around you. Do you see any souls less perfect, less wonderful than you?"

At this the Little Soul twirled around, and was surprised to see himself surrounded by all the souls in heaven. They had come from far and wide throughout the Kingdom, because they heard that the Little Soul was having an extraordinary *conversation with God.*

"I see none less perfect than I!" the Little Soul exclaimed. "Who, then, shall I have to forgive?"

Just then, another soul stepped forward from the crowd. "You may forgive me," said this Friendly Soul.

"For what?" the Little Soul asked.

"I will come into your next physical lifetime and do something for you to forgive," replied the Friendly Soul.

"But what? What could you, a being of such Perfect Light, do to make me want to forgive you?" the Little Soul wanted to know.

"Oh," smiled the Friendly Soul, "I'm sure we can think of something."

"But why would you want to do this?" The Little Soul could not figure out why a being of such perfection would want to slow down its vibration so much that it could actually do something "bad."

"Simple," the Friendly Soul explained, "I would do it because I love you. You want to experience your Self as Forgiving, don't you? Besides, you've done the same for me."

"I have?" asked the Little Soul.

"Of course. Don't you remember? We've been All Of It, you and I. We've been the Up and the Down of it, and the Left and the Right of it. We've been the Here and the There of it, and the Now and the Then of it. We've been the Big and the Small of it, the Male and the Female of it, the Good and the Bad of it. We've *all been the All of It*.

"And we've done it by *agreement,* so that each of us might experience ourselves as The Grandest Part of God. For we have understood that. . . .

"In the absence of that which You Are Not, that Which You ARE, is NOT.

"In the absence of 'cold,' you cannot be 'warm.' In the absence of 'sad,' you cannot be 'happy,' without a thing called 'evil,' the experience you call 'good' cannot exist.

If you choose to *be a thing, something or someone opposite to that has to show up somewhere in your universe* to make that possible."

The Friendly Soul then explained that those people are God's Special Angels, and these conditions God's Gifts.

"I ask only one thing in return," the Friendly Soul declared.

"Anything! *Anything*," the Little Soul cried. He was excited now to know that he could experience every Divine Aspect of God. He understood, now, The Plan.

"In the moment that I strike you and smite you," said the Friendly Soul, "in the moment that I do the worst to you that you could ever imagine—in that selfsame moment . . . *remember Who I Really Am.*"

"Oh, I won't forget!" promised the Little Soul. "I will see you in the perfection with which I hold you now, and I will remember Who You Are, always."

That is . . . that is an extraordinary story, an incredible parable.

And the promise of the Little Soul is the promise I make to you. *That* is what is unchanging. Yet have you, My Little Soul, kept this promise to others?

No. I'm sad to say I have not.

Do not be sad. Be happy to notice what is true, and be joyous in your decision to live a new truth.

For God is a work in progress, and so are you. And remember this always:

If you saw you as God sees you, you would smile a lot.

So go, now, and see each other as Who You Really Are.

Observe. *Observe. OBSERVE.*

I have told you—the major difference between you and highly evolved beings is that highly evolved beings *observe more.*

If you wish to increase the speed with which you are evolving, *seek to observe more.*

That in itself is a wonderful observation.

And I would have you now observe that *you, too,* are an event. You are a human, comma, *being.* You are a process. And you are, in any given "moment," the product of your process.

You are the Creator and the Created. I am saying these things to you over and over again, in these last few moments we have together. I am repeating them so that you will *hear them*, understand them

Now, this process that you and I are is eternal. It always was, is now, and always will be occurring. It needs no "help" from you in order to occur. It happens "automatically." And, when left alone, it happens *perfectly.*

There is another saying that has been placed into your culture by Werner Erhard—*life resolves itself in the process of life itself.*

This is understood by some spiritual movements as "let go and let God." That is a good understanding.

If you will just *let go,* you will have gotten yourself out of the "way." The "way" is The Process—which is called *life itself.* This is why all masters have said, "I am the life and the way." They have understood what I have said here perfectly. They *are* the life, and they *are* the way—the event in progress, The Process.

All wisdom asks you to do is trust The Process. That is, *trust God.* Or, if you wish, *trust yourself,* for Thou Art God.

Remember, We Are All One.

How can I "trust the process" when the "process"—*life*—keeps bringing me things I don't like?

> *Like* the things life keeps bringing you!
> Know and understand that you are bringing it to your Self.
> SEE THE PERFECTION.
>
> See it in *everything,* not just in things that *you* call perfect. I have carefully explained to you in this trilogy why things happen the way they happen, and how. You do not need to read that material again here—although it might do you benefit to review it often, until you understand it thoroughly.

Please—just on this one point—a summarizing insight. Please. How can I "see the perfection" of something that I experience as not perfect at all?

> *No one can create your experience of anything.*
> Other beings can, and *do,* co-create the exterior circumstances and events of the life you live in common, but the *one thing* that *no one else can do is cause you to have an experience* of ANYTHING you do not choose to experience.
> In this, you are a Supreme being. And no one—NO ONE—can tell you "how to be."
> The world can present you with circumstances, but only you decide what those circumstances mean.
> Remember the truth I gave you long ago.
> Nothing matters.

Yes. I'm not sure I fully understood it then. That came to me in an out-of-body experience in 1980. I recall it vividly.

> And what do you remember of it?

That I was confused at first. How could "nothing matter"? Where would the world be, where would *I* be, if nothing mattered at all?

What answer did you find to that very good question?

I "got" that nothing mattered intrinsically, in and of itself, but that I was adding meaning to events, and so, causing them to matter. I got this at a very high metaphysical level as well, giving me a huge insight about the Process of Creation itself.

And the insight?

I "got" that all is energy, and that energy turns into "matter"—that is, physical "stuff" and "occurrences"—according to how I thought about them. I understood, then, that "nothing matters" means that nothing turns *into* matter except as we choose for it to. Then I forgot that insight for over ten years, until You brought it to me again earlier in this dialogue.

> Everything I have brought you in this dialogue you have known before. I have given it to you before, all of it, through others whom I have sent you, or to whose teachings I have brought you. *There is nothing new here*, and you have nothing to learn. You have only to remember.
>
> Your understanding of the wisdom "nothing matters" is rich and deep, and serves you well.

I'm sorry. I cannot let this dialogue end without pointing out a glaring contradiction.

Which is—?

You have taught me over and over again that what we call "evil" exists so that we may have a context within which to experience "good." You have said that What I Am cannot be experienced if there is no such thing as What I Am Not. In other words, no "warm" without "cold," no "up" without "down," and so on.

That's right.

You have even used this to explain to me how I could see every "problem" as a blessing, and every perpetrator as an angel.

Correct again.

Then how come every description of the life of highly evolved beings contains virtually no "evil"? All you've described is paradise!

Oh, good. Very good. You are really thinking about all this.

Actually, Nancy pointed this out. She was listening to me read some of the material out loud to her and she said, "I think you need to ask about this before the dialogue is over. How do HEBs experience themselves as Who They Really Are if they've eliminated all the negative stuff from their lives?" I thought it was a good question. In fact, it stopped me cold. And I know You just said we didn't need any more questions, but I think You need to address this one.

Okay. One for Nancy, then. As it happens, it's one of the best questions in the book.

(Ahem.)

Well, it *is*. . . . I'm surprised you didn't catch this when we were talking about HEBs. I'm surprised you didn't think of it.

I did.

You did?

We are all One, aren't we? Well, the *part of me which is Nancy* thought of it!

Ah, *excellent!* And, of course, *true.*

So, Your answer?

I will return to My original statement.
In the absence of that which you are not, that which you are, is not.
That is, in the absence of cold, you cannot know the experience called warmth. In the absence of up, the idea of "down" is an empty, meaningless concept.
This is a truth of the universe. Indeed, it explains why the universe is the way it *is*, with its cold and its warmth, its ups and downs, and, yes, its "good" and its "evil."

Yet know this: *You are making it all up.* You are *deciding* what is "cold" and what is "warm," what is "up" and what is "down." (Get out in space and watch your definitions disappear!) You are *deciding* what is "good" and what is "evil." And your ideas about all these things have changed through the years—indeed, even through the *seasons.* On a summer day you would call 42°F "cold." In the middle of winter, however, you would say, "Boy, what a warm day!"

The universe merely provides you with a *field of experience*— what might be called a *range of objective phenomena.* You decide *what to label them.*

The universe is a whole system of such physical phenomena. And the universe is enormous. Vast. Unfathomably huge. *Endless,* in fact.

Now here is a great secret: It is not necessary for an opposite condition to exist *right next to you* in order to provide a contextual field within which the reality that you choose may be experienced.

The distance between contrasts is irrelevant. The entire universe provides the contextual field within which all contrasting elements exist, and all experiences are thus made possible. That is the *purpose* of the universe. That is its function.

But if I've never *experienced* "cold" in person, but merely see that it is "cold" somewhere else, very far away from me, how do I know what "cold" is?

You *have* experienced "cold." You have experienced *all of it.* If not in this lifetime, then in the last. Or the one before that. Or one of the many others. You *have* experienced "cold." And "big" and "small" and "up" and "down" and "here" and "there" and every contrasting element that there is. And these are burned into your memory.

You do *not have to experience them again if you* don't want to. You need merely remember them—know that they exist—in order to invoke the universal law of relativity.

All of you. All of you have experienced *everything.* That goes for all beings in the universe, not only humans.

You have all not only experienced everything, you *are* everything. You are ALL OF IT.

You are that which you are experiencing. Indeed, you are *causing* the experience.

I'm not sure I fully understand that.

I am about to explain it to you, in mechanical terms. What I want you now to understand is that what you are doing now is simply remembering everything you are, and choosing the portion of that which you prefer to experience in this moment, in this lifetime, on this planet, in this physical form.

My God, you make it sound so simple!

It *is simple*. You have separated your Self from the body of God, from the All, from the Collective, and you are becoming a member of that body once again. This is The Process called "re-membering."

As you re-member, you give your Self once again all the experiences of Who You Are. This is a cycle. You do this over and over again, and call this "evolution." You say that you "evolve." Actually, you RE-volve! Just as the Earth revolves around the sun. Just as the galaxy revolves around its center.

Everything revolves.

Revolution is the basic movement of all of life. Life energy *revolves*. That is what it *does*. You are in a truly *revolutionary movement*.

How do You *do* that? How do You keep finding words that make everything so clear?

It is you who are making it clear. You have done this by clearing up your "receiver." You've tuned out the static. You've entered into a new willingness to know. This new willingness will change everything, for you and for your species. For in your new willingness, you have become a true revolutionary—and your planet's greatest spiritual revolution has just begun.

It had better hurry. We need a new spirituality, *now*. We are creating incredible misery all around us.

That is because, even though all beings have already lived through all contrasting experiences, some *do not know it*. They have forgotten, and have not yet moved into full remembering.

With highly evolved beings this is not so. It is not necessary to have "negativity" right in front of them, in their own world, for them to know how "positive" their civilization is. They are "positively aware" of Who They Are without having to create negativity to prove it. HEBs merely notice who they are *not* by observing it *elsewhere in the contextual field.*

Your own planet, in fact, is one to which highly evolved beings look if they seek a contrasting field.

As they do so, they are reminded of how it was when *they* experienced what you are now experiencing, and they thus form an ongoing frame of reference through which they may know and understand what *they* are now experiencing.

Do you now understand why HEBs do not require "evil" or "negativity" in their own society?

Yes. But then why do we require it in ours?

You *DO NOT.* That is what I have been telling you throughout this whole dialogue.

You *do* have to live within a contextual field within which That Which You Are Not exists, in order for you to experience That Which You Are. This is the Universal Law, and you cannot avoid it. Yet you *are* living in such a field, right now. You do not have to create one. The contextual field in which you are living is called *the universe.*

You do not have to create a smaller contextual field in your own backyard.

This means that you can change life on your planet right now, and *eliminate all that you are not,* without endangering in any way your ability to know and experience That Which You Are.

Wow! This is the greatest revelation in the book! What a way to end it! So I *don't* have to keep calling forth the *opposite* in order to create and experience the next grandest version of the greatest vision I've ever had of Who I Am!

That is right. That is what I have been telling you from the very beginning.

But You didn't explain it in this way!

You would not have understood it until now.

You do *not* have to create the opposite of Who You Are and What You Choose in order to experience it. You merely need to observe that it has already been created—elsewhere. You need only remember that it exists. This is the "knowledge of the fruit of the Tree of Good and Evil" which I've already explained to you was not a curse, not the original sin, but what Matthew Fox has called *Original Blessing.*

And to remember that it exists, to remember that *you* have experienced it all before—everything that is—in physical form . . . all you have to do is look up.

You mean "look within."

No, I mean *just what I said.* LOOK UP. Look to the stars. Look to the heavens. OBSERVE THE CONTEXTUAL FIELD.

I have told you before, all you need to do to become highly evolved beings is to increase *your observational skills.* See "what's so," and then do "what works."

So, by looking elsewhere in the universe, I can see how things are in other places, and I can use those contrasting elements to form an understanding of Who I Am right here, right now.

Yes. This is called "remembering."

Well, not exactly. It is called "observing."

What do you think you are observing?

Life on other planets. In other solar systems, other galaxies. I suppose if we gathered sufficient technology, this is what we might observe. This is what I assume the HEBs have the ability to observe right now, given their advanced technology. You said Yourself that they are observing *us*, right here on Earth. So that is what we would be observing.

But what is it, *actually*, that you would be observing?

I don't understand the question.

Then I will give you the answer.
You are observing your own past.

What???

When you look up, you see the stars—as they were hundreds, thousands, millions of light-years ago. What you are seeing is *not actually there.* You are seeing what *was* there. You are seeing the past. And it is a past in which *you participated.*

Say again???

You were *there, experiencing* those things, *doing* those things.

I was?

Have I not told you that you have lived many lives?

Yes, but . . . but what if I were to travel to one of these places so many light-years away? What if I had the ability to actually go there? To be there "right now," in the very moment that I am not able to "see" on Earth for hundreds of light-years? What would I see then? Two "me's"? Are You saying that I would then see my Self, existing in *two places at once?*

Of course! And you would discover what I have told you all along—that time does not exist, and that you are not seeing "the past" at all! That it is *all happening NOW.*

You are also, "right now," living lives in what in Earth time, would be your future. It is the distance between your many "Selves" that allows "you" to experience discrete identities, and "moments in time."

Thus, the "past" that you re-member and the future that you would see, is the "now" that simply IS.

Whoa. That's incredible.

Yes, and it is true on another level as well. It is as I have told you before: *there is only One of us.* So when you look up at the stars you are seeing what you would call OUR PAST.

I can't keep up with this!

Hang on. There's one thing more I have to tell you.

You are *always* seeing what by your terms you would define as the "past," even when you are looking at what is right in front of you.

I am?

It is impossible to see The Present. The Present "happens," then turns into a burst of light, formed by energy dispersing, and that light reaches your receptors, your eyes, and *it takes time for it to do that.*

All the while that light is reaching you, life is *going on, moving forward.* The *next event is happening* while the light from *the last event is reaching you.*

The energy burst reaches your eyes, your receptors send that signal to your brain, which interprets the data and tells you what you are seeing. Yet that is not what is now in front of you at all. It is what you *think* you are seeing. That is, you are thinking about what you have seen, telling yourself what it is, and deciding what you are going to call it, while what is happening "now" is preceding your process, and awaiting it.

To put this simply, *I am always one step ahead of you.*

My God, this is *unbelievable.*

Now *listen.* The more *distance* you place between your Self and the physical location of any event, the *further into the "past" that event recedes.* Place yourself a few light-years back, and what you are looking at happened very, very long ago, indeed.

Yet it did *not* happen "long ago." It is merely physical *distance* which has created the illusion of "time," and allowed you to experience your Self as being both "here, now" all the while you are being "there, then"!

One day you will see that what you call time and space are *the same thing.*

Then you will see that *everything is happening right here, right now.*

This is . . . this is . . . *wild.* I mean, I don't know what to make of all this.

When you understand what I have told you, you will understand that *nothing you see is real.* You are seeing the *image* of what was once an event, yet even that image, that energy burst, is something you are interpreting. Your personal interpretation of that image is called your image-ination.

And you can use your imagination to create *anything*. Because—and here is the greatest secret of all—your image-ination *works both ways.*

Please?

You not only *interpret* energy, you *create it.* Imagination is a function of your mind, which is one-third of your three-part being. In your mind you image something, and it begins to take physical form. The longer you image it (and the more OF you who image it), the more physical that form becomes, until the increasing energy you have given it literally *bursts into light,* flashing an image of itself into what you call your reality.

You then "see" the image, and once again *decide what it is.* Thus, the cycle continues. This is what I have called The Process.

This is what YOU ARE. You ARE this Process.

This is what God IS. God IS this Process.

This is what I have meant when I have said, you are *both the Creator and the Created.*

I have now brought it all together for you. We are concluding this dialogue, and I have explained to you the mechanics of the universe, the secret of all life.

I'm . . . bowled over. I'm . . . flabbergasted. Now I want to find a way to apply all this in my daily life.

You *are* applying it in your daily life. You cannot *help* but apply it. This is *what is happening.* The only question will be whether you apply it *consciously or unconsciously,* whether you are at the effect of The Process, or are the cause of it. In everything, be *cause.*

Children understand this perfectly. Ask a child, "Why did you do that?" and a child will tell you. "Just because."

That is the only reason to do anything.

This is astounding. This is an astounding rush to an astounding ending to this astounding dialogue.

The most significant way in which you may consciously apply your New Understanding is to be the *cause* of your experience, not at the effect of it. And know that you *do not have to create the opposite of Who You Are in your personal space or personal experience* in order to know and experience Who You Really Are, and Who You Choose To Be.

Armed with this knowledge, you can change your life, and you can change your world.

And this is the truth I have come to share with all of you.

Whoa! Wow! I got it. *I got it!*

Good. Now know that there are three basic wisdoms that run through the entire dialogue. These are:

1. We Are All One.
2. There's Enough.
3. There's Nothing We Have To Do.

If you decided that "we are all one," you would cease treating each other the way you do.

If you decided that "there's enough," you would share everything with everyone.

If you decided that "there's nothing we have to do," you would stop trying to use "doingness" to solve your problems, but rather, move to, and come *from,* a state of being which would cause your experience of those "problems" to disappear, and the conditions themselves to thus evaporate.

This is perhaps the most important truth of all for you to understand at this stage in your evolution, and it is a good place to end this dialogue. Remember this always, and make it your mantra:

There's nothing I have to have, there's nothing I have to do, and there's nothing I have to be, except exactly what I'm being right now.

This does not mean that "having" and "doing" will be eliminated from your life. It means that what you experience yourself having or doing will spring *from* your being—not lead you *to* it.

When you come *from* "happiness," you do certain things because you *are* happy—as opposed to the old paradigm in which you did things that you hoped would *make* you happy.

When you come *from* "wisdom," you do certain things because you *are* wise, not because you are trying to *get* to wisdom.

When you come *from* "love," you do certain things because you *are* love, not because you want to *have* love.

Everything changes; everything turns around, when you come *from* "being," rather than seeking to "be." You cannot "do" your way to "being." Whether you are trying to "be" happy, be wise, be love—or be God—you cannot "get there" by doing. And yet, it is true that you *will* be doing wonderful things once you "get there."

Here is the Divine Dichotomy. The way to "get there" is to "be there." Just *be* where you choose to *get!* It's that simple. *There's nothing you have to do.* You want to be happy? *Be happy.* You want to be wise? *Be wise.* You want to be love? *Be love.*

That is Who You Are in any event.

You are My Beloved.

Oh! I just lost my breath! You have such a wondrous way of putting things.

It is the truth that is eloquent. Truth has an elegance that startles the heart to its own reawakening.

That is what these *Conversations with God* have done. They have touched the heart of the human race, and reawakened it.

Now they lead you to a critical question. It is a question all of humanity must ask itself. Can, and will, you create a new cultural story? Can and will you devise a new First Cultural Myth, upon which all other myths are based?

Is the human race inherently good, or inherently evil?

This is the crossroads to which you have come. The future of the human race depends on which way you go.

If you and your society believe you are inherently good, you will make decisions and laws that are life affirming and constructive. If you and your society believe that you are inherently evil, you will make decisions and laws that are life denying and destructive.

Laws that are life affirming are laws that allow you to be, do, and have what you wish. Laws that are life denying are laws that stop you from being, doing, and having what you wish.

Those who believe in Original Sin, and that the inherent nature of man is *evil*, claim that God has created laws which *stop* you from doing as you wish—and promote human laws (an endless number of them) that seek to do the same.

Those who believe in Original Blessing, and that the inherent nature of man is *good*, proclaim that God has created natural laws which *allow* you to do as you wish—and promote human laws that seek to do the same.

What is your viewpoint of the human race? What is your viewpoint of your Self? Left entirely to your own devices, do you see yourself as being able to be trusted? In everything? How about others? How do you view them? Until they reveal themselves to you, one way or the other, what is your basic assumption?

Now, answer this. Do your assumptions further your society in breaking *down*, or breaking *through*?

I see my Self as trustworthy. I never did before, but now I do. I have *become* trustworthy, because I have changed my ideas on the kind of person I am. I am also clear now on what God wants, and what God doesn't want. I am clear about You.

These *Conversations with God* have played a huge role in that change, in making that shift possible. And I now see in society what I see in myself—not something that is breaking down, but something that is breaking through. I see a human culture that is at last awakening to its divine heritage, aware of its divine purpose, and increasingly conscious of its divine Self.

If that is what you see, that is what you will create. Once you were lost, but now you are found. You were blind, but now you see. And this *has* been an amazing grace.

You have sometimes been apart from Me in your heart, but now We are whole again, and We can be forever. For what you have joined together, no one but you can put asunder.

Remember this: You are always a part, because you are never apart. You are always a part OF God, because you are never apart FROM God.

This is the truth of your being. We are whole. So now you know the whole truth.

This truth has been food for the hungry soul. Take, and eat of it. The world has thirsted for this joy. Take, and drink of it. Do this in re-membrance of Me.

For truth is the body, and joy is the blood, of God, who is love.

Truth.

Joy.

Love.

These three are interchangeable. One leads to the other, and it matters not in which order they appear. All lead to Me. All *are* Me.

And so I end this dialogue as it began. As with life itself, it comes full circle. You have been given truth here. You have been given joy.

You have been given love. You have been given here the answers to the largest mysteries of life. There is now only one question remaining. It is the question with which we began.

The question is not, to whom do I talk, but who listens?

Thank You. Thank You for talking to *all* of us. We have heard You, and we will listen. I love You. And as this dialogue ends, I *am* filled with truth, joy, and love. I am filled with You. I feel my Oneness with God.

That place of Oneness is heaven.

You are there now.

You are never *not* there, because you are never *not* One with Me.

This is what I would have you know. This is what I would have you take, at last, from this conversation.

And here is My message, the message I would seek to leave with the world:

My Children, who art in Heaven, hallowed is your name. Your kingdom is come, and your will is done, on Earth as it is in Heaven.

You are given this day your daily bread, and you are forgiven your debts, and your trespasses, exactly to the degree that you have forgiven those who trespass against you.

Lead your Self not into temptation, but deliver your Self from the evils you have created.

For thine *is* the Kingdom, and the Power, and the Glory, forever. Amen.

And amen.

Go now, and change your world. Go now, and be your Highest Self. You understand now all that you need to understand. You know now all that you need to know. You are now all that you need to be.

You never were anything less. You simply did not know this. You did not remember it.

Now you remember. Seek to carry this remembrance with you always. Seek to share it with all those whose lives you touch. For yours is a destiny grander than you might ever have imagined.

You have come to the room to heal the room. You have come to the space to heal the space.

There is no other reason for you to be here.

And know this: I love you. My love is always yours, both now, and even forever more.

I am with you always.

All ways.

Goodbye, God. Thank You for this dialogue. Thank You, thank You, *thank You.*

And you, My wonderful creation. Thank you. For you have given God a voice again—and a place in your heart. And that is all either of Us have ever really wanted.

We are together again. And it is very good.

Afterword

You have finished reading what I truly believe to be one of the most significant spiritual documents of our time. It is significant because of the impact that it has already made on our planet as of this writing (April, 2005), and the ever-increasing impact that I am certain it will continue to make in the years and decades ahead. Indeed, I believe that long after I have left this life, this message will live on. It has already touched the lives of more than seven million people. That number will reach 70 million, then 700 million, and go even beyond.

Is this boastful, or arrogant? I hope you do not consider it so. For me it is a simple statement of what I am sure is true: that this message was never meant for me alone, nor for a relative handful, but for the world entire.

I am humbly grateful to have been able to have played my small role—and it *was* a small role—in bringing this message forward. All I did was ask questions, the same questions we all ask, and then simply take down the answers. I am certain that I did not even take them down cleanly or purely or without internal distraction, and so I am due no special thanks or recognition, but must, in fact, ask the forgiveness of everyone for having done such an imperfect job with such an important task.

I am sure that, try as I might, I have inadvertently allowed my own feelings or thoughts to intrude upon the incoming communication, to invade the wisdom, to compromise the clarity, perhaps even to shape the nuance if not the substance, of the messages that were given to be shared here. I honestly believe that this happened rarely. The fact that it happened at all saddens me enormously. I humbly ask your pardon. If good intentions are any measure, I believe myself to have done the very best that any person could, given the extraordinary circumstances of this dialogue's emergence.

I leave you now to ponder the greatest truth to be found here, which is that the greatest truth shall not be found here at all but within your own heart, within your own soul, and within your own mind. Think, feel, and know the truth as it resides within you. For you are now, and shall always be, the highest source, the only authority, and the greatest and closest connection with God that there will ever be. Look not, then, outside yourself, but go within, within, always within, to find your Oneness with the Divine, to feel the love for which you yearn, and to know the peace that passes all understanding.

God is within you, with you always, and will never leave you, no matter what you have done, no matter what you are now doing, no matter what you may ever do. You cannot push God away, you cannot shove God away, you cannot require God to move away from you under any circumstances. You will never find God so angry or so disappointed or so judgmental or so righteous as to desert you, *ever.* You shall never be condemned to everlasting isolation, to say nothing of torture. You are held in the everlasting embrace of God through all eternity. *This* is the measure of God's love.

Please, please, if there is anything lasting that you take from this message, let it be this. If there is anything of value that this work has produced, let it be that the world's mind has been changed about God. At last.

I have been asked many times by reporters, television and radio interviewers, people in the audience at my lectures, in letters, calls, and e-mails: "If God could bring but one message to the world, what would it be?" My answer has always been the same. A simple five-word statement: *You've got me all wrong.*

Now, please, some brief closing comments before I leave you to ponder what you have read here.

First, there have been many people who have said, "If only I had come across something like this earlier! I wish, I just wish, that you could find a way to make this message available for young people, and for children."

I have. For teenagers, one can obtain *Conversations with God for Teens,* and for the very young I have produced two very special children's books, *The Little Soul and the Sun,* and its sequel, *The Little Soul and the Earth.*

Others have said, "I just wish you could make this message available to people who cannot afford to buy all these books. Too bad you can't just put some book in electronic form on the Internet that people might download for nothing."

I have. The free, electronic book *The Holy Experience*, based on the messages found here, may be downloaded at www.nealedonaldwalsch.com.

At this website you will also find news of the work being done by the nonprofit Conversations with God Foundation, as well as our sister organization, Humanity's Team.

The Conversations with God Foundation is engaged in producing educational materials, programs, and retreats for people who are interested in delving more deeply into the material found here, and learning how they can apply these messages to their daily lives. The Foundation also offers very special training for persons who feel they would like to teach this material. The Life Education Program has placed teachers on the ground in cities, towns, and villages around the world.

Humanity's Team is a global movement of more than 10,000 members at this writing. It is a true grass roots movement—what has been called "a civil rights movement for the soul, freeing humanity at last from the oppression of its belief in a violent, angry, and vindictive God." Its mission is to create the space of possibility for a new form of spirituality to emerge upon the earth—an expression of humanity's impulse to experience the Divine, without making others wrong for the way in which they are doing it.

Again, you may link to all of this through the portal at www.nealedonaldwalsch.com.

And now, a closing invitation. The one thing I have heard more than any other single reaction to the Conversations with God material is, "What can I do? I want to see everyone have access to this life-giving, spirit-renewing message! I want to become part of the change that can alter our world. What can I do?"

There is a great deal you can do. You can become a spiritual helper on our planet. You can become part of the change that you wish to see in the world. I invite you to go to the website listed above and check out a powerful little booklet, *PART OF THE CHANGE: Your Role as a Spiritual Helper.* This is a short but incisive handbook that outlines ten steps you can take right now to bring about change in your day-to-day experience and to become a spiritual way-shower for all of those whose lives you touch. I'll send an electronic copy to you by e-mail for free if you'll simply ask for it.

For now, thank you for finding your way to this special edition of the *CwG* trilogy. If you know of anyone who you think might benefit from the messages found here, please pass on your copy of this book. You can always get another, and you could bring immeasurable benefit to the life of someone about whom you care.

Blessings to you, now and always. May God be expressed in your life.

—*NDW*

Index

F

M